Lecture Notes in Computer Science 15896

Founding Editors

Gerhard Goos
Juris Hartmanis

Editorial Board Members

Elisa Bertino, *Purdue University, West Lafayette, IN, USA*
Wen Gao, *Peking University, Beijing, China*
Bernhard Steffen, *TU Dortmund University, Dortmund, Germany*
Moti Yung, *Columbia University, New York, NY, USA*

The series Lecture Notes in Computer Science (LNCS), including its subseries Lecture Notes in Artificial Intelligence (LNAI) and Lecture Notes in Bioinformatics (LNBI), has established itself as a medium for the publication of new developments in computer science and information technology research, teaching, and education.

LNCS enjoys close cooperation with the computer science R & D community, the series counts many renowned academics among its volume editors and paper authors, and collaborates with prestigious societies. Its mission is to serve this international community by providing an invaluable service, mainly focused on the publication of conference and workshop proceedings and postproceedings. LNCS commenced publication in 1973.

Osvaldo Gervasi · Beniamino Murgante ·
Chiara Garau · Yeliz Karaca ·
Maria Noelia Faginas Lago · Francesco Scorza ·
Ana Cristina Braga
Editors

Computational Science and Its Applications – ICCSA 2025 Workshops

Istanbul, Turkey, June 30 – July 3, 2025
Proceedings, Part XI

Editors
Osvaldo Gervasi
University of Perugia
Perugia, Italy

Chiara Garau
University of Cagliari
Cagliari, Italy

Maria Noelia Faginas Lago
University of Perugia
Perugia, Italy

Ana Cristina Braga
University of Minho
Braga, Portugal

Beniamino Murgante
University of Basilicata
Potenza, Italy

Yeliz Karaca
University of Massachusetts
Worcester, MA, USA

Francesco Scorza
University of Basilicata
Potenza, Italy

ISSN 0302-9743 ISSN 1611-3349 (electronic)
Lecture Notes in Computer Science
ISBN 978-3-031-97653-7 ISBN 978-3-031-97654-4 (eBook)
https://doi.org/10.1007/978-3-031-97654-4

© The Editor(s) (if applicable) and The Author(s), under exclusive license to Springer Nature Switzerland AG 2026

This work is subject to copyright. All rights are solely and exclusively licensed by the Publisher, whether the whole or part of the material is concerned, specifically the rights of translation, reprinting, reuse of illustrations, recitation, broadcasting, reproduction on microfilms or in any other physical way, and transmission or information storage and retrieval, electronic adaptation, computer software, or by similar or dissimilar methodology now known or hereafter developed.
The use of general descriptive names, registered names, trademarks, service marks, etc. in this publication does not imply, even in the absence of a specific statement, that such names are exempt from the relevant protective laws and regulations and therefore free for general use.
The publisher, the authors and the editors are safe to assume that the advice and information in this book are believed to be true and accurate at the date of publication. Neither the publisher nor the authors or the editors give a warranty, expressed or implied, with respect to the material contained herein or for any errors or omissions that may have been made. The publisher remains neutral with regard to jurisdictional claims in published maps and institutional affiliations.

This Springer imprint is published by the registered company Springer Nature Switzerland AG
The registered company address is: Gewerbestrasse 11, 6330 Cham, Switzerland

If disposing of this product, please recycle the paper.

Preface

The compiled 14 volumes (LNCS volumes 15886–15899) consist of the peer-reviewed papers from the 68 Workshops of the 2025 International Conference on Computational Science and Its Applications (ICCSA 2025), which was held between June 30 – July 3, 2025 in Istanbul (Türkiye). The peer-reviewed papers of the main conference tracks are published in a separate set made up of three volumes (LNCS 15648–15650).

The conference was held in a hybrid form, with the large majority of participants in presence, hosted by Galatasaray University, Istanbul, Türkiye. We enabled virtual participation for those who did not attend the event in person due to logistical, political and economic problems, by adopting a technological infrastructure via open-source software (jitsi + riot) and a commercial Cloud infrastructure.

With the 2025 edition, ICCSA celebrated its 25th anniversary, a quarter of a century as a memorable moment that is harmoniously aligned with Istanbul, an extraordinary city located at the crossroads and acting as a bridge connecting Asia and Europe, representing different cultures, beliefs as well as lifestyles, which highlights its intercultural fabric.

ICCSA 2025 marked another fruitful and thought-provoking academic event in the International Conferences on Computational Science and Its Applications (ICCSA) conference series, previously held in Hanoi, Vietnam (2024), Athens, Greece (2023), Málaga, Spain (2022), Cagliari, Italy (hybrid with a few participants in presence in 2021 and completely online in 2020), whilst earlier editions took place in Saint Petersburg, Russia (2019), Melbourne, Australia (2018), Trieste, Italy (2017), Beijing, China (2016), Banff, Canada (2015), Guimaraes, Portugal (2014), Ho Chi Minh City, Vietnam (2013), Salvador, Brazil (2012), Santander, Spain (2011), Fukuoka, Japan (2010), Suwon, South Korea (2009), Perugia, Italy (2008), Kuala Lumpur, Malaysia (2007), Glasgow, UK (2006), Singapore (2005), Assisi, Italy (2004), Montreal, Canada (2003), and (as ICCS) Amsterdam, the Netherlands (2002) and San Francisco, USA (2001).

Computational Science constitutes the main pillar of most present research, industrial and commercial applications, and plays a unique role in exploiting ICT innovative technologies, and the ICCSA conference series has, accordingly, provided ample opportunities to researchers and industry practitioners to discuss new ideas, to share complex problems and their solutions, and to shape new trends in Computational Science. As the conference mirrors society from a scientific point of view, this year's undoubtedly dominant theme was large language models, machine learning and Artificial Intelligence (AI) and their applications in the most diverse technological, economic and industrial fields, amongst the others.

The ICCSA 2025 conference was structured in six general tracks covering the fields of computational science and its applications: Computational Methods, Algorithms and Scientific Applications – High Performance Computing and Networks – Geometric Modeling, Graphics and Visualization – Advanced and Emerging Applications – Information Systems and Technologies – Urban and Regional Planning. In addition, the conference consisted of 68 workshops, focusing on topical issues of utmost importance to science, technology and society: from new computational approaches for earth science, to mathematical methods for image processing, new statistical and optimization methods, several Artificial Intelligence approaches, sustainability issues, smart cities and related technologies, to name some.

In the Workshops' proceedings, we accepted 362 full papers, 37 short papers and 2 Ph.D. Showcase papers from total of 1043 submissions (Acceptance rate 38.4%). In the Main Conference Proceedings, we accepted 71 full papers, 6 short papers and 1 Ph.D. Showcase paper from 269 submissions to the General Tracks of the Conference (with an acceptance rate of 29.9%). We would like to convey our sincere appreciation to the workshops' chairs and co-chairs and program committee members for their diligent work, commitment and dedication.

The success and consistent maintenance of the ICCSA conference series in general, and of ICCSA 2025 in particular, rely upon the support of many people: authors, presenters, participants, keynote speakers, workshop chairs, session chairs, organizing committee members, student volunteers, Program Committee members, Advisory Committee members, International Liaison chairs, reviewers and other individuals in various roles. Thus, we take this opportunity to wholehartedly thank each and everyone.

We additionally wish to thank publisher Springer for their agreement to publish the proceedings, besides sponsoring part of the best papers awards and for their kind assistance and cooperation during the editing process.

We would cordially like to invite you to refer to the ICCSA website https://iccsa.org, where you can find the relevant details regarding this academic endeavor and event of ours.

June 2025

Osvaldo Gervasi
Yeliz Karaca
Beniamino Murgante
Chiara Garau

A Welcome Message from the Organizers

The International Conference on Computational Science and Its Applications (ICCSA) reflects a culmination of meticulous and dedicated efforts and academic endeavors toward the progress of science and technology.

One of the most noteworthy aspects of ICCSA is its fostering of a collective spirit, bringing together a plethora of participants from all over the world. Correspondingly, this merging power manifests itself in the 25th anniversary of ICCSA, which is a quarter of a century, in Istanbul, Türkiye, which connects and acts as a bridge between two continents, namely Asia and Europe. This unique location in the world hosts the 25th year of ICCSA at Galatasaray University, located on Çırağan Avenue by Istanbul's Bosphorus, which is an established international university bestowed with a distinctive past of teaching tradition, research and education exceeding five centuries.

Istanbul, having served as the capital city of four empires, namely the Roman Empire (330–395), the Byzantine Empire (395–1204 and 1261–1453), the Latin Empire (1204–1261) and the Ottoman Empire (1453–1922), is an exceptional city of the Republic of Türkiye founded by Mustafa Kemal Atatürk.

Situated at a strategic location along the historic Silk Road, Istanbul is at the core of extending rail networks which span across Europe and West Asia along with the only sea route between the Black Sea and the Mediterranean.

The cultural, historical and economic pulses of the country are evident in Istanbul whose rooted origins have embraced varying beliefs, lifestyles and populace, which highlights the city's mosaic quality with blended fabric in a constant harmonious flow. This has enabled cultures to grow and be nurtured, which is profoundly rooted in its urban culture.

Computational Science constitutes the main pillar of most present research, industrial and commercial activities besides manifesting a unique role in exploiting and addressing innovative Information and Communication Technologies. Thus, the 25-year-old ICCSA conference series provides remarkable opportunities to get acquainted with leading researchers, scientists, scholars, practitioners and many more while exchanging innovative ideas and initiating new partnerships, associations and bonds.

With the hosting of Galatasaray University, I would personally and on behalf of the Local Organizing Committee, with the members Emre Alptekin, Gülfem Işıklar Alptekin, Cengiz Kahraman, Abdullah Çağrı Tolga and Ayberk Zeytin, like to convey our sincere gratitude and thanks to everyone who exerted their efforts in and contributed to the realization of ICCSA 2025. With these notes and remarks, welcome to Istanbul!

Cordially yours,
On behalf of the Local Organizing Committee.

June 2025   Yeliz Karaca

Organization

Honorary General Chairs

Bernady O. Apduhan			Kyushu Sangyo University, Japan
Kenneth C. J. Tan			Sardina Systems, UK

General Chairs

Yeliz Karaca				University of Massachusetts, USA
Osvaldo Gervasi				University of Perugia, Italy
David Taniar				Monash University, Australia

Program Committee Chairs

Beniamino Murgante			University of Basilicata, Italy
Chiara Garau				University of Cagliari, Italy
Ana Maria A. C. Rocha		University of Minho, Portugal
A. Çağrı Tolga				Galatasaray University, Turkey

International Advisory Committee

Jemal Abawajy				Deakin University, Australia
Dharma P. Agarwal			University of Cincinnati, USA
Rajkumar Buyya				Melbourne University, Australia
Claudia Bauzer Medeiros		University of Campinas, Brazil
Manfred M. Fisher			Vienna University of Economics and Business, Austria
Pierre Frankhauser			University of Franche-Comté/CNRS, France
Marina L. Gavrilova			University of Calgary, Canada
Sumi Helal					University of Florida, USA & Lancaster University, UK
Bin Jiang					University of Gävle, Sweden
Yee Leung					Chinese University of Hong Kong, China

International Liaison Chairs

Ivan Blečić	University of Cagliari, Italy
Giuseppe Borruso	University of Trieste, Italy
Elise De Donker	Western Michigan University, USA
Maria Noelia Faginas Lago	University of Perugia, Italy
Maria Irene Falcão	University of Minho, Portugal
Robert C. H. Hsu	Chung Hua University, Taiwan
Yeliz Karaca	University of Massachusetts Chan Medical School, USA
Tae-Hoon Kim	Zhejiang University of Science and Technology, China
Vladimir Korkhov	Saint Petersburg University, Russia
Takashi Naka	Kyushu Sangyo University, Japan
Rafael D. C. Santos	National Institute for Space Research, Brazil
Maribel Yasmina Santos	University of Minho, Portugal
Anastasia Stratigea	National Technical University of Athens, Greece

Workshop and Session Organizing Chairs

Beniamino Murgante	University of Basilicata, Italy
Chiara Garau	University of Cagliari, Italy

Award Chair

Wenny Rahayu	La Trobe University, Australia

Publicity Committee Chairs

Elmer Dadios	De La Salle University, Philippines
Nataliia Kulabukhova	Saint Petersburg University, Russia
Daisuke Takahashi	Tsukuba University, Japan
Shangwang Wang	Beijing University of Posts and Telecommunications, China

Local Organizing Committee Chairs

Emre Alptekin	Galatasaray University, Turkey
Gülfem Işıklar Alptekin	Galatasaray University, Turkey
Cengiz Kahraman	İstanbul Technical University, Turkey
A. Çağrı Tolga	Galatasaray University, Turkey
Ayberk Zeytin	Galatasaray University, Turkey

Technology Chair

Damiano Perri — University of Perugia, Italy

Program Committee

Vera Afreixo	University of Aveiro, Portugal
Vladimir Alarcon	Northern Gulf Institute, USA
Filipe Alvelos	University of Minho, Portugal
Debora Anelli	Polytechnic University of Bari, Italy
Hartmut Asche	Hasso-Plattner-Institut für Digital Engineering Ggmbh, Germany
Nizamettin Aydın	İstanbul Technical University, Turkey
Ginevra Balletto	University of Cagliari, Italy
Nadia Balucani	University of Perugia, Italy
Socrates Basbas	Aristotle University of Thessaloniki, Greece
David Berti	ART SpA, Italy
Michela Bertolotto	University College Dublin, Ireland
Sandro Bimonte	CEMAGREF, TSCF, France
Ana Cristina Braga	University of Minho, Portugal
Tiziana Campisi	Kore University of Enna, Italy
Yves Caniou	Université Claude Bernard Lyon 1, France
Alessandra Capolupo	Polytechnic University of Bari, Italy
José A. Cardoso e Cunha	Universidade Nova de Lisboa, Portugal
Rui Cardoso	University of Beira Interior, Portugal
Leocadio G. Casado	University of Almería, Spain
Mete Celik	Erciyes University, Turkey
Maria Cerreta	University of Naples Federico II, Italy
Ta Quang Chieu	Thuyloi University, Vietnam
Rachel Chien-Sing Lee	Sunway University, Malaysia
Birol Ciloglugil	Ege University, Turkey
Mauro Coni	University of Cagliari, Italy

Florbela Maria da Cruz Domingues Correia	Polytechnic Institute of Viana do Castelo, Portugal
Alessandro Costantini	INFN, Italy
Roberto De Lotto	University of Pavia, Italy
Luiza De Macedo Mourelle	State University of Rio De Janeiro, Brazil
Marcelo De Paiva Guimaraes	Federal University of Sao Paulo, Brazil
Frank Devai	London South Bank University, UK
Joana Matos Dias	University of Coimbra, Portugal
Aziz Dursun	Virginia Tech University, USA
Laila El Ghandour	Heriot-Watt University, UK
Rafida M. Elobaid	Canadian University Dubai, United Arab Emirates
Maria Irene Falcao	University of Minho, Portugal
Florbela P. Fernandes	Polytechnic Institute of Bragança, Portugal
Paula Odete Fernandes	Polytechnic Institute of Bragança, Portugal
Adelaide de Fátima Baptista Valente Freitas	University of Aveiro, Portugal
Valentina Franzoni	University of Perugia, Italy
Andreas Fricke	University of Potsdam, Germany
Raffaele Garrisi	Centro Operativo per la Sicurezza Cibernetica, Italy
Ivan Gerace	University of Perugia, Italy
Maria Giaoutzi	National Technical University of Athens, Greece
Salvatore Giuffrida	University of Catania, Italy
Teresa Guarda	Universidad Estatal Peninsula de Santa Elena, Ecuador
Sevin Gümgüm	Izmir University of Economics, Turkey
Malgorzata Hanzl	Technical University of Lodz, Poland
Maulana Adhinugraha Kiki	Telkom University, Indonesia
Clement Ho Cheung Leung	Chinese University of Hong Kong, China
Andrea Lombardi	University of Perugia, Italy
Marcos Mandado Alonso	University of Vigo, Spain
Ernesto Marcheggiani	Katholieke Universiteit Leuven, Belgium
Antonino Marvuglia	Luxembourg Institute of Science and Technology, Luxembourg
Michele Mastroianni	University of Salerno, Italy
Hideo Matsufuru	High Energy Accelerator Research Organization, Japan
Fernando Miranda	Universidade do Minho, Portugal
Giuseppe Modica	University of Reggio Calabria, Italy
Majaz Moonis	University of Massachusetts, USA
Nadia Nedjah	State University of Rio de Janeiro, Brazil
Paolo Nesi	University of Florence, Italy

Suzan Obaiys	University of Malaya, Malaysia
Marcin Paprzycki	Polish Academy of Sciences, Poland
Eric Pardede	La Trobe University, Australia
Ana Isabel Pereira	Polytechnic Institute of Bragança, Portugal
Damiano Perri	University of Perugia, Italy
Massimiliano Petri	University of Pisa, Italy
Telmo Pinto	University of Coimbra, Portugal
Alessandro Plaisant	University of Sassari, Italy
Maurizio Pollino	ENEA, Italy
Alenka Poplin	Iowa State University, USA
Marcos Quiles	Federal University of São Paulo, Brazil
Nguyen Huu Quynh	Thuyloi University, Vietnam
Albert Rimola	Universitat Autònoma de Barcelona, Spain
Humberto Rocha	University of Coimbra, Portugal
Marzio Rosi	University of Perugia, Italy
Lucia Saganeiti	University of L'Aquila, Italy
Francesco Scorza	University of Basilicata, Italy
Marco Paulo Seabra dos Reis	University of Coimbra, Portugal
Jie Shen	University of Michigan, USA
Francesco Tajani	Sapienza University of Rome, Italy
Rodrigo Tapia Mcclung	Centro de Investigación en Ciencias de Información Geoespacial, Mexico
Eufemia Tarantino	Polytechnic University of Bari, Italy
Sergio Tasso	University of Perugia, Italy
Ana Paula Teixeira	Universidade do Minho, Portugal
Yiota Theodora	National Technical University of Athens, Greece
Giuseppe A. Trunfio	University of Sassari, Italy
Toshihiro Uchibayashi	Kyushu University, Japan
Marco Vizzari	University of Perugia, Italy
Frank Westad	Norwegian University of Science and Technology, Norway
Fukuko Yuasa	High Energy Accelerator Research Organization, Japan
Ljiljana Zivkovic	Republic Geodetic Authority, Serbia

Workshops

Workshop on Advancements in Applied Machine-Learning and Data Analytics (AAMDA 2025)

Workshop Organizers
Alessandro Costantini	INFN, Italy
Daniele Cesini	INFN, Italy
Elisabetta Ronchieri	INFN, Italy
Barbara Martelli	INFN, Italy

Workshop Program Committee Members
Alessandro Costantini	Istituto Nazionale di Fisica Nucleare (INFN), Italy
Daniele Cesini	Istituto Nazionale di Fisica Nucleare (INFN), Italy
Elisabetta Ronchieri	Istituto Nazionale di Fisica Nucleare (INFN), Italy
Barbara Martelli	Istituto Nazionale di Fisica Nucleare (INFN), Italy
Luca Dell'Agnello	Istituto Nazionale di Fisica Nucleare (INFN), Italy

Advanced and Innovative Web Apps 2025 (AIWA 2025)

Workshop Organizers
Damiano Perri	University of Perugia, Italy
Osvaldo Gervasi	University of Perugia, Italy
Stelios Kouzeleas	International Hellenic University, Greece
Sergio Tasso	University of Perugia, Italy

Workshop Program Committee Members
David Berti	ART SpA, Italy
JungYoon Kim	Gachon University, South Korea
TaiHoon Kim	Zhejiang University of Science and Technology, China

Advanced Processes of Mathematics and Computing Models in Complex Data-Intensive Computational Systems (AMCM 2025)

Workshop Organizers

Yeliz Karaca	University of Massachusetts Chan Medical School and Massachusetts Institute of Technology, USA
Dumitru Baleanu	Lebanese American University, Lebanon
Osvaldo Gervasi	University of Perugia, Italy
Yudong Zhang	University of Leicester, UK
Majaz Moonis	University of Massachusetts Chan Medical School and Massachusetts Institute of Technology, USA

Workshop Program Committee Members

TaeHoon Kim	Zhejiang University of Science and Technology, China
Martin Bohner	Missouri University of Science and Technology, USA
Shuihua Wang	University of Leicester, UK
Khan Muhammad	Sungkyunkwan University, South Korea
Mahmoud Abdel-Aty	Sohag University, Egypt
Aziz Dursun	Virginia Polytechnic Institute and State University, USA
Kemal Güven Gülen	Namık Kemal University, Turkey
Akif Akgül	Hitit Üniversitesi, Turkey

Advanced Numerical Approaches for Assessment and Design of No-Tension Masonry Structures (ANAMS 2025)

Workshop Organizers

Antonino Iannuzzo	Universitá degli studi del Sannio, Italy
Carlo Olivieri	Universitá Telematica Pegaso, Italy
Andrea Montanino	CIMNE, Spain
Elham Mousavian	University of Edinburgh, UK

Workshop Program Committee Members

Pietro Meriggi	Roma Tre University, Italy
Francesca Perelli	University of Naples Federico II, Italy
Marialuigia Sangirardi	University of Oxford, UK
Sam Cocking	University of Cambridge, UK

Matteo Salvalaggio	University of Minho, Portugal
Vittorio Paris	University of Bergamo, Italy
Luigi Sibille	Norwegian University of Science and Technology, Norway
Natalia Pingaro	Politecnico di Milano, Italy
Martina Buzzetti	Politecnico di Milano, Italy
Generoso Vaiano	Pegaso Telematic University, Italy
Alessandra Capolupo	Politecnico di Bari, Italy
Amal Gerges	Università degli Studi di Cagliari, Italy
Fabian Orozco	National Autonomous University of Mexico, Mexico
Nathanael Savalle	Polytech Clermont and Université Clermont Auvergne, France
Luca Umberto Argiento	University of Naples Federico II, Italy
Bartolomeo Pantó	Durham University, UK

Unveiling the Synergies Between Air Quality and Climate PlAnning (AQCliPA 2025)

Workshop Organizers

Angela Pilogallo	University of L'Aquila, Italy
Luigi Santopietro	University of Basilicata, Italy
Filomena Pietrapertosa	IMAA CNR, Italy
Monica Salvia	IMAA CNR, Italy
Carlo Trozzi	IMAA CNR, Italy
Valeria Scapini	Central University of Chile, Chile

Workshop Program Committee Members

Lucia Saganeiti	IMAA-CNR, Italy
Lorena Fiorini	University of L'Aquila, Italy
Antonio Mazza	IMAA-CNR, Italy
Gabriele Nolè	IMAA-CNR, Italy
Carmen Guida	University of Naples "Federico II", Italy
Floriana Zucaro	University of Naples "Federico II", Italy
Sabrina Lai	University of Cagliari, Italy
Chiara Garau	University of Cagliari, Italy

Advancements in Spatial assessment of Socio-Ecological SystemS (ASSESS 2025)

Workshop Organizers
Daniele Cannatella	TU Delft, The Netherlands
Giuliano Poli	University of Naples Federico II, Italy
Eugenio Muccio	TU Delft, The Netherlands
Claudiu Forgaci	TU Delft, The Netherlands

Workshop Program Committee Members
Daniele Cannatella	TU Delft, The Netherlands
Giuliano Poli	University of Naples Federico II, Italy
Eugenio Muccio	University of Naples Federico II, Italy
Claudiu Forgaci	TU Delft, The Netherlands
Maria Cerreta	University of Naples Federico II, Italy
Maria Somma	University of Naples Federico II, Italy
Laura Di Tommaso	University of Naples Federico II, Italy
Sabrina Sacco	Politecnico di Milano, Italy
Piero Zizzania	University of Naples Federico II, Italy
Gaia Daldanise	CNR IRISS, Italy
Benedetta Grieco	University of Naples Federico II, Italy
Giuseppe Ciciriello	University of Naples Federico II, Italy
Marta Dell'Ovo	Politecnico di Milano, Italy
Francesco Piras	University of Cagliari, Italy
Diana Rolando	Politecnico di Torino, Italy
Stefano Cuntò	University of Naples Federico II, Italy
Ludovica La Rocca	University of Naples Federico II, Italy

Blockchain and Distributed Ledgers: Technologies and Applications (BDLTA 2025)

Workshop Organizers
Vladimir Korkhov	Saint Petersburg State University, Russia
Elena Stankova	Saint Petersburg State University, Russia
Nataliia Kulabukhova	Saint Petersburg State University, Russia

Workshop Program Committee Members
Adam Belloum	University of Amsterdam, the Netherlands
Dmitrii Vasiunin	Deutsche Telekom Cloud Services E.P.E., Greece
Serob Balyan	Osensus Arm LLC, Armenia
Suren Abrahamyan	Osensus Arm LLC, Armenia
Ashot Sergey Gevorkyan	NAS of Armenia, Armenia

Michal Hnatic	Univerzita Pavla Jozefa Šafárika v Košiciach, Slovakia
Michail Panteleyev	Saint Petersburg Electrotecnical University, Russia
Martin Vala	Univerzita Pavla Jozefa Šafárika v Košiciach, Slovakia
Nodir Zaynalov	Tashkent University of Information Technologies named after Muhammad al Khwarizmi, Uzbekistan
Michail Panteleyev	Saint Petersburg Electrotecnical University, Russia
Alexander Degtyarev	Saint Petersburg University, Russia
Alexander Bogdanov	St. Petersburg State University, Russia

Bio and Neuro Inspired Computing and Applications (BIONCA 2025)

Workshop Organizers

Nadia Nedjah	State University of Rio de Janeiro, Brazil
Luiza de Macedo Mourelle	State University of Rio de Janeiro, Brazil

Workshop Program Committee Members

Nadia Nedjha	State University of Rio de Janeiro, Brazil
Luiza de Macedo Mourelle	State University of Rio de Janeiro, Brazil
Luigi Maciel Ribeiro	State University of Rio de Janeiro, Brazil
Joelmir Ramos	Federal University of Rio de Janeiro, Brazil
Rogério Moraes	Brazilian Navy, Brazil
Marcos Santana Farias	Institute of Nuclear Energy, Brazil
Luneque Silva Jr.	Federal University of ABC, Brazil
Alan Oliveira	University of Lisboa, Portugal
Brij Bhooshan Gupta	Asia University, Taiwan

Computational and Applied Mathematics (CAM 2025)

Workshop Organizers

Maria Irene Falcão	University of Minho, Portugal
Fernando Miranda	University of Minho, Portugal

Workshop Program Committee Members

Fernando Miranda	University of Minho, Portugal
Graça Tomaz	Polytechnic of Guarda, Portugal
Helmuth Malonek	University of Aveiro, Portugal

Isabel Cacao	University of Aveiro, Portugal
João Morais	Autonomous Technological Institute of Mexico, Mexico
Lidia Aceto	University of Eastern Piedmont, Italy
Luís Ferrás	University of Porto, Portugal
M. Irene Falcão	University of Minho, Portugal
Patrícia Beites	University of Beira Interior, Portugal
Paulo Amorim	FGV EMAp, Brazil
Regina de Almeida	University of Trás-os-Montes e Alto Douro, Portugal
Ricardo Severino	University of Minho, Portugal

Computational and Applied Statistics (CAS 2025)

Workshop Organizer

Ana Cristina Braga	ALGORITMI Research Centre, LASI, University of Minho, Portugal

Workshop Program Committee Members

Adelaide Freitas	University of Aveiro, Portugal
Andreas Futschik	Johannes Kepler University Linz, Austria
Ana Cristina Braga	University of Minho, Portugal
Ângela Silva	University of Minho, Portugal
Arminda Manuela Gonçalves	University of Minho, Portugal
Carina Silva	Polytechnic Intitute of Lisbon, Portugal
Elisete Correia	University of Trás-os-Montes e Alto Douro, Portugal
Frank Westad	Norwegian University of Science and Technology, Norway
Isabel Natario	New University of Lisbon, Portugal
Irene Oliveira	University of Trás-os-Montes e Alto Douro, Portugal
Ivan Rodriguez Conde	University of Vigo, Spain
Joaquim Gonçalves	Instituto Politécnico do Cávado e do Ave, Portugal
Lino Costa	University of Minho, Portugal
Marco Reis	University of Coimbra, Portugal
Maria Filipa Mourão	Polytechnic Institute of Viana do Castelo, Portugal
Maria João Polidoro	Polytechnic Institute of Porto, Portugal
Martin Perez Perez	University of Vigo, Spain
Michal Abrahamowicz	McGill University, Canada
Vera Afreixo	University of Aveiro, Portugal

Werner G. Müller	Johannes Kepler University Linz, Austria
Bruna Silva Ramos	University Lusiada de Famalicão, Portugal
Inês Sousa	University of Minho, Portugal
Luís Miguel Rocha Matos	University of Minho, Portugal
Manuel Carlos Figueiredo	University of Minho, Portugal

Cyber Intelligence and Applications (CIA 2025)

Workshop Organizer

Gianni D'Angelo	University of Salerno, Italy

Workshop Program Committee Members

Gianni D'Angelo	University of Salerno, Italy
Francesco Palmieri	University of Salerno, Italy
Massimo Ficco	University of Salerno, Italy
Arcangelo Castiglione	University of Salerno, Italy

Computational Methods for Business Analytics (CMBA 2025)

Workshop Organizers

Cláudio Alves	Universidade do Minho, Portugal
Telmo Pinto	Universidade do Minho, Portugal

Workshop Program Committee Members

Abdulrahim Shamayleh	American University of Sharjah, United Arab Emirates
Ana Rocha	University of Minho, Portugal
Angelo Sifaleras	University of Macedonia, Greece
Cristóvão Silva	University of Coimbra, Portugal
José Valério de Carvalho	University of Minho, Portugal
Miguel Vieira	Universidade Lusófona, Portugal
Rita Macedo	Université de Lille, France
Ana Moura	Universidade de Aveiro, Portugal
Cristina Lopes	ISCAP, Portugal
Eliana Costa e Silva	Instituto Politécnico do Porto, Portugal

Computational Methods, Statistics and Industrial Mathematics (CMSIM 2025)

Workshop Organizers

Maria Filomena Teodoro	IST ID, Instituto Superior Técnico, Portugal
Marina Alexandra Pedro Andrade	ISCTE – Lisbon University Institute, Portugal
Paula Simões	University of Lisbon, Portugal
Teresa A. Oliveira	IST ID, Instituto Superior Técnico, Portugal

Workshop Program Committee Members

Amilcar Oliveira	Universidade Aberta and Universidade de Lisboa, Portugal
Victor Lobo	Escola Naval and NOVA IMS Almada, Portugal
António Pacheco	IST Universidade de Lisboa, Portugal
Eliana Costa	Escola Superior de Tecnologia e Gestão IPPorto, Portugal
Aldina Correia	Escola Superior de Tecnologia e Gestão IPPorto, Portugal
Fernando Carapau	University of Évora, Portugal
Ricardo Moura	Portuguese Naval Academy, Portugal
Ana Borges	Escola Superior de Tecnologia e Gestão IPPorto, Portugal
Cristina Lopes	ISCAP IPPorto, Portugal
Fernanda Costa	University of Minho, Portugal
Cabrita Carlos	IPBeja, Portugal
Maria Luísa Morgado	University of Trás os Montes e Alto Douro and University of Lisboa, Portugal
Rosário Ramos	Universidade Aberta, Portugal
Sofia Rézio	Iscal, Instituto Politécnico de Lisboa, Portugal
Matteo Sacchet	University of Turin, Italy
Marina Marchisio Conte	University of Turin, Italy
António Seijas-Macias	University of Coruña, Spain
Luís F. A. Teodoro	University of Glasgow, UK and University of Oslo, Norway
Christos Kitsos	University of West Attica, Greece
M. Filomena Teodoro	Universidade de Lisboa, Portugal
Marina A. P. Andrade	Instituto Universitário de Lisboa, Portugal
Paula Simões	Military Academy and Universidade Nova de Lisboa, Portugal
Teresa Oliveira	Universidade Aberta and Universidade de Lisboa, Portugal

Computational Optimization and Applications (COA 2025)

Workshop Organizers

Ana Rocha	ALGORITMI Research Centre, LASI, University of Minho, Portugal, Portugal
Humberto Rocha	ALGORITMI Research Centre, LASI, University of Minho, Portugal, Portugal

Workshop Program Committee Members

Florbela Fernandes	Polytechnic Institute of Bragança, Portugal
Clara Vaz	Polytechnic Institute of Bragança, Portugal
Ana Pereira	Polytechnic Institute of Bragança, Portugal
Filipe Alvelos	University of Minho, Portugal
Joana Dias	University of Coimbra, Portugal
Eligius M. T. Hendrix	University of Málaga, Spain
Emerson José de Paiva	Federal University of Itajubá, Brazil
Ana Paula Teixeira	University of Trás-os-Montes and Alto Douro, Portugal
Lino Costa	Universidade do Minho, Portugal

Coastal Cities Versus Inland Areas. Hypotheses for Sustainable Regeneration Through Ecosystem Services of 'Hooking' and Rehabilitation of Brownfield Sites (CoastalCities_VS_InlandAreas 2025)

Workshop Organizers

Celestina Fazia	Università di Enna Kore, Italy
Angrilli Massimo	University of Chieti-Pescara, Italy
Valentina Ciuffreda	University of Chieti-Pescara, Italy
Maurizio Oddo	Università di Enna Kore, Italy
Marcello Sestito	Università di Enna Kore, Italy
Clara Stella Vicari Aversa	University of Reggio Calabria, Italy

Workshop Program Committee Members

Alessandro Camiz	Università d'Annunzio, Italy
Thowayeb Hassan	King Faisal University, Saudi Arabia
Alessandro Barracco	Università Kore di Enna, Italy
Mario Morrica	University of Urbino, Italy
Mariana Ratiu	University of Oradea, Romania
Alanda Akamana	Mohammed VI Polytechnic University, Morocco
Kaoutare Amini Alaoui	Mohammed VI Polytechnic University, Morocco

Computational Astrochemistry 2025 (CompAstro 2025)

Workshop Organizers

Marzio Rosi	University of Perugia, Italy
Daniela Ascenzi	University of Trento, Italy
Nadia Balucani	University of Perugia, Italy
Stefano Falcinelli	University of Perugia, Italy

Workshop Program Committee Members

Dario Campisi	Università degli Studi di Perugia, Italy
Giacomo Giorgi	Università degli Studi di Perugia, Italy
Andrea Giustini	Università degli Studi di Perugia, Italy
Luca Mancini	Università degli Studi di Perugia, Italy
Albert Rimola	Universitat Autònoma de Barcelona, Spain
Gianmarco Vanuzzo	Università degli Studi di Perugia, Italy
Dimitrios Skouteris	Master-Tec, Italy
Piero Ugliengo	Università degli Studi di Torino, Italy
Franco Vecchiocattivi	Università degli Sudi di Perugia, Italy
Giacomo Pannacci	Università degli Studi di Perugia, Italy
Costanza Borghesi	Università degli Studi di Perugia, Italy
Marco Parriani	Università degli Studi di Perugia, Italy
Marta Loletti	Università degli Studi di Perugia, Italy
Fernando Pirani	Università degli Studi di Perugia, Italy
Andrea Lombardi	Università degli Studi di Perugia, Italy
Noelia Faginas Lago	Università degli Studi di Perugia, Italy
Paolo Tosi	Università di Trento, Italy
Cecilia Coletti	Università degli Studi Chieti-Pescara, Italy
Nazzareno Re	Università degli Studi Chieti-Pescara, Italy
Linda Podio	Osservatorio Astrofisico di Arcetri INAF, Italy
Claudio Codella	Osservatorio Astrofisico di Arcetri INAF, Italy
Gabriella Di Genova	Università degli Studi di Perugia, Italy

Computational Methods for Porous Geomaterials (CompPor 2025)

Workshop Organizers

Vadim Lisitsa	IPGG SB RAS, Russia
Evgeniy Romenski	IPGG SB RAS, Russia

Workshop Program Committee Members

Vadim Lisitsa	Institute of Petroleum Geology and Geophysics SB RAS, Russia
Evgeniy Romenski	Sobolev Institute of Mathematics SB RAS, Russia
Vladimir Cheverda	Sobolev Institute of Mathematics SB RAS, Russia
Tatyana Khachkova	IPGG SB RAS, Russia
Dmitry Prokhorov	IPGG SB RAS, Russia
Mikhail Novikov	Sobolev Institute of Mathematics SB RAS, Russia
Sergey Solovyev	Sobolev Institute of Mathematics SB RAS, Russia
Kirill Gadylshin	LLC RNBashNIPIneft, Russia
Olga Stoyanovskaya	Lavrentev Institute of Hydrodynamics SB RAS, Russia
Yerlan Amanbek	Nazarbaev University, Kazakstan

Workshop on Computational Science and HPC (CSHPC 2025)

Workshop Organizers

Elise de Doncker	Western Michigan University, USA
Hideo Matsufuru	High Energy Accelerator Research Organization, Japan

Workshop Program Committee Members

Elise de Doncker	Western Michigan University, USA
Hideo Matsufuru	High Energy Accelerator Research Organization (KEK), Japan
Fukuko Yuasa	KEK, Japan
Issaku Kanamori	RIKEN, Japan
Hiroshi Daisaka	Hitotsubashi University, Japan
Norikazu Yamada	KEK, Japan
Naohito Nakasato	University of Aizu, Japan
Robert Makin	Western Michigan University, USA

Cities, Technologies and Planning 2025 (CTP 2025)

Workshop Organizers

Giuseppe Borruso	University of Trieste, Italy
Beniamino Murgante	University of Basilicata, Italy
Malgorzata Hanzl	Lodz University of Technology, Poland
Anastasia Stratigea	National Technical University of Athens, Greece
Ljiljana Zivkovic	Republic Geodetic Authority, Serbia
Ginevra Balletto	University of Trieste, Italy

Workshop Program Committee Members

Giuseppe Borruso	University of Trieste, Italy
Beniamino Murgante	University of Basilicata, Italy
Malgorzata Hanzl	Lodz University of Technology, Poland
Anastasia Stratigea	National Technical University of Athens, Greece
Ljiljiana Zivkovic	Republic Geodetic Authority of Serbia, Serbia
Ginevra Balletto	University of Cagliari, Italy
Silvia Battino	University of Sassari, Italy
Mara Ladu	University of Cagliari, Italy
Maria del Mar Munoz Leonisio	University of Cádiz, Spain
Ahinoa Amaro Garcia	University of Las Palmas of Gran Canaria, Spain
Maria Attard	University of Malta, Malta
Enrico D'agostini	World Maritime University, Sweden
Francesca Krasna	University of Trieste, Italy
Brisol Garcia Garcia	Polytechnic University of Quintana Roo, Mexico
Tu Anh Trinh	UEH University, Vietnam
Giovanni Mauro	Università degli Studi della Campania, Italy
Maria Ronza	University of Naples Federico II, Italy
Massimiliano Bencardino	University of Salerno, Italy
Tomasz Bradecki	Silesian University of Technology, Poland
Dorota Kamrowska-Załuska	Gdańsk University of Technology, Poland
Iwona Jażdżewska	University of Lodz, Poland
Yiota Theodora	National Technical University of Athens, Greece
Apostolos Lagarias	University of Thessaly, Greece
George Tsilimigkas	University of the Aegean, Greece
Akrivi Leka	National Technical University of Athens, Greece
Maria Panagiotopoulou	National Technical University of Athens, Greece
Andrea Gallo	Ca' Foscari University of Venice, Italy
Francesca Sinatra	University of Trieste, Italy

Digital Transition: Effects on Housing Mobility, Market, Land Governance (DIGITRANS 2025)

Workshop Organizers

Fabrizio Battisti	University of Florence, Italy
Fabiana Forte	University of Campania, Italy
Orazio Campo	Sapienza University of Rome, Italy
Alessio Pino	Kore University of Enna, Italy
Carlo Pisano	University of Florence, Italy
Mariolina Grasso	Kore University of Enna, Italy

Workshop Program Committee Members

Fabrizio Battisti	University of Florence, Italy
Fabiana Forte	Università della Campania Luigi Vanvitelli, Italy
Orazio Campo	University of Rome "La Sapienza", Italy
Alessio Pino	Kore University of Enna, Italy
Carlo Pisano	University of Florence, Italy
Mariolina Grasso	Università Kore di Enna, Italy

Evaluating Inner Areas Potentials (EIAP 2025)

Workshop Organizers

Diana Rolando	Politecnico di Torino, Italy
Alice Barreca	Politecnico di Torino, Italy
Manuela Rebaudengo	Politecnico di Torino, Italy
Giorgia Malavasi	Politecnico di Torino, Italy

Workshop Program Committee Members

John Accordino	Virginia Commonwealth University, USA
Francesco Bruzzone	Università Iuav di Venezia, Italy
Maria Cerreta	Università degli Studi di Napoli Federico II, Italy
Maddalena Chimisso	Università degli Studi del Molise, Italy
Chiara Chioni	Università degli Studi di Trento, Italy
Annalisa Contato	Università degli Studi di Palermo, Italy
Cristina Coscia	Politecnico di Torino, Italy
Marta Dell'Ovo	Politecnico di Milano, Italy
Benedetta Di Leo	Università Politecnica delle Marche, Italy
Sara Favargiotti	Università degli Studi di Trento, Italy
Maddalena Ferretti	Università Politecnica delle Marche, Italy
Salvo Giuffrida	Università degli Studi di Palermo, Italy
Barbara Lino	Università degli Studi di Palermo, Italy
Umberto Mecca	Politecnico di Torino, Italy
Beatrice Mecca	Politecnico di Torino, Italy
Giuliano Poli	Università degli Studi di Napoli Federico II, Italy
Marco Rossitti	Politecnico di Milano, Italy
Alexandra Stankulova	Politecnico di Torino, Italy
Elena Todella	Politecnico di Torino, Italy
Asja Aulisio	Politecnico di Torino, Italy
Giulia Datola	Politecnico di Milano, Italy

Francesco Calabrò	Università degli Studi Mediterranea di Reggio Calabria, Italy
Valeria Saiu	Università degli Studi di Cagliari, Italy
Maria Rosa Trovato	Università di Catania, Italy

Econometric and Multidimensional Evaluation in Urban Environment (EMEUE 2025)

Workshop Organizers

Maria Cerreta	University of Naples Federico II, Italy
Carmelo Maria Torre	Polytechnic University of Bari, Italy
Pierluigi Morano	Polytechnic University of Bari, Italy
Simona Panaro	University of Naples Federico II, Italy
Felicia Di Liddo	University of Naples Federico II, Italy
Debora Anelli	University of Naples Federico II, Italy

Workshop Program Committee Members

Carmelo Maria Torre	Polytechnic University of Bari, Italy
Maria Cerreta	University of Naples Federico II, Italy
Pierluigi Morano	Polytechnic University of Bari, Italy
Francesco Tajani	Sapienza University of Rome, Italy
Simona Panaro	University of Naples Federico II, Italy
Felicia di Liddo	Polytechnic University of Bari, Italy
Debora Anelli	Sapienza University of Rome, Italy
Giuliano Poli	University of Naples Federico II, Italy
Maria Somma	University of Naples Federico II, Italy
Simona Panaro	University of Campania Luigi Vanvitelli, Italy
Laura Di Tommaso	University of Naples Federico II, Italy
Caterina Loffredo	University of Naples Federico II, Italy
Ludovica La Rocca	University of Naples Federico II, Italy
Sabrina Sacco	Politecnico di Milano, Italy
Piero Zizzania	University of Naples Federico II, Italy
Gaia Daldanise	CNR IRISS, Italy
Benedetta Grieco	University of Naples Federico II, Italy
Giuseppe Ciciriello	University of Naples Federico II, Italy
Marta Dell'Ovo	Politecnico di Milano, Italy
Daniele Cannatella	TU Delft University, The Netherlands
Eugenio Muccio	University of Naples Federico II, Italy
Sveva Ventre	University of Naples Federico II, Italy

Governance of Energy Transition: Environmental, Landscape, Social and Spatial Planning (ENERGY_PLANNING 2025)

Workshop Organizers

Mara Ladu	University of Cagliari, Italy
Ginevra Balletto	University of Cagliari, Italy
Emilio Ghiani	University of Cagliari, Italy
Alessandra Marra	University of Salerno, Italy
Roberto De Lotto	University of Pavia, Italy
Balázs Kulcsár	Chalmers University of Technology, Sweden

Workshop Program Committee Members

Riccardo Trevisan	University of Cagliari, Italy
Marco Naseddu	University of Cagliari, Italy
Giuseppe Borruso	University of Trieste, Italy
Andrea Gallo	University of Trieste, Italy
Francesca Sinatra	University of Trieste, Italy
Maria Attard	University of Malta, Malta
Tu Anh Trinh	UEH University Ho Chi Minh City, Vietnam
Marcello Tadini	University of Eastern Piedmont, Italy
Luigi Mundula	University for Foreigners of Perugia, Italy
Silvia Battino	University of Sassari, Italy
Maria del Mar Munoz Leonisio	University of Cádiz, Spain
Anna Richiedei	University of Brescia, Italy
Michele Pezzagno	University of Brescia, Italy
Federico Mertellozzo	University of Firenze, Italy
Marco Mazzarino	IUAV University Venice, Italy

Ecosystem Services in Spatial Planning for Climate Neutral Urban and Rural Areas (ESSP 2025)

Workshop Organizers

Sabrina Lai	University of Cagliari, Italy
Francesco Scorza	University of Basilicata, Italy
Corrado Zoppi	University of Cagliari, Italy
Beniamino Murgante	University of Basilicata, Italy
Carmela Gargiulo	University of Naples Federico II, Italy
Floriana Zucaro	University of Naples Federico II, Italy

Workshop Program Committee Members

Alfonso Annunziata	University of Basilicata, Italy
Ginevra Balletto	University of Cagliari, Italy
Ivan Blečić	University of Cagliari, Italy
Giuseppe Borruso	University of Trieste, Italy
Barbara Caselli	University of Parma, Italy
Maria Cerreta	University of Naples Federico II, Italy
Chiara Garau	University of Cagliari, Italy
Carmen Guida	University of Naples Federico II, Italy
Federica Isola	University of Cagliari, Italy
Francesca Leccis	University of Cagliari, Italy
Federica Leone	University of Cagliari, Italy
Silvia Rossetti	University of Parma, Italy
Luigi Santopietro	University of Basilicata, Italy
Carmelo Torre	Polytechnic of Bari, Italy

The 15th International Workshop on Future Information System Technologies and Applications (FiSTA 2025)

Workshop Organizers

Bernady O. Apduhan	Kyushu Sangyo University, Japan
Rafael Santos	Brazilian National Institute for Space Research, Brazil

Workshop Program Committee Members

Agustinus Borgy Waluyo	Monash University, Australia
Andre Ricardo Abed Grégio	Federal University of Paraná, Brazil
Eric Pardede	La Trobe University, Australia
Kai Cheng	Kyushu Sangyo University, Japan
Ching-Hsien Hsu	Asia University, Taiwan
Fenghui Yao	Tennessee State University, USA
Yusuke Gotoh	Okayama University, Japan
Alvaro Fazenda	Federal University of São Paulo, Brazil
Kazuaki Tanaka	Kyushu Institute of Technology, Japan
Tengku Adil	MARA Technological University, Malaysia
Toshihiro Yamauchi	Okayama University, Japan
Yasuaki Sumida	Kyushu Sangyo University, Japan
Earl Ryan Aleluya	MSU-Iligan Institute of Technology, Philippines
Cherry Mae G. Villame	MSU-Iligan Institute of Technology, Philippines
Anton Louise De Ocampo	Batangas State University, Philippines
Krishnamoorthy Ranganthan	Chennai Institute of Technology, India

Flow Management in Urban Contexts (FMUC 2025)

Workshop Organizers
Alessio Pino	Kore University of Enna, Italy
Giovanna Acampa	Kore University of Enna, Italy

Workshop Program Committee Members
Giovanna Acampa	University of Florence, Italy
Alessio Pino	Kore University of Enna, Italy
Mariolina Grasso	Università Kore di Enna, Italy
Fabrizio Battisti	University of Florence, Italy
Fabrizio Finucci	Roma Tre University, Italy
Antonella G. Masanotti	Roma Tre University, Italy
Daniele Mazzoni	Roma Tre University, Italy

Geographical Analysis, Urban Modeling, Spatial Statistics 2025 (Geog-And-Mod 2025)

Workshop Organizers
Beniamino Murgante	University of Basilicata, Italy
Giuseppe Borruso	University of Trieste, Italy
Hartmut Asche	University of Potsdam, Germany
Rodrigo Tapia McClung	CentroGeo, Mexico
Andreas Fricke	University of Potsdam, Germany

Workshop Program Committee Members
Giuseppe Borruso	University of Trieste, Italy
Beniamino Murgante	University of Basilicata, Italy
Hartmut Asche	University of Potsdam, Germany
Rodrigo Tapia-McClung	Centro de Investigación en Ciencias de Información Geoespacial (CentroGeo), Mexico
Andreas Fricke	University of Potsdam, Germany
Malgorzata Hanzl	Lodz University of Technology, Poland
Anastasia Stratigea	National Technical University of Athens, Greece
Ljiljiana Zivkovic	Republic Geodetic Authority of Serbia, Serbia
Ginevra Balletto	University of Cagliari, Italy
Silvia Battino	University of Sassari, Italy
Mara Ladu	University of Cagliari, Italy
Maria del Mar Munoz Leonisio	University of Cádiz, Spain
Ahinoa Amaro Garcia	University of Las Palmas of Gran Canaria, Spain
Maria Attard	University of Malta, Malta

Enrico D'agostini	World Maritime University, Sweden
Francesca Krasna	University of Trieste, Italy
Brisol García García	Polytechnic University of Quintana Roo, Mexico
Tu Anh Trinh	UEH University, Vietnam
Giovanni Mauro	Università degli Studi della Campania, Italy
Maria Ronza	University of Naples Federico II, Italy
Massimiliano Bencardino	University of Salerno, Italy
Andrea Gallo	Ca' Foscari University of Venice, Italy
Francesca Sinatra	University of Trieste, Italy
Salvatore Dore	University of Trieste, Italy

Geogames for Sustainable Development (Geogames 2025)

Workshop Organizer

Alenka Poplin	Iowa State University, USA

Workshop Program Committee Members

Alenka Poplin	Iowa State University, USA
Bruno Amaral de Andrade	Portucalense University, Portugal
Brian Tomaszewski	Rochester Institute of Technology, USA
Deepak Marhatta	Tribhuvan University, Nepal
Alessandro Plaisant	University of Sassari, Italy
David Schwartz	Rochester Institute of Technology, USA
Silvia Rossetti	University of Parma, Italy
Floriana Zucaro	University of Naples Federico II, Italy
Alfonso Annunziata	University of Basilicata, Italy
Reza Askarizad	University of Cagliari, Italy
Chiara Garau	University of Cagliari, Italy
Tanja Congiu	University of Sassari, Italy

Geomatics for Resource Monitoring and Management (GRMM 2025)

Workshop Organizers

Alberico Sonnessa	Politecnico di Bari, Italy
Eufemia Tarantino	Politecnico di Bari, Italy
Alessandra Capolupo	Politecnico di Bari, Italy

Workshop Program Committee Members

Umberto Fratino	Politecnico di Bari, Italy
Valeria Monno	Politecnico di Bari, Italy

Antonino Maltese	Università degli studi di Palermo, Italy
Athos Agapiou	Cyprus University of Technology, Cyprus
Michele Mangiameli	Università di Catania, Italy
Angela Gorgoglione	Universidad de la República de Uruguay, Uruguay
Roberta Ravanelli	University of Liège, Belgium
Ester Scotto di Perta	Università degli studi di Napoli Federico II, Italy
Giacomo Caporusso	CNR, Italy
Andrea Montanino	International Centre for Numerical Methods in Engineering of Barcelona, Spain
Antonino Iannuzzo	Università degli studi del Sannio, Italy
Alessandro Pagano	Politecnico di Bari, Italy
Francesco Di Capua	Università degli Studi della Basilicata, Italy
Albertini Cinzia	CNR-IREA, Italy
Alessandra Saponieri	Università degli studi del Salento, Italy
PierFrancesco Recchi	Università degli studi di Napoli Federico II, Italy
Vincenzo Totaro	Politecnico di Bari, Italy
Stefania Santoro	CNR Water Research Institute, Italy
Francesco Bimbo	University of Foggia, Italy
Cristina Proietti	Istituto Nazionale di Geofisica e Vulcanologia, Italy
Carla Cavallo	University of Salerno, Italy
Gaetano Falcone	Università degli Studi di Napoli Federico II, Italy
Valeria Belloni	Sapienza University of Rome, Italy
Alessandra Mascitelli	University of Chieti-Pescara, Italy

HERitage and CLIMAte neutrality. Resilient approach for nature centered/based sustainable cities (HERCLIMA 2025)

Workshop Organizers

Celestina Fazia	Università di Enna Kore, Italy
Angrilli Massimo	University of Chieti-Pescara, Italy
Clara Stella Vicari Aversa	University of Reggio Calabria, Italy
Dorina Camelia Ilies	University of Oradea, Romania
Mariana Ratiu	University of Oradea, Romania

Workshop Program Committee Members

Alessandro Camiz	Università d'Annunzio, Italy
Mario Morrica	University of Urbino, Italy
Thowayeb Hassan	King Faisal University, Saudi Arabia
Alessandro Barracco	Università Kore di Enna, Italy
Kaoutare Amini Alaoui	Mohammed VI Polytechnic University (UM6P), Morocco

Mariana Ratiu University of Oradea, Romania
Valentina Ciuffreda Università Chieti-Pescara, Italy

International Workshop on Information and Knowledge in the Internet of Things (IKIT 2025)

Workshop Organizers

Teresa Guarda	Universidad Estatal Península de Santa Elena, Ecuador
Luis Enrique Chuquimarca Jimenez	Universidad Estatal Península de Santa Elena, Ecuador
Gustavo Gatica	Universidad Andrés Bello, Chile
Filipe Mota Pinto	Polytechnic Institute of Leiria, Portugal
Arnulfo Alanis	Instituto Tecnológico de Tijuana, Mexico
Luis Mazon	Universidad Estatal Península de Santa Elena, Spain

Workshop Program Committee Members

Arnulfo Alanis	Instituto Tecnológico de Tijuana, Mexico
Bruno Sousa	University of Coimbra, Portugal
Carlos Balsa	Instituto Politécnico de Bragança, Portugal
Filipe Mota Pinto	Instituto Politécnico de Leiria, Portugal
Gustavo Gatica	Universidad Andrés Bello, Chile
Isabel Lopes	Instituto Politécnico de Bragança, Portugal
José-María Díaz-Nafría	Universidad a Distancia, Spain
Maria Fernanda Augusto	BiTrum Research Group, Spain
Maria Isabel Ribeiro	Instituto Politécnico Bragança, Portugal
Modestos Stavrakis	University of the Aegean, Greece
Simone Belli	Universidad Complutense de Madrid, Spain
Walter Lopes Neto	Instituto Federal de Educação, Brazil

International Workshop on territorial Planning to integrate Risk prevention and urban Ontologies (IWPRO 2025)

Workshop Organizers

Beniamino Murgante	University of Basilicata, Italy
Roberto De Lotto	University of Pavia, Italy
Elisabetta Maria Venco	University of Pavia, Italy
Caterina Pietra	University of Pavia, Italy

Workshop Program Committee Members

Stefano Borgo	Consiglio Nazionale delle Ricerche ISTC, Italy
Valentina Costa	Università di Genova, Italy
Hamid Danesh Pajouh	Middle East Technical University, Turkey
Ilaria Delponte	Università di Genova, Italy
Lorena Fiorini	Università de L'Aquila, Italy
Veronica Gazzola	Politecnico di Milano, Italy
Ghazaleh Goodarzi	Islamic Azad University, Iran
Michele Grimaldi	Università degli Studi di Salerno, Italy
Alessandra Marra	Università degli Studi di Salerno, Italy
Naghmeh Mohammadpourlima	Åbo Akademi University, Finland
Francesca Pirlone	Università di Genova, Italy
Silvia Rossetti	Università di Parma, Italy
Bahareh Shahsavari	University of Minnesota, USA
Ilenia Spadaro	Università di Genova, Italy
Maria Rosaria Stufano Melone	Politecnico di Bari, Italy

Regional Connectivity, Spatial Accessibility and MaaS for Social Inclusion (MaaS 2025)

Workshop Organizers

Mara Ladu	University of Cagliari, Italy
Ginevra Balletto	University of Cagliari, Italy
Gianfranco Fancello	University of Cagliari, Italy
Tanja Congiu	University of Sassari, Italy
Patrizia Serra	University of Cagliari, Italy
Francesco Piras	University of Cagliari, Italy

Workshop Program Committee Members

Marco Naseddu	University of Cagliari, Italy
Italo Meloni	University of Cagliari, Italy
Giuseppe Borruso	University of Trieste, Italy
Andrea Gallo	University of Trieste, Italy
Francesca Sinatra	University of Trieste, Italy
Maria Attard	University of Malta, Malta
Tu Anh Trinh	UEH University, Vietnam
Marcello Tadini	University of Eastern Piedmont, Italy
Luigi Mundula	University for Foreigners of Perugia, Italy
Silvia Battino	University of Sassari, Italy
Brunella Brundu	University of Sassari, Italy
Veronica Camerada	University of Sassari, Italy

Maria del Mar Munoz Leonisio	University of Cádiz, Spain
Anna Richiedei	University of Brescia, Italy
Michele Pezzagno	University of Brescia, Italy
Marco Mazzarino	IUAV University Venice, Italy

The Development of Urban Mobility Management, Road Safety and Risk Assessment (MANTAIN 2025)

Workshop Organizers

Antonio Russo	Università degli Studi di Enna, Italy
Corrado Rindone	University of Reggio Calabria, Italy
Antonio Polimeni	University of Messina, Italy
Florin Rusca	Politehnica University of Bucharest, Romania
Grigorios Fountas	Aristotle University of Thessaloniki, Greece
Antonio Comi	University of Rome Tor Vergata, Italy

Workshop Program Committee Members

Massimo Di Gangi	University of Messina, Italy
Orlando Marco Belcore	University of Messina, Italy
Antonio Polimeni	University of Messina, Italy
Socrates Basbas	Aristotle University of Thessaloniki, Greece
Claudia Caballini	Polytechnic of Torino, Italy
Efstathios Bouhouras	Aristotle University of Thessaloniki, Greece
Stefano Ricci	Sapienza University of Rome, Italy
Marina Zanne	University of Lubljana, Slovenia
Kh Md Nahiduzzaman	Mohammed VI Polytechnic University, Morocco
Alexsandra Deluka Tibljaš	University of Rijeka, Croatia
Guilhermina Torrao	Aston University, UK

Multidimensional Evolutionary Evaluations for Transformative Approaches (MEETA 2025)

Workshop Organizers

Maria Cerreta	University of Naples Federico II, Italy
Giuliano Poli	University of Naples Federico II, Italy
Maria Somma	University of Naples Federico II, Italy
Gaia Daldanise	CNR IRISS, Italy
Ludovica La Rocca	University of Naples Federico II, Italy

Workshop Program Committee Members

Maria Cerreta	University of Naples Federico II, Italy
Giuliano Poli	University of Naples Federico II, Italy
Maria Somma	University of Naples Federico II, Italy
Laura Di Tommaso	University of Naples Federico II, Italy
Sabrina Sacco	Politecnico di Milano, Italy
Piero Zizzania	University of Naples Federico II, Italy
Gaia Daldanise	CNR IRISS, Italy
Benedetta Grieco	University of Naples Federico II, Italy
Giuseppe Ciciriello	University of Naples Federico II, Italy
Marta Dell'Ovo	Politecnico di Milano, Italy
Daniele Cannatella	TU Delft, The Netherlands
Eugenio Muccio	University of Naples Federico II, Italy
Francesco Piras	University of Cagliari, Italy
Diana Rolando	Politecnico di Torino, Italy
Sveva Ventre	University of Naples Federico II, Italy
Caterina Loffredo	University of Naples Federico II, Italy
Ludovica La Rocca	University of Naples Federico II, Italy
Simona Panaro	University of Campania Luigi Vanvitelli, Italy

Building Multi-dimensional Models for Assessing Complex Environmental Systems (MES 2025)

Workshop Organizers

Vanessa Assumma	University of Bologna, Italy
Caterina Caprioli	Politecnico di Torino, Italy
Giulia Datola	Politecnico di Milano, Italy
Federico Dell'Anna	University of Bologna, Italy
Marta Dell'Ovo	Politecnico di Milano, Italy
Marco Rossitti	Politecnico di Milano, Italy

Workshop Program Committee Members

Vanessa Assumma	Università di Bologna, Bologna
Caterina Caprioli	Politecnico di Torino, Italy
Giulia Datola	DAStU Politecnico di Milano, Italy
Federico Dell'Anna	Politecnico di Torino, Italy
Marta Dell'Ovo	Politecnico di Milano, Italy
Marco Rossitti	Politecnico di Milano, Italy
Francesca Torrieri	Politecnico di Milano, Italy
Mariarosaria Angrisano	Università Telematica Pegaso, Italy
Maksims Feofilovs	Riga Technical University, Latvia

Danny Caprini	Politecnico di Milano, Italy
Giulio Cavana	Politecnico di Torino, Italy
Sebastiano Barbieri	Politecnico di Torino, Italy
Marta Bottero	Politecnico di Torino, Italy
Francesco Cosentino	Politecnico di Milano, Italy
Silvia Ronchi	Politecnico di Milano, Italy
Chiara Mazzarella	TU Delft, Netherlands
Marco Volpatti	Politecnico di Torino, Italy
Chiara D'Alpaos	Università degli Studi di Padova, Italy
Alessandra Oppio	Politecnico di Milano, Italy
Alessia Crisopulli	Politecnico di Milano, Italy
Domenico D'Uva	Politecnico di Milano, Italy
Giorgia Malavasi	Politecnico di Torino, Italy
Rubina Canesi	Università degli Studi di Padova, Italy
Elena Todella	Politecnico di Torino, Italy
Beatrice Mecca	Politecnico di Torino, Italy
Giulia Marzani	University of Bologna, Italy
Isabella Giovanetti	University of Bologna, Italy
Lucia Petronio	University of Bologna, Italy
Franco Corti	University of Padova, Italy
Salvatore De Pascalis	Politecnico di Milano, Italy
Valeria Vitulano	Politecnico di Torino, Italy
Lorenzo Diana	Università degli studi di Napoli Federico II, Italy
Maksims Feofilovs	Riga Technical University, Latvia
Marco De Luca	Politecnico di Torino, Italy
Ilaria Cazzola	Politecnico di Torino, Italy
Andrea De Toni	Politecnico di Milano, Italy
Eugenio Muccio	University of Naples Federico II, Italy
Giuliano Poli	University of Naples Federico II, Italy
Francesco Sica	University "La Sapienza" of Rome, Italy
Elena Di Pirro	Università degli Studi del Molise, Italy
Riccardo Alba	Università di Torino, Italy
Irene Regaiolo	Università di Torino, Italy
Francesca Cochis	Università di Torino, Italy

Modelling Liveable Cities: Techniques, Methods, Challenges, and Perspectives Behind the 'X-Minute' City (MLC 2025)

Workshop Organizers

Federico Mara	University of Pisa, Italy
Valerio Cutini	University of Pisa, Italy
Alessandro Araldi	Université Côte d'Azur, France

Flávia Lopes — Chalmers University of Technology, Sweden
Giovanni Fusco — Université Côte d'Azur, France

Workshop Program Committee Members

Simone Rusci — University of Pisa, Italy
Lorena Fiorini — University of L'Aquila, Italy
Chiara Di Dato — University of L'Aquila, Italy
Francesco Zullo — University of L'Aquila, Italy
Alfonso Annunziata — University of Basilicata, Italy
Beniamino Murgante — University of Basilicata, Italy
Alessandro Araldi — Universitè Côte d'Azur, France
Chiara Garau — University of Cagliari, Italy
Giampiero Lombardini — Università di Genova, Italy
Flavia Lopes — Chalmers University of Technology, Sweden
Giovanni Fusco — Universitè Côte d'Azur, France

Mathematical Methods for Image Processing and Understanding 2025 (MMIPU 2025)

Workshop Organizers

Ivan Gerace — Università degli Studi di Perugia, Italy
Gianluca Vinti — Università degli Studi di Perugia, Italy
Arianna Travaglini — Università degli Studi della Basilicata, Italy

Workshop Program Committee Members

Ivan Gerace — University of Perugia, Italy
Gianluca Vinti — University of Perugia, Italy
Arianna Travaglini — University of Basilicata, Italy
Marco Baioletti — University of Perugia, Italy
Marco Donatelli — University of Insubria, Italy
Anna Tonazzini — C.N.R. Pisa, Italy
Muhammad Hanif — Ghulam Ishaq Khan Institute of Engineering Sciences and Technology, Pakistan
Francesco Marchetti — University of Padua, Italy
Wolfgang Erb — University of Padua, Italy
Danilo Costarelli — University of Perugia, Italy
Francesco Santini — University of Perugia, Italy
Valentina Giorgetti — University of Perugia, Italy

Mobility Opportunities Bridging Inequalities: Social Inclusion and Gender Equity Initiatives Strategies Against Fragmentation and Complexity of Mobility (MOBIL-EGI 2025)

Workshop Organizers

Tiziana Campisi	University of Enna Kore, Italy
Guilhermina Torrao	Aston University, UK
Socrates Basbas	Aristotle University of Thessaloniki, Greece
Tanja Congiu	University of Sassari, Italy
Stefanos Tsigdinos	National Technical University of Athens, Greece
Florin Nemtanu	Politehnica University of Bucharest, Romania

Workshop Program Committee Members

Massimo Di Gangi	University of Messina, Italy
Orlando Marco Belcore	University of Messina, Italy
Francesco Russo	Mediterranean University of Reggio Calabria, Italy
Alexandros Nikitas	University of Huddersfield, UK
Marilisa Nigro	Rome Tre University, Italy
Kh Md Nahiduzzaman	Mohammed VI Polytechnic University, Morocco
Efstathios Bouhouras	Aristotle University of Thessaloniki, Greece
Antonio Comi	University of Rome Tor Vergata, Italy
Edouard Ivanjko	University of Zagreb, Slovenia
Osvaldo Gervasi	University of Perugia, Italy
Beniamino Murgante	University of Basilicata, Italy
Chiara Garau	University of Cagliari, Italy

MOdels and indicators for assessing and measuring the urban settlement deVElopment in the view of NET ZERO by 2050 (MOVEto0 2025)

Workshop Organizers

Lorena Fiorini	University of L'Aquila, Italy
Lucia Saganeiti	CNR-IMAA, Italy
Angela Pilogallo	CNR-IMAA, Italy
Alessandro Marucci	University of L'Aquila, Italy
Francesco Zullo	University of L'Aquila, Italy

Workshop Program Committee Members

Ginevra Balletto	University of Cagliari, Italy
Giuseppe Borruso	University of Trieste, Italy
Chiara Garau	University of Cagliari, Italy

Beniamino Murgante	University of Basilicata, Italy
Giulia Desogus	University of Cagliari, Italy
Ljiljana Zivkovic	Republic Geodetic Authority, Serbia
Luigi Santopietro	University of Basilicata, Italy
Ilaria Delponte	University of Genoa, Italy
Carmen Guida	University of Naples Federico II, Italy
Chiara Di Dato	University of L'Aquila, Italy

5th Workshop on Privacy in the Cloud/Edge/IoT World (PCEIoT 2025)

Workshop Organizers

Lelio Campanile	Università degli Studi della Campania Luigi Vanvitelli, Italy
Mauro Iacono	Università degli Studi della Campania Luigi Vanvitelli, Italy
Michele Mastroianni	Università degli Studi di Foggia, Italy

Workshop Program Committee Members

Arcangelo Castiglione	Università degli Studi di Salerno, Italy
Maria Ganzha	Warsaw University of Technology, Poland
Daniel Grzonka	Cracow University of Technology, Poland
Antonio Iannuzzi	Università degli Studi Roma Tre, Italy
Armando Tacchella	Università degli Studi di Genova, Italy
Biagio Boi	University of Salerno, Italy
Marco De Santis	University of Salerno, Italy
Fiammetta Marulli	Università degli Studi della Campania "L. Vanvitelli", Italy
Christian Riccio	Università degli Studi della Campania "L. Vanvitelli", Italy
Luigi Piero Di Bonito	Università degli Studi di Napoli Federico II, Italy

Preserving Our Past: Spatial and Remote Sensing Technologies for Cultural Heritage in a Changing Climate (POP 2025)

Workshop Organizers

Maria Danese	CNR-ISPC, Italy
Nicola Masini	CNR-ISPC, Italy
Rosa Lasaponara	CNR-IMAA, Italy

Workshop Program Committee Members

Maria Danese	CNR-ISPC, Italy
Nicola Masini	CNR-ISPC, Italy
Rosa Lasaponara	CNR-IMAA, Italy
Dario Gioia	CNR-ISPC, Italy
Giuseppe Corrado	Università degli Studi della Basilicata, Italy
Canio Sabia	CNR-ISPC, Italy

Processes, methods and tools towards RESilient cities and cultural and historic sites prone to SOD and ROD disasters (RES 2025)

Workshop Organizers

Elena Cantatore	Polytechnic University of Bari, Italy
Dario Esposito	Polytechnic University of Bari, Italy
Alberico Sonnessa	Polytechnic University of Bari, Italy

Workshop Program Committee Members

Elena Cantatore	Politecnico di Bari, Italy
Dario Esposito	Politecnico di Bari, Italy
Alberico Sonnessa	Politecnico di Bari, Italy
Valeria Belloni	Sapienza University of Rome, Italy
Michela Ravanelli	Sapienza University of Rome, Italy
Silvano Dal Sasso	University of Basilicata, Italy
Francesco Chiaravalloti	CNR - IRPI, Italy
Roberta Ravanelli	University of Liège, Belgium
Alessandra Mascitelli	University of Chieti-Pescara, Italy
Francesco Di Capua	University of Basilicata, Italy
Gabriele Bernardini	Università Politecnica delle Marche, Italy
Vito Domenico Porcari	University of Basilicata, Italy
Carmen Rosa Fattore	University of Basilicata, Italy
Stefania Santoro	Water Research Institute, Italy

Scientific Computing Infrastructure (SCI 2025)

Workshop Organizers

Vladimir Korkhov	Saint Petersburg State University, Russia
Elena Stankova	Saint Petersburg State University, Russia
Nataliia Kulabukhova	Saint Petersburg State University, Russia

Workshop Program Committee Members

Adam Belloum	University of Amsterdam, the Netherlands
Dmitrii Vasiunin	Deutsche Telekom Cloud Services E.P.E., Greece
Serob Balyan	Osensus Arm LLC, Armenia
Suren Abrahamyan	Osensus Arm LLC, Armenia
Ashot Sergey Gevorkyan	NAS of Armenia, Armenia
Michal Hnatic	Univerzita Pavla Jozefa Šafárika v Košiciach, Slovakia
Michail Panteleyev	Saint Petersburg Electrotecnical University, Russia
Martin Vala	Univerzita Pavla Jozefa Šafárika v Košiciach, Slovakia
Nodir Zaynalov	Tashkent University of Information Technologies named after Muhammad al Khwarizmi, Uzbekistan
Michail Panteleyev	Saint Petersburg Electrotecnical University, Russia
Alexander Degtyarev	Saint Petersburg University, Russia
Alexander Bogdanov	St. Petersburg State University, Russia

Ports and Logistics of the Future - Smartness and Sustainability (SmartPorts 2025)

Workshop Organizers

Andrea Gallo	Università degli Studi di Trieste, Italy
Gianfranco Fancello	University of Cagliari, Italy
Giuseppe Borruso	Università degli Studi di Trieste, Italy
Enrico D'agostini	World Maritime University, Sweden
Silvia Battino	Università degli Studi di Sassari, Italy
Veronica Camerada	Università degli Studi di Sassari, Italy

Workshop Program Committee Members

Giuseppe Borruso	University of Trieste, Italy
Beniamino Murgante	University of Basilicata, Italy
Ginevra Balletto	University of Cagliari, Italy
Silvia Battino	University of Sassari, Italy
Mara Ladu	University of Cagliari, Italy
Maria del Mar Munoz Leonisio	University of Cádiz, Spain
Ahinoa Amaro Garcia	University of Las Palmas of Gran Canaria, Spain
Maria Attard	University of Malta, Malta
Enrico D'agostini	World Maritime University, Sweden
Francesca Krasna	University of Trieste, Italy

Tu Anh Trinh	UEH University - Ho Chi Minh City, Vietnam
Giovanni Mauro	Università degli Studi della Campania, Italy
Maria Ronza	University of Naples Federico II, Italy
Massimiliano Bencardino	University of Salerno, Italy
Andrea Gallo	Ca' Foscari University of Venice, Italy
Francesca Sinatra	University of Trieste, Italy
Salvatore Dore	University of Trieste, Italy
Veronica Camerada	University of Sassari, Italy
Brunella Brundu	University of Sassari, Italy
Gianfranco Fancello	University of Cagliari, Italy
Marcello Tadini	University of Eastern Piedmont, Italy
Marco Mazzarino	IUAV University Venice
José Ángel Hernández Luis	University of Las Palmas de Gran Canaria, Spain
Marco Naseddu	University of Cagliari, Italy
Maurizio Cociancich	Adriafer, Italy
Giovanni Longo	University of Trieste, Italy
Luca Toneatti	University of Trieste, Italy
Martina Sinatra	University of Cagliari, Italy
Enrico Vanino	University of Sheffield, UK
Patrizia Serra	University of Cagliari, Italy
Agostino Bruzzone	University of Genoa, Italy
Marco Petrelli	University of Roma 3, Italy

Smart Transport and Logistics - Smart Supply Chains (SmarTransLog 2025)

Workshop Organizers

Francesca Sinatra	University of Trieste, Italy
Maria del Mar Munoz	Universidad de Cádiz, Spain
Brunella Brundu	University of Sassari, Italy
Patrizia Serra	University of Cagliari, Italy
Salvatore Dore	University of Trieste, Italy
Marco Naseddu	University of Cagliari, Italy

Workshop Program Committee Members

Giuseppe Borruso	University of Trieste, Italy
Beniamino Murgante	University of Basilicata, Italy
Ginevra Balletto	University of Cagliari, Italy
Silvia Battino	University of Sassari, Italy
Mara Ladu	University of Cagliari, Italy
Maria del Mar Munoz Leonisio	University of Cádiz, Spain
Ahinoa Amaro Garcia	University of Las Palmas of Gran Canaria, Spain

Maria Attard	University of Malta, Malta
Enrico D'agostini	World Maritime University, Sweden
Francesca Krasna	University of Trieste, Italy
Tu Anh Trinh	UEH University, Vietnam
Giovanni Mauro	Università degli Studi della Campania, Italy
Maria Ronza	University of Naples Federico II, Italy
Massimiliano Bencardino	University of Salerno, Italy
Andrea Gallo	Ca' Foscari University of Venice, Italy
Francesca Sinatra	University of Trieste, Italy
Salvatore Dore	University of Trieste, Italy
Veronica Camerada	University of Sassari, Italy
Brunella Brundu	University of Sassari, Italy
Gianfranco Fancello	University of Cagliari, Italy
Marcello Tadini	University of Eastern Piedmont, Italy
Marco Mazzarino	IUAV University Venice
José Ángel Hernández Luis	University of Las Palmas de Gran Canaria, Spain
Marco Naseddu	University of Cagliari, Italy
Maurizio Cociancich	Adriafer, Italy
Giovanni Longo	University of Trieste, Italy
Luca Toneatti	University of Trieste, Italy
Martina Sinatra	University of Cagliari, Italy
Enrico Vanino	University of Sheffield, UK
Patrizia Serra	University of Cagliari, Italy
Agostino Bruzzone	University of Genoa, Italy
Marco Petrelli	University of Roma 3, Italy

Smart Tourism (SmartTourism 2025)

Workshop Organizers

Silvia Battino	University of Sassari, Italy
Francesca Krasna	University of Trieste, Italy
Ainhoa Amaro	University of Las Palmas de Gran Canaria, Spain
Maria del Mar Munoz	University of Cádiz, Spain
Brisol García García	Polytechnic University of Quintana Roo, Mexico
Marta Meleddu	University of Sassari, Italy

Workshop Program Committee Members

Giuseppe Borruso	University of Trieste, Italy
Beniamino Murgante	University of Basilicata, Italy
Gianfranco Fancello	University of Cagliari, Italy
Mara Ladu	University of Cagliari, Italy

Martina Sinatra   University of Cagliari, Italy
Salvatore Dore   University of Trieste, Italy
Marco Mazzarino   IUAV University Venice, Italy
Veronica Camerada   University of Sassari, Italy
Brunella Brundu   University of Sassari, Italy
Maria Attard   University of Malta, Malta
Ginevra Balletto   University of Cagliari, Italy
Giovanni Mauro   University degli Studi della Campania, Italy
Salvatore Lampreu   University of Sassari, Italy
Maria Ronza   University of Naples, Italy
Massimiliano Bencardino   University of Salerno, Italy

Sustainable evolution of long-Distance frEight and paSsenger Transport (SOLIDEST 2025)

Workshop Organizers
Francesco Russo   University of Reggio Calabria, Italy
Andreas Nikiforiadis   Democritus University of Thrace, Greece
Orlando Marco Belcore   University of Messina, Italy
Antonio Comi   University of Rome Tor Vergata, Italy
Tiziana Campisi   Kore University of Enna, Italy
Aura Rusca   Politehnica University of Bucharest, Romania

Workshop Program Committee Members
Massimo Di Gangi   University of Messina, Italy
Orlando Marco Belcore   University of Messina, Italy
Antonio Polimeni   University of Messina, Italy
Socrates Basbas   Aristotle University of Thessaloniki, Greece
Efstathios Bouhouras   Aristotle University of Thessaloniki, Greece
Marina Zanne   University of Lubljana, Slovenia
Marilisa Nigro   Rome Tre University, Italy
Edoardo Marcucci   Molde University College, Norway
Eugen Rosca   Polytechnic University of Bucharest, Romania
Kh Md Nahiduzzaman   Mohammed VI Polytechnic University, Morocco
Beniamino Murgante   University of Basilicata, Italy
Chiara Garau   University of Cagliari, Italy

Sustainability Performance Assessment: Models, Approaches, and Applications Toward Interdisciplinary and Integrated Solutions (SPA 2025)

Workshop Organizers

Francesco Scorza	University of Basilicata, Italy
Sabrina Lai	University of Cagliari, Italy
Francesco Rotondo	Università Politecnica delle Marche, Italy
Jolanta Dvarioniene	Kaunas University of Technology, Lithuania
Michele Campagna	University of Cagliari, Italy
Corrado Zoppi	University of Cagliari, Italy

Workshop Program Committee Members

Federico Amato	University of Lausanne, Switzerland
Ferdinando Di Carlo	University of Basilicata, Italy
Maddalena Floris	University of Cagliari, Italy
Federica Isola	University of Cagliari, Italy
Giuseppe Las Casas	University of Basilicata, Italy
Federica Leone	University of Cagliari, Italy
Giampiero Lombardini	University of Genoa, Italy
Federico Martellozzo	University of Florence, Italy
Alessandro Marucci	University of L'Aquila, Italy
Ana Clara Moura	Universidade Federal de Minas Gerais, Brazil
Beniamino Murgante	University of Basilicata, Italy
Silviu Nate	Lucian Blaga University of Sibiu, Romania
Anastasia Stratigea	National Technical University of Athens, Greece
Francesco Zullo	University of L'Aquila, Italy
Luigi Santopietro	University of Basilicata, Italy
Benedetto Manganelli	University of Basilicata, Italy

Specifics of Smart Cities Development in Europe (SPEED 2025)

Workshop Organizers

Chiara Garau	University of Cagliari, Italy
Katarína Vitálišová	Matej Bel University, Slovak Republic
Marco Fanfani	University of Florence, Italy
Anna Vaňová	Matej Bel University, Slovak Republic
Kamila Borsekova	Matej Bel University, Slovak Republic
Paola Zamperlin	University of Florence, Italy

Workshop Program Committee Members

Claudia Loggia	University of KwaZulu-Natal, South Africa
Francesca Maltinti	University of Cagliari, Italy
Alessandro Plaisant	University of Sassari, Italy
Alenka Poplin	Iowa State University, USA
Silvia Rossetti	University of Parma, Italy
Gerardo Carpentieri	University of Naples Federico II, Italy
Carmen Guida	University of Naples Federico II, Italy
Floriana Zucaro	University of Naples Federico II, Italy
Anastasia Stratigea	National Technical University of Athens, Greece
Yiota Theodora	National Technical University of Athens, Greece
Giovanna Concu	University of Cagliari, Italy
Paolo Nesi	University of Florence, Italy
Emanuele Bellini	University of Roma Tre, Italy
Mana Dastoum	Polytechnic University of Madrid, Spain
Barbara Caselli	University of Parma, Italy
Martina Carra	University of Brescia, Italy
Alfonso Annunziata	University of Basilicata, Italy
Elisabetta Venco	University of Pavia, Italy
Caterina Pietra	University of Pavia, Italy
Enrico Collini	University of Florence, Italy
Luciano Alessandro Ipsaro Palesi	University of Florence, Italy

Smart, Safe, and Healthy Cities (SSHC 2025)

Workshop Organizers

Chiara Garau	University of Cagliari, Italy
Gerardo Carpentieri	University of Naples Federico II, Italy
Carmen Guida	University of Naples Federico II, Italy
Tanja Congiu	University of Sassari, Italy
Martina Carra	University of Brescia, Italy
Alenka Poplin	Iowa State University, USA

Workshop Program Committee Members

Rosaria Battarra	Istituto di Studi sul Mediterraneo, Italy
Barbara Caselli	University of Parma, Italy
Francesca Maltinti	University of Cagliari, Italy
Romano Fistola	Università degli Studi di Napoli Federico II, Italy
Alessandro Plaisant	University of Sassari, Italy
Silvia Rossetti	University of Parma, Italy
Marco Fanfani	University of Florence, Italy
Reza Askarizad	University of Cagliari, Italy

Floriana Zucaro	University of Naples Federico II, Italy
Anastasia Stratigea	National Technical University of Athens, Greece
Yiota Theodora	National Technical University of Athens, Greece
Giovanna Concu	University of Cagliari, Italy
Francesco Zullo	University of L'Aquila, Italy
Paola Zamperlin	University of Florence, Italy
Vincenza Torrisi	University of Catania, Italy
Tiziana Campisi	University of Enna Kore, Italy
Katarína Vitálišová	Matej Bel University, Slovakia
Tazyeen Alam	University of Cagliari, Italy
Mana Dastoum	Polytechnic University of Madrid, Spain
Martina Carra	University of Brescia, Italy
Alfonso Annunziata	University of Basilicata, Italy
Elisabetta Venco	University of Pavia, Italy
Caterina Pietra	University of Pavia, Italy

Smart and Sustainable Island Communities (SSIC 2025)

Workshop Organizers

Chiara Garau	University of Cagliari, Italy
Anastasia Stratigea	National Technical University of Athens, Greece
Yiota Theodora	National Technical University of Athens, Greece
Giovanna Concu	University of Cagliari, Italy

Workshop Program Committee Members

Milena Metalkova-Markova	University of Portsmouth, UK
Tarek Teba	University of Portsmouth, UK
Alenka Poplin	Iowa State University, USA
Gerardo Carpentieri	University of Naples Federico II, Italy
Carmen Guida	University of Naples Federico II, Italy
Floriana Zucaro	University of Naples Federico II, Italy
Silvia Rossetti	University of Parma, Italy
Barbara Caselli	University of Parma, Italy
Martina Carra	University of Brescia, Italy
Alfonso Annunziata	University of Basilicata, Italy
Maria Panagiotopoulou	National Technical University of Athens, Greece
Apostolos Lagarias	University of Thessaly, Greece
Paola Zamperlin	University of Florence, Italy
Vincenza Torrisi	University of Catania, Italy
Giuseppina Vacca	University of Cagliari, Italy
Roberto Minunno	Curtin University, Australia
Marco Zucca	University of Cagliari, Italy

Elisabetta Venco	University of Pavia, Italy
Caterina Pietra	University of Pavia, Italy
Pietro Crespi	Politecnico di Milano, Italy

From STreet Experiments to Planned Solutions (STEPS 2025)

Workshop Organizers

Silvia Rossetti	Università degli Studi di Parma, Italy
Angela Ricciardello	Kore University of Enna, Italy
Francesco Pinna	Università degli Studi di Cagliari, Italy
Chiara Garau	Università degli Studi di Cagliari, Italy
Tiziana Campisi	Kore University of Enna, Italy
Vincenza Torrisi	University of Catania, Italy

Workshop Program Committee Members

Martina Carra	University of Brescia, Italy
Barbara Caselli	University of Parma, Italy
Tanja Congiu	University of Sassari, Italy
Gabriele D'Orso	University of Palermo, Italy
Matteo Ignaccolo	University of Catania, Italy
Md Kh Nahiduzzaman	Mohammed VI Polytechnic University, Morocco
Muhammad Ahmad Al-Rashid	University of Malaya, Malaysia
Alessandro Plaisant	University of Sassari, Italy
Marianna Ruggieri	University of Enna Kore, Italy
Michele Zazzi	University of Parma, Italy

Sustainable Tourism Evaluations: approaches, methods and indicators (STEva 2025)

Workshop Organizers

Mariolina Grasso	Università Kore di Enna, Italy
Fabrizio Finucci	Roma Tre University, Italy
Daniele Mazzoni	Roma Tre University, Italy
Antonella G. Masanotti	Roma Tre University, Italy
Giovanna Acampa	University of Florence, Italy

Workshop Program Committee Members

Giovanna Acampa	University of Florence, Italy
Fabrizio Finucci	Roma Tre University, Italy
Mariolina Grasso	"Kore" University of Enna, Italy

Alberto Marzo	Ministero della Cultura, Italy
Antonella G. Masanotti	Roma Tre University, Italy
Daniele Mazzoni	Roma Tre University, Italy
Rocco Murro	Sapienza University of Rome, Italy
Claudio Piferi	University of Florence, Italy
Alessio Pino	"Kore" University of Enna, Italy
Nicoletta Setola	University of Florence, Italy
Laura Calcagnini	Roma Tre University, Italy
Antonio Magarò	Roma Tre University, Italy
Janos Ghyerghyak	University of Pécs, Hungary
Ágnes Borsos	University of Pécs, Hungary
Fabrizio Battisti	University of Florence, Italy

Sustainable Development of Ports (SUSTAINABLEPORTS 2025)

Workshop Organizers

Tiziana Campisi	University of Enna KORE, Italy
Giuseppe Musolino	University of Reggio Calabria, Italy
Efstathios Bouhouras	Aristotle University of Thessaloniki, Greece
Elen Twrdy	University of Ljubljana, Slovenia
Elena Cocuzza	University of Catania, Italy
Aura Rusca	Politehnica University of Bucharest, Romania

Workshop Program Committee Members

Massimo Di Gangi	University of Messina, Italy
Orlando Marco Belcore	University of Messina, Italy
Antonio Polimeni	University of Messina, Italy
Claudia Caballini	Polytechnic of Torino, Italy
Gianfranco Fancello	University of Cagliari, Italy
Marina Zanne	University of Lubljana, Slovenia
Stefano Ricci	Sapienza University of Rome, Italy
Beniamino Murgante	University of Basilicata, Italy
Chiara Garau	University of Cagliari, Italy

Theoretical and Computational Chemistry and Its Applications (TCCMA 2025)

Workshop Organizers

Noelia Faginas Lago	Università di Perugia, Italy
Andrea Lombardi	Università di Perugia, Italy
Marcos Mandado Alonso	University of Vigo, Spain

Workshop Program Committee Members

Noelia Faginas-Lago	University of Perugia, Italy
Andrea Lombardi	University of Perugia, Italy
Marcos Mandado	University of Vigo, Spain
Angeles Peña	University of Vigo, Spain
Luca Mancini	Universiy of Perugia, Italy
Massimiliano Bartolomei	CSIC, Spain
Cecilia Coletti	University of Chieti-Pescara, Italy
Iñaki Tuñón	Universidad de Valencia, Spain
Albert Rimola Gilbert	Universitat Autònoma de Barcelona, Spain
Stefano Falcinelli	University of Perugia, Italy
Dario Campisi	University of Perugia, Italy
Ernesto García Para	University of the Basque Country, Spain
Giacomo Giorgi	University of Perugia, Italy
Tomás González Lezana	IFF CSIC, Spain
Enrique M. Cabaleiro Lago	Universidade de Santiago de Compostela, Spain
Aurora Costales	Universidad de Oviedo, Spain
Angel Martin	Universidad de Oviedo, Spain
Jose Manuel	University of Vigo, Spain
Annarita Laricchiuta	CNR ISTP Bari, Italy
Fernando Pirani	University of Perugia, Italy

Transport Infrastructures for Smart Cities (TISC 2025)

Workshop Organizers

Francesca Maltinti	University of Cagliari, Italy
Mauro Coni	University of Cagliari, Italy
Benedetto Barabino	University of Brescia, Italy
Nicoletta Rassu	University of Cagliari, Italy
James Rombi	University of Cagliari, Italy

Workshop Program Committee Members

Francesco Pinna	University of Cagliari, Italy
Chiara Garau	University of Cagliari, Italy
Mauro D'Apuzzo	University of Cassino, Italy
Roberto Minunno	Curtin University, Australia
Tiziana Campisi	University of Enna Kore, Italy
Roberto Ventura	University of Brescia, Italy
Alessandro Plaisant	University of Sassari, Italy
Massimo Di Francesco	University of Cagliari, Italy

Vincenza Torrisi — University of Catania, Italy
Paola Zamperlin — University of Florence, Italy

Transforming Urban Analytics: The Impact of Crowdsourced Mapping and Advanced AI Techniques on Future Cities (Tr-UrbAna 2025)

Workshop Organizers
Ayse Giz Gulnerman Gengec — Ankara Hacı Bayram Veli University, Turkey
Müslüm Hacar — Tildiz Technical University, Turkey
Himmet Karaman — Istanbul Technical University, Turkey

Workshop Program Committee Members
Beniamino Murgante — University of Basilicata, Italy
Abdulkadir Memduhoğlu — Harran University, Turkey
Zeynel Abidin Polat — İzmir Katip Çelebi University, Turkey
Güzide Miray Perihanoğlu — Van Yüzüncü Yıl University, Turkey
Tugba Memisoglu Baykal — Ankara Hacı Bayram Veli University, Turkey

From structural to TRAnsformative-change of City Environment: challenges and solutions and perspectives (TRACE 2025)

Workshop Organizers
Pierluigi Morano — Polytechnic University of Bari, Italy
Maria Rosaria Guarini — Sapienza University of Rome, Italy
Francesco Sica — Sapienza University of Rome, Italy
Francesco Tajani — Sapienza University of Rome, Italy
Marco Locurcio — Polytechnic University of Bari, Italy
Debora Anelli — Polytechnic University of Bari, Italy

Workshop Program Committee Members
Felicia di Liddo — Politecnico di Bari, Italia
Valeria Saiu — Università di Cagliari, Italia
Emma Sabatelli — Sapienza Università di Roma, Italia
Antonella Roma — Sapienza Università di Roma, Italia
Giuseppe Cerullo — Sapienza Università di Roma, Italia
Lucia della Spina — Università di Reggio Calabria, Italia
Alejandro Segura de la Cal — Politecnico di Madrid, Spain
Yilsy Nuñez — Politecnico di Madrid, Spain
Gabriella Maselli — Università di Salerno, Italy
Maria Rosa Trovato — Università di Catania, Italy

Manuela Rebaudengo	Politecnico di Torino, Italy
Pierfrancesco De Paola	Università di Napoli Federico II, Italy
Daniela Tavano	Università della Calabria, Italy
Maria Saez	University of Granada, Spain
Paola Amoruso	LUM "Giuseppe Degennaro" University, Italy

Temporary Real Estate management: Approaches and methods for Time-integrated impact assessments and evaluations (TREAT 2025)

Workshop Organizers

Chiara Mazzarella	TUDelft, The Netherlands
Hilde Remoy	TUDelft, The Netherlands
Maria Cerreta	University of Naples Federico II, Italy

Workshop Program Committee Members

Chiara Mazzarella	TU Delft, The Netherlands
Hilde Remoy	TU Delft, The Netherlands
Maria Cerreta	University of Naples Federico II, Italy
Maria Somma	University of Naples Federico II, Italy
Simona Panaro	University of Campania Luigi Vanvitelli, Italy
Laura Di Tommaso	University of Naples Federico II, Italy
Caterina Loffredo	University of Naples Federico II, Italy
Ludovica La Rocca	University of Naples Federico II, Italy
Sabrina Sacco	Politecnico di Milano, Italy
Piero Zizzania	University of Naples Federico II, Italy
Gaia Daldanise	CNR IRISS, Italy
Benedetta Grieco	University of Naples Federico II, Italy
Giuseppe Ciciriello	University of Naples Federico II, Italy
Marta Dell'Ovo	Politecnico di Milano, Italy
Daniele Cannatella	TU Delft, The Netherlands
Eugenio Muccio	University of Naples Federico II, Italy
Sveva Ventre	University of Naples Federico II, Italy

Supporting the Transition to Ecological Economy in Cities Regeneration: Circular Model Tools for Reusing Architecture and Infrastructures (TReE 2025)

Workshop Organizers

Mariarosaria Angrisano	Pegaso University, Italy
Giulio Cavana	Politecnico di Torino, Italy
Francesca Buglione	CNR-ISPC, Italy

Antonia Gravagnuolo   CNR-ISPC, Italy
Piera Della Morte   Pegaso University, Italy

Workshop Program Committee Members
Giulia Datola   Politecnico di Milano, Italy
Vanessa Assumma   University of Bologna, Italy
Marco Volpatti   Politecnico di Torino, Italy
Sebastiano Barbieri   Politecnico di Torino, Italy
Caterina Caprioli   Politecnico di Torino, Italy
Marta Dell'Ovo   Politecnico di Milano, Italy
Federico Dell'Anna   Politecnico di Torino, Italy
Elena Todella   Politecnico di Torino, Italy
Danny Casprini   Politecnico di Milano, Italy
Grazia Neglia   Università Telematica Pegaso, Italy
Francesca Nocca   Università degli Studi di Napoli Federico II, Italy
Giulio Cavana   Politecnico di Torino, Italy
Francesca Buglione   CNR-IPSC, Italy
Marco Rossitti   Politecnico di Milano, Italy
Jhon Escorcia   Politecnico di Torino, Italy
Beatrice Mecca   Politecnico di Torino, Italy
Sara Biancifiori   Politecnico di Torino, Italy

Urban Digital Twins and Data Spaces: Shaping the Future of Sustainable Cities (TwinAbleCities 2025)

Workshop Organizers
Dessislava Petrova Antonova   Sofia University, GATE Institute, Bulgaria
Beniamino Murgante   University of Basilicata, Italy
Senthil Rajendran   RMSI, Bahrain
Tiziana Campisi   Kore University of Enna, Italy
Mila Koeva   University of Twente, The Netherlands

Workshop Program Committee Members
Dessislava Petrova-Antonova   Sofia University, Bulgaria
Mila Koeva   The University of Twente, The Netherlands
Beniamino Murgante   University of Basilicata, Italy
Senthil Rajendran   RMSI, Bahrain
Tiziana Campisi   Kore University of Enna, Italy

Urban Regeneration: Innovative Tools and Evaluation Model (URITEM 2025)

Workshop Organizers

Fabrizio Battisti	University of Florence, Italy
Giovanna Acampa	University of Florence, Italy
Orazio Campo	Sapienza University of Rome, Italy
Melania Perdonò	University of Florence, Italy

Workshop Program Committee Members

Fabrizio Battisti	University of Florence, Italy
Giovanna Acampa	University of Florence, Italy
Orazio Campo	University of Rome "La Sapienza", Italy
Melania Perdonò	Università degli Studi di Firenze, Italy

Urban Space Accessibility and Mobilities (USAM 2025)

Workshop Organizers

Chiara Garau	DICAAR, University of Cagliari, Italy
Alessandro Plaisant	University of Sassari, Italy
Barbara Caselli	University of Parma, Italy
Mauro D'Apuzzo	University of Cassino and Southern Lazio, Italy
Gabriele D'Orso	University of Palermo, Italy
Matteo Ignaccolo	University of Catania, Italy

Workshop Program Committee Members

Mauro Coni	University of Cagliari, Italy
Martina Carra	University of Brescia, Italy
Tiziana Campisi	University of Enna Kore, Italy
Tanja Congiu	University of Sassari, Italy
Francesca Maltinti	University of Cagliari, Italy
Silvia Rossetti	University of Parma, Italy
Barbara Caselli	University of Parma, Italy
Angela Pilogallo	University of L'Aquila, Italy
Lorena Fiorini	University of L'Aquila, Italy
Reza Askarizad	University of Cagliari, Italy
Francesco Pinna	University of Cagliari, Italy
Aime Tsinda	University of Rwanda, Rwanda
Youssef El Ganadi	International University of Rabat, Morocco
Marco Migliore	University of Palermo, Italy
Alessio Salvatore	Italian National Research Council, Italy
Giuseppe Stecca	Italian National Research Council, Italy

Paola Zamperlin	University of Florence, Italy
Vincenza Torrisi	University of Catania, Italy
Gerardo Carpentieri	University of Naples Federico II, Italy
Carmen Guida	University of Naples Federico II, Italy
Floriana Zucaro	University of Naples Federico II, Italy
Alfonso Annunziata	University of Basilicata, Italy
Elisabetta Venco	University of Pavia, Italy
Caterina Pietra	University of Pavia, Italy
Tazyeen Alam	University of Cagliari, Italy
Valerio Cutini	University of Pisa, Italy

UX Mobility 2025: Placing User Experience at the Center of Urban Mobility: Methods and Frameworks (UXM 2025)

Workshop Organizers

Carmen Guida	Università degli Studi di Napoli Federico II, Italy
Gerardo Carpentieri	Università degli Studi di Napoli Federico II, Italy
Federico Messa	Systematica srl, Italy
Lamia Abdelfattah	Systematica srl, Italy

Workshop Program Committee Members

Rosaria Battarra	Istituto di Studi sul Mediterraneo CNR, Italy
Romano Fistola	Università degli Studi di Napoli Federico II, Italy
Lucia Saganeiti	IMAA-CNR, Italy

Virtual Reality and Augmented reality and applications (VRA 2025)

Workshop Organizers

Damiano Perri	University of Perugia, Italy
Osvaldo Gervasi	University of Perugia, Italy
Chau Ma Thi	University of Engineering and Technology, Vietnam National University, Hanoi, Vietnam
Paolo Nesi	University of Florence, Italy
Pierfrancesco Bellini	University of Florence, Italy

Workshop Program Committee Members

David Berti	ART SpA, Italy
JungYoon Kim	Gachon University, South Korea

TaiHoon Kim	Zhejiang University of Science and Technology, China
Marcelo de Paiva Guimares	Federal University of São Paulo, Brazil
Sergio Tasso	University of Perugia, Italy

Workshop on Advanced and Computational Methods for Earth Science Applications (WACM4ES 2025)

Workshop Organizers

Luca Piroddi	University of Cagliari, Italy
Patrizia Capizzi	University of Palermo, Italy
Marilena Cozzolino	University of Molise, Italy
Sebastiano D'Amico	University of Malta, Malta
Chiara Garau	University of Cagliari, Italy
Giuseppina Vacca	University of Cagliari, Italy

Workshop Program Committee Members

Andrea Angelini	CNR ISPC, Italy
Ilaria Barone	Università degli Studi di Padova, Italy
Patrizia Capizzi	University of Palermo, Italy
Luigi Capozzoli	CNR, Italy
Alberto Carletti	University of Cagliari, Italy
Emanuele Colica	University of Malta, Malta
Marilena Cozzolino	Università del Molise, Italy
Sebastiano D'Amico	University of Malta, Malta
Chiara Garau	University of Cagliari, Italy
Luciano Galone	University of Malta, Malta
Peter Iregbeyen	University of Malta, Malta
Mariano Lisi	Basilicata Aerospace Cluster CLAS, Italy
Raffaele Martorana	Università di Palermo, Italy
Paolo Mauriello	Università del Molise, Italy
Veronica Pazzi	University of Florence, Italy
Raffaele Persico	Università della Calabria, Italy
Luca Piroddi	University of Cagliari, Italy
Sina Saneiyan	Binghamton University, USA
Mercedes Solla	Universidade de Vigo, Spain
Deodato Tapete	ASI, Italy
Giuseppina Vacca	University of Cagliari, Italy
Enrica Vecchi	University of Cagliari, Italy

Sponsoring Organizations

ICCSA 2025 would not have been possible without the tremendous support of many organizations and institutions, for which all organizers and participants of ICCSA 2025 express their sincere gratitude:

Galatasaray University, Istanbul, Türkiye
(https://gsu.edu.tr/en)

African Mathematical Union
(https://www.africanmathunion.org/)

Springer Nature Switzerland AG, Switzerland
(https://www.springer.com)

The University of Massachusetts, USA
(https://www.umass.edu/)

University of Perugia, Italy
(https://www.unipg.it)

University of Basilicata, Italy
(http://www.unibas.it)

Monash University, Australia
(https://www.monash.edu/)

Kyushu Sangyo University, Japan
(https://www.kyusan-u.ac.jp/)

Universidade do Minho
Escola de Engenharia

University of Minho, Portugal
(https://www.uminho.pt/)
Venue
ICCSA 2025 took place in: **Galatasaray University, Istanbul, Türkiye**

Additional Reviewers

Reviewers
The review tasks for each workshop have been carried out by the workshop Organizers and the members of the workshop Program Committee.

Plenary Lectures

Sky Safe with GAI and Post-quantum Computing

Elizabeth Chang

Professor of Cyber Security and Head of Discipline, University of the Sunshine Coast, Australia

Abstract. Professor Chang's talk in this presentation has two distinct parts. To start, she will introduce the landscape of cybersecurity development, attacks, threats, and vulnerabilities, as well as state-of-the-art cyber protection, cyber defence, and cyber incident prevention. This is followed by a discussion of the impact of Generative AI (GAI) and quantum-safe cryptographic computing, highlighting the major issues and challenges in research, education, and training. In conclusion, she will present a vision for Sky Safe solutions, aiming to achieve cyber resilience that supports business and economic stability, enhances human capabilities, and promotes environmental sustainability.

Disaster Preparedness and Risk Profiling in the Digital Era from Earth Observation Lens

Jagannath Aryal

Department of Infrastructure Engineering, University of Melbourne, Australia

Abstract. Natural hazards which turn into disasters result in severe losses of lives, infrastructure, and property. Disasters such as earthquakes and landslides and their impacts on transportation safety, infrastructure resilience, and displacement of people to new places are challenges. To address such challenges, earth observation data and intelligent methods can provide potential solutions in developing decision support systems. This talk will present the state of the art in Earth observation for disaster resilience using intelligent methods. In the Earth observation space, digitalisation has revolutionised the way we map, monitor, and develop decision support systems. Global case study examples covering earthquake-induced landslides from the Himalayan region will cover the digital capabilities. The digital capabilities will embrace object recognition, interpretation, and their accurate and precise capture to integrate into digital models. The developed digital models from representative case studies can be leveraged in other jurisdictions in profiling risks to protect lives and infrastructure and creating disaster preparedness in the era of digital age and digital economy.

Intelligent Image Enhancement for Real-World Applications in Adverse Atmospheric Conditions

Khan Muhammad

Department of Global Convergence, Sungkyunkwan University, South Korea

Abstract. The adverse impacts of atmospheric conditions such as haze, fog, and low-light environments pose significant challenges for real-world applications reliant on computer vision, including autonomous driving, surveillance, and remote sensing. This keynote explores cutting-edge advancements in intelligent image enhancement, drawing insights from two pivotal studies. The first introduces HazeSpace2M, a comprehensive dataset and novel classification-guided dehazing framework that improves image clarity across diverse atmospheric conditions, addressing the gap between synthetic and real-world dehazing performance. The second focuses on LoLI-Street, a benchmark for low-light image enhancement tailored to urban environments, extending beyond enhancement to enable robust object detection and scene understanding. Taken together, these contributions demonstrate how integrating domain-specific datasets, advanced algorithms, and performance benchmarks can significantly elevate the reliability of computer vision systems under challenging weather and lighting conditions. Attendees will gain valuable insights into the methodologies, datasets, and practical applications driving innovation in this field, with implications for research and industry alike.

In Memory of Carmelo Torre

Unfortunately, Professor Carmelo Torre, one of the cornerstones of the ICCSA Conference, passed away last December, leaving everyone stunned and deeply saddened. His loss has created a profound void within our academic community. Carmelo was not only a respected scholar and dedicated contributor to the success and growth of ICCSA, but also a generous colleague, mentor, and friend to many. His intellectual rigor, warm personality, and unwavering commitment to advancing research will be remembered with great admiration. As we continue the work he helped shape, we honor his legacy and the indelible mark he left on all of us. Carmelo Torre graduated in engineering at the Polytechnic of Bari with a thesis on urban planning under Dino Borri's guidance. He began his research career by collaborating with Franco Selicato. During his PhD at the University of Naples Federico II under Luigi Fusco Girard, he specialized in real estate market analysis and multi-criteria evaluation methods. He explored the social impacts of urban transformations with his lifelong friend Maria Cerreta. His first ICCSA participation was in Perugia in 2008, in the session Geographical Analysis, Urban Modeling, Spatial Statistics. Instantly captivated by the conference, his charisma enabled him to involve various Italian scientific communities, including those in real estate and statistics. ICCSA became a yearly commitment for him, where he valued the high editorial quality of the proceedings and the dynamic post-presentation discussions and debates he passionately and expertly enriched. In 2012, alongside Maria Cerreta and Paola Perchinunno, he organized the workshop Econometrics and Multidimensional Evaluation in the Urban Environment (EMEUE), fostering dialogue on critical topics. His influence steadily grew, drawing numerous research groups to ICCSA and establishing real estate and assessment as one of the conference's leading fields. A pillar of ICCSA, he was involved across all facets of the event. Torre's contributions to academic discourse were marked by intellectual rigor and innovative thinking. His conference interventions consistently challenged conventional wisdom, offering insights transcending disciplinary boundaries. Beyond the conference, he passionately advocated for equity and social justice. His left-leaning ideology, though firm, earned respect from those with differing views, thanks to his sincerity and loyalty. He was creative, generous, and always willing to help, even at a personal cost. Despite battling illness, he maintained his characteristic optimism, warmth, cheerfulness, and commitment, supported by his partner, Caterina Rinaldo. His legacy lives on in his ideas, dedication, and unmatched generosity.

Contents – Part XI

Smart, Safe, and Healthy Cities (SSHC 2025)

Assessing Walking Accessibility: A GIS-Based Analysis of Postal Services in the City of Naples 3
   Gerardo Carpentieri, Carmen Guida, and Valerio Martinelli

Land Suitability Analysis of Nature-Based Solutions for Climate Adaptation and Mitigation in the Sardinia Region, Italy 16
   Chiara Garau, Alfonso Annunziata, and Francesco Scorza

Leveraging Gamification in E-Commerce for Climate Change: A Persuasive Technology Acceptance Model (TAM) Approach 34
   Wei-Jie Phang and Chien-Sing Lee

Visibility Graph Analysis vs. Human Mobility Patterns: An Empirical Validation of Simulation-Based Analysis Using Space Syntax in Public Squares 51
   Reza Askarizad and Chiara Garau

Smart, Close, and Happy City: A Global Index for Measuring Urban Well-Being. The Case Study of the San Benedetto Neighbourhood, Cagliari (Italy) 69
   Alessia Torlini, Chiara Pinna, and Chiara Garau

From structural to TRAnsformative-change of City Environment : chal- lenges & solutions & perspectives (TRACE 2025)

Valuing Nature: Experimenting the GiVal Toolkit for the Economic Evaluation of Nature-Based Solutions in Milan 91
   Giulia Datola, Francesca Torrieri, Marta Dell'Ovo, and Alessandra Oppio

Understanding Airbnb Supply in Rome: Multivariate Analysis of Prices and Accommodation Patterns 107
   Maria Rosaria Guarini, Francesco Sica, Alejandro Segura-de-la-Cal, and Yilsy Núñez Guerrero

Quantifying the Loss of Property Value Due to Energy Inefficiency: A Stranded Asset Risk Assessment in the Real Estate Sector 122
   Daniela Tavano and Francesca Salvo

Rationalizing Evaluation Legal Models for Affordable Home Ownership
and Leasehold Interests in Italy 134
   *Marco Locurcio, Pierluigi Morano, Paola Amoruso, Felicia Di Liddo,
and Francesco Tajani*

A GIS-Based Spatial Evaluation Model for Planning Urban Regeneration
Investments 146
   *Francesco Tajani, Francesco Sica, Pierfrancesco De Paola,
Pierluigi Morano, and Giuseppe Cerullo*

A Set of Criteria for the Assessment of the Suitability of a Building to be
Converted for Use as a Healthcare Facility 158
   *Antonella Roma, Maria Rosaria Guarini, Marco Locurcio,
Felicia Di Liddo, and Pierluigi Morano*

Spatial Analysis of Urban Decay: Spillover Effects and Significant
Patterns for the City of Rome (Italy) 178
   *Pierluigi Morano, Debora Anelli, Francesco Tajani, Emma Sabatelli,
and Felicia Di Liddo*

Construction Cost Estimate and Building Information Modeling
in Renovation Projects Early Design Stages 195
   Pietro Bonifaci, Sergio Copiello, and Federico Panarotto

**Supporting the Transition to Ecological Economy in Cities
Regenera- tion: Circular Model Tools for Reusing Architecture and
Infrastructures (TReE 2025)**

Multi-criteria Decision Aiding for Adaptive Reuse of Cultural Heritage:
An Application in the City of Naples (Italy) 217
   Giulia Datola and Marta Bottero

Participatory Strategies for Supporting Decision Making in Cultural
Heritage Adaptive Reuse Interventions 234
   *Marta Bottero, Giulio Mondini, Sebastiano Barbieri,
Caterina Caprioli, and Federico Dell'Anna*

The Role of Urban Planning in Building the Circular Urban Model. The
Case of Naples 248
   Giuseppe Mazzeo

Adaptive Reuse of Religious Cultural Heritage: The Case Study
of the Church "Santissimo Nome di Gesù" in Turin (Italy) 266
   *Cavana Giulio, Angrisano Mariarosaria, Gravagnuolo Antonia,
Luigi Fusco Girard, and Bottero Marta*

Cultural and Creative Practices as Drivers of Circular Economy: A 9R
Framework Perspective 283
   Sabrina Pedrini and Maria Tartari

Building the Future While Preserving the Past: Digital Tools
and Community Engagement to "Re-Generate" Historic Buildings
in Post-Disaster Scenarios 299
   Mariarosaria Angrisano, Grazia Neglia, and Ippolita Mecca

Transport Infrastructures for Smart Cities (TISC 2025)

Interpretable Crash Severity Prediction Models to Improve Cyclist Safety 319
   *Giuseppe Cappelli, Sofia Nardoianni, Mauro D'Apuzzo,
   and Vittorio Nicolosi*

A Macroscopic and Physically-Based Relationship Between Bike Speeds
and Energy Expenditure During Commuting Trips 335
   *Giuseppe Cappelli, Sofia Nardoianni, Mauro D'Apuzzo, Heather Kaths,
   Vittorio Nicolosi, and Maria Teresa Iannattone*

Estimation of Pedestrian Flows with Open-Source Crowding Data:
An Integrated Model in Nomentano-Tiburtina District, Rome 350
   *Sofia Nardoianni, Giuseppe Cappelli, Mauro D'Apuzzo,
   Vittorio Nicolosi, and Mariano Pernetti*

Econometric Model for Forecasting Air Transport Demand: The Case
of Cagliari – Elmas Airport 368
   *Nicoletta Rassu, Mauro Coni, Riccardo Zedda, Kevin Panetto,
   and Francesca Maltinti*

Evaluating Skid Resistance of Indoor Pavements Using the Tortus
Tribometer and British Pendulum Tester: A Case Study 385
   *James Rombi, Marta Salis, Mauro Coni, Nicoletta Rassu,
   and Francesca Maltinti*

Road Accidents - Study of the Evolution and Mapping of Accidents
Within the Municipality of Cagliari – Italy 401
   *Nicoletta Rassu, Mauro Coni, James Rombi, Marta Salis,
   and Francesca Maltinti*

Traffic Light Control at Intersections in Case of Heterogeneous Traffic
Using Reinforcement Learning 419
   Do Thai Giang, Truong Cong Doan, and Phan Duy Hung

Web of Things Based Advanced Smart Parking Management Solution 432
  Luciano Alessandro Ipsaro Palesi, Matteo Naldi, and Paolo Nesi

Author Index 451

Smart, Safe, and Healthy Cities (SSHC 2025)

Assessing Walking Accessibility: A GIS-Based Analysis of Postal Services in the City of Naples

Gerardo Carpentieri(✉) ⓘ, Carmen Guida ⓘ, and Valerio Martinelli ⓘ

Department of Civil, Building and Environmental Engineering, University of Naples Federico II, Naples, Italy
`gerardo.carpentieri@unina.it`

Abstract. The current patterns of rapid urbanization pose significant challenges to social and economic inclusion. The planning of local services within urban environment is crucial in addressing issues of accessibility. The assessment and resolution of shortcomings depends on holistic assessment of disparities in accessibility.

This paper examines the accessibility of population to local services, with a particular focus on postal services in the city of Naples. In the Italian context, as in many other nations, national posts provide a broad range of essential logistical, financial and social services, making their accessibility a key factor in urban inclusion. In the case of Poste Italiane, in line with obligations under European and national law, the company explicitly states that the strategic positioning of its offices is essential to effective community service.

The study develops a modified Two Step Floating Catchment Area (2SFCA) methodology to measure the levels of accessibility to post offices during both morning and afternoon hours. The research aims to identify spatial disparities in service accessibility and to provide insights into improving urban planning and service distribution, particularly for more vulnerable population groups. The methodology used in this study is based on Geographic Information Systems (GIS) and considers the supply and demand of urban services as well as the mobility patterns and behavioral traits of the population.

The application of the 2SFCA methodology in Naples reveals significant variations in accessibility levels. The findings indicate that substantial portions of the population, particularly in the urban periphery, experience poor accessibility to post offices, and that spatial accessibility to services varies remarkably depending on the setting of opening hours by Poste Italiane.

The study underscores the importance of tailored urban strategies in ensuring equitable access to essential services, thereby enhancing the quality of life.

Keywords: Urban accessibility · Urban services · Post office

1 Introduction

In the current era of rapid urbanization and growing socio-economic disparities, one of the most pressing challenges facing cities is that of ensuring equitable access to essential services [1, 2]. The constant increase in urban populations can lead to critical failures in the performance and accessibility of the service networks necessary for daily life. Urban residents, particularly those in socio-economically marginalized and more distant areas, often face significant barriers in accessing essential services. The more vulnerable populations tend to be disproportionally affected by problems such as poor spatial distribution of services, which may then operate on limited hours and lack integration with sustainable transportation [3, 4]. Moreover, these are the same populations that also tend to lack awareness, education and logistical opportunities in accessing digital services [5, 6]. Adding to the shortcomings of traditional infrastructure, the digital divide thus further deepens the disparities in accessing essential services.

The complex interplay of inequalities in accessing essential services, ranging from issues of spatial and temporal distribution to technological exclusion, demands a comprehensive approach that not only addresses physical access but also considers the role of digital literacy and on-line service delivery. Within this scenario, the current research addresses the challenge of optimizing service distribution in urban environments, in this case with a particular application to the Italian national post, a provider of highly diversified financial-logistical-administrative services. The research provides a data-driven framework for assessing and improving service accessibility, aimed at not only at revealing the limitations of any current network, but also at supporting public and private stakeholders in overcoming the revealed challenges through concrete evidence-based proposals of solutions.

Central to this study is the recognition that the aims of urban inclusivity and service accessibility are deeply interconnected with issues of environmental responsibility and sustainable mobility [7, 8]. The challenges of inclusivity and accessibility to services are to be met by actions at the key levels of environmental and spatial planning, through integration with sustainable transport options, and even in details such as adjusting hours of operation and inter-relations with other services. The current research confronts the challenges head-on, offering a pathway to planning and development of urban environments where all residents, regardless of socio-economic context or mobility level, have equal access to vital services and where cities as a whole are more equitable and sustainable.

The current research examines the specific issue of accessibility to postal services. National postal networks are widespread across their territories, aimed at providing access to the entire population regardless of geographical location or socio-economic status. The posts of Europe are not limited to delivery services, instead having the potential offer of a wide range of services, from banking, mortgage, lending and financial management to money transfer, credit card and bill payment services, certification of documents and payment to government accounts, mobile phone subscriptions and energy services. Given this rich offer, postal services play a crucial role with respect to the entire population and in the daily lives of single individuals. Furthermore, national postal services operate under distinct regulatory frameworks, which shape their structure, distribution, delivery and accessibility to different societal sectors. Thus, in focusing on postal services, the current research explores the challenges and opportunities that arise in optimizing access to an important example of a widely used essential service.

The regulatory framework for postal services is outlined in European Directive 97/67/EC, which stipulates that Member States must guarantee permanent, accessible and universal postal service across their entire territory, meeting standards of quality at prices affordable to all citizens. To ensure comprehensive coverage, they may designate one or more entities as universal service providers. Such universal providers are classified as public utilities, obligated to ensure essential services for all citizens, independent of local territorial factors or economic issues.

In Italy, Legislative Decree No. 261/1999 transposes the provisions of the European Directive and assigns Poste Italiane S.p.A. the responsibility for delivering the universal service. The relationship between Poste Italiane and the state, represented by the Ministry of Economy and Finance, is regulated through five-year renewable program contracts. The proposed contracts, which specify the provision of services, are subject to further evaluation and approval by the Communications Regulatory Authority (AGCOM).

In the Italian context, Ministerial Decree 1444/68 regulates the urban planning of all collective spaces and facilities of common interest, including post offices. In particular, the General Regulatory Plans of all municipalities must ensure minimum distributions of green spaces and facilities for educational, religious, cultural, health, sport and administrative services – including postal services - per resident citizen. In total, the requirement for such spaces – including parking but excluding roadways - is a minimum non-negotiable provision of 18 m^2 per inhabitant.

Moreover, Ministerial Decree of 2008 "Approval of the general conditions for the provision of the universal postal service" clearly recognizes Poste Italiane as an essential service, held to the provision of equitable coverage across the national territory and setting out operational benchmarks in meeting universal obligations. In particular, Table 1 below, reports the criteria in the matter of distribution of access points to the universal service.

Table 1. Criteria on distribution of access points to the public postal network (DM 2008).

Access points to postal service	Service terms
One access point within a maximum of 3 km from the place of residence	For 75% of the population
One access point within a maximum of 5 km from the place of residence	For 92.5% of the population
One access point within a maximum of 6 km from the place of residence	For 97.5% of the population
At least one post office	For 96% of municipalities

2 Literature Review

This literature review aims to provide a critical analysis of the methodologies for measuring urban accessibility to neighborhood services, with a focus on the evolution from early cumulative measures and gravitational models to the adoption of the Two-Step Floating Catchment Area (2SFCA) method.

Early methodologies, based on cumulative measures and gravitational models [9], quantified the potential for supply-demand interaction by measuring the total number of opportunities in an area and weighting it by distance to population. Although useful as a first instrument of measurement, gravity-based formulations only consider the supply aspect of accessibility, neglecting fundamental aspects such as demand and the true travel times to reach the service, not necessarily quantified by distance alone. Such approaches were prone to overestimating accessibility due to uniformly weighting all opportunities, and also proceeded from the weak assumption of homogeneous population distribution. Moreover, the early gravity-based models suffered rigid dependence on administrative boundaries, meaning that the results of the spatial analysis depended on the zoning used (municipal, provincial, regional and so on), which typically does not reflect the true spatial heterogeneity [10]. The assumptions of uniform population distribution across the territory, equal accessibility for all the population of a given area, and the rigidity of the spatial conception, therefore all represented critical weaknesses [11]. Finally, there was a lack of analysis of correlation between opportunities available in an area and the potential demand of the population. Although subject to various criticisms, incidence-based gravitational measures have been the most widely used in studies regarding accessibility, because they provide an aggregate indicator of accessibility that is, to some extent, relatively easy to calculate and interpret [12].

Building on the state of the art, Radke & Mu [13] (2000) and later Luo & Wang [14] (2003) developed a gravity-based measure intended to overcome the limitations of earlier models, initially applying it to accessibility for medical services. Instead of relying on rigid administrative boundaries, the 2SFCA method (Two-Step Floating Catchment Area) introduces the concept of a "floating area", in which circular buffers are defined around each service point, based on a distance threshold d_0 beyond which an individual would not travel to the service. The concept of distance threshold establishes the margin from which accessibility suffers significant decrease, reflecting the lower propensity of users to travel to services that are too far away. This parameter, defined based on empirical evidence, assigns a decreasing value to users as distance increases, thus differentiating the impedance of distance throughout the catchment area. In this way, a specific "fluctuating" area is determined for each service location j, within which the potentially affected population is considered for the calculation of the supply-to-population ratio (R_j). The latter, defined as the number of services available at j divided by the population residing within distance d_0 from j, introduces the concept of user competition. Then, for each point of residence i, the method identifies all areas j accessible within the threshold d_0 and sums the relative R_j ratios to obtain the accessibility indicator A_i. The 2SFCA thus provides a dynamic, replicable indicator for more accurate measurement of accessibility, responding in particular to criticisms of traditional gravity models, which had not adequately considered heterogeneous population distribution and other factors of spatial variation.

Although the 2SFCA method was initially developed for measurement of spatial accessibility to primary health care, it has since been applied in respect of other services, in general as a convenient indicator of stresses arising from origin-destination relationships. Over the years, the method has been used to measure accessibility to work activities, to parks [15] and other urban amenities [16], to green areas [17], and more recently to postal services. In studies such as those conducted in Lyon [18] and rural Croatia [19], the 2SFCA indicator was found to support intuitive, replicable and easily interpreted analysis of the number and distribution of postal service branches, their hours of operation and the services offered, in relation to population density and distribution. Such results provide crucial support for decision-making in integrated urban planning, aimed at ensuring equitable access to services in line with national and European regulations. In general, the literature reveals the importance of integrated approaches that consider the interactions between land use, transportation systems and the characteristics of the individual services and populations. For these reasons, 2SFCA emerges as the most appropriate methodological approach for measurement of accessibility in complex urban settings, in support of urban design and intervention aimed at improving quality of life.

3 Methodology

This section describes the analytical framework applied to assess spatial inequalities in access to postal services in the city of Naples. The methodology, organized in four steps, is designed to ensure consistency, transparency, and replicability, in line with best practices in urban spatial analysis.

1. Data collection - This first step provided for the identification and acquisition of the spatial and alphanumeric data necessary for the study, including demographic data (population aged over 15), data on street networks and building footprints, and the spatial distribution of post offices. Most datasets were sourced from national and regional open data portals (ISTAT, OpenStreetMap and National Geoportal). Postal service data were manually geocoded from information provided on the Poste Italiane website (https://www.poste.it/cerca/index.html#/vieni-in-poste).
2. GIS Data processing - In this step, all collected data were organized within a GIS environment, i.e. the operational geodatabase. Population data were proportionally allocated to a grid of hexagonal cells (50 meters per side) based on building footprint [20]. The hexagonal grid ensured spatial accuracy and efficiency in distance computation [21, 22]. Street network data were refined and converted into a routable graph to support calculation of catchment areas and travel distances. Services and population data were spatially joined to the grid for subsequent computations of accessibility.
3. Accessibility measurement - The levels of accessibility were calculated using a modified Two-Step Floating Catchment Area (2SFCA) method, including a weighting coefficient (k) to reflect time-dependent availability of services (post offices open only part of the day). The method involved calculating supply-demand ratios for each post office, including at different times of day, and then assigning accessibility scores to each hexagonal cell using a Gaussian decay function.
4. Results interpretation and policy integration - The final step involved interpreting the resulting accessibility index in relation to spatial patterns of service provision and population distribution. Results were visualized through maps and statistical analysis, highlighting inequalities and potential service gaps. This evidence-based approach supports public decision-makers in designing equitable service planning policies, especially for vulnerable populations such as the elderly.

The method used to measure accessibility to postal services is a modified 2SFCA, specifically developed with respect to the research aim. The first step is to compute, for each post office j, a ratio Rj (Eq. 1) of supply and demand [20]. The supply of post services is quantified by the number of services available from each office (S_j); the demand is the sum of the population over 15 years old in location i, with Pi weighted to consider a walking-distance-decay function, W_{ij}, which is a function of the total distance. The distances between residential locations i and post offices j are estimated by Network Analyst and ArcGIS Pro, taking into account both walking and transit routes [23].

Although many offices of Poste Italiane are open from 8:30 a.m. to 7:30 p.m., some locations close in the afternoon, with significant impacts on accessibility. Hence, to consider the reduction of postal services during the afternoon, a k coefficient was introduced, varying between 0 and 1 in representation of the availability of services. The coefficient is a ratio of the services available Sj at a given time, relative to the number of services functioning in the morning.

For the second step, A_i, the accessibility of each hexagonal cell was obtained (as reported in Eq. 2) by summing the supply-demand ratios of the j postal offices serving the i cell — multiplied for the impedance function coefficients W_{ij}, to take into account both the spatial distribution of postal offices and the population.

$$R_j = \frac{S_j \bullet \left(\frac{S_j}{S}\right) \bullet k}{\sum P_i \bullet W_{ij}} \quad (1)$$

$$A_i = \sum R_j \bullet W_{ij} \quad (2)$$

The distance-decay function W_{ij} was introduced to reflect people's mobility habits: a Gaussian impedance function, whose values vary between 1 and 0, was used. This function's main characteristic is that it quickly decreases when time of travel is close to the maximum minutes supportable by each age category to access the service, in keeping with their physical capabilities [24].

$$W_{ij} = e^{-d_{ij}^2/\beta} \quad (3)$$

The coefficient β was set equal to 200 in order to best represent mobility attitudes of different population categories according to outcomes in the scientific literature [25–27].

The above methodology requires only open-source data, thereby ensuring full applicability in other territorial contexts.

Table 2 lists the alphanumeric and spatial data (vector and raster) sourcing for application of the GIS-based procedure.

4 Case Study

Naples is the third largest Italian city by population and the fifth in population density. As of 2020, the city has 908,082 inhabitants living within an area of 119,02 km^2, resulting in a density of 7,629 inhabitants per km^2 (ISTAT, 2025). The city is divided into 10 administrative municipalities and more informally into 12 quarters. Given the substantial urban dimensions and highly varied physical and social character of the different quarters, Naples seems a good choice for testing the modified 2SFCA.

Table 2. Alphanumeric and spatial input data.

Dataset	Format	Type of geometry	Source	Year
Population	Alphanumeric	–	ISTAT	2021
Census sections	Geometric	Polygon	ISTAT	2021
Walking street network	Vector	Polyline	OpenStreetMap	2023
Buildings and land use	Vector	Polygon	National Geoportal	2022
Post office locations	Vector/ alpha-numeric	Point	Poste Italiane (manual input)	2025

The center of Naples, featuring high population densities and many buildings of historic importance within intensely developed neighborhoods, consists of the quarters of Monte Calvario, San Giuseppe, Porto, and San Ferdinando. The peripheral quarters, developed mainly between the late-nineteenth and twentieth centuries, are characterized by more varied and sprawling urban development with buildings of lesser importance. Social and economic conditions vary significantly. The quarters of Posillipo, Vomero, and Chiaia, for example, are characterized by greater wealth and a higher quality of life, while residents of Pinera, Scampia, and Ponticelli are more likely to face economic disadvantages.

Within the 12 quarters there are a total of 61 Poste Italiane offices. Of these, 31 are open from 8:20 a.m. to 7:05 p.m., Monday to Friday, and Saturday from 8:20 a.m. to 12:35 p.m. The other 30 offices are open from 8:20 a.m. to 12:35 p.m., Monday to Saturday. All post offices offer basic post and parcel services but also additional services which may include current and checking accounts, teller and/or ATM cash deposit and withdrawal services, automatic deposit and payment services, postal money orders, loans, investment services, cash cards, acceptance of government vouchers, acceptance of tax and pension contributions, provision of pensions and welfare, payments of fines, administrative and utilities bills, various insurance services, electronic passport requests, digital identity services, fiber-optic internet and mobile telephone services, energy contracts. The number of these services in each office ranges from a minimum of seven to a maximum of eleven. Figure 1 shows the distribution of post offices in the municipalities of Naples.

The evaluation of walkability considers the category of individuals over 15 years of age who are resident in Naples (792,675), possessing the autonomy and legal right to assess most of the offered services. The results of the study would also be relevant for the population of younger individuals, able to utilize a more restricted range of services.

5 Results

The application of the modified 2SFCA method to the city of Naples yields important insights into the accessibility of postal services over the course of the day, in relation to their distribution throughout the entire urban area. The analysis reveals important

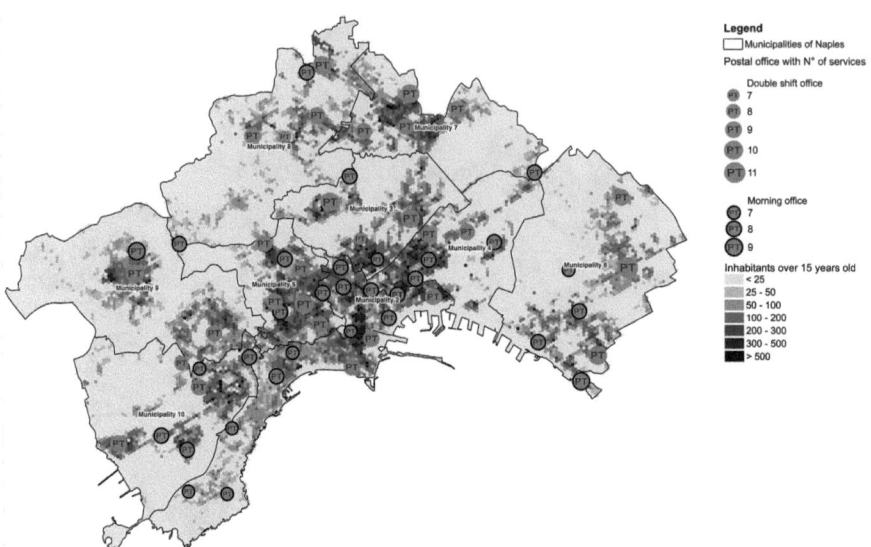

Fig. 1. City of Naples, distribution of post offices and residents over age 15 (elaboration of ISTAT data, 2021).

differences in service availability between the morning and afternoon scenarios and with respect to the varying population densities and socio-economic character of the different urban quarters.

During the morning hours (Fig. 2), when all 61 post offices are operational, accessibility levels are generally high across the city. The historic central and more affluent quarters, such as Vomero and Chiaia, show robust service coverage. Here, the majority of residents can access postal services within contained walking distances. These quarters benefit from a dense urban fabric and, during the morning hours, a high spatial concentration of services. The peripheral quarters, however, present a more heterogeneous scenario. While the analysis reveals acceptable levels of accessibility for certain quarters, others, particularly those with irregular urban structures, show reduced accessibility. The Gaussian impedance function reveals the potential for residents in these neighborhoods to experience lengthy travel distances to the nearest postal offices, therefore with impracticable levels of walkability.

In the afternoon (Fig. 3), accessibility is significantly impacted by the closure of 30 out of 61 post offices. The incorporation of the k coefficient within the model reveals a conspicuous diminution in service accessibility, particularly within peripheral districts where the offices remaining operational tend to be sparsely distributed. As demonstrated in Fig. 4, however, the decrease in available services tends to have a disproportionate overall impact on the more densely populated inner-city neighborhoods.

Furthermore, the network analysis conducted using ArcGIS Pro shows that in some municipalities, the remaining open offices would face a sharp increase in demand, potentially leading to extended waiting times and overcrowded facilities. This is particularly evident in high-density areas with fewer alternative service points. The afternoon scenario challenges the regulatory thresholds set by the Ministerial Decree of 2008, as the

Assessing Walking Accessibility: A GIS-Based Analysis 11

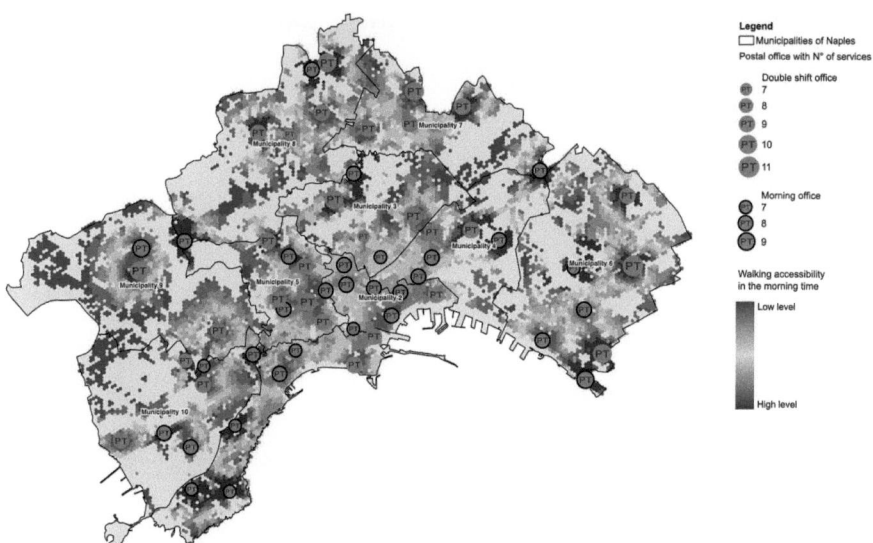

Fig. 2. The walking accessibility to post office during the morning time in the City of Naples, Italy.

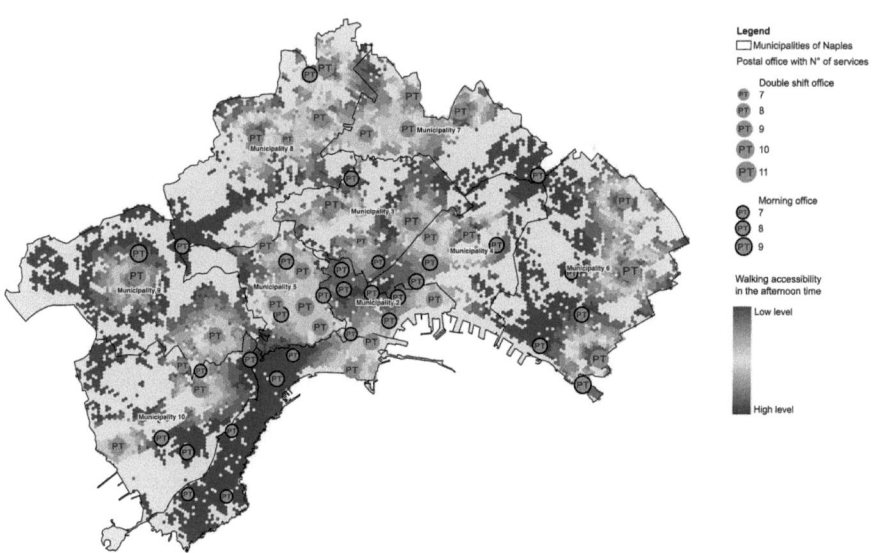

Fig. 3. City of Naples, walking accessibility to post offices during afternoon hours.

reduction in coverage results in longer walking distances to the nearest post office for significant portions of the population.

The variation in accessibility levels between the morning and afternoon scenarios is further illustrated in Fig. 4, which quantifies the number of inhabitants within each

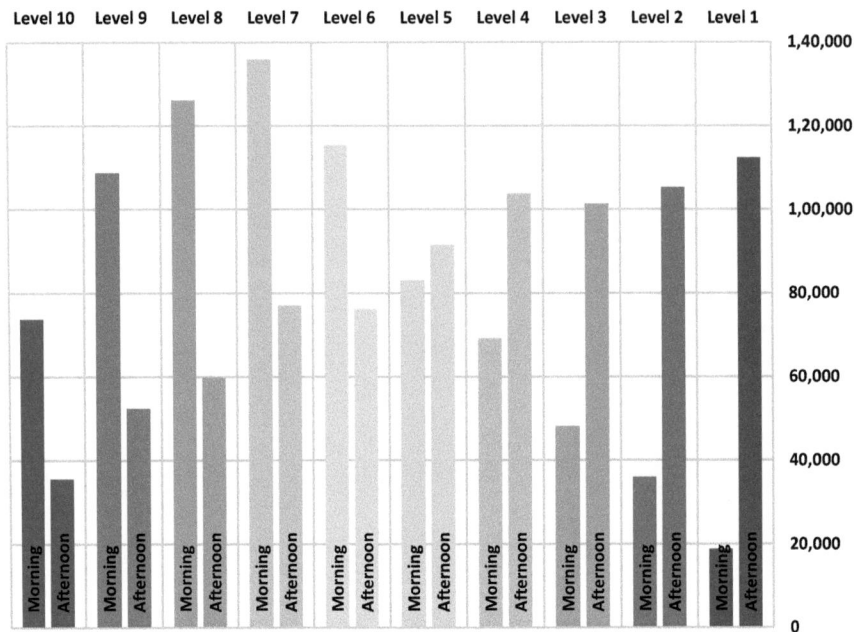

Fig. 4. Inhabitants per level of accessibility to postal services: comparison of morning to afternoon hours (respectively left/right columns).

accessibility level. The results indicate a clear shift: during the morning hours, a significant portion of the population benefits from high accessibility (Levels 10–7), whereas in the afternoon, a substantial number of residents experience a decline in accessibility. This is particularly evident in quarters with lower accessibility (Levels 1–4) with high numbers of affected inhabitants. The differences between these levels reveals the critical effect of operating hours on accessibility to urban public services, with implications for social equity and efficiency of the offered service.

Drawing on these insights, policymakers and urban planners can in general provide for enhanced connectivity to services, including through improvements in walkability, and promote sustainable active mobility, with particularly strong benefits in under-served areas. In particular, postal service providers can use this analysis in strategies for optimization of office locations, adjustments of operating hours, and better alignment of specific services with actual demand. Such integrated approaches address accessibility challenges both through general urban mobility planning and efficient management of the specific network, in this case for postal services.

6 Conclusions and Policy Implications

The results of this study underscore the necessity of developing integrated policies and planning tools that account for the multiple factors influencing urban accessibility. The accessibility of postal services in Naples is shaped by spatial, socio-economic and mobility-related constraints, requiring multidisciplinary approaches in urban service analysis and planning. The methodology applied in this study provides a valuable framework for identifying accessibility gaps and serves as a decision-making support for policymakers and urban planners.

Optimizing the spatial and temporal distribution of post offices, particularly in underserved districts, would significantly enhance the equity and efficiency of services. The insights from this study can be integrated into the general regulatory and sustainable mobility plans for the city of Naples, ensuring that postal services are considered alongside transportation, healthcare, and social infrastructure in spatial and functional planning.

This research is closely aligned with the Research to Business (R2B) paradigm, offering practical applications that bridge the gap between academic analysis and real-world decision-making, particularly in the planning of strategic service networks. By developing a data-driven framework for assessing accessibility to essential services, the study significantly contributes to processes of evidence-based decision-making. The insights gained can guide both public and private stakeholders in optimizing service distribution. The research objective is intimately linked with broader goals of sustainable mobility and urban inclusivity. Enhancing access to postal services, through scenarios such as improved spatial planning, adjusted operating hours, and better integration with sustainable transport options, can play a pivotal role in fostering more equitable urban environments. Ensuring that essential services are universally accessible, regardless of socio-economic status or mobility limitations, contributes to the creation of a more inclusive urban landscape, while simultaneously promoting sustainable and efficient mobility solutions.

Apart from walkability, future interventions should prioritize connectivity via public transportation systems, critically important to more vulnerable groups. For this reason, additional studies could evaluate the optimal location of postal services in relation to public transport, but also to other public services of key importance to underserved sectors.

Future research could expand on the current study by testing the methodology in other urban contexts, beginning with cities of similar socio-spatial characteristics, and by investigating walkability factors that influence accessibility for specific population groups, such as the elderly, considering variations across seasons and times of day. Further improvements to the methodology could involve the integration of additional sustainable transport modes, such as bike-sharing and micro-mobility, to refine the assessment of accessibility beyond walkability. Moreover, incorporating operational data on postal service supply and demand, including average waiting times, congestion levels, and availability of digital services, would provide a more comprehensive understanding of accessibility. The use of the accessibility index in analysis of spatial equity could also be refined by weighting the offer of different services per post office, assigning higher values to offices with multifunctional roles.

In general, it is clear that the development of web-based GIS tools facilitates the visualization and interpretation of accessibility patterns, enabling more effective decision-making. By integrating data-driven analysis into urban policy and planning, cities can enhance both the accessibility and inclusivity of essential services, ensuring that all residents, regardless of location or socio-economic status, benefit from fair and efficient provision of public services.

References

1. United Nations, Department of Economic and Social Affairs, Population Division: World Urbanization Prospects: The 2018 Revision, (2018). https://population.un.org/wup/assets/WUP2018-Report.pdf
2. Davis, M.: Planet of Slums. Verso (2006)
3. Neutens, T.: Accessibility, equity and health care: review and research directions for transport geographers. J. Transp. Geogr. **43**, 14–27 (2015). https://doi.org/10.1016/j.jtrangeo.2014.12.006
4. Delmelle, E.: Measuring the Spatial Equity of Transport Systems: Emerging Data Opportunities, pp. 31–46. Edward Elgar Publishing eBooks (2024). https://doi.org/10.4337/9781802201888.00009
5. Guida, C., Caglioni, M.: Urban accessibility: the paradox, the paradigms and the measures. A scientific review. TEMA J. Land Use Mobil. Environ. **13**(2), 149–168 (2020). https://doi.org/10.6092/1970-9870/6743
6. Scarponi, L., Abdelfattah, L., Gorrini, A., Valenzuela Cortés, C., Carpentieri, G., Guida, C., Zucaro, F., Andreola, F., Muzzonigro, A., Da Re, L., Gargiulo, E., Cañas, C., Walker, J., Choubassi, R.: Thematic review on women's perception of safety while walking in public space: the STEP UP project. Sustainability. **15**(21), 15636 (2023). https://doi.org/10.3390/su152115636
7. Litman, T.: Evaluating transportation equity. World Transp. Policy Pract. **8**(2), 50–65 (2002) https://trid.trb.org/view/726039
8. Pellicelli, G., Rossetti, S., Caselli, B., Zazzi, M.: Urban regeneration to enhance sustainable mobility. TEMA J. Land Use Mobil. Environ., 57–70 (2022). https://doi.org/10.6093/1970-9870/8646
9. Hansen, W.G.: How accessibility shapes land use. J. Am. Inst. Plann. **25**, 73–76 (1959)
10. Geurs, K.T., van Wee, G.P.: Accessibility evaluation of land-use and transport strategies: review and research directions. J. Transp. Geogr. **12**, 127–140 (2004). https://doi.org/10.1016/j.jtrangeo.2003.10.005
11. Dong, X., Ben-Akiva, M., Bowman, J., Walker, J.: Moving from trip-based to activity-based measures of accessibility. Transp. Res. A. **2**, 163–180 (2006). https://doi.org/10.1016/j.tra.2005.05.002
12. Xing, L., Liu, Y., Wang, B., Wang, Y., Liu, H.: An environmental justice study on spatial access to parks for youth by using an improved 2SFCA method in Wuhan, China. Cities. **96**, 102405 (2019). https://doi.org/10.1016/j.cities.2019.102405
13. Radke, J., Mu, L.: Spatial decomposition, modeling and mapping service regions to predict access to social programs. Geogr. Inf. Sci. **6**, 105–112 (2000). https://doi.org/10.1080/10824000009480538
14. Luo, W., Wang, F.: Spatial accessibility to primary care and physician shortage area designation: a case study in Illinois with GIS approaches. In: Khan, O.A., Skinner, R. (eds.) Geographic information systems and health applications, pp. 260–278. Idea Group Publishing, Hershey, PA, and London (2003). https://doi.org/10.4018/978-1-59140-042-4.ch015
15. Li, Z., Fan, Z., Song, Y., Chai, Y.: Assessing equity in park accessibility using a travel behavior-based G2SFCA method in Nanjing, China. J. Transp. Geogr. **96**, 103179 (2021). https://doi.org/10.1016/j.jtrangeo.2021.103179

16. Zhao, Z., Li, X., Xu, Y., Yang, S., Jiang, Y., Wang, S.: Evaluating spatial accessibility of cultural urban land use by using improved 2SFCA method in Xi'an, China. Heliyon. **8**(12), e11993 (2022). https://doi.org/10.1016/j.heliyon.2022.e11993
17. Qin, J., Liu, Y., Yi, D., Sun, S., Zhang, J.: Spatial accessibility analysis of parks with multiple entrances based on real-time travel: the case study in Beijing. Sustainability. **12**(18), 7618 (2020). https://doi.org/10.3390/su12187618
18. Mercier, A., Corvec, S.S., Ovtracht, N.: Measure of accessibility to postal services in France: a potential spatial accessibility approach applied in an urban region. Pap. Reg. Sci. **100**(1), 227–250 (2020). https://doi.org/10.1111/pirs.12564
19. Mostarac, K., Kavran, Z., Feletar, P.: Application of catchment area method for determining post office accessibility: case study Bjelovar-Bilogora county. Geoadria. **24**(1), 53–70 (2019). https://doi.org/10.15291/geoadria.2858
20. Carpentieri, G., Favo, F.: The end-use electric energy consumption in urban areas: a GIS-based methodology. An application in the city of Naples. TEMA J. Land Use Mobil. Environ. (2017b). DOAJ (DOAJ: Directory of Open Access Journals). https://doi.org/10.6092/1970-9870/5173
21. Lubamba, J.K., Radoux, J., Defourny, P.: Multimodal accessibility modeling from coarse transportation networks in Africa. Int. J. Geogr. Inf. Sci. **27**(5), 1005–1022 (2012b). https://doi.org/10.1080/13658816.2012.735673
22. Guida, C., Carpentieri, G.: Quality of life in the urban environment and primary health services for the elderly during the Covid-19 pandemic: an application to the city of Milan (Italy). Cities. **110**, 103038 (2021). https://doi.org/10.1016/j.cities.2020.103038
23. Carpentieri, G., Guida, C., Masoumi, H.E.: Multimodal accessibility to primary health services for the elderly: a case study of Naples, Italy. Sustainability. **12**(3), 781 (2020). https://doi.org/10.3390/su12030781
24. Bauer, J., Groneberg, D.A.: Measuring spatial accessibility of health care providers – Introduction of a variable distance decay function within the floating catchment area (FCA) method. PLoS One. **11**(7), e0159148 (2016). https://doi.org/10.1371/journal.pone.0159148
25. Kwan, M.P.: Space-time and integral measures of individual accessibility: a comparative analysis using a point-based framework. Geograph. Anal. **30**(3), 191–216 (1998). https://doi.org/10.1111/j.1538-4632.1998.tb00396.x
26. Palermo, A., Tucci, G., Chieffallo, L.: Definition of spatio-temporal levels of accessibility. Isochronous analysis of regional transport networks. TeMA - J. Land Use, Mobil. Environ. **18**(1), 23–38 (2025). https://doi.org/10.6093/1970-9870/11146
27. Pirselimoğlu Batman, Z., Ender Altay, E., Sengül, S.: The relationship between walkability and landscape values in transportation. Examination of landscape values in urban area transportation axes. TeMA - J. Land Use, Mobil. Environ. **17**(2), 285–308 (2024). https://doi.org/10.6093/1970-9870/10462

Land Suitability Analysis of Nature-Based Solutions for Climate Adaptation and Mitigation in the Sardinia Region, Italy

Chiara Garau[1], Alfonso Annunziata[2(✉)], and Francesco Scorza[2]

[1] Department of Civil and Environmental Engineering and Architecture (DICAAR), University of Cagliari, 09123 Cagliari, Italy
[2] Department of Engineering, University of Basilicata, 85100 Potenza, Italy
alfonso.annunziata@unibas.it

Abstract. The study investigates the improvement of urban ecological infrastructure via urban and peri-urban forestation initiatives. The study focuses on Blue and Green Infrastructure (BGI) in vulnerable urban areas as a relevant solution to fostering sustainable development and addressing climate change adaptation and mitigation. By integrating multi-criteria spatial analysis and statistical models, the study develops a replicable procedure to identify suitable areas for BGI interventions, ensuring optimised use of financial resources and maximising environmental, social, and economic benefits. The procedure is aimed at organising the information required for implementing the Geodesign process in the context of defining strategies for adaptation to and mitigation of climate alteration. It is applied to a case study in Sardinia, Italy. The study's findings demonstrate the relevance of the procedure to the spatialisation of public policies, enabling evidence-based decisions in the context of integrating mitigation and adaptation strategies into urban regeneration and sustainable development plans.

Keywords: Climate Change · Mitigation · Adaptation · Nature Based Solutions · Urban Forests · Sardinia

1 Introduction

The sustainable development of urban areas is a critical step for contributing to goals defined at global, regional, national, sub-national and local levels [1]. The trends of urbanisation and the persistence of unsustainable forms of production and consumption are responsible for the increasing role of cities as major drivers of climate alteration and as areas vulnerable to climate change impacts. Consequently, implementing transformative strategies for sustainable and resilient cities is central to enable integrated sustainable development and mitigation of and adaptation to climate alterations. The proposed study

---

This paper is the result of the joint work of the authors. 'Abstract', 'Methodology', 'Results' and 'Conclusions' were written jointly by all authors. Francesco Scorza wrote the 'Introduction', Chiara Garau wrote the 'Discussion' and Alfonso Annunziata the 'Literature review'.

© The Author(s), under exclusive license to Springer Nature Switzerland AG 2026
O. Gervasi et al. (Eds.): ICCSA 2025 Workshops, LNCS 15896, pp. 16–33, 2026.
https://doi.org/10.1007/978-3-031-97654-4_2

is part of a research on "Geodesign for climate change mitigation and adaptation in the Mediterranean region". Geodesign utilises a comprehensive methodology to investigate inter-systemic interactions across distinct spatial and temporal scales [2] and develops a structured and iterative process for enabling informed decisions [3–5]. As a result, Geodesign represents a valid tool to respond to issues determined by climate alteration [5, 6]. The proposed study focuses on urban ecological infrastructures and emphasises interventions of urban and peri-urban forestation. Expanding the urban ecological infrastructure is a strategy based on the nature-based solutions perspective. Interventions of urban and peri-urban forestation are relevant to provide environmental, social, and economic benefits, including improved climate resilience and climate regulation, carbon sequestration and storage, conservation of urban biodiversity and regeneration of public spaces for recreation and social activities. This research examines the identification of areas most suitable to interventions of Blue and Green Infrastructures (BGI) reinforcement. The objective is to contribute in the optimisation of limited financial resources and maximise the related environmental, social and economic benefits. This study adopted multi-criteria spatial analysis and statistical models to develop a replicable procedure aimed at: i) identifying vulnerable parts of urbanised areas most suitable to BGI development; ii) identifying clusters of urbanised land units presenting similar suitability levels. The proposed procedure is tested in the case study of the Sardinia Region, in Italy. The relevance of the study results from distinct aspects: i) defining the optimal location for interventions relevant to climate alteration adaptation and mitigation; ii) underlining the relevance of the spatial dimension in the definition of mitigation and adaptation strategies. As a result, the study contributes to enabling evidence-based decisions in the context of urban adaptation plan development and integrating mitigation/ adaptation criteria into urban regeneration and sustainable development plans. The article is organised into six sections: after the introduction, a review of the scientific literature is presented in Sect. 2. The methodology section describes data, tools, models and indicators utilised to implement the procedure. Section 4 presents the findings related to the identification of clusters of urbanised land units and the computation of a metric of site suitability. Section 5 discusses the findings from the analysis. Finally, the Conclusions delineate the significance of the study's results, the limits of the methodology, and the pertinent directions for the study's advancement. The study contributes to studies on the alignment of sustainable development and adaptation/ mitigation initiatives and the development of decision support model for the spatialization of mitigation and adaptation policies [7, 8].

2 Literature Review

2.1 Climate Alterations and Cities

Sustainable development is defined as a form of development that seeks to satisfy the requirements of both present and future generations. The United Nations 2030 Agenda for sustainable development outlines an ambitious vision on development articulated in a set of transformative goals and targets [9]. Contrasting climate alteration is recognised as a requirement for sustainable development. The Sustainable Development Goal (SDG) 11 also indicates the construction of safe, resilient and sustainable cities as a condition for sustainable development [9, 10]. The role of urban sustainable development as a driver of global sustainable development is reiterated by the New Urban Agenda [1, 11] and, at a regional level, by the Urban Agenda for The European Union [12] and the New Leipzig Charter [13]. Moreover, cities and urbanisation trends determine interdependent consequences relevant to climate alteration: emergence of urbanised areas as major sources of GHG (Greenhouse gasses) emissions [14, 15]; and increased vulnerability and exposure of urbanised areas to climate alteration impacts. The proportion of urban emissions on global emissions is significant and continues to increase [15, 16], from 25 $GtCO_2eq$ in 2015, equal to 62% of global emissions, to 29 $GtCO_2eq$ in 2020 equal to 62–72% of global emissions. Urban emissions are also influenced by urban structural factors, including urban form, density and size [17]. Consequently, trends in urban land use and urban form transformation influence future urban environmental impact and long-term mitigation potential. Moreover, interactions among modification in urban form, exposure and vulnerability and direct climate impacts can engender potential adverse impacts specific to individual urban areas [17]. For instance, temperature increase due to climate alterations can amplify the multi-scale adverse impacts of the urban heat island (UHI) [18, 19]. UHI refers to localised elevated temperature in the urban environment, determined by the material properties and spatial configuration of the built environment and heat release from urban functions [17]. Cities' levels of exposure to river, pluvial, sewer and coastal floods [17] are increased as a result of continued increase in global surface temperatures and urban structure modification resulting in land use conversion and soil sealing [20, 21]. Consequently, adaptation and mitigation measures in urban areas become central to mitigating climate change and enhancing resilience, as well as to urban sustainable development strategies. The 2030 Agenda [9], the New Urban Agenda [1], and the Urban Agenda for the EU [12, 13] advocate for the implementation of integrated policies aimed at enhancing resilience to catastrophes, as well as adapting to and mitigating climate change, as fundamental criteria for urban sustainable development. Specifically, combining mitigation actions and integrating Sustainable Development Goals can catalyse sustainable urban developmental trajectories. At the same time, interferences among mitigation options, and among mitigation, adaptation and sustainable development goals are to be considered [15]. For instance, a need emerge for defining optimal level of density so as to avoid fragmentation and reduction of blue and green infrastructure and consequent UHI intensification [22–24].

2.2 Adaptation and Mitigation Actions for Urban Areas

Key strategies for coupling mitigation, adaptation, and sustainable development benefits encompass land use diversity and density, intrinsic to the Transit Oriented Development, 15-minute city and Neighbourhood Unit models [25], electrification and decarbonisation of urban energy systems, improving buildings energy performance, transition to net-zero emissions materials in the construction sector [26, 27], increased mobility options, prioritising active travel and public transit, avoiding, minimising and recycling waste [28] and blue and green infrastructure [29]. Urban BGIs refer to a strategic perspective aimed at developing continuous and multi-functional structures of green and blue spaces [30]. Urban BGI is a form of Nature-based Solutions (NBS). NBS are solutions based on nature and use the metabolism of ecosystems as infrastructure to provide natural services [31], increasing climate resilience, generating co-benefits for society, and ensuring the protection, sustainable management and restoration of natural or modified ecosystems [32].Urban BGIs include a broad set of natural and semi-natural spaces including forests, agricultural land, urban green areas, private gardens, ponds, streams and single green elements (green roofs, green façades, street trees) [15, 30]. Urban BGIs produce benefits in terms of mitigation, adaptation and SDGs realisation [29, 33, 34]. In particular, urban forests provide reduced building energy use, reduced water use, conditions conducive to active travel, and carbon storage and sequestration [15]. Adaptation co-benefits include reduced local temperatures, reduced incidence of cardiovascular and respiratory diseases, flooding mitigation, improved air quality and biodiversity protection [35, 36]. Mitigation benefits, in terms of carbon sequestration, are estimated to be an average of 2.05 tCha-1y-1 in functional urban areas in the United States [37] and 2.67 tCha-1y-1 in a case study conducted in Madrid, Spain [38]. Teo et al. [39] estimate a global carbon sequestration potential of 82.4 (+ − 25.7) $MtCO_2ey^{-1}$. In terms of micro-climate regulation a tree cover of 16% of urbanised areas can result in a temperature decrease of 1 °C [35]. Lastly, urban forests are relevant to Sustainable Development goals and targets relative to the development of safe, resilient and sustainable cities: urban forest contribute, in fact, to developing a continuous infrastructure of open, inclusive, multi-purpose, usable safe open spaces, for promoting vibrant urban environment, improving air quality, quality of life and increasing resilience [1, 13]. The study presented in the subsequent sections outlines a procedure for evaluating the suitability of urban areas for forestation interventions at the census tract level, considering climatic, structural, and land use factors.

3 Methodology

The procedure combines spatial multicriteria analysis and statistical analysis to evaluate the suitability of urban areas in the Sardinia Region, to intervention of BGI development and, in particular, of urban forestation relevant to adapting to and mitigating climate alteration. The procedure is organised in six stages (Fig. 1): i) selection of relevant spatial units; ii) selection of relevant criteria and sub-criteria; iii) selection of pertinent indicators, indicators computation and normalisation; iv) computation of the load-factors for the sub-criteria and for the criteria, based on distinct scenarios; v) computation of a composite indicator for the selected criteria and of a composite indicator of land suitability (ISUF) for the proposed scenarios; vi) analysis of the spatial auto-correlation for the indicators related to the selected criteria and for the composite indicator of land suitability determined under the proposed scenarios.

3.1 Selection of Spatial Units

The census tracts from the 2021 National Census representing urbanised areas in the Sardinia Region (Fig. 2) are selected as the units of analysis [40]. Census tracts are selected based on the value of the categorial variable 'location type'. More precisely, census tracts labelled as urban centers, or urbanised clusters are selected as units of

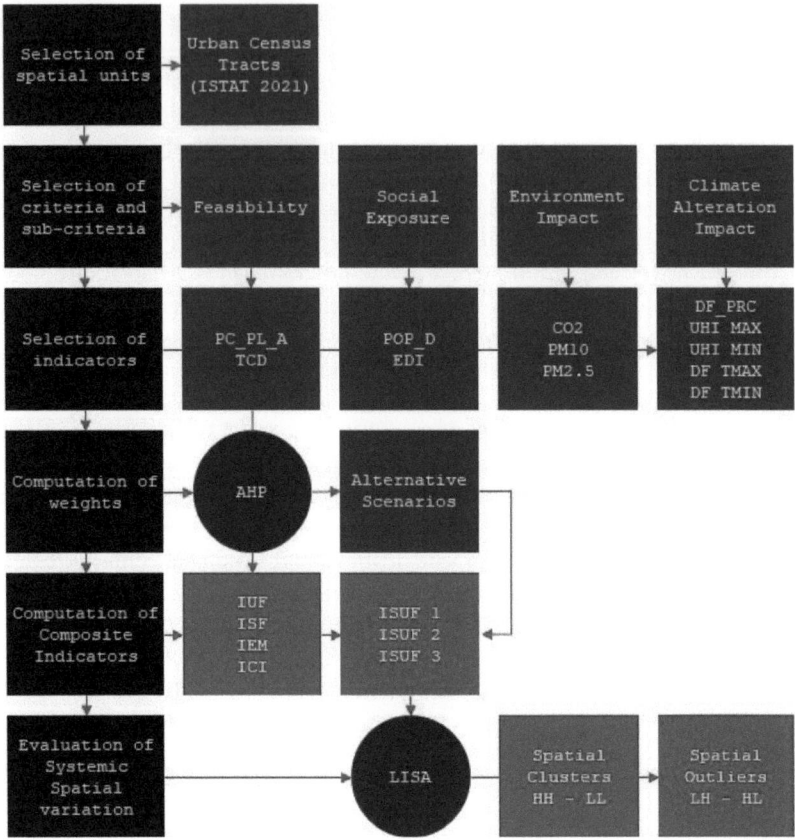

Fig. 1. Organization of the proposed procedure.

analysis. Selecting census tracts as units of analysis is instrumental to obtaining a granular representation of the spatial variability of conditions of suitability to specific mitigation and adaptation actions across an urban area.

3.2 Criteria and Sub-criteria Selection

The selection of criteria and sub-criteria is representative of the need to optimise the localisation of interventions for maximising benefits in terms of adaptation to and mitigation of climate alteration. The criteria refer to four dimensions: i) feasibility of the action; ii) social exposure; iii) Environmental impact of urbanised areas; iv) magnitude of climate alteration impacts.

The feasibility of the intervention is related to urban form factors, which represent the sub-criteria. These include the presence of plantable areas, and the tree cover density. The second criterion refers to the exposure of the population to climate alteration impacts mitigated by urban forests. The sub-criteria are population density and percentage of vulnerable individuals. Urbanised areas' environmental impact includes the sub-criteria

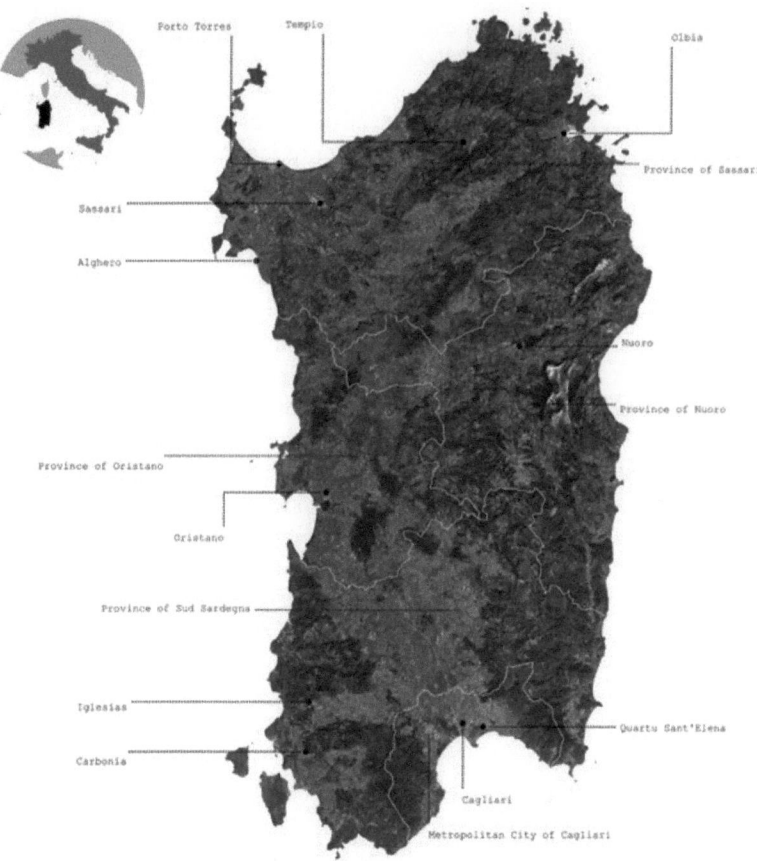

Fig. 2. Selection of the Area of Study.

intensity of CO_2 emissions, PM 10 concentration and PM 2.5 concentration. Lastly, the magnitude of climate alteration impacts includes the sub-criteria Variation of precipitation patterns, diurnal and nocturnal Urban Heat Island and variation of minimum and maximum temperatures. Localised elevated temperature, temperature increase, and precipitation variation represent, in fact, climate alteration impacts mitigated by urban forestation interventions.

3.3 Selection, Computation and Normalisation of the Indicators

The procedure is based on 12 indicators representing the selected sub-criteria. The presence of plantable areas is operationalised in terms of the ratio of permeable land, presenting a tree cover density minor than 50%, on the surface area of the i-th census tract. Information on land cover is derived from the CLCplus Backbone 2021 layer. The latter provides a detailed land cover inventory for the 2021 reference year, in the spatial resolution of 10 m, representing for each cell the dominant land cover among the 11 basic land cover classes [41]. Tree Cover Density is measured in terms of the average value, for each census tract, of tree cover density derived from the Layer Tree Cover Density (TCD) retrieved from the Copernicus Land Monitoring Service (CLMS). The TCD layer provides the level of tree cover density in a range from 0% to100% at pan-European level in the spatial resolution of 10 m for the 2018 reference year [42].

Population density is computed as the number of individuals per ha residing in the i-th census tract. Data related to resident population per census tract and census tract surface area are retrieved from the dataset Territorial Bases and Census Variables for the reference year 2021 of the Italian National Statistic Institute (ISTAT) [40]. The percentage of vulnerable individuals refers to the proportion of the elderly population for each census tract and it is operationalised in terms of the elderly dependency index. Elderly population is, in fact, vulnerable to temperature increase and localised elevated temperatures in urban areas, resulting from and amplified by climate alteration [15]. The Elderly Dependency Index is computed for each census tract as the ratio of the population of age superior to 65 years on the population of age comprised in the 15–64 years range. The CO_2 emissions intensity is computed as the mean value, for each census tract, of the value averaged over 12 months of cumulated CO_2 emissions. The indicator is based on the Anthropogenic emissions of CO_2 Layer retrieved from the global emission inventories of the Copernicus Atmosphere Monitoring Service [43]. The dataset provides the cumulated emission intensity from 12 sectors, measured in $KgCO_2$ m^{-2} s^{-1}, for the 2019 reference year, at a spatial resolution of 0.1°. The values are converted in tCO_2 Km^{-2} $year^{-1}$ and the raster layer is reprojected, resampled via a B-spline interpolation at a spatial resolution of 1 km and clipped to the area of interest. Similarly, PM10 and PM2.5 concentration levels are computed as the mean value for individual census tracts, of the annual average of concentration levels of PM10 and PM2.5, measured in micrograms per cubic meter of air ($\mu g/m^3$). Data are derived from the pm10, European air quality data for 2022, and from the pm2.5, European air quality data for 2022 [44]. The data set provides concentrations levels for PM2.5 and PM10 at a spatial resolution of 1 km. The raster layers are reprojected, resampled via a B-spline interpolation at a spatial resolution of 500 m and clipped to the area of interest. Average CO2 emission intensity and PM10 and PM2.5 concentration levels at census tracts level are computed via the zonal statistic function in a GIS environment, by averaging the related values of the cells comprised in the census tract. Precipitation regime alteration is computed, for the i-th census tract, as the variation among the average of annual precipitations in the 1970–2000 period and the average of estimated annual precipitations in the 2021–2040 period. Urban Heat Island during day and night hours are computed at census tract level respectively as the variation in maximum and minimum temperature averaged over the summer season among the i-th census tract and contiguous rural areas. Contiguous rural areas are defined via a multi-step procedure based on Wang et al. [45, 46]. The procedure includes creation of 12 buffers of the urban clusters at varying radii; selection of the area delimited by the boundaries of the 12th and ninth buffer; removal of areas covered by water; selection of areas with elevation ranging from −50 m to +50 m from the mean elevation of the relevant urban cluster. The radius of the i-th buffer is determined so that the area delimited by the boundaries of the i-th buffer and the i-th − 1 buffer is half the surface area of the related urban cluster. Minimum and Maximum temperature variation are computed, respectively, as the divergence among the mean summer maximum temperature and the summer minimum temperature averaged over the 1970–2000 period and the estimated mean summer maximum temperature and summer minimum temperature averaged over the 2021–2040 period. Subsequently, the maximum and minimum temperature variations for each census tract are calculated by averaging the corresponding values of the cells contained in the census tract. Precipitation data and Temperature data are derived from the Historical Climate Data and the Future Climate Data datasets of the WorldClim data service [47, 48]. Data are provided as raster grids at a spatial resolution of 1 Km. The raster layers are reprojected, resampled via a B-spline interpolation at a spatial resolution of 200 m and clipped to the area of interest. Data related to the 2021–2040 period derive from estimates computed under the Shared Socio-economic Pathway (SSP) 370, for the Global Climate Model (GCM) GISS-E2–1-G. SSP 370 refers to a scenario of moderate implementation of mitigation and adaptation actions in a context of resurgent nationalism, concerns about competitiveness and security, and regional conflicts [49, 50].

3.4 Weighting of Sub-criteria and Criteria

The weights of the criteria and the sub-criteria are determined via the Analytical Hierarchy Process (AHP), developed by Thomas Saaty in the 1970s [51]. It is a measurement procedure based on a process of problems' decomposition via the identification of an objective and the determination of the criteria, sub-criteria and alternatives relevant to realising the objective. AHP reduces the complexity of a problem via a pairwise comparison technique integrated into a multi-level structure: the multi-level structure is used to represent the problem and pairwise comparisons are used to determine relations among the variables comprised in a same level [51, 52]. In the discrete case the comparisons result in dominance matrices and in the continuous case in kernels of Fredholm operators. Comparisons are formalised in terms of a dominance factor c_{ij} representing the relative importance of element i compared to element j of the same level in relation to element k of the superior level. The dominance matrices are positive and reciprocal, e.g. $c_{ij} = 1/c_{ji}$. A qualitative evaluation, based on a semantic scale, can be provided if the dominance factor cannot be determined quantitatively. The value scale proposed by Saaty [53] enables the conversion of qualitative and comparative evaluations into quantitative terms. The matrix is an n*n structure, where n is the number of elements being compared. The value in row i and column j of the matrix indicates the relative importance of element i over element j concerning a variable k of the superior level. The comparison matrices are normalised by dividing each dominance factor c_{ij} by the sum of the values in the same column. The average of the values in row i of the normalised matrix represents the weight of the i-th element. The level of evaluations' consistency is determined by calculating the Consistency Ratio (CR). If CR is superior to 0.1 a re-examination of the judgements in the comparison matrix is often required. CR is given by the ratio between the Consistency Index (CI) and the Random Consistency Index (RCI). CI is obtained via Eq. 1:

$$CI = \frac{\lambda_{\max} - n}{n - 1} \qquad (1)$$

λ_{max} represents the principal eigenvalue of the comparison matrix. Lastly, the Random Consistency Index, is a predetermined value, and is a function of the number n of elements considered.

3.5 Computation of a Composite Indicator of Site Suitability

The computation of criteria's priorities considers the definition of distinct scenarios. In scenario 1 the Magnitude of Climate Alteration impacts is considered more important, and the feasibility of the action is considered of minor significance. In scenario 2 the feasibility of the action and the magnitude of climate alteration impacts are evaluated as more significant and impact on climate alteration is considered as the least important criterion. Lastly, in scenario 3, Social Exposure is prioritised over the remaining criteria. Concerning sub-criteria, the percentage of plantable areas and Tree Cover density are considered of equal importance in relation to the feasibility of the actions. Similarly, Population density and the Elderly Dependency Index are given equal priority concerning the level of social exposure to climate alteration impacts. Regarding urbanised areas' environmental impact, the concentration of PM10 and PM2.5 are considered of equal significance and more important compared to Intensity of CO_2 emissions. Benefits provided by urban forests in terms of reduction of particulate concentration and improved air quality [54] are considered more relevant to local urban populations compared to forests' contribution to mitigation via carbon sequestration, given the supralocal dimension of climate alteration. Regarding the magnitude of climate alteration impacts, the increase in minimum and maximum temperatures is considered more relevant compared to UHI and alteration in precipitation regimes. For each criterion, an index is calculated as the sum of the products of the pertinent sub-criteria metrics and their respective weights. The resulting indicators represent the suitability of the spatial units in relation to individual criteria: IUF formalises the feasibility of the intervention, ISF social exposure, IEM formalises urban environmental impacts and ICI measures the magnitude of relevant climate alteration impacts. Lastly, a composite indicator of land suitability (ISUF) is computed as the sum of the products of the criteria indexes and the respective weights determined for each alternative scenario.

3.6 Spatial Autocorrelation

A local Indicator of Spatial Association [55] is computed to evaluate the presence of systematic spatial variation in the Indicator of Land Suitability. Spatial autocorrelation statistics are designed to reject the null condition of spatial randomness in favour of an alternative of clustering. The selected Indicator is the Local Moran's I, computed via the GeoDa software tool, version 1.22 [56]. The Local Moran's I is computed, for a location i, as the product of the value of a variable and its spatial lag (see Eq. 2).

$$I = \frac{z_i * \sum_j w_{ij} * z_j}{\sum_i z_i^2} \quad (2)$$

The spatial lag of a variable measured at location i is formalised as the sum of the values measured at adjacent locations multiplied by a factor determined by a function of the distance of the adjacent locations from location i. If adjacent observations present similar data values the map indicates positive spatial autocorrelation. If adjacent observations tend to present contrasting values, then a negative spatial autocorrelation is observed. The direction of the relation is visualised via a plot, denominated a Moran scatterplot, that presents the spatial lag of the variable on the y-axis and the original variable on the x-axis. Significance is measured via a pseudo p-value derived from a conditional permutation procedure. As a result, given a location i, the values of the n-1 remaining observations are randomly permuted to generate a reference distribution. Subsequently, the p-value is computed as a function of the number of permutation (M) and the number of times the Local statistics computed from the random data sets is equal or superior to the observed statistic (R) (Eq. 3).

$$p = \frac{R+1}{M+1} \tag{3}$$

The evaluation of significance and of the location of individual observations in the Moran Scatterplot results in the identification of four types of clustering: observations presenting values above the mean, and adjacent to observations presenting similar values form a High-High (HH) cluster. Observations presenting values below the mean and adjacent to observations presenting values below the mean form a Low-Low (LL) cluster. High-Low (HL) and Low-High (LH) outliers refer respectively to observations presenting values above the mean adjacent to observations presenting contrasting values and observations presenting values below the mean adjacent to observations presenting values above the mean. An exploratory statistical analysis using the Average Comparison Chart is conducted to characterise the suitable areas under the alternative scenarios, enabling the identification of statistically significant differences in the mean values of selected sub-criteria between suitable and non-suitable census tracts.

4 Results

The computation of the composite indicator of land suitability under alternative scenarios indicate a general moderate condition of suitability of urban census tracts to interventions of urban forestation. More precisely, the indicator computed under scenario 1 indicates levels of suitability ranging from 0.197 to 0.582, a mean value of 0.374 and a median of 0.376. Under scenario 2, levels of suitability range from 0.181 to 0.646. The mean value is 0.432 and the median is equal to 0.430. Lastly, the composite indicator computed under scenario 3 presents values comprised in the interval 0.128–0.597, a mean value of 0.305 and a median of 0.303 (Fig. 3).

The Local Moran's I underlines significant spatial relations for scenario 1, indicated by a value of the statistic of 0.803, a moderate level of interdependence for scenario 2, indicated by a value of Local Moran's I of 0.476, and a modest spatial relation under scenario 3, indicated by a Local Moran's I equal to 0.330. Focusing on Scenario 1 (Fig. 2), a significant p-value (<0.005), derived from 999 permutations, is observed for 36.1% of urban census tracts, and adequate levels of significance, indicated by a p-value inferior to 0.05 is observed for 7730 census tracts, equal to 56.6% of the selected sample. The evaluation of the direction of the correlation indicates that 3822 census

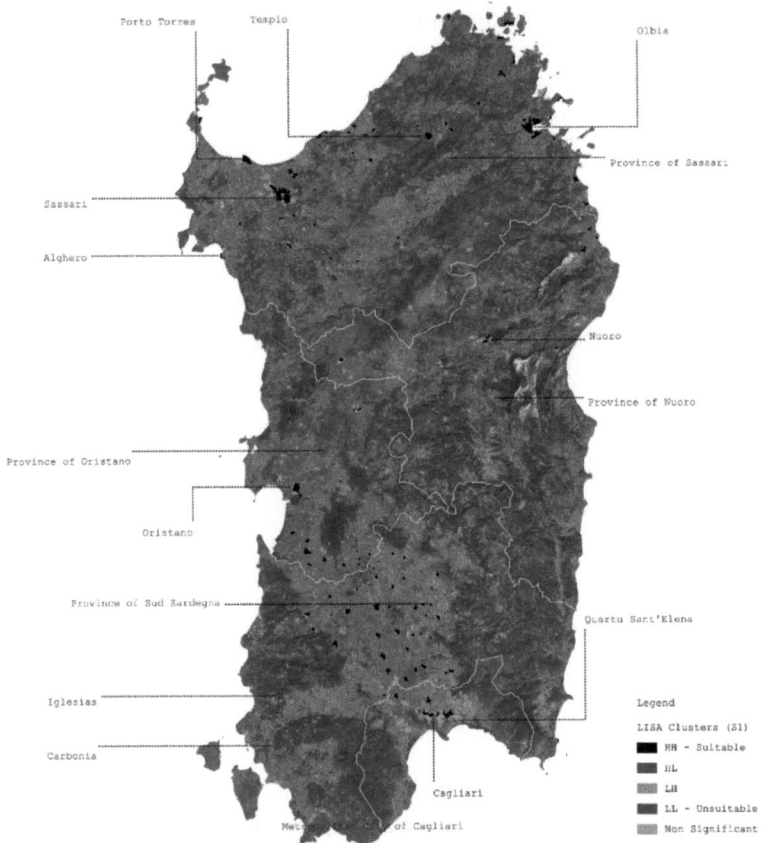

Fig. 3. Clusters Derived from Local Moran's I, under scenario 1. Census Tracts categorised as High-High Clusters are identified as Suitable Locations.

tracts, equal to 27.9% of the sample, present levels of suitability above the mean and positively related to levels of suitability observed at adjacent locations. As a result, 3822 census tracts are comprised in HH clusters. Vice versa, 3312 census tracts, equal to 24.2% of the sample, are comprised in LL clusters. Observations in LL clusters present levels of suitability below the mean and positively related to values computed at adjacent locations. A limited percentage of census tracts, equal respectively to 0.06% and 0.07% is categorised as spatial outliers, comprised in LH and HL clusters: 83 census tracts present values below the mean negatively related to values observed at adjacent locations (LH clusters) and 101 census tracts present values above the mean and are contiguous to locations presenting values below the mean (HL clusters). HH clusters are located in semi-central and periurban areas of main urbanised regions, including Cagliari, Oristano, Sassari and Olbia and in urban clusters in the Campidano Plain. LL clusters include urban centres in the Sulcis Iglesiente province and in mountainous internal areas in the Nuoro Province, and central compact districts and costal urbanised areas in the Metropolitan City of Cagliari (MCC). As a result, Considering plantable areas located in urban census tracts presenting values of the composite indicator of land suitability above the mean and adjacent to location presenting analogous values, a total surface area of 3490.11 ha is suitable to interventions of urban forestation, under scenario 1. Under Scenario 2, derived from prioritising criteria of feasibility and magnitude of climate alteration impact, 3218,28 ha of plantable areas are identified as suitable to interventions of urban forestation. Under Scenario 2 a distribution of suitable census tracts similar to Scenario 1 is observed. Suitable areas are located in peri-urban areas in the Metropolitan City of Cagliari and in urban Centres situated in the Campidano Plain. Spatial clusters of suitable areas are observed in the cities of Olbia and Tempio and in peri-urban districts in the urban areas of Sassari, Nuoro and Oristano. Under scenario 3, derived from prioritising social exposure criterion, a minor portion of plantable areas, equal to 2116,73 ha, is identified as suitable. Suitable areas are concentrated in periu-urban areas in the MCC, and in the urban areas of Sassari and Nuoro, in urbanised clusters in the Campidano Plain and in the cities of Olbia, Tempio and Porto Torres. Lastly, a significant systemic spatial variation is observed for criteria indicators IEM and ICI, as indicated by a local Moran's I statistic equal to, respectively, 0.990 and 0.961, and a mild spatial correlation for the IUF indicator, resulting in a value of 0.246 of the Local Moran's I. In particular, concerning the composite indicator of the magnitude of climate alteration impact, ICI, clusters of observations presenting values above the mean are located in Sassari and Nuoro Provinces, indicating a more relevant estimated alteration of climatic variables in the near future. Concerning urban areas' impact on climate alteration and air quality, formalised by the IEM indicator, clusters of observation presenting values above the mean, representative of elevated concentration of PM10, PM2.5 and Carbon emissions, comprise census tracts in the City of Cagliari, around industrial areas in the metropolitan City of Cagliari and in the urbanised area of the Campidano Plain.

5 Discussion

Several considerations emerge from the study's results. The first consideration concerns the potential benefit in terms of climate alteration mitigation resulting from the reforestation of plantable areas located in suitable urban census tracts. Given a surface area of suitable plantable areas of 3490.113 ha, under Scenario 1, and a carbon sequestration potential of urban forest of 2.67 tCha-1y-1 [38], the total estimated mitigation potential is equal to 9318.60 tCy^{-1}, or to 34168.21 $tCO_2e\ y^{-1}$. Estimated costs of implementing urban forestation interventions are equal to 152 million €, given a unitary cost of 43,485 € ha^{-1} derived from the Program for the conservation and valorisation of urban Green areas financed by the Italian Ministry of Environment and Energy Security (MASE). Under Scenario 2, the total estimated mitigation potential, in terms of Carbon sequestration amounts to 8592.81 tCy^{-1} or to 31506.96 $tCO_2e\ y^{-1}$. Estimated Cost of conversion of areas identified as suitable under Scenario 2 is equal to 140 million €. Under Scenario 3, estimated benefits, in terms of carbon sequestration are equal to 5651.66 tCy^{-1} or to 20722.76 $tCO_2e\ y^{-1.}$ Estimated costs of reforestation of suitable areas under Scenario 3 amount to 92 million €.

Concerning suitable locations, an exploratory analysis is conducted by using the Average Comparison Chart function of the GeoDa software tool, Version 1.22. Average

Comparison evaluates the significance of the divergence among the mean value of the j-th variable computed for a sub-set of observations and the mean value computed for the remaining observations. Significance is measured by the p-value derived from the f-statistic calculated for a regression including a binary variable equal to 1 for the observations included in the sub-set and to 0 for the remaining observations. Suitable census tracts, present average values of percentage of plantable areas, tree cover density, carbon emissions and estimated variation in precipitation below the mean of remaining census tracts. Vice versa, normalised indicators of density, concentration of PM10 and PM2.5, increase of minimum and maximum temperatures, and estimated UHI, computed for the suitable areas, present mean values above the mean of the remaining census tracts. As a result, reforestation of areas identified as suitable under Scenario 1 could optimise adaptation co-benefits resulting from improved air quality, micro-climate regulation, and provision of open, multi-purpose urban spaces. Suitable census tracts under Scenario 2 present mean values of Tree Cover Density, Carbon emissions, and reduction of precipitation below the mean of unsuitable census tracts. Vice versa, mean values of percentage of plantable areas, concentration of PM10 and PM2.5, magnitude of UHI conditions, temperature increase, and Surface Urban Heat Island and Land Surface Temperature are above the mean of unsuitable locations. As a result, prioritising reforestation of areas identified as suitable under Scenario 2 could result in optimising adaptation benefits in terms of air and surface temperature regulation and improved air quality. Suitable areas identified under scenario 3 present mean values of tree cover density and carbon emissions below mean values computed for the remaining census tracts, and mean values of percentage of plantable areas, population density, precipitation increase, concentration of PM10 and PM2.5, diurnal UHI conditions, diurnal and nocturnal temperature increase, Surface Urban Heat Island and Land Surface Temperature, above the mean of unsuitable locations. As a result, reforestation of plantable areas situated in suitable locations individuated under scenario 3 could result in optimising adaptation co-benefits related to improved air quality, air and surface temperature regulation, flooding mitigation, and creation of multi-purpose urban spaces.

6 Conclusions

The proposed study is part of a research project on "Geodesign for climate change mitigation and adaptation in the Mediterranean region". Geodesign envisages a structured and iterative process for enabling informed decisions. Geodesign utilises a systems-based perspective to investigate inter-systemic interactions across distinct spatial and temporal scales [2]. As a result, the iterative structure of Geodesign provides a valid tool to address the issues posed by climate alteration [5]. The proposed study aims to develop a procedure for structuring the information required for implementing the Geodesign process in the context of defining strategies of adaptation to and mitigation of climate alteration. The objective is to enable evidence-based decisions related to the localisation of adaptation and mitigation actions for urban areas. The study contributes to the scientific discourse on mitigation and adaptation by investigating the spatial dimension of policies and initiatives aimed at improving the resilience of urbanised areas. More precisely, the original contribution of the study consists in the development of a multi-stage procedure integrating multi-criteria spatial analysis and geostatistical models to enable the identification of urban lands suitable to the regeneration of urban BGIs. The relevance of the procedure consists in supporting the spatialisation of public policies, optimising the utilisation of limited financial resources and maximising social, economic and environmental benefits. In particular, the study tests and demonstrates the validity of the procedure for identifying suitable locations for urban reforestation interventions so as to maximise benefits in terms of mitigation of climate alteration and co-benefits in terms of adaptation and sustainable development: the conversion of permeable land in areas identified as suitable could result, in fact, in benefits in terms of carbon sequestration ranging from 20722.76 $tCO_2e\ y^{-1}$ under Scenario 3 to 34168.21 $tCO_2e\ y^{-1}$ under Scenario 1. Estimated Adaptation and Sustainable development co-benefits include improved air quality, regulation of air and surface temperature, mitigation of UHI, biodiversity conservation, restoration of ecosystems and creation of inclusive, safe, multi-functional public spaces. The future development of the study will focus on refining the set of indicators related to urban form factors, the impacts of climate alterations on urban areas, and the environmental impact of urbanised areas. It will also concern developing procedures for evaluating land suitability for specific adaptation and mitigation actions relevant to the urban and transport sectors in Mediterranean regions.

Acknowledgments. This study was supported by the research grant for the project "Geodesign for climate change mitigation and adaptation in the Mediterranean region" funded by Fondazione di Sardegna. This study was also partially supported within the "e.INS – Ecosystem of Innovation for Next Generation Sardinia" funded by the Italian Ministry of University and Research under the Next-Generation EU Programme (National Recovery and Resilience Plan – PNRR, M4C2, INVESTMENT 1.5 –DD 1056 of 23/06/2022, ECS00000038). In particular, the "Discussion" was funded by eINS. This study was also partially supported by the MUR through two projects, (1) SMART3R-FLITS: SMART Transport for Travelers and Freight Logistics Integration Towards Sustainability" (Project protocol: 2022J38SR9; CUP Code: F53D23005630006) and (2) PRIN 2022 PNRR project "GeoDesign for Climate URban nEutrality (GD-CURE) - P2022HENAY". This study reflects only the authors' views and opinions, and neither the European Union nor the European Commission nor The MUR can be considered responsible for them.

Disclosure of Interests. The authors have no competing interests.

References

1. Habitat, U.N.: New Urban Agenda. United Nations, New York (2017)
2. Steinitz, C.: A Framework for Geodesign: Changing Geography by Design (2012)
3. Scorza, F.: Training decision-makers: GEODESIGN workshop paving the way for New Urban Agenda. In: Lecture Notes in Geoinformation and Cartography. Springer, Berlin (2020). https://doi.org/10.1007/978-3-030-58811-3_22
4. Dastoli, P.S., Pontrandolfi, P., Scorza, F., Corrado, S., Azzato, A.: Applying geodesign towards an integrated local development strategy: the Val d'Agri case (Italy). In: Lecture Notes in Computer Science, pp. 253–262. Springer, Berlin (2022). https://doi.org/10.1007/978-3-031-10545-6_18
5. Steinitz, C., Orland, B., Fisher, T., Campagna, M.: Geodesign to address global change. In: Intelligent Environments, pp. 193–242. Elsevier, Amsterdam (2023). https://doi.org/10.1016/B978-0-12-820247-0.00016-3

6. Campagna, M.: Geodesign in the planning practice: lessons learnt from experience in Italy. J. Digit. Landsc. Archit. **7**, 496–503 (2022). https://doi.org/10.14627/537724048
7. Jin, S., Stokes, G., Hamilton, C.: Empirical evidence of urban climate adaptation alignment with sustainable development: Application of LDA. Cities. **136**, 104254 (2023). https://doi.org/10.1016/j.cities.2023.104254
8. Roest, A.H., Weitkamp, G., van den Brink, M., Boogaard, F.: Mapping spatial opportunities for urban climate adaptation measures in public and private spaces using a GIS-based decision support model. Sustain. Cities Soc. **96**, 104651 (2023). https://doi.org/10.1016/j.scs.2023.104651
9. United Nations: Transforming Our World: the 2030 Agenda for Sustainable Development (2015)
10. United Nations Department of Economic and Social Affairs: The 17 Goals (2015). https://sdgs.un.org/goals
11. Las Casas, G., Scorza, F., Murgante, B.: New urban agenda and open challenges for urban and regional planning. In: Calabrò, F., Della Spina, L., Bevilacqua, C. (eds.) New Metropolitan Perspectives. ISHT 2018, pp. 282–288. Springer, Cham (2019). https://doi.org/10.1007/978-3-319-92099-3_33
12. European Commission: European Urban Initiative (EUI) - Description of the Action (2021). https://ec.europa.eu/regional_policy/en
13. European Union: The New Leipzig Charter: The Transformative Power of Cities for the Common Good (2020). https://ec.europa.eu/regional_policy/en/newsroom/news/2020/12/12-08-2020-new-leipzig-charter-the-transformative-power-of-cities-for-the-common-good
14. Ribeiro, H.V., Rybski, D., Kropp, J.P.: Effects of changing population or density on urban carbon dioxide emissions. Nat. Commun. **10**, 3204 (2019). https://doi.org/10.1038/s41467-019-11184-y
15. Lwasa, S., Seto, K.C., Bai, X., Blanco, H., Gurney, K.R., Kılkış, Ş., Lucon, O., Murakami, J., Pan, J., Sharifi, A., Yamagata, Y.: Urban systems and other settlements. In: Shukla, P.R., Skea, J., Slade, R., Al Khourdajie, A., van Diemen, R., McCollum, D., Pathak, M., Some, S., Vyas, P., Fradera, R., Belkacemi, M., Hasija, A., Lisboa, G., Luz, S., Malley, J. (eds.) Climate Change 2022: Mitigation of Climate Change. Cambridge University Press, Cambridge and New York, NY (2022). https://doi.org/10.1017/9781009157926.010
16. Gurney, K., Kilkis, S., Seto, K., Lwasa, S., Moran, D., Riahi, K., Keller, M., Rayner, P., Luqman, M.: Greenhouse Gas Emissions from Global Cities Under SSP/RCP Scenarios, 1990 to 2100 (2021). https://doi.org/10.31223/x5z639
17. Dodman, D., Hayward, B., Pelling, M., Castan Broto, V., Chow, W., Chu, E., Dawson, R., Khirfan, L., McPhearson, T., Prakash, A., Zheng, Y., Ziervogel, G.: Cities, settlements and key infrastructure. In: Pörtner, H.-O., Roberts, D.C., Tignor, M., Poloczanska, E.S., Mintenbeck, K., Alegría, A., Craig, M., Langsdorf, S., Löschke, S., Möller, V., Okem, A., Rama, B. (eds.) Climate Change 2022: Impacts, Adaptation and Vulnerability, pp. 907–1040. Cambridge University Press, Cambridge and New York, NY (2022). https://doi.org/10.1017/9781009325844.008
18. Sabrin, S., Karimi, M., Fahad, M.G.R., Nazari, R.: Quantifying environmental and social vulnerability: role of urban Heat Island and air quality, a case study of Camden, NJ. Urban Clim. **34**, 100699 (2020). https://doi.org/10.1016/j.uclim.2020.100699
19. Mutzu Martis, M., Garau, C.: A literature review of the Urban Heat Island (UHI) phenomenon connected with smart cities paradigm. In: Gervasi, O., Murgante, B., Garau, C., Taniar, D., Rocha, C., A.M.A., and Faginas Lago, M.N. (eds.) Computational Science and Its Applications – ICCSA 2024 Workshops, pp. 3–17. Springer Nature, Cham (2024)
20. Skougaard Kaspersen, P., Høegh Ravn, N., Arnbjerg-Nielsen, K., Madsen, H., Drews, M.: Comparison of the impacts of urban development and climate change on exposing European

cities to pluvial flooding. Hydrol. Earth Syst. Sci. **21**, 4131–4147 (2017). https://doi.org/10.5194/hess-21-4131-2017
21. Avashia, V., Garg, A.: Implications of land use transitions and climate change on local flooding in urban areas: An assessment of 42 Indian cities. Land Use Policy. **95**, 104571 (2020). https://doi.org/10.1016/j.landusepol.2020.104571
22. McDonald, R.I., Aronson, M.F.J., Beatley, T., Beller, E., Bazo, M., Grossinger, R., Jessup, K., Mansur, A.V., Puppim de Oliveira, J.A., Panlasigui, S., Burg, J., Pevzner, N., Shanahan, D., Stoneburner, L., Rudd, A., Spotswood, E.: Denser and greener cities: Green interventions to achieve both urban density and nature. People Nat. **5**, 84–102 (2023). https://doi.org/10.1002/pan3.10423
23. Xu, L., Wang, X., Liu, J., He, Y., Tang, J., Nguyen, M., Cui, S.: Identifying the trade-offs between climate change mitigation and adaptation in urban land use planning: An empirical study in a coastal city. Environ. Int. **133**, 105162 (2019). https://doi.org/10.1016/j.envint.2019.105162
24. Pierer, C., Creutzig, F.: Star-shaped cities alleviate trade-off between climate change mitigation and adaptation. Environ. Res. Lett. **14**, 085011 (2019). https://doi.org/10.1088/1748-9326/ab2081
25. Ewing, R., Cervero, R.: "Does compact development make people drive less?" The answer is yes. J. Am. Plan. Assoc. **83**, 19–25 (2017). https://doi.org/10.1080/01944363.2016.1245112
26. Younis, A., Dodoo, A.: Cross-laminated timber for building construction: a life-cycle-assessment overview. J. Build. Eng. **52**, 104482 (2022). https://doi.org/10.1016/j.jobe.2022.104482
27. Ürge-Vorsatz, D., Khosla, R., Bernhardt, R., Chan, Y.C., Vérez, D., Hu, S., Cabeza, L.F.: Advances toward a net-zero global building sector. Annu. Rev. Environ. Resour. **45**, 227–269 (2020). https://doi.org/10.1146/annurev-environ-012420-045843
28. Gómez-Sanabria, A., Kiesewetter, G., Klimont, Z., Schoepp, W., Haberl, H.: Potential for future reductions of global GHG and air pollutants from circular waste management systems. Nat. Commun. **13**, 106 (2022). https://doi.org/10.1038/s41467-021-27624-7
29. Tate, C., Wang, R., Akaraci, S., Burns, C., Garcia, L., Clarke, M., Hunter, R.: The contribution of urban green and blue spaces to the United Nation's sustainable development goals: an evidence gap map. Cities. **145**, 104706 (2024). https://doi.org/10.1016/j.cities.2023.104706
30. European Environment Agency: Urban green and blue infrastructure planning (2021). https://climate-adapt.eea.europa.eu/en/metadata/adaptation-options/green-spaces-and-corridors-in-urban-areas
31. Nature (IUCN), I.U. for C. of: Nature-Based Solutions (2021). https://www.iucn.org/theme/nature-based-solutions
32. European Environment Agency: Nature-based Solutions in Europe: Policy, Knowledge and Practice for Climate Change Adaptation and Disaster Risk Reduction. European Environment Agency (2021)
33. Almaaitah, T., Appleby, M., Rosenblat, H., Drake, J., Joksimovic, D.: The potential of Blue-Green infrastructure as a climate change adaptation strategy: a systematic literature review. Blue-Green Syst. **3**, 223–248 (2021). https://doi.org/10.2166/bgs.2021.016
34. O'Regan, A.C., Nyhan, M.M.: Towards sustainable and net-zero cities: A review of environmental modelling and monitoring tools for optimizing emissions reduction strategies for improved air quality in urban areas. Environ. Res. **231**, 116242 (2023). https://doi.org/10.1016/j.envres.2023.116242
35. Marando, F., Heris, M.P., Zulian, G., Udías, A., Mentaschi, L., Chrysoulakis, N., Parastatidis, D., Maes, J.: Urban heat island mitigation by green infrastructure in European Functional Urban Areas. Sustain. Cities Soc. **77**, 103564 (2022). https://doi.org/10.1016/j.scs.2021.103564

36. Reis, C., Lopes, A.: Evaluating the cooling potential of urban green spaces to tackle urban climate change in Lisbon. Sustainability. **11**, 2480 (2019). https://doi.org/10.3390/su11092480
37. Nowak, D.J., Greenfield, E.J., Hoehn, R.E., Lapoint, E.: Carbon storage and sequestration by trees in urban and community areas of the United States. Environ. Pollut. **178**, 229–236 (2013). https://doi.org/10.1016/j.envpol.2013.03.019
38. Gómez-Villarino, M.T., Gómez Villarino, M., Ruiz-Garcia, L.: Implementation of urban green infrastructures in peri-urban areas: a case study of climate change mitigation in Madrid. Agronomy. **11**, 31 (2021). https://doi.org/10.3390/agronomy11010031
39. Teo, H.C., Zeng, Y., Sarira, T.V., Fung, T.K., Zheng, Q., Song, X.P., Chong, K.Y., Koh, L.P.: Global urban reforestation can be an important natural climate solution. Environ. Res. Lett. **16**, 034059 (2021). https://doi.org/10.1088/1748-9326/abe783
40. Istituto Nazionale di Statistica (ISTAT): Basi territoriali e variabili censuarie (2024). https://www.istat.it/notizia/basi-territoriali-e-variabili-censuarie/
41. Agency, E.E.: CLCplus Backbone 2021 (raster 10 m), Europe, 3-yearly, Jun. 2024 (2024). https://sdi.eea.europa.eu/catalogue/srv/api/records/71fc9d1b-479f-4da1-aa66-662a2fff2cf7?language=all
42. European Environment Agency: Tree Cover Density 2018 (raster 10 m), Europe, 3-yearly (2020). https://doi.org/10.2909/486f77da-d605-423e-93a9-680760ab6791
43. Copernicus Atmosphere Monitoring Service: CAMS Global Emission Inventories (2020). https://ads.atmosphere.copernicus.eu/datasets/cams-global-emission-inventories
44. European Environment Agency: European Air Quality Data (Interpolated Data) – Series (2023). https://www.eea.europa.eu/en/datahub/datahubitem-view/82700fbd-2953-467b-be0a-78a520c3a7ef
45. Wang, Y., Wang, H., Yao, F., Stouffs, R., Wu, J.: An integrated framework for jointly assessing spatiotemporal dynamics of surface urban heat island intensity and footprint: China, 2003–2020. Sustain. Cities Soc. **112**, 105601 (2024). https://doi.org/10.1016/j.scs.2024.105601
46. Chakraborty, T., Lee, X., Ermida, S., Zhan, W.: On the land emissivity assumption and Landsat-derived surface urban heat islands: a global analysis. Remote Sens. Environ. **265**, 112682 (2021). https://doi.org/10.1016/j.rse.2021.112682
47. Fick, S.E., Hijmans, R.J.: WorldClim 2: new 1-km spatial resolution climate surfaces for global land areas. Int. J. Climatol. **37**, 4302–4315 (2017). https://doi.org/10.1002/joc.5086
48. Gutowski Jr., W.J., Giorgi, F., Timbal, B., Frigon, A., Jacob, D., Kang, H.-S., Raghavan, K., Lee, B., Lennard, C., Nikulin, G., O'Rourke, E., Rixen, M., Solman, S., Stephenson, T., Tangang, F.: WCRP COordinated Regional Downscaling EXperiment (CORDEX): a diagnostic MIP for CMIP6. Geosci. Model Dev. **9**, 4087–4095 (2016). https://doi.org/10.5194/gmd-9-4087-2016
49. Fujimori, S., Hasegawa, T., Masui, T., Takahashi, K., Herran, D.S., Dai, H., Hijioka, Y., Kainuma, M.: SSP3: AIM implementation of shared socioeconomic pathways. Glob. Environ. Chang. **42**, 268–283 (2017). https://doi.org/10.1016/j.gloenvcha.2016.06.009
50. Li, X., Zhou, Y., Eom, J., Yu, S., Asrar, G.R.: Projecting global urban area growth through 2100 based on historical time series data and future shared socioeconomic pathways. Earth's Future. **7**, 351–362 (2019). https://doi.org/10.1029/2019ef001152
51. Saaty, T.L.: The Analytic Hierarchy Process. McGraw Hill, New York, NY (1980)
52. Saaty, R.W.: The analytic hierarchy process—what it is and how it is used. Math. Model. **9**, 161–176 (1987). https://doi.org/10.1016/0270-0255(87)90473-8
53. Saaty, T.L., Vargas, L.G.: Hierarchical analysis of behavior in competition: prediction in chess. Behav. Sci. **25**, 180–191 (1980). https://doi.org/10.1002/bs.3830250303
54. Pallozzi, E., Guidolotti, G., Mattioni, M., Calfapietra, C.: Particulate matter concentrations and fluxes within an urban park in Naples. Environ. Pollut. **266**, 115134 (2020). https://doi.org/10.1016/j.envpol.2020.115134

55. Anselin, L.: Local indicators of spatial association—LISA. Geogr. Anal. **27**, 93–115 (1995)
56. Anselin, L., Rey, S.J.: Modern Spatial Econometrics in Practice: A Guide to GeoDa, GeoDaSpace and PySAL. GeoDa Press, Chicago, IL (2014)

Leveraging Gamification in E-Commerce for Climate Change: A Persuasive Technology Acceptance Model (TAM) Approach

Wei-Jie Phang[(✉)] and Chien-Sing Lee

Sunway University, Bandar Sunway 47500, Selangor, Malaysia
phangweijie36@gmail.com

Abstract. The rising global population has intensified climate change, with 2022 evidencing the highest record of greenhouse gas emissions, at 53.79 billion metric tons. By 2024, the average surface temperature has also surpassed the 1.5-degree threshold. Despite increasing occurrences of climate change, there exists a gap between knowledge and acting towards mitigating climate change. This study integrates mini-games and gamification into an e-commerce mobile app as (in) direct persuasive mechanisms to reduce individual carbon footprints and increase willingness to mitigate/act. Hypotheses are: (1) climate change-oriented gamification in e-commerce will increase awareness of climate change; (2) gamification will encourage individuals and communities to act towards reducing climate change; (3) gamification, e-commerce, and a carbon footprint calculator will help reduce carbon footprint. Alpha-beta testing based on the Technology Acceptance Model, finds that the biggest difference between pre-post-game introduction is personal carbon footprint, followed by the level of willingness to engage with climate change, possible initiatives for mitigating climate change, and cause-effect purchase decisions in the 'Shop' feature. The transition from a simple calculator to a visualized carbon footprint report, the change of real-life challenges into interactive mini games, highlights the importance of direct contextualization and immediate relevance. However, the study faces limitations, due to small sample size, and reliance on generalized emission data, which affects the accuracy of the carbon footprint calculator.

Keywords: Design thinking · metaverse · climate change · carbon footprint · e-commerce-mini-games · gamification

1 Introduction

In recent years, climate change has grown into a critical global concern. Its adverse effects range from fluctuating weather conditions that jeopardize agricultural output, to escalating sea levels that heighten the perils of floods due to excessive rainfall [1, 2]. The World Health Organization has also reported that climate-induced floods have affected over 2 billion people globally from 1998 and 2017 [2].

Additionally, climate change has contributed to other natural disasters, including heatwaves, droughts, and storms, causing environmental destruction, and threatening human life [2]. Wildlife and ecosystems have also been significantly impacted, with climate-driven disruptions facilitating the spread of diseases among wildlife and the intrusion of non-native species [3]. Hence, the United Nations has regarded climate change as requiring urgent immediate action [4].

Despite the widespread awareness of climate change, the lack of accessible information on actions that contribute to individual carbon footprints hinders efforts to mitigate climate change [5]. This gap between awareness and action thus underscores the need for tools that help individuals understand and reduce their carbon footprints, fostering responsible behaviors to combat climate change. The use of technology has emerged as a possible method for educating users about climate change. Technologies such as Augmented Reality (AR) and Virtual Reality (VR) have gained popularity in their ability to create immersive learning. However, despite their potential, AR and VR remains as expensive solutions for widespread adoption, limiting their accessibility and scalability for educating about climate change [6].

In contrast, e-commerce has risen in popularity, with approximately 2.71 billion users globally [7]. Major platforms such as Shopee and Lazada have successfully utilized gamification strategies, offering rewards such as e-commerce coins for discounts to enhance user engagement and encourage positive behaviours. Building on this trend, this study proposes a solution that bridges the business (e-commerce) and tech (development of games and related innovations) sectors to address climate change. By leveraging e-commerce and gamification as tools for direct persuasion, the goal is to encourage users to act for climate change. Through gamification, users can virtually experience the positive consequences upon performing environmentally friendly behaviours, fostering intrinsic motivation. This process can lead to self-persuasion, where individuals internally adopt sustainable behaviours or attitudes, rather than relying on external incentives [8]. By doing so, the project aims to:

1. enhance individual awareness of climate change by educating users on their carbon footprint, emission sources, and environmental consequences,
2. increase individual or community efforts to reduce carbon footprint,

Specific aspects of investigation are based on two theories. First, Cognitive Load Theory (CLT) highlights that pattern identification helps learning, memory and understanding. Moreover, game mechanisms/elements decompose chunks of information into smaller parts [9]. Hence, complex information can become more digestible and easier to remember. Second, the Gamified Learning Theory (GLT) [10] suggests that game-like features, such as challenges, rewards, and feedback, can influence attitudes and behaviors in non-game contexts. Hence, it makes sense to utilize scenario-based challenges/games and gamification to achieve the above objectives.

The research questions formulated for this paper are as outlined:

1. Will climate change-oriented gamification in e-commerce increase awareness of climate change?
2. Will gamification in e-commerce encourage individuals and communities to act more towards reducing climate change?
3. Will gamification, e-commerce, and the integration of a carbon footprint calculator contribute to actions that would reduce carbon footprints?

2 Literature Review

2.1 Climate Change

The United Nations defines climate change as long-term alterations in temperature and weather patterns. This phenomenon is strongly linked to the release of GHGs, which are heat-trapping atmospheric gasses composed from carbon dioxide, methane, nitrous oxide, and other chlorofluorocarbon gasses [11]. Research has highlighted the importance of maintaining a balance of natural GHGs in Earth's atmosphere to support life, with carbon dioxide playing a key role in absorbing and radiating heat [12, 13]. However, human activities since the Industrial Revolution have significantly increased carbon dioxide emissions, contributing to global warming and climate change [11]. Statistics have shown that since 1990, carbon dioxide emissions have surged by over 60%, to 37.55 billion metric tons in 2023, marking the highest emission record to date [14].

Climate change results from a combination of natural phenomena and human activities [13]. Natural causes, like volcanic eruptions and tectonic movements, can influence Earth's temperature; however, their impact on climate change is minimal due to their slow pace [15]. In contrast, anthropogenic climate change, driven by human activities, is the main contributor to the observed increase in global warming. Specifically, activities such as the combustion of fossil fuels releases carbon dioxide into the atmosphere, significantly increasing carbon emissions. Human activities, including energy consumption in buildings for heating and cooling appliances, emit much carbon [16].

Moreover, population growth amplifies carbon emissions, as increased demand for consumer goods and agricultural products leads to requirements of higher industrial production, which are often powered by fossil fuels. Similarly, waste production (like food and yard waste), and transportation choices are significant contributors to GHG emissions [17, 18]. Landfill waste decomposition releases methane and carbon dioxide, collectively known as landfill gas [17]. Transportation is also largely dependent on petroleum-based fuels, which accounts for up to 15% of global GHG emissions [18].

2.2 Carbon Footprint

Carbon footprint refers to the total greenhouse gas emissions resulting from individual and business activities [19]. Greenhouse gases include methane, and nitrous oxide, which are carbon dioxide equivalents (CO_2e). The use of CO_2e standardizes the measurement of GHGs based on their different global warming potential (GWP), allowing for a consistent assessment of their collective impact [20].

To calculate carbon footprints, established protocols such as GHG Protocol and Life Cycle Assessments are used for organizations. ISO 14064 provides a standard method for quantifying organizational emissions, involving the multiplication of activity data by emission factors [20]. The World Wildlife Fund (WWF) and The Nature Conservancy, estimate personal carbon emissions.

Equation (1) is a generic formula for calculating the carbon footprint, where activity data is the quantitative measure of activities conducted (such as kilograms of waste disposed), while emission factor refers to the measure of emissions produced for every unit of activity (e.g., kg of CO_2e per ton of waste disposed).

$$Carbon\ Emission = Activity\ data \times Emission\ Factor \tag{1}$$

2.3 E-commerce

In recent years, e-commerce usage has increased tremendously due to its benefits offered [21]. According to Shopify, users aged 18 to 34 are the primary users for e-commerce, with 67% increasing their expenditure post-pandemic [22]. In Malaysia, the youth dominate e-commerce usage, with individuals below 20 taking up 27.4% of the total, and those in their 20 s making up 21.1% of the users [23]. To enhance user engagement, e-commerce such as Pinduoduo, Shopee, and Lazada have integrated gamification, for example Duo Duo Orchard, Shopee Bubble, and Lazland. Shopee is now the first among Southeast Asia's leading e-commerce platforms and is the most popular in Malaysia, with over 60 million visitors every month [24]. Hence, this study has chosen Shopee to emulate.

2.4 Games and Gamification

Games provide interactive experiences with predetermined rules, goals, a measurable progression system, and a clear conclusion to end the game [25]. In contrast, gamification involves integrating elements frequently found in games into non-gaming contexts to accomplish a particular goal or to encourage specific behaviors. Gamification plays a significant role, with research stating that it builds an environment where individuals are naturally driven to interact with content relevant to a specific domain, thereby facilitating behavior modification towards more desirable outcomes [26]. Common gamification elements include rewards, points, leaderboards, virtual currencies, and progress bars.

Gamification in E-commerce. Gamification in e-commerce is projected to be integrated into 87% of online stores within the next 5 years [27]. Numerous studies have highlighted the positive impacts of gamification in e-commerce. For example, a systematic review by Azmi et al. [28] found that rewards, badges, and leaderboards are the most implemented gamification elements, which contribute to successful integration in e-commerce. These elements, specifically rewards like coupons and discounts, have been found to exert a psychological effect on consumers, promoting loyalty and return visits. Similarly, another study supported the prominence of rewards, points, badges, and leaderboards in e-commerce gamification [29]. Numerous studies on Shopee's gamification features have demonstrated their effectiveness in enhancing user engagement, where participants reported increased satisfaction and interest as they accumulated rewards, triggering positive reinforcement for prolonged platform use [30–32]. Users also expressed their preference for challenges in games, noting that it motivated them to play longer, and contributed to their satisfaction and retention [30, 31].

Gamification for Climate Change. Douglas and Brauer [26] found that gamification in applications promoting sustainability and climate change awareness is more effective in encouraging sustainable behavior compared to other behavior modification techniques.

Specifically, apps that integrated rewards and feedback were more successful in engaging users than those focused solely on informational content. Another study emphasized the importance of combining emotional storytelling (pathos), ethical responsibility (ethos), and factual decision-making (logos) to enhance the impact of gamified climate change applications. Similarly, Novo et al. discovered that integrating gamification into sustainability apps increased users' environmental awareness and motivation for sustainable practices [33]. However, they noted that the lack of sufficient theoretical content limited participants' knowledge growth. Thus, these studies highlight the need to balance gamification elements with educational content to maximize its effectiveness.

3 Methodology

3.1 The Self-Determination Theory (SDT)

SDT identifies 3 core factors that drive human motivation and behavior, i.e., autonomy, competence, and social relatedness [34]. *Autonomy* refers to the need for individuals to feel self-governed. *Competence* refers to the need to feel successful in one's actions. SDT explains that people are more likely to engage in behaviors when they feel socially connected (social relatedness).

3.2 The Technology Acceptance Model (TAM)

The Technology Acceptance Model (TAM), introduced by Fred Davis, provides a theoretical framework for understanding how users adopt and engage with new technologies [35]. This study utilized constructs from TAM 1, 2 and 3 to evaluate user acceptance of the prototype (alpha testing) and its subsequent development (beta testing). As shown in Fig. 1, the evaluation framework was structured around key TAM constructs, including *perceived usefulness, perceived ease of use, attitude towards using, and behavioural intention to use.* Each construct was operationalized through a questionnaire, with responses collected using a 5-point Likert scale, ranging from "strong disagree" to "strongly agree".

3.3 Software Development Lifecycle

This project adopted an Iterative Incremental Prototyping Methodology. After initial ideation and problem definition, game features were derived from the literature reviewed, informed by Cognitive Load Theory and Gamified Learning Theory. These requirements were later translated into prototypes using Figma. Alpha testing was conducted on the prototypes to evaluate user acceptance and behaviour through a TAM-based questionnaire. The insights from the alpha testing informed design refinements, which were implemented into the development phase. Finally, the system underwent beta testing to validate its alignment with user needs using the same TAM framework.

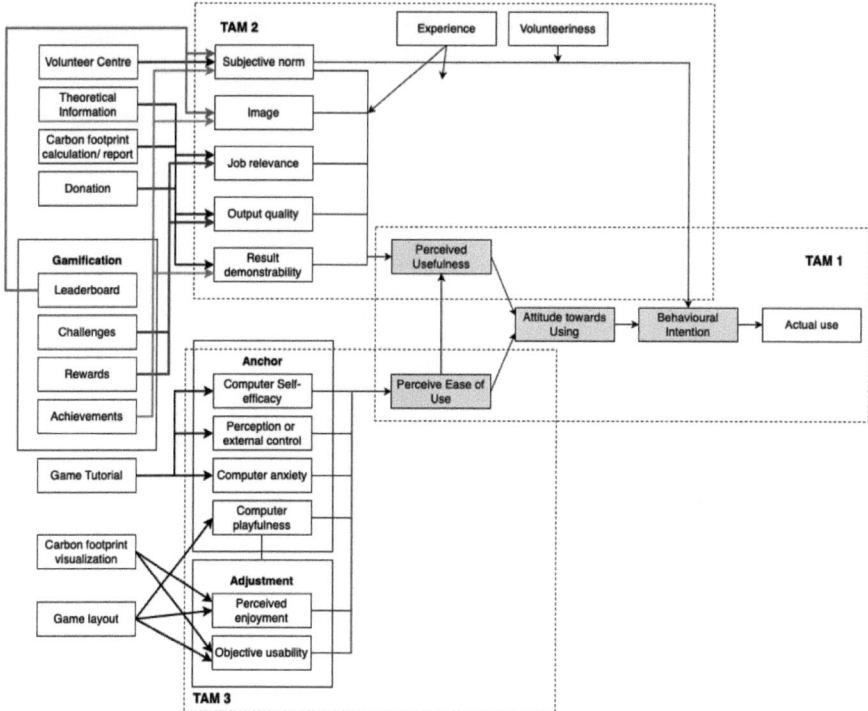

Fig. 1. TAM framework showing core constructs and relations to this study's key components.

3.4 Prototype Design

Figures 2 and 3 shows the app prototype. The game includes 5 main features: Shop, Challenges, Leader board, Achievements, and Coin Store. As shown in Fig. 3, the Leader board promotes engagement through point-based rankings, while the Challenges encourage real-world sustainable actions, such as using public transport, with rewards granted upon proof of completion. Purchases made in the Shop are reflected in the game's virtual environment (graphically and carbon footprint amount) to simulate their environmental impact; for example, buying an energy-related product updates the energy source in the user's in-game 'city'.

4 Results and Discussion

The survey was conducted via Google Forms and assessed participants' awareness and intentions before and after interacting with the game, in line with TAM constructs. The survey collected a total of 37 responses for alpha testing, and 40 for beta testing.

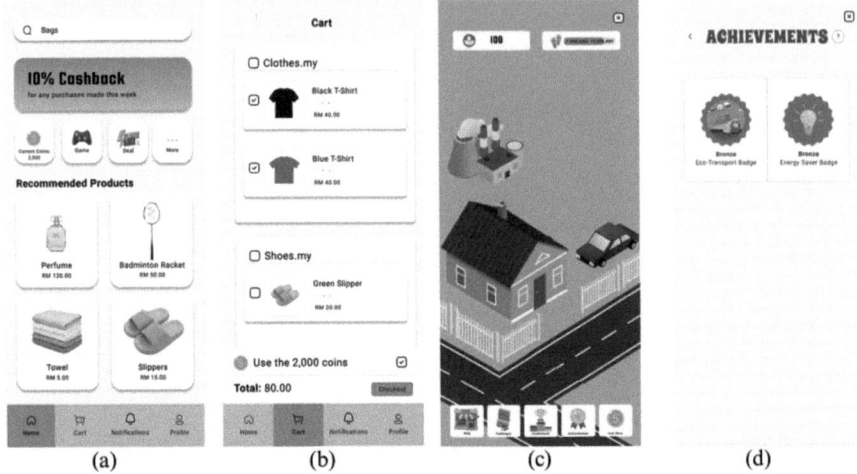

Fig. 2. Overview of the e-commerce and game prototype. (a) The e-commerce homepage, displaying coin balance, product listings, and access to the game. (b) Cart page where coins can be redeemed for discounts (1 coin = RM 0.01). (c) Game interface, accessed via the homepage. (d) Achievements page, accessed through the game menu.

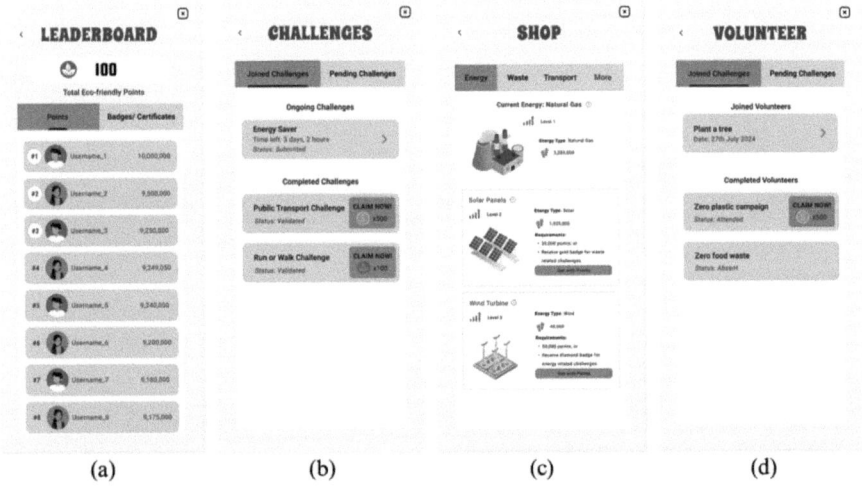

Fig. 3. Additional features of the game. (a) Leader board page displaying user rankings based on eco-points and achievements. (b) Challenges page showing ongoing and upcoming challenges with deadlines. (c) In-game Shop offering sustainable products categorized under energy, waste, transportation. (d) Volunteer page, showing available volunteer opportunities.

4.1 Alpha Testing

Results Based on TAM. Table 1 shows the results from alpha testing, with calculated average ratings from 1 to 5 (5 being the highest). For *perceived usefulness*, the average score for all measured factors of user's awareness exceeds 4 (post-introduction of the game), which is a very positive sign. The biggest difference between pre-post game introduction is attributed to awareness of personal carbon footprint (1.24). This difference may be due to contextualization and immediate visualization of the causes and consequences, or impacts based on the personal carbon footprint.

Table 1. Alpha Testing Results.

TAM construct	Item assessed	Mean		Difference
		pre-introduction	Post-introduction	
Perceived usefulness	Awareness of causes and consequences (Shop's theoretical information)	3.78	4.08	**0.30**
	Awareness of climate initiatives (Challenges/Donation/Volunteer)	3.59	4.11	**0.52**
	Awareness of personal carbon footprint (Progress Bar)	2.92	4.16	**1.24**
Perceived ease of use	Understandability of carbon footprint	–	3.95	–
	Comprehension of theoretical content	–	3.89	–
	Challenges/ Donation/ Volunteer	–	3.77	–
Attitude toward use	Challenges/ Donation/ Volunteer	–	4.19	–
	Shop feature	–	4.05	–
	Future game use	–	4.05	–
Behavioral intention to use	Reward-based challenges	–	4.08	–
	Donations/ Volunteer feature	–	3.41	–
	Willingness to use Climate Guardians	–	3.89	–
	Intention to use Shop	–	3.89	–

The carbon footprint calculation received the highest score for *perceived ease of use*. However, participants noted that the carbon footprint visualization appeared confusing. Since the calculation was displayed as a progress bar, it appeared to the participant that the goal was to fill the bar, when the objective was to reduce it. Overall, participants reported positive *attitudes towards using* Climate Guardians and its features, as indicated by the average scores.

For *behavioural intention to use*, the intention to engage in challenges received the highest score, suggesting a stronger preference for individual-based activities as compared to group-based activities (donation/ volunteer), which scored the lowest. In contrast, the Shop feature received a score of 3.89. Participants noted that overly wordy texts have reduced their engagement, which may have influenced this rating.

4.1.1 General Feedback

Participants provided feedback on the app. This was adapted to the developed app, as shown in Fig. 4. The key revisions made based on the alpha feedback were:

- Text-heavy sections were replaced with visual comics and graphics.
- Carbon footprint progress bar was changed to a pie chart with numerical data.
- Complex real-life tasks were redesigned as mini-games (e.g., trash sorting).
- Volunteer section was updated with direct organization's contact information.
- Donation achievements (certificates) were added to increase trust and encourage engagement.
- Game tutorial was added to improve ease of use.
- Carbon footprint reduction thresholds were added, for users to unlock rewards like coins to improve gameplay engagement.

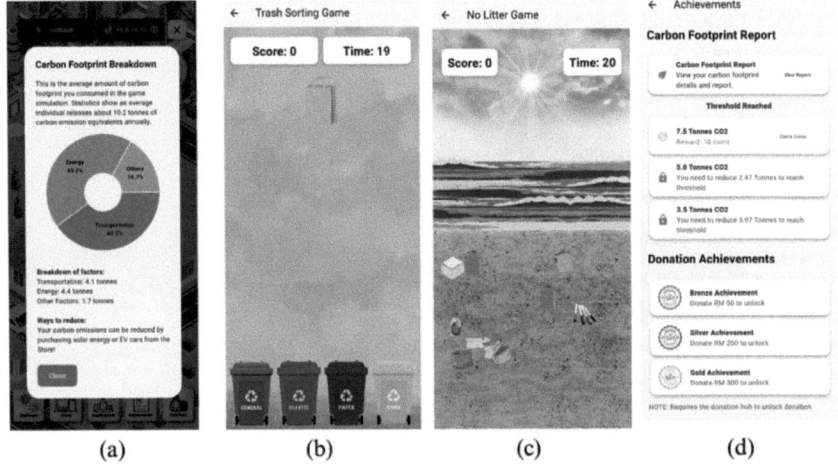

Fig. 4. Screenshot of developed app: carbon footprint calculation, mini games, and achievements. (a) Carbon footprint visualizations. (b) Trash sorting mini game. (c) Trash collection mini game. (d) Achievement page displaying carbon footprint reports, certificates or thresholds.

4.2 Beta Testing

Results Based on TAM. The comparison between the alpha and beta testing results shows consistent increase in scores (Table 3). In terms of *perceived usefulness*, the carbon footprint visualization and reports received the highest scores, indicating that visual tools like pie charts were effective in increasing user awareness of their carbon footprint and environmental impact (Table 3). The rewards-based challenges were also rated highly (4.10), reinforcing the motivational effect of rewards in maintaining participation. However, motivation by leader board scored relatively lower, at 3.85, suggesting that friendly competitions did not resonate as strongly with users.

For *perceived ease of use*, all features were rated above 4, suggesting positive user experiences in navigating the app. Regarding *attitudes towards using,* the reward-based challenges and theoretical content (in Shop) were the top 2 high scores. The largest improvement was observed in attitudes towards 'Shop', suggesting that changing text to graphic delivery of theoretical information improved user reception.

Additionally, for *behavioural intention to use*, the donation or volunteer center increased by 0.49 points compared to the alpha testing phase. This improvement suggests that changes, such as greater transparency and highlighting recipient organizations for donations may have increased user trust and usage intentions.

4.2.1 General Feedback

This section revealed that participants felt empowered to engage in climate change mitigation initiatives after using the game, with 40% agreeing, and 40% strongly agreeing, and an average score of 4.20. Thus, the results indicate a positive attitude towards taking action following the gameplay.

4.3 Discussion

4.3.1 Analysis of Research Question 1

Will climate-change-oriented gamification in e-commerce increase awareness and learning about climate change?

In line with the Gamified Learning Theory (GLT) [10] and Cognitive Load Theory (CLT) [9], the developed game has implemented **clear goals** through *donation thresholds* and *carbon footprint reduction targets*. Users also receive **immediate feedback** in mini games e.g., the trash sorting game, where they can immediately see whether their sorting of trash is correct or incorrect through addition or reduction of points and visual cues. Additionally, **continuous reinforcement** is present in the game. Rewards e.g., e-commerce *coins, virtual badges, and certificates* are awarded to users upon showing positive climate-related behaviors.

From Table 2, initially, average ratings for awareness of carbon footprint, and causes and consequences were below 4. But after/post-introduction of gamification elements, the scores increased to 4 and above, indicating increased awareness. This concurs with [36]'s findings. [36] find that goals, feedback and continuous reinforcement mechanisms increase awareness because an enjoyable learning process of the content and positive reinforcement encourages active engagement/deeper absorption and repeated participation; eventually leading to long-term retention of knowledge. Hence, climate change-oriented gamification in e-commerce, which are **goal-oriented**, and includes **challenges** with **immediate feedback** and **continuous reinforcements**, augmented by *carbon footprint visualizations*, and *donation opportunities*, can increase participants' awareness of climate change.

Table 2. Beta Testing: Change in Perceived Usefulness Before and After Game Introduction.

Pre-introduction of game		Post-introduction of game		Difference
Awareness of carbon footprint	2.7	Awareness of carbon footprint through visualization and report	4.23	1.53
Awareness of causes and consequences	3.65	Awareness of causes and consequences through Shop's theoretical information	4.10	0.45
Willingness to take climate change initiatives	3.35	Willingness to take initiatives after learning through challenges	4.18	0.83

4.3.2 Analysis of Research Question 2

Will gamification in e-commerce encourage individuals and communities to act more toward reducing climate change?

Autonomy. Table 2 indicates that initially, participants are only moderately willing to act (average score of 3.35). However, after integrating gamification in the e-commerce-cum-climate change game mobile app, willingness to engage in mitigation efforts increases to 4.18. This highlights that rewards (i.e., e-commerce coins) and achievements (i.e., certificates) serve as extrinsic motivators, or indirect persuasion mechanisms [37, 38]. Though certificates may act as external incentives, but over time, these extrinsic motivators can encourage self-persuasion by prompting users to reflect on their actions and internalize the value of sustainable behaviors. For example, earning a certificate for donations might initially be driven by the desire for recognition (extrinsic motivation), but reflecting on the achievement can lead individuals to see themselves as environmentally responsible, thus reinforcing intrinsic motivation. This is in accordance with [39], which suggests that rewards can positively influence users' game enjoyment, contributing to their intrinsic motivation to conduct climate actions.

Additionally, the intention to use the *donation* feature increases from 3.41 in alpha testing to 3.90 (Table 3, TAM Construct: Intention to Use) after introducing *certificates* as rewards in beta testing. The finding suggests that gamification elements in our integrated e-commerce-climate change game mobile app, has successfully increased motivation for climate action through our **direct and indirect persuasion** mechanisms.

Competence. Based on SDT [34], as users are increasingly aware, their competence level increases. Achievements, points and leader boards in the developed app function as tools that enhance user's competence, as they give immediate feedback and reinforces a sense of progress [37]. When users observe measurable increases in outcomes, they experience feelings of success and mastery. Consequently, users are more likely to take part in activities and persist in them, as they find the experience personally rewarding [37]. The increase in participants' sense of empowerment (score of 4.20, as mentioned under

Table 3. Beta Testing Results.

TAM construct	Item assessed	Mean Alpha	Mean Beta	Difference
Perceived usefulness	Awareness of carbon footprint (Visualization/ report)	4.16	4.23	0.07
	Awareness of climate initiatives (Challenges/ Donation/ Volunteer)	4.11	4.18	0.07
	Awareness of causes and consequences (Shop's theoretical information)	4.08	4.10	0.02
	Willingness to take initiatives (Challenges)	–	4.18	–
	Motivation to learn by Challenges' rewards	–	4.10	–
	Motivation by leader board	–	3.85	–
Perceived ease of use	Challenges	3.77	4.35	0.58
	Donation/ volunteer centre	3.77	4.20	0.43
	Acquisition and comprehension of theoretical information	3.89	4.20	0.31
	Ease of understandability of carbon footprint	3.95	4.25	0.30
Attitude towards using	Shop	4.05	4.23	0.18
	Challenges	4.19	4.25	0.06
	Future usage of game	4.05	4.10	0.05
	Volunteer Centre	4.19	4.20	0.01
Intention to use	Donation/Volunteer Centre	**3.41**	**3.90**	**0.49**
	Climate Guardians (the game)	3.89	4.10	0.21
	Shop	**3.89**	**4.03**	**0.14**
	Reward-based Challenges	4.08	4.20	0.12
	Carbon footprint visualizations	–	4.20	–

Beta Testing's General Feedback) suggests that gamification has increased user's belief and confidence in their ability to take climate change mitigation initiatives (autonomy).

Social Relatedness. Despite increased willingness and empowerment to act, participants rated the leader board's effectiveness moderately (3.85, in Table 3, TAM Construct: Perceived Usefulness), indicating that they would prefer not to compete, when it comes to climate change. *Social relatedness* (the need for connection) through actual contributions in action or donations is more meaningful. For instance, participants have rated an average score of 4.18 (Table 3) for their willingness to engage in real-life climate change mitigation initiatives after learning from the mini games. Thus, while gamification increases willingness to act through the SDT framework, enhancing the social aspects of the game, e.g. allowing collaborative challenges, can further foster a sense of collective purpose, engagement and motivation to act [36].

4.3.3 Analysis of Research Question 3

Will gamification, e-commerce, and the integration of a carbon footprint calculator contribute to actions that would reduce carbon footprints?

The integration of gamification and a carbon footprint calculator can foster accountability by providing a measurable outcome of user's in-game choices, with participants noting an increased awareness of their carbon footprint after interacting with it (average score of 4.23, see Table 3). This indicates that real-time feedback (increase/decrease in carbon footprint calculation) can positively influence user perception and understanding of their environmental impact, encouraging users to make more informed lifestyle changes. This finding is consistent with previous research by [40], which shows that awareness of one's carbon footprint is strongly correlated with increased carbon-reduction practices, as individuals are more inclined to adopt sustainable behaviours when they are aware of the issues and their implications.

This can also be explained by [41]'s study, which identifies that digital platform that offered environmental feedback, such as carbon footprint calculations can influence users to adjust their climate-related habits. [41] stated that their findings aligned with previous research, indicating that feedback could lead individuals to change their consumption, which could reduce emissions linked to consumption by 23%.

Additionally, the *donation* feature with achievements as motivators, provides a direct method for players to support climate action, where donations would go to organizations focused on carbon footprint reduction, such as those running recycling campaigns. The beta testing results showed an average intention to use score of 3.90 (Table 3). While this indicates a neutral-to-positive willingness to donate, it suggests that users had moderate motivation to support environmental causes. Although intention by itself does not ensure action, the inclusion of the donation mechanism appears promising, especially if future developments combined it with more social incentives or community-based objectives.

5 Conclusion

In conclusion, this research project demonstrates the potential of integrating mini games with gamification into e-commerce as an effective strategy to raise climate change awareness and reduce individual carbon footprints. By incorporating gamified elements such as rewards, badges, and a carbon footprint calculator, the app has successfully engaged users, promoting sustainable behaviors.

The findings have highlighted the positive impact of the app's carbon footprint calculator and interactive game simulations, which have notably increased participants' awareness of climate change and motivated them to engage in climate mitigation efforts. However, the use of leaderboards have not significantly increased motivation, suggesting that users prefer collaboration instead of competition, to address climate change. While leader boards create a sense of competition, participants might not have experienced a collaborative social environment to drive motivation. To address this, [36] suggests implementing social forums for users to share their experiences, connect with friends, and monitor peer's progress, to provide social support and accountability that sustains their motivation. [37] also suggests activities that would emphasize the significance of the player's involvement for the team activity, which may be communicated through an engaging narrative (a gamification element) in the game.

Thus, this study has confirmed the three hypotheses, that integrating e-commerce with a climate change game mobile app can drive actions that would reduce carbon footprints. Furthermore, knowledge enlightens the sense of purpose and drives action more than gamification elements themselves. These highlight the importance of design thinking grounded in more holistic understanding and design based on Game Learning Theory [10]-Krath et al.'s [36] goals, immediate feedback, continuous reinforcements and Self-Determination Theory's [34] competence, social-relatedness and autonomy. However, as the current study does not assess their long-term behaviour, future research can employ longitudinal studies to measure long-term adoption. We also hope to contribute to the United Nations Collaborative Program on Reducing Emissions from Deforestation and Forest Degradation in Developing Countries, albeit in an urban context.

Ultimately, this study concludes that the combination of gamification in e-commerce and educational games, along with tools, e.g., carbon footprint calculators, can contribute to reductions in carbon footprints. Above all, the transition from a simple calculator to a visualized carbon footprint report, the change of real-life challenges into interactive mini games, highlights the importance of direct contextualization and immediate relevance. Thus, gamification emerges as a viable alternative compared to more costly technologies, e.g., AR and VR.

6 Limitations and Future Work

The study recognizes several limitations. Firstly, the user base was relatively small (N = 37 for alpha testing, N = 40 for beta testing) and skewed towards younger demographics, which limits generalizability of the findings. Hence, the observed climate change initiatives might not extend to other age groups unless they were frequent e-commerce users. Additionally, the evaluation was conducted over a short period, measuring intention rather than actual behavioral change. While the data suggested an increase in climate-related awareness and short-term willingness to act, long-term behavioral intention remains uncertain. As such, future research should include longitudinal studies to assess whether users would maintain reduced consumption and altered purchasing habits over time.

Furthermore, due to time and resource constraints, the carbon footprint calculator relied on generalized emission factors from Europe and Malaysia, which may not accurately reflect individual user behaviors in Malaysia. Future work could improve the accuracy of the carbon footprint calculator by incorporating more localized data and personalized activity tracking. Moreover, employing game engines and Procedural Content Generation techniques could enhance the game's interactivity. Additional features, such as social and collaborative elements like team challenges, could be incorporated to emphasize the collective impact on climate change. Social media APIs could also be integrated to allow users to share their achievements or eco-friendly behaviors, providing social proof to motivate others to join in.

Acknowledgments. This study was funded by Sunway University. The authors would like to thank Sunway University for the resources and support given throughout the course of this project.

Disclosure of Interests The authors have no competing interests to declare that are relevant to the content of this article.

References

1. United Nations: 1.5°C: what it means and why it matters. https://www.un.org/en/climatechange/science/climate-issues/degrees-matter
2. Wu, Y., Martens, P., Krafft, T.: Public awareness, lifestyle and low-carbon city transformation in China: a systematic literature review. Sustainability. **14**, 10121 (2022). https://doi.org/10.3390/su141610121
3. Quratulann, S., Muhammad Ehsan, M., Rabia, E., Sana, A.: Review on climate change and its effect on wildlife and ecosystem. Open J. Environ. Biol. **6**, 008–014 (2021). https://doi.org/10.17352/ojeb.000021
4. United Nations: Climate change. https://www.un.org/en/global-issues/climate-change
5. United Nations Development Programme & Japan-Caribbean Climate Change Partnership: Knowledge Attitudes and Practice Study on Climate Change. (2016)
6. Al-Ansi, A.M., Jaboob, M., Garad, A., Al-Ansi, A.: Analyzing augmented reality (AR) and virtual reality (VR) recent development in education. Soc. Sci. Humanit. Open. **8**, 100532 (2023). https://doi.org/10.1016/j.ssaho.2023.100532
7. Shopify: Global Ecommerce Statistics: Trends to Guide Your Store in 2025 - Shopify Malaysia. https://www.shopify.com/my/enterprise/blog/global-ecommerce-statistics
8. Haveliwala, M.: Self-persuasion as habit change technique: Understanding the science behind adopting new habits and making them stick. EPRA Int. J. Multidiscip. Res. (IJMR). **7**(8), 258–265 (2021) https://eprajournals.com/IJMR/article/5725
9. Capatina, A., Juarez-Varon, D., Micu, A., Micu, A.E.: Leveling up in corporate training: Unveiling the power of gamification to enhance knowledge retention, knowledge sharing, and job performance. J. Innov. Knowl. **9**(3), 100530–100530 (2024). https://doi.org/10.1016/j.jik.2024.100530
10. Landers, R.N.: Developing a theory of gamified learning. Simul. Gaming. **45**, 752–768 (2014). https://doi.org/10.1177/1046878114563660
11. Nunez, C.: Carbon Dioxide in the Atmosphere is at a Record High. Here's What You Need to Know. https://www.nationalgeographic.com/environment/article/greenhouse-gases
12. Wadanambi, R., Wandana, L., Chathumini, K., Dassanayake, N., Preethika, D., Arachchige, U.: The effects of industrialization on climate change. J. Res. Technol. Eng. **1**, 86 (2020)
13. Lindsey, R.: Climate Change: Atmospheric Carbon Dioxide. https://www.climate.gov/news-features/understanding-climate/climate-change-atmospheric-carbon-dioxide
14. Tiseo, I.: Annual Carbon Dioxide (CO_2) Emissions Worldwide from 1940 to 2023. https://www.statista.com/statistics/276629/global-co2-emissions/
15. Turrentine, J.: What Are the Causes of Climate Change?. https://www.nrdc.org/stories/what-are-causes-climate-change#natural
16. United Nations: Home Energy. https://www.un.org/en/actnow/home-energy

17. Krause, M., Kenny, S., Stephenson, J., Singleton, A.: Quantifying Methane Emissions from Landfilled Food Waste. (2023)
18. Selçuk, I.Ş., Köktaş, A.M.: Transport sector energy use and carbon emissions: a study on sectoral fiscal policies. Ekonomika i Organizacja Logistyki. **5**, 17–30 (2020). https://doi.org/10.22630/eiol.2020.5.3.18
19. Selin, N.E.: Carbon Footprint (2013). https://www.britannica.com/science/carbon-footprint
20. Ministry of Mahaweli Development and Environment: A Guide for Carbon Footprint Assessment (2016)
21. Jain, V., Malviya, B., Arya, S.: An overview of electronic commerce (e-Commerce). J. Contemp. Issues Bus. Gov. **27**, 665–670 (2021)
22. Systems, N.: How Young Consumers Are Changing the eCommerce Landscape. https://www.newcastlesys.com/blog/how-young-consumers-are-changing-the-ecommerce-landscape
23. Malaysian Communications and Multimedia Commission: Malaysia: Online Shoppers by Age 2016., https://www.statista.com/statistics/878419/malaysia-online-shoppers-by-age/
24. Wong, K.X., Wang, Y., Wang, R., Wang, M., Oh, Z.J., Lok, Y.H., Khan, N., Khan, F.: Shopee: how does e-commerce platforms affect consumer behavior during the COVID-19 pandemic in Malaysia? Int. J. Account. Finan. Asia Pac. **6**, 38–52 (2023). https://doi.org/10.32535/ijafap.v6i1.1934
25. Becker, K.: What's the difference between gamification, serious games, educational games, and game-based learning? In: Academia Letters, p. 209 (2021). https://doi.org/10.20935/al209
26. Douglas, B.D., Brauer, M.: Gamification to prevent climate change: a review of games and apps for sustainability. Curr. Opin. Psychol. **42** (2021). https://doi.org/10.1016/j.copsyc.2021.04.008
27. CustomerGlu: Gamification in Ecommerce: The Best Way to Boost Sales (2022). https://www.customerglu.com/blogs/gamification-in-ecommerce. Accessed 3 Mar 2025
28. Azmi, L.F., Ahmad, N., Iahad, N.A.: Gamification elements in E-commerce—a review. In: 2021 International Congress of Advanced Technology and Engineering (ICOTEN). https://doi.org/10.1109/ICOTEN52080.2021.9493475
29. Putra Ramadhan, M.A.W., Sensuse, D.I., Suryono, R.R., Kautsarina, K.: Trends and applications of gamification in E-commerce: a systematic literature review. J. Inf. Syst. Eng. Bus. Intell. **9**, 28–37 (2023). https://doi.org/10.20473/jisebi.9.1.28-37
30. Ningtyas, L.A., Atmaja, F.T.: Optimizing customer engagement: the impact of gamification elements on customer stickiness in shopee games. Manag. Anal. J. **13**, 11–20 (2024). https://doi.org/10.15294/maj.v13i1.1385
31. Muhammad Athoillah, N., Hidayat, A.: Analysis of the role of gamification in influence shopping engagement: shopee e-commerce case study. Int. J. Econ. Bus. Innov. Res. **3**, 212–229 (2024)
32. Hermawan, J., Utami Tjhin, V.: The effect of gamification on customer engagement in e-commerce. J. Theor. Appl. Inf. Technol. **101**, 5952 (2023)
33. Novo, C., Zanchetta, C., Goldmann, E., Vaz, C.: The use of gamification and web-based apps for sustainability education. Sustainability. **16**, 3197–3197 (2024). https://doi.org/10.3390/su16083197
34. Ryan, R.M., Deci, E.L.: Self-determination theory. In: Encyclopedia of Quality of Life and Well-Being Research, vol. 1, pp. 1–7 (2022). https://doi.org/10.1007/978-3-319-69909-7_2 630-2
35. Mugo, D.G., Njagi, K., Chemwei, B., Ochwagi Motanya, J.: The technology acceptance model (TAM) and its application to the utilization of mobile learning technologies. Br. J. Math. Comput. Sci. **20**, 1–8 (2017). https://doi.org/10.9734/BJMCS/2017/29015

36. Krath, J., Schürmann, L., von Korflesch, H.F.O.: Revealing the theoretical basis of gamification: a systematic review and analysis of theory in research on gamification, serious games and game-based learning. Comput. Hum. Behav. **125**, 106963 (2021)
37. Sailer, M., Hense, J.U., Mayr, S.K., Mandl, H.: How gamification motivates: an experimental study of the effects of specific game design elements on psychological need satisfaction. Comput. Hum. Behav. **69**(69), 371–380 (2017). https://doi.org/10.1016/j.chb.2016.12.033
38. Fulton, J.: Theory of Gamification-Motivation (2019)
39. Hammady, R., Arnab, S.: Serious gaming for behaviour change: a systematic review. Information. **13**(3), 142 (2022). https://doi.org/10.3390/info13030142
40. Dash, D.K., Pradhan, P., Kumar, R.: Awareness and practices of carbon footprint reduction: a survey among postgraduate students. Curr. Res. J. Soc. Sci. Hum. **6**(1), 122–131 (2023). https://doi.org/10.12944/crjssh.6.1.10
41. Hoffmann, S., Lasarov, W., Reimers, H., Trabandt, M.: Carbon footprint tracking apps. Does feedback help reduce carbon emissions? J. Clean. Prod. **434**, 139981 (2023). https://doi.org/10.1016/j.jclepro.2023.139981

Visibility Graph Analysis vs. Human Mobility Patterns: An Empirical Validation of Simulation-Based Analysis Using Space Syntax in Public Squares

Reza Askarizad[1,2] and Chiara Garau[1(✉)]

[1] Department of Civil and Environmental Engineering and Architecture (DICAAR), University of Cagliari, Via Marengo 2, 09123 Cagliari, Italy
cgarau@unica.it

[2] Department of Urban and Regional Planning, Universidad Politécnica de Madrid, 28040 Madrid, Spain

Abstract. In recent decades, computational analytical approaches have revolutionised research in urban planning and design, offering new insights that traditional approaches omitted. Combining social science approaches with cutting-edge digital technologies, these developments help to simulate and forecast human behaviour in urban public places. Among them, Space Syntax constitutes a substantial framework; Visibility Graph Analysis (VGA) serves as an important tool for investigating socio-behavioural dynamics in the urban planning process. However, enquiries concerning the empirical validity of these simulations remain a critical issue. This work intends to expand the dialogue on validating simulation-based results using empirical research. It particularly scrutinises how agent-based simulations, guided by VGA's parameters, match observable human movement and socio-behavioural activities. The case study is "Bastione di Saint Remy", a historically and socially important urban square in Cagliari, Italy, noted for its energetic pedestrian bustle and attractive setting. This study aims to validate simulation tools by comparing agent-based simulation results with real-world mobility patterns, thus addressing gaps in their applicability and reliability. The methodology employs Space Syntax principles, utilising Depthmap software to conduct simulations, while human mobility patterns are analysed through systematic empirical observations. Although visual integration and visual connectivity show partial alignment with observed pedestrian movement, visual control and the visual clustering coefficient indicate a stronger correlation with human mobility and static behaviours. Furthermore, the study reveals underused areas within the square, therefore emphasising the necessity of further research on activating leftover spaces.

This paper is the result of the joint work of the authors. 'Abstract', 'Study Area', 'Methodology' and 'Results' were written jointly by the authors. RA wrote 'Agent-based simulation using space syntax' and 'Discussion and Conclusion'. CG wrote 'Introduction' and 'Human mobility patterns in urban public spaces'. CG coordinated and supervised the paper.

Keywords: Visibility Graph Analysis (VGA) · Space Syntax · Social activities · Human mobility · Movement patterns · Urban squares · Urban public spaces · Computational design · Bastione di Saint Remy

1 Introduction

Designing socially sustainable urban spaces depends critically on an awareness of and managing human movement patterns, especially in public squares where many events and interactions comply with [1–3]. These spaces serve as vital nodes within the urban fabric, facilitating pedestrian movement, social exchange, and architectural expression [4, 5]. People's movement through and within public squares greatly affects their capability to support dynamic socio-behavioural activities [6, 7], accessibility, and usability. Good control of human movement patterns guarantees that these areas are not only efficient but also socially viable and equitable, therefore promoting a balanced cohabitation of many user groups [8–11]. The spatial configuration of urban squares plays a critical role in shaping how individuals navigate and interact within them, highlighting the need for strategies that harmonise mobility with the socio-functional objectives of urban design [12]. Responding to these challenges, urban planners can design public spaces that improve connectivity, promote active participation, and foster the growth of liveable cities [13, 14]. Smart urban systems that enable computational analytical methods to have changed the discipline of urban planning and design significantly over the recent years, and innovative tools that study and predict human behaviour in complex urban environments will contribute to the transformation of this discipline [15, 16]. These methods enable planners and designers to simulate and analyse spatial configurations and their influence on mobility and social interactions, thus providing data-driven insights which are typically absent from traditional approaches [17–19]. Simulation-based studies such as Space Syntax are among the most prominent given their ability to reveal important interactions between human movement patterns and spatial layout [20–22]. The visual narrative of the flow of pedestrian movement in the urban environment can contribute to understanding people's mobility and urban activities, particularly those functions related to urban public spaces [23]. In this regard, one of the key features of Space Syntax, the Visibility Graph Analysis (VGA) has proven to be useful in examining human behaviour through the visual connection within urban spaces [24, 25]. This analytical approach permits the identification of potential hotspots, areas of significant pedestrian flow, and locations encouraging social interaction [26]. Expanding on these capabilities, Agent-Based Analysis simulates individual decision-making processes where agents reflect more fine-grained understanding of pedestrian movement patterns [27–29]. This approach gives valuable insights about how people move in urban environments, also how mobility patterns may change, and how they react to design interventions, by modelling the behaviours and interactions of virtual agents [30, 31] within a spatial framework. This new style of synthesis which is made possible by computational methods marks an important paradigm-based shift toward effective and responsive urban-drawing devices on-site, specifically in lively urban squares.

The evolution of computational simulation tools used for urban planning has witnessed exciting developments and widespread implementation even if doubts over their validity and reliability continue to be a pressing concern. While approaches such as agent-based analysis offer useful predictions about human mobility patterns, their results often lack empirical validation. This raises critical issues about how real are simulation-based outcomes with measures in real settings, especially when considering dynamic contexts such as public squares. In the absence of experimental evidence that can reflect the reality in urban form, results achieved from simulation are likely to yield fragmentary or even incorrect lessons and therefore be of little use as a practical mechanism in urban design. This gap highlights the importance of systematic contrasts between simulation-based analyses and actual patterns of human mobility. Agent-Based Analysis, a subset of VGA, can potentially address this problem by simulating the choices of individuals as they play the game of mobility. However, its performance in adequately depicting real-world dynamics is still restricted sampling. As computational tools have the potential to influence urban design practices in social sustainability goals, closing this gap is essential to improve their reliability and effectiveness.

This study focuses on the possible empirical validity of simulation-driven examination, specifically Agent Based Analysis within Space syntax, based on its performative congruence with real human mobilities and socio-behavioural activities observed in public squares. The study addresses two fundamental key questions: (1) How successfully does Agent-Based Analysis replicate real-world human movement? (2) How can employing this sort of simulation-based analyses inform socially sustainable urban design? On these questions, the research poses two hypotheses, (a) Agent-Based Analysis may effectively replicate real-world mobility patterns when spatial configurations are a primary determinant of movement, and (b) incorporating validated simulation tools into urban design processes could improve public squares in terms of functionality. In linking computational simulations with empirical observations, this work deepens the understanding of human behaviour in urban space.

The findings are expected to advance the application of simulation-based methodologies, offering meaningful guidance for urban designers, planners, and architects to create dynamic and socially engaging public environments.

2 Literature Review

2.1 Human Mobility Patterns in Urban Public Spaces

Human mobility patterns in urban public spaces have attracted considerable research interest due to their relevance in urban planning, transportation, and social behaviour analysis. One of the earlier studies by Jahromi et al. [32] conducted a simulation model using call detail data, GPS, and WiFi traces to analyse human mobility. Their findings revealed that the simulator is highly adaptable and effective at modelling spatio-temporal behaviour across different geographic and population scales. This adaptability underscores the potential of technology in understanding urban mobility and its integration with urban systems. However, these models face limitations in providing real-time data accuracy and capturing the complexity of social dynamics in urban environments.

Sun et al. [33] argued that urban dynamics are both predictable and stable, making them critical for forecasting urban behaviour and detecting anomalies. They contended that stable urban dynamics may enhance traffic management and planning. Yang et al.

[34] extended this idea by establishing a clear correlation between mobility behaviours and urban functional areas, emphasising the importance of spatial analysis for optimising urban planning. Nonetheless, these models often overlook the potential disruption of previously stable mobility patterns caused in urban forms, or the integration of mixed-use spaces. Kang et al. [35] highlighted the role of urban morphology in shaping mobility, suggesting that urban design significantly influences how people move through space. This perspective is confirmed by Santilli et al. [36], who demonstrated that hybrid forecasting models can accurately estimate pedestrian flows. While these models contribute significantly to planning, they may not fully capture the impact of emerging urban forms and newer mobility options.

The integration of sustainable mobility practices has also become a focal point in urban mobility studies. Sultan et al. [37] examined factors influencing mobility mode choice, revealing that barriers to adopting sustainable mobility remain despite infrastructure improvements. Their work emphasises the need for targeted planning to address those barriers. Mezoued et al. [38] adapted the Slow City concept to larger cities, with an emphasis on walking as a main transport mode. Adapting this model is essential for promoting sustainable mobility in densely populated urban areas. Nonetheless, a struggle exists in addressing the balance between pedestrian-centric areas as well as other urban transportation modes, especially micro-mobility vehicles, which Zhang et al. can pose challenges to road safety [39] noted. It's a contradiction in urban mobility planning, where expanding space for some modes of transportation is creating risks for others. Another important element of human mobility in urban areas is safety. Campisi et al. [40] noted that pedestrian safety is determined by many different factors including overall crossing patterns, quality of the infrastructure and traffic conditions. Their analysis showed that distracted pedestrians that use mobile phones were more prone to accidents, highlighting a critical issue in urban mobility. Although Bluetooth networks are a technological advancement for analysing pedestrian movement, the application of such technologies is ineffective in real-world settings despite their utility [41]. These advancements provide valuable insights but also highlight their weaknesses of relying solely on technological solutions without addressing broader social and infrastructural factors.

The built environment significantly influences human mobility, and numerous studies emphasised the important role of spatial configuration, land-use diversity, and urban attractiveness in the movement patterns. Yang et al. [42] contended that the residential built environment is as important—even, perhaps, more so—than the distance travelled or the number of stops in shaping human mobility. These insights highlight the role of urban design in promoting social interactions and improving urban quality of life. Zhang & Li [43] proposed an Activity Space-based Gravity model, which modelled the spatial temporal characteristics and the attractiveness of each urban region, significantly enhancing the prediction of human mobility flows. This advancement is a significant step towards more precise and efficient urban mobility models. Khotbehsara et al. [44] revealed that while in more urbanised regions other factors may play, urban land-use diversity and compatibility distinctly shape pedestrian mobility in low-density city environments.

However, despite these advancements, Chu et al. [45] suggest that existing models still struggle with issues of socio-economic segregation. Abbiasov et al. [46] found that despite the benefits of increasing access to local amenities on human mobility, it also often increases segregation, especially low-income residents, which may prove problematic for the large-scale adoption of concepts such as the 15-minute city. Indeed, this results in an important shortcoming of current research that tends to emphasise accessibility as a main imperative of urban mobility, while neglecting the influence of socio-economic disparities on mobility patterns and access to urban facilities.

In a nutshell, while substantial progress has been made in understanding human mobility patterns, a limited number of studies have integrated space syntax analysis or investigated the validity of agent-based models in this field. Despite the wide range of studies undertaken, there is a continued need for more comprehensive research that bridges the gap between spatial design, human behaviour, and socio-economic dynamics in urban mobility studies. The following subsection will evaluate such studies primarily focused on agent-based simulations using space syntax.

2.2 Agent-Based Simulation Using Space Syntax

Agent-based simulation, particularly when combined with space syntax, has become an effective tool for analysing human movement and behaviour in urban environments. This subsection summarises relevant research, discussing the benefits and drawbacks of combining these methodologies for understanding the relationship between spatial configuration and user movement patterns. Esposito et al. [47] demonstrated significant relationships between experimental approaches to spatial cognition and predictions based on space syntax, suggesting that the respective approaches may complement each other and collectively better inform our understanding of agent-based decisions and behaviours. Omer and Kaplan [48] stressed the usefulness of agent-based pedestrian volume models in an integrated space syntax framework, specifically in contexts with inconsistent correlations between street network and land-use patterns. This underlines why using agent-based models has the potential to address gaps in traditional space syntax approaches, particularly as they relate to evolving urban conditions.

In addition, Mara et al. [49] showed how, by integrating metrics from space syntax with agent-based modelling, the interactions between pedestrian behaviour, urban configurations, and environmental conditions can elucidate crime distributions. This approach highlights the flexibility of agent-based models across a wide range of use cases, such as pedestrian behaviours and crime reduction. Koutsolampros and Varoudis [50] proposed a hybrid model that includes non-player-character movement techniques leads to simulations behaving more "human-like" and follow realistic movement patterns. This is an advancement as a common critique of traditional space syntax model is that they fail to emulate nuanced human behaviour within complex spatial environments.

However, challenges still exist despite these advances. Chun et al. [51] conducted no statistically significant correlations between eco psychology theories, agent-based modelling and observed human behaviour. It highlights the complexity of spatial usage patterns for humans, and the difficulty in modelling them correctly.

Conversely, Tang and Hu [52] showed that agent-based simulations can be used to identify optimal pedestrian flow in urban spaces in a way that affords optimised access to public space which implies that these models can still provide value in process application especially in relevant urban contexts. Furthermore, research has illustrated how urban facility design shapes human mobility patterns and static social behaviours in public space. Such a configuration would create greater socially inclusive urban public spaces as incorporating more of visual connectivity and integration (with a reduced visual entropy and less visual cluster) and therefore offers more of urban vitality perspective [53].

Further research has investigated innovative approaches to agent-based modelling. For example, Yıldız and Çağdaş [54] calculated the attractiveness value of the urban space components based on their distance from the reference point and the attraction factor of the use, showing the effectiveness of this method in simulating temporal variations in user behaviour in public squares. Sobreira [55] also presented a simulation of inner-city squatter settlements demonstrating the ability of agent-based models to depict complicated urban systems, e.g. the role of the abundance of vacant land and the interactions of inhabitants. Turner and Penn [56] further enrich this discourse. They found that human movement could rather be fit well by a very simple movement rule based on a "random next step" that is influenced by the visual field at that location, and outperforms models based on destination. This is in line with Jiang and Jia's [57] conclusion on aggregating flow patterns being more influenced by configurations of the street network, as opposed to specific (and relatively natural) human behaviours, highlighting the primacy of spatial affordances in activating movement.

In contrast, Mohammed and Ukai [58] employed other spatial metrics like the space matrix and mixed-use index within agent-based models, offering urban planners a generalized tool to forecast urban land expansion. This highlights the possibilities of agent-based modelling as a bridge between spatial analysis and applied urban planning. The use of agent-based models in tourism and smart city applications opens further opportunities for these models. Wang et al. [59] used 3D isovist analysis alongside agent-based modelling to predict visitor flow volumes in tourism-oriented villages, offering implications toward optimising visitor behaviour. With the same view, researchers [60] investigated the application of smart city initiatives in the sector of urban architecture in order to improve pedestrian movement in separated urban zones as a solution for some constraints of traditional urban compositions.

Despite the significant advancements in integrating space syntax with agent-based modelling, a gap remains in empirically validating these simulations against real-world human mobility patterns. While a limited number of studies emphasise the accuracy of agent-based models in replicating observed behaviours, others highlight discrepancies that suggest the need for further refinement. This research addresses these gaps by empirically validating simulation-based analyses in a renowned public square of Cagliari in Italy, through a comparison with actual human mobility patterns. This study aims to provide a framework for evaluating and validating the effectiveness of agent-based simulations in urban planning by examining their interaction with real-world human mobility patterns, thereby enhancing the design of user-centric public spaces. Figure 1 illustrates a summary of the conducted literature review.

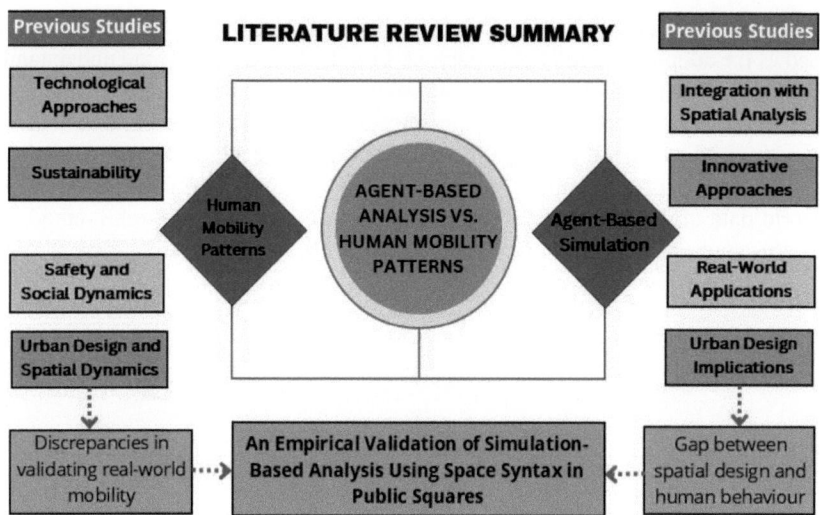

Fig. 1. Main themes and findings of the literature review, with the existing gap covered with this study.

3 Methodology

This study adopted a mixed-methods research strategy, integrating both quantitative and qualitative approaches. The quantitative aspect involves the simulation of spatial configurations using Space Syntax analysis. For this purpose, the authors used UCL Depthmap 10 software. Before conducting the syntactical analysis, a detailed urban map of the studied square was meticulously drawn to include all relevant elements and urban amenities that might influence the simulation of human mobility patterns.

This included both natural and artificial features, such as gardens, trees, lamp posts, seating areas, and other types of urban furniture, all of which were drawn using AutoCAD 10 software. The map was exported to DXF format and imported into Depthmap software for analysis. There were two main procedures in the analysis of spatial configuration: visual graph analysis (VGA) to evaluate the square's spatial attributes and an agent-based analysis that questioned the individual movements based on the environment's spatial configuration.

The analysis employed several VGA metrics to understand the square's visual structure and its influence on movement. Visual integration reveals how easily a space can be seen from all others, suggesting areas of higher usage. Visual connectivity counts direct sightlines, indicating immediate visual and, consequently, spatial access. The visual clustering coefficient shows how stable or disrupted the view is during movement, potentially identifying pause points. Visual control quantifies the ability to see and be seen, hinting at informal surveillance. Finally, gate count identifies locations where many potential paths converge, likely attracting spontaneous pedestrian flow [61, 62].

The qualitative phase involved empirical observations of how humans moved in the square to validate and ground-truth the agent-based simulations. The observations sought to measure the degree to which simulation results matched the actual pedestrian motion of the individuals found at the public square. In this study, static snapshots techniques are used as the adopted observational method. In order to analyse a broad understanding of human movement patterns a series of snapshots were taken from the top floor level. To ensure that external factors did not make an impact on this experiment, observations were done under good weather conditions. Lastly, a comparative analysis was undertaken to compare the agent-based simulations conducted in the Space Syntax framework with real-world data observed. Figure 2 shows the paradigm for the research methodology used in this study.

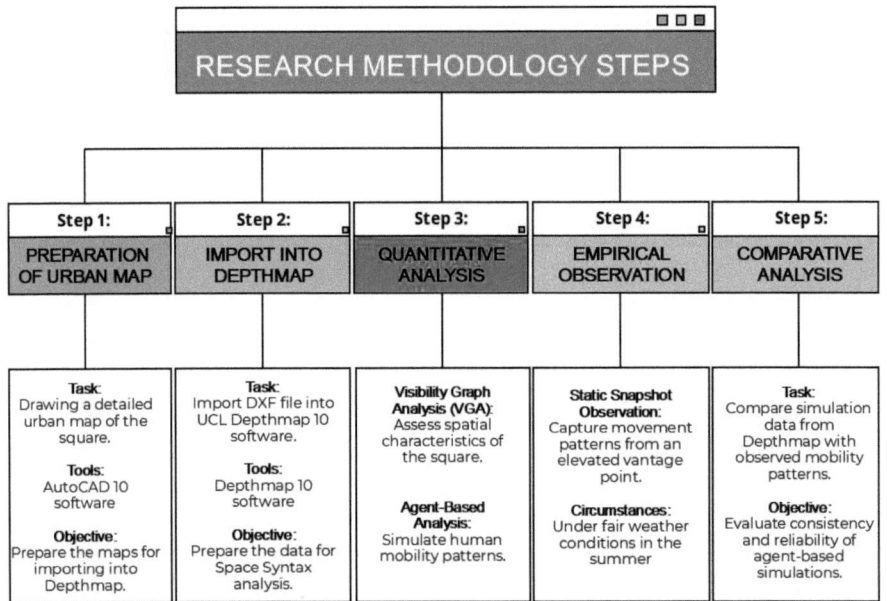

Fig. 2. Flowchart of research methodology illustrating the sequential steps from spatial configuration analysis to empirical validation.

4 The Area of Study: the "Bastione di Saint Remy"

The "Bastione di Saint Remy" is located in Cagliari, the capital of Sardinia, Italy (Fig. 3). Sardinia is known for its cultural heritage, traditional architecture, and natural beauty, and it has great importance in national and international tourism. Located in the historical Castello district, the "Bastione di Saint Remy" has a central location in Cagliari, boasting a strategic point of the city and the Gulf of Cagliari. The great Bastione di Saint Remy is a high monumental structure and urban square, built in the late 19th and early 20th centuries. It has grand arches, white limestone facades and an imposing staircase leading visitor up to an elevated terrace, all characteristics of neoclassical architecture. The structure is named after a notable figure from the time it was built, Baron Saint Remy. This landmark of architecture was once built to protect the city but has since been converted into a public space and a social center.

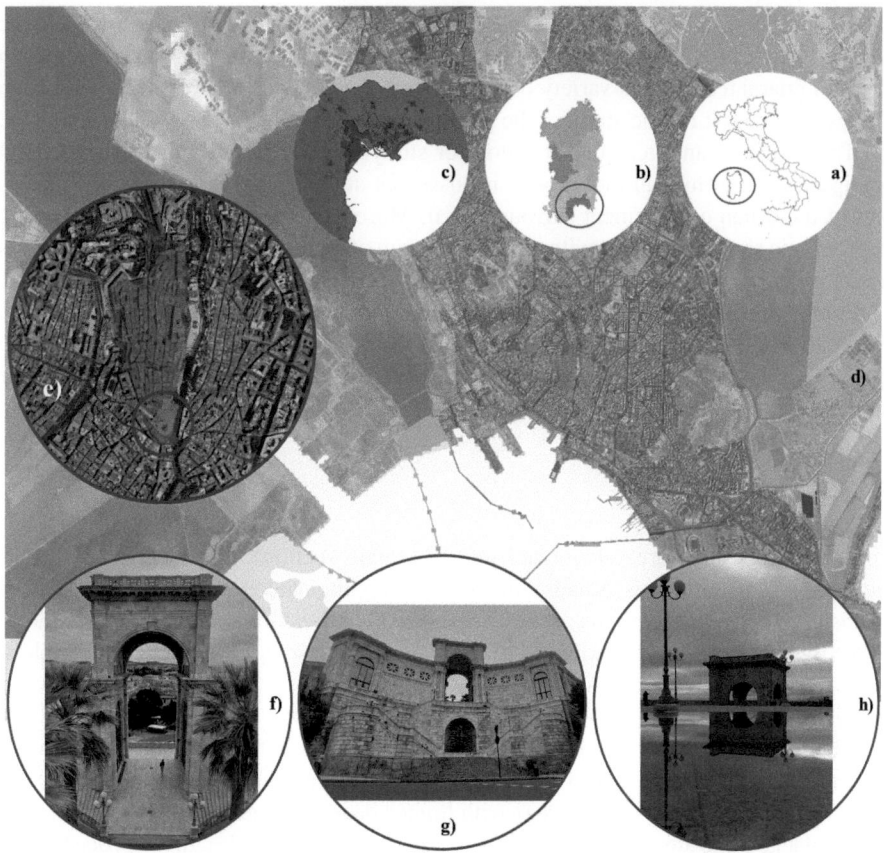

Fig. 3. Geographical location of the case study (a: Location of Sardinia in Italy; b: Location of Cagliari Metropolitan City in Sardinia; c: Location of Study Area in Cagliari; d: Location of Castello Neighbourhood in Cagliari; e: Location of Case Study in Castello Neighbourhood; f, g, h: Different views of Bastione di Saint Remy).

The square is an essential component of Cagliari's urban fabric, connecting the lower city to the Castello district. It is reached by a series of broad staircases (with elevators); it conduits pedestrian activity. At its highest point, the Bastione forms a large open terrace, a public gathering space.

Its panoramic views encompass the city, the harbour, and the surrounding hills, creating an unparalleled setting for both locals and visitors to enjoy. The Bastione is one of the most important tourist venues, and it is visited by many different people for its significance, architectural style, and lively atmosphere. It is an important place for cultural gatherings, markets, and social meetings. Particularly well-known for its magnificent views, it makes for an optimal place to observe both sunrise and sunset. It is best known for the relaxed nature, availability of cafes and seats, and as such is a warm place to socialise.

Due to being a historical monument, urban square, and social space, the Bastione di Saint Remy provides an ideal case study for this research. Its prominent location in Cagliari guarantees a great variety of users (both tourists and local residents) and is an interesting context for the study of the patterns of human mobility and social activities.

The square is an interesting location for studying the relationship between spatial configuration and human mobility as it possesses unique architectural features and is part of the urban environment surrounding it. Moreover, its identity as a placemaking and touristic site is consistent with the research aim of exploring how city design impacts where we play (stationary social activities) or go (movement of beings) in public places. Through empirical-led analysis by taking the Bastione di Saint Remy as a centre point, this study seeks to explore the everyday experiences and visions of those that shape the space. This data will then serve to verify whether simulated analysis predicts actual user mobility patterns and preferences.

5 Results

The obtained results are categorised into two main sections: empirical observations and Space Syntax analysis, along with their overlapping outcomes to assess the level of consistency between the two datasets. The empirical observations were conducted in July 2024. Based on the investigations and observations, the square experiences its highest pedestrian mobility around sunset. Consequently, the observations occurred between 8:00 p.m. and 9:00 p.m.

The method used for documenting behavioural maps in this study is based on the accumulation of crowds, which has been visualised using a black-coloured chromatic spectrum. In this visualisation, areas with higher pedestrian density are represented in darker black, while areas with lower density appear in lighter shades. In the Space Syntax analysis, various VGA metrics were employed to provide a comprehensive assessment of influential spatial factors. These metrics include visual integration, visual connectivity, visual clustering coefficient, visual control, and gate count analysis. In these visualisations, areas with higher numerical values are represented in warmer colours, while areas with quantitative values appear in cooler colours.

The findings from the VGA analysis at Bastione di Saint Remy indicate that visual integration is somewhat correlated with observed pedestrian mobility patterns. The highest integration value in this analysis was 19.57, recorded in front of the entrance stairs. While this value demonstrates a high level of consistency with observed mobility patterns, it also highlights additional potential spaces that could facilitate pedestrian movement (Fig. 4). Similarly, the visibility graph of connectivity yields comparable results, with the highest connectivity value reaching 4761, suggesting a moderate consistency with pedestrian mobility patterns (Fig. 5).

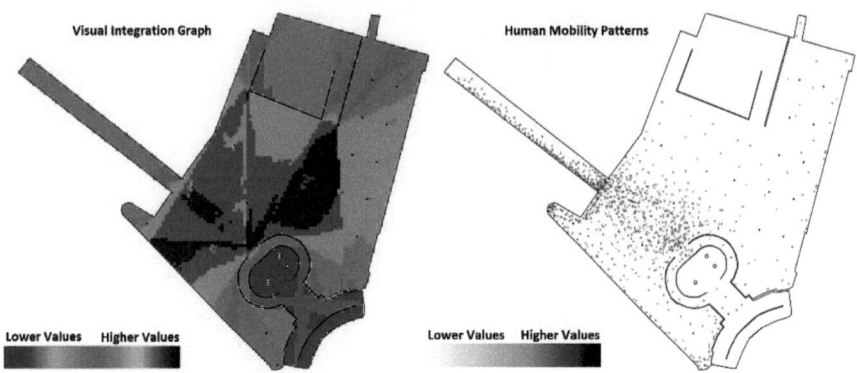

Fig. 4. Visual integration analysis of the study area and its comparison with human mobility patterns.

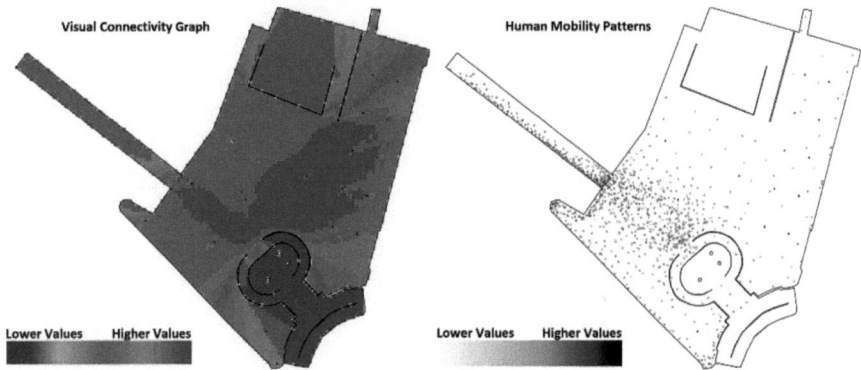

Fig. 5. Visual connectivity analysis of the study area and its comparison with human mobility patterns.

While integration and connectivity exhibited partial consistency with observed movement patterns, other variables—such as visual control and visual clustering coefficient—displayed greater alignment between the simulated models and real-world pedestrian behaviour. The results of visual control analysis indicate a significant correlation with observed pedestrian movement patterns, with the highest visual control value recorded at 1.68, validating the movement patterns within this public space (Fig. 6). Additionally, the visual clustering coefficient showed a high degree of correlation with stationary behaviours, with the highest quantitative value of 0.98 (Fig. 7). Notably, the gate count analysis—conducted using the agent-based tools of the software—revealed a complete inconsistency between the simulation results and the actual observed movement patterns within the public square (Fig. 8).

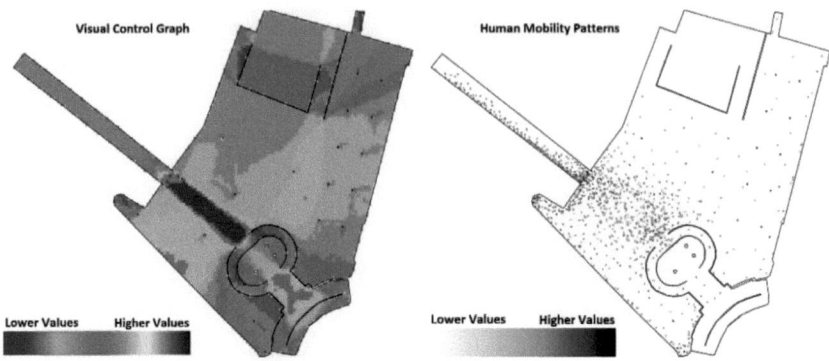

Fig. 6. Visual control analysis of the study area and its comparison with human mobility patterns.

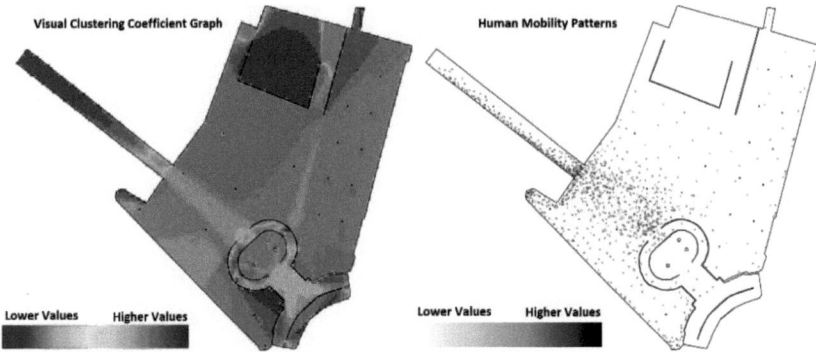

Fig. 7. Visual clustering coefficient analysis of the study area and its comparison with human mobility patterns.

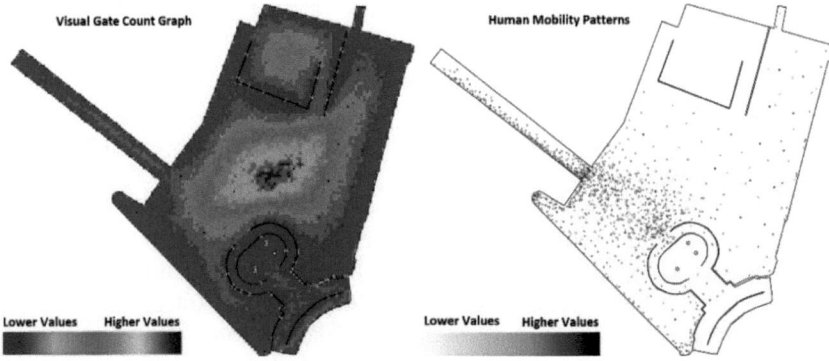

Fig. 8. Visual gate count analysis of the study area and its comparison with human mobility patterns.

6 Discussion and Conclusion

This study explores the viability of simulation-based approaches in predicting human mobility behaviours in real-life environments; it tests the empirical adequacy of these models in the field of Space Syntax, especially the agent-based analysis, at public squares i.e. a representative case study for geo-spatial settings. This relationship is also key to evaluate the accuracy of computational predictive models of the urban processes in urban studies and their applicability to provide relevant insights on evidence-based urban design.

The findings obtained shows that human mobility patterns follow spatial configuration and its topological relationships to some extent. Strikingly, the visual control showed great correlation with pedestrian flow patterns, supporting the theory of Jan Gehl [63] not only should urban spaces be designed in a way where we can see them, they should also promote the value of being seen by others. Finally, it was found that the visual clustering coefficient was highly correlated with stationary behaviours, suggesting that the metric has notable significance for socio-behavioural evaluations of public spaces. Conversely, the presence of the visual integration and connectivity metrics does not fully reflect human mobility trajectories, although some residual/unused spaces have been pin-pointed in the square and suggest more works on residual spaces and their activation in future studies.

Despite these insights, certain limitations should be acknowledged. Firstly, the study focuses on a single case study—Bastione di Saint Remy—meaning that the findings are intrinsically tied to its specific spatial and social context. Thus, dimensions such as functional characteristics, aesthetic experience, and daily activity rhythms might also affect pedestrian mobility besides the shape of the space itself. In addition, the observed data collection was limited to a specific time interval, which may not be entirely representative of the overall mobility pattern taking place within the study area. Future research should explore these elements in greater detail and consider other urban squares to improve the generalisability of the findings. Additionally, methods like ethnographic studies and participatory observations can help us better understand how users engage with public spaces.

The originality of this research is highlighted when comparing these results with prior studies. Whereas other studies demonstrated the contribution of visual integration and connectivity to pedestrian movement prediction [64–66], this study demonstrates that visual control and clustering coefficients may offer greater predictive power for socio-behavioural activities in certain public spaces. This distinction highlights the importance of context-specific analyses and the importance of methodological refinement in Space Syntax studies.

In conclusion, this work turns directly to the two substantive research questions. Firstly, it shows that Agent-Based Analysis based on Space Syntax has some degree of internal validation of real-life human movement patterns, where some metrics (such as visual control, clustering coefficient, integration, and connection) are better classifiers than others. Second, findings showing the effects of space use simulation analyses in urban use finding processes can help to achieve socially sustainable public space in such as areas with high activity and those that are not sufficiently activated urban settings. Further studies should extend these findings by improving simulation models and incorporating in particular further socio-spatial variables in order to develop predictive accuracy and practical application.

Acknowledgments. This study was supported by the MUR through two projects, (1) SMART3R-FLITS: SMART Transport for Travelers and Freight Logistics Integration Towards Sustainability" (Project protocol: 2022J38SR9; CUP Code: F53D23005630006) and (2) MOVING StEPS: MOVING from Street Experiments to adaptive Planned Solutions (Project protocol: 2022BLK9TS; CUP Code: F53D23005550006), both financed by the PRIN 2022 (Research Projects of National Relevance) program, funded by the European Union (NextGenerationEU). This study reflects only the authors' views and opinions, and neither the European Union nor the European Commission can be considered responsible for them.

References

1. Grieco, M.: Social sustainability and urban mobility: shifting to a socially responsible pro-poor perspective. Soc. Responsib. J. **11**(1), 82–97 (2015). https://doi.org/10.1108/SRJ-05-2014-0061
2. Gonzalez, M.C., Hidalgo, C.A., Barabasi, A.L.: Understanding individual human mobility patterns. Nature. **453**(7196), 779–782 (2008). https://doi.org/10.1038/nature06958
3. Noulas, A., Scellato, S., Lambiotte, R., Pontil, M., Mascolo, C.: A tale of many cities: universal patterns in human urban mobility. PLoS One. **7**(5), e37027 (2012). https://doi.org/10.1371/journal.pone.0037027
4. Lang, J., Marshall, N.: Urban Squares as Places, Links and Displays: Successes and Failures. Routledge, London (2016). https://doi.org/10.4324/9781315660707
5. Mehta, V.: Evaluating public space. J. Urban Des. **19**(1), 53–88 (2014). https://doi.org/10.1080/13574809.2013.854698
6. Jamei, E., Ahmadi, K., Chau, H.W., Seyedmahmoudian, M., Horan, B., Stojcevski, A.: Urban design and walkability: lessons learnt from Iranian traditional cities. Sustainability. **13**(10), 5731 (2021). https://doi.org/10.3390/su13105731
7. Cattell, V., Dines, N., Gesler, W., Curtis, S.: Mingling, observing, and lingering: everyday public spaces and their implications for well-being and social relations. Health Place. **14**(3), 544–561 (2008). https://doi.org/10.1016/j.healthplace.2007.10.007
8. Zhang, S., Hu, Z., Zhen, F., Kong, Y., Tong, Z.: Assessing the (in)equality of an x-minute city accounting for human mobility patterns. Transp. Res. Part A Policy Pract. **192**, 104354 (2025). https://doi.org/10.1016/j.tra.2024.104354
9. Pinna, F., et al.: A literature review on urban usability and accessibility to investigate the related criteria for equality in the city. In: Gervasi, O., et al. (eds.) Computational Science and Its Applications – ICCSA 2021. Lecture Notes in Computer Science, vol. 12958. Springer, Cham (2021). https://doi.org/10.1007/978-3-030-87016-4_38
10. Askarizad, R., He, J., Dastoum, M.: Gender disparity in public spaces of Iran: design for more inclusive cities. Cities. **158**, 105651 (2025). https://doi.org/10.1016/j.cities.2024.105651
11. Garau, C., Annunziata, A., Desogus, G., Rossetti, S.: Spatial smartness and (In)justice in urban contexts? The case studies of Cagliari and Parma, Italy. In: Marucci, A., Zullo, F., Fiorini, L., Saganeiti, L. (eds.) Innovation in Urban and Regional Planning. INPUT 2023, vol. 463. Springer, Cham (2024). https://doi.org/10.1007/978-3-031-54096-7_42
12. Simões Aelbrecht, P.: 'Fourth places': the contemporary public settings for informal social interaction among strangers. J. Urban Des. **21**(1), 124–152 (2016). https://doi.org/10.1080/13574809.2015.1106920

13. Elshater, A., Abusaada, H., Tarek, M., Afifi, S.: Designing the socio-spatial context urban infill, liveability, and conviviality. Built Environ. **48**(3), 341–363 (2022). https://doi.org/10.2148/benv.48.3.341
14. Soltani, S., Gu, N., Ochoa, J.J., Sivam, A.: The role of spatial configuration in moderating the relationship between social sustainability and urban density. Cities. **121**, 103519 (2022). https://doi.org/10.1016/j.cities.2021.103519
15. Mansourihanis, O., Maghsoodi Tilaki, M.J., Yousefian, S., Zaroujtaghi, A.: A computational geospatial approach to assessing land-use compatibility in urban planning. Land. **12**(11), 2083 (2023). https://doi.org/10.3390/land12112083
16. Huang, X.: Computational urban science needs to go beyond computational. Comput. Urban Sci. **4**(1), 18 (2024). https://doi.org/10.1007/s43762-024-00130-4
17. Ostwald, M.J., Lee, J.H.: Computational analytical methods for buildings and cities: space syntax and shape grammar. Buildings. **13**(7), 1613 (2023). https://doi.org/10.3390/buildings13071613
18. Pan, M., Shen, Y., Jiang, Q., Zhou, Q., Li, Y.: Reshaping publicness: research on correlation between public participation and spatial form in urban space based on space syntax—a case study on Nanjing Xinjiekou. Buildings. **12**(9), 1492 (2022). https://doi.org/10.3390/buildings12091492
19. Crooks, A., Castle, C., Batty, M.: Key challenges in agent-based modelling for geo-spatial simulation. Comput. Environ. Urban. Syst. **32**(6), 417–430 (2008). https://doi.org/10.1016/j.compenvurbsys.2008.09.004
20. Kim, Y.O., Penn, A.: Linking the spatial syntax of cognitive maps to the spatial syntax of the environment. Environ. Behav. **36**(4), 483–504 (2004). https://doi.org/10.1177/0013916503261384
21. Yamu, C., et al.: Bill Hillier's legacy: space syntax—a synopsis of basic concepts, measures, and empirical application. Sustainability. **13**(6), 3394 (2021). https://doi.org/10.3390/su13063394
22. Askarizad, R., Daudén, P.J.L., Garau, C.: Exploring the role of configurational accessibility of alleyways on facilitating wayfinding transportation within the organic street network systems. Transp. Policy. **157**, 179–194 (2024). https://doi.org/10.1016/j.tranpol.2024.09.001
23. Khotbehsara, E.M., et al.: The walkable environment: a systematic review through the lens of space syntax as an integrated approach. Smart Sustain. Built Environ., 1–27 (2025). https://doi.org/10.1108/SASBE-02-2024-0049
24. Lee, J.H., Ostwald, M.J., Zhou, L.: Socio-spatial experience in space syntax research: a PRISMA-compliant review. Buildings. **13**(3), 644 (2023). https://doi.org/10.3390/buildings13030644
25. Lee, J.H., Ostwald, M.J.: Latent Dirichlet Allocation (LDA) topic models for space syntax studies on spatial experience. City Territ. Archit. **11**(1), 3 (2024). https://doi.org/10.1186/s40410-023-00223-3
26. van Nes, A., Yamu, C.: Orientation and wayfinding: measuring visibility. In: Introduction to Space Syntax in Urban Studies. Springer, Cham (2021). https://doi.org/10.1007/978-3-030-72743-7
27. Moosavi, S.M., Cornadó, C., Askarizad, R.: Analyzing the influence of residents' socio-cultural reflections on the spatial configuration of historical persian residential architecture. Sustainability. **17**, 879 (2025). https://doi.org/10.3390/su17030879
28. DeAngelis, D.L., Diaz, S.G.: Decision-making in agent-based modeling: a current review and future prospectus. Front. Ecol. Evol. **6**, 237 (2019). https://doi.org/10.3389/fevo.2018.00237
29. An, L.: Modeling human decisions in coupled human and natural systems: review of agent-based models. Ecol. Model. **229**, 25–36 (2012). https://doi.org/10.1016/j.ecolmodel.2011.07.010

30. Cheliotis, K.: An agent-based model of public space use. Comput. Environ. Urban. Syst. **81**, 101476 (2020). https://doi.org/10.1016/j.compenvurbsys.2020.101476
31. Mara, F., Cutini, V.: Space syntax vs agent-based modelling in the maze of urban complexity: a critical comparison between top-down and bottom-up approaches and applications. In: International Conference on Innovation in Urban and Regional Planning. LNCS, vol. 3, pp. 585–596. Springer, Cham (2023). https://doi.org/10.1007/978-3-031-54118-6_52
32. Jahromi, K.K., Zignani, M., Gaito, S., Rossi, G.P.: Simulating human mobility patterns in urban areas. Simul. Model. Pract. Theory. **62**, 137–156 (2016)
33. Sun, J.B., Yuan, J., Wang, Y., Si, H.B., Shan, X.M.: Exploring space–time structure of human mobility in urban space. Physica A Stat. Mech. Appl. **390**(5), 929–942 (2011). https://doi.org/10.1016/j.physa.2010.10.033
34. Yang, X., Zhao, Z., Lu, S.: Exploring spatial-temporal patterns of urban human mobility hotspots. Sustainability. **8**(7), 674 (2016). https://doi.org/10.3390/su8070674
35. Kang, C., Ma, X., Tong, D., Liu, Y.: Intra-urban human mobility patterns: an urban morphology perspective. Physica A Stat. Mech. Appl. **391**(4), 1702–1717 (2012). https://doi.org/10.1016/j.physa.2011.11.005
36. Santilli, D., D'apuzzo, M., Evangelisti, A., Nicolosi, V.: Towards sustainability: new tools for planning urban pedestrian mobility. Sustainability. **13**(16), 9371 (2021). https://doi.org/10.3390/su13169371
37. Sultan, B., Katar, I.M., Al-Atroush, M.E.: Towards sustainable pedestrian mobility in Riyadh city, Saudi Arabia: a case study. Sustain. Cities Soc. **69**, 102831 (2021). https://doi.org/10.1016/j.scs.2021.102831
38. Mezoued, A.M., Letesson, Q., Kaufmann, V.: Making the slow metropolis by designing walkability: a methodology for the evaluation of public space design and prioritizing pedestrian mobility. Urban Res. Pract. **15**(4), 584–603 (2022). https://doi.org/10.1080/17535069.2021.1875038
39. Zhang, C., Du, B., Zheng, Z., Shen, J.: Space sharing between pedestrians and micro-mobility vehicles: a systematic review. Transp. Res. Part D: Transp. Environ. **116**, 103629 (2023). https://doi.org/10.1016/j.trd.2023.103629
40. Campisi, T., Otković, I.I., Šurdonja, S., Deluka-Tibljaš, A.: Impact of social and technological distraction on pedestrian crossing behaviour: a case study in Enna, Sicily. Transp. Res. Proc. **60**, 100–107 (2022). https://doi.org/10.1016/j.trpro.2021.12.014
41. Angel, A., Cohen, A., Dalyot, S., Plaut, P.: Estimating pedestrian traffic with Bluetooth sensor technology. Geo-spat. Inf. Sci. **27**(5), 1391–1404 (2024). https://doi.org/10.1080/10095020.2023.2247446
42. Yang, X., Li, J., Fang, Z., Chen, H., Li, J., Zhao, Z.: Influence of residential built environment on human mobility in Xining: a mobile phone data perspective. Travel Behav. Soc. **34**, 100665 (2024). https://doi.org/10.1016/j.tbs.2023.100665
43. Zhang, X., Li, N.: An activity space-based gravity model for intracity human mobility flows. Sustain. Cities Soc. **101**, 105073 (2024). https://doi.org/10.1016/j.scs.2023.105073
44. Khotbehsara, E.M., Somasundaraswaran, K., Kolbe-Alexander, T., Yu, R.: The influence of spatial configuration on pedestrian movement behaviour in commercial streets of low-density cities. Ain Shams Eng. J. **16**(1), 103184 (2025). https://doi.org/10.1016/j.asej.2024.103184
45. Chu, C., Zhang, H., Wang, P., Lu, F.: Simulating human mobility with a trajectory generation framework based on diffusion model. Int. J. Geogr. Inf. Sci. **38**(5), 847–878 (2024). https://doi.org/10.1080/13658816.2024.2312199
46. Abbiasov, T., Heine, C., Sabouri, S., Salazar-Miranda, A., Santi, P., Glaeser, E., Ratti, C.: The 15-minute city quantified using human mobility data. Nat. Hum. Behav. **8**(3), 445–455 (2024). https://doi.org/10.1038/s41562-023-01770-y

47. Esposito, D., Santoro, S., Camarda, D.: Agent-based analysis of urban spaces using space syntax and spatial cognition approaches: a case study in Bari, Italy. Sustainability. **12**(11), 4625 (2020). https://doi.org/10.3390/su12114625
48. Omer, I., Kaplan, N.: Using space syntax and agent-based approaches for modeling pedestrian volume at the urban scale. Comput. Environ. Urban. Syst. **64**, 57–67 (2017). https://doi.org/10.1016/j.compenvurbsys.2017.01.007
49. Mara, F., Altafini, D., Cutini, V., Malleson, N.: Simulation to forecast crime patterns: comparing space syntax and agent-based models in exploring pedestrian movement and visibility. Environ. Plan. B Urban Anal. City Sci. (2024)
50. Koutsolampros, P., Varoudis, T.: Assisted agent-based simulations: Fusing non-player character movement with Space Syntax. In: Proceedings of the 11th International Space Syntax Symposium, vol. 11, pp. 164–161. Instituto Superior Tecnico Departamentode Engenharia Civil, Arquitetura e Georrecursos (2017)
51. Chun, J., Psarras, S., Koutsolampros, P.: Agent-based simulation for 'choice of seats': a study on the human space usage pattern. In: Proceedings of the 12th International Space Syntax Symposium. International Space Syntax Symposium, Beijing (2019)
52. Tang, M., Hu, Y.: Pedestrian simulation in transit stations using agent-based analysis. Urban Rail Transit. **3**(1), 54–60 (2017). https://doi.org/10.1007/s40864-017-0053-5
53. Askarizad, R., He, J.: The role of urban furniture in promoting gender equality and static social activities in public spaces. Ain Shams Eng. J. **16**(2), 103250 (2025). https://doi.org/10.1016/j.asej.2024.103250
54. Yıldız, B., Çağdaş, G.: Fuzzy logic in agent-based modeling of user movement in urban space: definition and application to a case study of a square. Build. Environ. **169**, 106597 (2020). https://doi.org/10.1016/j.buildenv.2019.106597
55. Sobreira, F.: Squatter settlements consolidation: spatial analysis in an agent-based environment. In: Proceedings of the 4th International Space Syntax Symposium, pp. 16–11. University College London, London (2003)
56. Penn, A., Turner, A.: Space syntax based agent simulation. In: Proceedings of the 1st International Conference on Pedestrian and Evacuation Dynamics, pp. 99–114. University of Duisburg (2001)
57. Jiang, B., Jia, T.: Agent-based simulation of human movement shaped by the underlying street structure. Int. J. Geogr. Inf. Sci. **25**(1), 51–64 (2011). https://doi.org/10.1080/13658811003712864
58. Mohammed, A.M., Ukai, T.: Agent-based modelling for spatiotemporal patterns of urban land expansion around university campuses. Model. Earth Syst. Environ. **9**(1), 1119–1133 (2023). https://doi.org/10.1007/s40808-022-01551-y
59. Wang, S., Huang, Y., Li, T.: Understanding visitor flow and behaviour in developing tourism-service-oriented villages by space syntax methodologies: a case study of Tabian rural cection of Qingshan Village, Hangzhou. J. Asian Archit. Build. Eng. **24**, 1–20 (2024). https://doi.org/10.1080/13467581.2024.2349737
60. Askarizad, R., Dastoum, M., Garau, C.: Street puppet theatre shows on the façades of commercial buildings as a novel stimulator for social gatherings in smart cities. Buildings. **14**(9), 2950 (2024). https://doi.org/10.3390/buildings14092950
61. Turner, A.: Depthmap: a program to perform visibility graph analysis. In: Proceedings of the 3rd International Symposium on Space Syntax, vol. 31, pp. 12–31 (2001)
62. Al Sayed, K., Turner, A., Hillier, B., Lida, S., Penn, A.: Space Syntax Methodology. Bartlett School of Architecture, London (2014)
63. Gehl, J.: Life Between Buildings, Translated by J. Koch, New York (1987)
64. Can, I., Heath, T.: In-between spaces and social interaction: a morphological analysis of Izmir using space syntax. J. Hous. Built Environ. **31**, 31–49 (2016). https://doi.org/10.1007/s10901-015-9442-9

65. Zerouati, W., Bellal, T.: Evaluating the impact of mass housings' in-between spaces' spatial configuration on users' social interaction. Front. Archit. Res. **9**, 34–53 (2020). https://doi.org/10.1016/j.foar.2019.05.005
66. Bendjedidi, S., Bada, Y., Meziani, R.: Urban plaza design process using space syntax analysis: El-Houria plaza, Biskra, Algeria. Int. Rev. Spat. Plan. Sustain. Dev. **7**, 125–142 (2019). https://doi.org/10.14246/irspsda.7.2_125

Smart, Close, and Happy City: A Global Index for Measuring Urban Well-Being. The Case Study of the San Benedetto Neighbourhood, Cagliari (Italy)

Alessia Torlini, Chiara Pinna, and Chiara Garau(✉)

Department of Civil and Environmental Engineering and Architecture (DICAAR), University of Cagliari, via Marengo 2, 09123 Cagliari, Italy
cgarau@unica.it

Abstract. This study explores the relationship between proximity and urban well-being, by combining qualitative and quantitative analyses of emotional perceptions of happiness at the neighbourhood level with an investigation of physical factors that measure spaces accessibility, services functionality, and citizens' social perceptions. The main goal is to enhance ongoing research on the Smart, Close and Happy City to create a "Global Index for Measuring Urban Well-Being", beginning with the human-scale "15-minute city" model. This research emphasises the need for an interdisciplinary approach that addresses the methodological gap present in traditional literature, which tends to separate the spatial analysis of urban infrastructures from the study of social dynamics. The methodology used for the overall assessment of neighbourhood proximity and urban well-being combines objective data with the subjective perceptions of users of the urban space regarding proximity, safety, comfort, well-being and spatial appreciation. The application of the adopted method on the San Benedetto (CA) neighbourhood highlights the importance of connecting the physical and emotional dimensions in evaluating the design effectiveness of a human-scale urban context.

Keywords: Happy City · Smart City · Healthy City · Accessibility · Walkability · Emotions · Proximity · Urban Happiness · Measuring Happiness · Urban Well-Being · Pedestrianisation · urban planning · 15-minute city · Cagliari

1 Introduction

The prevailing model of the "smart city", mostly centred on technological innovation and energy efficiency, risks of intensifying inequities while overlooking human well-being and the community dimension. In contrast to this vision, the importance of fundamental principles such as sustainability, circularity and proximity re-emerges, capable of

---

This paper is the result of the joint work of the authors. 'Abstract', 'San Benedetto Neighbourhood in Cagliari (Italy)' and 'Results' were written jointly by the authors. AT and CG wrote 'City of Proximity'. CP and CG wrote the 'Introduction'. CG wrote 'Methodological approach' with sub-paragraphs, 'Global Index for Measuring Urban Well-Being'. and 'Discussion and Conclusions'. CG coordinated and supervised the paper.

© The Author(s), under exclusive license to Springer Nature Switzerland AG 2026
O. Gervasi et al. (Eds.): ICCSA 2025 Workshops, LNCS 15896, pp. 69–87, 2026.
https://doi.org/10.1007/978-3-031-97654-4_5

orienting urban planning towards a more inclusive and resilient model. This article continues ongoing research on the smart and happy city, which investigates the complex relationship between the urban environment and emotional well-being [1]. In particular, this work focuses on the role of proximity, a concept that extends beyond physical proximity to services, including the social, emotional, and relational dimensions of the city experience.

The concept of proximity considers the 15-min city model proposed by Carlos Moreno [2], which has developed from the 1923 idea of the neighbourhood unit [3, 4]. It represents an attempt to actualise the aforementioned concepts, fostering the development of self-sustaining communities where inhabitants may fulfil their daily requirements efficiently. However, Moreno is not the only theoretician who has contributed to outlining the concept of the city on a human scale [4]; renowned personalities such as Ildefonso Cerdà, Jane Jacobs, Jan Gehl, Christopher Alexander, Léon Krier, Jeff Speck, and Salvador Rueda have historically and contemporaneously underscored the significance of designing urban environments that prioritise human and environmental well-being.

The key research question examines the impact of proximity on social cohesion and the sense of belonging within a neighbourhood: does proximity to public spaces, essential services, cultural activities, and shared meeting places enhance social interactions, fortify neighbourhood connections, and foster a collective identity? Conversely, can urban fragmentation, not sufficient public places, and distance from services contribute to resident isolation, undermine the social fabric, and heighten feelings of alienation? In this perspective, this paper intends to validate a global index for measuring urban well-being that measures the impact of proximity to services, as well the urban happiness perception, while also considering its effect on social cohesiveness. The San Benedetto neighbourhood in Cagliari will serve as a case study for this analysis. The authors aim to provide useful tools for planning more human, inclusive and resilient cities, where proximity becomes a key factor for individual and collective well-being.

This article therefore aims to demonstrate how proximity to quality services and places positively influences perceptions of urban well-being, emphasising the role of human-scale planning in enhancing psychological well-being and fostering the sense of belonging of citizens. To accomplish this objective, this paper after this introduction, presents Sect. 2 in which is analysed the Proximity City notion. Section 3 delineates a methodological approach for evaluating and quantifying the urban proximity. Section 4 tests the applicability of a new index to quantitatively assess urban proximity; this is followed by a qualitative analysis that investigates the subjective perception of citizens (Sect. 5). Followed by the results applied to the case study (Sects. 6 and 7), and the definition of the global index for measuring urban well-being (Sect. 8). Section 9 discusses the future prospects of the research.

2 City of Proximity

The concept of urban proximity, central to the current debate on urban development, encourages to critically reassess relationships between a new smartness of a city and the urban landscape. Proximity extends beyond the physical dimension, including the depth of social connections, accessibility to services, and the vitality of public areas, thereby demonstrating remarkable complexity. While not an explicit goal of the 2030 Agenda, proximity is a fundamental notion. It enhances health and well-being (Goal 3) via accessible health services and "walkability," fosters sustainable and inclusive cities (Goal 11) by mitigating pollution and promoting social cohesion and diminishes disparities (Goal 10) by ensuring equitable opportunities. In accordance with the Agenda, proximity guarantees dignity for everyone and fosters resilient communities. Jane Jacobs examined the intangible element of proximity in her book "The Death and Life of Great American Cities" [5]. Her understanding of proximity is inherently connected to the notion of diversity, suggesting a synthesis of functions and a dynamic network of interactions that particularly flourish along lively and pedestrian-friendly streets. For Jacobs, the possibility of moving on foot is an essential factor in fostering connections and facilitating spontaneous observation. According to Jeff Speck [6], proximity is intricately connected to walkability, shaped and governed by the urban fabric, which must be structured to ensure the utility of walking, safety concerning environmental and physical elements, and comfort through a harmonious combination of buildings and landscape. The author also presents information about economic savings and advantages pertaining to health and environmental sustainability directly associated with the concepts of proximity.

Furthermore, the architect and urban planner Jan Gehl, in "Life in the City" [7] articulates his concept of a human-scale city as the most effective and sustainable settlement model, emphasising the connection between urban life and architectural structures. The author examines the challenges urban planning must confront to enhance the city's liveability, citizen well-being and sociability, and to foster walkability. The notion of the 15-minute City, advocated by Carlos Moreno, effectively reemphasises the importance of proximity, which is essential for urban well-being. Nonetheless, Saverio Mecca underscores the danger of this term devolving into a simple and idealised conception of self-sufficient neighbourhoods [8]. While the 15-minute City offers the promise of enhanced accessibility to essential services, it is imperative to acknowledge the intricate nature of urban environments, requiring meticulous planning across several scales and efficient coordination across various governance levels. Salvador Rueda's "superblock" [9] concept provides a fundamental unit for the urban environment, focused on active and public mobility, as well as diversity and proximity, including both physical access to services and immaterial aspects related to the satisfaction of human needs. The organisation of urban spaces based on the idea of proximity is a crucial aspect in establishing a more efficient, ecological, and accessible transportation system for everyone. Combining services and activities in limited spaces promotes the use of sustainable transportation methods, enhances public transport efficiency, reduces private automobile use, and optimises urban logistics management. An urban planning approach that prioritises proximity is essential for developing human-scale cities that address community needs while mitigating pollution, transportation congestion, and enhancing both physical and mental well-being.

A city that adopts these values transforms into a more equal, inclusive, sustainable, healthy, and resilient environment. A city where proximity includes not just distance but also the quality of life. Proximity encompasses not just physical proximity but also an emotional connection derived from the diversity and complexity of urban environments. This subjective connection to diversity is essential for directing emotional experiences, as it may affect the emotional state, experience, and behaviour of individuals inside a space. Positive experiences in stimulating situations foster resilience, sustainability, social responsibility, and quality of life [10]. In the age of digitalisation and globalisation, both physical and emotional proximity have significantly diminished, resulting in a contemporary type of alienation. To mitigate this tendency, Franco Arminio [8, p. 194] advocates for a return to proximity via "walking", a slow and contemplative reflective practice that facilitates reconnection with the land and its inhabitants. This method fosters enhanced awareness and appreciation of places, rediscovering their uniqueness and beauty.

3 Methodological Approach

The method's definition focusses on estimating a neighbourhood's intervention potential based on its proximity, which may be measured qualitatively and quantitatively. The success of an approach that integrates both quantitative and qualitative research is extensively shown in several reputable academic publications [11–16].

In Italy and Europe, recent years have seen the establishment of many indices for assessing proximity, enabling the qualitative and quantitative identification of significant concerns and potential solutions to enhance proximity connections. The "15 Minute City Index" [17] is recognised as an urban planning measurement aimed at implementing the "15-minute city" model; this index comprises forty-nine indicators across thirteen service categories linked to population density and land use (Environment, Safety, Health, Food, Education, Entertainment, Public offices, Soft mobility, Fast mobility, Economy, Housing, Sports, and Culture).

Other indices identified in the literature include (i) the Inclusive Accessibility by Proximity Index (IAPI) [18], which assesses pedestrian and cyclist accessibility by evaluating the quality of spaces and routes, as well as citizen perceptions through tests and questionnaires; (ii) the NExt proXimity Index (NEXI) [19], which examines accessibility to services within a fifteen-minute walking distance; (iii) the High Quality of Social Life (HQSL) [20], which analyses social life quality through six fundamental functions (Living, Working, Supplying, Caring, Learning, Enjoying) based on interviews and data collection; and the Urban Diversity Index, which quantifies the diversity of urban services and activities grounded in biodiversity theory.

Although using varied methodologies, these indicators seek to qualitatively and quantitatively evaluate urban proximity. A prominent indication of proximity is the accessibility of an urban agglomeration, defined as the capacity and easy access of reaching a location, which is directly affected by its spatial arrangement. In literature, this metric is often assessed using the Space Syntax approach [21], which examines the city as a network of open spaces and how geometric and topological attributes influence its accessibility, hence affecting social, economic, and environmental factors. However, the literature lacks an approach that links indicators measuring proximity with urban happiness.

As a result, the methodology was organised into the following phases: (1) general framework of all environmental variables and contributions that influence human-environment interactions and definition of the indices that contribute to the evaluation of the "neighbourhood proximity index"; (2) identification of indicators and sub-indicators at the neighbourhood scale related to the respective indices; (3) research of methodologies and typical urban planning tools and selection of software (QGIS, DepthmapX) and methods of calculating the sub-indicators; (4) exclusion of non-applicable sub-indicators, whose evaluation procedure requires the provision of devices and software not directly available; (5) definition of a qualitative analysis to support and validate the results of the calculation process of the proximity index, which can also provide an overview of the needs, desires and critical issues perceived by users of the place; (6) comparison between the results of the quantitative and qualitative analysis; (7) definition of the "global index for measuring urban well-being", which systematises the "emotional perception index of the degree of happiness" [1] and the "neighbourhood proximity index". The next paragraph shows the definition of the indices that contribute to the evaluation of the "neighbourhood proximity index", seeing in detail how the indicators and sub-indicators were formulated.

4 Neighbourhood Proximity Index

The "Neighborhood Proximity" Index is expressed in formula 1 and incorporates the synthetic indices of "Accessibility" (I_A), "Social Perception" (I_{SP}), and "Functionality" (I_F), which are defined based on activities considered essential for a satisfying neighbourhood experience: walking, cycling, easily accessing services, fostering social connections, and utilising pleasant and functional spaces.

$$Inp = \frac{(Ia + Isp + If)}{3} \qquad (1)$$

4.1 Accessibility Index

Accessibility refers to the ease of accessing locations and the degree to which land use and transport systems facilitate this via a combination of travel modes, particularly emphasising the concepts of walkability and cycling. The latter are examined by using radii of 400 and 700 m, respectively, from the central node for the computation of the indicators. The selection of these numbers is justified by the observation that, in macro-scale situations, the metric radius used for for space syntax analysis often ranges from 400 to 800 m [22] (Table 1).

Table 1. Definition of the Index of "Accessibility".

Index	Indicators	Attributes	Sub-Indicators	Calculation Methods
Accessibility	a) Availability of services	Local Services [23]	Normalised distance from centroid space to secondary functions $r = 700$ m $r = 400$ m	$Dist_{norm} = \left(1 - \frac{cost-50}{Du-50}\right)$
	b) Availability of public transport	Nodes of the local public transport network [25]	Normalised distance from centroid space to nodes of LPT networks $r = 700$ m $r = 400$ m	$Dist_{norm\_LPT} = \text{MAX}\left[1 - \frac{Di-50}{Du-50}\right]$
	c) Availability of green areas and areas used as parks	Configuration of the urban system [25]	Normalised distance from centroid space to nodes $r = 700$ m $r = 400$ m	$Dist_{norm} = \left(1 - \frac{cost-50}{Du-50}\right)$
	d) Potential as a destination	Urban system configuration [23–26]	Normalised angular integration $r = 700$ m $r = 400$ m	$NAIN = \frac{NC^{1.2}}{TD}$
	e) Potential as a transit space	Configuration of the urban system [23, 27, 28]	Normalised angular choice $r = 700$ m $r = 400$ m	$NACH = \frac{\log CH + 1}{\log TD + 3}$

4.2 Social Perception Index

The social perception of space is linked to the notion that human behaviours are influenced to differing degrees by perception. Space serves as a collection of locations, defined by individuals through utilisation, social perception, or a combination of both, encompassing various interpersonal relationships—whether positive or negative, characterised by meets or conflicts, emotionally charged or merely coexistent [29] (Table 2).

Table 2. Definition of the Index of "Social Perception".

Index	Indicators	Attributes	Sub-indicators	Calculation methods
Social perception	a) Vitality	Perceived liveliness [5]	Amenities	Number of Feature Types Amenities = 4 Score 1 Amenities = 3 Score 0.6 Amenities = 2 Score 0.3 Amenities = 1 Score 0.1
			Presence of urban points of attraction	Yes = 1 No = 0.1

(continued)

Table 2. (*continued*)

Index	Indicators	Attributes	Sub-indicators	Calculation methods
	b) Meeting acquaintances (spatial proximity)	Probability of frequent encounters [23–26]	Normalised angular integration r = 200 m	$NAIN = \frac{NC^{1.2}}{TD}$
	c) Knowing (situational proximity)	Casual Meet-Up Occasions [23]	Normalised distance from centroid space to services of urban scale	Distance from primary uses of urban scale R100 = 1 R200 = 0.8 R300 = 0.6 R700 = 0.3 R > 700 = 0.1

4.3 Functionality Index

The functionality is assessed concerning the practicality of pedestrian and cycling pathways and the availability of high-quality street furniture, designed to provide inhabitants solutions that enhance everyday life by making it more enjoyable and practical (Table 3).

Table 3. Definition of the Index of "Functionality".

Index	Indicators	Attributes	Sub-indicators	Calculation methods
Functionality	a) Movement	Usability of pedestrian – cycle – vehicular surfaces [23]	Cross-section	$L = \frac{P0(P^2 - 16*A)}{4}^{0.5}$
			Slope	$P = \left(\frac{z_{range}}{S_{length}}\right)$
			Obstacles	No = 1 Rare = 0.5 Some = 0.3 Numerous = 0.1
			Condition	Optimal = 1 Good = 0.5 Inadequate = 0.3 Deficient = 0.1
	b) Comfort	Usability of the benches [7, 23, 30, 31]	Density	Yes = 1 No = 0.1
			Position	Front of buildings = 1 Marginals = 0.6 Isolated = 0.1
			View	Figurable space and diversity of uses = 1 Figurable space or diversity of uses = 0.6 Generic space = 0.1

(*continued*)

Table 3. (*continued*)

Index	Indicators	Attributes	Sub-indicators	Calculation methods
			Seating comfort	Supports = 1 Backrest = 0.6 Seat = 0.1
		Usability of toilets [23]	Presence	Yes = 1 No = 0.1
			Distance	Distance d ≤ 50 m = 1 50 m < d ≤ 100 m = 0.7 100 m < d ≤ 200 m = 0.5 200 m < d ≤ 400 m = 0.3 d > 400 m = 0.1
			Condition	Good = 1 Adequate = 0.5 Deficient = 0.1
			Accessibility	Yes = 1 No = 0.1
		Usability of services for users with disabilities	Presence	Yes = 1 No = 0.1
			Condition	Good = 1 Adequate = 0.6 Deficient = 0.1
	c) Potential as a parking space	Usability of parking spaces [7, 30–32]	Presence of punctual and defined elements along the border, elements of mediation between internal and external space	Yes = 1 No = 0.1
			Presence of spaces that can potentially be converted through street experiments	Yes = 1 No = 0.1

5 Qualitative Analysis

To confirm the findings derived from the software's graphic processing, a qualitative evaluation questionnaire was developed among residents, visitors, or passersby within the neighbourhood. The well acknowledged saturation principle for sampling was used [11–16]. The questionnaire titled "Perceived Happiness, Accessibility, and Safety in the Neighbourhood," consisting of 32 questions organised into sections for simplicity of comparison with quantitative analysis findings, was developed and distributed. The categories addressed 1) accessibility to local services and transportation; 2) perceived safety; 3) comfort, aesthetic appeal, sociability, and overall satisfaction. The authors concentrate on 7 of the 32 questions that mainly examine factors of perceived proximity. These 7 questions are:

(I) How do you evaluate the provision of neighbourhood services? (Please give a rating from 1 Insufficient to 5 Excellent).
(II) Do you believe that getting to the services on foot is: (Please provide a rating from 1 to 5; 1 = Difficult; 5 = Simple). Briefly state the reason: ____.
(III) Within the neighbourhood you move more: • by car • by public transport • on foot or by bicycle. Briefly state the reason____.
(IV) If you move more on foot or by bicycle, how do you evaluate the ease of movement? (Please provide a rating from 1 to 5; 1 = Very difficult; 5 = Very easy) Briefly state the reason: ____.
(V) Do you think public transport is efficient for getting to or from the neighbourhood and getting around it? (Please provide a rating from 1 to 5; 1 = Not very efficient; 5 = Very efficient). Why? ____.
(VI) Do you think that the number of parking spaces for cars in the neighbourhood is sufficient? (Please give a rating from 1 to 5; 1 = Not at all; 5 = Excellent)
(VII) Do you think that the presence of public green spaces is sufficient? (Please provide a rating from 1 to 5; 1 = Insufficient; 5 = More than sufficient).

The next section presents the case study under examination on which the qualitative-quantitative method was defined and validated.

6 San Benedetto Neighbourhood in Cagliari (Italy)

The San Benedetto neighbourhood, in Cagliari (Sardinia), is a dynamic and densely populated neighbourhood. In 2022, the population was 7,921 residents, constituting nearly 5% of the city's total, with a density of 18,929 inhabitants per square kilometre. This urban configuration makes it an advantageous research location for examining walkability, accessibility, and resident well-being. Moreover, San Benedetto is distinguished for its variety of services. The attractiveness of the neighbourhood is further accentuated by the pedestrian flow generated by commercial activities, the historical value of some sites and the presence of two important urban landmarks: the Civic Market and the subway station.

Figure 1 shows the San Benedetto neighbourhood, in Cagliari (Sardinia).

The authors' subsequent section organises the data, emphasising the need of integrating quantitative and qualitative studies to get a comprehensive knowledge of the neighbourhood's urban proximity and its advantages.

7 Results

The quantitative analysis performed using QGIS, considers the central square of the neighbourhood as the reference node for the evaluation of distances and it led to the following results. The neighbourhood's average accessibility, assessed from the perspective of foot users, generated an inadequate evaluation mostly associated with the availability of amenities, urban transportation, and green spaces, as well as park areas situated at a considerable distance from the central hub (Fig. 2a). Concerning cycling users, a good level of accessibility emerges due to mostly positive opinions referring to the various sub-indicators (Fig. 2b).

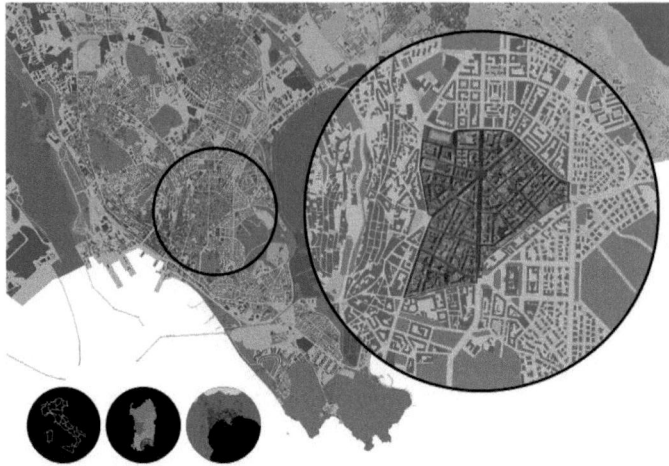

Fig. 1. San Benedetto Neighbourhood in Cagliari, Italy (authors' elaboration).

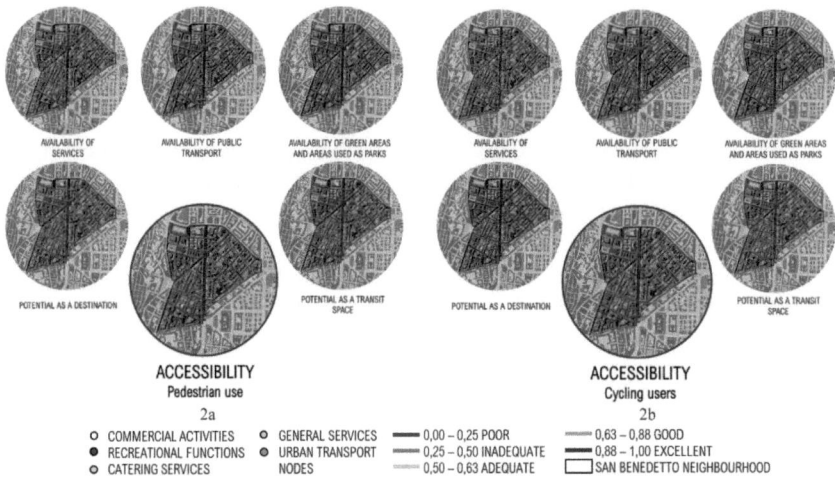

Fig. 2. Accessibility analyses (2.a Pedestrian use; 2.b Cycling use). Source: authors' elaboration.

Overall, the global accessibility of the neighbourhood (Fig. 3), determined by the average levels of pedestrian and cycling accessibility, produces an adequate rating.

As highlighted in the previous paragraph, the functionality index is given by the combination of different factors: 1) circulation, or rather the practicability of pedestrian and cycle paths; 2) the provision of quality street furniture, capable of offering citizens solutions that simplify daily life, making it more pleasant and practical. This criterion can for example be characterised by the usability of toilets also for disabled people; 3) the potential of the public space as a car park. In a nutshell, the functionality, linked to the indicators "Movement", "Comfort" and "Potential as a parking space", is inadequate (Fig. 4). Explaining in detail, "Movement" is the main way to gain experience of spaces,

GLOBAL ACCESSIBILITY

— 0,00 – 0,25 POOR   — 0,63 – 0,88 GOOD
— 0,25 – 0,50 INADEQUATE   — 0,88 – 1,00 EXCELLENT
— 0,50 – 0,63 ADEQUATE   ☐ SAN BENEDETTO NEIGHBOURHOOD

Fig. 3. Global Accessibility.

and it is strongly dependent on the characteristics of the surfaces that can facilitate or hinder it. For this reason, the spatial component investigated for the study of movement is the surface of cycle (Fig. 5a) and pedestrian paths (Fig. 5b), and the related attribute is the "Usability of surfaces".

FUNCTIONALITY

— 0,00 – 0,25 POOR   — 0,63 – 0,88 GOOD
— 0,25 – 0,50 INADEQUATE   — 0,88 – 1,00 EXCELLENT
— 0,50 – 0,63 ADEQUATE   ☐ SAN BENEDETTO NEIGHBOURHOOD

Fig. 4. Functionality. Source: authors' elaboration.

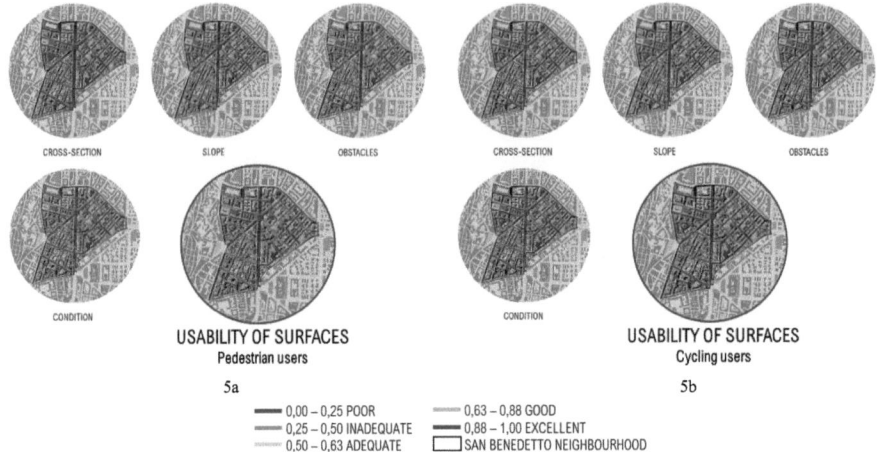

Fig. 5. Movement - usability of surfaces (a. Pedestrian users; b. Cycling users). *Source:* authors' elaboration.

The "Comfort" indicator is constituted by the sub-indicators "Usability of benches", "Usability of services for users with disabilities" and "Usability of toilets". Figure 6 shows the sub-indicators "Usability of benches". The work for sub-indicators has been done for all of them, but due to space limitations, only this example is reported. Figure 7 shows the indicator of Comfort.

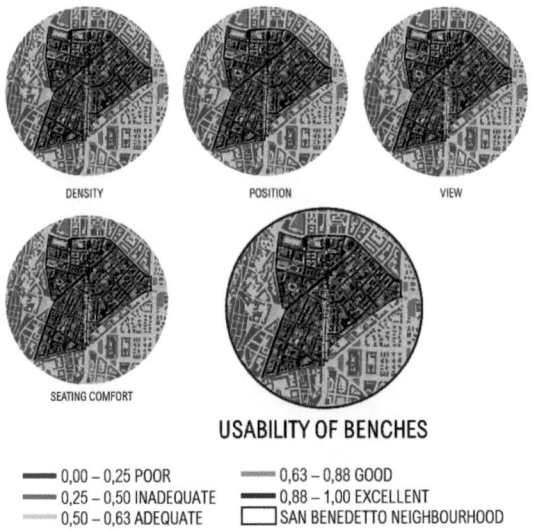

Fig. 6. The sub-indicator "Usability of benches".

The last indicator that is connected with functionality is the "potential as a parking space" (Fig. 8) and is identified with the presence of border elements and spaces

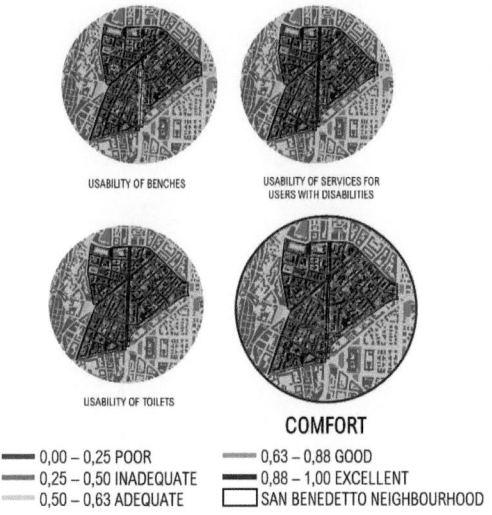

Fig. 7. The "Comfort" indicator. *Source:* authors' elaboration.

potentially convertible with Tactical Urban Planning interventions or street experiments [33–35].

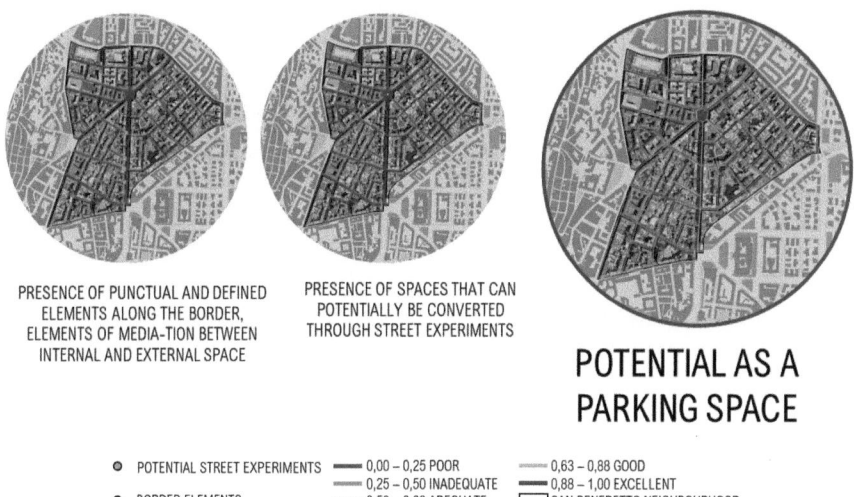

Fig. 8. The "Potential as a parking space" indicator. *Source:* authors' elaboration.

The social perception of the neighbourhood (Fig. 9), based on the average of the indicators "Vitality", "Meeting acquaintances (spatial proximity)" and "Knowing (situational proximity)" reflects a good level. Indeed, the situational proximity, a factor affecting prospects for casual meetings, is optimal due to the presence of the San Benedetto Market, a service on a metropolitan scale.

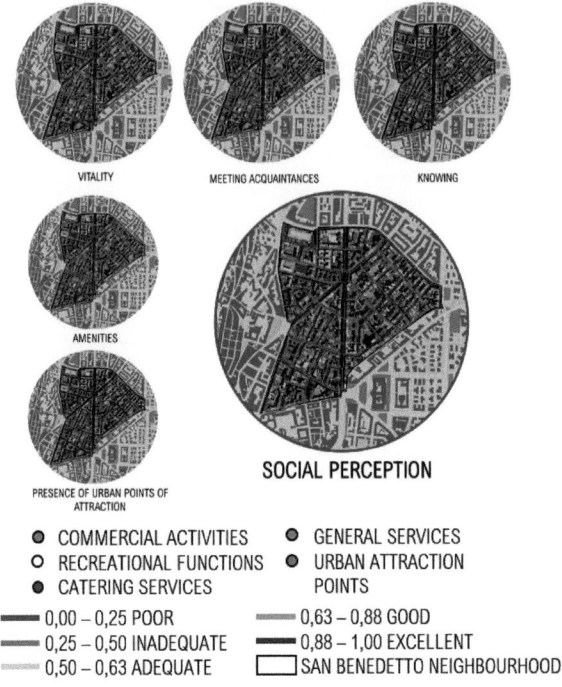

Fig. 9. Social perception.

The average of the "Accessibility", "Social Perception" and "Functionality" indices allows us to determine the "Neighbourhood Proximity Index" (Fig. 10).

The data obtained from the quantitative analysis were integrated with the information collected through the questionnaire "Perceived Happiness, Accessibility, and Safety in the Neighbourhood," conducted among the residents of the San Benedetto neighbourhood.

The questionnaire, distributed over 30 days, collected 117 responses. The research focused on the most representative responses, revealing a diverse age distribution: 33.3% aged 31–45 years, 30.8% aged 46–60 years, 21.4% aged 18–30 years, and 14.5% aged beyond 60 years.

A majority of participants (57.3%) reside in San Benedetto. The survey showed that the availability of neighbourhood services is mostly good/excellent and that reaching these services on foot is easy (52.2%), indicating among the reasons the proximity, the optimal distribution and the efficiency of the public transport service.

On the other hand, those who complain about difficulties in accessing services on foot, report the presence of architectural barriers, high car traffic, persistent construction sites and lack of supermarkets. 76.1% of the sample stated that they move around the neighbourhood mostly on foot or by bicycle, compared to 12.8% who move by car and 11.1% by public transport.

Fig. 10. Neighbourhood Proximity Index. Source: authors' elaboration.

The ease of movement on foot or by bicycle did not register any extremely critical evaluation, however, those who complain of difficulty in movement justify their choice by denouncing dangerous cycle paths, chaotic traffic and double-row parking.

Users of the neighbourhood evaluate the public transport service positively, highlighting the good connection with the rest of the city. Despite the temporary suspension of the tram service, many users recognise the potential of the MetroCagliari once the extension of the route is completed.

The neighbourhood has chaotic traffic flow, characterised by very congested roadways and inadequate parking facilities. 31.6% of the sample perceives the availability of public green areas as scarcely sufficient, while 46.2% express overall dissatisfaction.

8 Global Index for Measuring Urban Well-Being

By integrating the conclusions of the article on urban happiness [1] with the analysis of the literature and the considerations brought forward in the present study, it is possible to create a complete framework to evaluate "neighbourhood happiness" in a holistic way.

This approach, which leads to the definition of the Global Index of for Measuring Urban Well-Being allows to correlate the data on happiness, as well as the data on proximity with the indicators of subjective well-being of the residents. From the average of the "Neighbourhood Proximity Index" and the "Emotional Perception Index of the

Degree of Happiness", it follows that the neighbourhood of San Benedetto is "adequately happy".

Figure 11 shows the representation of the Global Index of for Measuring Urban Well-Being.

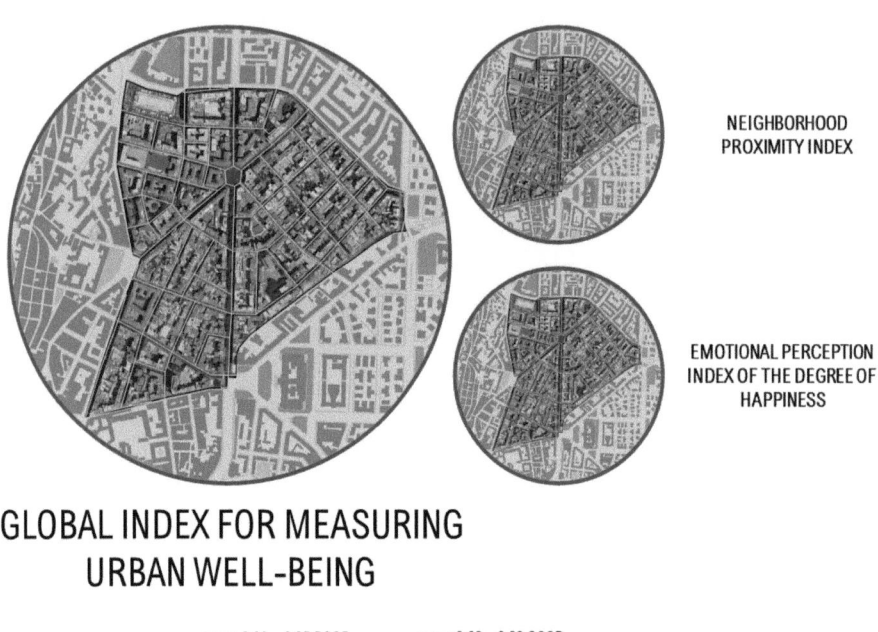

Fig. 11. Global Index for Measuring Urban Well-Being. Source: authors' elaboration.

9 Discussion and Conclusions

This study explores the crucial link between urban proximity and residents' well-being, integrating the qualitative and quantitative analysis of the emotional perception of happiness with the investigation of the physical factors needed to measure the accessibility of spaces, the functionality of services and the social perception of citizens. The primary objective was to develop a global index for measuring urban well-being, a tool to quantify and compare the level of satisfaction and well-being of the population in specific urban contexts.

The results support the hypothesis that proximity to services and spaces of socialisation positively affects social cohesion and the sense of belonging. On the other hand, urban fragmentation and distance from such services are correlated with phenomena of social isolation. However, the spatial analysis revealed in some areas a potential discrepancy between the objective evaluation of infrastructures and the emotional perception of residents, underlining the multifactorial nature of well-being and the concept of urban happiness.

The analysis finds that achieving an optimal assessment can be limited by factors such as the lack of areas dedicated to pedestrians, which limits the usability of the space; the difficulty of accessing and using some essential services; the high intensity of vehicular traffic, which negatively affects air quality and safety and the lack of adequate safety measures, which negatively influences the perception of well-being of residents.

Therefore, the results obtained support the need for an interdisciplinary approach that integrates spatial analysis with the study of socio-cultural dynamics and confirming the need to qualitatively and quantitatively consider both objective parameters, such as proximity, and subjective indicators, such as the perception of happiness and quality of life.

Furthermore, the importance of pedestrianisation and an efficient organisation of the road system is emphasised, considering the mobility needs of the entire city to improve and re-educate the habits of users and plan a sustainable mobility network.

For the future, the research may be replicated in other neighbourhoods of the city or in other contexts, using the same indicators or integrating them with new ones that include the well-being of particular vulnerable categories of users. In addition, it is suggested to deepen the study of the relationship between proximity and perception of urban space, especially in crisis situations. It is also important to examine the impact of digital technologies, develop models to predict the effects of urban policies, compare the results in different contexts, involve citizens in planning, analyse the perceptions of different social groups and study the effect of specific urban micro interventions. In fact, the implementation of urban investigation methodologies that integrate the analysis of individual and collective perceptions, in relation to socio-cultural factors and personal experiences, represents a necessary evolution to understand and modulate the use of urban spaces, and this approach goes beyond mere physical evaluation, favouring the understanding of experiential interactions between users and the environment. In this sense, the idea of implementing playful technological activities to be done outdoors, designed and configured as effective analysis tools of perception, sense of belonging and collective identity, is supported. This approach would also contribute to a deeper and more participatory understanding of the urban context, promoting its safety and enhancement.

The comparison of different analysis methodologies, as demonstrated in this study, is therefore an essential element for a holistic understanding of urban well-being. The integration of quantitative and qualitative data, together with the analysis of individual and collective perceptions, allows for the development of more effective and targeted urban policies, capable of responding to the real needs of citizens and promoting more inclusive and sustainable cities.

Acknowledgements. This study was partially supported within the "e.INS – Ecosystem of Innovation for Next Generation Sardinia" funded by the Italian Ministry of University and Research under the Next-Generation EU Programme (National Recovery and Resilience Plan – PNRR, M4C2, INVESTMENT 1.5 –DD 1056 of 23/06/2022, ECS00000038). In particular, the "Methodological approach" was funded by eINS. This study reflects only the authors' views and opinions, and neither the European Union nor the European Commission can be considered responsible for them. This study was also partially supported by the project "RAMÉ RegCITIES: spatial analyses foR co-creAting the future of sMartest and happiEst REGions/CITIES. Comparisons between Cagliari in Italy and Des Moines in the US", founded by the program "Bando 2023 Mobilità Giovani Ricercatori (MGR)", financed by the Autonomous Region of Sardinia (under the Regional Law of 7 August 2007, n. 7 "Promotion of Scientific Research and Technological Innovation in Sardinia"). This study was also partially supported by the MUR through the project "SMART3R-FLITS: SMART Transport for Travellers and Freight Logistics Integration Towards Sustainability" (Project protocol: 2022J38SR9; CUP Code: F53D23005630006), financed with the PRIN 2022 (Research Projects of National Relevance) program. We authorise the MUR to reproduce and distribute reprints for Governmental purposes, notwithstanding any copyright notations thereon. Any opinions, findings, and conclusions, or recommendations expressed in this material are those of the authors and do not necessarily reflect the views of the MUR.

References

1. Torlini, A., Pinna, C., Garau, C.: Smart, close, and happy city: a global index for measuring urban well-being. the case study of the san benedetto neighbourhood, Cagliari (Italy). In: Gervasi, O., (eds.) 25th International Conference on Computational Science and Its Applications (ICCSA 2025), ICCSA 2025, LNCS15898, pp.1–19. Springer, Cham (2026). https://doi.org/10.1007/978-3-031-97657-5_9. (2025, in press)
2. Moreno, C.: La ville du quart d'heure: pour un nouveau chrono-urbanisme. La Tribune (2016)
3. Yamu, C., Garau, C.: The 15-min city: a configurational approach for understanding the spatial, economic, and cognitive context of walkability in Vienna. In: International Conference on Computational Science and Its Applications, pp. 387–404. Springer International Publishing, Cham (2022)
4. Gaglione, F., Zucaro, C.G.F., Cottrill, C.: 15-minute neighbourhood accessibility: a comparison between Naples and London. Eur. Transp. Trasp. Eur. **85**, 1–16 (2021)
5. Jacobs, J.: The Death and Life of Great American Cities. Vintage Books a Division of Random House, INC, New York (1961)
6. Speck, J.: Walkable City: How Downtown can Save America, One Step at a Time. Farrar, Straus and Giroux (2012)
7. Gehl, J.: Cities for People. Island Press (2013)
8. Mecca, S.: Prossimità. Il benessere nella città del futuro. Didapress, Firenze (2023)
9. Rueda, S.: Per una pianificazione ecosistemica della città, pp. 47–55. Quodlibet (2019)
10. Brunner, L.M., et al.: Emotional experiences of urban walking environments: an application of the circumplex model of affect. J. Transp. Health. **42**, 102008 (2025)
11. Glaser, B.G., Strauss, A.L.: The discovery of grounded theory: strategies for qualitative research. Aldine, New York (1967)
12. Annunziata, A., Garau, C.: Understanding kid-friendly urban space for a more inclusive smart city: The case study of Cagliari (Italy). In: Computational Science and Its Applications–ICCSA 2018: 18th International Conference, Melbourne, VIC, Australia, July 2–5, 2018, Proceedings, Part III, vol. 18, pp. 589–605. Springer International Publishing (2018)
13. Garau, C., Annunziata, A., Coni, M.: A methodological framework for assessing practicability of the urban space: the survey on conditions of practicable environments (SCOPE) procedure applied in the case study of Cagliari (Italy). Sustainability. **10**(11), 4189 (2018)
14. Garau, C., Annunziata, A.: Smart city governance and children's agency: an assessment of the green infrastructure impact on children's activities in Cagliari (Italy) with the tool "opportunities for children in urban spaces (OCUS)". Sustainability. **11**(18), 4848 (2019)

15. Hennink, M., Hutter, I., Bailey, A.: Qualitative Research Methods. Sage (2020)
16. Garau, C., Annunziata, A.: Supporting children's independent activities in smart and playable public places. Sustainability. **12**(20), 8352 (2020)
17. Enel X Italia S.r.l: 15 Minute City Index. https://www.enelx.com/it/it/istituzioni/sostenibilita/open-data-pubblica-amministrazione/15-minutes-city-index
18. Lanza, G., Carboni, L.: Un indice per progettare la città dei 15 minuti: Inclusive Accessibility by proximity index – IAPI. DiTe (2023) https://www.dite-aisre.it/un-indice-per-progettare-la-citta-dei-15-minuti-inclusive-accessibility-by-proximity-index-iapi/
19. AA: Le città italiane sono già 15 minuti? Il Next Proximity Index: un modo innovativo e scalabile per misurarlo, basato su open data. Ambiente e non solo. https://ambientenonsolo.com/le-citta-italiane-sono-gia-15-minuti-il-next-proximity-index-un-modo-innovativo-e-scalabile-per-misurarlo-basato-su-open-data/
20. Moreno, C., Gallo, C., Chabaud, D., Masson, I.: The 15-minute City Model: an Innovative Approach to Measuring Quality of Life in Urban Settings. Research Gate (2023) https://www.researchgate.net/publication/369943086_ETI_Chair_White-Paper-3_EN
21. Yamu, C., Van Nes, A., Garau, C.: Bill Hillier's legacy: Space syntax—A synopsis of basic concepts, measures, and empirical application. Sustainability. **13**(6), 3394 (2021)
22. Van Nes, A., Yamu, C.: Introduction to Space Syntax in Urban Studies. Springer (2021)
23. Garau, C.: Università degli studi di Cagliari, Facoltà di Ingegneria e Architettura, Corso di Pianificazione Ambientale AA 2021/2022. (2022)
24. Bavelas, A.: Modelli di comunicazione in gruppi orientati al compito. J. Acoust. Soc. Am. **22**, 725–730 (1950)
25. Sabidussi, G.: The centrality index of a graph. Psychometrika. **31**, 581–603 (1966)
26. Hillier, B., Hanson, J.: The Social Logic of Space. Cambridge University Press (1984)
27. Freeman, L.C.: A set of measures of centrality based on betweenness. Sociometry. **40**(1), 35–41 (1977)
28. Freeman, L.C.: Centrality in social networks conceptual clarification. Soc. Netw. **1**, 215 (1978-1979)
29. Gazzola, A.: Uno sguardo diverso. La percezione sociale dello spazio naturale e costruito. Franco Angeli (2011)
30. Gehl, J.: Open Space: People Space. Taylor & Francis (2007)
31. Gehl, J.: Life between buildings: using public space. Island Press (2011)
32. Lydon, M., Garcia, A. (2011). Urbanistica Tattica: azioni a breve termine, cambiamenti a lungo termine
33. Garau, C., Pirisino, M.S., Pinna, F.: A literature review on street experiments: a preliminary step towards adaptive planned solutions from bottom-up experiments. In: International Conference on Computational Science and Its Applications, pp. 184–196. Springer Nature Switzerland, Cham (2024)
34. Acierno, A.: Agopuntura e urbanistica tattica nella rigenerazione delle città. *Territorio della Ricerca su Insediamenti e Ambiente*. Riv. Int. Cult. Urban. **12**(23), 7–16 (2019)
35. Lorenzelli, V.: Placemaking: Creare luoghi vivi, amati, attraenti. Gruppo 24 Ore (2024)

From structural to TRAnsformative-change of City Environment: chal- lenges & solutions & perspectives (TRACE 2025)

Valuing Nature: Experimenting the GiVal Toolkit for the Economic Evaluation of Nature-Based Solutions in Milan

Giulia Datola[1(✉)][iD], Francesca Torrieri[2][iD], Marta Dell'Ovo[1][iD], and Alessandra Oppio[1][iD]

[1] Department of Architecture and Urban Studies (DAStU), Politecnico di Milano, 20133 Milan, Italy
{giulia.datola,marta.dellovo,alessandra.oppio}@polimi.it
[2] Department of Architecture Built Environment and Construction Engineering (DABC), Politecnico di Milano, 20133 Milan, Italy
francesca.torrieri@polimi.it

Abstract. Urban environments are particularly affected by climate change impacts, such as Urban Heat Island (UHI), which leads to tangible consequences for the well-being and health of citizens. In this context, several national and international policies promote the implementation of Nature-Based Solutions (NBS) in urban contexts to provide a sustainable strategy for climate change mitigation and adaptation. However, the integration of these solutions into strategic urban planning remains a challenge, particularly due to the difficulty of evaluating their economic value. This study investigates the suitability of the Green Infrastructure Valuation toolkit (GiVal) as a preliminary tool for the economic assessment of NBS in urban environments. The tool has been applied for the economic evaluation of a reforestation project in the city of Milan, aligned with key goals of the city's Climate and Air Plan. Based on the Benefit Transfer method, the GiVal tool estimates the economic value of a wide range of benefits. The proposed application underlines both the strengths and the criticalities of the GiVal tool. According to the obtained results and the recognised strengths and criticalities, it can be addressed that this tool is an effective preliminary evaluation framework which enables the identification of the benefits provided by the analysed NBS.

Keywords: Economic evaluation · Nature-Based Solution (NBS) · Total Economic Value (TEV)

1 Introduction

The climate change phenomenon is exposing societies to many stresses and risks [1, 2]. Urban environments are particularly vulnerable to climate change effects, as both the direct and indirect impacts affect social, economic, and environmental aspects [3–5]. One of the main impacting phenomena is represented by the Urban Heat Island (UHI), which leads to tangible consequences for the well-being and health of citizens [3]. In this context, Nature-Based Solutions (NBS) are proposed as strategic interventions to foster sustainable and resilient urban development [6], as well as to implement operative mitigation and adaptation strategies by maximising the interactions between natural and built environments [7–10]. Therefore, the implementation of NBS in the urban context, such as urban forestry and Sustainable Urban Drainage Systems (SUDS) can offer multiple benefits, including reduced flood risk, improved water quality, better air quality, and the mitigation of UHI effects [11].

Within this premise, the introduction of NBS in urban contexts is supported by different policies, ranging from the international level with the European Green Deal and the Sustainable Development Goals (SDGs), to the national level with the Italian Recovery and Resilience Plan (PNRR). These policies frame NBS as effective urban regeneration strategies, owing to their ability to simultaneously provide a range of environmental, social, and economic benefits [12].

Despite the abovementioned supporting policies and the general interest in the concept of NBS, the strategic planning and the operative implementation of NBS in urban context are not emerging as priorities in urban action to tackle climate and multidimensional challenges. This condition is mainly due to difficulties in evaluating the benefits of these solutions in monetary terms [13], as well as in estimating implementation and maintenance costs [9, 14]. The estimation of costs and benefits associated with NBS interventions is a critical issue for their integration into strategic urban planning processes. According to this state-of-the-art, this research is mainly based on this research question Q_1 *"How can the benefits of Nature-Based Solutions (NBS) in urban areas be effectively evaluated in monetary terms to inform and support strategic planning processes?"*. In this framework, the present research explores and tests the Green Infrastructure Valuation toolkit (GiVal) for developing the ex-ante evaluation of the generated economic value of NBS interventions in the urban context, thus addressing its suitability in supporting decision-making in the early stages of urban planning.

This tool has been applied to assess the economic value of an urban reforestation project in the city of Milan, designed to mitigate the UHI effect. Some adjustments have been made to the input data (Sect. 3) to enable a context-specific assessment as much as possible and to consider the difference in the currency. The proposed application permits to recognize of both the strengths and criticalities of the GiVal tool in assessing the economic value of NBS in urban environments.

The present paper is structured as follows. Section 2 is dedicated to the introduction of the concept of NBS and to the description of the economic evaluation of natural capital to address its main methodological background. This section also lists the most relevant tools developed for the economic evaluation of natural resources and Green Infrastructure (GI). Section 3 contains the description of the application of the GiVal toolkit to the considered case study, also underlying the adjustments made. Section 4 critically discusses and analyses the obtained results, focusing on both the strengths and criticalities of the adopted tools. Section 5 summarises the contents of the proposed study and discusses the possible implementation of the GiVal toolkit.

2 Nature-Based Solution and Economic Evaluation of Natural Capital

2.1 Nature-Based Solution Definition

The concept of Nature-Based Solution (NBS) is an umbrella term which has been introduced in 2008 [15]. Since the first introduction, several definitions of NBS have been proposed in both academic and political contexts. One of the most shared definitions is that provided by the European Commission [16], which describes NBS as *"solutions inspired and supported by nature that are cost-effective, provide environmental, social, and economic benefits, and enhance resilience. These solutions introduce more diverse nature and natural processes into cities, landscapes, and seascapes through locally adapted, resource-efficient, and systemic interventions"*. Given the variety of existing definitions, this research adopts the one previously mentioned, as it emphasizes the multidimensional and multifunctional nature of NBS. Accordingly, the study aims to evaluate the economic benefits of NBS from a holistic perspective.

2.2 Economic Evaluation of Natural Capital

Economic evaluation refers to the assignment of monetary values to non-market assets, goods and services. Non-marketed goods and services are those that are not directly traded in the marketplace, such as natural resources, clean air, or neighbourhood amenities [17]. If a good or service contributes positively to human well-being, it holds economic value.

Over time, the economic evaluation of environmental goods has undergone significant theoretical development, leading to the formulation of the Total Economic Value (TEV) concept [18]. According to Pearce and Turner (1990) [19], the TEV consists of two principal components represented by the use and non-use values (Fig. 1).

Specifically, the use value refers to three main components:

1. Direct use value is related to the benefits derived from tangible goods that can be consumed, harvested, or directly experienced;
2. Indirect use value refers to the benefits provided by Ecosystem Services (ES) and natural functions that support human well-being;
3. Option value can be considered as a particular type of use value that reflects the importance of preserving the possibility of utilising certain resources or services in the future.

Non-use can also be divided into two components:

1. Bequest value, which reflects the importance of preserving the natural capital and ecosystems for the benefit of future generations;
2. Existing value refers to the satisfaction or moral benefit individuals derive simply from knowing that a natural asset or ecosystem exists, regardless of any intention to use it.

Different evaluation techniques are available for estimating the TEV. These methods can be divided into two main categories (Fig. 1), the Revealed Preference (RP) and the Stated Preference (SP) [17, 19, 20].

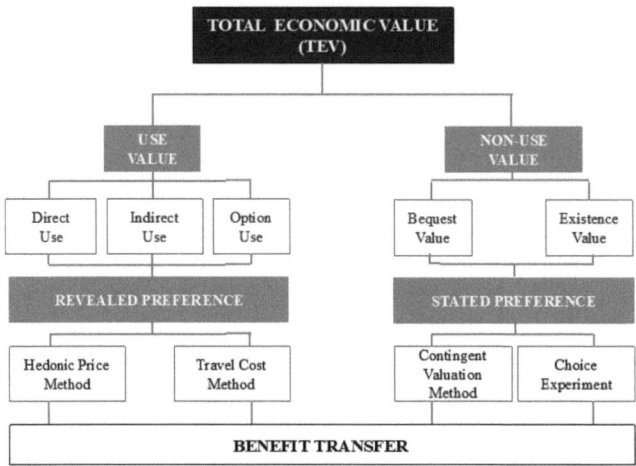

Fig. 1. Total Economic Value components and evaluation methodologies (elaboration from Pearce et al., 2002).

The RP methods derive economic values from choices and behaviours observed in related markets. These methods assume that people's preferences are indirectly revealed through their market decisions. The most widely used RP techniques are the Hedonic Price (HP) method and the Travel Cost Method (TCM). The HP is based on the measurement of the change in the value of an asset caused by an environmental characteristic in labour or property markets. Accordingly, amenity and disamenity can be derived from the difference in the value of a property, which corresponds to the Willingness to Pay (WTP) for the improvement of a given environmental quality. Assuming that environmental characteristics are reflected in property prices, it is possible to isolate the value of these individual characteristics, but this depends on the amount of data available on property prices, which must be adequate for the level of detail desired [21]. The TCM estimates value based on the travel expenses (including time and money) incurred by individuals to access natural sites, such as parks, forests, or lakes. These costs reflect the demand and value people place on these experiences [22]. The RP methods are mainly used for estimating the use value.

On the other hand, SP methods use hypothetical market scenarios to directly elicit individuals' WTP for specific environmental improvements or to avoid degradation. These approaches are especially useful for capturing non-use values that cannot be directly observed through actual market behavior [23]. The main techniques within this category include the Contingent Valuation Method (CVM) and the Choice Experiment (CE). The CVM uses structured surveys to directly ask individuals how much they would be WTP for a defined improvement in environmental quality or to avoid a particular form of degradation. As noted in the literature, it is the most commonly applied method for estimating non-use values [24]. On the other hand, the CE presents respondents with a series of hypothetical alternatives, each described by different attributes and levels. By analysing the choices individuals make, researchers can estimate the marginal value of individual ecosystem attributes and the trade-offs people are willing to accept [25].

As shown in Fig. 1, the results derived from SP and RP are often used to implement the Benefit Transfer (BT) method [26]. The BT is an economic valuation method that applies monetary estimates, like WTP, from one context (evaluation area) to another (the policy site) using statistical and econometric methods [27]. It is commonly used in ex-ante evaluation and policy analysis when time or resources prevent new primary valuation studies [27]. BT is typically divided into two approaches: (1) point transfer, which applies a single estimate directly or with simple adjustments, and (2) function transfer, which uses statistical models derived from multiple studies [28, 29]. The point transfer is the simplest approach, but it requires strong similarity between sites to be reliable. On the other hand, the function transfer is often based on meta-analysis, offering thus greater flexibility by generating valuation functions that consider variations in site characteristics and methodological factors. In general, the function transfer process involves the definition of the valuation objective, compiling and screening relevant studies, extracting key variables, building a meta-regression model, and applying the resulting function to the policy site. This approach enhances the robustness and generalizability of economic valuation in support of environmental and policy decision-making [30, 31].

Both Revealed Preference (RP) and Stated Preference (SP) methods have their respective strengths and limitations. RP methods are grounded in actual observed behavior, providing robust estimates of use values, but their application is often constrained by the availability and quality of market data. In contrast, SP methods offer greater flexibility and can capture a broader spectrum of values, including non-use values, but they may be subject to biases due to the hypothetical nature of survey responses.

Therefore, the choice of method should be context-dependent, taking into account the specific type of ES being evaluated, the availability of relevant data, and the overarching policy or management objectives [32].

2.3 Available Toolkit for the Economic Evaluation of Natural Capital in an Urban Context

The methodologies proposed by the appraisal discipline for the economic evaluation of the benefits of green solutions and natural capital are increasingly supported by several tools proposed by European projects and various research institutions. These tools are designed to quantify in monetary terms the benefits of GI. They also support Cost-Benefit Analysis (CBA), policy formulation, and stakeholder engagement, ultimately making the evaluation process more accessible and actionable for planners, decision-makers, and practitioners. Table 1 presents an overview of some of the most widely used tools for the economic evaluation of GI and NBS. They are described according to the purpose, the evaluation methodology and the evaluation output. As illustrated by Table 1, many of these tools are designed to translate ecological outcomes into monetary terms, facilitating their integration into economic decision-making.

This research selected the GiVal tool among others for two main reasons. Firstly, it adopts the BT as its basic methodological approach, which permits the estimated values to be adapted and applied to different contexts with appropriate adjustments. Secondly, the GiVal tool provides an evaluation output of the Net Present Value (NPV), enabling the quantification of the benefits of the NBS intervention in monetary terms. Therefore,

Table 1. List of the most relevant tools for the economic evaluation of GI and NBS in urban contexts.

Tool	Developer	Purpose	Evaluation methodology	Evaluation output
Economic evaluation of GI investment through discounted benefits	Natural Economy Northwest	Support economic appraisal of GI investments by local authorities and planners	Benefit transfer from empirical literature and UK government sources	Economic evaluation of GI investment through the Net Present Value (NPV)
InVEST	Natural Capital Project	Model and map ES under different land-use scenarios	Biophysical models with optional economic valuation via market prices, avoided cost, or BT	Spatial maps and quantitative estimation of services like carbon storage, urban cooling, etc. Monetary values only for some selected models
i-Tree	U.S. Forest Service	Quantify urban forest benefits for planning and management	Biophysical modeling and economic valuation via market/avoided cost	Monetary estimation for air pollution removal, carbon sequestration, and energy savings
BEST	CIRIA (UK)	Estimate benefits of SuDS and other GI interventions	Multi-criteria analysis with economic proxies and unit values from literature	Monetary valuation of flood mitigation, water quality, amenity, health and biodiversity

it permits to response to the main research question Q_1, as it provides strategic insights into the feasibility of the intervention to strategically support the urban planning process.

3 Application

3.1 Case Study

As declared in Sect. 1, this research aims to address the suitability of the GiVal tool for estimating the economic value of urban forestation for the city of Milan. The objective is to evaluate its capacity to provide a preliminary economic assessment that can support the early-stage planning and definition of this type of intervention.

The case study under evaluation focuses on the proposal of the implementation of NBS as a suitable strategy for revitalising vacant green spaces [11], as well as a suitable intervention for UHI mitigation. Specifically, the case study refers to the urban forestation intervention project aimed at regenerating the neglected green area located in Via dei Canzi, in the city of Milan (Fig. 2). This intervention aligns with the strategic objectives of the Climate and Air Plan of the city of Milan [33]. This plan proposes and suggests several actions to implement urban regeneration, mitigation and adaptation strategies through the integration of NBS or GI in the context of the city of Milan, as specifically underlined by objectives 4.2 "Urban cooling and reduction of the heat island phenomenon" and objective 4.3 "Milan, sponge city".

Fig. 2. Territorial framework of the intervention area with a specific focus on UHI.

In this perspective, urban forestation is recognised as a combined intervention, according to the fact that it can mitigate emissions through increasing carbon storage [11], as well as adapting the urban environment to the growing impacts of heat waves, reducing local average temperatures and the heat island effect [34]. The designed intervention proposed for Via dei Canzi directly supports these two objectives. The area was selected due to its high degree of soil sealing and limited vegetation cover, conditions that significantly improve the UHI effects. By increasing permeable surfaces and vegetation, the intervention contributes to the targets of climate neutrality by 2050 and urban cooling by 2030, as established in the Climate and Air Plan.

3.2 The GiVal Toolkit

The GiVal toolkit [35] has been developed to support preliminary project appraisal by identifying the potential impacts of both proposed GI interventions and existing green assets. It provides a structured framework for the economic evaluation of GI projects, such as urban reforestation, by estimating a broad range of environmental, social, and economic benefits.

It supports the development of indicative Cost-Benefit Analysis (CBA) by integrating monetised, quantitative, and qualitative impacts, and it permits the estimation of the TEV through the BT method.

In detail, it evaluates eleven benefit categories, each grounded in ES functions and linked to policy objectives:

- Climate change adaptation and mitigation;
- Water and flood management;
- Place and communities;
- Health and wellbeing;
- Land and property values;
- Investment;
- Labor productivity;
- Tourism;
- Recreation and leisure;
- Biodiversity;
- Land management.

Each benefit is supported by a logic model that considers the connection between the GI intervention and its expected outputs and outcomes, using value transfer methods and evidence from case studies and empirical research. The tool is mainly based on two key case studies that inform its valuation parameters. The first is the study by Garrod and colleagues, 2003 [36], which provides average values for forestry and woodland benefits. The second reference is the work commissioned by the Department for Communities and Local Government (DCLG), which offers insights into the scale of external, non-use benefits that GI can deliver [37].

The Excel-based calculator provided by the toolkit includes multiple interlinked worksheets that guide users through the valuation process and help consolidate the results into a structured economic appraisal. Here are described the spreadsheets mainly related to the project description and the project evaluation:

- Project Data Sheet. It is the sheet used to fill in the baseline information about the project. It includes details such as the type and size of the GI intervention, land use characteristics, site location, population density, and assumptions about visitor numbers. These parameters are directly connected to the benefit calculation tools to provide an evaluation fitted to the details of the project;
- Cost-Benefit Analysis (CBA) Sheet. This sheet combines the results from the different benefit modules and compares the total value of the benefits with the project's capital and operational costs. However, it has to be specified that the capital and the operational costs of the project are not calculated with the support of this tool, they have to be estimated separately and filled in;
- Summary of Economic Value. This sheet presents all monetised benefits by benefit category, in discounted present value terms over the defined appraisal period.

3.3 Applying the GiVal Toolkit for the Economic Evaluation of Urban Reforestation Intervention in the City of Milan

Before describing the application and the adjustment made, it is necessary to underline that the GiVal toolkit has been selected among the other proposed tools (Table 1) according to the fact that is based on the BT method, which makes it possible to use estimated values derived from similar case studies (Sect. 2). As well, it permits to respond to the main research question Q_1 (Sect. 1).

The preliminary steps implemented for the GiVal tool application for the economic evaluation of the urban forestation intervention in the city of Milan concerns firstly the identification of the benefits to consider following intervention objectives, and secondly, the arrangement of some input data contained in the values library to ensure the evaluation context-based as much as possible and to consider the difference in the currency.

First, the relevant benefits have been identified. In this context, the tourism spreadsheet has not been considered, as the necessary information is not available at the current stage of project development. Similarly, the spreadsheets related to the labour productivity and land management benefits have not been considered, according to the fact that these benefits are calculated based on the number of employees and site maintenance. Therefore, this calculation sheet has not been filled and considered for the evaluation according to the fact because the input data are too detailed and specific for the current stage of project development.

Secondly, it is essential to note that the economic values established in the Excel-based calculator to assess the benefits are expressed in pounds sterling [£]. Moreover, the monetary values refer to different years (e.g., 2006, 2007, 2012, and 2018) than the valuation year. For this reason, all the amounts have been first converted from pounds sterling [£] to euros [€] using the exchange rates provided by the Bank of Italy for the respective reference years.[1] Subsequently, the amounts in euros were adjusted to 2024 values using the appropriate updating coefficients. According to these adjustments, the performed calculation have been made directly in euros [€].

Thirdly, some of the input data, both from the values library spreadsheet and other sources used to describe the project context, have been tuned to ensure the assessment reflects the specific characteristics of the intervention.

These adjustments were necessary because several default values in the tool are based on data from the UK context. Specifically, the made changes are described as follows:

- Average household energy consumption (electricity) for cooling. The calcolator originally included an input value in kWh/year based on average UK data. This value has been replaced to better reflect the Italian context, using data provided by ENEA.[2] A value of 2000 kWh/year was entered, representing an average between the estimated consumption of new buildings (1000–1500 kWh/year) and older buildings (2000–2500 kWh/year);
- Average household energy consumption (gas) for heating. As in the previous case, the value originally included in the spreadsheet referred to average consumption in

---

[1] https://tassidicambio.bancaditalia.it/terzevalute-wf-ui-web/converter
[2] Energy Efficiency Unit Department, Rapporto Annuale sull'Efficienza Energetica 2024

the UK. This input was replaced with data from ENEA, reflecting the Italian context. The updated value entered is 10,700 kWh/year;
- Commercial electricity price. The original value was replaced with the average electricity price in Italy, set at 0.17 €/kWh according to ARERA[3];
- In the climate spreadsheet, the values for the percentage of buildings with air-conditioned [%] and the yearly air conditioning use [Hrs/yr] have been modified to better reflect the application context. The percentage has been set at 50%, and the yearly usage has been set at 540 h/year based on data provided by ENEA;
- In the water spreadsheet, the value for annual rainfall was updated, with 125.25 mm/year as provided by ENEA. This estimate reflects the seasonal distribution of rainfall, which is generally heavier during the winter months;

In the property spreadsheet, the input for the average property price has been based on the average market value in the OMI zone where the project area is located. Specifically, the OMI zone is the "D13 - Lambrate, Rubattino, Rombon". In this context, the valuation referred to civil residential properties in standard condition has been considered, with market values ranging from 2,900 €/m^2 to €4,000 €/m^2. Therefore, the average value equal to 3,450 €/m^2 has been estimated and used for the evaluation.

4 Discussion of Results

This section describes and critically analyses the results obtained by applying the GiVal toolkit for the economic evaluation of the forestation intervention in the city of Milan.

First of all, it is necessary to underline that the tool sets a discount rate of 3.5% and the Excel-calculator sheet is organised to set a a time horizon of 50 years at least.

Both values have been considered appropriate for this assessment. The 50-year period aligns with the typical life cycle of forestation projects within the necessary and required ordinary and extraordinary maintenance costs [38]. As well, the discount rate equal to 3.5% complies with European guidelines for the evaluation of GI [39].

Based on the project data, the values provided in the toolkit's library, and the adjustments made to specific inputs (Sect. 3), the GiVal toolkit estimates an NPV for the benefits equal to € 409,245.

This amount reflects benefits related to climate change adaptation and mitigation, water management and flood alleviation, place and community enhancement, health and well-being, land and property value improvements, and recreation.As described before (Sect. 3), the benefits associated with labour productivity, land management, and tourism have not been included in this calculation, as the relevant data are not available at this stage of the project.

Moreover, the benefits related to biodiversity have been estimated as 0 € (Table 2). This is because, in the toolkit, the biodiversity-related benefits are calculated only for the areas specifically designated for nature and wildlife conservation. Considering that the NBS intervention under evaluation is an urban forestation intervention, this typology of intervention is not engaged in the category considered by the tool for the evaluation of biodiversity benefits. This aspect critically underlines the difficulty of considering the specific characteristics of NBS intervention in the urban context.

---

[3] Autorità di Regolazione per Energia Reti e Ambiente, 2025

Table 2. Economic benefits of urban forestation intervention evaluated with the GiVal toolkit.

Benefit	Economic value [€]
Climate Change adaptation and mitigation	17,878
Water management and flood alleviation	162
Place and communities	30,974
Health and well-being	203,910
Land and property values	7,396
Labor productivity	0
Tourism	0
Recreation and leisure	148,925
Biodiversity	0
Land management	0
TOT	**409,245**

Table 2 summarises the monetary contribution of each of the benefits considered, as reported in the "Summary of Economic Value" spreadsheet.

The evaluation provided by the tool, which estimates the monetary value of each benefit separately, is particularly useful for understanding which dimensions are most enhanced by the proposed NBS intervention. This perspective can also support ex-ante comparison and monitoring, helping to assess whether the project is moving in the right direction from the early stages.

Concerning costs, the tool does not provide any information or input data for estimating the implementation and maintenance expenses of the intervention. However, these are essential for properly developing the Cost-Benefit Analysis (CBA) and calculating the NPV, which requires both discounted costs and benefits. The costs have to be estimated separately and manually entered into the calculation tool.

In this case, the implementation and ordinary maintenance costs have been assessed in another study proposed by Torrieri and colleagues (2025) [40]. Therefore, the costs estimated through the Prezziario della Regione Lombardia have been implemented in the CBA spreadsheet.

Table 3 synthesises the estimated costs for the considered NBS intervention for urban forestation.

Table 3. Synthesis of estimation cost for forestation intervention (Torrieri et al., 2025).

	Cost [€]	Source
Implementation cost	563,056 €	Prezziario Regione Lombardia, 2023
Maintenance cost	150,759 €/year	Prezziario Regione Lombardia, 2023

The estimated costs have been entered into the CBA spreadsheet, and the discounted amount of costs has been calculated using a discount rate of 3.5%, using a 20-year time horizon consistent with the benefits evaluation. The time horizon has been set to 20 years, according to the fact that only ordinary maintenance costs.

Based on these inputs, the total amount of the discounted cost, considering both implementation and ordinary maintenance costs, amounts to € 2,360,080. Extraordinary maintenance costs have been excluded at this preliminary stage, as the Lombardy Region price list expresses extraordinary maintenance in €/tree, and at this preliminary stage of the project, the exact number of trees to be planted is not yet defined.

Table 4 summarises the estimated discounted amount for both benefits and costs and shows their combination for calculating the final NPV of the intervention.

Table 4. Synthesis of discounted costs and benefits and the estimated NPV.

	[€]
Discounted Benefits	409,245
Discounted Costs	−2,360,080
NPV	1,950,835

As can be observed, the final NPV is negative. It is also important to highlight that a relevant number of benefits have not been included in the evaluation due to the current state of development of the project. In particular, the benefits related to labour productivity, land management and tourism have not been considered, although their inclusion would likely lead to a significant increase in the total estimated benefits. Additionally, concerning the biodiversity benefits, the applied toolkit only accounts for those areas specifically designated for nature and wildlife conservation, limiting the estimation of these benefits in the urban context. It reveals that the model does not fully reflect the characteristics of urban-scale interventions.

Considering the GiVal toolkit as a support tool for project design in its early stages, the obtained results should suggest a downsizing of the intervention area (3.36 hectares), given the high implementation and maintenance costs of an urban forestation project and the limited economic value of the benefits compared to the initial investment.

However, in the context of public interventions that generate long-term benefits, such as NBS and urban forestation, the choice of the discount rate becomes particularly important. This is the rationale at the basis of the test carried out to address how the NPV changes with a lower discount rate. Specifically, the test explored the variation in NPV when applying a 2% discount rate. This discount rate has been chosen based on a 2006 study that advocated the use of a discount rate equal to 1.4% to evaluate the long-term costs and benefits of climate change mitigation actions [41].

Using the discount rate of 2%, an NPV of −1,592,431 € has been estimated. This result highlights and confirms that not estimating some benefits penalises in a significant manner the final NPV against a significant investment. Furthermore, a more structured and detailed sensitivity analysis is required to precisely determine which item among discount rate, benefits and costs has the greatest impact on NPV. Also, the use of decreasing discount rates over time could be considered according to the long-term benefits concerning the implementation of urban forestation.

5 Conclusions

This research aims to answer the main research questions Q_1: *"How can the benefits of NBS in urban areas be effectively evaluated in monetary terms to inform and support strategic planning processes?"*. Therefore, this application applies the GiVal toolkit to address its suitability for developing the preliminary economic evaluation of NBS in urban environments. The toolkit has been applied to estimate the economic value of an urban forestation intervention in Via dei Canzi, Milan, in alignment with the key objectives outlined in the City of Milan's Climate and Air Plan.

One of the main challenges in this field is the integration of environmental benefits into traditional CBA, a process that often requires expertise not easily accessible to many stakeholders [8]. The GiVal toolkit aims to bridge this gap by providing an accessible, evidence-based framework for estimating the potential benefits of GI interventions [35]. The proposed application permits underlining of both strengths and critical issues concerning the examined tool.

The most evident strength is that the GiVal tool offers a valuable initial insight into the spectrum of benefits provided by NBS and GI. It permits the identification of the different types of benefits related to the analysed NBS, ranging from leisure and recreation to less immediately tangible ones such as climate regulation, health and well-being, and property value increases. This categorisation supports the alignment of the intervention with the broader strategic goals of the local government. The second strength is represented by the robust methodological framework at the basis. By using the BT method [19], the toolkit enables a structured and methodologically consistent estimation of economic benefits even when context-specific valuation data is lacking. Moreover, the required input data are relatively easy to obtain from public or open-access databases, enabling context-based adjustments that enhance the reliability and applicability of the results (Sect. 3).

On the other hand, some criticalities have to be discussed. First of all, the default economic values within the toolkit are expressed in British pounds [£] and they are referred to periods which are different from the date of evaluation. Therefore, in the proposed application, all monetary values have been converted using exchange rates provided by the Bank of Italy and updated to 2024, to perform calculations in euros [€] and to be able to compare the benefits estimated by the tool with the costs estimated previously [40]. Moreover, it has to be underlined that these adjustments can introduce inconsistencies or errors without proper adjustments.

However, the main criticality concerns the absence of cost estimation support, within the lack of a module for preliminary estimating implementation, maintenance, and operational costs [8]. As a result, the tool cannot be used to perform a full CBA unless users provide costs estimated externally.

Furthermore, this tool is not able to properly consider the specific features and benefits provided by NBS implemented in urban contexts. As underlined in Sect. 4, the tool only considers those areas specifically designated for nature and wildlife conservation for estimating the biodiversity benefits. In this sense, the NBS referred to the urban forestation cannot be considered for this estimation, thus limiting the estimation of these specific benefits in urban contexts.

The GiVal toolkit has been designed as a support tool for project design in its early stages for the preliminary identification and evaluation of the benefits of NBS interventions. However, considering that this tool evaluates long-term benefits, the issue of the choice of discount rate is fundamental [41], as the possibility of using a decreasing rate over time, given the wide period of benefits. Therefore, considering the peculiarities of the application described in this paper, the development of an in-depth sensitivity analysis is considered fundamental in the future phases of the research to understand which aspects among the discount rate, costs and benefits influence mostly the NPV. This analysis is even more necessary given the lack of estimating some benefits as NBS implemented on an urban scale (Sect. 4).

Moreover, some future research should be addressed to implement and integrate cost estimation modules (implementation and operational costs) in the GiVal toolkit to better support the early-stage planning of NBS in an urban context within a comprehensive perspective of costs and benefits [42, 43].

Acknowledgements. Francesca Torrieri carried out this research within the PRIN project "Nature for sustainable cities: planning cost-effective and just solutions for urban issues (NatSolis) - 2022ZLE8HC".

References

1. Carter, T.R., Benzie, M., Campiglio, E., et al.: A conceptual framework for cross-border impacts of climate change. Glob. Environ. Chang. **69**, 102307 (2021). https://doi.org/10.1016/j.gloenvcha.2021.102307
2. Olivieri, F., Sassenou, L.-N., Olivieri, L.: Potential of nature-based solutions to diminish urban heat island effects and improve outdoor thermal comfort in summer: case study of Matadero Madrid. Sustainability. **16**, 2778 (2024). https://doi.org/10.3390/su16072778
3. Romanello, M., van Daalen, K., Anto, J.M., et al.: Tracking progress on health and climate change in Europe. Lancet Public Health. **6**, e858–e865 (2021). https://doi.org/10.1016/S2468-2667(21)00207-3
4. Faivre, N., Fritz, M., Freitas, T., et al.: Nature-based solutions in the EU: Innovating with nature to address social, economic and environmental challenges. Environ. Res. **159**, 509–518 (2017). https://doi.org/10.1016/j.envres.2017.08.032
5. Gómez Martín, E., Máñez Costa, M., Egerer, S., Schneider, U.A.: Assessing the long-term effectiveness of nature-based solutions under different climate change scenarios. Sci. Total Environ. **794**, 148515 (2021). https://doi.org/10.1016/j.scitotenv.2021.148515
6. Raymond, C.M., Frantzeskaki, N., Kabisch, N., et al.: A framework for assessing and implementing the co-benefits of nature-based solutions in urban areas. Environ. Sci. Policy. **77**, 15–24 (2017). https://doi.org/10.1016/j.envsci.2017.07.008
7. Cohen-Shacham, E., Andrade, A., Dalton, J., et al.: Core principles for successfully implementing and upscaling Nature-based Solutions. Environ. Sci. Policy. **98**, 20–29 (2019). https://doi.org/10.1016/j.envsci.2019.04.014

8. Dumitru, A., Garcia, I., Zorita, S., et al.: Approaches to monitoring and evaluation strategy development. In: Evaluating the Impact of Nature-based Solutions. A Handbook for Practitioners. EU Publications Office (2021)
9. European Commission: Nature-based Solutions: State of the Art in EU-Funded Projects. Publications Office of the European Union (2020)
10. Rossitti, M., Torrieri, F.: Circular economy as 'catalyst' for resilience in inner areas. Sustain. Mediterr. Constr., 64–67 (2021)
11. Masiero, M., Biasin, A., Amato, G., et al.: Urban forests and green areas as nature-based solutions for brownfield redevelopment: a case study from Brescia Municipal Area (Italy). Forests. **13**, 444 (2022). https://doi.org/10.3390/f13030444
12. Wickenberg, B., McCormick, K., Olsson, J.A.: Advancing the implementation of nature-based solutions in cities: a review of frameworks. Environ. Sci. Policy. **125**, 44–53 (2021). https://doi.org/10.1016/j.envsci.2021.08.016
13. Oppio, A., Caprioli, C., Dell'Ovo, M., Bottero, M.: Assessing ecosystem services through a multimethodological approach based on multicriteria analysis and cost-benefits analysis: a case study in Turin (Italy). J. Clean. Prod. **472**, 143472 (2024). https://doi.org/10.1016/j.jclepro.2024.143472
14. Sowińska-Świerkosz, B., García, J.: What are nature-based solutions (NBS)? Setting core ideas for concept clarification. Nat. Based Solut. **2**, 100009 (2022). https://doi.org/10.1016/j.nbsj.2022.100009
15. Tarantino, G., Bottero, M.C., Datola, G., Arco, E.: Implementation of Nature-Based Solutions (Nbs) for Urban Heat Island (Uhi) Mitigation Restoration of Green Brownfields in the City of Milan (2024)
16. European Environment Agency: Nature-based Solutions in Europe: Policy, Knowledge and Practice for Climate Change Adaptation and Disaster Risk Reduction (2021)
17. Pearce, D., Ozdemiroglu, E., Bateman, I.J., et al.: Economic Valuation with Stated Preference Techniques. Edward Elgar Publishing (2002)
18. Roscelli, R.: Manuale di estimo. Valutazioni economiche ed esercizio della professione. UTET Università (2014)
19. Pearce, D.W., Turner, R.K.: Economics of Natural Resources and the Environment. Johns Hopkins University Press (1990)
20. Freeman, A.M., Herriges, J.A., Kling, C.L.: The Measurement of Environmental and Resource Values: Theory and Methods. Taylor & Francis (2014)
21. Croci, E., Lucchitta, B., Penati, T.: Valuing ecosystem services at the urban level: a critical review. Sustainability. **13**, 1–16 (2021). https://doi.org/10.3390/su13031129
22. Clawson, M., Knetsch, J.L.: Economics of outdoor recreation. In: Resources for the Future. Wiley (1966)
23. Bateman, I.J., Carson, R.T., Day, B., et al.: Economic Valuation with Stated Preference Techniques. Edward Elgar Publishing (2002)
24. Mitchell, R.C.: Using Surveys to Value Public Goods, pp. 7–9 (2013). https://doi.org/10.4324/9781315060569
25. Louviere, J.J., Hensher, D.A., Swait, J.D., Adamowicz, W.: Combining sources of preference data. In: Stated Choice Methods, pp. 227–251. Cambridge University Press (2000)
26. Wilson, M.A., Hoehn, J.P.: Valuing environmental goods and services using benefit transfer: the state-of-the art and science. Ecol. Econ. **60**, 335–342 (2006). https://doi.org/10.1016/j.ecolecon.2006.08.015
27. Zhou, J., Wu, J., Gong, Y.: Valuing wetland ecosystem services based on benefit transfer: a meta-analysis of China wetland studies. J. Clean. Prod. **276**, 122988 (2020). https://doi.org/10.1016/j.jclepro.2020.122988

28. Stanley, T.D., Jarrell, S.B.: Meta-regression analysis: a quantitative method of literature surveys. J. Econ. Surv. **3**, 161–170 (1989). https://doi.org/10.1111/j.1467-6419.1989.tb00064.x
29. Boyle, K.J., Bergstrom, J.C.: Benefit transfer studies: myths, pragmatism, and idealism. Water Resour. Res. **28**, 657–663 (1992). https://doi.org/10.1029/91WR02591
30. Johnston, R., Rolfe, J., Rosenberger, R., Brouwer, R.: Benefit Transfer of Environmental and Resource Values: A Guide for Researchers and Practitioners, Springer, Berlin (2015)
31. Mehvar, A., Filatova, T., de Ruyter van Stevenickc, E., et al.: Quantifying economic value of coastal ecosystem services: a review. J. Mar. Sci. Eng. **6**, 5 (2018). https://doi.org/10.3390/jmse6010005
32. Bateman, I., Mace, G., Fezzi, C., et al.: Economic analysis for ecosystem service assessments. Environ. Resour. Econ. **48**, 177–218 (2011)
33. Comune di Milano (2023) Piano AriaClima
34. Abhijith, K.V., Kumar, P., Gallagher, J., et al.: Air pollution abatement performances of green infrastructure in open road and built-up street canyon environments—a review. Atmos. Environ. **162**, 71–86 (2017). https://doi.org/10.1016/j.atmosenv.2017.05.014
35. Ashton, R., Baker, R., Dean, J., et al.: Building natural value for sustainable economic development. In: The Green Infrastructure Valuation Toolkit User Guide, p. 83 (2011)
36. Willis, K., Garrod, G., Scarpa, R., et al.: The Social and Environmental Benefits of Forests in Great Britain. Centre for Research in Environmental Appraisal & Management (2003)
37. England, N., Heritage, E.: Valuing and Funding Green Infrastructure, pp. 1–16 (2016)
38. Bonsignori R, Senes G (2022) Soluzioni progettuali tipo di infrastrutture verdi per la gestione delle acque meteoriche
39. Commission E (2014) Guide to Cost-Benefit Analysis of Investment Projects
40. Torrieri, F., Datola, G., Dell'Ovo, M., et al.: Integrating spatial analysis, ecosystem services and cost analysis for nature-based solution (NBS) planning in the urban context. Aestimum. (in press)
41. Stern, L.N.: Stern Review: The Economics of Climate Change. United Kingdom (2006)
42. del Giudice, V., Passeri, A., Torrieri, F., de Paola, P.: Risk analysis within feasibility studies: an application to cost-benefit analysis for the construction of a new road. Appl. Mech. Mater. **651–653**, 1249–1254 (2014). https://doi.org/10.4028/www.scientific.net/AMM.651-653.1249
43. del Giudice, V., Passeri, A., de Paola, P., Torrieri, F.: Estimation of risk-return for real estate investments by applying Ellwood's model and real options analysis: an application to the residential real estate market of Naples. Appl. Mech. Mater. **651–653**, 1570–1575 (2014). https://doi.org/10.4028/www.scientific.net/AMM.651-653.1570

Understanding Airbnb Supply in Rome: Multivariate Analysis of Prices and Accommodation Patterns

Maria Rosaria Guarini[1(✉)] [iD], Francesco Sica[1] [iD], Alejandro Segura-de-la-Cal[2] [iD], and Yilsy Núñez Guerrero[3] [iD]

[1] Department of Architecture and Design, Sapienza University of Rome, Via Flaminia 359, 00196 Rome, Italy
mariarosaria.guarini@uniroma1.it
[2] Department of Architectural Constructions and Their Control, Polytechnic University of Madrid, Av. de Juan de Herrera 6, 28040 Madrid, Spain
alejandro.segura@upm.es
[3] Department of Organization Engineering, Business Administration and Statistics, Polytechnic University of Madrid, C. de José Gutiérrez Abascal 2, 28006 Madrid, Spain

Abstract. The repercussions resulting from the succession of unregulated tourist activities, exemplified by overtourism, are also evident in the residential market, particularly within the short-term rental sector. These are commercial environments whose developmental rules and evolution over time frequently do not adhere to standards of normalcy and traceability of their characteristics across various spatial scales, from neighbourhood to city. This arises from the unpredictability of price creation processes at a regional level concerning (e.g.) the target demographic that requires short-term renting.

The phenomenon of short-term rentals in the city is investigated in this article, with the primary attention being placed on the qualities that are unique to this phenomenon in terms of demand, supply, and spatial considerations. Rome is utilized as the case study. The primary evidence across various analytical scales (urban area, municipality, city) is emphasized, examining their empirical relationships concerning the relevant territorial setting.

Keywords: Airbnb · short-term renting · multivariate analysis

1 Introduction

Mass tourism is a phenomenon that is progressively proliferating globally. In European, particularly in Italy, locales and cities (e.g., Rome, Florence and Venice), the repercussions of over tourism are manifest, associated with the influx of visitors to historical and cultural sites concentrated in relatively confined areas, often marked by severely limited spaces. The emergence and expansion of sharing economy platforms have significantly enhanced mass tourism by altering the accessibility/utilization of tourism resources and services. One viable alternative to long-term hotel stays is home-sharing, also known as short-term renting [1].

Eurostat data on collaborative economy platforms indicates a substantial increase in short-term rentals in tourist cities from 2018 to 2023 [2]. This trend has been fueled in part by the rise of collaborative economy platforms that facilitate the free or paid sharing of goods and services between private individuals [3]. After a record-breaking 2019 with 512 million overnight stays, the number of annual guest nights in short-term accommodation booked through online platforms in the European Union (EU) contracted by 47% in 2020 (272 million) due to the COVID pandemic, according to EUROSTAT statistics on the "Collaborative economy platforms". However, 2023 saw a strong rebound, with over 719 million overnight stays. Italy (+27.5%) and Greece (+21.6%), in particular, are showing growth from 2022 year to 2023 that surpasses the overall growth of the EU. With about seven million overnight stays in 2023, Italy also topped the list of countries with the most international tourists. Based on these statistics, Rome ranked second among the four platforms for overnight stays in 2023 with 12.5 million, just behind Paris with 19.3 million. Barcelona, Lisbon, and Madrid followed with 10.9 million, 10.5 million, and 9.5 million, respectively. In all, out of all the overnight stays in the EU booked through the four platforms, which total 719 million, 8.7 percent, or 62.8 million, occurred in these five cities. Figure 1 shows the number of guest stays in the European Union from 2018 to 2023.

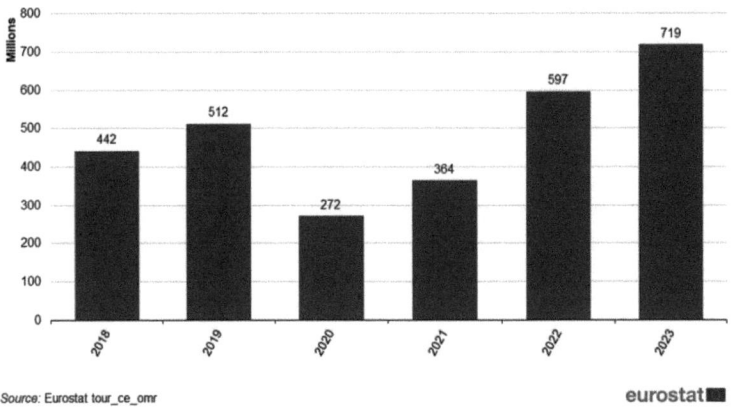

Fig. 1. Annual guest nights in the EU, 2018–2023. *Source*: [4].

As a result of the proliferation of collaborative economy platforms, a considerable number of homeowners have opted to rent out their residential units on a short-term basis using platforms. This is done with the intention of generating substantial profits in the shorter term, as opposed to relying on traditional long-term leases [5]. The potential for a more lucrative source of income motivated individuals to invest in real estate by acquiring new properties for the short-term rental market, often at prices exceeding their true value. The primary entities in this market consist of five global companies (Airbnb, Booking.com, Expedia/VRBO, Tripadvisor, and Tujia), who collectively represented over seventy-five percent of the sales in this global market in 2019 [6]. As of 2025, Airbnb is the preeminent platform for short-term rentals globally, featuring over eight million active listings from more than five million hosts throughout over 240,000 countries and cities [7].

The purpose of this study is to analyse the supply, demand, and locational characteristics via Airbnb that are related with the short-term rental market in Rome. The paper is structured as follows: Sect. 2 provides a review of the sector literature on the impacts of Airbnb on the residential market (2.1) and a description of the proposed analysis methodology (2.2). Section 3 presents the results of the investigation and Sect. 4 the discussion.

2 Materials and Methods

2.1 How Airbnb is Influencing the Housing Market: Literature Survey

The absence of regulation in this economic sector has resulted in numerous (predominantly adverse) consequences in prominent tourist destinations, which have been thoroughly examined in scholarly literature. Zervas, Proserpio, and Byers (2017) demonstrated that Airbnb's entry into the Texas hotel business adversely affected it, revealing that a 1% increase in Airbnb listings led to a 0.05% decline in quarterly hotel revenues [8].

Several authors have indicated that the proliferation of short-term rentals has exacerbated tourist pressure, resulting in a diminished availability of affordable housing for residents and contributing to the gentrification of specific neighbourhoods, where residents are supplanted by tourists, thereby causing significant alterations and distortions in the residential property market for both purchasing and renting [9]. Other scholars have demonstrated that these effects are more pronounced in urban centres, where tourist attractions are prevalent, resulting in a heightened concentration of short-term rental accommodations and subsequently causing an unequal development of supply and demand [9]. The spread of collaborative economy platforms has brought about profound changes in the tourism accommodation sector. The academic literature on this topic has demonstrated the varying degrees of substitutability between the hotel market and short-term rentals, depending on the services offered, which differ significantly and target distinct customer segments. Yoong, K., Woltering, R.-O., and Heo, C.Y., in their study focusing on the cities of Barcelona, London, and Paris, explored the impact of home-sharing platforms such as Airbnb on the hotel industry. They found that the severity of the effect varies depending on the market, the hotel segment, and the type of Airbnb listing [10]. Yang and Mao, utilizing an extensive dataset encompassing 28 locations in the United States, demonstrated that a 1% rise in hotel room rates resulted in a 1397% increase in the availability of accommodations on Airbnb [11].

Another element that has been brought to light in the literature is the concentration of supply in the hands of "professional" hosts who provide management services for multiple flats at the same time. This has the potential to have substantial consequences on urban dynamics, overtourism, and the behavior of operators [6]. Several authors have focused on the importance, relationships, and influences between content created directly by hosts (Market-Generated Content – MGC) and that created by guests (User-Generated Content – UGC); these factors influence both consumer intentions and choices, as well as hosts' marketing strategies on platforms, consequently affecting the prices and characteristics of properties listed in the short-term rental market [12–16]. To mitigate the impact of the unregulated proliferation of short-term rental accommodations in tourist locales, some countries (e.g., Italy) and cities (e.g., London, Paris, Barcelona) have implemented legislation. Scholars examining the ramifications of Airbnb's presence on local communities have investigated legal and tax implications, as well as the means and consequences of enacting home-sharing ordinances (HSOs) to control the short-term rental industry [17].

As stated by Morales et all., the impact of Airbnb listings on a city as a whole is concentrated in the municipalities closest to tourist attractions, so Airbnb listings can influence how housing prices behave. In these districts, Airbnb listings can be identified as a factor driving up long-term rental prices [18].

The examination of pricing and availability of short-term rental housing is especially pertinent given the transition in housing utilization, from a conventional real estate asset influenced by standard market variations to an investment asset assessed through alternative valuation metrics, including tourist influx, occupancy rates, or associated services. These features that introduce greater price volatility are framed within the development of financialization models as described by [19].

2.2 Methodology

Subsequent to that theoretical framework, this research aims to describe the tourist rental market in the city of Rome from the perspective of pricing in the supply displayed on the Airbnb platform, providing an overview of the current situation of Airbnb listings. Data was collected, preprocessed, and analyzed using descriptive statistical techniques, variance analysis, and machine learning classification models. Several software tools were employed, including Excel, SPSS, and QGIS, to comprehensively describe the phenomenon under study.

The classification tree technique is a supervised machine learning method that seeks to partition the feature space into a smaller number of subspaces using a series of decision rules, ensuring that the response variable values are similar within each subspace. Used for both classification and regression tasks. It builds binary trees that recursively partition the dataset into increasingly homogeneous groups, using criteria such as Gini impurity for classification or mean squared error for regression. The tree grows in a greedy fashion and may be pruned afterward to prevent overfitting. The classification tree technique is highly valued for its interpretability, flexibility, and robustness. It can capture non-linear relationships and variable interactions without prior assumptions and handles both numerical and categorical data, while being resistant to outliers and missing values. These features make CART particularly useful when the goal is to describe and understand patterns in data in a clear and structured way. In this study, the CART algorithm was applied, which is used for both classification and regression tasks. Cross-validation strategies and model selection techniques were implemented to maximize performance while maintaining interpretability, thereby preventing overfitting.

Dataset. This study utilizes publicly accessible secondary data from Inside Airbnb, which includes records of 12 characteristics of the tourist rental market in the city of Rome. The dataset comprises 125,390 records, divided into four time periods spanning from the last quarter of 2023 to the third quarter of 2024. To ensure data quality and reliability, a cleaning process was conducted to remove corrupted, anomalous, missing, or duplicate records. Missing values were not imputed; instead, irrelevant data were eliminated and missing or outlier values were systematically addressed. The integration of different datasets resulted in a consolidated table covering the final quarter of 2023 and three quarters of 2024. We have used data from the last year openly available on the Inside Airbnb website, which is sufficient for the purposes of the exploratory study being analyzed in this research.

Variables. The dataset provides information on various aspects of the Airbnb short-term rental market in Rome, including different types of hosts, rental prices, host characteristics, minimum nights, number of reviews, availability, room type, and geolocation data to identify neighborhoods and urban zones of the city, among other attributes. For the analysis, rental price was used as the dependent variable, while the remaining characteristics served as predictors. It is important to note that there is no information available on the capacity of the accommodation, nor the start date of the offer on the accommodation platform.

3 Results

The analyses applied to the data set were firstly a study of EDA (descriptive analysis) and the testing of the hypotheses of normality (the variables do not present normality), homoscedasticity, independence, among others, with the objective of verifying whether the data set requires substantial transformations in some of its variables.

It can be observed that the price variable presents a percentage of missing or missing data, which reduces the data set of this variable to 112,000 observations. A collinearity and multicollinearity analysis of the variables that report on reviews (number_of_reviews, number_of_reviews_ltm, last_review, reviews_per_month) was carried out, with the result that all four variables show collinearity, which could undermine the model's stability and reliability. Therefore, following methodological criteria, three of the variables were excluded, retaining only the one that demonstrated the highest theoretical relevance and best statistical performance according to the Variance Inflation Factor (VIF) and significance tests. This decision helped reduce informational redundancy, enhance coefficient interpretability, and prevent distortions in the parameter estimates. For research purposes we have worked only with the variable number of reviews ltm, to avoid redundancy of information. In general, the frequency tables corresponding to the categorical variables Room_type and neighbourhoods and urban zones are as follows:

The Table 1 shows the existence of high price variations depending on the location and type of accommodation. It can be seen that the rental offer on Airbnb is highly concentrated in Entire Home typologies 76.2% followed by Private Room 22.5%, with hotel room or shared room alternatives representing 1.3% of the offer in Rome. At the neighborhood level, the supply is concentrated in the historic center of Rome, accounting for over 50% of the total supply among all housing alternatives.

The progressive increase in prices is significant for the period analyzed, with an average growth of 24% across the entire city, driven by a 36% increase in the historic

Table 1. List of Airbnb accommodation offerings for the third quarter of 2024, segmented by neighborhood as well as by type of establishment (Entire home/apt, Hotel room, Private room, Shared room).

Municipality	Entire home/apt		Hotel room		Private room		Shared room	
	Av.Price	%	Av.Price	%	Av.Price	%	Av.Price	%
I Centro Storico	**280**	**51.%**	**220**	**71.2%**	**194**	**49.0%**	**87**	**38.7%**
II Parioli/Nomentano	176	6.8%	106	3.2%	114	7.3%	58	5.0%
III Monte Sacro	212	1.7%	113	1.4%	84	1.9%	32	1.7%
IV Tiburtina	195	1.5%			79	2.7%	37	1.7%
V Prenestino/Centocelle	102	4.6%			74	5.1%	50	22.7%
VI Roma delle Torri	164	0.8%			77	1.2%	31	4.2%
VII San Giovanni/Cine.	207	7.7%	137	8.8%	106	9.3%	26	5.0%
VIII Appia Antica	162	2.5%	175	2.1%	110	3.3%	38	2.5%
IX Eur	215	1.3%	90	0.4%	94	1.0%		
X Ostia/Acilia	216	3.3%			97	2.0%	96	5.0%
XI Arvalia/Portuense	152	2.0%	152	0.4%	102	2.3%	37	6.7%
XII Monte Verde	183	5.6%	109	3.2%	126	4.8%	34	2.5%
XIII Aurelia	205	6.7%	172	8.1%	154	6.4%	27	0.8%
XIV Monte Mario	213	2.3%	117	1.1%	94	2.1%		
XV Cassia/Flaminia	170	1.8%	145	0.4%	97	1.5%	231	3.4%
Total	**233**	**22,927**	**198**	**285**	**150**	**6755**	**69**	**119**

The average rental price per night is indicated, as well as the percentage share of the supply by the neighborhood in relation to the total supply in Rome for each type of accommodation. *Source*: Own elaboration.

center. Only two districts show higher growth rates: 48% in Municipality VI (Roma delle Torri) and 46% in Municipality XIV (Monte Mario), both of which have a very limited supply. In fact, Municipality VI has the lowest number of listings in the entire city, with 279 properties in the third quarter of 2024. Additionally, it is worth noting that the average growth is influenced by the listing of atypical properties in these districts, featuring very high prices exceeding €1000 per night - a pattern that differs from the general trend observed in overall price growth.

Figure 2 illustrates the weight and spatial distribution of each type of property listed on Airbnb for the third quarter of 2024. These data align with those presented in Table 1 and highlight the significant predominance of entire home listings compared to other accommodation types on the platform. Section A shows a wide distribution of this type across the city center of Rome, with a share exceeding 50%. Outside the city center, listings are concentrated in neighborhoods bordering the *Vatican* area to the west and the *Termini* railway station to the east. Section B, which refers to hotel and aparthotel offerings, reveals their limited presence in the overall supply, along with their higher concentration within the historical center. Given the nature of these establishments, this category encompasses a broad range — from units with private bathrooms to guesthouses or boutique hotel concepts — generally lacking traditional hotel services such as on-site dining. Section C of Fig. 2 shows the distribution of private rooms (with or without private bathrooms), a category again concentrated in the historical center, with notable presence around *Termini* and the *Vatican* areas. Finally, Section D displays the distribution of shared rooms, which are mainly concentrated around the *Termini* railway station.

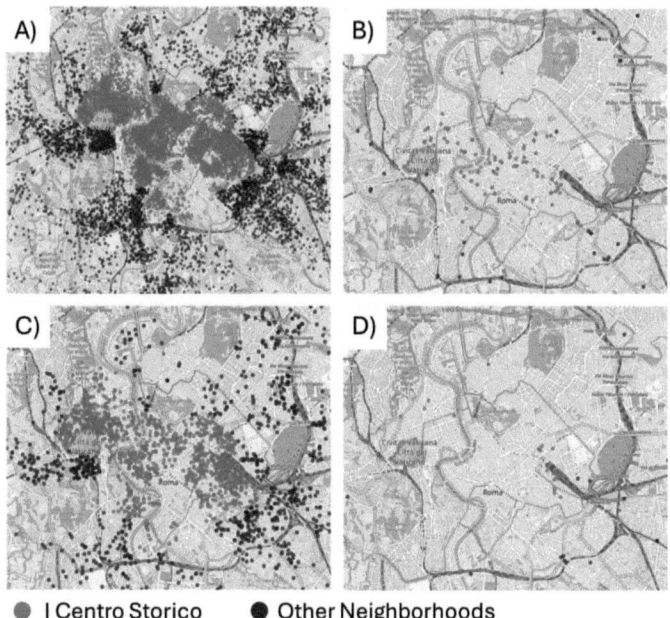

Fig. 2. Map of Rome showing the spatial distribution of Airbnb listings by room type. Fig. A presents the supply of Entire home/apartment, B shows hotel rooms, C refers to private rooms, and finally, and D illustrates shared rooms

The descriptive statistics for the quantitative variables are presented in the following table.

To verify if the data presents significant differences in terms of price in the 4 quarters under analysis, an analysis of variance (One-Way ANOVA) was applied, resulting in a (p-value) of less than 0.05, which indicates that there are significant differences in the price variable between the 4 quarters. The test carried out indicates that in the quarters 2023-Q4 and 2024-Q1 the prices vary between them and in comparison, with the other three quarters, the quarters 2024-Q2 and 2024-Q3 do not present a variation between them in terms of prices, but they do vary from the quarters 2023-Q4 and 2024-Q3. The results are shown in Table 2.

On demonstrating that there are price differences between the quarters of the year through the analysis of variance (ANOVA) and the graph of price differences by quarter. We proceed to carry out the supervised classification analysis by quarters, in order to be able to detect what differentiates each time of the year in terms of prices.

Table 2. Average price differences by quarters.

Quarter	N° cases	Mean	Deviation	Min-Max
2023-Q4	27,376	172,37	712,362	8–80.000
2024-Q1	26,543	187,00	625,570	10–80.000
2024-Q2	28,510	207,82	522,857	10–64.000
2024-Q3	30,086	213,37	653,220	8–72.000

Classification trees were constructed using the CRT (Classification and Regression Trees) method with "price" as the dependent variable. Machine learning technique is applied for each quarter. The Table 3 below shows a summary of the results obtained.

Table 3. Summary of CTRs.

	2023 Q4	2024 Q1	2024 Q2	2024 Q3
Average price	172,37	187	207,82	213,37
First segmentation variable	Mínimum nights	neighbourhood	neighbourhood	neighbourhood
Relevant variables	Number of reviews ltm, availability 365, room type	Number of reviews ltm, availability 365, room type.	Number of reviews ltm, room type, availability 365	Number of reviews, availability 365, room type
Higher average price	2360,39 Nodo 2	908,39 Nodo 8	1235,55 Nodo 8	880,87 Nodo 8
Minimum average price	95,12 Nodo 8	83,9 Nodo 14	78,90 Nodo 14	89,58 Nodo 14
Points of division	Minimun nights <= 362, >362, Number of reviews ltm, <= 0.5, > 0.5, availability 365, <= 365, > 365, room type	Neighbourhood Number of reviews ltm, <= 0.5, > 0.5, availability 365, <= 365, > 365, room type	Neighbourhood Number of reviews ltm, <= 0.5, > 0.5, room type, availability 365, <= 365, > 365	Neighbourhood Number of reviews, <= 0.5, > 0.5, availability 365, <= 365, > 365, room type
Singularity	23 cases with very high price in Node 2	few cases, high prices in Node 8	56 cases with very high price in Node 8	88 cases high prices in Node 8

- Tree 2023Q4 is unique in that it starts by dividing by minimum_nights, it identifies a clear difference between short and long term rentals with properties with stays over 362 nights, in this Q4 2023 analysis the number_of_reviews_ltm is very relevant.

- Tree 2024Q1 the first segmentation variable is neighborhood and shows the concentration of accommodation in the neighborhood I. The outliers are less extreme than in other trees; it is the most balanced and has a shallower depth.
- Tree 2024Q2 the first segmentation variable is neighborhood and clearly shows how more reviews lower the price, shows better differentiation by room_type. Outlier (Node 8) is very clear and bounded, the most structured and clear, and behaves more predictably and logically.
- Tree 2024Q3 is again segmented with neighborhood as the first variable, it is highlighted that few reviews raise the price. availability_365 generates strong outliers.

In the segmentations made in the classification trees for the different quarters, it can be seen the need to further detail the analysis by urban areas, due to the fact that the municipality with the highest presence of accommodation is the *Centro Storico* of Rome, which gives rise to the question of whether Municipality I presents significant differences by urban areas in terms of accommodation prices and the concentration of accommodation.

When the analysis was carried out using the classification tree technique, an adjustment was made to the territorial segmentation of the lodgings, moving from a division by municipality to a classification based on specific urban zones within each municipality. The results obtained indicate that the urbanistic zone variable is not a determining factor in the variation of lodging prices. This conclusion is supported by the data presented in Table 4.

Table 4. Importance of independent variable of CTRs.

Independent variable	Normalized importance [%]
Availability_365	100,0
Number_of_reviews_ltm	38,1
Minimum_nights	34,7
Room_type	29,3
Z_URB	0,1

Although the results obtained indicate that the urbanistic zone variable is not a determining factor in the variation of lodging prices, it is important to consider these findings in a relative manner. The analysis carried out was of a general nature, so it cannot be ruled out that, when examining the distribution of urban areas within each municipality individually, different results may be obtained in which this variable have a significant impact. In this sense, future research will study each municipality in more detail, allowing for a more detailed evaluation of the influence of urban zones on the determination of lodging prices. This first analysis is therefore a starting point for more specific studies.

Prices in the *Centro Storico* neighborhood are significantly higher than in all other neighborhoods, as shown in Fig. 3. This difference, both in average price and in the availability of property listings, is reflected in the fact that *Centro Storico* is the only neighborhood above the average, while the other fourteen neighborhoods remain below that level in the third quarter of 2024. These price differences are evident across all types of available accommodations, both in terms of averages and data dispersion, with a high number of outliers observed particularly in the cases of "entire home/apartment" and "private room" listings.

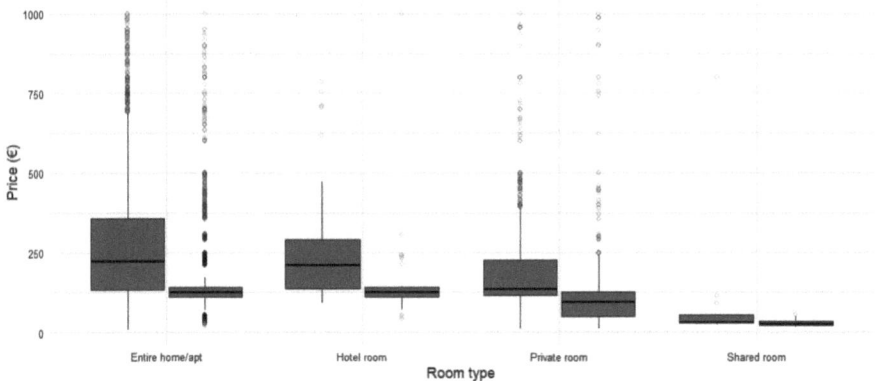

Fig. 3. Boxplot diagram showing the price distribution for each type of listing, with the city center of Rome segmented on the left and the remaining neighborhoods on the right.

The next notable aspect concerns reviews associated with listings. Table 5 shows the average price as the number of reviews increases, considering values of 0 (no reviews), 1, 2, 10, and the case labeled 100*, which represents the average for listings with 90 to 109 reviews, due to the lower number of individual data points available to calculate a reliable mean. A general decrease in prices is observed as the number of reviews increases, with the lowest average prices corresponding to the highest number of available reviews. For "entire home/apartment" listings, average prices decrease by between 45% and 57% when comparing listings with no reviews to those with around 100 reviews. These reductions are even greater for "private room" listings, ranging from 51% to 65%. A similar trend is observed for "hotel room" and "shared room" types, with proportionally larger reductions when the initial prices are lower. This pattern is exemplified in the third quarter of 2024, during which the price differences between listings with 0 reviews and those with approximately 100 reviews show a decrease of 50% for "entire home/apartment," 57% for "hotel room," 51% for "private room," and 77% for "shared room". In the analysis, segmentation by room type is necessary due to the different configurations of the supply. The use of aggregated data leads to an increased weight of lower-priced offerings, such as shared-use rooms, resulting in average data showing a larger decrease than what is actually observed for each room type.

Finally, the analysis of property concentration yields representative results for the city of Rome, both in terms of specific points in time for each quarter and in the temporal evolution of the data. From a point-in-time perspective, there is a notable level of concentration in the supply, where the 33,833 listings are distributed among 18,445 user accounts, resulting in an average of 1.83 listings per account. The user with the highest

Table 5. Evolution of rental prices according to the number of reviews over the past year on the Airbnb platform. *Source*: Own elaboration.

		Number of Reviews				
		0	1	2	10	100*
Entire Home/Apartment	2023 Q4	261	236	194	179	112
	2024 Q1	275	214	200	186	135
	2024 Q2	299	259	223	190	163
	2024 Q3	338	241	224	215	170
Hotel Room	2023 Q4	268	165	149	89	
	2024 Q1	213	178	135	114	
	2024 Q2	244	194	176	119	
	2024 Q3	246	239	240	107	
Private room	2023 Q4	203	132	113	82	71
	2024 Q1	192	127	117	110	77
	2024 Q2	200	155	144	95	91
	2024 Q3	197	146	147	124	97
Shared Room	2023 Q4	125	42	40	29	
	2024 Q1	75	35	85	43	
	2024 Q2	106	53	49	30	
	2024 Q3	112	43	64	26	

number of properties — 302 in the third quarter of 2024 — accounts for 0.89% of the total Airbnb supply in Rome for that quarter. The top 10 users by number of properties, with a combined total of 1032, represent 3.05%, while the top 100 users control 3455 listings, accounting for 10.21%. From a temporal perspective, there has been an increase in concentration over the last four quarters. For example, the share of listings held by the top 10 accounts increased from 2.86% to 3.05%, while the share held by the top 100 accounts rose from 9.46% to 10.21%, indicating a trend toward greater concentration. In this regard, not only is there a continued growth of accounts managing multiple properties throughout the period, but also the emergence of new accounts that, within two to three quarters, go from managing zero properties to managing between 10 and 32.

Figure 4 shows the existence of accounts with a large number of housing units, which, however, are widely distributed without a noticeable high concentration in specific areas. The historical center of Rome — delimited by the Vatican to the west, *Termini* railway station to the east, *Villa Borghese* to the north, and the neighborhoods of *Trastevere* and *Testaccio* to the south — concentrates the supply of these hosts.

Fig. 4. Spatial representation of the dwellings managed by the five most representative host_id accounts.

4 Discussion and Conclusions

The study's primary objective of elucidating the key spatial-logistic attributes of the short-term rental market in Rome is corroborated by results that align with existing literature, encompassing aspects such as supply, room type, year-round availability, minimum stay requirements, user ratings, and property concentration. This analysis indicates a substantial majority of housing supply in the city's historic centre, where prices are markedly elevated compared to other neighbourhoods. The price of accommodation is directly correlated with the property's availability and inversely correlated with the number of reviews. However, no relationship has been observed between accommodation prices and the number of properties owned by a given *host_id*.

The minimum number of nights booked influences the prices in the last quarter of the year it can be observed that only 0.1% of the accommodations represent long term rentals, accommodations with fewer reviews have an higher average price. Properties with full availability during the year and which are complete flats tend to have higher prices.

For the first quarter of the year, the municipality where the accommodation is located starts to be decisive, Municipality I concentrates the highest prices of the accommodation offered with average prices of 224.76, with Municipality X joining this municipality. Likewise, accommodation in the in the historic center with less than 0.5 in number of reviews in the last year has prices of 345.55 higher than the average of the Municipalities I, X. High availability (365 days) correlates with higher prices, accommodation with fewer reviews has a higher average price. Properties with full availability throughout the year and which are complete flats tend to have higher prices.

The accommodations with the lowest average prices in Municipality I and X, are those with reviews above 0.5 and the whole flats stand out with a higher average price than the other room types.

In the second quarter, the Municipality I *Centro Storico* of the city of Rome concentrates the highest prices of the accommodations offered with average prices of 260. Likewise, the accommodations in the historic center with less than 0.5 in number of reviews in the last year have prices of 377 higher than the average of Municipality I. The minimum number of nights influences prices in the last quarter of the year, with accommodation with fewer reviews having a higher average price. Properties with full availability in the year and which are full flats tend to have higher prices.

The accommodations with the lowest average prices in Municipality I are those with reviews above 0.5 and the whole flats stand out with a higher average price than the other types of room type. Node 2, which concentrates accommodation outside the *Centro Storico*, shows that accommodation with 1.5 or more reviews in the last year has lower prices than those with fewer reviews in the last year. It can also be observed that the type of accommodation influences the average price, being higher for whole flats than for other types of accommodation, so that the availability and type of accommodation make the difference in the deep branches.

In the quarter 2024Q3, the Municipality I corresponding to the *Centro Storico* entre of the city of Rome concentrates the highest prices of the accommodations offered with average prices of 260. Also, the accommodations of the *Centro Storico* with less than 0.5 in number of reviews in the last year have prices of 377 higher than the average of the Municipality I.

The results open up future lines of research with potential impact both temporally and spatially. Extending the temporal horizon of the analysis would allow for the observation of long-term trends in this type of housing supply and could also enable comparisons in relation to regulatory changes affecting the sector. On the spatial side, further developing the analysis at the level of urban zones may provide greater depth to the study [20–23]. Another promising line of inquiry lies in comparing the results obtained for Rome with those of other cities, at the Italian, European, and international levels.

Disclosure of Interests. The authors have no competing interests to declare that are relevant to the content of this article.

Attribution of the parts of the text is the result of the joint work of all authors and will be attributed equally.

References

1. Quattrone, G., Proserpio, D., Quercia, D., Capra, L., Musolesi, M.: Who benefits from the sharing economy of Airbnb? In: WWW 2016: Proceedings of the 25th International Conference on World Wide Web, pp. 1385–1394. ACM, New York (2016)
2. Eurostat: Short-stay accommodation offered via online collaborative economy platforms – monthly data. https://ec.europa.eu/eurostat/statistics-explained/index.php?title=Short-stay_accommodation_offered_via_online_collaborative_economy_platforms_-_monthly_data. Accessed 30 Mar 2025

3. Guttentag, D., Smith, S., Potwarka, L., Havitz, M.: Why tourists choose Airbnb: a motivation-based segmentation study. J. Travel Res. **57**(3), 342–359 (2018). https://doi.org/10.1177/0047287517696980
4. Eurostat: Short-stay accommodation offered via online collaborative economy platforms. https://ec.europa.eu/eurostat/statistics-explained/index.php?title=Short-stay_accommodation_offered_via_online_collaborative_economy_platforms. Accessed 30 Mar 2025
5. Barron, K., Kung, E., Proserpio, D.: The Effect of Home-Sharing on House Prices and Rents: Evidence from Airbnb. https://ssrn.com/abstract=3006832
6. Giannoni, S., Brunstein, D., Guéniot, F., Jouve, J.: Multichannel distribution strategy of Airbnb hosts. Ann. Tour. Res. Empir. Insights. **2**(1), 100017 (2021). https://doi.org/10.1016/j.annale.2021.100017
7. Airbnb: About Us. https://news.airbnb.com/about-us/. Accessed 28 Mar 2025
8. Zervas, G., Proserpio, D., Byers, J.W.: The rise of the sharing economy: estimating the impact of Airbnb on the hotel industry. J. Market. Res. **54**(5), 687–705 (2017). https://doi.org/10.1509/jmr.15.0204
9. Wachsmuth, D., Weisler, A.: Airbnb and the rent gap: gentrification through the sharing economy. Environ. Plan. A. **50**(6), 1147–1170 (2018). https://doi.org/10.1177/0308518X18778038
10. Yoong, K., Woltering, R.-O., Heo, C.Y.: Revisiting Airbnb's disruption of hotels: Uneven impacts across markets, segments, and accommodation types. Int. J. Hosp. Manag. **126**, 104073 (2025). https://doi.org/10.1016/j.ijhm.2024.104073
11. Yang, Y., Mao, Z.: Welcome to my home! an empirical analysis of Airbnb supply in US cities. J. Travel Res. **58**(8), 1274–1287 (2019). https://doi.org/10.1177/0047287518815984
12. Chen, D., Bi, J.-W.: Cue congruence effects of attribute performance and hosts' service quality attributes on room sales on peer-to-peer accommodation platforms. IJCHM. **34**(10), 3634–3654 (2022). https://doi.org/10.1108/IJCHM-10-2021-1275
13. Wang, H., Liang, C., Zhu, Y., Zhou, M.: Congruence in communication and customer booking decision: a cognitive heuristic perspective. Int. J. Bus. Commun. **61**, 703–721 (2024). https://doi.org/10.1177/23294884231157561
14. Zhang, L., Ma, Y., Mahmood, R., Pan, X.: Balancing consistency and incongruence: Influences on consumer booking intentions in the sharing economy. Tour. Manag. **109**, 105134 (2025). https://doi.org/10.1016/j.tourman.2025.105134
15. Chen, D., Zhang, W., Bi, J.-W., Qiu, H., Lyu, J.: Hosts' online affinities and their impacts on the number of online reviews on peer-to-peer platforms. Tour. Manag. **100**, 104817 (2024). https://doi.org/10.1016/j.tourman.2023.104817
16. Filieri, R., Raguseo, E., Vitari, C.: Extremely negative ratings and online consumer review helpfulness: the moderating role of product quality signals. J. Travel Res. **60**, 699–717 (2021). https://doi.org/10.1177/0047287520916785
17. Briel, D., Dolnicar, S.: The evolution of Airbnb regulation – An international longitudinal investigation 2008–2020. Ann. Tour. Res. **87**(15), 102983 (2021)
18. Morales-Alonso, G., Núñez, Y.M.: Dragging on multilisting: the reason why home-sharing platforms make long-term rental prices increase and how to fix it. Technol. Forecast. Soc. Chang. **174**, 121297 (2022). https://doi.org/10.1016/j.techfore.2021.121297
19. de la Cal, S., Alejandro: Análisis del Proceso de Capitalización del Sector Inmobiliario Español. Tesis (Doctoral), E.T.S. de Edificación (UPM) (2024). https://doi.org/10.20868/UPM.thesis.81421
20. Guarini, M.R., Ghiani, G., Sica, F., Tajani, F.: Which minimum indicator set of sustainability may be utilized in urban assessments? Meta-evidence gained through a systematic literature review. Sustainability. **17**, 3221 (2025). https://doi.org/10.3390/su17073322

21. Tajani, F., Sica, F., De Paola, P., Morano, P.: A networking-economic model to enhance the cultural value in small towns. In: Smart and Sustainable Built Environment (2024). https://doi.org/10.1108/SASBE-08-2023-0233
22. Sica, F., De Paola, P., Tajani, F., Doko, E.: Spatial–temporal ontology of indicators for urban landscapes. Land. **14**(1), 72 (2025). https://doi.org/10.3390/land14010072
23. Guarini, M.R., Roma, A., Sabatelli, E., Segura-de-la-Cal, A.: Intrinsic and extrinsic attributes in real estate pricing: Insights for sustainable urban planning strategies. Land Use Policy. **153**, 107543 (2025). https://doi.org/10.1016/j.landusepol.2025.107543

Quantifying the Loss of Property Value Due to Energy Inefficiency: A Stranded Asset Risk Assessment in the Real Estate Sector

Daniela Tavano(✉) and Francesca Salvo

Department of Environmental Engineering, University of Calabria, Via Pietro Bucci, Cubo 46b, 87036 Rende, Italy
daniela.tavano@unical.it

Abstract. This study examines the economic implications of energy inefficiency in the real estate sector, focusing on the risk of asset stranding resulting from evolving regulatory and market conditions. Considering the European Union's Directive (EU) 2024/1275 and increasing market preferences for energy-efficient buildings, properties with substandard energy performance face growing devaluation risks. This study presents a quantitative framework for assessing the loss of property value resulting from energy inefficiency. The model incorporates three key dimensions: market devaluation, excess operational costs, and CO_2 emission-related penalties. Through market analysis and financial discounting techniques, this framework evaluates the cumulative financial impact of energy underperformance over a defined time horizon. The results indicate that inefficient buildings are becoming increasingly vulnerable to economic obsolescence, particularly as energy prices increase and carbon pricing mechanisms are implemented. These findings underscore the urgency of energy retrofit interventions to mitigate financial losses and preserve asset value. This study contributes to the ongoing climate-aligned real estate investment discourse and provides a decision-support tool for property owners, investors, and policymakers.

Keywords: Energy Inefficiency · Stranded Assets · Real Estate Valuation · Hedonic Pricing Model · Carbon Pricing

1 Introduction

The real estate sector is crucial in addressing climate change, accounting for over one-third of the global greenhouse gas emissions. This industry is under mounting pressure to decarbonize, making climate change a strategic priority. According to research from the Carbon Risk Real Estate Monitor and the Global Real Estate Sustainability Benchmark, buildings are responsible for 37% of the global carbon emissions [1]. However, only 15% of global real estate assets are aligned with the 1.5 °C target outlined in the Paris Agreement [2]. These findings underscore the urgent need for more ambitious and comprehensive decarbonization across the entire sector.

At the European level, approximately 75% of buildings are classified as energy-inefficient [3]. In Italy, the situation is particularly severe: approximately 60% of residential buildings, representing over 12 million structures and more than 31 million housing units, were built before 1976, when energy efficiency regulations were either minimal or non-existent [4, 5]. Furthermore, more than 70.4% of these buildings fall into the lowest energy performance categories ("E," "F," and "G"), while only 11% exceed class "B" (i.e., "A1" to "A4"), highlighting a pressing need for modernization to meet contemporary energy efficiency standards.

Regulatory frameworks are key drivers of the shift toward a more sustainable built environment. In this context, the European Union formally adopted the "Green Homes" Directive (EPBD – Energy Performance of Buildings Directive), officially titled Directive (EU) 2024/1275 and published in the Official Journal of the European Union on May 8, 2024 [6]. This legislation is a cornerstone of the EU's "Fit for 55" climate package, aiming to fully decarbonize the building stock by 2050 [6]. This directive focuses on large-scale renovations and significant improvements in building energy performance.

Key measures mandated by the directive for Italy and other EU member states include:

- **New private buildings**: From 2030 onward, all new private buildings must satisfy zero-emission standards. Public buildings must comply with this requirement by 2028 [7].
- **Residential buildings**: An average reduction of 16% in energy consumption is required by 2030, with a target of 20–22% by 2035 [7].
- **Non-residential buildings**: These must reduce energy consumption by 16% by 2030 and by 26% by 2033 [7].

By implementing these measures, the EU aims to align the real estate sector with the climate objectives of the Paris Agreement and the European Green Deal, fostering a transition to a more energy-efficient future [7].

Despite its ambitious targets, the EPBD does not impose direct penalties on property owners who fail to comply with prescribed timelines. There are also no explicit bans on selling or renting properties that do not meet these standards. However, this regulatory leniency does not shield noncompliant buildings from market dynamics. Stricter efficiency standards have already led to a decline in market interest for properties that do not meet new benchmarks. These assets are becoming increasingly unattractive to buyers and tenants, many of whom prioritize sustainable buildings with lower operating costs.

Several events, such as the COVID-19 pandemic, the war in Ukraine, and the rise in energy costs, made people pay more attention to the energy performance of their property. At the same time, the exponential growth in the sustainability theme and the growing interest in the environmental, social, and governance (ESG) criteria have resulted in a greater appreciation for properties that comply with these new standards. As a direct consequence, all the buildings inappropriate in terms of energy efficiency could face the risk of economic obsolescence. These properties, in fact, are characterized by high operating costs and, for this reason, are becoming less attractive for supply and demand; this aspect risks fuelling the so-called "stranded assets". A stranded asset refers to an investment that prematurely loses value owing to shifts in the market, regulations, or environmental conditions.

Several factors contribute to the stranded asset risk in real estate:

- **Regulatory pressure**: As energy performance standards tighten, noncompliant buildings risk becoming unmarketable and losing value.
- **Shifting market preferences**: Tenants and buyers are increasingly favoring certified green properties and marginalizing less efficient ones.
- **Financial implications**: Properties with poor energy performance may face challenges in securing financing, especially as financial institutions adopt stricter ESG investment criteria [8–12].
- **Climate-related risks**: Buildings dependent on fossil fuels are more vulnerable to devaluation, especially when considering transitional and physical risks related to climate change, such as floods, wildfires, and landslides [13].
- **Technological advancement**: The falling costs of clean technologies such as solar panels and heat pumps further diminish the appeal of inefficient buildings.

The financial impact of stranded assets can be significant to property owners, lenders, and institutional investors. Transitioning to zero-emission buildings may necessitate substantial investment in retrofitting and alternative heating systems. Without a clear and well-managed transition strategy, institutions may face asset write-downs and financial losses associated with such properties.

2 Aim

This study aims to develop a quantitative model to measure the loss of property value caused by energy inefficiency, with a particular focus on stranded asset risks. The proposed model integrates three key dimensions: market devaluation owing to poor energy performance, excess operational costs compared to energy-efficient buildings, and penalties related to CO_2 emissions. By analyzing the real estate market and applying financial discounting techniques, this study seeks to provide a decision-support tool for property owners, investors, and policymakers. The goal consists of providing a tool for assessing the urgency and cost-effectiveness of energy retrofit interventions, thus contributing to the transition toward a more sustainable and resilient building stock.

3 Literature Review

3.1 The Relationship Between Energy Performance and Value of a Property

The theme of the relationship between energy performance and property value is gaining increasing importance in real estate sector research. The increasing interest in climate change effects and building energy efficiency has led many homeowners, investors, and policymakers to gain a better insight into the impact of energy performance on property value. Many studies have shown that energy efficiency is a parameter that can positively affect the property value; this has reflected on a higher demand for energy-efficient buildings in different markets [14–17]. For instance, studies conducted in Sweden and Italy highlighted that properties having a better energy efficiency level tend to get higher prices [15, 18].

The energy performance of a building can be certified through a document known as the "Energy Performance Certificate" (EPC). Based on this document, in possession of any property for sale, potential buyers or tenants can compare the energy performance of buildings displayed on the market. The role of the EPCs is to promote energy saving in the residential sector and, at the same time, to provide a means to improve the environmental performance of the residential buildings sector [19]. There are conflicting views as to whether or not EPCs have an impact on property values. Still, it is indeed demonstrated that they can change households' attitudes towards environmental performance [19].

Hedonic pricing models have been used several times to explore how energy performance affects property values. They examine the influence of the different characteristics of a property on its price, among which is also energy efficiency [20, 21]. By analyzing sales data together with property characteristics, these models are able to determine how EPCs influence the value of residential properties [17, 22]. In essence, they help to quantify the percentage change in property values related to energy performance [17]. It's also important to note that a property's location and the trends in the local market can play a significant role in shaping the connection between energy performance and property value. Booker found that the local market's response to sustainability is the missing link between environmental performance and property value [23]. This means that the value placed on energy performance may vary depending on regional factors and market conditions [23]. The architectural, typological, and physical-technical attributes of a building can also affect how energy performance influences property prices. Barreca et al. (2021) found that the joint effect of building energy performance and the above attributes is poorly studied [24]. This study explored how energy performance and various features affect property prices through spatial analyses conducted on a sample of housing properties from Turin's real estate market, along with several subsamples [24]. Numerous studies have identified a positive correlation between energy efficiency and property values. Davis et al. (2015) used a hedonic pricing specification to find a small but positive relationship between improved energy performance and higher selling prices in the Belfast housing market [17]. A study conducted by Duarte and Chen showed that, in a short period, the energy premium for multi-family dwellings in the metropolitan area of Barcelona showed a positive trend [25]. This result suggests that buyers are willing to pay more for energy-efficient homes, as this effect translates into potential energy savings and environmental benefits associated with these properties.

3.2 Stranded Asset Risk and Energy Inefficiency in Real Estate

The idea of stranded assets, which represent assets that have undergone sudden or premature write-downs or depreciations or that have become liabilities [26], is now highly significant, as the trend towards a low-carbon economy continues [27]. This risk arises when properties lose their economic viability due to various factors, such as climate change policies and changing market preferences, and, as a result, goods have difficulty producing economic returns due to changes in environmental conditions and societal expectations [28].

The concept of stranded assets is crucial for understanding the long-term economic viability of real estate investment. Leskinen et al. (2020) highlight that property values fully reflect environmental performance properties and motivate mainstream investors to adopt sustainable features [26]. This means that, as environmental awareness grows and regulations become tighter, the value of energy-inefficient properties may decline significantly, resulting in financial losses for owners and investors.

Several factors contribute to the increasing risk of real estate assets becoming stranded because of energy inefficiency.

Intensifying Minimum Energy Efficiency Standards (MEES): Governments worldwide are enforcing stricter energy efficiency regulations for buildings. Booker emphasized that commercial structures with low Energy Performance Certificate (EPC) ratings could be considered unsustainable, lose value, and fall into obsolescence, especially following the UK's Minimum Energy Efficiency Standards (MEES) enacted in April 2018 [23].

Growing Environmental Awareness: Increasing public awareness of climate change and building environmental impact drives the demand for energy-efficient properties. Waters and Elder's research has shown that investment in eco-friendly innovation can be fully justified, as house purchasers have demonstrated a willingness to pay as much as $15,000 for energy-efficient homes [19].

Technological Advancements: The rapid advancement of energy-efficient technology has made older, inefficient buildings obsolete. Current research focuses on new investments and innovative opportunities for enhancing energy efficiency in building stocks, aiming to quickly realize widespread zero-energy building (ZEB) standards [29].

Energy Price Volatility: Variations in energy prices can significantly influence building operating expenses, rendering energy-inefficient properties less appealing to both tenants and buyers. According to Fekete and Baranyai (2024), energy performance certificates substantially affect a property's perceived market value [30].

3.3 Cost and Carbon Pricing Impact on Real Estate Depreciation

Depreciation, regarding real estate, denotes the slow decrease in a property's value as time passes, influenced by factors such as physical wear and tear, functional obsolescence, and external economic conditions. Energy inefficiency is becoming an increasingly significant depreciation driver, particularly as operating costs rise and regulations become more stringent. The rise of carbon pricing mechanisms amplifies this trend, making properties with high carbon footprints less appealing to investors and tenants. There are several reasons why real estate assets might lose value, and energy inefficiency is a significant concern.

Physical Deterioration: the value of the property tends to decrease over time due to the aging of materials and normal wear, especially in cases where maintenance has been poor.

Functional Obsolescence: the property tends to become less attractive for potential buyers or future tenants, due to outdated systems or presence of non-modern services.

Economic Obsolescence: property values can be reduced due to several external factors, such as changes in market conditions and growing environmental concerns.

Energy Inefficiency: buildings tend to lose value when the carbon emissions related to energy consumption are too high, due to high energy consumption and limited use of renewable energy (excessive dependence on fossil sources).

Carbon Pricing Mechanisms: different carbon taxes (or even cap-and-trade systems) tend to increase operating costs for energy-intensive buildings, resulting in faster depreciation.

The net operating income of a property is strongly influenced by high energy costs (necessary to heat, cool, and illuminate the house). As a result, buildings that are energy inefficient and therefore subject to higher costs become less attractive for buyers and lessors. It is therefore obvious that the depreciation of real estate is strongly influenced by the continuous increases in energy prices, which, together with energy inefficiency, generate a significant increase in operating costs associated with the property itself. On this basis, action to upgrade existing buildings with energy-efficient technologies is very useful in order to reduce depreciation risks and increase the value of real estate [31]. In addition to the economic aspect, the energy upgrading of a building contributes to reducing carbon dioxide emissions, as Mecca et al. (2020) note that the real estate sector is responsible for approximately 39% of global energy-related CO_2 emissions [32]. These enhancements can decrease energy usage, cut operational expenses, and enhance the appeal of a property to both tenants and buyers.

4 Quantifying "Stranded Asset" Risk Due to Energy Inefficiency

4.1 Framework Overview

This study presents a quantitative framework for formally evaluating the financial impact of energy inefficiency in the real estate sector. It measures the potential loss of inefficient buildings across a defined timeline and under specific market and regulatory conditions. This method incorporates three components.

- **Market Devaluation:** Captures the expected reduction in asset value resulting from energy performance noncompliance [33–36].
- **Excess Operational Costs:** These represent the present value of additional utility expenses incurred by inefficient properties compared with benchmark buildings.
- **CO_2 Emission Costs**: Measures the discounted cost of excess carbon emissions under assumed carbon pricing schemes.

The mathematical formulation is as follows:

$$R_{SA} = \left(V_{benchmark} - V_{actually}\right) + \sum_{t=1}^{T} \frac{\Delta C_{Op}}{(1+r_{Op})^t} + \sum_{t=1}^{T} \frac{\Delta C_{Em}}{(1+r_{Em})^t} \quad (1)$$

where R_{SA} refers to the expected monetary loss resulting from the market and regulatory disadvantage of energy-inefficient buildings, expressed as a deterministic estimate in euros, rather than a probabilistic risk measure; $V_{benchmark}$ is the market value of an energy-efficient benchmark property; $V_{actually}$ is the current market value of the inefficient building; ΔC_{Op} is the annual operational cost differential (benchmark vs. inefficient building); ΔC_{Em} is the annual emission cost differential (benchmark vs. inefficient building); T is the time horizon for cost savings evaluation; r_{Op} is the discount rate applied to operational cost differentials (ΔC_{Op}), representing the financial time preference of private actors (property owners, investors) (it reflects standard financial discounting practices, incorporating opportunity cost of capital, inflation, and risk premiums associated with energy prices); r_{Em} is the discount rate applied to CO_2 emission differentials (ΔC_{Em}), representing a societal discount rate consistent with climate policy evaluations. This rate captures the ethical imperative to account for long-term, intergenerational impacts of carbon emissions.

In this study, the benchmark served as the reference condition against which the market value, operational costs, and CO_2 emissions of inefficient buildings were compared. The benchmark value, together with its associated operational and environmental parameters, is scenario dependent and reflects regulatory, market, and technological trajectories. To ensure methodological robustness and policy relevance, the benchmark can be defined in alignment with the recast Energy Performance of Buildings Directive (EPBD) (Directive EU 2024/1275), which sets targets for decarbonizing the European building stock [37].

4.2 Data Sources and Variables

The calculation of each component relies on three distinct data layers, which are examined individually in the following paragraphs:

Market Valuation Data

The first component of the "Stranded Asset" Risk refers to the market devaluation associated with the energy inefficiency of a building. Properties with lower energy performance tend to experience a progressive decline in market value over time compared with more energy-efficient buildings. This phenomenon is particularly relevant in a context where the demand for low-emission and energy-efficient buildings is growing rapidly, pushing both investors and buyers to prefer assets with superior energy performance.

The following expression captures this market depreciation:

$$\Delta V = V_{benchmark} - V_{actually} \qquad (2)$$

where $V_{benchmark}$ represents the market value of the energy-efficient benchmark. This value can be estimated through market analysis or comparative methods, using data with similar properties and better energy ratings. $V_{actually}$ is the current market value of the inefficient buildings.

The difference between these two values quantifies the value loss attributable exclusively to the building's substandard energy performance, assuming that all other physical and locational attributes are constant.

Operational Cost Differential

The operational cost differential measures the annual economic burden resulting from an inefficient building's excess energy consumption compared with that of an energy-efficient benchmark building. This term is computed as the difference between the actual and benchmark annual utility bills using data contained in the Certificate of Energy Performance (abbreviated as "APE" in Italy). Specifically, the following fields are relevant (Table 1).

Table 1. "APE" Field relevant to quantify "Stranded Asset" Risk.

Description	Usage in the Model
Total primary non-renewable energy demand, in kWh/m²/year (EPgl,nren)	Multiply by surface area and unit energy cost to estimate
Fuel type used (e.g., gas, electricity)	Determines the unit energy price (€/kWh)
Heated floor area of the building	Used to scale the energy performance index to total consumption
Official energy class (e.g., F, G)	Identifies current and benchmark classes

The operational cost differential is quantified in the following way:

$$\Delta C_{Op} = \Delta Ec \bullet P_{en} = \left(Ec_{actually} - Ec_{benchmark}\right) \bullet P_{en} \quad (3)$$

with:

$$Ec_{actually} = EPgl, nren_{actually} \bullet Area_{heat} \quad (4)$$

$$Ec_{benchmark} = EPgl, nren_{benchmark} \bullet Area_{heat} \quad (5)$$

where $Ec_{actually}$ is the energy consumption of the inefficient building, $Ec_{benchmark}$ is the energy consumption of an energy-efficient benchmark property $EPgl, nren_{actually}$ is the total primary non-renewable energy demand of the inefficient building, $EPgl, nren_{benchmark}$ is the total primary non-renewable energy demand of an energy-efficient benchmark property, $Area_{heat}$ is the heated floor area of the building, P_{en} is the energy price.

CO_2 Emissions and Carbon Pricing

The emission data were calculated based on the energy mix used in the building (e.g., natural gas and electricity) and standard emission factors (in kg CO_2 per kWh). The annual emission gap ΔEm is monetized through current or projected carbon prices from regulatory frameworks (e.g., the EU ETS and voluntary carbon markets):

$$\Delta C_{Em} = \Delta Em \bullet P_{CO_2} = \left(Em_{actually} - Em_{benchmark}\right) \bullet P_{CO_2} \quad (6)$$

where $Em_{actually}$ is the annual emission value of the inefficient building, $Em_{benchmark}$ is the annual emission value of an energy-efficient benchmark property, P_{CO_2} is the carbon price.

5 Discussion and Conclusion

The findings of this study indicate that energy inefficiency represents a real economic threat to the real estate sector, resulting in the gradual devaluation of buildings that do not perform well in terms of energy efficiency. The interplay between decreased market value, increased operational expenses, and stricter carbon pricing policies significantly undermines the appeal of inefficient buildings, making them less desirable for buyers and investors. During a rapid energy transition, remaining in lower-energy classes imposes greater financial pressure on property owners and increases the likelihood that these buildings will become stranded assets—properties that lose value irreversibly due to their failure to meet evolving regulatory and market requirements.

The analysis has shown that, on the one hand, direct market devaluation reflects the increasing demand for high-performance buildings. However, rising operational expenses and environmental penalties associated with carbon taxation systems make managing low-performance properties progressively more burdensome. Moreover, the evolving European regulatory framework, which gradually enforces compliance with stricter energy-efficiency standards, further accelerates the depreciation trend for buildings that fail to implement timely retrofit interventions.

To truly make a difference, adopting risk-mitigation strategies through energy retrofitting is essential. Not only does upgrading buildings support environmental sustainability, but it also significantly contributes to preserving and boosting real estate value. Property owners should look closely at the opportunity to invest in energy-efficient solutions, understanding that the financial benefits from reduced operational costs and improved market appeal far outweigh the initial investment in upgrades. Similarly, investors and financial institutions should incorporate energy-related depreciation risk into their valuation models, considering energy efficiency as a crucial factor in real estate risk management. Integrating market devaluation, operational cost differentials, and CO_2 emission penalties into a unified valuation framework demonstrates the multifaceted nature of the risks posed by energy underperformance. The proposed model provides a replicable and data-driven approach for quantifying this risk, enabling stakeholders to anticipate value erosion and make informed decisions.

It is essential to clarify that the model proposed in this study does not refer to costs associated with energy retrofit because its purpose is not to assess the financial feasibility of interventions, but rather to quantify the economic risk of maintaining energy inefficient buildings in their current state. The estimated loss can be interpreted as the financial exposure property owners would face without timely energy upgrades. While the financial sustainability of retrofit interventions is certainly relevant for private actors, this dimension does not fall within the scope of this research. Future study developments could incorporate investment costs for retrofitting and public incentive schemes to assess the potential trade-off between avoided losses and upfront expenses. In addition, future research could enhance the model's applicability by including dynamic policy scenarios, regional market differences, and behavioral factors that influence investor and consumer responses to energy efficiency.

Simultaneously, public policy is crucial in supporting the real estate sector's transition toward more sustainable standards. Tax incentives, subsidies for retrofitting, and clear, stable regulations are indispensable tools to guide the market through this transformation, thereby minimizing the risk of economic loss and promoting the development of a resilient building stock that aligns with the decarbonization goals.

References

1. Bösche, J.: A concept for measuring real estate sustainability from the investors' perspective. VJH. **90**, 19–42 (2021). https://doi.org/10.3790/vjh.90.4.19
2. Global Warming of 1.5 °C —
3. Rapporto Annuale Efficienza Energetica 2023, ENEA (2023)
4. *Norme per il contenimento del consumo energetico per usi termici negli edifici.* 373 (1976)
5. Morano, P., Tajani, F., Di Liddo, F., Guarnaccia, C.: The value of the energy retrofit in the Italian housing market: two case-studies compared. WSEAS Trans. Bus. Econ. **15**, 249–258 (2018)
6. Versolmann, I.: The Development of Energy Policy in the European Union: Continuity, Critical Junctures and Change. Routledge/UACES contemporary European studies; Routledge, Abingdon, Oxon; New York, NY (2025)
7. Piaia, E., Turillazzi, B., Di Giulio, R., Sebastian, R.: Advancing the decarbonization of the construction sector: lifecycle quality and performance assurance of nearly zero-energy buildings. Sustainability. **16**, 3687 (2024). https://doi.org/10.3390/su16093687
8. Aich, S., Thakur, A., Nanda, D., Tripathy, S., Kim, H.-C.: Factors affecting ESG towards impact on investment: a structural approach. Sustainability. **13**, 10868 (2021). https://doi.org/10.3390/su131910868
9. Cadamuro Morgante, F., Gholamzadehmir, M., Sdino, L., Rosasco, P.: How to invest in the "Market of Sustainability": evaluating the impacts of a real estate investment across ESG criteria [Investire Nel "Mercato Sostenibile": Valutare Gli Impatti Di Un Investimento Immobiliare Attraverso i Criteri ESG]. Valori e Valutazioni. **33**, 65–84 (2023). https://doi.org/10.48264/VVSIEV-20233306
10. McCabe, J. ESG and Real Estate 2023
11. Nanda, A.: ESG in real estate investment: issues for the future. In: Brears, R.C. (ed.) The Palgrave Encyclopedia of Urban and Regional Futures, pp. 513–517. Springer International Publishing, Cham (2022) ISBN 978-3-030-87744-6
12. Robinson, S., McIntosh, M.G.: A literature review of environmental, social, and governance (ESG) in commercial real estate. J. Real Estate Lit. **30**, 54–67 (2022). https://doi.org/10.1080/09277544.2022.2106639
13. Del Giudice, V., Salvo, F., De Paola, P., Del Giudice, F.P., Tavano, D.: Ex-ante flooding damages' monetary valuation model for productive and environmental resources. Water. **16**, 665 (2024). https://doi.org/10.3390/w16050665
14. Popescu, D., Bienert, S., Schützenhofer, C., Boazu, R.: Impact of energy efficiency measures on the economic value of buildings. Appl. Energy. **89**, 454–463 (2012). https://doi.org/10.1016/j.apenergy.2011.08.015
15. Cerin, P., Hassel, L.G., Semenova, N.: Energy performance and housing prices: does higher dwelling energy performance contribute to price premiums? Sustain. Dev. **22**, 404–419 (2014). https://doi.org/10.1002/sd.1566
16. Chegut, A., Eichholtz, P., Holtermans, R., Palacios, J.: Energy efficiency information and valuation practices in rental housing. J. Real Estate Finance Econ. **60**, 181–204 (2020). https://doi.org/10.1007/s11146-019-09720-0
17. Davis, P.T., McCord, J.A., McCord, M., Haran, M.: Modelling the effect of energy performance certificate rating on property value in the Belfast Housing Market. Int. J. Hous. Mark. Anal. **8**, 292–317 (2015). https://doi.org/10.1108/IJHMA-09-2014-0035
18. Micelli, E., Giliberto, G., Righetto, E., Tafuri, G.: Urban disparities in energy performance premium prices: towards an unjust transition? Land. **13**, 224 (2024). https://doi.org/10.3390/land13020224

19. Waters, M., Elder, B.: Green values and the UK residential market: the impact of energy performance certificates on property value. In: Proceedings of the Proceedings of the 14th Annual European Real Estate Society Conference—London, UK. ERES, London, UK (27 June 2007)
20. De Ruggiero, M., Salvo, F., Tavano, D., Zinno, R.: When green turns into value. In: Abastante, F., Bottero, M., D'Alpaos, C., Ingaramo, L., Oppio, A., Rosato, P., Salvo, F. (eds.) Urban Regeneration Through Valuation Systems for Innovation, pp. 279–289. Green Energy and Technology; Springer International Publishing, Cham (2022) ISBN 978-3-031-12813-4
21. De Ruggiero, M., Manganelli, B., Marchianò, S., Salvo, F., Tavano, D.: Comparative and evaluative economic analysis of ground mounted photovoltaic plants. In: Mondini, G., Oppio, A., Stanghellini, S., Bottero, M., Abastante, F. (eds.) Values and Functions for Future Cities, pp. 181–199. Green Energy and Technology; Springer International Publishing, Cham (2020) ISBN 978-3-030-23784-4
22. Davis, P., McCord, M.J., McCluskey, W., Montgomery, E., Haran, M., McCord, J.: Is energy performance too taxing?: A CAMA approach to modelling residential energy in housing in Northern Ireland. J. Eur. Real Estate Res. **10**, 124–148 (2017). https://doi.org/10.1108/JERER-06-2016-0023
23. Booker, Y.: Assessing the impact of the intensifying UK minimum energy efficiency standards (MEES) on regional office rental values. Int. J. Urban Sci. **24**, 152–172 (2020). https://doi.org/10.1080/12265934.2019.1651669
24. Barreca, A., Fregonara, E., Rolando, D.: EPC labels and building features: spatial implications over housing prices. Sustainability. **13**, 2838 (2021). https://doi.org/10.3390/su13052838
25. Marmolejo-Duarte, C., Chen, A.: The evolution of energy efficiency impact on housing prices. An analysis for metropolitan Barcelona. Rev. Constr. **18**, 156–166 (2019). https://doi.org/10.7764/RDLC.18.1.156
26. Leskinen, N., Vimpari, J., Junnila, S.: A review of the impact of green building certification on the cash flows and values of commercial properties. Sustainability. **12**, 2729 (2020). https://doi.org/10.3390/su12072729
27. Campiglio, E., Van Der Ploeg, F.: Macrofinancial risks of the transition to a low-carbon economy. Rev. Environ. Econ. Policy. **16**, 173–195 (2022). https://doi.org/10.1086/721016
28. Muldoon-Smith, K., Greenhalgh, P.: Suspect foundations: developing an understanding of climate-related stranded assets in the global real estate sector. Energy Res. Soc. Sci. **54**, 60–67 (2019). https://doi.org/10.1016/j.erss.2019.03.013
29. Ruggeri, A.G., Gabrielli, L., Scarpa, M., Marella, G.: What is the impact of the energy class on market value assessments of residential buildings? An analysis throughout Northern Italy based on extensive data mining and artificial intelligence. Buildings. **13**, 2994 (2023). https://doi.org/10.3390/buildings13122994
30. Fekete, D.E., Baranyai, E.: Impact of the 2022 energy crisis on the importance of energy performance certificates for the real estate market. Financ. Econ. Rev. **23**, 106–134 (2024). https://doi.org/10.33893/FER.23.1.106
31. Sica, F., Tajani, F., Cerullo, G.: An evaluation model for an optimal decarbonisation process in the built environment. Built Environ. Proj. Asset Manag. **15**, 51–66 (2025). https://doi.org/10.1108/BEPAM-05-2024-0126
32. Mecca, U., Moglia, G., Piantanida, P., Prizzon, F., Rebaudengo, M., Vottari, A.: How energy retrofit maintenance affects residential buildings market value? Sustainability. **12**, 5213 (2020). https://doi.org/10.3390/su12125213
33. Salvo, F., Romita, T., De Ruggiero, M., Tavano, D.: Residential tourism and real estate appraisal: Turismo Residenziale e Valutazione Immobiliare. Valori e Valutazioni. **25**, 53–58 (2020)

34. Salvo, F., De Ruggiero, M., Tavano, D.: Social variables and real estate values: the case study of the city of Cosenza. In: Napoli, G., Mondini, G., Oppio, A., Rosato, P., Barbaro, S. (eds.) Values, Cities and Migrations, pp. 173–186. Green Energy and Technology; Springer International Publishing, Cham (2023) ISBN 978-3-031-16925-0
35. Benvenuti, A., Salvo, F., Tavano, D.: The mortgage lending value (MLV): proposal for a new calculation procedure. Aestimum. **83**, 21–31 (2024). https://doi.org/10.36253/aestim-14725
36. Salvo, F., Dell'Ovo, M., Tavano, D., Sdino, L.: Valuation approaches to assess the cultural heritage. In: Bevilacqua, C., Calabrò, F., Della Spina, L. (eds.) New Metropolitan Perspectives. Smart Innovation, Systems and Technologies, vol. 178, pp. 1746–1754. Springer International Publishing, Cham (2021) ISBN 978-3-030-48278-7
37. Koengkan, M., Silva, N., Fuinhas, J.A.: Assessing energy performance certificates for buildings: a fuzzy set qualitative comparative analysis (fsQCA) of Portuguese municipalities. Energies. **16**, 3240 (2023). https://doi.org/10.3390/en16073240

Rationalizing Evaluation Legal Models for Affordable Home Ownership and Leasehold Interests in Italy

Marco Locurcio[1](✉) ⓘ, Pierluigi Morano[1] ⓘ, Paola Amoruso[2] ⓘ, Felicia Di Liddo[1] ⓘ, and Francesco Tajani[3] ⓘ

[1] Department of Civil, Environmental, Land, Building Engineering and Chemistry (DICATECh), Polytechnic University of Bari, Bari 70126, Italy
marco.locurcio@poliba.it

[2] Department of Engineering, LUM "Giuseppe Degennaro" University, Bari, Casamassima 70010, Italy

[3] Department of Architecture and Design, "Sapienza" University of Rome, Rome 00196, Italy

Abstract. With reference to the issue of the evaluation of the purchase prices for leasehold properties, in Italy the transfer of properties built as part of regulated housing initiatives is restricted by a series of constraints, the removal of which entails a set of fees to be borne by the housing lessees. This study, starting from an analysis of similar tools applied in other European territorial contexts, provides a methodological approach for estimating these fees while simultaneously considering the framework established by the current regulations, the trends in the residential market, and the inflation dynamics.

Keywords: Social housing · real estate · surface right

1 Introduction

Economic public housing, also known as public or social housing, is a key element in the housing policies of many European countries. This sector aims to provide affordable housing for low- and middle-income groups, thereby contributing to social cohesion and citizens' well-being. The size and the management of public housing vary significantly among European countries. On average, about one-fifth of European households reside in social housing. However, the percentage of social housing within the total stock markedly differs from country to country. For instance, in Italy, public residential housing accounts for approximately 3.5% of the total housing stock, with about 900,000 units managed by public entities and municipalities [1]. Generally, the public housing sector in Europe faces several challenges, including funding shortages, maintenance and management issues, and a growing demand that surpasses the available supply. These problems have been exacerbated by public housing divestment policies initiated in the 1990s, by leading to a steady decrease in available housing.

To address these challenges, the European Union and individual Member States are implementing various strategies. The European Commission, for instance, recognizes the housing as a fundamental infrastructure for urban economic growth and citizens' wellbeing, promoting policies and funding aimed at supporting social and affordable housing [2]. For instance, the affordable housing initiative guides the New European Bauhaus (NEB), which is a policy and funding initiative that makes green transition in built environments enjoyable, attractive and convenient. The core values of the New European Bauhaus are represented by sustainability, aesthetics and inclusiveness, combining the social paradigm with the ecological transition [3].

Analyzing in more detail the interpretation and management of social housing at a European level, there are three common elements across EU Member States in defining social housing: *i) Mission*: considered to be of general interest; *ii) Objective*: to increase supply of affordable housing by constructing, managing or purchasing social housing; *iii) Target:* target groups are defined in terms of socio-economic status or the presence of vulnerabilities. Beyond the aforementioned similarities, there is no common official definition for the term "social housing" across Europe, and not all EU Member States even use this term as exemplified: in Austria the terms either "Limited-Profit Housing" or "People's Housing" are used; in Denmark either "Common Housing" or "Not-for-Profit Housing" are implied; in France "Housing at Moderate Rent"; in Germany "Housing Promotion"; in Spain "Protected Housing"; in Sweden "Public Utility Housing" [4–6].

Beyond semantic differences, social housing policies in Europe vary significantly across the countries, in terms of the diversity of the strategies reflecting different historical, economic, and social approaches. This heterogeneity of policies, together with the peculiarities of the specific context, leads to huge differences in the amounts of social housing built in each country.

2 Aim

With reference to the Italian context, this study aims to explore the transformation of the surface right - obtained as leasehold property - into full ownership for housing units built in Public Economic and Social Housing Plan (PEEP) areas, by comparing the market dynamics with the conventional evaluation principles applied according with the legal appraisal. Specifically, the regulations allowing this transformation introduce a series of coefficients (hereinafter defined as $\alpha = 0.6$ and $\beta = 0.5$), without providing any explanation of how they are determined.

This study seeks to offer a guideline for determining these coefficients through a compensatory approach [7] that takes into account the evolution of the property market, the financial investment trends, and the inflation index variations. The objective of the proposed approach is to neutralize the initial advantages granted to leaseholders of housing units built in PEEP areas, by considering the evolution of the property market and the broader economy from the date of the housing assignment (i.e. starting date of the leasehold) to the date of transformation of the surface right into full ownership. The proposed approach aims to achieve greater equity in the determination of these coefficients, by incorporating the specificities of the local contexts in which interventions are carried out.

The work is organized as follows. In Sect. 3 an overview of affordable housing regulations in the European and Italian context is framed. In Sect. 4 the method for the appropriate evaluation of the coefficients to be applied in the legal formula for the transformation of the surface right in full ownership is illustrated. In Sect. 5 the conclusions of the work are drawn.

3 Economic and Social Housing in Italy: History and Main Tools

From the outlined framework, it emerges that social housing develops across Europe according to heterogeneous models that reflect different national contexts, although common factors persist. In the Italian context, social housing has its roots in the early twentieth century, when the State and housing cooperatives began constructing dwellings for the working class. During the Fascist period (1922–1943), popular neighborhoods were built to improve the housing conditions of the lower-income population. After World War II, Italy faced a housing crisis due to accelerated urbanization and post-war reconstruction, which led to a significant increase in housing demand. Due to the scarcity of affordable housing, the Italian government developed housing policies aimed at constructing homes for low-income social groups. Specifically, Law No. 167 of April 18, 1962 (amended and integrated by Laws No. 904 of July 21, 1965, and No. 865 of October 22, 1971) introduced the establishment of the Economic and Popular Housing Plans (PEEP) [8–10]. These plans regulated the zoning of areas designated for the construction of affordable or public housing, as well as related infrastructure and social services, including green spaces. For the first time the law made expropriation for public utility useable for these areas, establishing a monetary compensation lower than the market value, set at the areas' value on the market two years before the adoption of the PEEP plan. The intention was to allow municipalities, IACP (Public Housing Institutes), and social housing developers—who could be allocated the buildable land—to purchase more central areas at a relatively low cost and equip them with all the necessary social services, which had to be included in the same zoning plan.

In the following years, Article 35 of Law No. 865 of October 22, 1971, regulated the allocation of these areas, providing for two distinct regimes: full ownership transfer, which permanently transferred the land to private individuals, and surface rights, which allowed beneficiaries (leaseholders) to construct and own the buildings while the public entity retained the ownership of the land for a period ranging from 60 to 99 years [9]. In Italy, the surface right remains one of the most widely used legal tools in urban planning and public housing projects.

Within economic and popular housing, land granted under surface rights is generally assigned by the Municipality to specific cooperatives or construction companies for a fixed period (60 to 99 years) [10]. These companies and cooperatives, after constructing the buildings, transfer the leasehold right of the housing units at subsidized prices to individuals who satisfy specific income requirements.

Articles 952–956 of the Italian Civil Code regulate the surface right, defined as a legal institution allowing an individual (the "*superficiary*") to build, maintain, and use a structure on land owned by another entity (the "*landowner*") [11]. This legal tool creates a clear distinction between *the grantor*, who owns the land, and *the grantee*, who holds the surface rights. The grantee does not own the land but is permitted to use superficial property for economic purposes.

The surface right can be established through: *i)* contract, either for consideration or free of charge. If for consideration, payment can be made in a lump sum or through periodic installments, such as an annual concession fee; *ii)* will (testamentary disposition); *iii)* adverse possession (usucapion), upon recognized legal requirements.

In the following years, Article 31 of Law No. 448 of December 23, 1998, introduced the possibility for municipalities to transfer full ownership of land included in PEEP areas that had been previously granted under surface rights [12]. The transformation of surface rights into full ownership allows housing assignees to purchase the land on which their housing units are built.

This process takes place following a proposal from the municipality and the acceptance of individual housing assignees, in exchange for payment determined according to the Law No. 448/1998 and formalized through a public deed [12]. The amount to be paid is calculated based on a conventional method established by Law No. 448/1998 [12]. However, this valuation process does not always adequately reflect the actual market conditions of the specific area, which can lead to significant disparities in treatment depending on the context in which the land is located. Moreover, while the aspects related to the specificities of the surface right from a legal perspective and its transfer have been extensively addressed [13], the purely evaluative aspects have been less explored [14, 15], probably because they fall within the scope of the "legal" appraisal [16].

4 Method

The development of affordable and public housing in Italy, supported by the legislative framework established by the PEEP law, essentially provided that the municipal administration would expropriate land from private owners and transfer it to cooperatives, which were responsible for the actual construction of the housing units. These units were subsequently assigned to beneficiaries (often cooperative members), individuals with specific income and asset requirements that made access to the free housing market more difficult.

The land designated for the development of affordable and public housing was allocated by the municipality to concessionaires, with 60% granted under a surface right (meaning the municipality retained ownership of the land) and the remaining 40% transferred as full ownership.

This distinction led to different restrictions on the housing units, particularly regarding their sales. For both types of housing, there were time-based restrictions on the transfer of the corresponding property rights (especially if potential buyers did not satisfy certain income or asset criteria) and a prohibition on selling above the maximum allowable price. In addition to these restrictions, housing units with the surface right were subject to an additional constraint: according to the agreements between the municipality and the leaseholders, upon expiration of the concession period (typically 99 years), the surface right would be extinguished, and the landowner - the municipality - would become the owner of the building. Alternatively, there was an option to renew the leasehold for a maximum of another 99 years, subject to the payment of a fee.

Over the years, the legislator has introduced a series of regulations aimed at facilitating the removal of the restriction related to the maximum sale price, allowing housing units to be bought and sold at market prices, as well as the transformation of the surface right into full ownership. Given the advantages originally granted to the initial leaseholders, the legislator has established monetary amounts that those wishing to remove these restrictions must pay to the administration for their elimination.

The current regulatory framework, specifically Law No. 448 of December 23, 1998 – Public Finance Measures for Stabilization and Development (as amended by Law No. 108/2021 and Decree-Law No. 21/2022) [17], states that the transformation of the surface right into full ownership occurs upon payment of a fee ($C_{c.48}$) determined through Eq. (1):

$$C_{c.48} = (60\% \cdot MV_{area} - C_o) \tag{1}$$

where

- MV_{area} is the market value of the asset, that is, the market value of the buildable land at the date of the transfer agreement;
- C_o are the charges for granting the surface right, revalued based on the variation in the consumer price index for blue- and white-collar households (ISTAT-FOI), as determined by the Italian National Institute of Statistics (ISTAT) [18], occurring between the month in which these charges were paid and the month in which the land transfer agreement is executed.

The removal of the restriction on the maximum sale price, as defined by Decree No. 151 of September 28, 2020 – Regulation on the removal of price constraints affecting properties built under the regulated housing scheme [19], establishes that the fee for the removal of maximum sale price restrictions (CRV) is determined through Eq. (2):

$$CRV = C_{c.48} \cdot Q_M \cdot 0.5 \frac{(ADC - ATC)}{ADC} \tag{2}$$

where

- Q_M is the millesimal share of the property unit;
- ADC is the number of years of the duration of the agreement;
- ATC is the number of years, or fraction thereof, that have passed from the agreement until the maximum duration of the agreement.

In the case of an agreement concerning the transfer of the surface right with a duration between 60 and 99 years, Eq. (2) becomes:

$$CRVs = CRV \cdot 0.5$$

In this study, the rationale behind these fees and the coefficients is questioned, in relation to the evolution of the property market and the trend of inflation.

The amount of fees paid by leaseholders to the municipal administration should be equal to the expropriation compensation paid to the original property owners, i.e. an amount that, over the last 50 years, has undergone significant changes due to numerous appeals and rulings by the Court of Cassation [20]. Currently, the compensation is equal to the market value of the expropriated buildable area, potentially reduced by 25% when the expropriation is aimed at implementing socio-economic reform interventions [21]. This amount should be distributed based on the percentages of the surface right and full ownership, as well as the market value differences between the housing units.

The market value of a property with the surface right, in the absence of specific legal provisions which were not present at the time this right was established, is equal to the initial accumulation of constant, deferred, and limited annual amounts, corresponding to the rental fees. Similarly, the market value of a property with full ownership, determined through the income capitalization method, is equal to the ratio between the annual amounts and the capitalization rate (Eq. (3)):

$$\Delta MV = \frac{MV_{SUP,M} - MV_{PRO,M}}{MV_{PRO,M}} = \left(a\frac{q^n - 1}{q^n r} - \frac{a}{r}\right)\frac{r}{a} = r\frac{q^n - 1}{q^n r} - 1 \quad (3)$$

where:

- $MV_{SUP,M}$ is the market value of the property with the surface right at the date of signing the concession;
- $MV_{PRO,M}$ is the market value of the property with full ownership at the date of signing the concession;
- a is the annual rent;
- r is the interest rate equal to the capitalization rate;
- $q = 1 + r$ is the unit amount;
- $n = ADC - ATC$ is the remaining duration of the concession.

In the absence of data related to the different charges paid by owners of the property/surface right, the proposed approach assumes that the difference in value is established according to the logic borrowed from financial mathematics. Therefore, given the charges O paid by the leaseholder to the municipality (function of the expropriation compensation), hypothesizing that the difference in charges borne by the leasehold and by the landlord is on the basis of the difference in value and considering the different percentage distribution of the areas, Eq. (4) can be obtained:

$$\begin{cases} 60\% \cdot O_{SUP} + 40\% \cdot O_{PRO} = O \\ \frac{O_{SUP} - O_{PRO}}{O_{PRO}} = \Delta MV \end{cases} \quad (4)$$

in which:

- O_{SUP} are the charges borne by the leaseholder;
- O_{PRO} are the charges borne by the landlord.

From the second formula of Eq.(4):

$$O_{SUP} - O_{PRO} = O_{PRO} \cdot \Delta MV \Rightarrow O_{SUP} = O_{PRO} \cdot (1 + \Delta MV)$$

which replaced in the first one in Eq. (4) allows to obtain O_{PRO}:

$$60\% \cdot O_{PRO} \cdot (1 + \Delta MV) + 40\% \cdot O_{PRO} = O \Rightarrow O_{PRO} = \frac{O}{1 + 60\% \cdot \Delta MV}$$

Valid if $1 + 60\% \cdot \Delta MV \neq 0$.

Consequently, O_{SUP} is equal to Eq. (5):

$$O_{SUP} = \frac{O}{1 + 60\% \Delta MV} \cdot (1 + \Delta MV) \tag{5}$$

According to the current regulatory provisions, the market value of full-owned housing units is, therefore, equal to the difference between the market value of similar properties (MV) and the fee for the removal of the maximum transfer price constraints, whereas for those with surface rights, the consideration for the transformation of the institution into full ownership right should also be deducted from the previous formula, i.e.:

$$MV_{PRO} = MV - CRV$$

$$MV_{SUP} = MV - CRVs - C_{c.48}$$

In the outlined framework, the question arises as to whether, in light of the ISTAT-FOI index [18] trend and the property market, the approach given by the law is fair and does not penalise or facilitate the assignees of housing with surface rights compared to those of housing in full ownership and to the residential real estate market dynamics.

Starting from average data provided by Scenari Immobiliari [22], the graph in Fig. 1 hypothesizes, with reference to the saleable gross surface unit of the accommodation and through a series of assumptions useful for determining the introduced parameters, the trend in nominal values for the entire duration of the concession, of the market value (MV), of the average value of properties transferred in ownership (MV_{PRO}), of the value of accommodations with surface rights calculated according to market logic ($MV_{SUP, M}$) and according to the current legislation (MV_{SUP}).

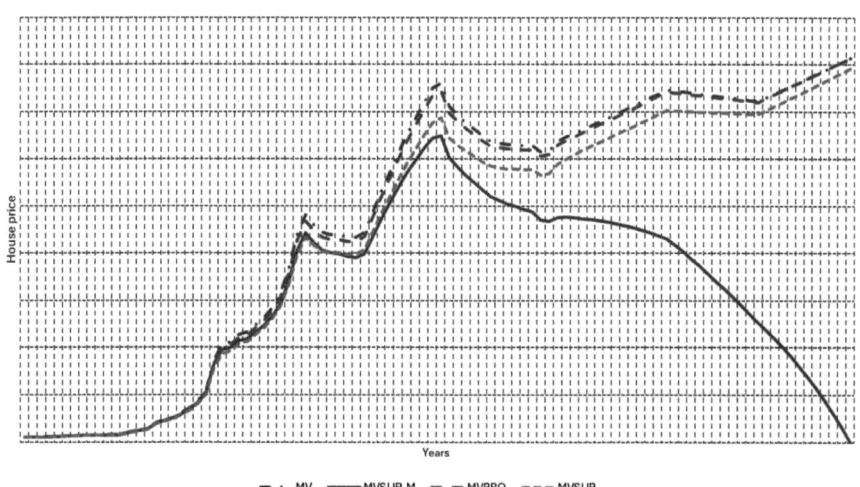

Fig. 1. Hypotheses about the trend of MV, MV_{PRO}, $MV_{SUP, M}$ and MV_{SUP}.

In Fig. 1 the hypotheses about the trend of MV, MV_{PRO}, $MV_{SUP, M}$ e MV_{SUP} are reported.

The prevailing behavior, in line with expectations, is:

$$MV > MV_{PRO} > MV_{SUP} > MV_{SUP,M}$$

Over time MV_{PRO} tends to MV up to be equal at the end of the $(ADC = ATC)$, since:

$$MV_{PRO} = MV - CRV = MV - C_{c.48} \cdot Q_M \cdot 0.5 \cdot \frac{(ADC - ATC)}{ADC} = MV - C_{c.48} \cdot Q_M \cdot 0.5 \cdot \frac{(ADC - ADC)}{ADC} = MV$$

The trend of MV_{SUP} is negatively influenced by the growth of real estate market values and positively by the increase in the ISTAT-FOI index [18] and the passing of the years, whereas $MV_{SUP, M}$ will be equal to 0 at the end of the concession.

Returning to the defined question, the limitations imposed on the transfer of properties were generated by the benefits recognized to the assignees deriving from a subsidized price paid for the areas.

Three alternative scenarios are assumed: *i)* purchase of the property at the market value; *ii)* assignment of the housing in ownership with the benefits and consequent limits recognized in the cases of the social and affordable housing and following investment of the "saved" amount in a "safe" investment (e.g. postal savings certificates, government bonds, etc.) at a compound interest rate i and *iii)* assignment of the housing in surface right and following investment as the previous case *(ii)*.

The fees introduced by the current regulations (CRV, $CRVs$ e $C_{c.\,48}$) which remove the initial advantage for the assignees should be identified.

Therefore:

$$\begin{cases} (MV_{area,0} - O_{PRO})(1+i)^n = CRV \\ (MV_{area,0} - O_{SUP})(1+i)^n = CRVs + C_{c.48} \end{cases} \quad (6)$$

The two terms on the left in Eq. (6) represent the monetary relief recognized to the assignees (in full ownership and with surface rights) with respect to market values, whereas, the two terms on the right in Eq. (6) constitute the relative fees as defined by the law.

Rewriting the fees of the law referred to the property unit of saleable gross surface and generalizing the introduced coefficients, the following relationships are obtained:

$$C_{c.48} = (\alpha \cdot MV_{area} - C_o)$$

$$CRV = \beta \cdot C_{c.48} \frac{(ADC - ATC)}{ADC}$$

$$CRVs = \beta \cdot CRV$$

Replacing the first equation into the second one and the second into the third:

$$CRV = \beta(\alpha \cdot MV_{area} - C_o)\frac{(ADC - ATC)}{ADC}$$

$$CRVs = \beta^2(\alpha \cdot MV_{area} - C_o)\frac{(ADC - ATC)}{ADC}$$

$$\begin{cases} (MV_{area,0} - O_{PRO})(1+i)^n = \beta(\alpha \cdot MV_{area} - C_o)\frac{(ADC-ATC)}{ADC} \\ (MV_{area,0} - O_{SUP})(1+i)^n = (\alpha \cdot MV_{area} - C_o)\left[\beta^2\frac{(ADC-ATC)}{ADC} + 1\right] \end{cases}$$

For greater representation easiness:

$$(1+i) = p$$

$$\frac{(ADC-ATC)}{ADC} = A$$

Therefore, the previous system becomes Eq. (7):

$$\begin{cases} (MV_{area,0} - O_{PRO})p^n = \beta(\alpha \cdot MV_{area} - C_o)A \\ (MV_{area,0} - O_{SUP})p^n = (\alpha \cdot MV_{area} - C_o)(\beta^2 \cdot A + 1) \end{cases} \quad (7)$$

Thus, an auxiliary variable is defined:

$$X = (\alpha \cdot MV_{area,0} - C_o)$$

and Eq. (7) can be rewritten according to Eq. (8):

$$\begin{cases} (MV_{area,0} - O_{PRO})p^n = \beta \cdot X \cdot A \\ (MV_{area,0} - O_{SUP})p^n = X(\beta^2 \cdot A + 1) \end{cases} \quad (8)$$

From the first expression of Eq. (8), X is obtained:

$$X = \frac{(MV_{area,0} - O_{PRO})p^n}{\beta \cdot A}$$

This relationship can be replaced into the second expression of Eq. (8):

$$(MV_{area,0} - O_{SUP})p^n = \frac{(MV_{area,0} - O_{PRO})p^n}{\beta \cdot A}(\beta^2 \cdot A + 1)$$

By multiplying both equation members by $\beta \cdot A$:

$$(MV_{area,0} - O_{SUP})p^n \cdot \beta \cdot A = (MV_{area,0} - O_{PRO})p^n(\beta^2 \cdot A + 1)$$

Hence, the right-hand side of the equation can be developed:

$$(MV_{area,0} - O_{SUP})p^n \cdot \beta \cdot A = (MV_{area,0} - O_{PRO})p^n \cdot \beta^2 \cdot A + (MV_{area,0} - O_{PRO})p^n$$

After moving on the left side of the equation the right part of the formula, the division by $p^n \neq 0$ and by $A \neq 0$ can be carried out:

$$(MV_{area,0} - O_{PRO})\beta^2 - (MV_{area,0} - O_{SUP})\beta + \frac{(MV_{area,0} - O_{PRO})}{A} = 0$$

Thus, a quadratic equation in the form of $a \cdot \beta^2 + b \cdot \beta + c = 0$ is obtained, in which:

$$a = (MV_{area,0} - O_{PRO})$$

$$b = -(MV_{area,0} - O_{SUP})$$

$$c = \frac{(MV_{area,0} - O_{PRO})}{A}$$

Whose resolution is:

$$\beta_{1,2} = \frac{-b \pm \sqrt{b^2 - 4ac}}{2a}$$

After determining β, X and consequently α, can be determined:

$$X = \frac{(MV_{area,0} - O_{PRO})p^n}{\beta A}$$

$$X = (\alpha \cdot MV_{area,0} - C_o) \Longrightarrow \alpha = \frac{X + C_o}{MV_{area,0}}$$

In this way, consistently with the formal structure introduced by the current legislation concerning the elimination of the constraints related to the maximum transfer price and the transformation of the surface right into full ownership, the coefficients α and β that allow to remove the initial monetary advantage recognized to the assignees in light of the evolution of the residential property market and the trend of inflation, are determined.

5 Conclusions

The social and affordable housing interventions that have been implemented in Italy since the 1970s through the PEEP plans have imposed a series of limitations on the transfer of the housing units, in accordance with the concessions granted to the assignees of such properties [23]. The main restrictions concern the maximum selling price (so-called maximum transfer price) and the presence, for some of these housing, of the surface right of instead of the ownership one.

Over the years, the need to remove such constraints has arisen in order to allow the assignees to fully dispose of the housing and to be able to place it on the free market. The legislator has intervened on several occasions in determining the contributions aimed at deleting the aforementioned constraints, through a series of expressions that do not adequately consider the context in which the properties are located, i.e. the trend of the residential property market, and the overall trend of the purchasing power of the population, measured by the inflation.

In the present research, while maintaining the formal structure of the equations included in the current legislation for the removal of such constraints, a methodological approach that also considers the trend of the property market and the ISTAT-FOI index has been proposed. The developed approach aims to ensure a fair tool that at the same time: *i)* takes into account the local specificities of the context in which the properties are located; *ii)* considers the evolution of recorded inflation; *iii)* compensates for the advantage of the housing assignees compared to those who purchased at market prices. The approach assumes that, in light of economic developments, the initial conditions (in terms of income and assets) that had guaranteed the assignees access to affordable and social housing are no longer valid. Future developments of the present research could involve the inclusion of additional elements that also take into account the income of the assignees at the date of removal of the aforementioned constraints. Furthermore, by applying the proposed approach to a series of case studies related to different Italian cities, it would be possible to evaluate the size of the coefficients to be applied in the legal formula and propose an abacus valid on a national scale. In this way, the objective is to generate a coefficients map that highlights the local specificities, thereby eliminating potential inequities arising from the use of context-independent coefficients.

Acknowledgments. The research has been carried put within the PRIN research project entitled "Digitalized life-cycle management of historic bridges by an integrated monitoring and modelling CDE platform – HBridgeIM (Historic Bridge Information Modelling)" (Grant number 2022744YM9).

References

1. Housing Europe. The State of Housing in Europe 2023
2. European Commission. Affordable Housing Initiative. 2023
3. European Union: New European Bauhaus. https://new-european-bauhaus.europa.eu/about/about-initiative_en
4. European Parliament: Directorate General for Internal Policies. Social Housing in the European Union (2013)
5. European Economic and Social Committee: Social housing in the EU - decent, sustainable and affordable. In: 592th Plenary Session. Brussels, 4-5 Dec 2024
6. OECD Affordable Housing Database: PH4.2. Social Rental Housing Stock. Accessed 16 Apr 2024
7. Trembecka, A.: The benefit principle in determining compensation for real estate expropriation. Geomat. Environ. Eng. **17**(2), 89–104 (2023)
8. Law No. 167 of April 18, 1962. Italian Official Gazette No. 111, 30 April 1962
9. Law No. 904 of July 21, 1965. Italian Official Gazette No. 190, 31 July 1965
10. Law No. 865 of October 22, 1971. Italian Official Gazette No. 276, 30 Oct 1971
11. Italian Civil Code, Articles 952–956. Italian Official Gazette No. 7, 4 April 1942
12. Law No. 448 of December 23, 1998, Article 31. Italian Official Gazette No. 302, 29 Dec 1998
13. Magri, M., Scilhanick, E.: Diritto di superficie. CEDAM editore (2006)
14. Carbonara, S., Stefano, D.: The transformation of surface rights into property rights. A financial resource for rebalancing municipal budgets. The case of Pescara. In: Morano, P., Oppio, A., Rosato, P., Sdino, L., Tajani, F. (eds.) Appraisal and Valuation, pp. 91–101. Green Energy and Technology. Springer International Publishing, Cham (2021)
15. De Mare, G., Nestico', A.: Il diritto di superficie nelle trasformazioni urbane: profili estimativi (2010)
16. Patel, M.B., Patel, D.A.: Empirical analysis of real estate disputes. J. Leg. Aff. Disput. Resolut. Eng. Constr. **15**(11), 04522037–04522031 (2023)

17. Law No. 448 of December 23, 1998 – Public Finance Measures for Stabilization and Development. Italian Official Gazette No. 302, 29 Dec 1998
18. National Statistical Institute (ISTAT): https://www.istat.it/tag/foi/. Accessed 18 Mar 2025
19. Decree No. 151 of September 28, 2020 – Regulation on the removal of price constraints affecting properties built under the regulated housing scheme. Italian Official Gazette No. 280, 10 Nov 2020
20. Civil Court of Cassation, United Sections, Judgment No. 500 of July 22, 1999; Civil Court of Cassation, Section I, Judgment No. 148 of April 30, 1999; Civil Court of Cassation, Section I, Judgment No. 349 of October 24, 2007; Civil Court of Cassation, Section I, Judgment No. 348 of October 24, 2007; Civil Court of Cassation, Section I, Judgment No. 181 of 2008
21. Presidential Decree No. 327 of June 8, 2001 – Consolidated Text of Legislative and Regulatory Provisions on Expropriation for Public Utility. Italian Official Gazette No. 189, 16 Aug 2001
22. Scenari Immobiliari. https://www.scenari-immobiliari.it/. Accessed 15 Mar 2025
23. Tajani, F., Morano, P.: Concession and lease or sale? A model for the enhancement of public properties in disuse or underutilized. WSEAS Trans. Bus. Econ. **11**, 787–800 (2014)

A GIS-Based Spatial Evaluation Model for Planning Urban Regeneration Investments

Francesco Tajani[1], Francesco Sica[1], Pierfrancesco De Paola[2], Pierluigi Morano[3], and Giuseppe Cerullo[1](✉)

[1] Department of Architecture and Design, "Sapienza" University of Rome, 00196 Rome, Italy
giuseppe.cerullo@uniroma1.it
[2] Department of Industrial Engineering, University of Naples Federico II, 80125 Naples, Italy
[3] Department of Civil, Environmental, Land, Building Engineering and Chemistry (DICATECh), Polytechnic University of Bari, 70126 Bari, Italy

Abstract. In recent years, the attention towards the use of artificial intelligence techniques, applied across various sectors (from logistics to urban planning, from healthcare to real estate valuation), has highlighted two divergent aspects in the implementation of these tools: on one hand, the advantages that can arise from their intrinsic ability to process big data, in order to enhance efficiency, innovation, and precision, providing strategic benefits to those involved in decision-making processes; on the other hand, the issues related to the possibility of controlling the generated outputs, when it comes to managing and interpreting black boxes that are difficult to be verified. In the field of territorial intervention valuation, the use of "rapid" estimation models, easily replicable even by less experienced users, represents an added value in identifying the best design solutions, especially in public/private partnership operations, so as to define win-win paths for the involved parties. Borrowing from the economics the principles of the urban rent, a procedure for evaluating the temporal evolution of area incidence factors, applied to the city of Rome (Italy), has been proposed. The results, geo-referenced in a GIS environment, provides for an easy-to-consult graphical interface to identify urban areas to be prioritized. The integration of the proposed method with an elastic net regression analysis has allowed the identification of the socio-economic variables that have most influenced the appreciation/depreciation of territorial areas, serving as a useful support for investment decisions (both public and private) and for urban intervention planning choices.

Keywords: Urban rent · GIS · Valuation · Urban regeneration · elastic net regression · spatial analysis · temporal analysis

1 Introduction

At European level, the New Urban Agenda [1] and the Sustainable Development Goal (SDG) No. 11 consider the urbanization the main territorial development policy [2, 3], by recognizing a predominant role to regeneration initiatives able of pursuing the targets of sustainable and resilience development and to bridge the gap between the different zones of the cities in terms of social and urban quality. In line with the continuous social and productive changes that have been characterizing the cities' dynamicity, the importance assumed by regeneration within the urban governance justifies the cogence to develop effective tools for the preliminary assessment of territorial interventions and for their monitoring [4]. These tools are expected to be capable of supporting decision-making processes, by adequately taking into account the locational factors of the project site and the local community needs [5]. In the current context, the economic measures introduced by governments within the National Recovery and Resilience Plan require the elaboration of new operational guidelines at the territorial, urban and architectural scale for the urban requalification, in order to support the decision-making processes of the Public Administrations and to effectively manage the obtained funding [6]. Therefore, the definition of evaluation techniques through which the project solutions can be appropriately analyzed has become fundamental, in order to avoid the failure of the provided investments.

In recent years, the potential and the opportunities arising from the application of artificial intelligence techniques have been universally acknowledged: in all sectors — from logistics [7, 8] to urban planning [9], from healthcare [10] real estate appraisal [11] — the advantages that have been derived from the intrinsic capacity to process big data have been correlated with the possibility of raising the levels of efficiency, innovation, and precision, providing those involved in decision-making processes with strategic benefits [12, 13].

On the other hand, the issues related to the risk of losing control over the generated outputs remains open, as well as the perplexities related to the complexity of managing and interpreting black boxes that are difficult to be verified. In the context of evaluating territorial interventions, the development of "rapid" estimation models, i.e. clear, transparent and easily replicable even by less experienced users, undoubtedly represents an added value in identifying optimal design solutions, especially in public/private partnership operations [14, 15], in order to define *win-win* paths for the actors involved, enabling the monitoring of project progress, as well as its flexibility in adapting to the dynamics associated with changes in the needs and the demands of the local communities [16].

2 Aim

The research presents a twofold objective.

In primis, borrowing the economic prodromes of the urban rent principles [17–21], a procedure for assessing the temporal evolution of area incidence factors has been proposed, by employing this economic parameter as a *proxy* for the locational preferences of the community in a specific territorial context. The increase/decrease of this factor over time, represented in a GIS environment in order to provide a simple and quick-to-consult graphical interface, has allowed for the identification of urban areas that have experienced an appreciation over time and, simultaneously, those that have been affected by a reduction in market attractiveness.

The simplicity of calculating the area incidence factors will allow, through their updating in a GIS environment, to ensure transparency, clarity, and continuity in the analysis of changes in preferences within the considered urban context, thus enabling the rapid identification—also through feedback from the needs and the demands expressed by the local communities following surveys in the reference territory — of the areas requiring the most attention and monitoring.

Then, by integrating the georeferenced outputs with an appropriate econometric analysis, it has become possible to highlight the socio-economic variables that have most influenced the appreciation/depreciation of the urban areas examined. The final results from the integration of the two phases described — *i)* estimation of temporal area incidence factors and their georeferencing, *ii)* identification of the socio-economic variables most relevant to the evolution of the area incidence factors and, therefore, the locational appreciation of the community — provide a valuable support for decision-making in territorial investment, by assisting the stakeholders (both public and private) involved in the planning processes of urban regeneration interventions.

The research is structured as follows. Section 3 describes the developed method, constituted by the two steps i) and ii) described above. Section 4 illustrates the application of the method to the case study of the city of Rome (Italy): taking into account the temporal period between the years 2015 and 2023, the evolution of the annual values of the area incidence factors is outlined and represented in thematic maps in GIS environment; then, through the implementation of an elastic net regression, the most significant socio-economic variables on the area incidence factors (i.e. on the market appreciation of the local communities) are identified. Finally, in Sect. 5 the conclusions of the work are discussed.

3 Method

The developed method consists of two phases:

i). estimation of temporal area incidence factors and their georeferencing in a GIS environment;
ii). analysis of the socio-economic variables that influence the phenomena of evolution of the area incidence factors and, therefore, the locational appreciation of the community.

Phase i). With reference to the Italian territory, the determination of the area incidence factors is carried out at the "microzone" municipal level, replicating the methodology proposed by Guerrieri [22] and applied on the entire national territory by Tajani et al. [23]. According to the Italian Presidential Decree 138/1998 and ensuing the Regulation issued by the Economy and Finance Ministry, a "microzone" is defined as «a portion of the municipal territory […] that is homogeneous in terms of location, urban-style, historical-environmental, socioeconomic characteristics, as well as the endowment of urban services and infrastructures»: therefore, the "microzone" is a macro-area of the territorial municipality in which the locational factors (i.e. accessibility, presence of services, building characteristics, green areas, pedestrian zones, etc.) contribute to the market price formation in a uniform manner. For each microzone of the entire national territory, the Italian Revenue Agency determines and half-yearly updates and publishes the average market values (i.e. quotations) for each intended uses.

Assuming that, within a municipal territory, the minimum quotation for the residential intended use ($V_{m,min}$, expressed in €/m^2) which has been recorded among all the microzones contributing to forming the municipal area, represents the threshold amount at which it has become profitable to build new housing units (i.e., coinciding with the absolute rent, equal to the cost of production gross of a normal profit expected by an ordinary investor [24–26]), the differential rent generated in microzones with higher market quotations (V_m, measured in €/m^2) is an expression of the incidence of the area, i.e. its weight in the determination of the market value of the built property.

Therefore, for the *i-th* microzone of the *j-th* municipality under investigation, the area incidence factor ($INC_{(i,j)}$, measured in %) has been evaluated using Eq. (1):

$$INC_{(i,j)} = \frac{V_{m(i,j)} - V_{m,min(j)}}{V_{m(i,j)}} \qquad (1)$$

Once the *INC* coefficients have been determined for different time periods and represented in a GIS environment, it has become possible to analyse the temporal evolution of the appreciation/depreciation of the examined territorial areas, as well as to calculate and graph the differentials (ΔINC) in the value of the area incidence factors, in order to quickly identify the areas that have increased in value and those that, due to substantial depreciation, require the most attention.

Phase ii). Following the outputs obtained in phase i) and based on the available data within the urban context under analysis, an econometric analysis can be developed to identify the socio-economic variables that may have had the most significant impact on the changes in zonal preferences by local communities. The outputs of this analysis will be able to provide useful indications on the needs that, more than the others, have been perceived as cogent by the community that will be affected by possible investments on the territory, and therefore will allow to guarantee a support to the decision-makers in the planning processes of urban interventions.

4 Case Study

The developed method as been implemented for the microzones of the city of Rome. Since the analysis aims to elucidate the locational preferences of urban communities, for the calculation of the area incidence factors through Eq. (1) the published quotations for residential use have been taken into account, in order to detect the appreciation/depreciation due to the purchase choices of the subjects who, prevalently, buy for direct use (and therefore not for investment purposes). The time frame for analysing the evolution of the area incidence factors has been from 2015 to 2023. Overall, the analysed microzones — those for which quotations related to residential use are published — are 169. In order to provide a tool that can be easily and quickly consulted and interpreted, the outputs obtained from the application of Eq. (1) for each microzone and each year of the investigation have been georeferenced in a GIS environment (Figs. 1, 2, 3, 4, 5, 6, 7, 8 and 9), whereas Fig. 10 displays the map of the differentials of the area incidence factors between 2023 and 2015.

The results obtained have led to interesting considerations. While between 2015 and 2019, there has been a general increase in the area incidence factors within the municipal territory — characterized by an average value of approximately 45% in 2015, 47% in 2016, 52% in 2017, 53% in 2018 and 55% in 2019 —, between 2020 and 2021 the coefficients have experienced a decline — from 54% to 50% —, evidently caused by the effects of the COVID-19 pandemic. In the years 2022 and 2023, the area incidence factors have increased once again, although they have not reached the values recorded in the pre-pandemic years. Observing the graph in Fig. 10, which shows the differential of the coefficient values between 2023 and 2015, it has emerged that, while the historic centre of Rome has maintained its appreciation over the years, the peripheral areas, benefiting from *i)* the effects of smart working, *ii)* public municipal investment policies aimed at improving service quality in less central areas, and *iii)* the absence of the current overtourism phenomenon — which has led many potential buyers to prefer locations further from the historic city —, have mainly experienced a significant increase in the market attractiveness. At the same time, the graph in Fig. 10 allows for the identification of areas — all suburban ones — that require attention, where a significant reduction in the value of the area incidence factors has been observed, due to the lack of infrastructure and services and/or social issues.

In order to outline possible intervention strategies for the municipal territory based on the temporal-spatial outputs obtained, and by consulting the data available from the National Institute of Statistics (ISTAT) [27] and the Urbistat website [28], eleven socio-economic indicators (Table 1) have been identified for each of the 169 study microzones in the city of Rome, with reference to the year 2023. These indicators have been used as explanatory variables for the area incidence factor (*INC*) in the year 2023 through the implementation of a regression analysis.

Specifically, the variables are:

- disposable income per capita (R), which represents the ratio between the gross disposable income of consumer households and the total number of people residing in the reference area, expressed in euros;
- unemployment rate (U), defined as the ratio of the number of individuals seeking employment to the total labour force, expressed as a percentage;
- population density (D), expressed as the ratio between the number of people residing in a specific area and the surface area of that area, measured in inhabitants per square kilometers;
- presence of foreigners (F), referring to the population composed of individuals with non-Italian citizenship or stateless persons habitually residing in Italy, calculated as a percentage of the total population;
- housing maintenance expenses (M), representing the average annual amount allocated to the maintenance and improvement of private housing and residential buildings, expressed in euros per capita per year;
- ambulatory service expenses (A), representing the annual cost incurred for access to territorial ambulatory health services, expressed in euros per inhabitant per year;

- hospital service expenses (H), measuring the annual amount spent on hospital services, expressed in euros per inhabitant per year;
- transport service expenses (T), including costs for both public and private transportation, such as buses, trains, and other modes used for daily or specific journeys, expressed in euros per capita per year;
- leisure and cultural service expenses (C), which include expenditures for recreational, cultural, and entertainment activities, such as cinema, theatre, museums, and other cultural events, expressed in euros per capita per year;
- education expenses (E), relating to costs for education, such as tuition fees for schools and universities, educational materials, and other learning activities, expressed in euros per capita per year;
- social protection expenses (P), which include financial resources allocated to services such as unemployment benefits, pensions, support for individuals with disabilities, and other welfare programs, expressed in euros per capita per year.

In Table 2, the main descriptive statistics — mean value, minimum value, maximum value, and standard deviation — of the variables of the model to be defined have been reported, while in Table 3, the correlation matrix of the variables has been presented. Analyzing the Pearson indices in Table 3, a high positive correlation of the dependent variable (i.e. *INC*) with all considered explanatory variables is observed, except for the indicators unemployment rate (U), population density (D) and presence of foreigners (F): therefore, these three indicators can be excluded from the development of the regression model. Furthermore, it has been observed that the socio-economic variables are characterized by a significant correlation among themselves, a phenomenon that could lead to collinearity problems. In order to prevent overfitting in the analysis data, an elastic net regression [29, 30], has been implemented, optimized through a ten-fold cross-validation which has been aimed at minimizing prediction error while ensuring an appropriate balance between model complexity and generalizability. This approach has been employed to reduce the effect of each predictor in the model and, consequently, to stabilize the regression function, as it is particularly suitable for datasets affected by multicollinearity.

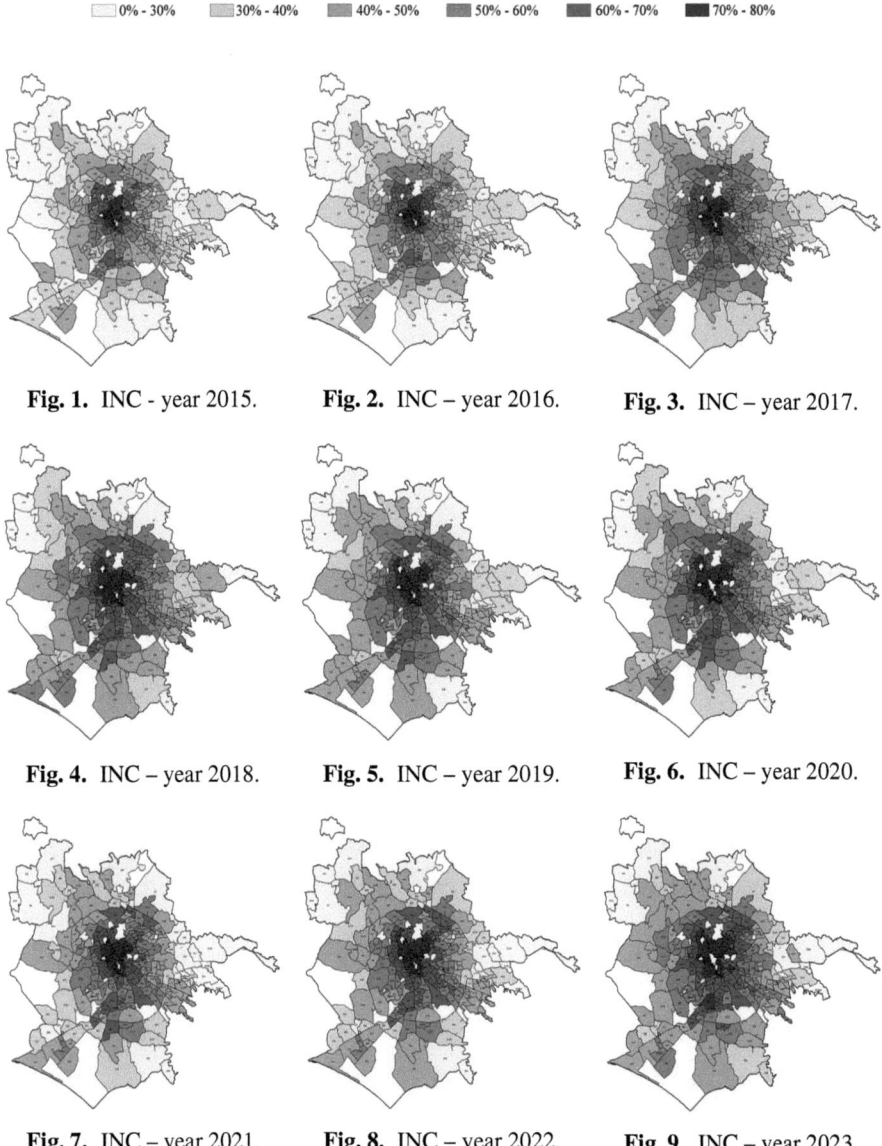

Fig. 1. INC - year 2015.   **Fig. 2.** INC – year 2016.   **Fig. 3.** INC – year 2017.

Fig. 4. INC – year 2018.   **Fig. 5.** INC – year 2019.   **Fig. 6.** INC – year 2020.

Fig. 7. INC – year 2021.   **Fig. 8.** INC – year 2022.   **Fig. 9.** INC – year 2023.

The output obtained is reported in Eq. (2), where the regression has identified the following relevant variables: the disposable income per capita (R), the leisure and cultural service expenses (C), the education expenses (E) and the social protection expenses (P).

$$INC = 24.857 + 0.000279 \cdot R + 0.007229 \cdot C + 0.023206 \cdot E + 0.136194 \cdot P \qquad (2)$$

The determination coefficient R^2 of the Eq. (2) is equal to 0.89, indicating a high statistical significance of the determined model. The function obtained thus shows that, based on the socio-economic indicators recorded, four variables have been identified as the most influential on the locational preferences of local communities. Among them, the decisive contribution has been provided by the social protection expenses (82.53%). The weights of the education expenses (12.78%) and the leisure and cultural service expenses (4.51%) are smaller, while the influence of the disposable income per capita on the area incidence factors is nearly negligible (0.17%).

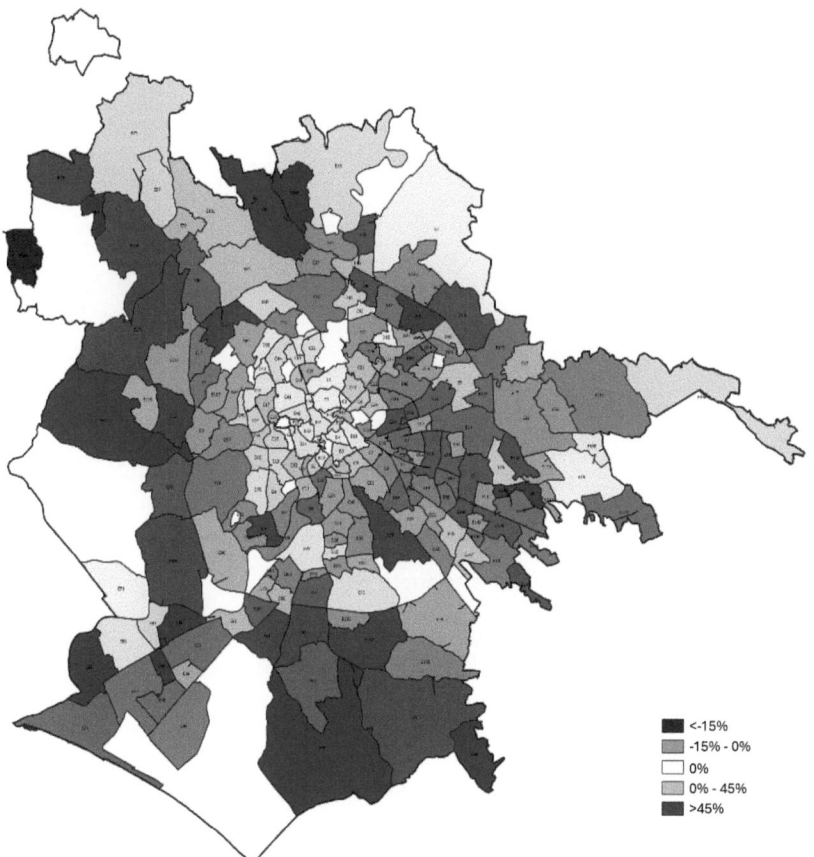

Fig. 10. ΔINC 2015–2023.

Table 1. Socio-economic variables for the regression analysis.

Variable	Acronym	Measurement unit
Disposable income per capita	R	€
Unemployment rate	U	% of the total population
Population density	D	inhabitants/km^2
Presence of foreigners	F	% of the total population
Housing maintenance expenses	M	€ per capita/year
Ambulatory service expenses	A	€ per capita/year

(*continued*)

Table 1. (*continued*)

Variable	Acronym	Measurement unit
Hospital service expenses	H	€ per capita/year
Transport service expenses	T	€ per capita/year
Leisure and cultural service expenses	C	€ per capita/year
Education expenses	E	€ per capita/year
Social protection expenses	P	€ per capita/year

Table 2. Descriptive statistics of the variables.

Variable	Average	Min.	Max	Stand. dev.
INC [%]	56.00	10.00	85.00	15.07
R [€]	25,241.00	9745.00	65,398.00	8849.29
U [%]	8.78	1.20	43.10	6.46
D [inh./km^2]	5843.00	1.50	97,037.00	8217.97
F [%]	13.55	2.70	35.70	6.72
M [€/year]	180.00	43.47	540.50	79.38
A [€/year]	397.00	195.00	924.00	115.90
H [€/year]	112.00	23.74	342.89	50.79
T [€/year]	340.53	168.60	787.00	98.15
C [€/year]	632.63	24.03	2208.74	347.25
E [€/year]	204.00	3.21	784.11	126.50
P [€/year]	127.00	93.27	214.39	19.19

Table 3. Correlation matrix.

	R	U	D	F	M	A	H	T	C	E	P	INC
R	1	0.06	0.31	0.09	0.98	0.99	0.99	0.99	0.99	0.99	0.99	**0.83**
U	0.06	1	−0.25	0.57	0.06	0.07	0.07	0.06	0.06	0.05	0.06	**−0.18**
D	0.31	−0.25	1	−0.05	0.32	0.31	0.31	0.31	0.31	0.31	0.31	**0.31**
F	0.09	0.57	−0.05	1	0.08	0.10	0.11	0.10	0.09	0.08	0.09	**0.01**
M	0.98	0.06	0.32	0.08	1	0.98	0.98	0.98	0.98	0.97	0.97	**0.81**
A	0.99	0.07	0.31	0.10	0.98	1	0.99	0.99	0.99	0.98	0.99	**0.82**
H	0.99	0.07	0.31	0.11	0.98	0.99	1	0.99	0.99	0.98	0.99	**0.82**
T	0.99	0.06	0.31	0.10	0.98	0.99	0.99	1	0.99	0.99	0.99	**0.83**
C	0.99	0.06	0.31	0.09	0.98	0.99	0.99	0.99	1	0.99	0.99	**0.83**
E	0.99	0.05	0.31	0.08	0.97	0.98	0.98	0.99	0.99	1	0.99	**0.83**
P	0.99	0.06	0.30	0.09	0.97	0.99	0.99	0.99	0.99	0.99	1	**0.83**
INC	**0.83**	**−0.18**	**0.31**	**0.01**	**0.81**	**0.82**	**0.82**	**0.83**	**0.83**	**0.83**	**0.83**	1

5 Conclusions

According to the current and global aim to pursue the diffusion of smart cities, the importance to provide effective preliminary assessment tools for urban planning policies constitutes a relevant focus of attention. Although the potential and opportunities that can arise from the use of artificial intelligence techniques have been recognized in the field of real estate valuation and urban planning support [31], the risk associated with the loss of control over the outputs generated by big data processing has been acknowledged, as well as the perplexity related to the complexity of managing and interpreting black boxes that are difficult to verify.

In this context, a user-friendly and easily replicable valuation model has been developed and tested in the present research, thanks to the graphical representation of outputs in a GIS environment, which are also intelligible to less experienced users. The methodology underlying the illustrated model borrows the prodromes of the urban rent theory for the assessment of the area incidence factors, i.e. the coefficients that express the importance that the local communities attribute to the set of the locational factors that characterize a homogeneous market area. Applied to the microzones that define the municipal territory of the city of Rome, the determination of the differential urban rent (i.e. of the different area incidence factors) has allowed for the explicit identification of the temporal variations in the appreciation of different areas by the local communities, and thus for the quick identification — also through the visualization on maps — of the territorial areas that, more than others, demonstrate the need for urban regeneration initiatives.

The developed model for the city of Rome could serve as a useful reference for both public and private operators in urban intervention planning priorities: the analysis conducted reveals that, between 2015 and 2023, on one hand, there has been a decline in preference for the suburban areas of the city (such as the Tor Bella Monaca neighbourhood), due to insufficient infrastructure and/or services and/or social inclusion issues; on the other hand, many peripheral areas, compared to the central ones where no relevant variations in the appreciation have been recorded, have experienced significant increases in desirability, as consequence of the widespread adoption of smart working following the COVID-19 pandemic and, therefore, a greater preference for areas that offer better livability, both in terms of available services and the absence of the overtourism phenomenon that inevitably affects the central areas.

The implementation of an elastic net regression, using the area incidence factors as the dependent variable alongside eleven socio-economic variables collected for the studied micro-zones, has allowed for the identification of the indicators that most influence, in the year 2023, the area incidence factors, which serve as proxies for the housing choices of local communities. The final regression model selects only four socio-economic variables as those that are truly explanatory of the formation of the area incidence factor values: the disposable income per capita, the leisure and cultural service expenses, the education expenses and the social protection expenses.

By comparing the contribution of each of these four indicators, it had been observed that, in the city of Rome, the areas that had been most economically valued have been primarily associated with higher expenditure on social protection, followed by spending on education and leisure and cultural services: this output can provide for a valuable support in the planning of upcoming urban regeneration interventions in the city of Rome, highlighting the imperative need to include, in the various proposed and to-be-implemented design solutions, the programming of services that would meet the needs revealed by the carried out analysis.

Therefore, the results could support the choice processes for effective strategic lines of territorial development, constituting a further point of view for the investigation of the urban territory, which could integrate a context analysis for an overall exam of the strengths and the criticalities of the considered case study.

Although the model has been tested in the specific context of Rome, it demonstrates strong potential for transferability to other urban settings, insofar as it is grounded in standardized socio-economic indicators and GIS-based spatial analysis. Its practical application in different contexts, however, may be constrained by the availability, quality, and consistency of the pertinent territorial data.

Future research insights may concern the application of the method to other (national and/or international) case studies, in order to test its reliability and to deepen its potentialities in terms of practical implications. In this sense, comparative analysis could be carried out, in order to verify the obtained results and investigate the outputs within the specific territorial context.

Note. The current study has been developed within the current research P.R.I.N. Project 2022: "INSPIRE—Improving Nature-Smart Policies through Innovative Resilient Evaluations", Grant number: 2022J7RWNF.

References

1. UN-Habitat: The New Urban Agenda, Nairobi, Kenya (2016)
2. Affairs: Sustainable Development Goals Report 2024, United Nations, S.L (2024)
3. Goal 11. Department of Economic and Social Affairs, https://sdgs.un.org/goals/goal11. Accessed 21 Mar 2025
4. Santopietro, L., Solimene, S., Lucchese, M., Di Carlo, F., Scorza, F.: An economic appraisal of the SE(C)AP public interventions towards the EU 2050 target: The case study of Basilicata region. Cities. **149**, 104957 (2024). https://doi.org/10.1016/j.cities.2024.104957
5. Morano, P., Tajani, F., Di Liddo, F., Ranieri, R., Amoruso, P.: The contribution of the most influencing factors on the housing rents: an analysis in the city of Milan (Italy). In: Gervasi, O., Murgante, B., Misra, S., Garau, C., Blečić, I., Taniar, D., Apduhan, B.O., Rocha, A.M.A.C., Tarantino, E., Torre, C.M. (eds.) Computational Science and Its Applications – ICCSA 2021, pp. 63–76. Springer International Publishing, Cham (2021). https://doi.org/10.1007/978-3-030-86979-3_5
6. Morano, P., Tajani, F., Di Liddo, F., Amoruso, P.: The public role for the effectiveness of the territorial enhancement initiatives: a case study on the redevelopment of a building in disuse in an Italian small town. Buildings. **11**, 87 (2021). https://doi.org/10.3390/buildings11030087
7. Woschank, M., Rauch, E., Zsifkovits, H.: A review of further directions for artificial intelligence, machine learning, and deep learning in smart logistics. Sustainability. **12**, 3760 (2020). https://doi.org/10.3390/su12093760
8. Toorajipour, R., Sohrabpour, V., Nazarpour, A., Oghazi, P., Fischl, M.: Artificial intelligence in supply chain management: a systematic literature review. J. Bus. Res. **122**, 502–517 (2021). https://doi.org/10.1016/j.jbusres.2020.09.009
9. Chaturvedi, V., de Vries, W.T.: Machine learning algorithms for urban land use planning: a review. Urban Sci. **5**, 68 (2021). https://doi.org/10.3390/urbansci5030068
10. Secinaro, S., Calandra, D., Secinaro, A., Muthurangu, V., Biancone, P.: The role of artificial intelligence in healthcare: a structured literature review. BMC Med. Inform. Decis. Mak. **21**, 125 (2021). https://doi.org/10.1186/s12911-021-01488-9
11. Alsawan, N.M., Alshurideh, M.T.: The application of artificial intelligence in real estate valuation: a systematic review. In: Hassanien, A.E., Snášel, V., Tang, M., Sung, T.-W., Chang, K.-C. (eds.) Proceedings of the 8th International Conference on Advanced Intelligent Systems and Informatics 2022, pp. 133–149. Springer International Publishing, Cham (2023). https://doi.org/10.1007/978-3-031-20601-6_11

12. Kok, N., Koponen, E.-L., Martínez-Barbosa, C.A.: Big data in real estate? From manual appraisal to automated valuation. J. Portf. Manag. **43**, 202–211 (2017). https://doi.org/10.3905/jpm.2017.43.6.202
13. Han, S., Ko, Y., Kim, J., Hong, T.: Housing market trend forecasts through statistical comparisons based on big data analytic methods. J. Manag. Eng. **34** (2018). https://doi.org/10.1061/(ASCE)ME.1943-5479.0000583
14. Morano, P., Anelli, D., Tajani, F., Roma, A.: The Real Estate Risk Assessment: An Innovative Methodology for Supporting Public and Private Subjects Involved into Sustainable Urban Interventions. In: Lecture Notes in Computer Science (including subseries Lecture Notes in Artificial Intelligence and Lecture Notes in Bioinformatics). 14109 LNCS, pp. 414–426 (2023). https://doi.org/10.1007/978-3-031-37120-2_27
15. Battisti, F., Guarini, M.R.: Public interest evaluation in negotiated public-private partnership. Int. J. Multicriteria Decis. Mak. **7**, 54 (2017). https://doi.org/10.1504/IJMCDM.2017.085163
16. Santopietro, L., Scorza, F.: Voluntary planning and city networks: a systematic bibliometric review addressing current issues for sustainable and climate-responsive planning. Sustainability. **16**, 8655 (2024). https://doi.org/10.3390/su16198655
17. Einaudi, L.: Questioni intorno all'imposta sulle aree edilizie. Roux e Viarengo (1900)
18. Grilli, C.: La rendita edilizia nelle moderne metropoli. Riv. Int. Sci. Soc. Discipl. Ausil. **53**, 329–380 (1910)
19. Famularo, N.: La stima dei fabbricati. Edizioni Calderini (1959)
20. Morano, P., Tajani, F., Anelli, D.: Urban planning variants: a model for the division of the activated "plusvalue" between public and private subjects [Interventi in variante urbanistica: un modello per la ripartizione tra pubblico e privato del "plusvalore" conseguibile]. Valori Valutazioni. **28**, 31–48 (2021). https://doi.org/10.48264/VVSIEV-20212804
21. Morano, P., Tajani, F., Anelli, D.: A decisions support model for investment through the social impact bonds. In: The case of the city of Bari (Italy). [Un modello a supporto delle decisioni per gli investimenti attuati mediante i Social Impact Bond. Il caso della città di Bari] (2020)
22. Guerrieri, G.: Il mercato della casa: domanda, offerta, tassazione e spesa pubblica. Carocci, Roma (2022)
23. Tajani, F., Manganelli, B., Sica, F., De Paola, P., D'Ugo, D.: A rational method for the quick assessment of the areas' weights applied to the Italian context. in: Gervasi, O., Murgante, B., Garau, C., Taniar, D., C. Rocha, A.M.A., and Faginas Lago, M.N. (eds.) Computational Science and Its Applications – ICCSA 2024 Workshops. pp. 66–77. Springer Nature Cham (2024). doi:https://doi.org/10.1007/978-3-031-65318-6_5
24. Carbone, F.: Ordinarietà: applicazione, implicazioni ed integrazioni. Aestimum, 195–221 (2021). https://doi.org/10.13128/AESTIM-8685
25. Camagni, R.: Rendita urbana e redistribuzione | La rendita immobiliare come prodotto finanziario: la valorizzazione dell'ex Zecca dello Stato. In: Redistribuzione della rendita urbana: teoria e attualità, pp. 15–25 (2019)
26. Camagni, R.: Perequazione urbanistica "estesa", rendita e finanziarizzazione immobiliare: un conflitto con l'equità e la qualità territoriale. Sci. Reg. **2014**(2), 29–44 (2014)
27. Istat.it: https://www.istat.it/. Accessed 24 Mar 2025
28. UrbiStat: Geomarketing & Market Research. https://www.urbistat.com/ita/. Accessed 24 03 2025
29. Zou, H., Hastie, T.: Regularization and variable selection via the elastic net. J. R. Stat. Soc., B: Stat. Methodol. **67**, 301–320 (2005). https://doi.org/10.1111/j.1467-9868.2005.00503.x
30. Yalpır, Ş., Yalpır, E.: Comparative evaluation of the performance of different regression models in land valuation. Adv. GIS. **4**, 10–14 (2024)
31. Rampini, L., Cecconi, F.R.: Artificial intelligence algorithms to predict Italian real estate market prices. J. Prop. Invest. Finance. **40**, 588–611 (2021). https://doi.org/10.1108/JPIF-08-2021-0073

A Set of Criteria for the Assessment of the Suitability of a Building to be Converted for Use as a Healthcare Facility

Antonella Roma[1](✉) , Maria Rosaria Guarini[1] , Marco Locurcio[2],
Felicia Di Liddo[2] , and Pierluigi Morano[2]

[1] Department of Architecture and Design, "Sapienza" University of Rome, Rome 00196, Italy
antonella.roma@uniroma1.it

[2] Department of Civil, Environmental, Land, Building Engineering and Chemistry, Polytechnic University of Bari, Bari 70125, Italy

Abstract. The COVID-19 pandemic highlighted the structural criticality of health systems at the international level and acted as a catalyst for their transformation. In Italy, under Mission 6 - Health, the NRRP envisages the strengthening of territorial healthcare by constructing two types of facilities: Community Homes Facilities (CHFs) and Community Hospitals (CHFs). The regulations allow these healthcare facilities to be built from scratch or by reusing existing buildings, an option that fits into a circular economy framework that favors urban regeneration processes and limits land consumption. The selection of buildings suitable for conversion is a complex decision-making process that requires a rigorous methodological approach capable of integrating both the intrinsic characteristics of the buildings and the extrinsic characteristics of the territorial context. This research, through a systematic review of the literature and regulatory frameworks, proposes five evaluation criteria to assess the degree of suitability of a building to undergo a re-functionalization process in favor of CHFs. The adoption of this methodological framework provides evidence-based support to policymakers and urban planners, facilitating informed site selection and contributing to an effective and sustainable reorganization of territorial healthcare.

Keywords: Healthcare facilities · Site selection · reuse of the building · Evaluation criteria · CHFs

1 Introduction

The public health emergency caused by COVID-19 (C19) in 2020 has posed significant challenges to healthcare facilities worldwide, affecting their operational, managerial and care delivery capacities. In the European context, National Health Systems (NHS) have been forced to address critical issues related to the scarcity of financial resources, the inadequacy of health infrastructures, the lack of appropriate technological equipment and the shortage of health workers. In Italy, the pandemic has been one of the most significant health crises that the country has faced in recent history: hospitals have had to deal with overcrowding in intensive care units and the reduction in their capacity to provide routine health services, with direct consequences for the management of non-C19-related diseases [1].

The systemic and structural criticalities that emerged during the pandemic spread are the direct implication of the policies carried out by the government over time [2]. The Italian NHS was established in 1978, ensuring universal healthcare coverage as a fundamental right for all citizens, regardless of individual financial capacity [3]. Despite the remarkable goal the NHS has faced growing economic crises. Since the 1990s, several reforms have been introduced to improve the efficiency and sustainability of the system. The most significant has been the decentralization of the NHS, shifting financial, managerial, and healthcare delivery responsibilities from the central government to the regions [4]. Under this model, the role of the government has been redefined as a regulatory and supervisory body, primarily for establishing the Essential Levels of Care (LEA) that each region must ensure for its population. While the primary objective of the reform was to strengthen the financial sustainability of the healthcare network, the outcomes of decentralization have been different and heterogeneous. Significant demographic, economic, and administrative disparities among regions, associated with variations in infrastructural resources, have exacerbated regional inequalities in healthcare service efficiency and expenditure levels. In particular, southern Italy regions have faced greater challenges in maintaining financial stability, leading to substantial budget deficits [5]. Consequently, the central government has intervened by implementing financial recovery plans aimed at containing healthcare expenditure in deficit-stricken regions [6, 7]. These policies have had the effect of progressively weakening the NHS and its structural limitations have become particularly evident during the health emergency. The pandemic has highlighted the need for the NHS to undergo a process of transformation in order to adequately manage potential health crises and respond effectively to ongoing demographic and epidemiological changes [8–11].

In this context, the European Union (EU) introduced the Next Generation EU, a temporary (2021–2027) financial instrument to rebuild Europe and mitigate the economic and social damage caused by C19. In order to access these funds, Italy developed the National Recovery and Resilience Plan (NRRP), which is structured into 7 missions, each representing a thematic area with a package of measures to be adopted [12, 13]. Mission 6, titled "Healthcare," focuses on strategies to modernize, digitalize, and enhance the inclusivity of healthcare infrastructures, ensuring equitable access to care and strengthening territorial healthcare services. One of the government's key objectives is to restructure community-based healthcare by establishing "Proximity Networks," i.e. facilities providing primary and intermediate healthcare services. These networks aim to solve the minimal healthcare communities' needs, alleviating pressure on hospitals [14]. Under the NRRP, the government initially has planned to establish 1350 community health facilities (CHF), 400 community hospitals (CH), and 600 local operating centers (LOC) by 2026. However, both the increase in raw material prices and the rise in energy prices in 2022 led to a significant increase in construction costs, which inevitably compromised the original NRRP targets. In response, on 7 August 2023, the European Commission has approved a revised version of the NRRP submitted by the Italian government to adjust and scale down the original objectives. Specifically, the revised targets include the establishment of 1038 CHFs ($-\Delta$ 312), 307 CHs ($-\Delta$ 97), and 400 LOCs ($-\Delta$ 200) [15].

To facilitate the planning phases of these new healthcare infrastructures, the National Agency for Regional Healthcare Services (AGENAS), in collaboration with the Department of Architecture, Built Environment and Construction Engineering (ABC) and the Design & Health Lab of the Polytechnic of Milan, has developed the *"Documento di indirizzo per il metaprogetto della Casa di Comunità"* [16] and the *"Documento di indirizzo per il metaprogetto dell'Ospedale di Comunità"* [17]. The purpose of these documents is to provide operational guidelines, based on the current legislative framework and community needs, to technical offices and designers involved in planning and designing CHFs and CHs. A fundamental aspect emphasized in these guidelines is the necessity of conducting preliminary analyses at both territorial and local scales to inform the decision-making process regarding the localization of these new healthcare facilities. To ensure fair and widespread access to CHFs and CHs, site selection should be based on strategic criteria that consider territorial specificities, rather than merely relying on quantitative criteria such as the population catchment area defined by sector regulations [18]. Indeed, localization plays a crucial role in the success of the new community-based healthcare model, but in the absence of adequate decision-support tools, the site selection is often handled on a case-by-case basis, leading to discretionary choices that risk making territorial inequalities greater [19].

Furthermore, the sector regulations provide two options for establishing CHFs and CHs: the construction of new buildings or the repurposing of disused structures. The latter option, following the principles of the circular economy, represents an opportunity to optimize financial resources and reduce the environmental impact of new infrastructure projects [20]. The reuse of disused buildings offers multiple benefits, including urban regeneration, reduction of consumption of natural land, and improvement of energy efficiency. The repurposing of existing structures is a particularly suitable solution for CHFs, as these facilities have relatively low architectural and technological complexity and moderate size requirements, making them easier to integrate into buildings originally designed for other functions.

2 Aim

The planning of CHFs and CHs represents a multidimensional decision-making issue that involves multiple disciplines and a wide range of stakeholders. Addressing this complexity requires the adoption of evaluation tools that integrate both qualitative and quantitative variables, thereby enabling a comprehensive representation of the decision-making problem while considering the specific constraints of the territorial context in which the assessment is developed. Furthermore, it is essential to ensure a balanced representation of the interests of the various stakeholders involved in the operation, including the state, regional authorities, local health agencies and the local population [19].

This study is part of the outlined framework. The objective is to propose a set of criteria to assess the suitability of existing buildings for conversion into healthcare facilities. In particular, the research aims to develop a structured criteria abacus to support decision-making processes concerning the functional repurposing of disused buildings for the establishment of CHFs.

The identification of the evaluation criteria set has been conducted in two stages. Firstly, a thorough review of sectoral regulations has been carried out, identifying the organizational, qualitative and technological standards for territorial healthcare structures. This ensured the inclusion of assessment criteria that met legislative requirements. In the second step, a comprehensive review of national and international academic literature on the localization of various types of healthcare facilities has been performed. This analysis aimed to determine established evaluation strategies that could serve as a foundation, adaptable to the specific context of CHFs.

In this sense, the goal of the present study is to identify the key evaluation criteria, systematically classified into categories (building-related, socio-demographic, epidemiological, economic, and territorial), to verify the feasibility of repurposing disused buildings within a valorization and functional transformation strategy. The methodological approach implemented in this research integrates regulatory aspects, empirical evidence and findings from previous studies aligned with the same objective, to provide Decision-Makers (DMs) with a practical support tool.

The results of the review process are presented in Sect. 3 of the paper. The obtained outputs led to the selection of five criteria, which are further detailed into sub-criteria that address critical issues in the planning phase of healthcare interventions aimed at the functional reconversion of degraded or unused buildings into CHFs. Finally, Sect. 4 outlines the study's conclusions and potential future research developments.

3 Identification of Criteria for Functional Reconversion of a Disused Building into a CHFs

Investment decisions regarding healthcare facility planning require extensive consideration, as the outcome of these choices can significantly impact the quality and effectiveness of healthcare services [21, 22]. In the context of the reorganization of territorial healthcare in Italy, Ministerial Decree No. 77 of 2022 defines CHFs as "physical and easily identifiable facilities where citizens can access healthcare and social-healthcare services with a healthcare focus" [23]. The regulation thus emphasizes the role of CHFs as recognizable territorial healthcare hubs, designed to become a reference point for the community ensuring widespread and accessible healthcare services. In order to achieve these objectives adequately, DMs have to identify a suitable localization for these facilities within the urban context, to guarantee that CHFs are easily accessible and rationally distributed across the national context. Beyond the issue of siting, it is also necessary to assess whether CHFs should be the result of an ex-novo project or integrated into existing buildings. The second approach (i.e. the reconversion of an existing asset for health use) could potentially expedite intervention implementation timelines and reduce land consumption, thereby promoting the regeneration of the built environment.

In this context, DMs need to adopt a structured methodological approach that facilitates a rational choice process for the planning of healthcare facilities (in general) and CHFs (in particular). The analyses should support both the identification of an appropriate localization for these facilities and the assessment of the feasibility of repurposing disused buildings for the new function. From this perspective, this research aims to develop a set of evaluation criteria to guide this decision-making process.

A narrative review of academic literature and sector-specific regulations has been carried out. The analysis of national and international empirical evidence is aimed at identifying criteria already used to address the challenges of siting healthcare facilities and repurposing disused real estate assets. The review has included studies on various types of healthcare facilities, with the objective of selecting a broad set of criteria that can be adapted to the evaluations of specific CHFs. The analysis has highlighted that the siting of newly built healthcare facilities has been extensively studied, whereas the repurposing of existing buildings for healthcare purposes remains an underexplored topic. To address this knowledge gap, the review has also included articles analyzing adaptive reuse in general, selecting from them only those criteria applicable to the planning of CHFs. The literature investigation has been conducted consulting major academic databases, i.e. Scopus, Google Scholar and PubMed, using keywords such as "siting healthcare facilities," "community healthcare facilities," "hospital site selection," and "adaptive reuse of buildings". The review has included only English-language articles that explicitly identified evaluation criteria in consistency with the research objectives. Furthermore, related articles and their bibliographies have been examined. This process of review ultimately has resulted in the selection of 40 scientific papers.

Concurrently, an analysis of the regulatory framework has been undertaken, with particular emphasis on Ministerial Decree No. 77 of 2022 [23] and the guidelines for the meta-project [16]. A qualitative analysis of regulatory documents has been developed to extract evaluation criteria that would be useful for the planning phase of CHFs.

The methodological approach adopted, in conjunction with the processing of the obtained results, has allowed the identification of five evaluation criteria, which have been further articulated into sub-criteria measurable through specific indicators. The criteria are intended to be adopted by public administration, policymakers and designers in the planning of CHFs, with the scope of ensuring decision-making based on a systematic and multidimensional approach.

The criteria identified are described below: i) Territorial context characteristics, ii) Site area (in the case of new constructions) and building characteristics (in the case of the refurbishment of disused buildings), iii) Sociodemographic characteristics, iv) Epidemiological aspects and v) Economic issues (see Fig. 1).

The **"Territorial context characteristics"** criterion comprises sub-criteria that allow the analysis of the specific features of the urban context in which a healthcare facility is planned to be included. The examination has highlighted that accessibility to healthcare facilities is an essential requirement to ensure equitable access to healthcare services and to reduce territorial inequalities. Homogeneous distribution of facilities enables an effective response to the growing healthcare needs of the population [24, 25]. In addition to the dimension of physical accessibility, further evaluation fields include the environmental quality of the urban context and the analysis of the pre-existing healthcare network.

The **"Site Area and Building Characteristics"** criterion incorporates sub-criteria designed to evaluate the physical characteristics of the building to be functionally transformed. Given that the majority of the selected articles focus on the construction of new

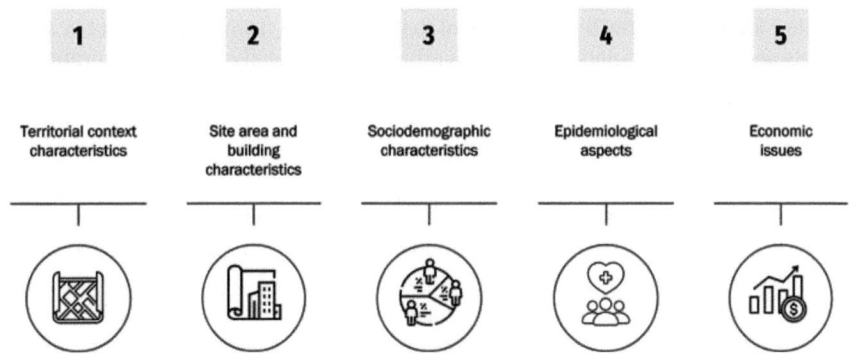

Fig. 1. Criteria for assessing the suitability of disused buildings for repurposing into healthcare use.

healthcare facilities, additional sub-criteria have been included to assess the suitability of the site for new developments.

Two further fundamental criteria for guiding investment decisions related to the establishment of healthcare facilities concern the analysis of the **"Sociodemographic characteristics"** and **"Epidemiological aspects"** of the target population (catchment area). By assessing these aspects, it is possible to understand the composition and distribution of the population that will benefit from the intervention.

Finally, the assessment of the economic and financial feasibility of a project concerns the analysis of the **"Economic issues"** associated with the initiative. The cost of the intervention, the level of community support and the modalities of funding are key factors in determining the economic sustainability of the project.

The criteria described are further divided into sub-criteria, each of which can be measured by indicators. In order to ensure a systematic presentation of the results of the narrative review, five tables have been elaborated (one for each criterion). Each table shows: i) the sub-criteria identified for the assessment of the criterion, ii) the indicators used to measure the sub-criteria, and iii) the bibliographic sources from which the systematized information is derived. It should be noted that the terminology used in the tables reflects the results of the review carried out in this research and, where possible, similar concepts have been grouped under a single definition.

3.1 Territorial Context Characteristics

The identification of the most suitable localization site for a healthcare facility must be based on a thorough analysis, both at the territorial and local levels. It is essential to adopt an assessment approach that makes it possible to examine the characteristics of an urban area in terms of potential and possible critical points in order to select the site that best meets the operational and functional needs of a health facility. The NRRP promotes the concept of 'proximity to healthcare', which requires that CHFs are planned taking into account the characteristics of the urban context, urban infrastructures, environmental quality and integration with the existing healthcare network.

Table 1 summarizes the findings related to this criterion from the review of academic literature and sector regulations. Specifically, from the analysis 15 measurable sub-criteria through quantitative and qualitative indicators have been identified.

Accessibility is the most important requirement to be considered in health facility planning operations. Soltani et al. [30] define accessibility as the ease with which a service can be reached within a reasonable time and at a reasonable cost. One of the first aspects to be analyzed is therefore the infrastructure efficiency of the reference urban area, assessed by the presence and distance of bus, tram, metro stops and railway stations from the structure. In addition to public transport, many studies analyze the efficiency of the road network linking residential areas to the health facility. In this context, Vahidnia et al. [52] use GIS systems to analyze road networks and calculate the length and average travel time (based on traffic information) to reach the facility. This type of data is particularly relevant for planning emergency services, for which it is essential to minimize the travel time to reach them. The assessment of major roads is also essential for the planning of community health centers, especially if they are to serve areas without public transport.

Another aspect to be taken into account is the existing and planned hospital network in the urban context. Ministerial Decree No. 77 of 2022 emphasizes the importance of integrating the functions of CHFs with the other care sectors, in order to ensure the cohesion of health services and the sharing of knowledge between professionals. Empirical evidence shows that the analysis of the existing health network is carried out using indicators such as the number and/or presence of health facilities in the urban context being evaluated. However, to guarantee a more accurate and comprehensive analysis, the consideration of other indicators, such as the type of facilities included in the area (hospitals, clinics, outpatient clinics) and their mode of financing (private, public, mixed) should be carried out. An analysis of this type makes it possible to characterize the range of services on the reference territory, to avoid duplication of services and compensate for any shortcomings [27]. Environmental quality is another field examined by empirical evidence. The concentration of air pollutants (e.g. PM10, O3, NO2), which is particularly high in urban areas, and noise pollution can have an impact on the well-being of patients during hospitalization. For this reason, several studies suggest avoiding proximity to (polluting and noisy) industrial activities that reduce the environmental quality of the urban context. In addition to being affected by environmental conditions, healthcare facilities also have an impact on the ecosystem. For example, the management of hospital wastewater is a major issue: the existence of an adequate sewerage network is essential [46]. Moreover, hydrogeological risk plays a crucial role in the choices processes related to the health facilities interventions. The distance from rivers and canals is used as an indicator to assess the risk of flooding, which could affect operational management and patient safety [56].

3.2 Site Area and Building Characteristics

The 'Site and building characteristics' criterion is structured into 17 sub-criteria, as shown in Table 2. These sub-criteria fall into two main categories: i) the assessment of the specific characteristics of a building undergoing functional change, and ii) the analysis of the site designated for the construction of a new healthcare facility.

Table 1. Sub-criteria and indicators of territorial context characteristics.

Territorial context characteristics		
Sub-criteria	Indicators	Source
Urban development center	Dummy (presence/absence)	[26, 27]
Potential of the area to become an attractive center	Dummy (presence/absence)	[19, 27–29]
Accessibility	Public, private, and soft mobility and number of parking spaces (availability; distance)	[19, 27–42]
	Bus stops (no.; distance)	[26, 43–46]
	Subway stops (no.; distance)	[43–45]
	Tram stops (no.; distance)	[43, 45]
	Taxi stops (no.; distance)	[46]
	Railway station (distance)	[43, 45, 47–50]
	Arterial roads and main roads (distance)	[26, 28, 30, 32, 33, 36, 40, 44, 45–55, 57, 58]
	Average annual daily traffic of roads leading to the facility (no. vehicles/year)	[32, 40, 43, 45]
	Travel time to the facility (minutes)	[30, 32, 35, 42, 52, 53, 57]
Existing healthcare facilities	Healthcare facilities (no.)	[19, 26, 27, 31, 33, 35, 40, 45, 59]
	Healthcare facility (distance)	[30, 31, 34–36, 44–49, 51, 53–55, 57]
	Frequency of visitation for health services, Healthcare spending and health insurance payment (%)	[43]

(*continued*)

Table 1. (*continued*)

Territorial context characteristics			
		Types of healthcare services provided, size, clientele and funding mechanism	[43, 59]
		Health market growth rate (%)	[31, 40, 59]
		Capacity/availability of healthcare facilities (ratio between no. beds/inhabitants)	[31, 33, 35, 39, 40, 45]
		Equity of access to health services	[57]
Services		Services present within a defined distance from the site (no.)	[19, 28, 29, 60]
		Offices (distance)	[44]
		Banks/ Post Offices (distance)	[27, 29, 44]
		Schools (distance)	[26, 27, 37, 44, 45, 47]
		Shopping centers/shops (distance)	[26, 37, 40, 41, 51, 57, 61]
		Place of cult (distance)	[26, 37, 44]
		Fire station (distance)	[18, 37, 44, 53, 54]
Sewerage system		Dummy (presence/absence)	[19, 26, 29, 30, 32, 43, 44, 46, 61]
Wastewater treatment system		Dummy (presence/absence)	[45]
Green areas		Parks/gardens (presence, distance)	[19, 26, 27, 30, 34, 38, 44, 45, 48, 54, 57, 60]
Hydrogeological/hydraulic instability		Rivers and canals (presence/absence)	[18, 26, 37, 44]

(*continued*)

Table 1. (*continued*)

Territorial context characteristics			
	Rivers and canals (distance)	[46, 49–51, 53, 55, 56, 58]
Natural disaster risk zones	Faults, volcanoes (distance)	[39, 40, 42, 44, 54, 56]
Air pollution	Contraction of specific pollutants (PM10, O3, NO2)	[18, 19, 26–30, 33, 38–40, 48, 52]
Noise pollution	Sound pressure level (Leq, Lden, dB)	[18, 19, 26–30, 32, 38–40, 46]
Water pollution	Contraction of specific pollutants (microbiological and chemical contamination, physic-chemical parameters)	[38–40]
Unhealthy industries	Industrial activities (presence/absence)	[18, 26, 45, 48, 53, 57]
Residential area	City center or densely populated areas (distance)	[30, 32, 33, 44, 47, 49, 50, 54, 55, 58]

In this sense, it should be recalled that, although the primary objective of this research is to identify criteria for assessing the suitability of a disused building for conversion into a healthcare facility, empirical evidence suggests that most studies focus on newly constructed projects. Therefore, to ensure a comprehensive review and to avoid overlooking potentially relevant factors, the study also includes criteria for evaluating site localization.

The construction of a new health facility involves significant costs, making the renovation of an existing building a potentially advantageous alternative [65]. However, this is not always the "best" solution and it is essential to analyze the potential criticalities associated with a renovation project, such as: i) the lack of suitable properties for conversion within the identified territorial context, ii) the excessive renovation costs due to the state of maintenance of the property, and iii) the disagreements among the stakeholders involved in the operation [66]. A thorough analysis of these aspects is fundamental to ensure the technical and economic feasibility of the interventions and to prevent any potential problems from compromising the success of the initiative.

The first aspect to consider in the redevelopment of disused real estate assets concerns the maintenance condition of the building, as severely deteriorated states of preservation may entail significant investment costs, thereby reducing the economic viability

Table 2. Sub-criteria and indicators of building and area characteristics.

Site area and building characteristics		
Sub-criteria	Indicators	Source
Area suitability	Contaminated area (dummy)	[19, 26, 27, 37, 40, 41, 45, 46, 50, 52, 56–58, 61]
Size and shape of the land	The ratio of site area to square meters of health facility (no.)	[19, 26–30, 46, 53]
Historical and artistic constraints	Constrained building (dummy)	[60]
Land use	Compatibility with the land-use plan: presence of urban constraints (dummy)	[19, 26, 27, 30, 32, 35, 38, 46, 47, 50, 56–59]
Site slope	Slope index (%)	[30, 45, 48, 56, 58]
Area flexibility	Possibility for future expansion (residual buildability index)	[28–30, 35, 37, 39–42, 46, 48, 61]
Water and electricity	Existence and functioning of water and electricity connections (dummy, qualitative assessment)	[30, 32, 33, 35, 37, 40, 41, 43, 45, 61]
Property size	m^2	[60]
Building Condition and Maintenance Status	Qualitative assessment of elements (floors, walls and ceilings, fixtures, electrical system, water system and sanitation, heating system, common areas)	[62–64]
Compliance with fire prevention regulations	Presence of compartmentalization systems with REI characteristics (dummy)	[60]
Compliance with seismic regulations	Seismic vulnerability index; compliance with current regulations (dummy)	[60]

(*continued*)

Table 2. (*continued*)

Site area and building characteristics		
Sub-criteria	Indicators	Source
Economic obsolescence	Estimated cost of refurbishment (€/m^2)	[63]
Physical obsolescence	Age of the building (years)	[63]
Functional adequacy	Layout flexibility: modular structural system (dummy)	[60, 63, 64]
Energy efficiency	Thermal transmittance; roof insulation; ground connection; energy certification; carbon footprint (kgCO$_2$e/m^2/year)	[60, 63]
Presence and adequacy of technical systems	Compliance and functionality of Heating, Ventilation & Air Conditioning, water supply, sanitary, and electrical systems (%)	[60]

of the intervention. In this context, Diana L., et al. [62] propose a qualitative assessment approach for the criterion *"building condition and maintenance status"*, based on the evaluation of specific functional components such as floors, walls and ceilings, fixtures, installations and common areas. These elements are rated on a scale ranging from "mediocre" to "poor." Notably, a building lacking electrical and plumbing systems is classified as being in critical condition. Similarly, Langstone C. et al. [63] introduce the concept of *"physical obsolescence"* to assess the condition of a building, a parameter primarily determined by the age of the structure and the lack of regular maintenance. Another fundamental aspect to be examined is *"functional adequacy"*: a modular supporting structure facilitates any building intervention necessary to adapt it to new functional requirements. In addition, the guidance documents for the meta-project of CHFs [16, 60] emphasize that healthcare facilities must comply with current fire prevention and structural safety regulations. In particular, buildings must be constructed with a structure and compartmentalization systems with REI characteristics, as specified by the legislative references, to limit the potential spread of fire.

Another crucial factor is the energy efficiency of the building, in line with the objectives of the 2030 Agenda and the European Green Deal [67–69]. The need to launch a decarbonization process that includes the built environment is demonstrated by the fact that the building sector is responsible for 40% of the EU's energy consumption and 36% of its annual greenhouse gas emissions from the energy sector [70–72]. In this context, academic literature and regulations propose various indicators to assess the energy efficiency of a building, including envelope transmittance, ground connection and roof insulation. In addition, the Energy Performance Certificate (EPC) provides a summarized classification of the building's efficiency, which can be used as part of the overall assessment of the property.

Beyond building-specific sub-criteria, the characteristics of the site in the case of new-build projects should be analyzed for an effective exam of the alternatives. In particular, a systematic analysis is required to verify the suitability of the site, in terms of soil compaction, potential contamination, land slope and the compatibility of the urban area with the hosting of a healthcare facility under urban planning regulations.

3.3 Sociodemographic Characteristics and Epidemiological Aspects

The socio-demographic characteristics and epidemiological aspects criteria are structured into sub-criteria, organized in Tables 3 and 4, which describe the reference social context.

The analysis of the demographic composition assumes a key role in defining the catchment area of a health facility and understanding the health needs of the communities [43]. Among the most commonly used indicators in empirical research, population density serves as a crucial parameter because it allows an estimate of the potential demand for healthcare that the facility will have to meet [30]. However, population density provides only an aggregate assessment, which requires further investigation to ensure effective planning of health services. An indicator in this regard is the age distribution of the population, with particular attention to the elderly population (>65 years), as they have a higher incidence of health conditions and consequently a greater need for medical use.

In addition to the demographic structure, the design of a health facility must take into account the epidemiological characteristics of the target area. The literature examines the prevalence of chronic and acute diseases in the population, as well as behavioral risk factors such as smoking prevalence, which can have a significant impact on healthcare demand and service delivery [43].

3.4 Economic Issues

Economic sustainability should be verified within the project assessment phase. It involves the analysis of a set of sub-criteria aimed at evaluating the economic-financial dimensions of the initiative. The literature review has allowed us to identify five sub-criteria, which are summarized in Table 5.

The literature reviewed mainly focuses on the cost of land purchase (in the case of an ex-novo project) and the total investment cost. A relevant aspect to be considered is the ownership of the land or building: if the land is publicly owned, the total cost of the intervention can be significantly reduced, as the burden of acquisition is avoided. For this reason, the legal nature of ownership is included in the indicators analyzed.

From a broader perspective of economic analysis, it is also crucial to consider the community support level for the project development.

Table 3. Sub-criteria and indicators of sociodemographic characteristics.

Sociodemographic characteristics		
Sub-criteria	Indicators	Source
Demographics	% of elderly (>65 years); age index	[32, 43, 46]
	Current population in the target area (no. of inhabitants)	[26, 27, 30–36, 39, 50, 58, 59]
	Estimated future population (% annual population growth rate)	[31, 32, 35, 39, 42]
	Population distribution by age groups (no.)	[26, 30, 31, 33–35, 40, 45, 59]
	Current population density (inhab./km^2)	[30–32, 34–37, 40–42, 44–46, 48, 50, 52, 53, 56, 58, 59, 61]
	Estimated future population density (inhab/km^2)	[30, 31]
	Net migration rate (%)	[32, 33]
Socio-economics	% of low-income families; per capita income (€/capita)	[30, 31, 33, 35, 37, 40, 41, 43, 45, 61]

Table 4. Sub-criteria and indicators of epidemiological aspects.

Epidemiological aspects		
Sub-criteria	Indicators	Source
Healthcare demand	Population aged (> 65 years) (no.)	[19, 27]
	Elderly with chronic diseases such as diabetes (%)	[43]
	Smokers (%)	[43]
	Physical activity rate (%)	[43]
	Community health status (% of population with disease)	[45]

Table 5. Sub-criteria and indicators of economic aspects.

Economic aspects		
Sub-criteria	Indicators	Source
Land ownership status	Public/private (%)	[19, 26, 27, 30, 37, 40–42, 45, 61]
Land cost	€/m^2	[19, 26, 27, 30–32, 34–37, 39, 40, 45, 46, 48, 52, 57, 59, 61]
Financial support	Source and availability of funds (descriptive analysis)	[30, 33, 39, 40, 42, 43, 45]
Community support	Participatory approach through surveys and focus groups (qualitative assessment)	[30, 43]
Investment cost	€/m^2	[28, 29, 31, 32, 34–37, 39–41, 43, 45, 59, 61]

4 Conclusions and Future Insights

Over time, Italy has favored a hospital-centered model, translating into the health services predominantly provided by hospitals. During the health crisis, this management model has not been able to adequately address the health needs of the population. The intervention strategies outlined by the government in the NRRP aim to reform the territorial healthcare system through the establishment of CHFs and CHs, which will provide respectively primary and intermediate care services. The regulations stipulate that these types of facilities can be established in existing, disused buildings through re-functionalization projects. Such interventions offer several advantages, including the regeneration of the existing building stock and the reduction of natural land consumption [73, 74]. To maximize the benefits of the limited available financial resources, investment decisions related to the development of these facilities need to be supported by operational tools that effectively orient the decision-making process. The key tasks to be undertaken during the planning phase of community health facilities include the identification of a strategic localization and the assessment of the feasibility of repurposing abandoned buildings.

The present research has examined both national and international academic literature as well as current regulations regarding the planning of community-based healthcare facilities. The review has aimed to select evaluation criteria that can support both the choice of a suitable site for health hubs and the verification of the feasibility of disused buildings for their functional reconversion for health purposes. The systematization of the collected contributions has led to the identification of 5 main evaluation criteria, which analyze the characteristics of the urban context, demographic and epidemiological aspects, the economic issues of the project and the characteristics of the building to be converted.

The identified criteria do not focus on the specificities of CHFs. Therefore, future research developments may include expanding and refining the criteria set to better and specifically represent the functional, design and operational characteristics of community-based health facilities. In addition, based on the research findings, further insight can concern the development of a decision support system to guide public administrators in the planning and implementation of community health hubs. The design of these facilities is a multi-dimensional choice problem involving different disciplines and multiple stakeholders. In order to effectively address this complexity, the adoption of Multi-Criteria Analysis techniques is proposed [75, 76]. These methods allow the integration of both quantitative and qualitative variables, the consideration of specific territorial constraints and the balancing of the interests of different involved subjects. Furthermore, given the spatial nature of some of the relevant variables, the use of GIS-based systems is envisaged. The expected outcome is the definition of a practical and flexible tool to support strategic decision-making in the context of the territorial health reform promoted by the current funding measures.

Note: This research was funded by the Type 1 research project (year 2024), entitled "Possible evolutions of economic analyses to support project evaluations in the health sector", supported by the Sapienza, University of Rome and it was developed within the project "MISTRAL - a toolkit for dynaMic health Impact analysiS to predicT disability-Related costs in the Ag"-HORIZON-HLTH-2022-ENVHLTH04 - Grant Agreement Project n. 101,095,119 of the Polytechnic of Bari (Italy).

References

1. Bosa, I., Castelli, A., Castelli, M., Ciani, O., Compagni, A., Galizzi, M., Garofano, M., Ghislandi, S., Giannoni, M., Marini, G., Vainieri, M.: Response to COVID-19: was Italy (un)prepared? Health Econ. Policy Law. **17**(1), 1–13 (2022)
2. Mauro, M., Giancotti, M.: Italian responses to the COVID-19 emergency: overthrowing 30 years of health reforms? Health Policy. **125**(4), 548–552 (2021)

3. Ricciardi, W., Tarricone, R.: The evolution of the Italian national health service. Lancet. **398**(10317), 2193–2206 (2021)
4. Mauro, M., Maresso, A., Guglielmo, A.: Health decentralization at a dead-end: towards new recovery plans for Italian hospitals. Health Policy. **121**(6), 582–587 (2017)
5. Tediosi, F., Gabriele, S., Longo, F.: Governing decentralization in health care under tough budget constraint: what can we learn from the Italian experience? Health Policy. **90**(2–3), 303–312 (2009)
6. De Belvis, A.G., Ferrè, F., Specchia, M.L., Valerio, L., Fattore, G., Ricciardi, W.: The financial crisis in Italy: implications for the healthcare sector. Health Policy. **106**(1), 10–16 (2012)
7. Parlamento Italiano Homepage: https://leg16.camera.it/561?appro=94. Accessed 10 Mar 2025
8. De Belvis, A.G., Meregaglia, M., Morsella, A., Adduci, A., Perilli, A., Cascini, F., Scarpetti, G., et al.: Italy: health system review. Health Syst. Transit. **24**(4), 1–236 (2022)
9. Jazieh, A.R., Kozlakidis, Z.: Healthcare transformation in the post-coronavirus pandemic era. Front. Med. **7**, 429 (2020)
10. Bustacchini, S., Abbatecola, A.M., Bonfigli, A.R., Chiatti, C., Corsonello, A., Di Stefano, G., Lattanzio, F., et al.: The Report-AGE project: a permanent epidemiological observatory to identify clinical and biological markers of health outcomes in elderly hospitalized patients in Italy. Aging Clin. Exp. Res. **27**, 893–901 (2015)
11. Atella, V., Piano Mortari, A., Kopinska, J., Belotti, F., Lapi, F., Cricelli, C., Fontana, L.: Trends in age-related disease burden and healthcare utilization. Aging Cell. **18**(1), e12861 (2019)
12. European Commission: https://commission.europa.eu/strategy-and-policy/recovery-plan-europe_it. Accessed 2 Mar 2025
13. Italia Domani: https://www.italiadomani.gov.it/content/sogei-ng/it/it/home.html. Accessed 02 03 2025
14. Filippini, T., Vinceti, S.R.: Italian National Recovery and resilience plan: a healthcare renaissance after the COVID-19 crisis? Acta Biomed. **92**(6), e2021463 (2021)
15. Ministero della Salute: https://www.pnrr.salute.gov.it/portale/pnrrsalute/dettaglioContenutiPNRRSalute.jsp?lingua=italiano&id=5805&area=PNRR-Salute&menu=investimenti. Accessed 2 Mar 2025
16. AGENAS: https://www.agenas.gov.it/comunicazione/primo-piano/2127-documento-di-indirizzo-per-il-metaprogetto-della-casa-della-comunit%C3%A0. Accessed 02 Mar 2025
17. AGENAS: https://www.agenas.gov.it/comunicazione/primo-piano/2160-documento-di-indirizzo-per-il-metaprogetto-dell-ospedale-di-comunit%C3%A0. Accessed 2 Mar 2025
18. Gola, M., Fior, M., Arruzzoli, S., Galuzzi, P., Capolongo, S., Buffoli, M.: A research method for locating community healthcare facilities in Italy: how to guarantee healthcare for all. J. Integr. Care. **32**(1), 98–114 (2024)
19. Dell'Ovo, M., Oppio, A., Capolongo, S., Dell'Ovo, M., Oppio, A., Capolongo, S.: Approaching the location of healthcare facilities: how to model the decision problem. In: Decision Support System for the Location of Healthcare Facilities: SitHealth Evaluation Tool, pp. 53–79 (2020)
20. Tajani, F., Morano, P.: Concession and lease or sale? A model for the enhancement of public properties in disuse or underutilized. WSEAS Trans. Bus. Econ. **17**, 18 (2014)
21. Gul, M., Guneri, A.F.: Hospital location selection: a systematic literature review on methodologies and applications. Math. Probl. Eng. **2021**(1), 6682958 (2021)
22. Baran, E.: An innovative fuzzy TOPSIS method to determine the location of a new hospital. Int. J. Eng. Sci. Appl. **2**(4), 133–136 (2018)
23. Gazzetta ufficiale: https://www.gazzettaufficiale.it/eli/id/2022/06/22/22G00085/SG. Accessed 04 Mar 2025

24. Jausovec, M., Korpnik, N., Gabrovec, B., Klemencic, V.S.: Siting of healthcare care facilities based on the purpose of their operation, demographic changes, environmental characteristics, and the impact on public health. Appl. Sci. **12**(1), 379 (2021)
25. McGrail, M.R., Humphreys, J.S.: Measuring spatial accessibility to primary care in rural areas: Improving the effectiveness of the two-step floating catchment area method. Appl. Geogr. **29**(4), 533–541 (2009)
26. Dell'Ovo, M., Capolongo, S., Oppio, A.: Combining spatial analysis with MCDA for the siting of healthcare facilities. Land Use Policy. **76**, 634–644 (2018)
27. Dell'Ovo, M., Frej, E.A., Oppio, A., Capolongo, S., Morais, D.C., de Almeida, A.T.: Multicriteria decision making for healthcare facilities location with visualization based on FITradeoff method. In: Decision Support Systems VII. Data, Information and Knowledge Visualization in Decision Support Systems: Third International Conference, ICDSST 2017, Namur, Belgium, May 29–31, 2017, Proceedings 3, pp. 32–44. Springer International Publishing (2017)
28. Sen, H.: Hospital location selection with ARAS-G. Eurasia Proc. Sci. Technol. Eng. Math. **1**, 359–365 (2017)
29. Şen, H., Demiral, M.F.: Hospital location selection with grey system theory. Eur. J. Econ. Bus. Stud. **2**(2), 66–79 (2016)
30. Soltani, A., Marandi, E.Z.: Hospital site selection using two-stage fuzzy multi-criteria decision-making process. J. Urban Environ. Eng. **5**(1), 32–43 (2011)
31. Al Mohamed, A.A., Al Mohamed, S., Zino, M.: Application of fuzzy multicriteria decision-making model in selecting pandemic hospital site. Future Bus. J. **9**(1), 14 (2023)
32. Miç, P., Antmen, Z.F.: A healthcare facility location selection problem with fuzzy TOPSIS method for a regional hospital. Eur. J. Sci. Technol.., Avrupa Bilim ve Teknoloji Dergisi. **16**, 750–757 (2019)
33. Şahin, T., Ocak, S., Top, M.: Analytic hierarchy process for hospital site selection. Health Policy Technol. **8**(1), 42–50 (2019)
34. Gazi, K.H., Momena, A.F., Salahshour, S., Mondal, S.P., Ghosh, A.: Synergistic strategy of sustainable hospital site selection in saudi arabia using spherical fuzzy mcdm methodology. J. Uncertain Syst. **17**(03), 2450004 (2024)
35. Senvar, O., Otay, I., Bolturk, E.: Hospital site selection via hesitant fuzzy TOPSIS. IFAC-PapersOnLine. **49**(12), 1140–1145 (2016)
36. Chiu, J.E., Tsai, H.H.: Applying analytic hierarchy process to select optimal expansion of hospital location: The case of a regional teaching hospital in Yunlin. In: 2013 10th International Conference on Service Systems and Service Management, pp. 603–606 (2013)
37. Chatterjee, D.: Can fuzzy extension of Delphi-analytical hierarchy process improve hospital site selection? Int. J. Intercult. Inf. Manag. **4**(2–3), 113–128 (2014)
38. Ahmed, A.H., Mahmoud, H., Aly, A.M.M.: Site suitability evaluation for sustainable distribution of hospital using spatial information technologies and AHP: a case study of upper Egypt, Aswan City. J. Geogr. Inf. Syst. **8**(05), 578 (2016)
39. Adalı, E.A., Tuş, A.: Hospital site selection with distance-based multi-criteria decision-making methods. Int. J. Healthc. Manag. **14**(2), 534–544 (2021)
40. Yılmaz, M., Atan, T.: Hospital site selection using fuzzy EDAS method: case study application for districts of Istanbul. J. Intell. Fuzzy Syst. **41**(2), 2591–2602 (2021)
41. Chatterjee, D., Mukherjee, B.: Potential hospital location selection using AHP: a study in rural India. Int. J. Comput. Appl. **71**(17), 1–7 (2013)
42. Jalaliyoon, N., Arastoo, A., Pirouti, A.: Land selection: using multiple criteria decisions making. Int. J. Acad. Res. Manag. (IJARM). **4**(1), 14–23 (2015)
43. Kim, J.I., Senaratna, D.M., Ruza, J., Kam, C., Ng, S.: Feasibility study on an evidence-based decision-support system for hospital site selection for an aging population. Sustainability. **7**(3), 2730–2744 (2015)

44. Eldemir, F., Onden, I.: Geographical information systems and multicriteria decisions integration approach for hospital location selection. Int. J. Inf. Technol. Decis. Mak. **15**(05), 975–997 (2016)
45. Fardi, K., Ghanizadeh, G., Bahadori, M., Chaharbaghi, S., Shokouh, S.M.H.: Location selection criteria for field hospitals: a systematic review. Health Promot. Perspect. **12**(2), 131 (2022)
46. Abdullahi, S., Mahmud, A.R.B., Pradhan, B.: Spatial modelling of site suitability assessment for hospitals using geographical information system-based multicriteria approach at Qazvin city, Iran. Geocarto Int. **29**(2), 164–184 (2014)
47. Halder, B., Bandyopadhyay, J., Banik, P.: Assessment of hospital sites' suitability by spatial information technologies using AHP and GIS-based multi-criteria approach of Rajpur–Sonarpur Municipality. Model. Earth Syst. Environ. **6**, 2581–2596 (2020)
48. Tripathi, A.K., Agrawal, S., Gupta, R.D.: Comparison of GIS-based AHP and fuzzy AHP methods for hospital site selection: a case study for Prayagraj City, India. GeoJournal. **87**(5), 3507–3528 (2021)
49. Ajaj, Q.M., Shareef, M.A., Jasim, A.T., Hasan, S.F., Noori, A.M., Hassan, N.D.: An AHP-based GIS for a new hospital site selection in the Kirkuk Governorate. In: 2019 2nd International Conference on Electrical, Communication, Computer, Power and Control Engineering (ICECCPCE), pp. 176–181 (2019)
50. Almansi, K.Y., Shariff, A.R.M., Kalantar, B., Abdullah, A.F., Ismail, S.N.S., Ueda, N.: Performance evaluation of hospital site suitability using multilayer perceptron (MLP) and analytical hierarchy process (AHP) models in Malacca, Malaysia. Sustainability. **14**(7), 3731 (2022)
51. Sharmin, N., Neema, M.N.: A GIS-based multi-criteria analysis to site appropriate locations of hospitals in Dhaka City. Hospital. **8**(4), 8–12 (2013)
52. Vahidnia, M.H., Alesheikh, A.A., Alimohammadi, A.: Hospital site selection using fuzzy AHP and its derivatives. J. Environ. Manage. **90**(10), 3048–3056 (2009)
53. Rahimi, F., Goli, A., Rezaee, R.: Hospital location-allocation in Shiraz using geographical information system (GIS). Shiraz E Med. J. **18**(8), e57572 (2017)
54. Kaveh, M., Kaveh, M., Mesgari, M.S., Paland, R.S.: Multiple criteria decision-making for hospital location-allocation based on improved genetic algorithm. Appl. Geomat. **12**, 291–306 (2020)
55. Rezayee, M.: Hospital site selection in Iskandar Malaysia using GIS-multi criteria analysis. Int J Basic Sci Appl Comput. **2**(10), 8–15 (2020)
56. Yu, M., Hu, S.Y., Cai, J.M., Guo, P.N., Li, H.B., Xing, H.G.: A comprehensive evaluation method for the site selection of new healthcare facilities in geological hazard-prone areas. Front. Earth Sci. **11**, 1121690 (2023)
57. Beheshtifar, S., Alimoahmmadi, A.: A multiobjective optimization approach for location-allocation of clinics. Int. Trans. Oper. Res. **22**(2), 313–328 (2015)
58. Almansi, K.Y., Shariff, A.R.M., Abdullah, A.F., Syed Ismail, S.N.: Hospital site suitability assessment using three machine learning approaches: evidence from the gaza strip in Palestine. Appl. Sci. **11**(22), 11054 (2021)
59. Wu, C.R., Lin, C.T., Chen, H.C.: Optimal selection of location for Taiwanese hospitals to ensure a competitive advantage by using the analytic hierarchy process and sensitivity analysis. Build. Environ. **42**(3), 1431–1444 (2007)
60. Capolongo, S., Buffoli, M., Gola, M., Mangili, S., Brambilla, A., Brusamolin, E., Picco, M., et al.: Metaprogetto per Case della Comunità e Ospedali di Comunità. In: Criteri di progettazione architettonico-funzionale e organizzativi. [Meta 2 e 3 (2022)
61. Ramani, K.V., Mavalankar, D., Patel, A., Mehandiratta, S.: A GIS approach to plan and deliver healthcare services to urban poor: a public private partnership model for Ahmedabad City, India. Int. J. Pharm. Healthc. Mark. **1**(2), 159–173 (2007)

62. Diana, L., D'Auria, S., Acampa, G., Marino, G.: Assessment of disused public buildings: Strategies and tools for reuse of healthcare structures. Sustainability. **14**(4), 2361 (2022)
63. Langston, C., Wong, F.K., Hui, E.C., Shen, L.Y.: Strategic assessment of building adaptive reuse opportunities in Hong Kong. Build. Environ. **43**(10), 1709–1718 (2008)
64. Bullen, P., Love, P.: Factors influencing the adaptive re-use of buildings. J. Eng. Des. Technol. **9**(1), 32–46 (2011)
65. Elrod, J.K., Fortenberry, J.L.: Adaptive reuse in the healthcare industry: repurposing abandoned buildings to serve medical missions. BMC Health Serv. Res. **17**, 5–14 (2017)
66. Elrod, J.K., Fortenberry, J.L.: Advancing indigent healthcare services through adaptive reuse: repurposing abandoned buildings as medical clinics for disadvantaged populations. BMC Health Serv. Res. **17**, 5–14 (2017)
67. European Commission: European Green Deal. https://commission.europa.eu/strategy-and-policy/priorities-2019-2024/european-green-deal_it. Accessed 24 Mar 2025
68. United Nations homepage: https://unric.org/it/agenda-2030/. Accessed 24 Mar 2025
69. Tajani, F., Anelli, D., Di Liddo, F., Morano, P.: An innovative methodology for the assessment of the social discount rate: an application to the European states for ensuring the goals of equitable growth. In: Smart and Sustainable Built Environment (2023)
70. Tajani, F., Sica, F., Morano, P., Locurcio, M., Roma, A.: An evaluation method of the building decarbonization process at the international level. In: International Conference on Computational Science and Its Applications, pp. 126–142. Springer Nature Switzerland, Cham (2024)
71. Sica, F., Tajani, F., Cerullo, G.: An evaluation model for an optimal decarbonization process in the built environment. Built Environ. Proj. Asset Manag. **15**(1), 51–66 (2025)
72. Tajani, F., Morano, P., Di Liddo, F., Doko, E.: A model for the assessment of the economic benefits associated with energy retrofit interventions: an application to existing buildings in the Italian territory. Appl. Sci. **12**(7), 3385 (2022)
73. Locurcio, M., Tajani, F., Anelli, D.: Sustainable urban planning models for new smart cities and effective management of land take dynamics. Land. **12**(3), 621 (2023)
74. Tajani, F., Morano, P., Di Liddo, F.: The optimal combinations of the eligible functions in multiple property assets enhancement. Land Use Policy. **99**, 105050 (2020)
75. Guarini, M.R., Battisti, F., Chiovitti, A.: A methodology for the selection of multi-criteria decision analysis methods in real estate and land management processes. Sustainability. **10**(2), 507 (2018)
76. Guarini, M.R., Sica, F., Tajani, F., Sabatelli, E., Anelli, D.: A strategic multidirectional approach for picking indicator systems of sustainability in urban areas. Urban Sci. **8**(3), 107 (2024)

Spatial Analysis of Urban Decay: Spillover Effects and Significant Patterns for the City of Rome (Italy)

Pierluigi Morano[1], Debora Anelli[2], Francesco Tajani[2], Emma Sabatelli[2(✉)], and Felicia Di Liddo[1]

[1] Department of Civil, Environmental, Land, Building Engineering and Chemistry (DICATECh), Polytechnic University of Bari, Bari 70126, Italy
{pierluigi.morano,felicia.diliddo}@poliba.it

[2] Department of Architecture and Design, "Sapienza" University of Rome, Rome 00196, Italy
{debora.anelli,francesco.tajani,emma.sabatelli}@uniroma1.it

Abstract. Contemporary cities face multiple complex challenges, including those related to the social, environmental, and economic aspects of urban decay. This phenomenon represents a critical issue for both built and non-built environments, potentially compromising the achievement of sustainable urban development goals. The spatial patterns of urban decay contain valuable information for developing targeted policies and understanding the causes and effects of its territorial distribution, revealing how urban areas interact and influence each other. The aim of this study is to identify the spillover effects and the most significant spatial patterns of urban decay in the city of Rome (Italy). The application of spatial correlation techniques, such as the bivariate Moran's index, enables the identification of significant relationships between key aspects of urban decay, using a set of indicators capable of representing the social, environmental, and economic dynamics of the phenomenon in Rome.

The results confirm the necessity of considering the spatial dimension of phenomena such as urban decay in urban planning, taking into account the interactions between different areas. Specifically, within the Grande Raccordo Anulare (GRA), which includes the historic center and consolidated residential areas of the city, the analysis has shown that some critical issues are concentrated in specific areas but generate spillover effects in adjacent zones. These findings support the implementation of priority urban regeneration strategies, providing an objective and comprehensive framework to facilitate the achievement of sustainable urban development goals.

Keywords: Urban decay · spatial analysis · spatial correlation · GIS-based decision support system · sustainable planning · socio-spatial inequalities

1 Introduction

With the intensification of urbanization, the quality of the urban environment is becoming increasingly important in ensuring people's well-being and promoting sustainable development. However, contemporary cities face significant challenges related to the geographic concentration of economic, social, and environmental distress [1]. These phenomena, often localized in specific urban areas, pose a growing threat to social cohesion and the balanced development of metropolitan regions [2].

In particular, urban decay represents one of the most critical manifestations of these dynamics, emerging as a multidimensional phenomenon that affects both consolidated urban areas and peripheral zones [3]. The presence of abandoned buildings [4, 5], declining property values [6], and rising crime rates [7] are interconnected issues that can further marginalize specific urban areas, following well-defined spatial patterns [8].

A particularly relevant aspect is its spillover effect [9]: decay tends to spread to adjacent areas, generating a negative spiral that progressively affects larger portions of the territory. This process amplifies social and economic inequalities, with effects extending beyond the most affected areas, compromising the overall balance of the urban fabric [10].

The assessment of complex issues such as urban decay, in which geographic space plays a fundamental role, must necessarily consider the spatial dimension [11]. Economic, social, and environmental factors contributing to decay are not uniformly distributed across the territory [12]. To fully understand the spread dynamics of urban decay and their impact on urban areas, it is essential to identify significant patterns that describe the spatial association among the different components of the phenomenon. Analyzing spatial dynamics is crucial to identifying critical areas where multiple issues coexist, enabling the development of targeted strategies to mitigate the phenomenon [13].

Spatial correlation analysis represents a key tool for this type of investigation, allowing for the detection of non-random patterns in the territorial distribution of urban decay indicators. Through spatial correlation techniques, such as the bivariate Moran's index, it is possible to analyze relationships between physical-environmental, social, and economic indicators, assessing both global associations across the study area and local patterns in specific zones [14].

These analyses not only facilitate the understanding of the mechanisms driving urban decay but also provide operational tools to support the planning of effective urban regeneration interventions. Such interventions can counteract the negative effects of urban decay and reverse detrimental trends in the territory [15].

2 Aim

Urban decay is not randomly distributed but follows spatial patterns that influence its spread and impact. However, the spatial relationships between indicators remain largely unexplored, limiting the ability to identify significant patterns and cause-effect relationships useful for urban planning.

This research analyzes urban decay in the city of Rome through a spatial approach, with the primary objective of identifying and interpreting spatial relationships between different indicators of decay using spatial correlation techniques.

In particular, the local bivariate Moran's index will be used to:

- Identify significant clusters of urban decay.
- Explore how the spatial distribution of decay varies depending on the analyzed component (physical-environmental, economic and social).

- Assess the influence of the number of contiguous elements (urban zones) on the stability and reliability of the final outputs.

The analysis will be conducted on the 106 urban zones within Rome's Grande Raccordo Anulare (GRA), using updated territorial data related to the three main components of urban decay.

The results will provide an objective framework to support urban planning, facilitating the identification of priority areas for regeneration interventions and offering valuable insights for sustainable development strategies.

The remainder of the research is structured as follows: Section 3 provides an overview of studies that employ spatial analyses in different thematic areas; Section 4 describes the proposed methodology; Section 5 presents the selected case study. Section 6 discusses the obtained results, including specific examples, while Sect. 7 contains the conclusions and future developments.

3 Background

Spatial analysis, particularly spatial correlation analysis, are widely used in various research fields, including territorial, economic, environmental and social sciences, thanks to the development of advanced methodologies and the integration of GIS tools.

These techniques are extensively applied in real estate market studies to understand the spatial dynamics of housing prices and identify residential submarkets [16].

Bor-Ming, H [17]. employs spatial analysis to examine the housing market in the Tainan Metropolis, using Moran's index to assess the spatial correlation of house prices and Local Indicators of Spatial Association (LISA) to define submarkets by analyzing the spatial concentration of higher and lower prices. Similarly, Yang et al. [18] evaluate the spatial correlation between accessibility to urban vibrancy centers and housing prices in Chengdu, China. This study first identifies urban vibrancy spaces based on social media data and calculates dynamic accessibility over time, subsequently analyzing its spatial correlation with housing prices using the local bivariate Moran's index.

In Italy, Barreca et al. [19] study the relationship between urban vibrancy and the real estate market in the city of Turin. The study uses a neighborhood service index as a proxy for urban vibrancy and investigates the presence of spatial correlation by calculating Moran's index and LISA to reveal different types of spatial correlations. Another study by Barreca et al. [13] focuses on the relationship between social and territorial vulnerability and the real estate market, combining a hedonic approach with spatial analysis techniques to measure the correlation between vulnerability indicators and property values using the local Moran's index.

Spatial analyses are also applied in urban planning. García-Ayllón and Franco [20] use Moran's index to analyze the spatial correlation between urban growth planning models and the increased flood risk in the city of Murcia, in southeastern Spain. Mi et al. [21] employ the local bivariate Moran's index to examine the interaction between topographic gradients and habitat quality within the Chang-Zhu-Tan urban agglomeration.

Murgante et al. [14] measure urban shrinkage phenomena and their effects in the deindustrialized city of Taranto by assessing key urban shrinkage indicators. In this study, Moran's index is used to evaluate global spatial correlation, while LISA statistics identify local patterns of the phenomenon. Additionally, the same authors have applied various spatial correlation techniques, including Kernel Density, Moran's index, and Getis-Ord index, to identify priority intervention areas in urban regeneration programs. These studies were conducted in the city of Bari, with particular attention to social indicators [22], and in both Bari and Taranto, focusing on urban renewal strategies [23].

4 Methodology

To examine the dependence and spatial association between urban decay indicators, spatial correlation analysis was employed, a statistical technique that identifies non-random spatial patterns in the distribution of one or more variables. This analysis allows for determining whether the examined variables exhibit a random, clustered, or dispersed spatial arrangement.

The principle underlying this technique is that geographic phenomena are often not randomly distributed but follow a spatial logic linked to the physical proximity of geographic units. This concept, known as Tobler's First Law of Geography, states that *"everything is related to everything else, but near things are more related than distant things"* [24]. To analyze such spatial relationships, specific measures such as Moran's Index [25] and Geary's Index [26] are used to calculate global spatial correlation across the entire dataset and local correlation to detect patterns in specific areas.

In this study, Moran's Index was chosen as one of the most widely used tools for spatial analysis. This index measures spatial association by comparing the value of a variable in a given area with the weighted average of values in neighboring areas, using a spatial weight matrix to define proximity relationships [27]. To explore the relationship between two variables, the bivariate Moran's Index was applied, allowing verification of whether the values of a variable X in one area are spatially correlated with the values of another variable Y in surrounding areas [28].

The index ranges from -1 to $+1$, where a value close to $+1$ indicates a strong positive correlation (high values of X in an area are associated with high values of Y in neighboring areas), while a value close to -1 indicates a strong negative correlation (high values of X in an area are associated with low values of Y in neighboring areas). A value close to 0 indicates no correlation, suggesting a random distribution of indicators [22].

The indicators selected for this analysis were normalized on a scale from 0 to 1 to ensure consistency in variable comparisons. The analysis was conducted on two scales: global, to detect correlations across the entire city, and local, to highlight specific patterns among urban areas. At the local scale, the local bivariate Moran's Index was used to assess whether a given area exhibits similar or dissimilar values compared to its surrounding areas [29]. This approach allowed for identifying high- or low-intensity clusters and outliers, based on a spatial weight matrix that defines the proximity relationships between the analyzed areas.

The analysis began with the calculation of the global bivariate Moran's Index, which revealed low levels of global correlation. Subsequently, a local analysis was conducted to identify significant patterns in specific areas.

The calculation of the local bivariate Moran's Index enabled the identification of five categories of spatial association:

- High-High (HH): areas with high values for both indicators;
- Low-Low (LL): areas with low values for both indicators;
- High-Low (HL): areas with high values of X associated with low values of Y;
- Low-High (LH): areas with low values of X associated with high values of Y;
- Not significant: areas without statistically significant relationships between the indicators.

To define proximity relationships between urban areas, a spatial weight matrix was constructed using the K-nearest neighbors (KNN) method, which considers the k closest areas in terms of distance as neighbors. The KNN method was chosen as it avoids problems related to dimensional heterogeneity among urban areas (which have very different surface areas) and ensures that each area has the same number of neighbors, improving result comparability. The k value in the spatial weight matrix determines how many neighboring elements are considered for each unit of analysis (in this case, the urban zones of Rome).

Since the results of spatial analyses can be sensitive to the choice of the weight matrix, a robustness test was conducted by varying the k value. Specifically, the analysis was repeated for different k values (ranging from 10 to 100), allowing an assessment of how granularity affects cluster stability.

With low k values (e.g., $k = 10$), the analysis emphasized relationships between very close areas, resulting in high variability in clusters.

With high k values (e.g., $k > 80$), spatial relationships were broader, reducing local fluctuations and allowing for the identification of more robust and consistent patterns.

This approach was applied to various pairs of indicators representing the three main components of urban decay: physical-environmental, economic, and social. The analysis was repeated by reversing the roles of variables X and Y to further investigate relationships and potential cause-effect dynamics between indicators.

For the calculation of indices and the geovisualization of results, GeoDa, a software for spatial analysis and geographic modeling, was used [30].

5 Case Study

The case study focuses on the city of Rome, a complex urban environment characterized by a significant variety of social, economic, and environmental dynamics.

The analysis considered the areas within the Grande Raccordo Anulare (GRA), which include the historic center and the city's consolidated residential zones. The areas inside the GRA concentrate the majority of the population, economic activities, and urban infrastructure. These areas are marked by strong contrasts: central districts with high cultural and tourist attractiveness coexist with peripheral zones facing significant challenges in terms of quality of life and urban development [31].

For this research, the chosen territorial unit of analysis was the urban zones, an official administrative subdivision of the municipal territory that allows for the analysis of spatial phenomena at an intermediate scale between neighborhoods and municipal districts. Specifically, the study considered 106 urban zones located within the GRA.

A few urban decay indicators were selected to capture various aspects of the phenomenon, taking into account the three fundamental components that characterize it:

physical-environmental, economic, and social. These indicators were selected on the basis of literature and the socio-economic and environmental context of the city of Rome.

Physical-environmental component:

A. Building vacancy rate (%)
B. Average age of recent housing stock (years)
C. Number of sites containing asbetos per unit area(n/km^2)
D. Pollutante missions (µg/m^3)

Economic component:

E. Functional mix (n)
F. Public expenditure on urban decor interventions 2017–2023 (€)
G. Percentage change in residential property values 2017–2023 (%)
H. Percentage change in commercial property values 2017–2023 (%)
I. Percentage change in tertiary property values 2017–2023 (%)
J. Real estate market intensity trend (IMI) 2017–2023 (%)

Social component:

K. Disposable income (€/year)
L. Unemployment rate (%)
M. Education rate (%)
N. Number of Public Housing units (n)
O. Number of urban decay reports (n)

For the physical-environmental component, building-related data (indicators A and B) were collected using the Urbistat geomarketing software, which references data from the latest update of the ISTAT census. Information on the presence of asbestos (indicator C) was obtained from a regional mapping initiative, while pollutant emission data (indicator D) were sourced from the Regional Environmental Protection Agency of Lazio, considering major outdoor air pollutants.

For the economic component, real estate market indicators (G, H, I, and J) were obtained by constructing historical series based on data collected from the Real Estate Market Observatory (REMO) of the Italian Revenue Agency for the period 2017–2023. The functional mix indicator (E) was calculated using Shannon's entropy index based on economic activity data gathered through Urbistat. The public expenditure indicator for urban decor (F) was developed using information available on the OpenCUP portal, summing public investments allocated to urban decor-related interventions over the same period as the real estate market data (2017–2023).

For the social component, data on disposable income (K), unemployment rates (L), and education rates (M) were acquired through the Urbistat software. The number and location of Public Housing units (N) were obtained by cross-referencing data from Roma Capitale with those from the Territorial Company for the public Residential Construction of the Municipality of Rome. The number of urban decay reports (O) was gathered through resident surveys.

A summary table (Table 1) presents the pairs of indicators considered for the spatial correlation analysis and the results of the global-scale correlation analysis.

Table 1. Urban decay indicators and global spatial correlation analysis results.

Component	Indicators		Bivariate global Moran's index
	X	Y	
Physical-environmental	A	C	−0,030
	A	D	0,004
	B	C	0,217
	B	D	0,013
Economic	E	G	0,099
	E	H	0,038
	E	I	0,158
	E	J	-0,04
	F	G	0,022
Social	N	K	-0,058
	N	L	-0,027
	N	M	-0,004
	N	O	-0,008

6 Results

6.1 General Considerations

Based on the results obtained from the calculation of the local bivariate Moran's I index, a sensitivity analysis of the clusters was conducted by varying the k value. This analysis revealed significant changes in the distribution and stability of the clusters.

For instance, the "High-High" cluster showed a steady increase as k increased, indicating that at a broader scale, it is possible to identify more areas characterized by high values of positive indicators, such as high disposable income and high education levels. Specifically, for the indicator pair E - G, the "High-High" cluster increased from 32 ($k = 10$) to 106 ($k = 100$), stabilizing beyond this value. In general, this pattern was observed for almost all indicator pairs, except for some combinations, such as E - J and A - D.

The "Low-High" cluster was found to be the most unstable, showing significant variations at intermediate k levels, suggesting that transition areas between decay and development consolidate at higher granularities.

Conversely, the "Low-Low" cluster tended to shrink as k increased, reflecting a polarization of decay areas into more defined units. This behavior suggests that policies targeting such areas should be more focused and structural.

Distinct trends emerged for certain indicator pairs. For example, in the case of E - G, the increase in the "High-High" cluster with rising k highlights the positive role of functional space distribution in the real estate market. Simultaneously, the "Low-Low" cluster decreased, suggesting a concentration of decay areas into more specific zones. For the N - M pair, the increase in the "High-High" cluster with higher k values indicates a correlation between public housing and high education levels, while the reduction of the "Low-Low" cluster suggests that areas with low values for both indicators become less widespread at a broader scale.

In the k ranges where the frequency of certain clusters (e.g., High-High or Low-Low) stabilizes, more explanatory k values can be identified. For the High-High cluster, for example, an increase and stabilization can be observed from $k = 80$ onwards across different analyses. The Low-Low cluster tends to decrease to zero or disappear entirely in many cases for $k \geq 50$, suggesting that significant clusters are mainly concentrated in the High-High and Low-High categories.

6.2 Results of the Physical-Environmental Component

From the analysis conducted, regarding the vacancy rate of residential buildings, the spatial relationships with the presence of asbestos and pollutant emissions appear to be limited. Although some significant correlations were observed, particularly for the number of sites containing asbestos, where some cases of positive spatial correlation were recorded, the geographical distribution suggests that building vacancy and environmental management are weakly interconnected in this case. The average age of the recent housing stock proved to be more relevant, with direct correlations to the presence of asbestos. Areas with older buildings tend to be located near sites containing asbestos, especially in central areas. In terms of pollutant emissions, the spatial relationships are weak, suggesting that the age of buildings has limited influence on the air quality in the surrounding areas.

The results of the analysis allowed for the identification of different distribution clusters of the indicators. For each cluster, it was possible to provide an interpretation, and the related operational implications derived from the results. The number of clusters and their location varies depending on the value of k.

As an example, a summary table (Table 2) is provided, which includes these considerations for the pair of indicators: building vacancy rate (A), considered as X, and the number of sites containing asbestos per unit of area (C), considered as Y.

Table 2. Clusters obtainable from the calculation of the local bivariate Moran's I index between indicators A and C.

Cluster	Description	Interpretation	Implications
High-High	Areas with high vacancy rate and high presence of asbestos	Highly degraded areas due to abandonment and poor maintenance	Urgent intervention required for environmental remediation and building recovery
Low-Low	Areas with low vacancy rates and low presence of asbestos	Well-maintained areas, with potential for new investments	Monitoring to prevent further degradation

(*continued*)

Table 2. (*continued*)

Cluster	Description	Interpretation	Implications
Low-High	Areas with few vacant buildings but high presence of asbestos	Potential environmental problems inherited from historic buildings	Prioritize environmental remediation
High-Low	Areas with many vacant buildings but low presence of asbestos	Decay linked to building abandonment	Rehabilitation programs for repurposing buildings

6.3 Results of the Economic Component

The analysis of spatial correlations between functional mix and changes in property values (residential, commercial, and tertiary) highlights that economic dynamics are primarily concentrated in central areas. Zones characterized by high functional diversity tend to show a significant variation in property values in the surrounding areas (High-High cluster). However, inverse correlations emerge in peripheral areas: in these zones, high levels of functional diversity do not always correlate with positive changes in property values, suggesting divergent economic dynamics compared to the urban center. A particular case concerns public spending on urban decor, which mainly shows inverse correlations. Therefore, it can be said that the variation in residential property values is minimally influenced spatially by proximity to urban zones where urban decor improvement interventions have been made. On the other hand, it appears that for a certain number of urban areas within the historical center, there is a high spatial correlation between the two indicators.

The table (Table 3) below shows the interpretation of the clusters obtainable from the spatial correlation analysis between functional mix (E) as X and the percentage change in residential property values 2017–2023 (G) as Y.

Table 3. Clusters obtainable from the calculation of the local bivariate Moran's I index between indicators E and G.

Cluster	Description	Interpretation	Implications
High-High	Areas with high functional diversification and strong positive changes in residential property values	The functional mix contributes to an increase in residential value, thanks to a balance between residences, commerce, and services	Successful models to replicate in less dynamic areas
Low-Low	Areas with low functional mix and weak or negative residential changes	Areas with low attractiveness, where limited diversification hinders development	Encourage interventions to improve functional diversification and make areas more attractive

(*continued*)

Table 3. (*continued*)

Cluster	Description	Interpretation	Implications
Low-High	Areas with low functional mix but positive residential changes	Areas where the residential market grows independently of functional diversification	Analyze the reasons for residential success to improve functional balance
High-Low	Areas with high functional mix but negative residential changes	Areas where diversification does not generate improvements in the real estate market, possibly due to infrastructure deficiencies	Evaluate infrastructure and available services to maximize the benefits of functional mix

6.4 Results of the Social Component

The analysis of social indicators in relation to public housing reveals a prevalence of inverse correlations. For example, a low number of public housing units is often associated with poorer social conditions, such as low incomes or high unemployment rates, in nearby areas. Similarly, an inverse relationship is observed with the education rate: areas with fewer public housing units tend to be surrounded by areas with higher levels of education rate. On the other hand, areas characterized by a direct correlation, where a high number of public housing units coincides with better social conditions, are mainly concentrated in central areas, although they are fewer in number. Regarding urban decay reports, it is noted that areas with a high number of public housing units are often associated with a higher number of reports in neighboring areas, a phenomenon particularly evident in central zones.

For the social component, the table (Table 4) with the interpretation of the clusters obtainable from the correlation analysis between the number of public housing units (N) as X and disposable income (K) as Y is provided.

Table 4. Clusters obtainable from the calculation of the local bivariate Moran's I index between indicators N and K.

Cluster	Description	Interpretation	Implications
High-High	Areas with a high concentration of public housing associated with relatively high incomes	Indicates efficient management of public housing, with positive effects on average income	Replicate models of socio-economic integration in other areas
Low-Low	Zones with low income and a low number of public housing units	Exclusive residential areas that limit access for the most vulnerable social groups	Expand public housing to reduce spatial inequalities

(*continued*)

Table 4. (*continued*)

Cluster	Description	Interpretation	Implications
Low-High	Zones with high income and a low number of public housing units	Possible exclusion of middle- to low-income groups from the housing market	Promote social inclusion policies to prevent urban segregation phenomena
High-Low	Areas with a high presence of public housing but low incomes	Socially disadvantaged areas, where public housing fails to mitigate economic issues	Integrate housing policies with economic and social support programs

6.5 Cluster Map with k = 50

The spatial correlation analysis with the bivariate local Moran's index was conducted, as mentioned in the methodology section, for several values of k, where changes in k correspond to a different number and distribution of clusters.

Three examples of cluster maps obtained for $k = 50$ are provided, one for each component identified to analyze the phenomenon.

For the physical-environmental component, the map resulting from the spatial correlation analysis between the vacancy rate of buildings (A) considered as X and the number of asbestos-containing sites per unit of surface (C) as Y is shown (Fig. 1).

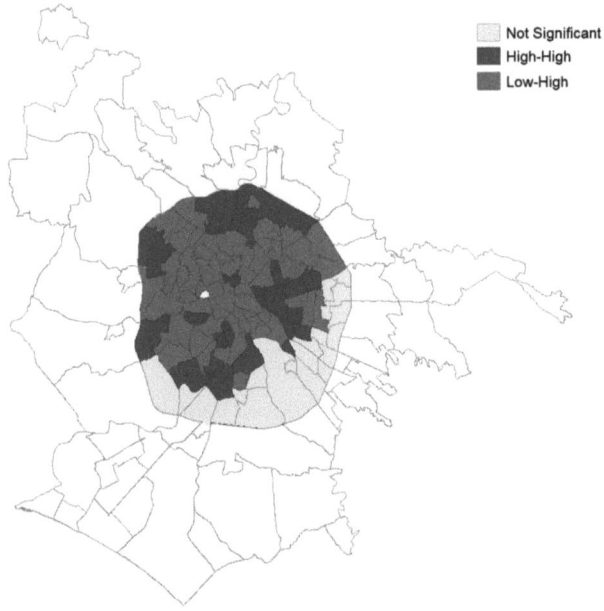

Fig. 1. Map of clusters obtained from the calculation of the local bivariate Moran's index between indicators A and C with $k = 50$.

In the figure, it can be observed that with a parameter $k = 50$, the analysis revealed that, out of 106 urban zones, 80% of the territory exhibits statistical significance, while for the remaining 20%, the results are not statistically significant. This suggests a random distribution or a high variability of the indicators.

The zones with statistical significance are divided into two clusters: High-High and Low-High. The majority of the zones, accounting for 53%, belong to the Low-High cluster, indicating an inverse spatial correlation: in areas with a low vacancy rate of residential buildings, a high number of asbestos-containing sites are found in the surrounding areas. These zones are relatively evenly distributed across the territory, unlike the High-High cluster, which covers 27% of the considered area and is more irregularly dispersed across different parts of the city.

The Moran's index reaches its lowest values in the central areas of the city, such as *Esquilino* (−0.76), *Flaminio* (−0.74), *Centro Storico* (−0.67), *Prati*, and *Celio* (−0.66). These negative values suggest that in central zones, the relationship between building vacancy and asbestos presence is weak or even absent. Conversely, areas characterized by a strong positive correlation show an uneven distribution within the GRA. The highest value is recorded in the urban zone of *Tor Fiscale* (0.93), located southeast of the urban center, while other high values are observed in *Casal Bruciato* (0.79) and *Testaccio* (0.77). These more peripheral areas may be characterized by poorly maintained buildings, where the presence of asbestos is more likely to be associated with a higher vacancy rate.

For the economic component, the map resulting from the spatial correlation analysis between functional mix (E) as X and the percentage variation in residential property values from 2017 to 2023 (G) as Y is presented (Fig. 2).

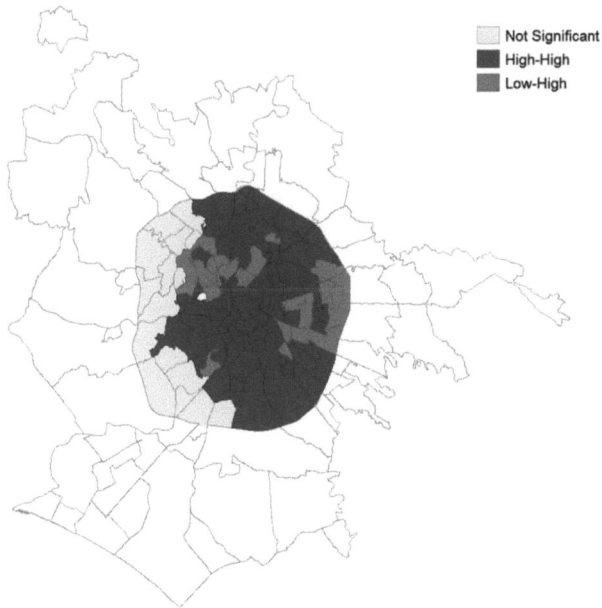

Fig. 2. Map of clusters obtained from the calculation of the local bivariate Moran's index between indicators E and G with $k = 50$.

The analysis conducted with $k = 50$ revealed that, out of 106 urban zones analyzed, only 15% exhibited a spatial correlation that was not statistically significant. Most of the areas belong to the High-High cluster (67 zones), while the remaining 23 fall into the Low-High cluster.

The zones characterized by a direct spatial correlation (High-High), where high levels of functional mix correspond to significant increases in residential property values in the surrounding areas over the past seven years, cover 63% of the analyzed territory and are relatively evenly distributed. However, the positive values of the Moran Index are not particularly high: the maximum value is recorded in the *Università* urban zone (0.59), while other notable values are found in the *Esquilino* and *XX Settembre* zones (0.50). In most cases, the index ranges between 0.10 and 0.15. This may suggest that, although functional diversification is linked to variations in property values, the effect is not strong enough to produce a significant impact.

The zones belonging to the Low-High cluster, where low economic activity diversification corresponds to high increases in residential property values, cover 22% of the analyzed areas and show a more irregular distribution. Two main concentrations can be identified: one in the central area and another in a peripheral area located east of the urban core. Finally, the zones where the correlation is negative present some extreme values, particularly in *Casetta Mistica* (−1.00) and *Tor Fiscale* (−0.88). Other less pronounced negative values are found in the *Omo* zone (−0.53) and the *Centro Direzionale Centocelle* (−0.45), while the most recurrent values range between −0.36 and − 0.21.

In the case of the social component, the map resulting from the spatial correlation analysis between the number of public housing units (N) as X and disposable income (K) as Y is reported (Fig. 3).

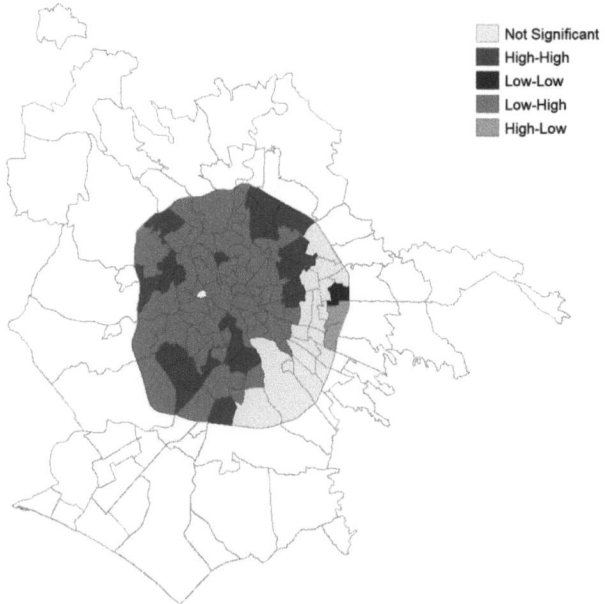

Fig. 3. Map of clusters obtained from the calculation of the local bivariate Moran's index between indicators N and K with $k = 50$.

The analysis conducted with k = 50 on the 106 urban zones showed that only 17% of them do not exhibit a spatially significant correlation. Most of the zones belong to the Low-High cluster (62 zones), while 23 zones fall into the High-High cluster. Additionally, there are two zones in the High-Low cluster and one in the Low-Low cluster, located near the GRA in the eastern part of the city.

The zones are characterized by an inverse spatial correlation (Low-High), where a low number of public housing units corresponds to high disposable income values in the surrounding areas, cover 58% of the analyzed territory and are relatively evenly distributed. However, Moran's index values remain moderate: the highest value is recorded in the *XX Settembre* and *Villa Borghese* areas (-0.25), followed by *Parioli* and Prati (-0.24). Most negative values fall within the range of -0.19 to -0.10.

Conversely, the zones with a direct spatial correlation (High-High), characterized by a high number of public housing units associated with relatively high incomes, show a more heterogeneous distribution across the territory, covering 22% of the area. In these zones, the highest Moran's index value is recorded in the Pineto area (1.00), followed by *Tufello* (0.68), while other areas, such as *Casal Bruciato*, exhibit lower values (0.30). Nonetheless, the most positive index values remain relatively low, ranging between 0.01 and 0.07.

7 Conclusions

Urban decay is a complex phenomenon resulting from the interaction of environmental, economic, and social factors, which manifest through non-random spatial dynamics. Its distribution across the territory is influenced by processes of concentration and diffusion that can exacerbate existing issues. In this context, spatial correlation analysis serves as an essential tool to understand the relationships between the variables contributing to decay and to identify significant patterns that can guide urban regeneration strategies. Urban planners and policymakers can use the results to develop regeneration strategies or targeted interventions, particularly in areas that have significant spillover effects.

This research implements a spatial correlation analysis using the bivariate Moran's index for the city of Rome. This analysis highlights the presence of significant clusters in the distribution of urban decay indicators, demonstrating how certain issues are concentrated in specific areas and can generate spillover effects in adjacent zones.

The stabilization of the High-High cluster beyond $k = 80$ suggests that urban decay in Rome follows large-scale spatial patterns, characterized by:

- Persistent and non-fragmented critical zones requiring coordinated interventions.
- Spillover effects of urban decay, making interventions in single neighborhoods insufficient.
- A minimum intervention scale that must cover entire urban areas rather than isolated points.

This suggests that highly critical urban zones tend to exhibit similar characteristics across a vast area rather than being scattered in a fragmented manner. Urban planning must therefore consider that decay is structured on a broad scale and requires regeneration efforts across extensive areas rather than isolated solutions.

The analysis results show that some areas exhibit decay patterns manifesting simultaneously across all three components (physical-environmental, economic, and social). In particular, the zones of Tormarancia, Testaccio, Serpentara, Casal Boccone, and Casal Bruciato belong to the High-High cluster in all three cases, indicating the presence of environmental issues (such as high building vacancy rates and asbestos presence) alongside a dynamic economic context characterized by a high functional mix and strong variations in residential property values. Conversely, the zones of Prati, Della Vittoria, Medaglie d'Oro, Farnesina, Parioli, Flaminio, Salario, and Trieste belong to the Low-High cluster across all components. These areas are distinguished by significant variations in residential property values but a low level of functional diversification. Additionally, the limited presence of public housing, combined with higher income levels, may exacerbate housing exclusion dynamics, reducing accessibility opportunities for economically vulnerable populations [32].

The findings confirm the need for an urban regeneration approach that considers interactions between indicators [33] and enables more effective intervention strategies by identifying areas where decay is most prevalent [34]. Specifically, urban regeneration policies should: i) promote functional diversification in declining areas to stimulate the real estate market; ii) optimize public housing management, as its concentration in economically disadvantaged areas without accompanying social inclusion policies and urban improvements may fail to enhance social conditions; iii) incentivize environmental remediation in historic areas to reduce environmental degradation [35–39].

The use of the local bivariate Moran's index also demonstrated how the granularity of the analysis influenced the identification of critical areas, with implications for defining the optimal intervention scale.

This research focused on the areas within Rome's GRA, future developments will extend the analysis to the entire city to capture the spatial dynamics characterizing even the most peripheral zones.

Note

The present study has been developer within the current "Sapienza" University Research Initiation Project 2024 entitled "A decision support model for the risk assessment of urban decay in urban regeneration interventions" and the current research P.R.I.N. Project 2022: "INSPIRE—Improving Nature-Smart Policies through Innovative Resilient Evaluations", Grant number: 2022J7RWNF.

References

1. Errante, L. Qualità dell'abitare urbano: un modello interpretativo per lo spazio pubblico. (2019)
2. Locurcio, M., Tajani, F., Anelli, D.: Sustainable urban planning models for new smart cities and effective management of land take dynamics. Land. **12**(3), 621 (2023)
3. Mireku, S.A., Abubakari, Z., Martinez, J.: Dimensions of urban blight in emerging southern cities: a case study of accra-ghana. Sustainability. **13**(15), 8399 (2021)
4. Martínez, C.F., Hodgson, F., Mullen, C., Timms, P.: Walking through deprived neighbourhoods: meanings and constructions behind the attributes of the built environment. Travel Behav. Soc. **16**, 171–181 (2019)

5. Vallebueno, A., Lee, Y.S.: Measuring urban quality and change through the detection of physical attributes of decay. Sci. Rep. **13**(1), 17316 (2019)
6. Maghelal, P., Andrew, S., Arlikatti, S., Jang, H.S.: Assessing blight and its economic impacts: a case study of Dallas, TX. WIT Trans. Ecol. Environ. **181**, 187–197 (2014)
7. Pinto, A.M., Ferreira, F.A., Spahr, R.W., Sunderman, M.A., Govindan, K., Meidutė-Kavaliauskienė, I.: Analyzing blight impacts on urban areas: a multi-criteria approach. Land Use Policy. **108**, 105661 (2021)
8. Razouk, H.: Integrating Domain Knowledge for the Analysis of Urban Blight Indicators Using NLP and Causal Data Science. (Doctoral dissertation, TU Graz) (2023)
9. Lokhande, T., Xie, Y.: Spatial spillover effects of urban decline in Southeast Michigan. Appl. Geogr. **158**, 103031 (2023)
10. Sun, W., Huang, Y., Spahr, R.W., Sunderman, M.A., Sun, M.: Neighborhood blight indices, impacts on property values and blight resolution alternatives. J. Real Estate Res. **41**(4), 555–604 (2019)
11. Cordera, R., Chiarazzo, V., Ottomanelli, M., dell'Olio, L., Ibeas, A.: The impact of undesirable externalities on residential property values: spatial regressive models and an empirical study. Transp. Policy. **80**, 177–187 (2019)
12. Anelli, D., Morano, P., Tajani, F., Sabatelli, E.: Impacts of urban decay on the residential property market: an application to the city of Rome (Italy). In: Computational Science and Its Applications – ICCSA 2024 Workshops: Hanoi, Vietnam, July 1–4, 2024, Proceedings, Part VIII, pp. 36–48. Springer International Publishing (2024)
13. Barreca, A., Curto, R., Rolando, D.: Assessing social and territorial vulnerability on real estate submarkets. Buildings. **7**(4), 94 (2017)
14. Murgante, B., Rotondo, F.: A geostatistical approach to measure shrinking cities: the case of Taranto. In: Statistical Methods for Spatial Planning and Monitoring, pp. 119–142 (2013)
15. Murgante, B., Danese, M., Las Casas, G.: Analyzing neighbourhoods suitable for urban renewal programs with autocorrelation techniques. In: Advances in Spatial Planning, pp. 165–178 (2012)
16. Basu, S., Thibodeau, T.G.: Analysis of spatial autocorrelation in house prices. J. Real Estate Financ. Econ. **17**, 61–85 (1998)
17. Bor-Ming, H.: Analisi della dipendenza spaziale dei prezzi delle abitazioni e dei sottomercati abitativi nella Tainan Metropolis, Taiwan. In: Territorio Italia, pp. 11–24 (2012)
18. Yang, L., Zhang, B., Zhang, X., Zhang, S., Yin, L.: Exploring the spatial correlation between accessibility to urban vibrancy centers and housing price from a time-dynamic perspective. GIScience Remote Sens. **60**(1), 2232191 (2023)
19. Barreca, A., Curto, R., Rolando, D.: Urban vibrancy: An emerging factor that spatially influences the real estate market. Sustainability. **12**(1), 346 (2020)
20. García-Ayllón, S., Franco, A.: Spatial correlation between urban planning patterns and vulnerability to flooding risk: a case study in murcia (Spain). Land. **12**(3), 543 (2023)
21. Mi, Y., Li, S., Wang, Z.: Spatial distribution and topographic gradient effects of habitat quality in the Chang-Zhu-Tan Urban Agglomeration, China. Sci. Rep. **14**(1), 22563 (2024)
22. Murgante, B., Casas, G.L., Danese, M.: Where are the slums? New approaches to urban regeneration. In: Social Computing, Behavioral Modeling, and Prediction, pp. 176–186. Springer US, Boston, MA (2008)
23. Murgante, B., Scorza, F.: Correlazione Spaziale e Pianificazione del Territorio: Principi ed Applicazioni (2023)
24. Tobler, W.R.: A computer model simulating urban growth in the detroit region. Econ. Geogr. **46**, 234–240 (1970)
25. Moran, P.A.: Notes on continuous stochastic phenomena. Biometrika. **37**(1/2), 17–23 (1950)
26. Geary, R.C.: The contiguity ratio and statistical mapping. Incorpor. Stat. **5**(3), 115–146 (1954)

27. Locurcio, M., Morano, P., Tajani, F., Di Liddo, F.: An innovative GIS-based territorial information tool for the evaluation of corporate properties: an application to the Italian context. Sustainability. **12**(14), 5836 (2020)
28. Chen, Y.: An analytical process of spatial autocorrelation functions based on Moran's index. PLoS One. **16**(4), e0249589 (2021)
29. Anselin, L.: Local indicators of spatial association—LISA. Geogr. Anal. **27**(2), 93–115 (1995)
30. Anselin, L., Syabri, I., Kho, Y.: GeoDa: an introduction to spatial data analysis. In: Handbook of Applied Spatial Analysis: Software Tools, Methods and Applications, pp. 73–89. Springer, Berlin, Heidelberg (2009)
31. Tajani, F., Sica, F., Morano, P., Guarini, M.R., Cerullo, G.: Neighbourhood markets as driving force of suburbs' urban regeneration: the case of the city of rome (Italy). In: International Symposium: New Metropolitan Perspectives, pp. 418–428. Springer Nature Switzerland, Cham (2024)
32. Locurcio, M., Tajani, F., Morano, P., Torre, C.M.: A fuzzy multi-criteria decision model for the regeneration of the urban peripheries. In: New Metropolitan Perspectives: Local Knowledge and Innovation Dynamics Towards Territory Attractiveness Through the Implementation of Horizon/E2020/Agenda2030–Volume 1, pp. 681–690. Springer International Publishing (2019)
33. Morano, P., Anelli, D., Tajani, F., Roma, A.: The real estate risk assessment: an innovative methodology for supporting public and private subjects involved into sustainable urban interventions. In: Computational Science and Its Applications-ICCSA 2023 Workshops, pp. 414–426. Springer International Publishing (2023)
34. Tajani, F., Anelli, D., Di Liddo, F., Morano, P.: An innovative methodology for the assessment of the social discount rate: an application to the European states for ensuring the goals of equitable growth. Smart Sustain. Built Environ. **13**(5), 1281–1309 (2024)
35. Santopietro, L., Solimene, S., Lucchese, M., Di Carlo, F., Scorza, F.: An economic appraisal of the SE (C) AP public interventions towards the EU 2050 target: the case study of Basilicata region. Cities. **149**, 104957 (2024)
36. Morano, P., Tajani, F., Di Liddo, F., Amoruso, P.: A feasibility analysis of energy retrofit initiatives aimed at the existing property assets decarbonisation. Sustainability. **16**(8), 3204 (2024)
37. Tajani, F., Morano, P.: Concession and lease or sale? A model for the enhancement of public properties in disuse or underutilized. WSEAS Trans. Bus. Econ. **17**, 18–28 (2014)
38. Anelli, D., Ranieri, R.: Resilience of complex urban systems: a multicriteria methodology for the construction of an assessment index. In: Calabrò, F., Della Spina, L., Bevilacqua, C. (eds.) New Metropolitan Perspectives. NMP 2022. Smart Innovation, Systems and Technologies, vol. 319, pp. 690–701. Springer, Cham (2022)
39. Manganelli, B., Anelli, D., Tajani, F., Morano, P.: Capitalization rate and real estate risk factors: an analysis of the relationships for the residential market in the city of Rome (Italy). Real Estate Manag. Valuat. **32**(3), 101–115 (2024)

Construction Cost Estimate and Building Information Modeling in Renovation Projects Early Design Stages

Pietro Bonifaci[1]( ), Sergio Copiello[1], and Federico Panarotto[2]

[1] Department of Architecture and Arts, University IUAV of Venice,
Santa Croce 191, Venice, Italy
{pietro.bonifaci,sergio.copiello}@iuav.it

[2] Department of Cultural Heritage, University of Padua, piazza Capitaniato 7, Padua, Italy
federico.panarotto@unipd.it

Abstract. The evaluation and control of building costs accompany real estate projects from the initial planning phase to the end of the construction stage. Each phase of project development is associated with distinct estimation methodologies, characterized by an increasing level of accuracy as the design progresses. Estimating construction costs during the early design stages is one of the most critical challenges in real estate and infrastructure investment planning. At these stages, detailed cost estimates based on bills of quantities are always unfeasible, as project information is typically limited to concise descriptions of functions and dimensions. Consequently, assessments rely on parametric methods, which involve identifying one or more reference buildings with similar characteristics to the planned one, using historical data on its costs as a basis for estimation. The cost of the reference buildings can be sourced from market monitors or specialized publications, such as building cost inventories. These inventories, in addition to providing construction costs divided by groups of work items, typically include key dimensional data, works brief description, and project excerpts. This study presents the results of BIM modeling for one of the buildings included in an inventory widely used in Italy, aiming to explore the potential of this technology to enhance cost estimate accuracy in the early design stages. The accuracy of parametric estimates based on data from the inventory and those derived from the BIM model is validated by comparison with a case study, for which the construction cost has been assessed through a bill of quantities.

Keywords: Building Information Modeling · Parametric construction cost estimate · Real estate investment planning

1 Introduction

The assessment and control of construction costs is an activity that involves the building process from the initial phases of investment planning to the conclusion of the construction and the commissioning of the property. In the architecture, engineering, and construction industry - and in the manufacturing sector, more generally - each phase of project development is paired with different cost estimation methodologies. The choice of the methodology to be used depends on the availability of information in each project phase and on the purpose of the assessment. The literature has provided various classifications of cost estimation methodologies with reference to the phases of product development [1, 2]. Regarding the construction industry, and based on a classification provided by [3], Aram et al. [4] have identified two categories related to the maturity level of project definition. The first one, suitable for use in the early design stages, comprises intuitive and analogical techniques, through which project costs are estimated based on historical data from similar projects. The second category, used in late design stages, includes analytical methods, which involve breaking down the construction to calculate its cost as the sum of the prices of its individual components or operations.

The accuracy of cost estimates is expected to increase as the project progresses: the more information is provided, the more precise the assessment becomes. AACE (Association for the Advancement of Cost Engineering) International [5] has developed a matrix that illustrates the general relationship between project development maturity, categorized into five classes based on the percentage of complete project definition, and the expected accuracy range of estimates for each phase. The relationship is shown in the following Fig. 1.

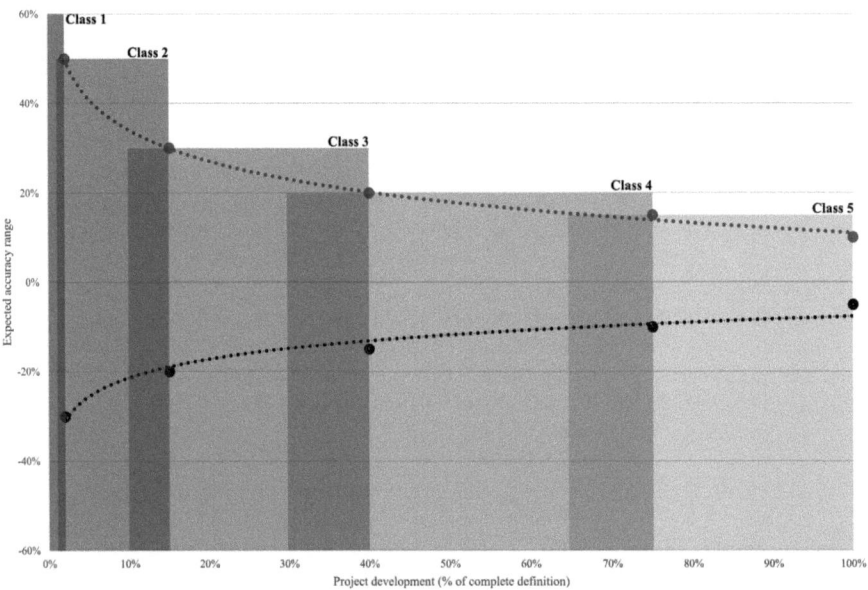

Fig. 1. Expected accuracy range based on maturity level of project definition (source: AACE International [5]).

Estimating construction costs during the early design stages is one of the most critical challenges in real estate investment planning [6–8]. Indeed, despite the limited design information and unpredictable external factors [3], early estimates significantly influences a projects success or failure as 70%–80% of the total building costs are determined at this stage, leaving little room for adjustments in later phases [6, 7].

If we assume that early design stages correspond to class five and four of the classification proposed by AACE, project information are often limited to location, building typology, functional space requirements, number of stories, preliminary room layouts, design criteria report, or technical memorandum by division of works, and the accuracy level of estimates can range from $-30\%/-20\%$ to $+30\%/+50\%$, depending on the projects complexity, degree of definition, availability of reference data, and also including an appropriate contingency[1] definition.

The purpose of this research is to verify whether the adoption of BIM (Building Information Modeling) design can improve the accuracy of construction cost estimates in the early design stages, with particular reference to renovation projects. In fact, although some studies highlight the need to deepen the use of BIM for cost estimation – the so-called fifth dimension of BIM [9, 10] – in the early design stages [11–14], much of the literature has primarily focused on using this technology for detailed cost estimation in late design stages [15], including the analysis of costs related to alternative design scenarios [16], improving quantity take-off activities [17, 18], reducing errors when drafting bills of quantities [19], and monitoring project progression [20].

To assess the potential of using BIM to enhance the accuracy of estimates during early design stages, the case study of a dwelling renovation will be analyzed. The cost, estimated through a bill of quantities in the late design stages, will serve as the benchmark for comparing early estimates made using traditional methods and those based on BIM model.

The paper is organized as follows: Sect. 2 provides a description of the cost estimation methodology in early design stages; Sect. 3 presents the application of a BIM-based design for cost estimation in the early design stages; Sect. 4 describes the case study and the application of traditional and BIM-based approaches for cost estimate. In Sect. 5, results of the application are discussed. Finally, Sect. 6 draws conclusions and outlines further developments.

2 Cost Assessment in Early Design Stages

As introduced earlier, the methodologies most frequently used for cost estimation in early design stages can be categorized as analogical techniques, such as historical unit prices, functional space unit price [5], superficial area [21], and elemental [22] methods, to name a few. These methods, through the identification of a reference parameter that allows the linking of technical information to economic data by associating unit costs with physical characteristics [1, 2, 23], allow cost estimation by comparing historical cost data of similar buildings (comparables) to the one to be built (subject). In general, the application of analogical methodologies involves the following steps.

---

[1] "An amount added to an estimate to allow for items, conditions, or events for which the state, occurrence, or effect is uncertain and that experience shows will likely result, in aggregate, in additional costs. Typically estimated using statistical analysis or judgment based on past asset or project experience" [29 p. 31].

1. Identification of the comparable(s) with construction characteristics similar to the subject. The construction cost and the main dimensional, functional, and physical data of the comparable(s) must be known. Comparable(s) can be identified by consulting the technical and economic documentation of similar constructions, or through specialized publications, such as the inventories of building typologies and construction costs.
2. Selection of the parameter to be used for the estimation. The parameter is chosen based on the typology of the subject, such as gross floor area for residential buildings, the number of parking spaces for garages, or the number of rooms for hotels and other accommodation facilities.
3. Calculation of the unit cost, obtained by dividing the total cost of the comparables by the identified parameter quantity.
4. Estimation of the subject's construction cost, obtained by multiplying the parametric cost from step 3 by the parameter quantity of the subject.

The superficial area method, used in this research, assumes that the reference parameter is the surface area of the building (in this research, the gross floor area – GFA). Therefore, the construction cost of the subject is assessed by multiplying the parametric cost (€/m² of GFA) of the comparable by the GFA of the subject.

If adequate information on costs and construction characteristics of both the subject and the comparables are available, an alternative procedure known as the elemental method may be used. This method "considers the major elements of a building and provides an order of cost estimate based on an elemental breakdown of the building project" [22 p. 29].

This approach requires the buildings (subject and comparable) to be divided into their major elements, the dimensions of which must be known. Moreover, the unit cost of each element must also be known for the comparables. The construction cost of the subject is then assessed by summing the unit cost of each element multiplied by the corresponding quantity, according to the following equation:

$$Cc = \sum_{i=1}^{n} Eq_i \times Ec_i \qquad (1)$$

where: Cc is the construction cost of the subject; Eq_i is the quantity of the i element of the subject; Ec_i is the unit construction cost of the ith element of the comparable(s).

The cost of the reference buildings can be sourced from market monitors or specialized publications, such as building cost inventories. In Italy, the most widely used information sources for the parametric estimation of construction costs [24] is the Price list of building typology and related construction costs published by the Milan Board of Engineers and Architects [25]. The inventory provides, based on the actual costs of various types of works (new construction, renovation, maintenance, etc.) and different building types, a breakdown of construction costs by elements. Moreover, a description of the works, reference drawings, and the main dimensional data are provided. However, the dimensional data are limited to the key parameters typical of each specific building type: for residential buildings, the gross floor area and volume; for industrial buildings, the volume; for hotels, the number of rooms, and so on. The cost of all building elements is then related to a single parameter – such as the gross floor area in residential buildings – which makes this information suitable for applying the superficial area method.

The application of the elemental method requires the costs of various elements be linked to their characteristic dimensions, as it is fundamentally a multi-parametric estimation approach. For instance, the parametric cost of windows and frames is not related to the gross floor area but rather to the surface area of the windows themselves, and the same principle applies to other elements. Consequently, detailed information on the dimensions of various elements is required for both the comparable(s) and the subject.

To obtain information regarding the dimension of the various elements of the construction for the application of the elemental method, a BIM model was created based on the documentation of one of the cases included in the inventory. The modeling process is discussed in the next section.

3 BIM Design for Parametric Cost Assessment

3.1 Overview on BIM Potentialities for Cost Assessment

At every stage of a building design process, BIM technology enables the extraction of precise calculations of quantities and spatial data, which can be used for cost estimation [26]. In advanced project phases, BIM-based models serve as a reliable tool for obtaining detailed quantity data, allowing for accurate cost estimates. Patrick MacLeamy, one of the pioneers in the theoretical development of the BIM methodology, emphasized that its use has the greatest impact in the early design phases [26]. A key advantage of BIM in this decision-making process is its ability to adapt and parametrically modify the project while maximizing integration across different disciplines. This enhances the speed of development and ensures more effective cost estimation. The automation of precise quantity calculations in parametric 3D models - where parameters, both dimensional and non-dimensional, can be easily adjusted - has made BIM-based approaches among the most widely adopted [16]. In traditional 3D CAD systems, every geometric aspect of an element must be manually adjusted by the user. In contrast, parametric modeling allows the shape or geometry of a component to update automatically in response to contextual changes and predefined user settings. In this approach, geometry adjusts dynamically based on the rules governing its definition [26]. Another crucial aspect of this methodology is its ability to automatically generate a network of relationships between BIM objects. This enables the reciprocal association of specific attributes - e.g. length, area, and cost - between model elements, such as the wall-window, wall-room, or wall-floor relationships.

Current BIM design tools automatically incorporate these functionalities and adopt what is known as "object-based parametric modeling". These features allow for precise and reliable quantity take-off in the more advanced design phases, as well as the generation of detailed as-built drawings. The process of extracting quantitative information relies on standard tools that query the model to obtain accurate geometric data. These tools often include dedicated quantity surveying functions within common BIM software, enabling the analysis of any model component - for instance, extracting all properties of a single wall layer. However, when performing quantity estimation in the early design stages, standard BIM authoring tools may present limitations due to their lack of customization. If the built-in functionalities do not adequately meet specific requirements, Visual Programming Languages (VPLs) can be employed [27]. These tools, often integrated within BIM software, enhance their capabilities by combining geometric modeling functions with algorithm creation. Unlike traditional programming, VPLs allow users to develop scripts through graphical manipulation of elements rather than written code, making them accessible to professionals without coding expertise [28]. In this specific case, the need to associate building spaces with their corresponding architectural components - such as walls, doors, and windows - required the development of a custom script. This script, interacting automatically with the BIM environment, can extract the required geometric quantities.

3.2 The Use of BIM in This Study

The modeling process of the reference building was carried out in two distinct steps. The first involved creating the geometries using a well-established parametric modeling approach, while the second focused on developing a script to extract the required quantities and process them through algebraic operations. The modeling began by defining a lower and an upper level, which, in BIM practice, establish a typical parametric modeling space that can be easily updated. Next, walls - consisting of a single generic layer - were created between these two levels, along with the openings they accommodate. Doors and windows were inserted using a library of modifiable objects, which can be easily adjusted through dedicated parameters. Finally, rooms were placed within the model. These were automatically recognized by the software as enclosed spaces defined by walls. Each room was then assigned a unique number and name based on its function, enabling the extraction of key dimensional data for the interior spaces. The resulting building model allows for easy geometric updates by modifying parameters, facilitating the exploration of different design scenarios.

The developed script begins by automatically acquiring all rooms within the model. Through a sort list operation, it organizes and groups them into specific housing units while identifying all spatially related elements. This process enables the identification

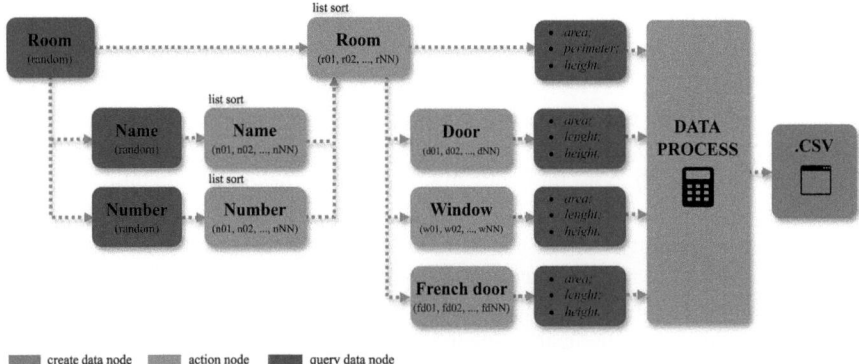

Fig. 2. Script workflow diagram.

and classification of all walls within the perimeter of each room, along with their associated openings. Once this operation is complete, the script extracts all relevant parameters linked to the architectural components - such as surface area, perimeter, height, and width - and combines them through algebraic operations with cost data to generate the required quantity estimates. Finally, all collected data is compiled into a CSV (Comma-Separated Values) file and exported in the common XLSX format (Fig. 2). The script runs automatically, ensuring that any updates to the model parameters are reflected real-time in the quantity calculations. This process represents a fully automated approach to quantity take-off for buildings modeled in a BIM environment.

4 Case Study

To verify whether the additional information obtained from the BIM model of a reference building actually results in more accurate cost estimates during the early design stages of renovation projects, a case study is developed. The process includes the following stages (Fig. 3). Firstly, a detailed cost estimate of a residential renovation project, used as the subject, is carried out through the preparation of a bill of quantities. The second phase involves identifying a reference building to be used as comparable from the aforementioned price list. Then, cost estimates are carried out using the superficial area method, and, after creating the BIM model of the comparable, the elemental method is applied. Finally, the accuracy of the parametric estimates is evaluated using the results of the bill of quantities as benchmark.

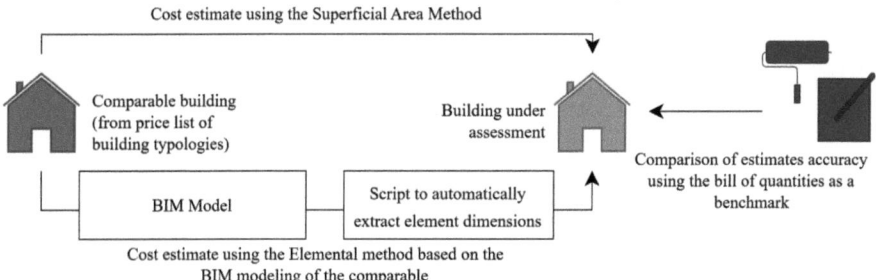

Fig. 3. Methodology workflow diagram.

4.1 Description and Cost Benchmark

The case study concerns the renovation of a flat located on the mezzanine floor of a condominium with ten residential units, built in 1927. For the purposes of this study, it is assumed that it is located on the outskirts of a medium-sized city in the Veneto region, northeast Italy, in an area characterized by good accessibility. The apartment consists of one living room, a kitchen, two bedrooms, one bathroom, and a small corridor. The gross floor area is 79 m^2, while the net floor area is 62.5 m^2. Fig. 4 shows the floor plan of the flat.

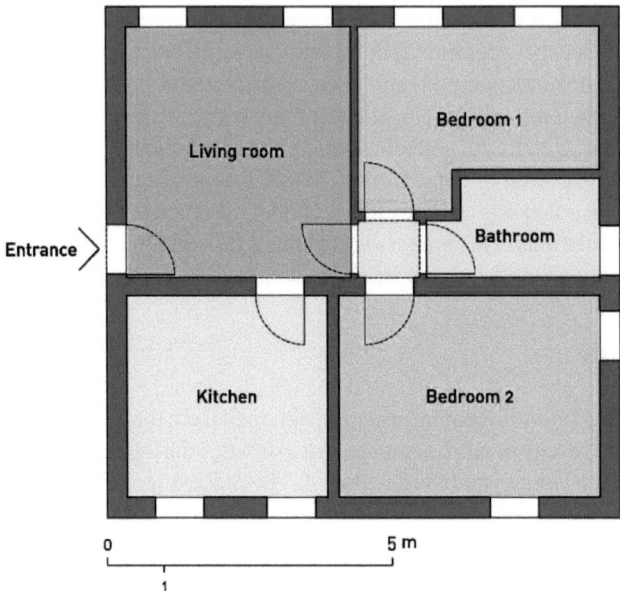

Fig. 4. Floor plan of the case study.

The renovation includes the following work: laying of internal wall and ceiling plaster; construction of screeds and installation of floors, with wooden flooring in the bedrooms and the small hallway, and tiled flooring in the other rooms; installation of tile cladding on the kitchen and bathroom walls; painting of internal walls; replacement of windows and doors. For the purposes of this study, costs related to demolition and the installation of heating, water, and electrical systems were not included. In order to identify the renovation cost to be used as a benchmark, a bill of quantities for the works was prepared, using the Public Works Price List of the Veneto Region, 2024 edition, as a reference. Table 1 provides a summary of work items, quantities, unit prices, and cost estimate obtained through the bill of quantities. The total renovation cost thus obtained is 42,166.59 €.

4.2 Superficial Area Method Based on Cost Inventory Data

The cost estimation using the superficial area method first requires identifying a suitable comparable within the mentioned price list of building typologies. Comparable A.8, renovation of a penthouse in a downtown area, was selected as it shares similar characteristics to those expected for the subject in terms of the breakdown of the work. Indeed, the costs of the comparable are broken down into a series of work categories that group together typical bill-measured items.

Table 1. Summary of the estimate from the bill of quantities.

Work	Quantity	Rate (€/UoM)	Total (€)
Providing and laying in position of two-coat interior plaster, applied at any height on vertical, horizontal, with an average total thickness of 20 mm. The area measured is the internal net surface area of walls (excluding doors and windows) and ceilings. (m^2)	269.76	27.08	7,305.10
Painting with washable paint for interior walls. The area measured is the internal net surface area of walls (excluding doors and windows) and ceilings. The area of bathroom and kitchen walls with tile cladding is also excluded. (m^2)	226.36	11.99	2,714.06
Reinforced concrete screed 10 cm thick. The area measured is the net area of floors. (m^2)	62.40	44.77	2,793.65
Providing and laying in position of first-choice ceramic floor tiles in the bathroom and the kitchen. The area measured is the net area of floors. (m^2)	16.90	50.49	853.28
Providing and laying in position of first-choice ceramic floor tiles in the living room. The area measured is the net area of floors. (m^2)	17.00	96.29	1,636.93
Providing and laying in position of oak wood flooring in bedrooms and the corridor. The area measured is the net area of floors. (m^2)	28.50	201.01	5,728.79
Providing and laying in position of oak wood skirting board in bedrooms and the corridor. The length measured is the perimeter of the room excluding doors. (m)	29.90	22.01	658.10
Providing and laying in position of first-choice ceramic skirting board in the living room. The length measured is the perimeter of the room excluding doors. (m)	13.95	50.12	699.17
Providing and laying in position of first-choice ceramic cladding tiles in the bathroom and the kitchen. The area measured is the internal net surface area of all walls cladded with ceramic tiles (excluding doors and windows). (m^2)	40.34	50.49	2,036.77
Providing and laying in position of aluminum windows with double glazing, including all the necessary components. The area measured is the net area of windows. (m^2)	13.01	653.70	8,501.35
Providing and laying in position of aluminum shutters. The area measured is the net area of windows. (m^2)	13.01	452.80	5,888.66
Providing and laying in position of internal wood doors including all the necessary components. The area measured is the net area of doors. (m^2)	10.71	312.86	3,350.73
TOTAL			42,166.59

Table 2 shows the comparable cost distribution across the various works categories and the unit cost referred to the gross floor area. Works categories considered for the subject cost estimation are highlighted using bold font and refer to the renovation works listed in Sect. 4.1.

Table 2. Construction costs of the comparable.

n.	Work category	Cost (€)	Unit Cost (€/m² GFA)
1	Scaffolding	1,49,641	
2	Demolitions and removals	27,370	
3	Reinforced concrete works and load-bearing masonry	1,26,978	
4	Roof	59,433	
5	Internal walls and insulation	37,822	
6	**Plaster**	**36,220**	**69.65**
7	Plasterboards suspended ceilings	4,377	
8	**Ceramic floors (in living area)**	**40,382**	**77.66**
9	**Wood floors (in sleeping area)**	**21,784**	**41.89**
10	**Traditional ceramic floors (in bathrooms and kitchens)**	**4,443**	**8.54**
11	**Ceramic cladding in bathrooms and kitchens**	**12,728**	**24.48**
12	**Painting**	**15,364**	**29.55**
13	**Doors**	**24,760**	**47.62**
14	Skylights	24,657	
15	**Windows**	**50,440**	**97.00**
16	Heating and cooling system	1,90,272	
17	Bricklayer support to heating and cooling system inst.	40,790	
18	Water system	57,021	
19	Bricklayer support to water system inst.	18,321	
20	Electrical system	75,515	
21	Bricklayer support to elettrical system inst.	37,216	
22	Lifts extension	1,23,784	
23	Bricklayer support to lifts extension	34,932	
TOTAL (€)		1,214,250	
GFA (m²)		520	
Total Unit Cost (€/m²)		2,335	
Total Unit Cost of works considered for estimation (€/m²)			396.39

The selected comparable, in fact, included additional works not relevant to the case study, such as roof reconstruction, installation of lifts, changes to the internal room layout, and so on. For the identified work categories, the unit cost has been calculated by dividing the total cost by the gross floor area of the comparable.

Table 3. Superficial area method cost estimate.

Work category	Unit cost (€/m² GFA)	Cost (€/m²)
Plaster	69.65	5,502.35
Ceramic floors (in living area)	77.66	6,135.14
Wood floors (in sleeping area)	41.89	3,309.31
Traditional ceramic floors (in bathrooms and kitchens)	8.54	674.66
Ceramic cladding in bathrooms and kitchens	24.48	1,933.92
Painting	29.55	2,334.45
Doors	47.62	3,761.98
Windows	97.00	7,663.00
TOTAL	396.39	31,314.81

The cost estimation was then carried out by applying the unit costs thus obtained to the subject gross floor area. As a result, the total renovation cost of the building under assessment using the superficial area method amounts to 31,314.81 €, derived from the product of the sum of the unit costs of the various work categories (396.39 €/m²) and its gross floor area (79 m²). Table 3 presents the results of the parametric estimation using the superficial area method.

4.3 Elemental Method Based on the BIM Modeling of the Comparable

Using dimensional information and technical drawings provided by the price list, a BIM model of the comparable was created. Figs. 5 and 6 show a sample view of the BIM model and the floor plan as issued in the price list.

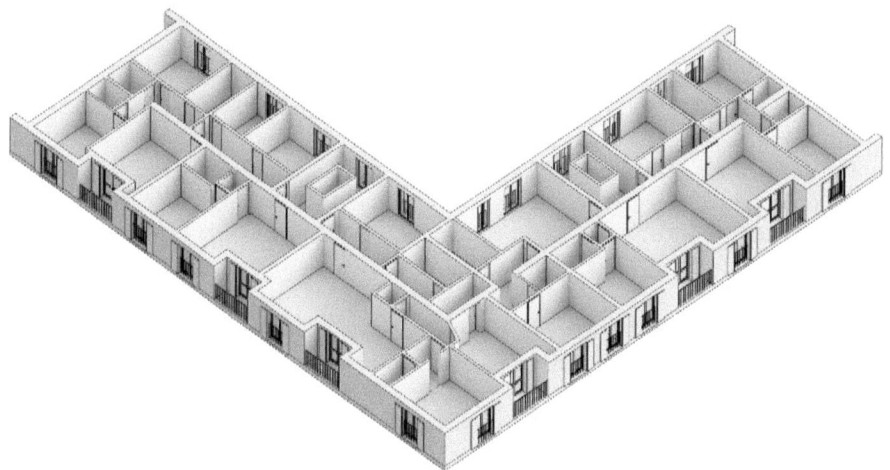

Fig. 5. BIM model of the comparable building.

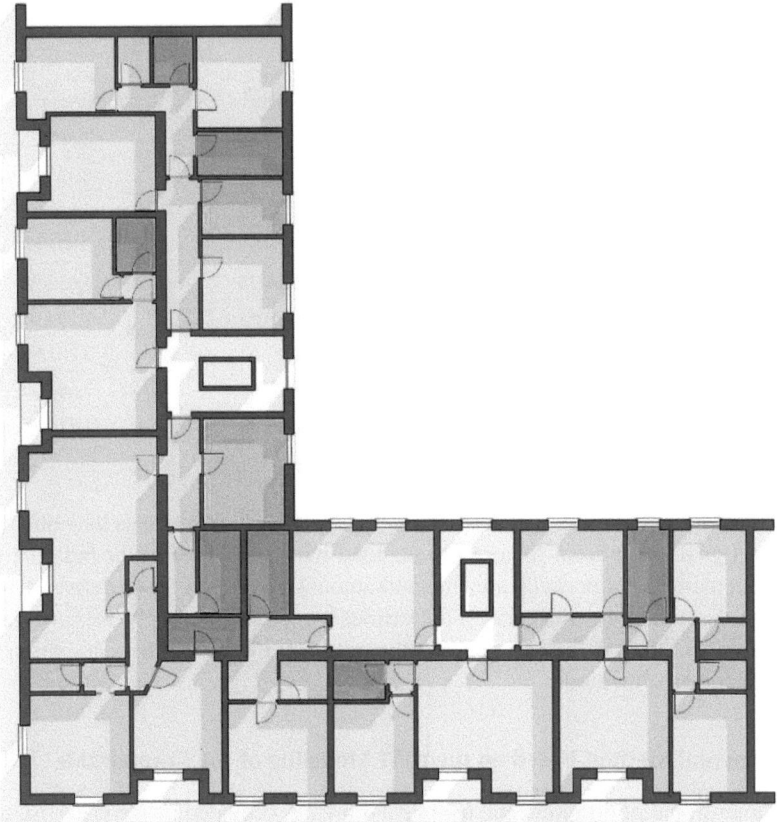

Fig. 6. Floor plan of the comparable building.

Then, by means of the script described in Sect. 3, it was possible to extract the dimensional details of the individual elements of the construction, in order to apply the elemental method for the cost estimate. The information extracted through the script, divided for each individual room of the reference building, is presented in an aggregated form in Table 4.

The costs of the reference building elements can therefore be related to the actual dimensions of the elements themselves. For example, the cost of plastering is divided by the sum of the Net walls surface area and Floors and ceilings surface area, the cost of painting is divided by the sum of the Painted net walls surface area and Floors and ceilings surface area, and so on. This allows for the calculation of their unit cost, as shown on the left side of Table 5. The parametric costs thus obtained are then applied to the dimensions of the elements of the building under assessment to obtain the estimate shown in the right part of the same table. Therefore, using the elemental method based on the BIM Modeling, the total renovation cost of the subject amounts to 44,838.83 €.

Table 4. Extraction of dimensions from the reference building elements.

Information	Description	Dimension
A - Room	Room identification code	–
B - Use	Room intended use	–
C - Room perimeter	Gross perimeter of the rooms (m)	535.17
D - Average height	Rooms average height (m)	2,2
E - Gross walls surface area	Total gross walls surface area (m^2)	1,177.37
F - Doors	Total number of doors (nr.)	82.00
G - Doors surface area	Total net surface area of doors (m^2)	137.76
H - Windows	Total number of windows (nr.)	20.00
I - Windows surface area	Total net surface area of windows (m^2)	44.46
L - French doors	Total number of French doors (nr.)	6.00
M - French doors surface area	Total net surface area of French doors (m^2)	15.12
N - Net walls surface area*	Total net walls surface area (m^2)	980.03
O - Tile cladding	Total surface area of walls cladded with tiles (m^2)	190.33
P - Painted net walls surface area**	Total painted net walls surface area (m^2)	789.70
Q - Floors and ceilings surface area	Total floor surface area of rooms (m^2)	410.37
R - Ceramic floors surface area	Total surface area of rooms with ceramic floor (m^2)	57.65
S - Non-ceramic floors surface area	Total surface area of rooms with non-ceramic floor (m^2)	352.72

* The surface area of doors, windows, and French doors is excluded (used, for example, to quantify plastering).
** The surface area of doors, windows, and French doors and that of tile cladding is excluded (used to quantify paintings).

Table 5. Unit costs of reference building elements.

	Comparable			Subject	
Work category (The letters refer to the elements described in Table 4)	Cost (€)	El. Dim. (m^2)	Unit Cost (€/m^2)	El. Dim. (m^2)	Cost (€)
Plaster - N + Q	36,220	1,421.06	25.49	269.76	6,876.18
Ceramic floors - R	40,382	226.41	178.36	17.00	3,032.12
Wood floors - S	21,784	126.31	172.46	28.50	4,915.11
Traditional ceramic floors - R	4,443	57.65	77.07	16.90	1,302.48
Ceramic cladding - O	12,728	261.36	48.70	40.34	1,964.56

(*continued*)

Table 5. (*continued*)

Work category (The letters refer to the elements described in Table 4)	Comparable			Subject	
	Cost (€)	El. Dim. (m²)	Unit Cost (€/m²)	El. Dim. (m²)	Cost (€)
Painting - P + Q	15,364	1,247.71	12.31	226.36	2,786.49
Doors – G	24,760	75.60	327.51	10.71	3,507.63
Windows - I + M	50,440	64.14	786.40	26.01	20,454.26
		TOTAL			44,838.83

5 Discussion

The tables below compare the results of the estimates obtained through the application of the three methods. The cost items in the bill of quantities have been grouped to align with the work categories identified for the reference building. Using the values from the bill of quantities as a benchmark, Table 6 shows the deviations for the superficial area method, while Table 7 presents those for the elemental method, both in absolute values and percentage terms. The following Fig. 7 shows the comparison of the percentage deviation from the benchmark of the two methods estimates.

Table 6. Comparison between bill of quantities and superficial area method estimates.

Work category	Cost benchmark (€)	Cost Sup. area meth. (€)	Absolute deviation (€)	% deviation
Plaster	7,305.10	5,502.35	-1,802.75	−24.68%
Ceramic floors	3,097.19	6,135.14	3,037.95	98.09%
Wood floors	7,662.83	3,309.31	−4,353.52	−56.81%
Traditional ceramic floors	1,609.89	674.66	−935.23	−58.09%
Ceramic cladding in bathrooms and kitchens	2,036.77	1,933.92	−102.85	−5.05%
Painting	2,714.06	2,334.45	−379.61	−13.99%
Doors	3,350.73	3,761.98	411.25	12.27%
Windows	14,390.02	7,663.00	−6,727.02	−46.75%
TOTAL	42,166.59	31,314.81	−10,851.78	−25.74%

Table 7. Comparison between bill of quantities and elemental method estimates.

Work category	Cost benchmark (€)	Cost element meth (€)	Absolute deviation (€)	% deviation
Plaster	7,305.10	6,876.18	−428.92	−5.87%
Ceramic floors	3,097.19	3,032.12	−65.07	−2.10%
Wood floors	7,662.83	4,915.11	−2,747.72	−35.86%
Traditional ceramic floors	1,609.89	1,302.48	−307.41	−19.10%
Ceramic cladding in bathrooms and kitchens	2,036.77	1,964.56	−72.21	−3.55%
Painting	2,714.06	2,786.49	72.43	2.67%
Doors	3,350.73	3,507.63	156.90	4.68%
Windows	14,390.02	20,454.26	6,064.24	42.14%
TOTAL	42,166.59	44,838.83	2,672.24	6.34%

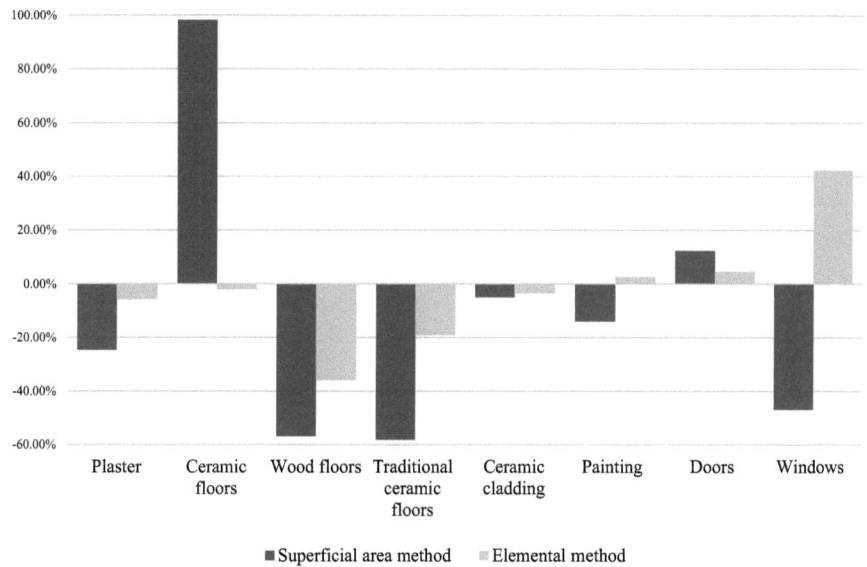

Fig. 7. Comparison of the percentage deviation from the benchmark of the two methods estimates.

Regarding the superficial area method, the cost categories with the largest deviations are those related to flooring, all of which are more than 50% higher than the benchmark (with ceramic flooring in the living area showing a percentage difference of +98.09%), and the external windows and doors category (−46.75%). The latter also shows a significant deviation in the elemental method estimate, although with opposite sign (+42.14%). This result may be due to the fact that the costs of the reference building, although updated annually, refer to a building constructed in 2004, and thus to technologies, particularly for windows and insulation, whose performance may no longer be applicable given the evolution of energy efficiency regulations. As for flooring, the elemental method yields more accurate results, especially for ceramic flooring, while for wooden floors it shows a greater underestimation (though smaller than that of the superficial area method), likely due to issues related to the quality of finishes (even though the same type of wood – oak – was chosen for both the subject and the comparable building). The best elemental method estimates are obtained for all the work related to walls (plastering, painting, and cladding), and for internal doors, for which the deviation from the benchmark is below 5%. As for the total cost, the elemental method estimate shows an overall deviation from the benchmark of 6.34%, which is a quarter of the absolute deviation of the superficial area method (−25.74%). From a timing perspective, the development of the BIM model required approximately two hours of work by an expert in modeling. The creation of the script took about four hours. The replication of the method requires only the development of additional BIM models, while the script operates independently and data processing is performed instantaneously.

Therefore, the elemental method based on BIM modeling seems to have significant potential for improving the accuracy of building renovation cost estimates in the early design stages.

6 Conclusions and Further Development

The research compared two methods for parametric construction cost estimate in early design stages. Starting from one of the most commonly used information sources in Italy for early design cost assessment, a BIM model and a script were developed to extract a larger amount of information on dimensions of the elements composing a construction identified as comparable. This allowed to assess the renovation costs of a sample property using both the superficial area method and the elemental method. By comparing the results of the two methods with the cost estimate carried out through the preparation of a detailed bill of quantities, it was concluded that the elemental method allows for a more accurate estimate, deviating by +6.34% from the expected costs, whereas the estimate performed with the superficial area method showed a significantly larger deviation of −25.75%. The latter aligns with the tolerances identified in the literature regarding the accuracy of estimates in the early design stages, while the former approaches the accuracy expected in late design stages. The results may be due to the choice of the case study: the renovation works (where the dimensions of the subject's elements are known beforehand and are only partially defined during the design phase, whereas in new constructions the dimensions of some elements in the early design stages may be entirely unknown), as well as the relative simplicity of the analyzed renovation project.

Future developments of the research aim, on one hand, to extend these analyses to more complex cases of building rehabilitation and new construction, and on the other hand, to test the creation of BIM models for comparables that include cost information, leveraging parametric modeling to allow for the inclusion of cost information and support more accurate estimates in early design stages.

References

1. Duverlie, P., Castelain, J.M.: Cost Estimation During Design Step: Parametric Method versus Case Based Reasoning Method. (1999)
2. Salmi, A., David, P., Blanco, E., Summers, J.D.: A review of cost estimation models for determining assembly automation level. Comput. Ind. Eng. **98**, 246–259 (2016). https://doi.org/10.1016/j.cie.2016.06.007
3. Niazi, A., Dai, J.S., Balabani, S., Seneviratne, L.: Product cost estimation: technique classification and methodology review. J. Manuf. Sci. Eng. **128**(2), 563–575 (2006). https://doi.org/10.1115/1.2137750
4. Aram, S., Eastman, C., Beetz, J.: Qualitative and Quantitative Cost Estimation: A Methodology Analysis. In: Computing in Civil and Building Engineering (2014), pp. 381–389. American Society of Civil Engineers, Reston, VA (2014). https://doi.org/10.1061/9780784413616.048
5. AACE International: Recommended practice 56R-08. Cost Estimate Classification System-as Applied in Engineering, Procurement, and Construction for the Building and General Construction Industries. TMC Framework: 7.3 - Cost Estimating and Budgeting. Morgantown, WV (2020)
6. Andersen, B., Samset, K., Welde, M.: Low estimates – high stakes: underestimation of costs at the front-end of projects. Int. J. Manag. Proj. Bus. **9**, 171–193 (2016). https://doi.org/10.1108/IJMPB-01-2015-0008
7. Johansen, A., Sandvin, B., Torp, O., Økland, A.: Uncertainty analysis – 5 challenges with today's practice. Procedia. Soc. Behav. Sci. **119**, 591–600 (2014). https://doi.org/10.1016/j.sbspro.2014.03.066
8. Welde, M., Odeck, J.: Cost escalations in the front-end of projects–empirical evidence from Norwegian road projects. Transp. Rev. **37**, 612–630 (2017). https://doi.org/10.1080/01441647.2016.1278285
9. Mayouf, M., Gerges, M., Cox, S.: 5D BIM: an investigation into the integration of quantity surveyors within the BIM process. J. Eng. Des. Technol. **17**, 537–553 (2019). https://doi.org/10.1108/JEDT-05-2018-0080
10. Mesároš, P., Smetanková, J., Mandičák, T.: The fifth dimension of BIM - Implementation survey. In: IOP Conference Series: Earth and Environmental Science. Institute of Physics Publishing (2019). https://doi.org/10.1088/1755-1315/222/1/012003
11. Yang, S.W., Moon, S.W., Jang, H., Choo, S., Kim, S.A.: Parametric method and building information modeling-based cost estimation model for construction cost prediction in architectural planning. Appl. Sci. **12**, 9553 (2022). https://doi.org/10.3390/app12199553
12. Cheung, F.K.T., Rihan, J., Tah, J., Duce, D., Kurul, E.: Early stage multi-level cost estimation for schematic BIM models. Autom. Constr. **27**, 67–77 (2012). https://doi.org/10.1016/j.autcon.2012.05.008
13. Cassandro, J., Mirarchi, C., Zanchetta, C., Pavan, A.: Enhancing accuracy in cost estimation: structured cost data integration and model validation. J. Inf. Technolo. Constr. **29**, 1293–1325 (2024). https://doi.org/10.36680/j.itcon.2024.058

14. Elghaish, F., Abrishami, S., Hosseini, M.R., Abu-Samra, S.: Revolutionising cost structure for integrated project delivery: a BIM-based solution. Eng. Constr. Archit. Manag. **28**, 1214–1240 (2020). https://doi.org/10.1108/ECAM-04-2019-0222
15. Babatunde, S.O., Perera, S., Ekundayo, D., Adeleye, T.E.: An investigation into BIM-based detailed cost estimating and drivers to the adoption of BIM in quantity surveying practices. J. Financ. Manag. Prop. Constr. **25**, 61–81 (2020). https://doi.org/10.1108/JFMPC-05-2019-0042
16. Fazeli, A., Dashti, M.S., Jalaei, F., Khanzadi, M.: An integrated BIM-based approach for cost estimation in construction projects. Eng. Constr. Archit. Manag. **28**, 2828–2854 (2021). https://doi.org/10.1108/ECAM-01-2020-0027
17. Alathamneh, S., Collins, W., Azhar, S.: BIM-based quantity takeoff: current state and future opportunities. Autom. Constr. **165**, 105549 (2024). https://doi.org/10.1016/j.autcon.2024.105549
18. Wu, S., Wood, G., Ginige, K.: A technical review of BIM based cost estimating in UK quantity surveying practice, standards and tools. Electron. J. Inf. Technol. Constr. **19**, 535–563 (2014)
19. Ying, T.Y., Kamal, E.M.: The revolution of quantity surveying profession in building information modelling (Bim) era: The malaysian perspective. Int. J. Sustain. Constr. Eng. Technol. **12**, 185–195 (2021). https://doi.org/10.30880/ijscet.2021.12.01.019
20. Raja Taihairan, R.B., Ismail, Z.: BIM: Integrating Cost Estimates at Initial/Design Stage. Int. J. Sustain. Constr. Eng. Technol. **6**, 62–74 (2015)
21. Ashworth, A., Perera, S.: Cost Studies of Buildings. Routledge (2015). https://doi.org/10.4324/9781315708867
22. Royal Institution of Chartered Surveyors: New rules of measurement NRM 1: Order of cost estimating and cost planning for capital building works, London (2021)
23. Hegazy, T., Ayed, A.: Neural network model for parametric cost estimation of highway projects. J. Constr. Eng. Manag. **124**, 210–218 (1998). https://doi.org/10.1061/(ASCE)0733-9364(1998)124:3(210)
24. Copiello, S., Bonifaci, P.: Depreciated replacement cost: Improving the method through a variant based on three cornerstones. Real Estate Manag. Valuat. **26**, 33–47 (2018). https://doi.org/10.2478/remav-2018-0014
25. Milan Board of Engineers and Architects: Prezzi Tipologie Edilizie. Dei - Tipografia del Genio Civile, Roma (2019)
26. Sacks, R., Eastman, C., Lee, G., Teicholz, P.: BIM Handbook. Wiley (2018). https://doi.org/10.1002/9781119287568
27. Salzano, A., Parisi, C.M., Acampa, G., Nicolella, M.: Existing assets maintenance management: Optimizing maintenance procedures and costs through BIM tools. Autom. Constr. **149**, 104788 (2023). https://doi.org/10.1016/j.autcon.2023.104788

28. Cavalliere, C., Dell'Osso, G.R., Favia, F., Lovicario, M.: BIM-based assessment metrics for the functional flexibility of building designs. Autom. Constr. **107**, 102925 (2019). https://doi.org/10.1016/j.autcon.2019.102925
29. AACE International: Recommended practice No. 10S-90. In: Cost Engineering Terminology. TMC Framework: General Reference, Morgantown, WV (2024)

Supporting the Transition to Ecological Economy in Cities Regenera- tion: Circular Model Tools for Reusing Architecture and Infrastructures (TReE 2025)

Multi-criteria Decision Aiding for Adaptive Reuse of Cultural Heritage: An Application in the City of Naples (Italy)

Giulia Datola[1] and Marta Bottero[2]

[1] Department of Architecture and Urban Studies (DAStU), Politecnico di Milano, 20133 Milan, Italy
giulia.datola@polimi.it

[2] Interuniversity Department of Regional and Urban Studies and Planning (DIST), Politecnico di Torino, Turin, Italy
marta.bottero@polito.it

Abstract. The paper explores the adaptive reuse paradigm for revitalising unmovable cultural heritage assets. More in detail, this research addresses a real-world evaluation demand concerning the assessment of different adaptive reuse strategies for the requalification of the hospital building in Naples (Italy). According to the complexity and multi-perspective nature of the research topic and the evaluation demand, an integrated and multimethodological evaluation framework has been proposed. Different adaptive reuse strategies have been evaluated by combining the SWOT analysis, the Stakeholder analysis and the PROMETHEE method to address and manage the complexity, multidimensionality and multi-values nature of the evaluation demand. The obtained results underline that the final ranking of the proposed adaptive reuse scenarios is based on a multidimensional and multi-perspective evaluation, supporting thus Decision-Makers in identifying the most suitable scenario for the renovation of the unmovable cultural heritage asset according to the intervention objectives.

Keywords: Adaptive reuse · PROMETHEE · Cultural Heritage

1 Introduction

The paradigm of adaptive reuse is considered a promising approach for the preservation and requalification of Cultural Heritage (CH) assets [1–5]. It permits changes in the use of existing buildings, following the requirements of both the new owner and the community [6–8]. The main purpose of this paradigm is to protect the building through the preservation of its historical and heritage significance and improving the environmental, economic and social conditions [9]. Thus, different dimensions, values and objectives, that range from the cultural aspects to the aesthetic and economic ones, have to be considered in this context [10, 11]. Therefore, the adaptive reuse of CH is a real-world complex decision-making process [12, 13]. In this sense, the decision process concerning interventions on CH should be made based on a multidimensional set of criteria and the preferences of the stakeholders involved [14]. However, studies dealing with the complexity of the decision process of adaptive reuse of CH assets are quite recent [15–17]. Therefore, the topic of defining a proper evaluation method for assessing is still less explored and fragmented [3, 18]. In this context, the current research demand concerns the development of a comprehensive assessment framework, which has to include multidimensional values [18]. In the literature, many scholars have proposed several assessment frameworks to evaluate adaptive-reuse strategies to properly support the decision-making process [18]. The suggested evaluation frameworks can be mainly categorised into three different groups:

- the mixed method;
- the Multi-Criteria Decision Aiding (MCDA);
- the Preference-Measurement Model (PMM) [18].

Concerning the MCDA, some valuable studies can be reported to introduce the methodological background of applying these techniques for CH adaptive reuse assessment. Salerno proposes an MCDA to evaluate projects of adaptive reuse for CH assets, supporting the choice of the intervention strategy [19]. Dezio and colleagues apply MCDA with Geographic Information System (GIS) to support the decision process in identifying suitable buildings for the adaptive reuse approach [20]. Bottero and colleagues propose the PROMETHEE method to assess the tangible and intangible aspects of cultural heritage [11, 21]. Della Spina applies MCDA to classify adaptive reuse strategies of unused CH assets and to support Decision-Makers Decision Makers (DMs) in the implementation of development strategies, to generate new economic, cultural and social values [22]. Torrieri and colleagues develop an integrated evaluation model, based on MCDA and a financial model to support the choice of alternative reuse of an ancient monastery in Mugnano Municipality, according to the multidimensional impacts of investment and intervention in CH [23]. Angrisano and colleagues propose the application of the SOCRATES Multi-Criteria evaluation method to assess CH adaptive reuse projects, integrating environmental, social, economic, and cultural dimensions [17]. Garavagnuolo and colleagues apply the TOPSIS method to assess the adaptive reuse of a historical building in Salerno (Italy) [16].

The present paper addresses a real-world evaluation demand, which concerns the evaluation of different adaptive-reuse strategies for the requalification of the hospital of the city of Naples. For this purpose, a multi-methodological evaluation framework [24] which combines the SWOT analysis, the Stakeholder analysis and the PROMETHEE [25, 26] method has been proposed to address the complexity, multidimensionality and multi-perspective nature of evaluation demand. The paper is organised as follows: Sect. 2 describes the considered evaluation techniques; Sect. 3 describes the application of the multimethodological approach; Sect. 4 illustrates and comments the evaluation results; Sect. 5 concerns the conclusion of the work within some critical reflections of the proposed methodology and reasoning about the future challenge of this research topic.

2 Proposed Multi-methodological Assessment Framework

2.1 SWOT Analysis

The SWOT analysis is a technique to support the decision process. It was introduced by the economist Albert Humphrey, who proposed the implementation of the SWOT analysis in the field of business economics [27]. Over the years, its application has been extended to different fields, both private and public. Currently, the SWOT analysis is a common tool in spatial planning and the assessment of regional programs [28]. The acronym SWOT refers to Strengths, Weaknesses, Opportunities, and Threats. This analytical method is used to examine the positive and negative aspects, both internal and external, of a particular initiative. Specifically, strengths and weaknesses are internal characteristics of the context that the policy or project can directly influence. On the other hand, opportunities and threats stem from the broader external environment and are generally beyond the direct control of the intervention. The SWOT analysis thus permits the data collection and management concerning the specific decision problem according to the logical procedure at the basis.

2.2 Stakeholders Analysis

The Stakeholder Analysis concerns the identification of all the subjects involved in the decision process, especially when dealing with public policies [34, 35]. Thus, the stakeholder analysis is a fundamental step in strategic planning and sustainability assessment, due to its ability to identify conflicting interests at an early stage of the process. From a practical point of view, stakeholder analysis concerns the identification and classification of stakeholder groups. Indeed, stakeholders have access to and can mobilize different types of resources (i.e., political, economic, legal, and cognitive resources), determining thus different categories (i.e., political actors, bureucratic actors, special interest, general interest, and experts.), following their resources [34]. The target of this analysis is to develop a strategic view of the community and institutional context of the decision process, underlying the relationships between the different actors and the issues they care about most.

2.3 PROMETHEE Method

The PROMETHEE methods refer to the MCDA techniques that are widely applied to address real-world decision-making problems. Specifically, PROMETHEE is an outranking method [29]. These methods are based on the pairwise comparison of a finite set of alternatives to rank them concerning a set of multidimensional criteria. The PROMETHEE technique was introduced by Brans and colleagues [25] and after improved by Brans and Vincke [30]. In the real-world decision problems, PROMETHEE methods are widely used to address several issues, like (1) environmental and energy management, (2) water management, (3) business and financial management, (4) logistics, transportation, and urban transformation [31, 32], among others.

PROMETHEE methods are based on specific principles that can be summarised as follows: (a) the set of criteria is finite; (b) criteria are not hierarchically structured; (c) the parameters of the decision model can be precisely defined. Specifically, the PROMETHEE has normally been applied to rank a finite set of m alternative actions A = {a, b, ..., m} concerning a finite set of k criteria G = {g_1, g_2, ..., g_k}, also involving several Decision Makers (DMs) [33]. These techniques permit to evaluate and rank of a set of alternatives, identifying those variables that affect the ranking, also analysing the differences and similarities between alternatives. To evaluate alternatives using the PROMETHEE method, the process starts by comparing actions against each criterion, reflecting the DMs preferences. This is achieved through pairwise comparisons to give local scores, which are subsequently aggregated into global scores, resulting in either a partial pre-order (PROMETHEE I), a complete pre-order rank (PROMETHEE II), or an interval pre-order rank (PROMETHEE III). However, complex decision problems typically involve multiple and multidimensional criteria, making it impossible to simultaneously optimise all of them. Consequently, additional information is needed to establish the Preference (P) threshold, the Indifference (I) threshold, and the dominance graph [26]. Decision Makers (DMs) have thus to provide preference information regarding the variables and parameters involved in the evaluation model, either directly or indirectly. Therefore, they are required to assign weights to the criteria and specify the shape of the preference functions.

PROMETHEE methods identify a function P_j for each criterion j, that represents the degree of preference of action (a) over action (b) about criterion g_j. This function is grounded on the difference in their evaluation $g_j(a)$–$g_j(b)$ which is a non-decreasing function. The degree of preference has been obtained from the Decision Makers (DMs) preference function, which transforms the difference in the evaluation of the two alternatives into a numerical scale between 0 and 1. The value 1 is assigned in the case of a strong preference for alternative (a) over alternative (b), whereas the value 0 is used to represent the indifference between alternative (a) and alternative (b). Six typical preference functions are proposed by literature, that can be summarised as follows: (1) Usual criterion, (2) quasi criterion (U-shape), (3) criterion with linear preference (V-shape), (4) level criterion, (5) linear criterion, and (6) Gaussian criterion [26, 30].

The final step of the PROMETHEE methodology is evaluating how much action (a) is preferred to action (b), considering all of the criteria. An overall preference index $\Pi(a,b)$ is calculated for this assessment. $\Pi(a,b)$ performs the intensity of preference of (a) over (b) and it is calculated by a weighted sum through this formula:

$$\Pi(a, b) = \sum_{j=1}^{k} w_j P_j(a, b) \qquad (1)$$

where $\Pi(a,b)$ represents the overall preference intensity of (a) over (b), with respect to all of the k criteria, w_j is the weight of criterion j and P_j (a,b) is the preference function of (a) over (b) about criterion j. It is important to underline that $\Pi(a,b) \sim 0$ represents a weak global preference for (a) over (b), whereas $\Pi(a,b) \sim 1$ shows a strong global preference for (a) over (b). The weights $w_j > 0$ represent the importance and the relevance of each criterion within the decision problem.

Since each alternative action is compared to the others, it is possible to define both a positive outranking flow $\Phi+(a)$ and a negative outranking flow $\Phi-(a)$ that can be defined:

$$\Phi^+(a) = \frac{1}{n-1} \sum_{b \in A} \Pi(a, b) \tag{2}$$

$$\Phi^-(a) = \frac{1}{n-1} \sum_{b \in A} \Pi(a, b) \tag{3}$$

Specifically, $\Phi+(a)$ represents the global preference for action (a) compared to all the other actions and determines how the alternative (a) outranks the others. The higher is $\Phi+(a)$, the better alternative (a) is compared to the others. Whereas $\Phi-(a)$ represents the global weakness of the actions (a) about all the other actions and it expresses how the alternative (a) is outranked by the others. Furthermore, these two flows can be combined to obtain the net outranking flow $\Phi(a)$:

$$\Phi(a) = \Phi^+(a) - \Phi^-(a) \tag{4}$$

The higher the net flow, the better the alternative is.

3 Application

3.1 Case Study

The present research proposes the application of the PROMETHEE method to evaluate and rank four different adaptive reuse strategies for the requalification of the hospital building in Naples (Southern Italy). Specifically, this building is located in the historical centre of the city of Naples (Fig. 1).

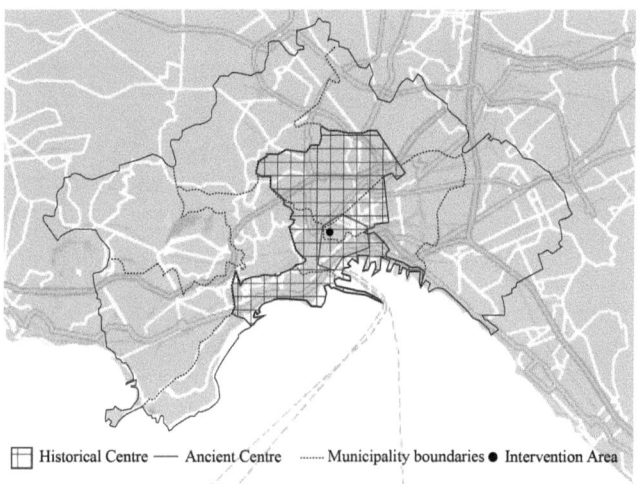

Fig. 1. Territorial framework.

One part of this building is currently used for a medical university, while the other part has no specific function, standing in neglected conditions. This state of the art also has negative impacts on the socio-economic conditions of the surrounding area. Several projects have been proposed during the last decade to requalify both the building and the neighbourhood to improve not only the physical condition of the unmovable asset but also the general socio-economic features of the interested area. However, none of the strategies proposed so far has been identified as suitable to overcome the above-mentioned issues through a multidimensional and comprehensive approach. All the proposed requalification scenarios were mainly focused on economic income, neglecting the social and environmental aspects.

The proposed multimethodological approach has been applied to address all the elements engaged. In detail, the SWOT and the stakeholder analysis are focused on collecting all the information of the area to identify the strategic elements to consider both in the alternative design and evaluation.

3.2 SWOT Analysis

Figure 2 illustrates the SWOT analysis performed for the decision-problem under analysis.

STRENGTHS	WEAKNESSES
- Link to the other areas of the city through the metri line 1 and 2 - Presence in the areas of numerous universities - Historical and cultural relevance of the site (Decumano street) - Presence of archeological sends - Accessibility of the area through other part of the historical center	- Degradation of the hospital structures - Lack of parking - Absence of accomodation for students - Absence of services for the community - Absence of recreational areas and facilities
OPPORTUNITIES	**THREATS**
- Unclusion of new activities for young people and students - Restitution of a unique structure to the block, promising a new vital space in the neighborhood - Creation of the recreational area and urban green spaces - Valorization of the archeological sends and creation of a network with other historical sites in the city - Provisionn of public services for local community	- Difficulties in sending historical resources for the operation - Lack of consensus from the inhabitants - Absence of private investors

Fig. 2. SWOT Analysis for the adaptive reuse of the hospital building in Naples (Guarini, 2019).

The SWOT analysis (Fig. 2) offers a comprehensive overview of the endogenous and exogenous factors that distinguish the context in which the hospital building is located. Among the strengths, the high level of accessibility of the area through public transportation can be highlighted. As well, the proximity to several universities and archaeological sites underlines the strategic value of the intervention area.

However, some relevant weaknesses have to be addressed, including the current degradation of infrastructure, the lack of essential services, and the absence of both recreational areas and accommodations for students.

Therefore, some opportunities can be identified to stress the strengths and overcome the weaknesses. For instance, the potential for activating new functions aimed at young people and students, through the reuse of existing spaces and the creation of urban green areas. As well, the valorisation of the archaeological site to integrate it into a broader cultural network to attract both interest and investment.

However, some potential threats could affect the renovation process. These include uncertainty in securing historical funding, limited private investment, and possible resistance from the local population, which can underestimate the importance of inclusive planning and stakeholder engagement.

3.3 Stakeholders Circle Analysis

This study applies the Stakeholder Circle Methodology to map the stakeholders involved. This technique has been developed by Bourne [34], and it analyses and maps the stakeholders according to their proximity, power, and interest. According to these criteria, this methodology permits the identification of the key players of the analysed decision-making process. Table 1 lists the stakeholders engaged in the examined decision process, with specific reference to their level, typology, resources, and objectives.

On the other hand, Fig. 3 represents the performed circle analysis. Stakeholders have been mapped considering (1) their power, which is represented by the dimension of the wedge they occupy, (2) their proximity, which is figured out by the concentric circles, and (3) their urgency, which is illustrated by the depth of the wedge. Through this analysis, it was possible to determine the role and the position of different stakeholders. In detail, the Napoli Municipality, architects, and private investors can be considered the key players of this decision-making process. Their power and proximity are relevant, and the urgency of the Napoli Municipality and architects reaches the goal. Instead, MiBAC, hospital personnel, actual residents of the area, and students have medium power, proximity, and urgency. On the other hand, actual residents of neighbouring, the associations, UNESCO, the European Community, media and public opinion, and tourists have a low power, interest, and urgency. Therefore, this analysis has been fundamental to determining the position of the public and private stakeholders according to the goal, as well as clarifying their objectives and interests.

Table 1. Identification of the stakeholders involved in the decision process (Guarini, 2019).

Stakeholders	Level	Typology	Resources	Objectives
European Community	European	Politic / Bureaucratic	Political Legal	Political consensus and verification of normative observance
UNESCO	European	Politic / Bureaucratic	Political/legal	Political consensus and economic income
MiBAC (Superintendence of archeologic and landscape assets)	Council	Public / Bureaucratic	Political Economic Legal	Political consensus and economic income
Campania Region	Regional	Public / Bureaucratic	Political Economic Legal	Political consensus and economic income
Napoli Municipality	Council	Public / Bureaucratic	Political Economic Legal	Political consensus and economic income; improvement of the social, urban, and economic aspects of the considered area
IV Municipality	Local	Public / Bureaucratic	Political Economic Legal	Political consensus and economic income; improvement of the social, urban, and economic aspects of the considered area
"Amici dei musei di Napoli" association	Local	Special interest	Cognitive Social	Interest in the development of cultural and recreational activities
Private investor	Local	Special interest	Cognitive Social	Maximization of the economic income
"Borgo Dante e Decumani" Association of workers, artisans, and local dealers	Local	Special interest	Cognitive Social	Interest in the development of new activities to make the area more attractive, and also to improve their activity income
"I sedili di Napoli" association of artisans and cultural researchers	Local	Special Interest	Cognitive Social	Interest in the restoration of the historical and cultural assets
Students	Local	Special interest	Cognitive Social	Creation of new spaces for studying
Actual residents	Local	Special Interest	Cognitive Social	Creation of new spaces for the community and improvement of the actual conditions
Hospital personnel	Local	Special Interest	Cognitive Social	Maintaining the hospital service and improving the actual conditions
Actual residents of neighbouring areas	Local	Special Interest	Cognitive Social	Creation of new spaces for the community and improvement of the actual conditions
Architects	Local	Expert	Cognitive	Development of intervention strategies
Tourists	Local	Special Interest	Cognitive Social	Interest in improving the actual conditions
Media and public opinion	Regional Local	General Interest	Cognitive Political	Influencing public opinion

3.4 Identification of Alternative Adaptive Reuse Scenarios

The alternative scenarios have been designed considering the multidimensional and multi-value decision process, recognised through the performed SWOT and stakeholder analysis. Furthermore, these scenarios have also been differentiated from each other to give both the municipality and the developer a wide range of choices, to better respond to the real needs.

The four scenarios can be described as follows:

1. Scenario 0 (Business as usual). This scenario corresponds to the state of the art, without any interventions, foreseeing the maintenance of the actual function of the medical university in one part of the building, and leaving the other part empty;

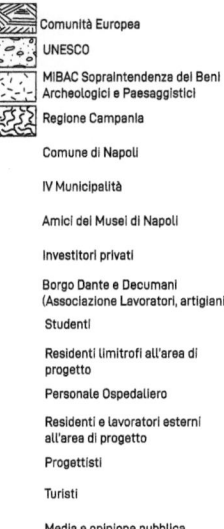

Fig. 3. Stakeholder Circle Analysis (Guarini, 2019).

2. The Community Hub. This project aims to fill the social and economic needs of the area. This strategy proposes requalification and adaptation interventions of the hospital building to create new spaces for the community. This scenario proposes the realisation of productive working spaces, characterised by the adaptability of their layout. The main objective is promoting community engagement by improving social innovation and inclusion;
3. The Student House. This scenario responds to the necessity of a new student house in the centre of the city of Naples. This project designs both public and private spaces to satisfy the requirements of both students and tourists;
4. The Archaeological and Cultural Park. This project provides the creation of an archaeological and cultural park to valorise the historical presence located both in this building and in the adjacent urban area.

3.5 Development of the PROMETHEE Method

3.5.1 Evaluation Criteria

The four scenarios have been evaluated according to a multidimensional set of criteria that refer to the environment, urban, social, and economic dimensions. Table 2 lists the criteria applied for the evaluation, which have been selected to engage in the evaluation from both public and private perspectives. The social criteria address the objectives and interests of citizens, tourists, and users. Whereas, the economic criteria consider the perspective of the private investors with a focus on the investment cost and profitability.

Table 2. List of multidimensional criteria applied for scenarios evaluation (Guarini, 2019).

Dimension	Criteria	Description
Environment	C_1 Permeable Surface / Territorial surface	The ratio between permeable surfaces and the overall territorial surface of the program [-]
	C_2 New green areas	Total of area designed to new green areas [square meters]
Urban	C_3 Architectonic Intervention	Restored area of the hospital [square meters]
	C_4 Archaeological Area	The revitalized portion of the archaeological area [square meters]
Social	C_5 Lodgings	Surface for residential functions [square meters]
	C_6 Sport and recreation area	Surfaces for sport and recreation activities [square meters]
	C_7 Didactics and cultural area	Surfaces for education and cultural activities [square meters]
	C_8 Mixitè Index	The index that describes the functional mix of the area [0-1]
	C_9 Co-working and labs	The surface of the structures for workshops, meetings, and training courses [square meters]
	C_{10} Healthcare assistance	Number of spaces designed for health assistance [number of people]
Economic	C_{11} New Jobs	Number of new jobs created [number]
	C_{12} Intervention cost	The total cost of the program [€]
	C_{13} Profitability	Income generated by the project [€]
	C_{14} Opening hours	Opening hours of the structure [number]

3.6 Application of PROMETHEE Method

Defined the evaluation criteria, the assessment has been performed according to the PROMETHEE method, following these steps:

1. Construction of the performance matrix. For each alternative, the performance over the set of criteria has been estimated;
2. Identification of the preference function P_j (a,b). For each criterion j, the Preference function (P) and Indifference (Q) threshold have been established. More in detail, the linear function has been selected for criteria C_1, C_2, C_6, C_7, C_9, C_{10}, and C_{12}. The level function has been chosen for criteria C_3, C_4, C_5, C_8, C_{11}, C_{13}, and C_{14};
3. Weighting the considered criteria. For this evaluation, the Simos' card method has been applied to determine the importance of different criteria [35]. For this purpose, a multidisciplinary panel of experts have been asked to weight criteria to represent and include in the evaluation the objectives of the identified stakeholders (Table 1). In detail, the panel of experts is composed of an expert in building restoration, to include the vision and objective of the private investor, a technician from Municipal Authority to assess the importance of criteria in according to the current municipality regulation, the city councillor, who represents the opinion, needs and requests of the community, both residents (workers, artisans, students) and tourists, and the superintendence of archaeology, who includes in the evaluation the principles of the UNESCO and also the interests of the local cultural initiatives. According to the Simos' card method, experts are given a set of pre-made cards representing each criterion (Table 2) and

asked to rank criteria from the least important to the most important. Moreover, it is also possible to differentiate the importance of the criteria through the addition of white cards between them. Thus, the greater the difference, the higher the number of white cards [36]. Figueira and Roy reviewed this method, introducing the z value [35]. This value represents how many times the last criterion is considered more important than the first, thus, z expresses a fixed interval between the criteria's weights [35]. In this application, the normalised weights have been calculated through the Simos-Roy-Figueira (SRF) procedure, to consider both criteria and the blank cards position. Figure 4 illustrates what emerged from the weighting procedure, underlying the different points of view of the four involved experts.

Moreover, both similarities and differences can be addressed among the declared weights, which can be justified for the different expertise and background of the involved experts.

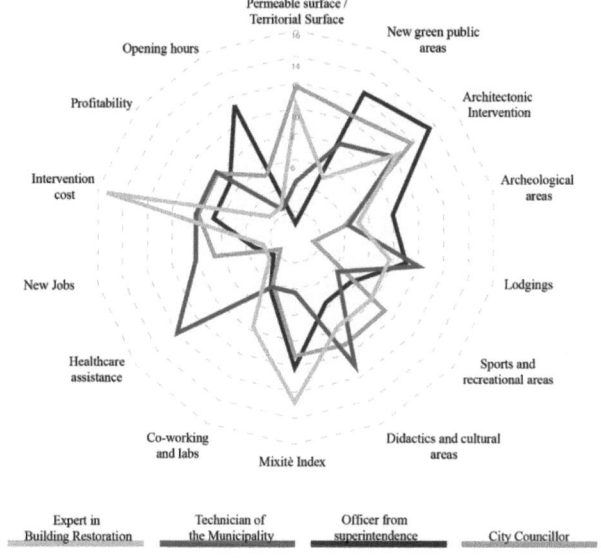

Fig. 4. Radar graph of experts' weights (Guarini, 2019).

Concerning the similarities, the criteria "C_3 architectonic intervention" and "C_8 mixitè index" have been evaluated as very important by all experts, underlying the urgency in renovating the physical aspect of the building, as well as the requirement in revitalising the intervention area according to social and economic dimensions. On the other hand, the criteria "C_{12} investment cost" and "C_{10} Health assistance" have been evaluated differently. The expert in building restoration evaluates the criterion "C_{12} investment cost" as highly important, according to its expertise and background, which reflects the necessity of proposing an intervention affordable according to the available investment budget. Instead, the technician of the municipality, the city councillor and the officer from the superintendence assessed this criterion as medium and low important. These weights underline the interests of the municipality and the city councilor to represent the citizens' interests and needs, as well as the officer superintendence in proposing an intervention in line with the requirements to respect the historical characteristics of the unmovable CH asset.

4 Results

Calculation of the overall preference index $\Pi(a,b)$, performing both the positive $\Phi+$ (a) and negative Φ-(b) outranking flows, and the comparison of the obtained outranking flows to define the complete ranking of the alternatives. In detail, the final ranking has been obtained through the implementation of the PROMETHEE method. Figures 4 and 5 show, respectively, the multi-actors' comparative rankings and the final ranking. The multi-actors comparative ranking (Fig. 5) shows that the Community Hub is the most preferred by the expert in restoration, by the technician of the municipality and by the superintendence officer. Whereas the city councillor prefers the Archaeological Park. It is interesting to notice that the restoration expert, the municipality technician and the superintendence officer have prioritised in their assessment the aspects related to mixité (criterion C_8) and architectural intervention (criterion C_3). This evaluation led them to appreciate more the community hub strategy, which excludes the construction of the new building and minimises the cost of intervention. As well, the city councillor assigned great importance to the presence of green areas (criterion C_2) and recreational facilities (criterion C_6). The evaluation performed by the city councillor identified the archaeological park scenario as the most preferable one, according to the fact that this scenario aims at valorising the open spaces of the intervention area.

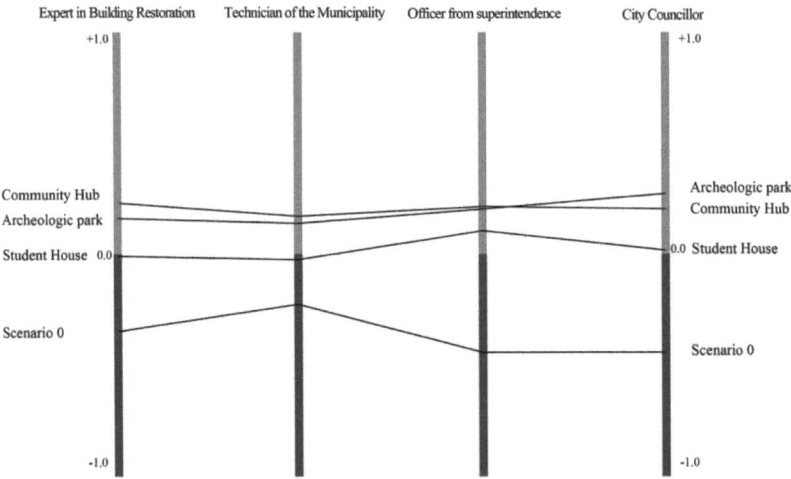

Fig. 5. Multi-actors comparative ranking (Guarini, 2019)

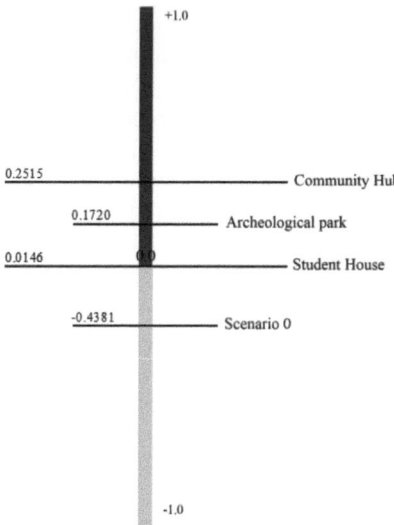

Fig. 6. Final ranking (Guarini, 2019).

Therefore, considering the experts' overall preferences, the preferred scenario is the Community Hub (Fig. 6). This final ranking shows the positive outranking flow that expresses how an alternative outranks all the others. Thus, it expresses its power and its outranking character. The higher the positive outranking, the better the alternative [37]. The obtained result is due to the Community Hub scenario's performance in different of the considered criteria. It has the best performance in many of the considered evaluation criteria, such as sport and recreation area, educational and cultural area, the mixité index, working space, new jobs, and profitability. Therefore, this scenario can satisfy the interests and objectives of both public and private stakeholders, according to its performance.

Moreover, it is possible to address that the scenario of the archaeological park has good performance in many of the considered criteria, but it presents the highest intervention cost, which is a criterion to minimise. As well, the archaeological park does not include any space dedicated to teaching and culture, which is an aspect considered very important by the involved experts. Scenario 0, the business as usual, is the least preferable scenario, according to the fact that it does not propose any intervention, without any improvement of the socio-economic conditions of the interested area.

5 Conclusion

The present research explores the issues and challenges of the evaluation of adaptive reuse strategies for unmovable CH assets. This research proposes a multimethodological evaluation framework to address the real-world evaluation demand for the renovation of the Policlinico, located in the historical centre of the city of Naples (Italy) [38]. The proposed evaluation framework integrates SWOT analysis, stakeholder analysis, and the

PROMETHEE method. The SWOT and stakeholder analysis have been applied to analyse the intervention context and the decision process, by systematising the information of the area of interventions, as well as identifying the different engaged stakeholders within their objectives and interests according to the project goal. These analyses have also been applied to define the multidimensional set of criteria for assessing the adaptive reuse strategies by taking into account the multidimensionality and the multiple values [39]. For this purpose, a multidisciplinary panel of experts were involved in weighing the different criteria, to determine their relevance according to the evaluation objective, as well as to guarantee the consideration of the perspectives of the involved stakeholders [31, 40]. According to the complexity of the addressed topic of CH adaptive reuse, the illustrated case study can be considered as a relevant application in considering and managing the multifaceted issues, which represent tangible real-world decision problems. This application underlines the suitability of the PROMETHEE method to support real-world complex decisions, considering its ability to compare the different alternatives considering the opinions of the different experts involved [41], as well as its implementation for adaptive reuse strategies evaluation in the context of CH. Moreover, the illustrated case study performed an evaluation which considers both the public and the private perspectives. This was possible by the engagement of a multidisciplinary panel of experts that represents the perspective of the developer, the public administration, and the citizens. The obtained results suggest that the proposed model provides an effective tool to support decision-making in highly complex contexts. It enhances transparency throughout the process and helps clarify the factors affecting the decision dynamics, facilitating the formulation of shared and inclusive development strategies [42].

Furthermore, some reflections can be made to set future research in this research context. First of all, the development and implementation of sensitivity analysis should be added to verify the robustness of the outputs of the evaluations, to better justify the final decision [11, 43]. Secondly, the financial analysis should be integrated into the multimethodological evaluation framework to estimate the cost of intervention and the cash flow to calculate the necessary economic resources to develop the selected intervention [44], as well as the Cost-Benefit Analysis (CBA) to calculate the economic cost, the cash flow and also the benefit of the strategy in the social and environmental field. Moreover, principles and criteria of the Circular Economy (CE) paradigm will be integrated into the proposed evaluation framework to be aligned with the recommendations of the European Commission (EC) [16].

Acknowledgement. This paper is based on the thesis work titled *"RE-INSULA. L'applicazione di una metodologia MCDA come strumento per analizzare ipotesi di adaptive reuse per il Primo Policlinico di Napoli"* by Sofia Guarini, with the supervision of Professor Marta Bottero and Professor Mauro Berta, Politecnico di Torino, Italy.

References

1. Bullen, P.A., Love, P.E.D.: Adaptive reuse of heritage buildings. Struct. Surv. (2011). https://doi.org/10.1108/02630801111182439

2. Plevoets, B., Van Cleempoel, K.: Adaptive reuse as a strategy towards conservation of cultural heritage: A literature review. In: WIT Transactions on the Built Environment (2011)
3. Foster, G., Saleh, R.: The circular city and adaptive reuse of cultural heritage index: measuring the investment opportunity in Europe. Resour. Conserv. Recycl. **175**, 105880 (2021). https://doi.org/10.1016/j.resconrec.2021.105880
4. Foster, G., Saleh, R.: The adaptive reuse of cultural heritage in European circular city plans: a systematic review. Sustainability. **13**, 2889 (2021). https://doi.org/10.3390/su13052889
5. Dell'ovo, M., Bassani, S., Stefanina, G., Oppio, A.: Memories at risk. How to support decisions about abandoned industrial heritage regeneration. Valori Valutazioni. **2020**, 107–115 (2020)
6. Fusco Girard, L., Gravagnuolo, A.: Circular economy and cultural heritage/landscape regeneration. In: Circular Business, Financing and Governance Models for a Competitive Europe, vol. 17, (2017). https://doi.org/10.6092/2284-4732/5472
7. McCoy, N., Latham, D.: Creative re-use of buildings. APT Bull. **32**, 77 (2001). https://doi.org/10.2307/1504746
8. Stanganelli, M., Torrieri, F., Gerundo, C., Rossitti, M.: A Strategic Performance-Based Planning Methodology to Promote the Regeneration of Fragile Territories Lecture Notes in Civil Engineering, vol. 146, pp. 149–157 (2021). https://doi.org/10.1007/978-3-030-68824-0_16
9. Wilkinson, S.J., James, K., Reed, R.: Using building adaptation to deliver sustainability in Australia. Struct. Surv. (2009). https://doi.org/10.1108/02630800910941683
10. Klamer, A.: The values of cultural heritage. In: Handbook on the Economics of Cultural Heritage (2013)
11. Bottero, M., D'Alpaos, C., Oppio, A.: Ranking of adaptive reuse strategies for abandoned industrial heritage in vulnerable contexts: a multiple criteria decision aiding approach. Sustainability. **11**, 785 (2019). https://doi.org/10.3390/su11030785
12. Della Spina, L.: Historical cultural heritage: Decision making process and reuse scenarios for the enhancement of historic buildings. In: Smart Innovation, Systems and Technologies (2019)
13. Ciomek, K., Ferretti, V., Kadziński, M.: Predictive analytics and disused railways requalification: insights from a post factum analysis perspective. Decis. Support. Syst. **105**, 34–51 (2018). https://doi.org/10.1016/j.dss.2017.10.010
14. Bottero, M.: A multi-methodological approach for assessing sustainability of urban projects. Manag. Environ. Qual. Int. J. **26**, 138–154 (2015). https://doi.org/10.1108/MEQ-06-2014-0088
15. Gravagnuolo, A., Angrisano, M., Girard, L.F.: Dismissed Historic Buildings and New Reuse Strategies: The Case of Edifici Mondo in the City of Salerno (Italy) Lecture Notes in Networks and Systems, pp. 214–224 (2024)
16. Gravagnuolo, A., Angrisano, M., Bosone, M., et al.: Participatory evaluation of cultural heritage adaptive reuse interventions in the circular economy perspective: a case study of historic buildings in Salerno (Italy). J. Urban. Manag. **13**, 107–139 (2024). https://doi.org/10.1016/j.jum.2023.12.002
17. Angrisano, M., Nocca, F., Scotto Di Santolo, A.: Multidimensional evaluation framework for assessing cultural heritage adaptive reuse projects: the case of the seminary in Sant'Agata de' Goti (Italy). Urban Sci. **8**, 50 (2024). https://doi.org/10.3390/urbansci8020050
18. Bottero, M., Datola, G., Fazzari, D., Ingaramo, R.: Re-thinking detroit: a multicriteria-based approach for adaptive reuse for the corktown district. Sustainability. **14**, 8343 (2022). https://doi.org/10.3390/su14148343
19. Salerno, E.: Identifying value-increasing actions for cultural heritage assets through sensitivity analysis of multicriteria evaluation results. Sustainability. **12**, 9238 (2020). https://doi.org/10.3390/su12219238

20. Dezio, C., Dell'Ovo, M., Oppio, A.: The antifragile potential of line tourism: towards a multimethodological evaluation model for Italian inner areas cultural heritage. In: Smart Innovation, Systems and Technologies, pp. 1819–1829 (2021)
21. Bottero, M., Dell'Anna, F., Nappo, M.: Evaluating Tangible and Intangible Aspects of Cultural Heritage: An Application of the PROMETHEE Method for the Reuse Project of the Ceva–Ormea Railway, pp. 285–295. Green Energy and Technology (2018)
22. Della Spina, L.: Adaptive sustainable reuse for cultural heritage: a multiple criteria decision aiding approach supporting urban development processes. Sustainability. **12**, 1363 (2020). https://doi.org/10.3390/su12041363
23. Torrieri, F., Fumo, M., Sarnataro, M., Ausiello, G.: An integrated decision support system for the sustainable reuse of the former monastery of "Ritiro del Carmine" in campania region. Sustainability. **11**, 5244 (2019). https://doi.org/10.3390/su11195244
24. Bottero, M., Oppio, A., Bonardo, M., Quaglia, G.: Hybrid evaluation approaches for urban regeneration processes of landfills and industrial sites: the case of the Kwun Tong area in Hong Kong. Land Use Policy. **82**, 585–594 (2019). https://doi.org/10.1016/j.landusepol.2018.12.017
25. Brans, J.P., Macharis, C., Kunsch, P.L., et al.: Combining multicriteria decision aid and system dynamics for the control of socio-economic processes. An iterative real-time procedure. Eur. J. Oper. Res. **109**, 428–441 (1998). https://doi.org/10.1016/S0377-2217(98)00068-X
26. Brans, J.-P., Mareschal, B., Figueira, J., et al.: Promethee methods. In: Multiple Criteria Decision Analysis: State of the Art Surveys, pp. 163–186 (2005)
27. Madsen, D.: SWOT analysis: a management fashion perspective. Int. J. Bus. Res. **16**, 39–56 (2016). https://doi.org/10.18374/IJBR-16-1.3
28. Halepoto, I.A., Sahito, A.A., Uqaili, M.A., et al.: Multi-criteria assessment of smart city transformation based on SWOT analysis. In: 2015 5th National Symposium on Information Technology: Towards New Smart World (NSITNSW), pp. 1–6. IEEE (2015)
29. Corrente, S., Figueira, J.R., Greco, S.: The SMAA-PROMETHEE method. Eur. J. Oper. Res. **239**, 514–522 (2014). https://doi.org/10.1016/j.ejor.2014.05.026
30. Brans, J., Vincke, P.: A preference ranking organization method: the PROMETHEE method for MCDM. Manag. Sci. **31**, 647–656 (1985)
31. Behzadian, M., Kazemzadeh, R.B., Albadvi, A., Aghdasi, M.: PROMETHEE: a comprehensive literature review on methodologies and applications. Eur. J. Oper. Res. **200**, 198–215 (2010). https://doi.org/10.1016/j.ejor.2009.01.021
32. Abastante, F., Caprioli, C., Gaballo, M.: The economic evaluation of projects as a structuring discipline of learning processes to support decision-making in sustainable urban transformations. Int. J. Sustain. Dev. Plan. **17**, 1297–1307 (2022). https://doi.org/10.18280/ijsdp.170427
33. Roy, B., Damart, S.: The uses of cost- benefit analysis in public transportation decision-making in France. Transp. Policy. **16**, 200 (2009)
34. Bourne, L., Walker, D.H.T.: Project relationship management and the Stakeholder Circle™. Int. J. Manag. Proj. Bus. **1**, 125–130 (2008). https://doi.org/10.1108/17538370810846450
35. Figueira, J., Roy, B.: Determining the weights of criteria in the ELECTRE type methods with a revised Simos' procedure. Eur. J. Oper. Res. **139**(2), 317–326 (2002). https://doi.org/10.1016/S0377-2217(01)00370-8
36. Siskos, E., Tsotsolas, N.: Elicitation of criteria importance weights through the Simos method: a robustness concern. Eur. J. Oper. Res. **246**, 543–553 (2015). https://doi.org/10.1016/j.ejor.2015.04.037
37. Brans, J.-P., Mareschal, B.: Promethee methods. In: Figueira, J., Greco, S., Ehrogott, M. (eds.) Multiple Criteria Decision Analysis: State of the Art Surveys, pp. 163–186. Springer, New York (2005)

38. Augusto, M., Lisboa, J., Yasin, M., Figueira, J.R.: Benchmarking in a multiple criteria performance context: an application and a conceptual framework. Eur. J. Oper. Res. **184**(1), 244–254 (2008). https://doi.org/10.1016/j.ejor.2006.10.052
39. Schito, J., Jullier, J., Raubal, M.: A framework for integrating stakeholder preferences when deciding on power transmission line corridors. EURO J. Decis. Process. **7**, 159–195 (2019). https://doi.org/10.1007/s40070-019-00100-w
40. Assumma, V., Bottero, M., Monaco, R.: Landscape economic attractiveness: an integrated methodology for exploring the rural landscapes in piedmont (Italy). Land. **8**(7), 105 (2019). https://doi.org/10.3390/land8070105
41. Steinhilber, S., Geldermann, J., Wietschel, M.: Renewables in the EU after 2020: a multi-criteria decision analysis in the context of the policy formation process. EURO J. Decis. Process. **4**, 119–155 (2016). https://doi.org/10.1007/s40070-016-0060-x
42. Rossitti, M., Torrieri, F.: Action research for the conservation of architectural heritage in mariginal areas: the role of evaluation / La ricerca azione per la conservazione del patrimonio architettonico in aree marginali: il ruolo della valutazione. Valori Valutazioni. **30**, 3–44 (2022). https://doi.org/10.48264/vvsiev-20223002
43. Assumma, V., Bottero, M., De Angelis, E., et al.: Scenario building model to support the resilience planning of winemaking regions: The case of the Douro territory (Portugal). Sci. Total Environ. **838**, 155889 (2022). https://doi.org/10.1016/j.scitotenv.2022.155889
44. Rossitti, M., Oppio, A., Torrieri, F.: The financial sustainability of cultural heritage reuse projects: an integrated approach for the historical rural landscape. Sustainability. **13**, 13130 (2021). https://doi.org/10.3390/su132313130

Participatory Strategies for Supporting Decision Making in Cultural Heritage Adaptive Reuse Interventions

Marta Bottero(✉) [image], Giulio Mondini [image], Sebastiano Barbieri [image], Caterina Caprioli [image], and Federico Dell'Anna [image]

Dipartimento Interateneo di Scienze, Progetto e Politiche del Territorio (DIST), Politecnico di Torino, Viale Mattioli, 39, 10125 Turin, TO, Italy
{marta.bottero,sebastiano.barbieri,caterina.caprioli, federico.dellanna}@polito.it,
giulio.mondini@formerfaculty.polito.it

Abstract. Participation is a multifaceted process that has become increasingly popular in projects and scenarios where the needs of the community have to be included in the decision-making process. In the context of cultural heritage management, these approaches are essential to ensure that the perspectives of all stakeholders are reflected in the proposed strategies. This paper traces the participatory process employed in the design of new functions for Villa Carpeneto, a historic building in the metropolitan area of Turin, Italy. The objective was to involve local stakeholders in order to facilitate social learning and improve the legitimacy and effectiveness of the decision-making process.

To explore possible scenarios for the reuse, the study adopted an integrated approach that combined several steps. It started with a historical review and an examination of the broader territorial context. This was followed by a participatory phase involving the local community. First, a workshop was organized to open a dialogue with local stakeholders. Later, a questionnaire was distributed to collect more structured feedback on possible future uses from residents. The findings highlight how involving communities in the decision-making process can support the sustainable reuse of heritage sites and strengthen the long-term value of shared planning.

Keywords: Participatory Planning · Cultural Heritage · Decision-making · Reuse

1 Introduction

The notion of participation is a multifaceted and open-ended concept, with a number of meanings and interpretations, that spans from public engagement to direct involvement in decisions [1]. Within this framework, participatory processes have become increasingly popular and have been embedded into research and project activities [2]. These processes have the potential to act as a bridge between global governance frameworks, national and regional objectives, and local realities [3]. This would ensure the development of inclusive and equitable strategies that are both practical and sensitive to territorial issues. They can be also an effective method of preventing "top-down" approaches that ignore context, leading to more relevant and sustainable outcomes [4].

The interest on this topic is also testified by the numerous studies that have investigated how stakeholders are involved [5–9]. Additionally, several authors have specifically advocated for more participatory approaches to better reflect the needs and viewpoints of stakeholders [10–12]. The inclusion of stakeholders in decision-making processes has the aim to increase social learning and trust-building, which should improve decision-makers' comprehension and application of stakeholders' perspectives and objectives [2].

There is now a large body of research on the subject, which attempts to consider stakeholder participation at different stages of the process and using different methods [13, 14]. Stakeholders' participation makes it possible to obtain more credible, legitimate and effective information and strategies compared to traditional research and expert work [15, 16]. In particular, the results produced have generally more direct effects on decision-making processes [2].

In the context of cultural and building heritage, the incorporation of public discussion presents a multifaceted landscape of opportunities and challenges, due to the fact that local identity, memory, and power dynamics are profoundly intertwined. Participation was experienced through a variety of methods and approaches. These include citizen participation, co-creative designs, collaborative mechanisms, and community-based initiatives [1]. This cooperation becomes fundamental in the implementation of protection and valorization policies and strategies, where institutions take the final decisions, but where local communities and citizens' associations, as the primary stakeholders of the territory, must actively participate and collaborate. Indeed, the proper use, conservation, and enhancement of this heritage are inextricably linked to popular involvement and participation. It is imperative to encourage users of the territory to reclaim the role played in the formation of a shared, collective identity and as a catalyst for cultural and economic development [17]. In this regard, the involvement of different population categories enables the implementation of strategic actions to be tailored to meet the needs of each group [18].

In light of these considerations, participatory processes are regarded as pragmatic strategies to ensure more effective, sustainable, and meaningful heritage conservation for present and future generations [19]. In this regard, it is imperative to overcome the challenges posed by these processes through an inclusive approach founded on trust, the sharing of expertise and resources, and the acknowledgement of communities' pivotal role in the preservation of their heritage.

Within this framework, the present work adopts a mixed approach [20–22], in order to integrate systematically quantitative and qualitative data in a real-world decision-making process [23, 24]. The decision-making process regards the exploration of alternative scenarios for the reuse of an historical building, called Villa Carpeneto, and its surroundings, located in the municipality of La Loggia, close to the city of Turin (Italy). In particular, the analysis starts with a detailed investigation into the territorial context in which the Villa Carpeneto is located, as well as the historical and planning system of the building. After the analysis of the state of the art, different community engagement methods are integrated. In particular, a workshop is organized for open discussions and collaborative exchanges among various stakeholders. Then, a structured survey is used to collect empirical data on residents' choices for future uses of the Villa Carpeneto spaces. A working group composed of academic experts was set up to review and discuss the outcomes of the territorial analysis, the workshop, and the structured survey. Rather than applying formal quantitative techniques, the team focused on identifying key needs and opportunities by analyzing the frequency and consistency of responses. This collaborative reflection helped structure potential functions for the villa, ensuring they respond to local priorities and the specific territorial context.

After this introduction, the paper is structured as follows. Section 2 presents the community engagement methods adopted for the participatory process of Villa Carpeneto. Section 3 regards the application of the methodologies previously presented. This section starts with the description of the territorial contexts and characteristics of the building. Then, the paper goes into depth on the description of the deliberative workshops and the survey-based analysis. Section 4 illustrates the results and findings obtained from the participatory engagement process. In Sect. 5, conclusive remarks and future perspectives are highlighted.

2 Community Engagement Methods

Over the last few decades, participatory approaches in conservation research have grown and evolved. They have moved beyond token forms of consultation, and now include a wide range of inclusive, co-designed methods that allow people to contribute meaningfully to decision-making [25, 26].

There are many ways to involve people, depending on the goal and the level of participation required. Structured tools, such as questionnaires and standardized observations, are useful for collecting data from many respondents and identifying common trends [27]. However, they often provide limited opportunities for participants to express their idea [28]. In contrast, more open-ended methods, like focus groups, interviews, or workshops, allow for deeper discussions and shared learning between researchers and communities [29]. Ethnographic tools, such as participant observation, are helpful in building trust and understanding local experiences [30]. In addition, creative techniques like storytelling, photo elicitation, and oral histories make it possible to explore the emotional and symbolic meanings people attach to places [31]. Spatial tools, including participatory GIS and volunteered geographic information (VGI), give communities the ability to map and visualize their values, needs, and future priorities [32].

For the Villa Carpeneto regeneration, we decided to use two complementary methods: a community workshop and a structured questionnaire. This approach allowed us to combine the depth and spontaneity of group discussion with the comparability of collected survey data.

In practice, we started with a workshop that brought together around seventy people from La Loggia and nearby municipalities. The aim was to reflect collectively on broader urban issues, identify shortcomings in infrastructure and cultural facilities, and encourage dialogue across local boundaries. Only after this first step did we focus more on Villa Carpeneto. A structured questionnaire was used to collect insights on possible future uses of the villa and its surroundings.

This two-phase approach helped us reach different segments of the population. The workshops gave participants the chance to discuss their priorities and co-create ideas in a collaborative setting. Meanwhile, the questionnaire allowed us to involve more people, including those who could not attend the events, including residents of nearby municipalities, and to compare responses systematically. This combination of methods aligns with recognized standards in participatory research and underlines the importance of adapting tools to the specific phase of the process, available resources, and the characteristics of the target population.

3 Application

3.1 Territorial and Urban Context of Villa Carpeneto

La Loggia is a municipality of 8724 inhabitants [33] in the metropolitan city of Turin. It is located about 6 km south of Turin and is part of the so-called second belt, strategically located with respect to some of the main connection arteries of the metropolitan area (Fig. 1). The municipality covers an area of 12.79 km^2 and borders the municipalities of Vinovo, Moncalieri and Carignano. This territory offers cultural services and facilities that are characteristic of the regional historical-artistic heritage, such as the Galli Castle and the della Rovere Castle (in Vinovo). The two municipalities also have libraries, primary schools and two big commercial centers, whose services are not only offered to the citizens of La Loggia but also to the neighboring municipalities. The surrounding area, covering about 14 municipalities in a radius of 10 km from the Villa Carpeneto, is equally composed in terms of services, with a few exceptions within the larger agglomerations. The municipalities in this territory are characterized by diversified population, and the presence of small and medium centres located primarily in plain regions. Moncalieri has the highest with a population of more than 56,000 individuals, followed by Carmagnola and Orbassano with a population of 28,000 and 23,000 respectively. Osasio and Castagnole Piemonte are some of the smaller centres with less than 3000 individuals [33].

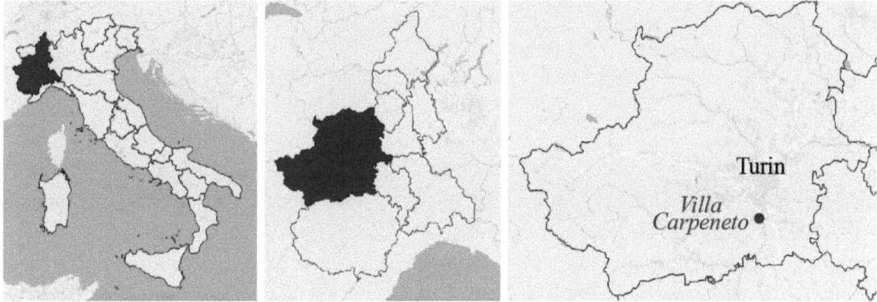

Fig. 1. Geographical location of Villa Carpeneto, La Loggia (TO).

From the hospitality point of view, the accommodation capacity is rather limited in most municipalities, with a clear prevalence of small facilities. Carmagnola and Moncalieri stand out for the largest number of accommodation facilities and beds available. Tourist presences are mainly concentrated in Moncalieri, which records over 110,000 overnight stays, followed by Orbassano and Candiolo [34].

Focusing on the area around La Loggia (Fig. 2), the river Po represents a very important and identifying element. The Parco Naturale del Po Piemontese is a natural area that develops thanks to this important watercourse, extending in a north-south direction. In addition to protecting biodiversity, it also offers the possibility of several cycling and walking routes along the river to the north. Within this area, we also find a Special Protection Zone (SPA) that coincides with a Site of Community Importance (SCI) called Lanca di Santa Marta. These places are fundamental to the local ecological network, contributing to the conservation of biodiversity and offering spaces for sustainable land use.

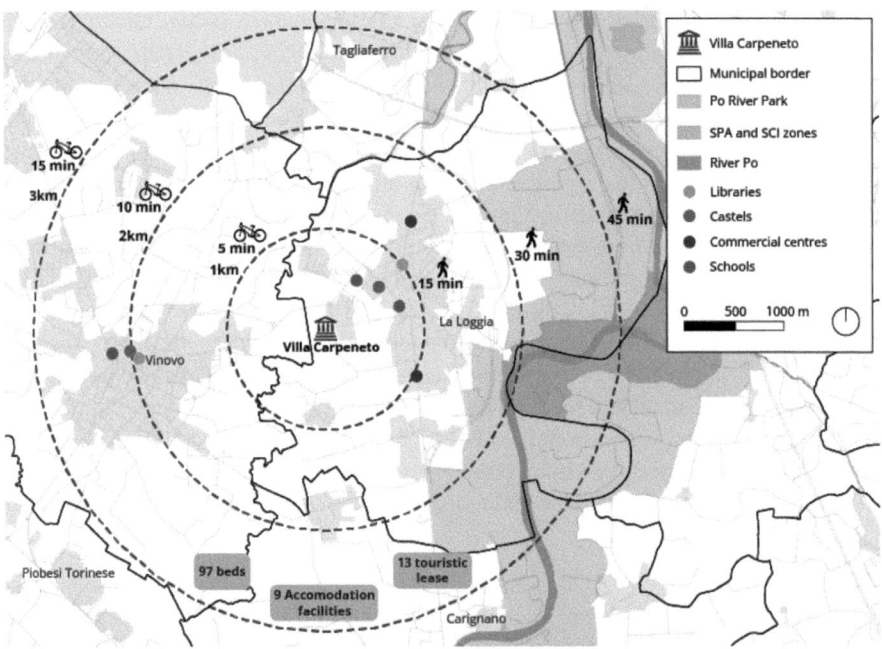

Fig. 2. Local context Villa Carpeneto.

Villa Carpeneto is located west of the town center, right on the municipal boundary of La Loggia. This building is an architectural property of cultural interest, recognized by the Italian Cultural Heritage and Landscape Code (Leg. Decree No. 42/2004). The current city plan places the Villa in the sub-area of the town which includes the rural pertinences of the complex. The regulations of the plan designated this area exclusively for public services and green spaces, while for the historic building, the maximum restoration and conservative renovation is allowed as the maximum intervention.

Vehicular access to the Villa is provided by provincial street no.145, which connects La Loggia with nearby Vinovo. Bicycle and pedestrian access are instead provided by the entrance boulevard, which starts from the center of the village and leads to the Villa's entrance gate. The areas surrounding the Villa Carpeneto complex are mostly natural or agricultural. Near the Villa, there are residential blocks and a large industrial complex.

The villa is surrounded by a modest communication network, mainly vehicular, that efficiently connects it with Turin. Its proximity to two major infrastructures, such as Turin's bypass (*Tangenziale Sud*) and the Turin-Savona highway, allow for a rapid connection not only with southern Piedmont and Liguria Region, but with all the other main highways.

If on a road level the Villa is in a favorable position, this is not the case for connections by local public transport. La Loggia is mainly connected to Turin by suburban buses, which are running at low frequencies. In addition, Moncalieri has a railway station served by four lines of the Metropolitan Railway Service (SFM), but it is not efficiently connected to the municipality of La Loggia.

This difference between public and private transport is very evident from the travelling times from the Villa to the relevant elements of the area. In Figs. 3 and 4, accessibility to the main mobility nodes, historic centers, cultural and environmental assets was studied. In particular, accessibility by private transport shows how most of the identified elements fall within average travel times of one hour. Whereas with public transport, travel times increase due to the lack of interconnection between mobility nodes. In fact, the same destinations that used to be reachable within one hour are reachable in about two hours by public transport.

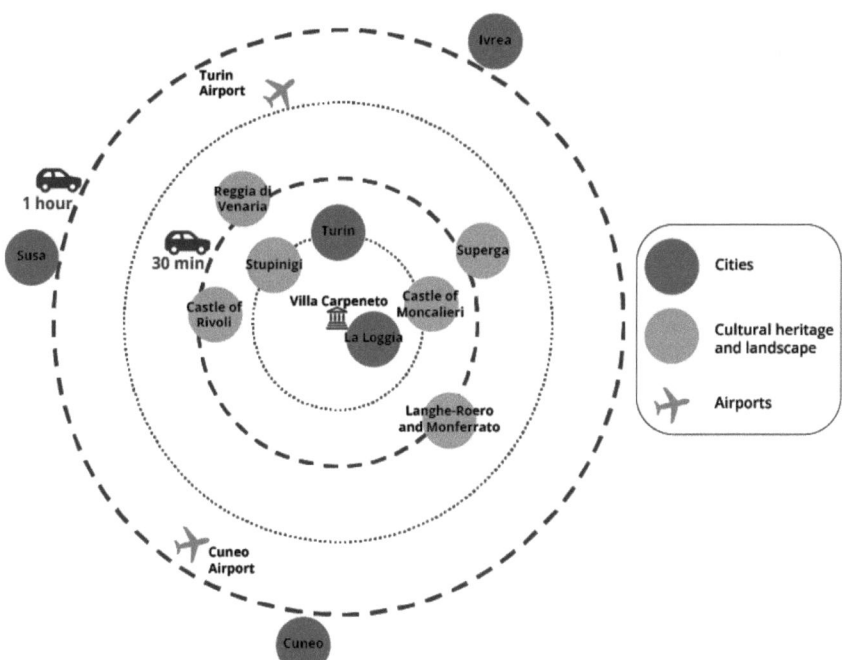

Fig. 3. Travel time from Villa Carpeneto to the main elements in the territory by private vehicle.

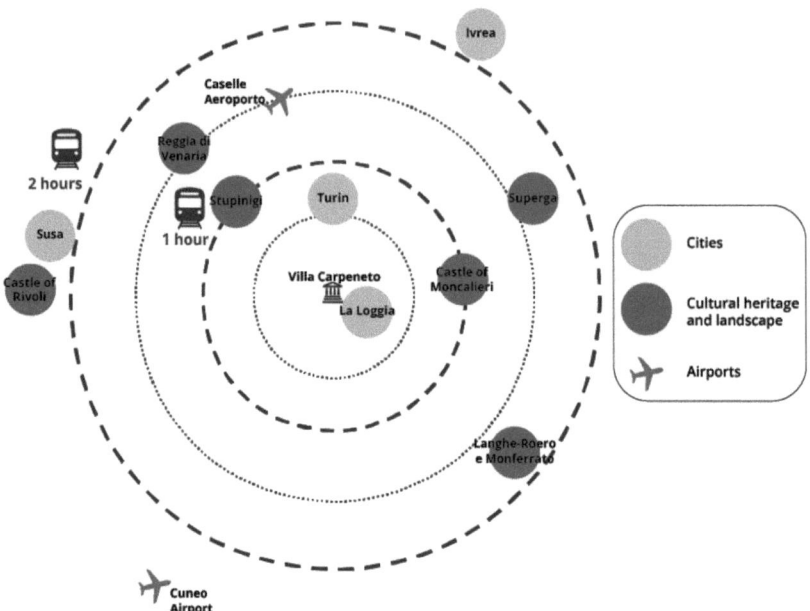

Fig. 4. Travel time from Villa Carpeneto to the main elements in the territory by Local Public Transport.

3.2 Analysis of the Current State and Potential of the Villa

The Villa Carpeneto is a historic building located in the municipality of La Loggia, Turin. The symbolic nature of this building encouraged the municipality to acquire it in 2024. This complex is now in a poor state of conservation due to a long period of total lack of maintenance and vandalism, which has compromised many of the valuable architectural elements present. In addition, the spaces have become overgrown with invasive vegetation. These conditions make some parts of the complex inaccessible and they complicate the assessment of the villa's true condition (Fig. 5).

From the outside, it is possible to get a general idea of the spaces available throughout the complex. The main access to the east is marked by a large gate that shows no visible signs of structural compromise.

Inside the complex is the former caretaker's house with an attached greenhouse (to the south) and, on the opposite side of the courtyard, the farmhouse (to the north). These spaces are currently difficult to access and show extensive damage, including the deterioration of the plaster and the presence of encroaching vegetation.

The aulic block of the villa (located to the west) is the element of greatest architectural value and the one that shows the most evident signs of deterioration. Both externally and internally, there are visible signs of vandalism and looting of architectural elements and furnishings considered to be of value. Externally, the main loggia has lost its balustrade, while the interior has been stripped of its precious majolica and parquet flooring. The stucco decorations, although slightly damaged, have survived and can be seen in many of the rooms. Some valuable elements such as the fireplaces, the woodwork in the library

Fig. 5. Current status of Villa Carpeneto (July 2024).

(although badly damaged) and the banister of the iconic "shell" staircase have been preserved.

Finally, the chapel, located between the Aulic block and the farmhouse, retains its original configuration and wooden pews, although the sacred furnishings are missing.

From a structural point of view, throughout the villa there are critical problems in the wooden horizons of the upper floors and the roof, which have been damaged by vegetation infiltration. Particularly noteworthy is a significant vertical crack in the loggia on the first floor, which could indicate structural failure.

Among the open spaces surrounding the complex, the gardens are now deprived of the original traces of Russell Page's design due to the uncontrolled growth of invasive vegetation. The large avenue leading to the town center is now inaccessible, but the original trees are still there, and it will be possible to restore the cycle-pedestrian path that has been hidden by vegetation over time. On the other hand, the large portal that gives access to the avenue from the urban fabric is badly damaged.

From the perspective of reusing the spaces described above, a number of functions and activities have been identified that are considered compatible and offer great opportunities for recovery. These functions are preliminary ideas that emerged from discussions with the municipality and considerations regarding the functionality of the available spaces, and they will be juxtaposed with the outcomes of the workshop. Among the options that emerged, recreational and cultural activities such as workshops, a library, a venue for exhibitions and events, and ceremonies are certainly possibilities for the villa's outdoor space; accommodation and restoration activities seem appropriate for spaces such as the farmhouse, while the chapel could be reused for exhibitions, events, and small-scale ceremonies.

On the other hand, activities preferable in the open air are considered excellent for the garden of the villa, such as an open-air cinema or other events that can combine culture and entertainment, as well as sports activities. Finally, some tourist services could be provided in the areas of the former caretaker's house and the greenhouses.

3.3 Community Workshops

The community workshop was a key methodological step to initiate dialogue and gather local knowledge in a structured but informal way. To foster an open and inclusive discussion environment, participants were organized into small heterogeneous groups, each composed of individuals with different roles and interest in the area. In the center of each table, a large paper board served as the main tool for discussion. Participants were asked to write on sticky note their responses to a series of predefined, open-ended questions. The first question, "What is missing in the area?", aimed to identify gaps in infrastructure, public services, and underused spaces in the southern part of the Turin metropolitan area, where La Loggia is located. It served as a starting point for collective analysis. The second question, "What would you like for the future?", invited participants to define their priorities based on the needs previously identified. Finally, "Where should these initiatives be implemented?" encouraged them to translate their ideas into practical proposals by pointing to specific locations in La Loggia and nearby municipalities. Together, these prompts supported a structured reflection on local challenges, desired improvements, and concrete opportunities for development.

Facilitators were present to support the process. Their role was not to guide the discussion, but to ensure that discussions remained accessible and respectful and that all voices were heard. This approach encouraged an interactive dynamic, allowing participants to contribute individually, and to expand the discussion through spontaneous conversation.

3.4 Survey-Based Analysis

After the workshop, a structured survey was launched to collect more systematic information on how the local community in the southern metropolitan area of Turin envisions the future use of Villa Carpeneto. The aim was to better understand preferences among the proposed functions and ensure that any future intervention reflects the everyday needs and expectations of residents.

The questionnaire was designed to be clear and easy to complete. It began with a section on participants' awareness of the villa, asking whether they knew its history, had visited the site, or were familiar with its current condition. The next part asked participants to evaluate different possible functions for the villa, such as cultural, educational, recreational, or social uses, and to indicate which ones they considered most relevant.

A further section collected general demographic information, allowing for comparisons across age groups, education levels, and places of residence.

Finally, an open-ended space was included for comments or suggestions, offering participants the opportunity to share more personal opinions or new ideas not covered in the predefined categories. To reach a wide and diverse audience, the survey was distributed both online and on paper. The digital version was shared through social media and the municipality's mailing lists, while printed copies were made available directly by the local administration.

4 Key Insights from Community Engagement

4.1 Community Workshop Outcomes

In November 2024, a workshop was held in La Loggia to actively involve the local community in rethinking the future of Villa Carpeneto. About seventy people participated, including residents, association representatives, local businesses, and delegates from neighboring municipalities (Fig. 6).

Fig. 6. Participation meeting of November in La Loggia (TO), Italy.

During the workshop, participants expressed several concerns about the area. One of the most common concerns was the scarcity of public infrastructure and shared community spaces. Participants stressed the absence of accessible areas where families, young people and residents in general can gather, relax or engage in cultural and recreational activities. There was a strong call for creating a multifunctional place that can host cultural events, educational initiatives and social interactions. Recurring suggestions included the creation of a public library, exhibition spaces and places for local assemblies.

The importance of promoting a stronger local identity also emerged, with several participants calling for stronger links between local schools and Turin-based cultural institutions. Other proposals focused on innovation and inclusion, with ideas such as training hubs for young people, environmental research centers and coworking spaces for local professionals.

Culture and leisure were consistently cited as strategic levers for local development. Inspired by the experiences of neighboring municipalities, residents proposed outdoor cinemas, community festivals, and thematic markets. Sports and wellness activities were also appreciated, not only for their recreational benefits, but also for their potential in improving social cohesion and contributing to the local economy.

Finally, the improvement of public transportation and the development of cycling infrastructure were considered essential to improve daily mobility and promote more sustainable modes of transportation.

Villa Carpeneto was often mentioned as the perfect place to host many of these ideas. It was envisioned as a cultural and social center, with areas for exhibitions, a small municipal theater, and a public library. The surrounding green area was seen as a space for outdoor workshops, performances and family events.

4.2 Survey Findings

The survey was completed by 126 people. Most of them were residents of La Loggia (78 percent), while the rest were from neighboring municipalities in the southern part of the Turin metropolitan area (22 percent). The questionnaire was available both online and in paper format to facilitate everyone's participation. The group of respondents was diverse in terms of age and education, with a majority between the ages of 35 and 54 and a balanced number with a high school diploma or college degree. This suggests an engaged and reflective community interested in local development.

When asked about potential future uses of the villa, respondents expressed strong support for cultural and artistic functions. Proposals included temporary exhibition spaces, collaborations with cultural institutions, and venues for concerts and public events. Educational uses also featured prominently: the villa was envisioned as a place where traditional crafts could intersect with emerging technologies, creating opportunities for intergenerational learning and attracting professionals with specialized skills.

A number of responses emphasized the enhancement of public spaces and community life. Suggestions included the creation of botanical gardens, pedestrian and bicycle paths, outdoor cinemas, and local markets. Special attention was also given to the needs of families and vulnerable groups, with proposals for daycare services, inclusive learning environments and intergenerational centers.

Another important theme was the potential for sustainable economic models. Several interviewees suggested that parts of the villa could be used for private events, such as weddings or conferences, as a means of generating revenue without compromising the cultural integrity of the site. Others suggested the creation of a café or restaurant with local products as a way to attract visitors and stimulate the local economy.

5 Discussion and Conclusions

This contribution presented a participatory decision framework aiming at supporting the exploration of alternative scenarios of reuse of an historical building. The building called Villa Carpeneto is considered a symbol of the municipality of La Loggia, where it is located. For this reason, the involvement of the citizens and all relevant stakeholders in the decision-making process became fundamental. After the detailed investigation of the Villa Carpeneto, as well as its relationship with the surroundings and the territorial context, a two-step community engagement approach was proposed. Firstly, open discussions and collaborative exchanges among the various stakeholders were exploited in open discussions. Secondly, empirical data on residents' opinions and preferences on the future of the Villa Carpeneto were collected through a structured survey.

The entire process increased the sense of shared ownership and involvement, ensuring that the people who are going to benefit the most from the restoration of the villa have a say in it. Additionally, the process followed highlighted how the evolution of the territory and its actualization should aim at ambitious goals based on a participatory approach, that considers the cultural, socio-economic and environmental heritage that will be left to future generations. In this regard, the most effective way to intervention is through an integrated approach, that makes use of a collaborative effort between different entities with the aim of achieving a shared goal. In this way, the local development can achieve multiple benefits, spanning the enrichment of individual lives and their well-being, the strengthening of the community social capital and economic growth, the revitalization of urban and rural areas, the promotion of sustainable tourism, and the attractiveness of the territory.

Future perspectives of the research will regard the elaboration of the data of the survey according to the Best-Worst Scaling (BWS) approach [35]. The community's preferences regarding the future development of Villa Carpeneto were asked specifically according to the logic of BWS. In BWS, people rate a set of three or more elements on a subjective scale, selecting the best and the worst ones. The identification of the most and least preferred should be more reliable than ranking all the elements, as required, for example, by the ranking method of conjoint analysis [36]. Using BWS, it will be possible to obtain more precise and quantitative results on the future uses of the Villa Carpeneto, according to the preferences expressed by the citizens. Moreover, the results will be used to propose real project proposals for the redevelopment of the building, that takes into account the social, economic and environmental aspects in play. An implementation plan for the interventions will be defined through a detailed timetable of the activity. This will consider the costs and sources of funding, as well as the involvement of the various stakeholders and the procedures for implementation.

Acknowledgments. The work presented in the publication has been developed by the authors within the research project "Reuse scenarios for the Villa Carpeneto (La Loggia)" carried out by the Interuniversity Department of Regional and Urban Studies and Planning (DIST), Politecnico di Torino (Scientific coordinators: prof. Marta Bottero and prof. Giulio Mondini). Part of the study was funded by MUR – DM 117/2023 (project PNRR-NGEU).

References

1. Colomer, L., Pastor Pérez, A.: City governance, participatory democracy, and cultural heritage in Barcelona, 1986–2022. Hist. Environ.: Policy Prac. **15**, 81–100 (2024). https://doi.org/10.1080/17567505.2023.2298546
2. Veisi, H., Jackson-Smith, D., Arrueta, L.: Alignment of stakeholder and scientist understandings and expectations in a participatory modeling project. Environ. Sci. Policy. **134**, 57–66 (2022). https://doi.org/10.1016/j.envsci.2022.04.004
3. Howard, T.: From international principles to local practices: a socio-legal framing of public participation research. Environ. Dev. Sustain. **17**, 747–763 (2015). https://doi.org/10.1007/s10668-014-9572-3
4. Dellinger, M.: Ten years of the Aarhus convention: how procedural democracy is paving the way for substantive change in national and international environmental law. Colo. Env't L. J. **23** (2012)
5. Tobias, S., Ströbele, M.F., Buser, T.: How transdisciplinary projects influence participants' ways of thinking: a case study on future landscape development. Sustain. Sci. **14**, 405–419 (2019). https://doi.org/10.1007/s11625-018-0532-y
6. Klenk, N.L., Meehan, K.: Transdisciplinary sustainability research beyond engagement models: toward adventures in relevance. Environ. Sci. Policy. **78**, 27–35 (2017). https://doi.org/10.1016/j.envsci.2017.09.006
7. Brennan, M., Rondón-Sulbarán, J.: Transdisciplinary research: exploring impact, knowledge and quality in the early stages of a sustainable development project. World Dev. **122**, 481–491 (2019). https://doi.org/10.1016/j.worlddev.2019.06.001
8. Bracken, L.J., Bulkeley, H.A., Whitman, G.: Transdisciplinary research: understanding the stakeholder perspective. J. Environ. Plan. Manag. **58**, 1291–1308 (2015). https://doi.org/10.1080/09640568.2014.921596
9. Rossitti, M., Oteri, A.M., Torrieri, F.: The social value of built heritage: an interdisciplinary discourse. Built Herit. **9**, 5 (2025). https://doi.org/10.1186/s43238-025-00173-4
10. González-Rosell, A., Blanco, M., Arfa, I.: Integrating stakeholder views and system dynamics to assess the water–energy–food nexus in Andalusia. Water (Basel). **12**, 3172 (2020). https://doi.org/10.3390/w12113172
11. Mach, K.J., Lemos, M.C., Meadow, A.M., et al.: Actionable knowledge and the art of engagement. Curr. Opin. Environ. Sustain. **42**, 30–37 (2020). https://doi.org/10.1016/j.cosust.2020.01.002
12. Voinov, A., Bousquet, F.: Modelling with stakeholders. Environ Model Softw. **25**, 1268–1281 (2010). https://doi.org/10.1016/j.envsoft.2010.03.007
13. Dell'Ovo, M., Torrieri, F., Oppio, A.: How to Model Stakeholder Participation for Flood Management, pp. 67–75 (2018)
14. Bottero, M., Bragaglia, F., Caruso, N., et al.: Experimenting community impact evaluation (CIE) for assessing urban regeneration programmes: the case study of the area 22@ Barcelona. Cities. **99**, 102464 (2020). https://doi.org/10.1016/j.cities.2019.102464
15. Cash, D.W., Clark, W.C., Alcock, F., et al.: Knowledge systems for sustainable development. Proc. Natl. Acad. Sci. **100**, 8086–8091 (2003). https://doi.org/10.1073/pnas.1231332100
16. Bottero, M., Assumma, V., Caprioli, C., Dell'Ovo, M.: Decision making in urban development: the application of a hybrid evaluation method for a critical area in the city of Turin (Italy). Sustain. Cities Soc. **72**, 103028 (2021). https://doi.org/10.1016/j.scs.2021.103028

17. Cerquetti, M., Romagnoli, A.: Toward Sustainable Innovation in Tourism: The Role of Cultural Heritage and Heritage Communities, pp. 33–50 (2022)
18. Ferretti, V., Bottero, M., Mondini, G.: Decision making and cultural heritage: an application of the multi-attribute value theory for the reuse of historical buildings. J. Cult. Herit. **15**, 644–655 (2014). https://doi.org/10.1016/j.culher.2013.12.007
19. Marucci, M.: Culture-led Urban Regeneration Projects: Participatory Good Practices in Europe. In: Working paper series of DiSSE. Department Sapienza Università di Roma (2025)
20. Creswell, J.W., Plano Clark, V.L.: Designing and Conducting Mixed Methods Research. Sage, CA, Thousand Oaks (2011)
21. Oppio, A., Dell'Ovo, M.: Cultural Heritage Preservation and Territorial Attractiveness: A Spatial Multidimensional Evaluation Approach, pp. 105–125 (2021)
22. Assumma, V., De Luca, C.: Assessing the value of cultural landscapes through the integration of biophysical-economic valuation, risk assessment and cost-benefit analysis. In: Computational Science and Its Applications – ICCSA 2024 Workshops, pp. 78–93. Springer (2024)
23. Caprioli, C., Bottero, M., De Angelis, E.: Combining an agent-based model, hedonic pricing and multicriteria analysis to model green gentrification dynamics. Comput. Environ. Urban. Syst. **102**, 101955 (2023). https://doi.org/10.1016/j.compenvurbsys.2023.101955
24. Rossitti, M., Torrieri, F.: Action research for the conservation of architectural heritage in mariginal areas: the role of evaluation / La ricerca azione per la conservazione del patrimonio architettonico in aree marginali: il ruolo della valutazione. Valori Valutazioni. **30**, 3–44 (2022). https://doi.org/10.48264/VVSIEV-20223002
25. Arnstein, S.R.: A ladder of citizen participation. J. Am. Inst. Plann. **35**, 216–224 (1969). https://doi.org/10.1080/01944366908977225
26. Newing, H., Brittain, S., Buchadas, A., et al.: 'Participatory' conservation research involving indigenous peoples and local communities: fourteen principles for good practice. Biol. Conserv. **296**, 110708 (2024). https://doi.org/10.1016/j.biocon.2024.110708
27. La Riccia, L., Assumma, V., Bottero, M.C., et al.: A contingent valuation-based method to valuate ecosystem services for a proactive planning and management of cork oak forests in Sardinia (Italy). Sustainability. **15**, 7986 (2023). https://doi.org/10.3390/su15107986
28. Murali, R., Bijoor, A., Thinley, T., et al.: Indigenous governance structures for maintaining an ecosystem service in an agro-pastoral community in the Indian Trans Himalaya. Ecosyst. People. **18**, 303–314 (2022). https://doi.org/10.1080/26395916.2022.2067241
29. Warren, C.A.: Qualitative interviewing. In: Handbook of Interview Research: Context and Method, pp. 83–101. Sage Publications, Thousand Oaks (2002)
30. Chua, L., Schreer, V., Thung, P.H.: Using Ethnographic Research for Social Engagement: A Toolkit for Orangutan (and other) Conservationists. University of Cambridge (2022)
31. Swanson, S.S., Ardoin, N.M.: Communities behind the lens: a review and critical analysis of visual participatory methods in biodiversity conservation. Biol. Conserv. **262**, 109293 (2021). https://doi.org/10.1016/j.biocon.2021.109293
32. Fagerholm, N., Raymond, C.M., Olafsson, A.S., et al.: A methodological framework for analysis of participatory mapping data in research, planning, and management. Int. J. Geogr. Inf. Sci. **35**, 1848–1875 (2021). https://doi.org/10.1080/13658816.2020.1869747
33. Istituto Nazionale di Statistica: ISTAT (2024). https://www.istat.it/. Accessed 6 Jan 2025
34. Osservatorio Turistico della Regione Piemonte: Movimenti turistici dei clienti negli esercizi ricettivi. In: Dati comunali - Anno 2024 (2025)
35. Finn, A., Louviere, J.J.: Determining the appropriate response to evidence of public concern: the case of food safety. J. Public Policy Mark. **11**, 12–25 (1992). https://doi.org/10.1177/074391569201100202
36. Bottero, M., Bravi, M., Caprioli, C., et al.: New Housing Preferences in the COVID-19 Era: A Best-to-Worst Scaling Experiment, pp. 120–129 (2021)

The Role of Urban Planning in Building the Circular Urban Model. The Case of Naples

Giuseppe Mazzeo[✉]

Pegaso University, Centro Direzionale, Isola F2, 80143 Naples, Italy
giuseppe.mazzeo@unipegaso.it

Abstract. The paper aims to explore how urban planning can approach city development by focusing on the reuse of urban spaces and the process of rebuilding the city from within. In doing so, urban planning will face specific situations that must be addressed on a case-by-case basis, potentially defining distinct methods for constructing a circular urban development model.

The paper analyzes a specific area of the city of Naples characterized by the presence of zones that are part of the historic urban center and more recent areas belonging to both consolidated and unconsolidated expansions. The area is examined in relation to transformation areas where significant changes in land use and urban form are either underway or planned.

Keywords: Naples · Urban requalification · Circular urban model

1 Introduction and Methodology of Research

The aim of the paper is to explore how the concept of the circular economy can be applied to urban regeneration and redevelopment, using the city of Naples as a case study. It investigates how principles of circularity – though not always explicitly named – have historically influenced urban planning in Italy, and how they can now be consciously integrated into modern urban strategies to create more sustainable, resilient, and inclusive cities. This paper aims to explore how urban planning can approach city development by focusing on the reuse of urban spaces and the process of rebuilding the city from within. In doing so, urban planning will face specific situations that must be addressed on a case-by-case basis, potentially defining distinct methods for constructing a circular urban development model.

Urban planning, from the early 1900s until the 1970s–80s, was primarily characterized by actions aimed at urban expansion. This process affected all the most advanced nations, characterizing a period of strong economic and social burst and leading to a significant rise in the wealth and well-being of European and Western countries.

The urban expansion process has come to an end over the past few decades for several reasons. On one hand, in many parts of Italy and Europe, it has saturated the available territorial spaces. On the other hand, population growth has slowed in many areas, affecting the expansion processes of cities. Furthermore, the evolution of economic

© The Author(s), under exclusive license to Springer Nature Switzerland AG 2026
O. Gervasi et al. (Eds.): ICCSA 2025 Workshops, LNCS 15896, pp. 248–265, 2026.
https://doi.org/10.1007/978-3-031-97654-4_16

systems and innovations in sectors such as mobility have resulted in the multiplication of cases of abandonment and degradation of many urbanized areas within city structures.

This process also affects the historical parts of the city, where very different phenomena, often in stark opposition, are concentrated. On one hand, there is the use of central urban areas as spaces of prestige, wealth, and exclusivity; on the other, there is the deterioration caused by abandonment and the lack of use and maintenance of urban spaces.

The paper analyzes a specific area of the city of Naples characterized by the presence of zones that are part of the historic urban center and more recent areas belonging to both consolidated and unconsolidated expansions. The area is examined in relation to transformation areas where significant changes in land use and urban form are either underway or planned. The analysis of the case study aims to determine whether these transformation processes take into account principles related to sustainability and the circular economy and whether they are compatible with the existing urban structure, which – particularly in the historic area – developed in periods and for functions very different from those currently present.

The paper represents the first step in a broader analysis. Further steps are planned, focusing on a deeper examination of the study's main critical aspects. The research starts with the urban evolution of the city and ultimately proposes a system of potential interventions. These interventions will apply the concepts of sustainability and urban circularity as guiding principles to support urban policies and planning.

To carry out this research project, the methodology follows the structure below:

1. Theoretical framework and literature review to establish the conceptual foundation for the circular economy and its relevance to urban planning. This step conducts a systematic literature review of academic sources on circular economy, urban regeneration, and urban planning history, also analyzing relevant policy documents and planning regulations.
2. Historical-comparative analysis to understand how circular economy principles have implicitly influenced past urban planning practices. This involves examining historical urban plans and redevelopment initiatives, comparing planning goals, land use changes, and redevelopment approaches across different time periods, and identifying implicit circular economy principles such as reuse, preservation, and densification.
3. Case study method to conduct an in-depth analysis of a specific area undergoing urban transformation.
4. Policy and planning document analysis, to assess how current urban transformation efforts incorporate circular economy principles.

2 Literature

The circular economy is a model of production and consumption, which involves sharing, leasing, reusing, repairing, refurbishing and recycling existing materials and products as long as possible. In this way, the life cycle of products is extended [1].

The literature on circular economy is extensive. The main idea of circular economy is to retain the value of resources and to prevent the use of virgin materials and waste outputs, not only by recycling and reusing, but primarily by reducing the need for resources [2]. Corvellec et al. [3] present a reasoned account of the critiques addressed to the circular economy and circular business models. Kirchherr et al. [4] confirm this and present 114 circular economy definitions which were coded on 17 dimensions. From these definitions derive that the main aim of the circular economy is considered to be economic prosperity, followed by environmental quality; its impact on social equity and future generations is barely mentioned.

Geissdoerfer et al. [5] deepens the connections between circular economy and sustainability highlighting that similarities and differences between both concepts remain ambiguous. Also Korhonen et al. [6] deepen the limitations of the concept of circular economy and conduct a critical analysis of the concept from the perspective of environmental sustainability.

An answer to the doubts come from Morseletto [7] that examines which targets can facilitate the transition towards a circular economy starting from 10 common circular economy strategies (i.e. recover, recycling, repurpose, remanufacture, refurbish, repair, re-use, reduce, rethink, refuse).

Specific attention is on the relationships between circular economy and the city. Petit-Boix and Leipold [8] sustain that cities are implementing a number of initiatives that aim to turn them into sustainable circular systems, also if whether these initiatives achieve their sustainability goals is largely unknown. For the authors cities encourage strategies relating to urban infrastructure, with an additional focus on social consumption aspects, such as repair and reuse actions. Research has yet to assess urban planning strategies, essential for defining the impacts of other urban elements.

Bolger and Doyon [9] sustain that the continuous growth of the cities is supported by systems of production and consumption that contribute to the depletion of natural resources and pollution of the environment. The circular economy model offers an alternative to the predominant take-make-dispose economic system. In particular, the role of strategic planning can facilitate a circular economy in urban settings. Using a comparative case study of the municipalities of Melbourne, Australia and Malmö, Sweden, the authors sustain that strategic urban planning can translate circular economy objectives into actions within specific urban areas, although barriers still exist to fully integrating the circular economy model.

Lakatos et al. [10] sustain that cities play a focal role in facilitating the transition towards circularity through the closing of the loops, recirculation, technical innovation, policy elaboration and citizens' support. Circular economy applied at the urban level still needs effort and innovation to successfully pass the transition phase from the linear economy. The authors develop a framework model that can be adapted in other cities to facilitate their transition to circular cities. Other authors [2] highlight that climate efficiency in cities cannot be improved simply by replacing the old structures with new ones, because both the construction and operation phases cause major resource and energy consumption. The review of literature is the basis for deepening three approaches for the adoption of circular economy in the built environment: (1) Management for sustainable cities; (2) Urban services and consumer practices aligned with circular economy; and (3) Cleaner production and construction. In the management of sustainable cities, the literature highlights self-correcting 'adaptive management cycle' with the phases of planning, implementation and evaluation.

As seen, an extension of the concept of circular economy is its application to the city [11]. Applying it to the city seems natural when considering that the circular economy is a theoretical framework aimed at deepening the understanding of production and consumption processes in relation to their increasing sustainability. In the traditional economy, production and consumption are closely linked to the concept of waste. Implementing circular economy processes grants a high level of sustainability, as its production and use do not naturally end in landfill disposal but rather in its transformation into a new product.

This process can be applied to urban structures in relation to the expansion of actions for regenerating degraded urban areas, repurposing abandoned spaces, improving energy efficiency, and implementing more sustainable waste management systems.

A settlement, and particularly a historic center, inherently applies the concept of a circular economy. While it may be debated whether this occurs at the micro level of buildings, it is undeniable that it happens at a macro level (districts, neighborhoods, and urban centers).

Urban centers are structures situated in a specific location where adaptation processes have been continuous over time since their foundation. They constitute an active artificial space, undergoing constant transformation – whether rapid or gradual, visible or subtle.

A city, therefore, can be considered a typical example of a circular economy, where space undergoes an initial transformation at a given time and a series of subsequent changes. These may include additions and modifications to volumes and functions within the space, yet the overall structure remains functional.

Why is it important to explore these aspects? Because the fundamental issue of urban structures, in their oldest or newest parts, is now the compatibility – both in terms of the functions they can accommodate and the use of spaces and volumes.

After the most critical period (from the second half of the nineteenth century to the first half of the last century), during which the central parts of cities were seen as urban structures to be modernized, often through radical interventions, we now face protection regulations that become stricter as the historical value of an area increases, preventing drastic transformations. However, the issue of adapting these spaces to functional evolution and the impacts that this evolution brings remains unresolved.

3 Theoretical Background

3.1 Transformations in Urban Structures: The Urban Planning Perspective

The restoration of historic centers was a topic of great cultural significance in the 1960s and 1970s, a period in which the protection of urban structures inherited from previous eras became more prominent, also due to the continuous destructive interventions on historic centers occurring at the time.

The radical transformation of morphology and functional stratification within urban centers was considered a "normal" operation for a long time, acquiring negative connotations only after World War II, when a cultural movement more focused on preserving even the smallest historical testimonies gained prominence over perspectives that favored unrestricted intervention.

Modern urban planning has complemented straightforward restoration efforts with new tools that have enhanced intervention capabilities based on the assumption that the focus is not solely on restoring physical structures but rather on the overall revitalization of the system formed by physical structures, relational frameworks, and socio-economic elements that interact with one another and enable coordinated intervention on the built environment.

This means that proposed tools no longer have merely a local relevance but are strongly connected to the urban scale, as they can influence the roles different urban sectors assume within city centers and add layers of meaning to interventions on built environments. Additionally, the cultural contributions that urban planning has assimilated in recent years have increased the significance and value of tools that were already influential in the economic and social framework of our post-industrial society.

The city can be analyzed from many perspectives: as a concrete expression of collective life, as a product of economic forces acting within the territory, as a political and social incubator, as a material trace of the past, and as the foundation of the future. Different evolutionary periods (both past and present) coexist within the city, adapting with varying degrees of ease. The awareness that the historical heritage present in cities enriches the entire social structure is a relatively recent achievement.

The urban planning debate on the preservation and restoration of older structures has been ongoing for a long time, beginning in the post-war reconstruction phase, when awareness of the need to preserve historic centers developed.

To the question of why restoration is necessary, one can respond with the theoretical assumption that the city is a system in which all elements are interrelated, to the extent that interventions on one part affect the entire organism, and the transformations achieved through restoration and enhancement of pre-existing elements represent a significant cultural enrichment for the urban community.

The evolution of theories and practices of urban intervention over the last century has facilitated a gradual shift from purely substitutional interventions to conservative interventions, and ultimately to interventions focused on the revitalization of structural elements and connective tissue [12].

After World War II, Italy was engaged in a difficult reconstruction effort. One consequence of this process was, on the one hand, the concentration of speculative activities in city center areas and, on the other, the neglect of other areas that were also affected by war destruction but were less economically attractive.

The total lack of control over reconstruction efforts provoked a strong reaction in defense of historic city centers. The "conservationist" stance was the most successful among various cultural groups (Nuova Italia, Associazione Nazionale Centri Storici, etc.) that emerged in the 1950s to protect the historical and artistic heritage.

The conservationist position excluded the possibility that historic centers could undergo modifications and adaptations, adhering to a cultural approach that prohibited any transformation within historic districts. This perspective effectively enforced stagnation in ancient areas while demonstrating marked indifference toward the rest of the urbanized territory.

According to conservationist views, only the ancient city deserved protection, and consequently, all urban planning interventions following nineteenth-century methodologies were condemned as destructive to centuries-old urban fabrics and detrimental to traditional living standards and social relationships shaped by local conditions. The expansion of tertiary functions within historic centers was considered highly harmful, as was the encroachment of modern urban developments that, by increasing surrounding populations, would render preservation impossible and, in a sense, pollute the historical character of the center.

By completely freezing any possible transformation of the historic center, it was effectively turned into a monument in its entirety, preserved as a testimony to past civilizations. This extreme position reflected a historical-cultural approach incapable of grasping the dynamic nature of urban evolution and development, prioritizing aesthetic and visual values over functional and economic ones, which ultimately weakened and rendered conservation efforts impractical.

Even at the time, the limitations of such a one-sided view of conservation were evident to those who saw the city as an evolving organism, in which the physical manifestations of each historical period serve as indicators of the civilization's progress. From this perspective, the preservation of the built fabric and architectural heritage needed to be framed within a broader discourse that addressed factors such as urban decay (understood as both a loss of functionality and the imposition of sterile insertions into unprepared contexts) [13], the interactive relationship between conservation and urban development, the necessity of defining urban transformation directions, the social relationship between center and periphery, and the challenges posed by urban services and exchange flows.

With Law 457 of August 5, 1978, particularly under Title IV, building and urban restoration were regulated for the first time by national legislation. The law delegated municipalities to identify areas subject to restoration. Within these areas, five types of interventions were defined under Article 31 [14].

The most advanced element of the law is its consideration of urban decay as a condition that affects not only historic city centers but the city as a whole. This broadened understanding of decay opened the door to interventions beyond historic centers, potentially fostering new relationships between different urban areas by addressing their interactions and altering urban development factors.

The scope of restoration activities was further expanded when applied not only to ancient urban fabric but also to more recent structures, thereby incorporating all built environments into conservation efforts, regardless of their intended use. This approach prioritizes the reuse of developed land over the consumption of new territory.

Law 493/1993, issued to accelerate investments and support employment, assigned urban renewal the role of facilitating a broad range of interventions aimed not only at restructuring limited urban areas (through projects encompassing building restoration, infrastructure integration, and environmental improvement) but also at the urban requalification of larger urban zones, addressing mobility (mass rapid transit, enhancement of local public transport) and parking.

The primary objective of this tool is the requalification of public residential assets built in the post-war period, which are generally in significant decay, along with the related urban services (both punctual and network-based), individual demand facilities, and urban furnishings.

In addition to the Urban Recovery Plan, the Urban Requalification Program (Ministerial Decree of December 21, 1994) was introduced, aimed primarily at addressing socio-economic, building, urban, and environmental degradation frequently found in peripheral or semi-central areas of large cities.

The Urban Requalification Program is similar in purpose to the Integrated Intervention Program introduced by Article 16 of Law 179/1992. It allows for territorial interventions that include planning efforts aligned with general regulatory plans, identifying implementing parties (both public and private), securing necessary financial resources, and establishing execution timelines.

The transition from the concept of recovery to that of redevelopment has recently undergone a further evolution, with the growing use of the concept of urban regeneration. On this issue, the national parliament is also working to define specific legislation [15], while the term has already been incorporated into various regional regulations. According to the unified bill project, "urban regeneration" refers to "a systematic set of urban and building transformations in urban areas and building complexes characterized by urban, building, environmental, or socio-economic degradation, which do not lead to land consumption, and follow criteria that employ methodologies and techniques related to environmental sustainability. This also includes actions for the reversible renaturalization of consumed land, the recovery of lost ecosystem services through de-impermeabilization, remediation, enhancement of ecological-environmental potential, and urban biodiversity".

3.2 The Circular Model and the Urban Trasformations

In the circular economic model, maintaining the value of products, materials, and resources is crucial. This must be achieved for as long as possible while minimizing waste production. The model is structured to extend the useful life of goods and eliminate or reduce waste.

In an urban context, the product's value translates into the city's image, the value of materials corresponds to the quality of the physical system (buildings, infrastructure, etc.), and resource value reflects the functionality of the city's systems.

These factors define the uniqueness of the urban system. They are not static but evolve, grow, and improve over time. At the same time, this uniqueness is also built on the level of space reuse and minimal waste generation.

It can be stated that regeneration processes are processes to which an innovative intervention model, such as the one linked to the urban circular economy, can be applied.

The introduction of the circular economy model applied to cities focuses on regeneration rather than consumption, the reuse of existing spaces, and resource optimization. Specifically, key concepts in the reuse of abandoned or not abandoned spaces include:

- Regeneration of buildings and spaces to adapt them to new functions.
- Utilization of disused areas for sustainable infrastructures such as new public transport systems, spaces for sustainable mobility, or urban green areas.

- Reducing resource consumption, both in terms of resources for constructing new buildings and resources for using them (land, energy, materials).

A strategic approach to circular urban planning is required for this transition. Several conditions are considered necessary for this approach to succeed:

- Context-specific planning that emphasizes the importance of developing urban plans tailored to each city or urban area, based on local characteristics. There is no one-size-fits-all solution. Regeneration and reuse needs vary depending on the context.
- Involvement of local communities, highlighting their role in the planning process. Citizen engagement is essential to ensure that interventions meet the population's real needs, creating spaces that promote social cohesion.
- Innovative technologies for sustainable planning, exploring both analytical methods (urban digital twins, real-time monitoring, etc.) and intervention strategies (smart cities, apps, etc.) that can optimize the management and planning of urban resources, making the city more efficient and less polluting.
- Attention to the conditions of the city green services, with the promotion of policies addressed to the growing of the green areas and to the promotion of the ecosystem services.

4 Case-Study

4.1 Naples and Its Central-Eastern Area

Naples is a highly interesting case for understanding the significance of a historic center in the evolutionary processes of a large urban area. The historical center has a clear impact on the city, especially when considering its ongoing economic relevance in the tertiary sector and, more recently, in tourism. For this specific work, the paper analyzes a specific portion of the city located in the central-eastern area (Fig. 1).

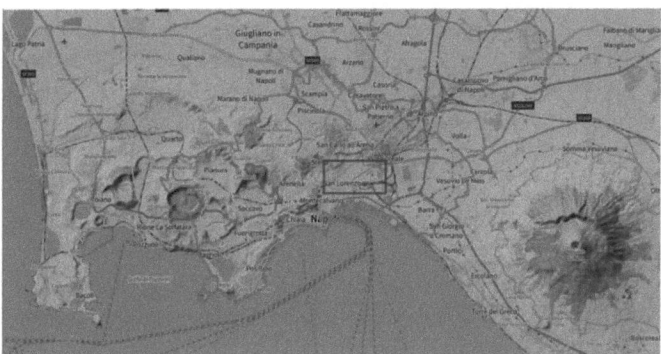

Fig. 1. Naples Municipality (orange) and surrounding territories. The case study area is indicated with a blue rectangle. Source: Author on Openstreetmap, 5/12/2024.

The wealth of architectural heritage makes it a unique case at both national and international levels. The interventions that have altered the face of this part of the city tell a singular story. Beginning with the cholera epidemic of 1884, the interventions reshaped the urban and social fabric without radically transforming it (Fig. 2).

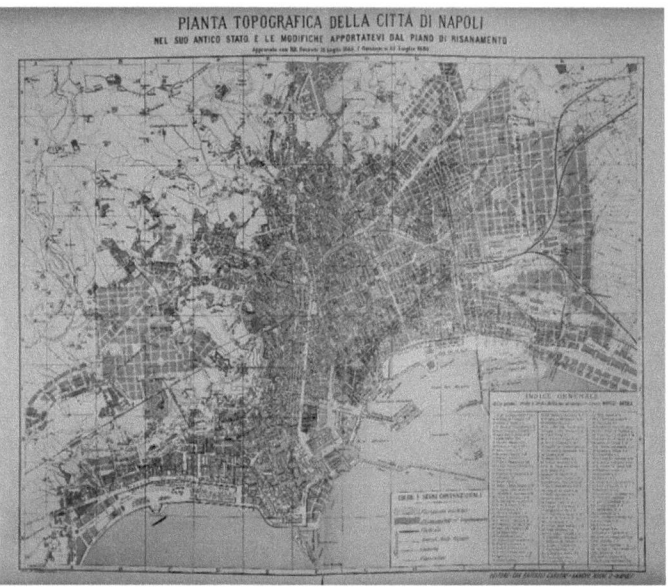

Fig. 2. The Risanamento in Naples. Intervention in the historic center and new urban expansions. Source: [16].

Other localized interventions affected its configuration after World War II, despite several attempts to alter its structure significantly. In recent decades, the introduction of rapid transit networks has changed the way people access and experience these urban spaces.

Today, Naples' historic center appears to have achieved a balance, thanks in part to urban planning tools that regulate its protection and transformation. This is not entirely true. On one hand, the set of rules governing its transformation is constantly tested by interventions of various scales, while on the other hand, significant phenomena – especially tourism – act as a slow but continuous process that tends to further weaken the resident social fabric.

The historic center of Naples is a complex system where an extensive network of monumental sites integrates seamlessly with the non-monumental urban fabric. The coexistence of these two building types has lasted for centuries in a symbiotic relationship. Buildings, churches, convents, and other structures are part of the residents' everyday experience. While they are not immune to occasional neglect, they remain recognized elements of the urban landscape.

The fabric of today's historic center began forming during the urban transformations of the medieval period. From that time on, the city underwent continuous changes that transformed the historic core without overwhelming it, at least until the early nineteenth century. At that point, the mechanisms of urban development changed, and the city began to expand based on much more radical real estate and industrial interests than in earlier periods [17, 18].

Until the early nineteenth century, the city's growth was characterized by a high degree of uniformity. From the nineteenth century onward, urban development accelerated and often profoundly affected both the built city and its surrounding areas. Interventions in the 19th and 20th centuries were carried out according to well-defined urban designs with new planning, typological, and distribution rules. Although different from earlier practices, these interventions succeeded in shaping new, strong elements that contributed to the city's image, following a model applied in many other European cities of the same period (Fig. 3).

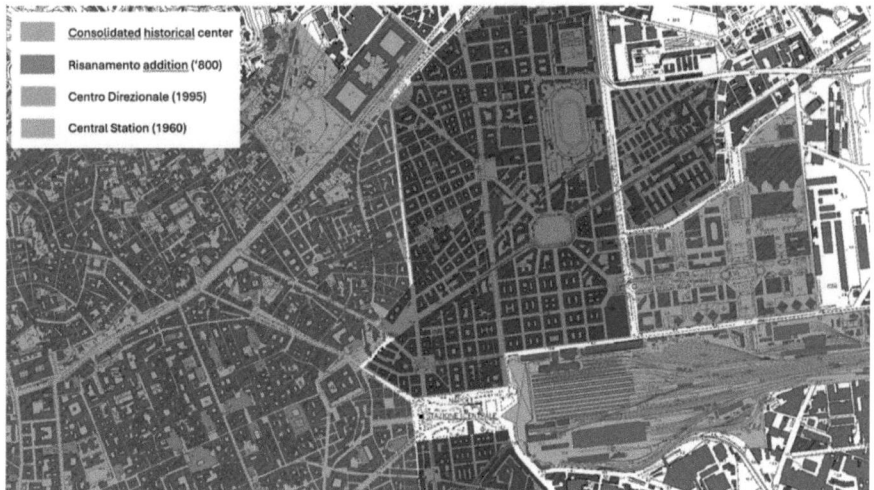

Fig. 3. Naples study area. From the historic center on the west to the Risanamento addiction and over. Source: Author.

The process that led to what is considered the city's historical development was formally recognized by the 2001 General Urban Plan (PRG) of Naples. This plan extended the boundaries of the historic center to include areas developed during the 19th and early 20th centuries, encompassing all urban fabrics preceding the post-World War II period. These areas are considered consolidated, representing a mature relationship between buildings and their surroundings, and are therefore subject to specific conservation regulations.

In the context of the historic center, the PRG of Naples adopts "typological classification" [19, 244] not only as a repository of knowledge to guide interventions but also as a "reading method" for urban fabrics. Its detailed approach allows for a direct transition from the General Master Plan to interventions on individual structures, without requiring additional operational planning tools.

The central-eastern area includes both parts of the ancient city and sections of the more recent city, which are still considered part of the historic center due to their pre-World War II origins.

4.2 Uses and Functions in the Study Area

In the field of research, significant interest is focused on the central-eastern area of the city. The analysed area is defined by key boundaries: to the North, the Albergo dei Poveri; to the South, the Central Station; to the East, the Centro Direzionale; and to the West, the city's historic center. It is a vast area characterized by the historic center to the west, the eastern part of the city to the east, and a central transitional area distinguished by its typical nineteenth-century urban expansions, which are regular and focused on maximizing real estate value.

While the historic center is a gem protected by UNESCO for its features and uniqueness, the eastern zone is the result of an entirely opposite urban development - lacking urban quality and any recognizable design. The central part, which separates these two areas, embodies both the merits and flaws of the western and eastern zones and does not seem to have its own distinct identity, other than being a generic urban expansion.

This area serves as a paradigmatic example of urban transformation processes within the city of Naples. The territory is partly stratified over time – primarily in the historic center – and partly unstratified, as it is of more recent formation. The latter includes largely regular urban grids shaped by the late nineteenth-century Risanamento [20–22], alongside spaces with functions that remain undefined. This means that ongoing transformations in this part of Naples could be highly significant and have a major impact on the city's overall image. The Centro Direzionale and the Central Station area are key components of this district (Figs. 4 and 5).

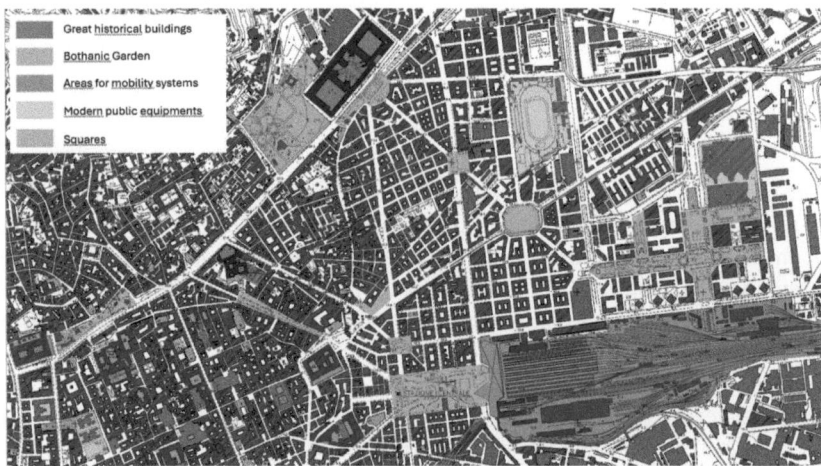

Fig. 4. Neaples study area. Main historical and modern poles. Source of the basic cartography [23].

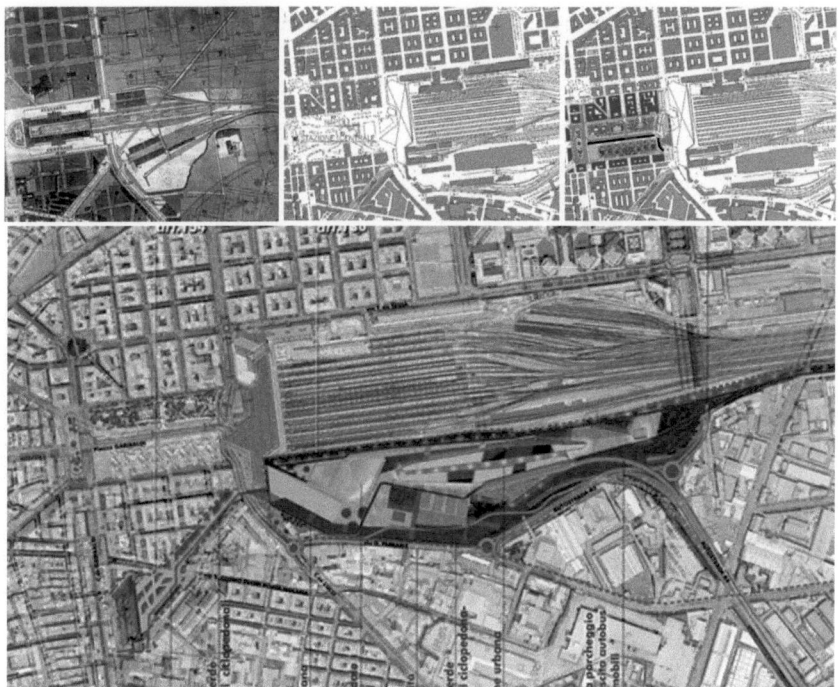

Fig. 5. Central Station area. Transformations from the second half of the Nineteenth century to today and over, with the Napoli Porta Est project.

The described area is characterized by prominent historical and architectural elements, strong consolidated urban stratifications, as well as more recently developed sections of varying quality, still undergoing consolidation.

As a result, urban transformations here can be highly impactful, steering towards objectives that not only enhance the quality of the existing urban fabric but also improve the city's resilience to climate change. This perspective aligns with the vision of a self-regenerating city, aimed at strengthening its adaptability and overall capacity for resistance.

The redevelopment of Piazza Garibaldi, completed in 2015, was designed by architect Dominique Perrault as part of the opening of the Garibaldi station of the Naples Metro Line 1. The intervention begins with the construction of the new underground station and extends to the surface, where the square was redesigned to include a 360 x 165-meter open space, covered by a system of steel tree-like structures. The project started from the renewal of critical infrastructure and expanded to the urban realm in an area that experiences a traffic flow of approximately 50 million people per year. The surrounding urban fabric is also undergoing significant regeneration programs.

In 2023, a Program Agreement was signed between the Campania Region, the Municipality of Naples, FS Sistemi Urbani, RFI, and EAV for the "Development of the Naples Garibaldi-Porta Est Complex Intermodal Node and Urban Regeneration of Adjacent Railway Areas". Pursuant to this agreement, the Campania Region and FS Sistemi Urbani launched an international design competition for the creation of the overall masterplan of the intervention, named "Napoli Porta Est" (Fig. 6).

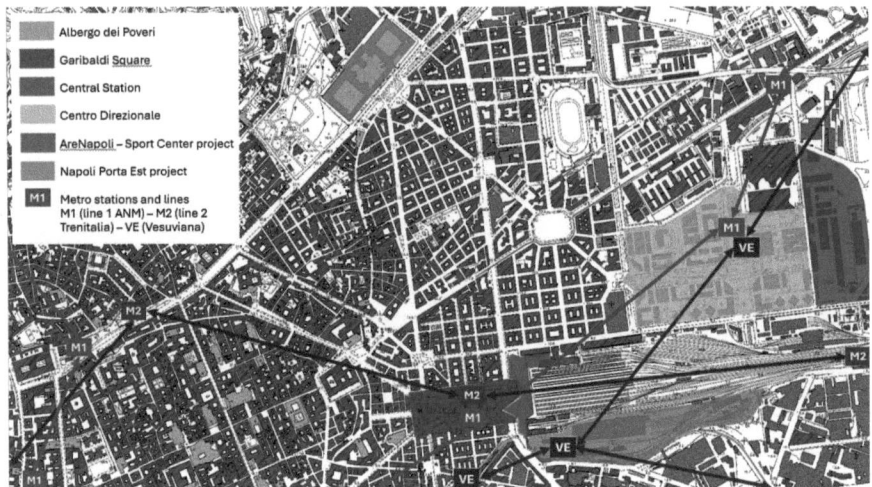

Fig. 6. Neaples study area. Mobility poles (metro and railways) and redevelopment areas.

The urban implementation plan derived from the project must be submitted for review and approval by the Municipality of Naples. The design competition, awarded to Zaha Hadid Architects in February 2025, covers an area exceeding 200,000 square meters. It focuses on the urban regeneration of the former FS freight yard at Centrale/Garibaldi station, with the integration of new mixed-use public-private functions and the new headquarters of the Campania Region; the reconnection of the redevelopment area with the surrounding urban fabric; the development of a pedestrian and cycling network equipped with green spaces and urban facilities; a new configuration of road infrastructure to improve urban and extra-urban traffic flows related to the new Garibaldi-Porta Est intermodal hub; the design of high-energy-efficiency solutions and enhancement of ecological and environmental quality.

A third strategic intervention concerns the redevelopment of the Centro Direzionale, designed by Japanese architect Kenzō Tange and completed in 1995. The area currently suffers from inadequate maintenance and outdated infrastructure, particularly the underground parking facilities beneath the central platform. Over the years, the area has also experienced a decline in activity within the towers, despite the introduction of new services and businesses. The planned opening of the Line 1 metro station in early 2025 is expected to act as a catalyst for the area's overall regeneration, improving connectivity with the rest of the city and initiating a comprehensive upgrading process for the entire complex.

A fourth major intervention involves the former wholesale fruit and vegetable market area, located east of the Centro Direzionale between Poggioreale and Gianturco. This area is currently subject to a project financing procedure for the development of Are-Napoli, a large multifunctional venue with a capacity of over 15,000 seats for concerts and 13,000 for sporting events.

The projected opening is scheduled for 2026, the year in which Naples will serve as the Sport European Capital. This new facility aims to fill a critical gap in the city's existing infrastructure for large-scale events. AreNapoli is part of a broader urban regeneration strategy for the eastern areas, including Naples' former industrial zone and the adjacent Piazza Garibaldi area. Its strategic location near the future metro station will ensure high accessibility and is expected to contribute significantly to the revitalization of the eastern sector of the city.

The socio-economic and environmental data of the city of Naples are generally negative. The city is usually ranked in the lower positions of national rankings, although it must be said that these rankings are typically based on provincial or metropolitan area data. This situation represents a vulnerability for the city, as the broader metropolitan area reduces the overall quality of the territory [24, 25]. In the 2024 Quality of Life ranking by Il Sole 24 Ore [26], the city is positioned 106th, or second-to-last. Its position varies across different categories: it ranks last for wealth and consumption, 65th for demographics and society, 101st for environment and services, and 68th for culture and leisure.

These data, along with others recently published (for example, Legambiente places Naples 103rd in the Ecosistema Urbano ranking [27], show the persistence of a state of crisis in the city despite the efforts made and ongoing to improve its overall quality.

5 Elements of Discussion

The considerations introduced in the previous sections have demonstrated the existence of a close relationship between processes of urban regeneration and redevelopment and theories connected to the principles of the circular economy. As shown in other studies [28–30], the analyses conducted have highlighted the possible interrelations between these two sectors, because both increasingly aim toward an organization of planning and operational actions that is strongly influenced by principles of sustainability and resource consumption reduction.

A relevant point of interest lies in the fact that the process of transition towards the use of an urban circular model has specific social and economic impacts. Circular urban regeneration processes create new economic opportunities (new forms of entrepreneurship and jobs in sectors such as building retrofitting, sustainable architecture, and green mobility services), improve social inclusion, and enhance quality of life through positive social impacts and the creation of new public, accessible, and green spaces.

However, critical elements persist and cannot be ignored. Gentrification phenomena often accompany regeneration processes, resulting in social simplification and the marginalization of low-income and low-education groups. Regeneration means investment and transformation of areas, which leads to rising housing, service, and goods costs, ultimately forcing low-income residents out. These aspects are by no means secondary and must be carefully considered when planning and transforming the city into a highly sustainable system. Many of the criticisms directed at these processes, especially from groups and political forces less sensitive to sustainability issues, focus on the increase in costs that these processes entail and the fact that these cost increases are economically unsustainable for large segments of the population.

There is also the difficulty of changing habits and lifestyles, which affects the speed at which more innovative and sustainable approaches can take root within social systems. One of the main criticisms of European policies on environmental sustainability is that they are based primarily on technocratic processes with predefined deadlines established in a top-down manner, with little consideration for external constraints. These constraints, mainly of an economic and social acceptability nature, can reduce or even block the full implementation of this process.

This has an additional political consequence: the growing rejection of such environmental policies by increasingly large segments of the population, who perceive them as elitist rather than the result of a careful analysis of the population's primary needs. Although these paths are taken based on evidence that currently makes them seem like an unavoidable choice, this perception is not shared by broad sections of the population.

Thus, it can be said that the process can succeed – though certainly not with a 100% probability – if there are two conditions:

– It must originate from the bottom up and be continuously supported over time by those who will be the primary agents of change, namely the citizens.
– It must be financed with public resources, with the goal of maximizing the benefits for the entire population, given that, as mentioned earlier, these processes significantly impact the economy of individuals and families.

Without these conditions, the process seems unlikely to succeed, especially in a situation where the economy is moving toward goals in which sustainability is becoming an increasingly marginal factor.

Despite this, the ongoing process still appears to be moving toward the development of good practices that can be applied, adapted, and reused in other contexts. The process has a clear, practical, and experimental value in the urban sphere and is heading in what seems to be an unavoidable direction—one that must be pursued regardless of the pressures stemming from climate change and meteorological crises.

It is a process that rightfully becomes part of the broader urban evolution processes that, over the centuries, have introduced elements of innovation in how cities are built and how their services and activities function.

In this context, several Italian and international case studies are particularly noteworthy for having started to apply circular economy models to urban planning and management tools. Among them, the following examples can be highlighted: Copenhagen, with its carbon neutrality strategy and extensive use of regenerated green spaces, Amsterdam, a pioneer in adopting a circular economy model in urban management, including the redevelopment of port areas, and Milan, with the focus on the redevelopment of former industrial areas and the creation of new public spaces, such as the Porta Nuova and CityLife projects.

6 Conclusions

The aim of this paper was to explore the possible applications of the circular economy concept to urban regeneration and redevelopment initiatives. To this end, the paper analyzed general principles, which were then applied to a case study of an area in the city of Naples.

The study highlighted how the concept of circularity, even if not explicitly stated, was already present within planning instruments, particularly in the implementation tools developed following the enactment of Law 1150 of 1942, the main national urban planning law. This becomes particularly evident in subsequent phases, when the preservation of historical urban structures became a central theme in urban planning debates, leading to the enactment of regulations on urban renewal in 1978. Over time, additional regulations followed, expanding the scope of urban recovery and redevelopment measures. These evolved into a system of urban planning tools aimed at guiding cities towards more equitable, modern, and functional conditions.

The evolution towards urban regeneration and redevelopment tools highlights a dual perspective on the relationship between urban interventions and the application of the circular economy concept.

On one hand, circularity can be considered a fundamental principle underlying recovery, redevelopment, and urban regeneration efforts, even though it was not explicitly recognized as such at the time. This implies that early recovery actions can be seen as precursors to the concept of circularity, despite their unawareness of this pioneering role.

On the other hand, the circular economy concept can be fully applied only to the more recent evolutions of urban regeneration, where interventions focus on existing spaces while incorporating sustainability and urban resilience considerations. This is achieved through innovative methodologies and technologies that minimize resource waste and create more sustainable urban spaces capable of addressing climate change challenges and urban polarization.

The case study analysis supports these considerations. The historical part of Naples underwent radical transformations during the 19th and early 20th centuries, with little regard for preservation. It was only from the 1980s onwards, with the adoption of the new city master plan, that interventions in the historic center shifted towards conservation and enhancement of existing structures.

Conversely, transformations in non-historical areas were far more radical, often with little consideration for their spatial context. This may explain why Naples' eastern zone remains an unsettled area undergoing significant transformations.

One can only hope that future actions will adopt the best national and international practices and apply them to Naples, successfully integrating planning and transformation with sustainability and circularity in the use of space and resources.

Overall, the paper confirms the urgent need for a paradigm shift – moving away from the classical, post-expansionist model towards a more sustainable approach that enhances and regenerates existing urban areas, creating cities that are more resilient, inclusive, and environmentally balanced. In this process, the role of innovative public policies is crucial in promoting reuse and urban regeneration, with the ultimate goal of fostering a sustainable and circular development model.

As stated in paragraph 1, the paper represents a first step in an ongoing research project. Further development of the research will include a deeper application of methodological steps 1 to 4, as well as the addition of two further components not yet developed. The first is the evaluation criteria and framework development, to create a framework for assessing the compatibility of circular economy principles with urban regeneration strategies. This may involve using matrices or evaluative frameworks based on criteria such as material reuse, land optimization, heritage preservation, socio-economic inclusion, and climate adaptation. The second is the building of recommendations, to integrate findings and propose a model or set of guidelines for circular urban planning. This will involve comparing historical and current practices, identifying best practices, and offering policy recommendations for incorporating circular economy principles into future urban regeneration efforts.

References

1. European Parliament: Circular Economy: Definition, Importance and Benefits (2023). https://www.europarl.europa.eu/topics/en/article/20151201STO05603/circular-economy-definition-importance-and-benefits#:~:text=What%20is%20the%20circular%20economy,products%20as%20long%20as%20possible. Accessed 10 Jan 2025
2. Joensuu, T., Edelman, H., Saari, A.: Circular economy practices in the built environment. J. Clean. Prod. **276**, 124215 (2020)
3. Corvellec, H., Stowell, H.F., Johansson, N.: Critiques of the circular economy. J. Ind. Ecol. **26**(2), 421–432 (2021)
4. Kirchherr, J., Reike, D., Hekkert, M.: Conceptualizing the circular economy: an analysis of 114 definitions. Resour. Conserv. Recycl. **127**, 221–232 (2017)
5. Geissdoerfer, M., Savaget, P., Bocken, N.M.P., Hultink, E.J.: The Circular Economy—a new sustainability paradigm? J. Clean. Prod. **143**, 757–768 (2017)
6. Korhonen, J., Honkasalo, A., Seppälä, J.: Circular economy: the concept and its limitations. Ecol. Econ. **143**, 37–46 (2018)
7. Morseletto, P.: Targets for a circular economy. Resour. Conserv. Recycl. **153**, 104553 (2020)
8. Petit-Boix, A., Leipold, S.: Circular economy in cities: reviewing how environmental research aligns with local practices. J. Clean. Prod. **195**, 1270–1281 (2018)
9. Bolger, K., Doyon, A.: Circular cities: exploring local government strategies to facilitate a circular economy. Eur. Plan. Stud. **27**(11), 2184–2205 (2019)
10. Lakatos, E.S., Yong, G., Szilagyi, A., Clinci, D.S., Georgescu, L., Iticescu, C., Cioca, L.-I.: Conceptualizing core aspects on circular economy in cities. Sustainability. **13**(14), 7549 (2021)
11. Ellen MacArthur Foundation: Cities in the Circular Economy: An Initial Exploration (2017). https://www.ellenmacarthurfoundation.org/cities-in-the-circular-economy-an-initial-exploration. Accessed 7 May 2025
12. Council of Europe: Convention for the Protection of the Architectural Heritage of Europe (1985). https://rm.coe.int/168007a087. Accessed 7 May 2025
13. Cervellati, P.L., Scannavini, R. (eds.): Bologna, politica e metodologia del restauro. Il Mulino, Bologna (1973)
14. Bonaccorsi, P.: Il recupero del patrimonio edilizio esistente. Edizioni delle Autonomie, Roma (1982)
15. Di Costanzo, C.: I disegni di legge sulla rigenerazione urbana (2024). https://www.osservatoriosullefonti.it/rubriche/fonti-statali/4617-osf-2-2024-stato1. Accessed 10 Jan 2025

16. D'Ambra, R.: Napoli antica illustrata. Raffaele Cardone, Napoli (1889)
17. De Seta, C.: Napoli. Laterza, Bari-Roma (1999)
18. Ghirelli, A.: Storia di Napoli. Einaudi, Torino (2006)
19. Comune di Napoli: Piano Regolatore Generale. Relazione (2021) https://www.comune.napoli.it/flex/cm/pages/ServeBLOB.php/L/IT/IDPagina/1025. Accessed 07 May 2025
20. Mazzeo, G.: Naples. Cities. **26**(6), 363–376 (2009)
21. Manzo, E.: Il "Risanamento" di Napoli. Dal progetto urbano alla scala architettonica. Atti Rass. Tecn. **1**, 113–122 (2018)
22. Amorosi, V.: Sventrare Napoli. Il caso del "risanamento" tra legislazione e narrazione. In: X Convegno Nazionale della ISLL – Italian Society for Law and Literature. Università degli studi di Napoli Federico II (2023)
23. Regione Campania: Cartografia tecnica regionale, Foglio 447123, Napoli Stazione Centrale. https://sit2.regione.campania.it/content/cartografia. Accessed 02 Feb 2025
24. Mazzeo, G., Papa, R.: Characteristics of sprawl in the Naples Metropolitan Area. Indications for Controlling and Monitoring Urban Transformations. In: Murgante, B., Misra, S., Rocha, A.M.A.C., Torre, C., Rocha, J.G., Falcão, M.I., Taniar, D., Apduhan, B.O., Gervasi, O. (eds.) Computational Science and Its Applications - ICCSA 2014. 14th International Conference. Guimarães, June 30–July 3, 2014. Proceedings, Part II. Lecture Notes in Computer Science, vol. 8580, pp. 520–531. Springer International Publishing, Cham (2014)
25. Mazzeo, G., Russo, L.: Aspects of land take in the metropolitan area of Naples. TEMA J. Land Use Mobil. Environ. **9**(1), 89–107 (2016)
26. Sole 24 Ore: Qualità della vita 2024 (2024). https://lab24.ilsole24ore.com/qualita-della-vita/napoli. Accessed 08 Feb 2025
27. Laurenti, M., Trentin, M.: Ecosistema urbano 2024. Rapporto sulle performance ambientali delle città, Legambiente, Roma (2024) https://www.legambiente.it/wp-content/uploads/2021/11/Ecosistema-Urbano_libro2024.pdf. Accessed 13 Feb 2025
28. Conejos, S., Yung, E.H.K., Chan, E.H.W.: Evaluation of urban sustainability and adaptive reuse of built heritage areas: a case study on conservation in Hong Kong's CBD. J. Des. Res. **12**(4), 260–279 (2014)
29. Robiglio, M.: The adaptive reuse toolkit. How cities can turn their industrial legacy into infrastructure for innovation and growth. In: Urban and Regional Policy Paper 38, pp. 5–38 (2016)
30. Gaballo, M., Mecca, B., Abastante, F.: Adaptive reuse and sustainability protocols in Italy: relationship with circular economy. Sustainability. **13**(14), 8077 (2021)

Adaptive Reuse of Religious Cultural Heritage: The Case Study of the Church "Santissimo Nome di Gesù" in Turin (Italy)

Cavana Giulio[1](✉) [ID], Angrisano Mariarosaria[2] [ID], Gravagnuolo Antonia[2] [ID], Luigi Fusco Girard[3,4] [ID], and Bottero Marta[1] [ID]

[1] Interuniversity Department of Regional and Urban Studies and Planning (DIST), Politecnico di Torino, 39, Viale Mattioli, 10125 Turin, TO, Italy
giulio.cavana@polito.it
[2] Institute of Heritage Science, National Research Council (CNR-ISPC), 80143 Naples, Italy
[3] Department of Engineering, Pegaso Telematic University, 80143 Naples, Italy
[4] University of Naples Federico II, 80143 Naples, Italy

Abstract. Religious cultural heritage represents a considerable part of Europe"s overall cultural heritage. In fact, Europe is home to over 500.000 religious structures, including churches, chapels, synagogues, mosques, cathedrals, monasteries and convents. Many religious buildings are in a state of abandonment due to the reduction of religious practices, the processes of secularization and demographic ageing. Circular Adaptive reuse of religious cultural heritage can be a feasible approach to give new life to this heritage through new functional uses that respond to the contemporary needs of the city and its inhabitants. The aim of this work is to present the preliminary results of a research project that targets the identification of evaluation processes and methods to study the possible adaptive reuse strategies for abandoned religious built heritage. The contribution presents the first results of a participatory process to co-construct the problem situation of the potential reuse identify and analyze possible adaptive reuse alternatives of the Church of Santissimo Nome di Gesù in Turin (Italy), with the objective of transforming this abandoned religious building into a resource that can contribute to the improvement of the well-being of the local community.

In particular, the paper aims to examine how the historical, architectural and cultural characteristics of the church can be preserved, while identifying new functional uses that meet the contemporary needs of the city and its inhabitants.

Keywords: Reuse of cultural heritage · circular economy · co-programming · co-participation · SWOT analysis

1 Introduction

Religious cultural heritage represents a considerable part of Europe"s overall cultural heritage, encompassing both tangible and intangible aspects. In fact, Europe is home to over 500.000 religious" structures, including churches, chapels, synagogues, mosques, cathedrals, monasteries and convents [1].

However, with the processes of secularization, a part of this heritage is characterized by non-use, and thus degradation due to lack of maintenance.

Following the processes of demographic decrease and ageing, the increasing urbanization and consequential depopulation of religious centers, as well as the decline of traditional religious practice, there is a growing need to identify new uses for buildings once used for worship. These uses, non-liturgical or religious, should be congruent with the "intrinsic value" of the religious heritage, its significance and social value for communities [2–7].

Heritage of religious interest in secularized Western countries has become an economically onerous commitment in terms of property maintenance and management. This is also due to the extinction of numerous church entities and the transformation of religious practices [8].

ICOMOS already in 2005, in its General Assembly, had promoted a resolution on the reuse of this extraordinary heritage, recognizing the significance of the value of the "spirit of places" [2].

A question that frequently arises is: what is the future of this religious heritage, especially when it is abandoned? How can cultural, historical and artistic values be safeguarded? What functional reuse can respect their original "sense" or meaning, i.e. that "inspiration" that gave physical form and generated these particular spaces?

The most frequently proposed functions for the reuse of religious heritage assets are related to tourism. The so-called "economy of experience" [9] has played a role here. However, tourism often does not offer a regenerative perspective: it tends to be "consumerist" of cultural heritage and, in some cases, even destructive of values [2, 10]. Furthermore, tourism may not always be a solution in marginal areas, smaller and peripheral centers.

On the other hand, the museum destination, although it may have cultural value, very often does not guarantee adequate profitability to at least cover the maintenance costs. Consequently, after a few years, the "museum church" may remain "empty" of life.

On the other side, alternative uses that have enabled the regeneration of religious cultural heritage have often been linked to productive functions [11]. For example, the spaces of Benedictine and Cistercian monasteries, which were also economic engines in their territory, have been reused as laboratories for the production of pharmaceutical, food and cosmetic products, using natural resources from neighboring territories and the traditional, still innovative knowledge of the monastic orders.

Although the abandonment of religious heritage is pervasive throughout Europe, a number of good practices of reuse and regeneration also emerge from several previous studies [12–15].

In this perspective, in a previous study by the authors [16], an analysis of specific cases of reuse of religious heritage (Catacombs of San Gennaro in Naples, Italy; Le Scalze in Naples, Italy; the Carmen Convent in Spain and the Domenikanenkerk in the Netherlands) was conducted, which highlighted the importance of co-design and co-planning processes for the choice of new functions for religious buildings through the involvement of the local community. Community involvement ensured that projects were adapted to local needs and values, promoting a strong sense of ownership and commitment. Furthermore, the new uses attributed to these churches have triggered both the creation of new jobs and an increase in tourist visits and, above all, the involvement of the third sector [17].

Co-designing and co-programming processes are emerging as necessary actions to ensure the sustainable reuse of abandoned religious heritage, because the participation of the local community and the involvement of stakeholders enhances the likelihood that projects meet the needs of the local population, strengthening the link with the territory [18]. Fostering participation, is also beneficial for a more informed evaluation of the technical, procedural, economic, and managerial obstacles that could be faced in each problem situation [19]. Furthermore, a proper participatory approach to the Cultural Heritage discourse has been also stressed as a way to mitigate the risk of top-down conservationist approach [20]. Indeed, also the Faro Convention stressed the need for the participation of other organizations other than only public institution [21] in a spirit of co-responsibility based on cooperation and collaboration of the different entities involved in the management and preservation of the common good [22]. This aspect is further substantiated by a more practical argument related to the scarcity of resources of the Public Administration which is negatively affected by the state of unused or sub-used assets constituting a cost for them. In this sense, public–private partnership, and the integration of the Third Sector in particular, could represent an innovative way to compensate inability (or lack of interest) of the central authority to provide specific services in the field of Cultural Heritage management while pursuing civic, solidarity, and social utility purposes [20, 23].

The approach of reusing abandoned and underused cultural assets is part of a "circular city" approach, through the recovery of buildings and urban areas that have exhausted their original function [24, 25]. The circular economy can be applied at the urban and the single building level, increasing the sustainability of interventions both environmentally and in terms of long-term management and sharing with the community. Thus, a "circular" approach to the adaptive reuse of religious cultural heritage can be feasible to give new life to this heritage through new functional uses that respond to the contemporary needs of the city and its inhabitants.

This article presents the first PRIN-TReE research project results (Grant PRIN 2022 No. 2022TN5M7F) aiming at identifying evaluation methods and processes that can help decision makers in defining adaptive reuse strategies of the cultural built heritage. The aim of this first part of the research project is to identify and analyze possible adaptive reuse strategies for abandoned religious heritage, with specific reference to the case study of the Church of Santissimo Nome di Gesù in Moncalieri, in the metropolitan area of Turin (Italy), with the objective of transforming this abandoned religious building into a resource that can contribute to the improvement of the well-being of the local community. The lessons learnt from the real case application will be used to identify possible drawbacks to current practices and to study a generalized methodology to support the decision makers in adaptive reuse projects. Within this larger objective, the aim of this paper is to apply a problem structuring method (SWOT analysis) as a preliminary tool to support the decision-maker in identifying a possible space of solution for the reuse of the asset grounded on the specificity of the territory in which it is inserted. In particular, this work describes the preliminary results of the participatory workshop conducted with experts in the fields of urban regeneration, restoration, urban design, economics, as well as with informed third sector entities operating on the territory to co-analyze the problem situation of the reuse of the abandoned case study, and set the direction for further steps towards the identification of adaptive reuse strategies. The workshop aimed at examining how the historical, architectural and cultural characteristics of the church can be preserved while identifying the new functional uses that meet the contemporary needs of the city and its inhabitants. The paper is structured as follows: in Sect. 2 the case study is presented; Sect. 3 presents the methodology; Sect. 4 presents the results and Sect. 5 discusses them; finally, in Sect. 6 conclusions are drawn.

2 Case Study and Problem Situation

The case study analyzed is the Chiesa del Santissimo Nome di Gesù (Church of the Holy Name of Jesus). The church is located in the town of Moncalieri (see Fig. 1), part of the Metropolitan City of Turin (Italy). In the northern part, the town is characterized by a hilly terrain, while in the South-Eastern part several water bodies are present.

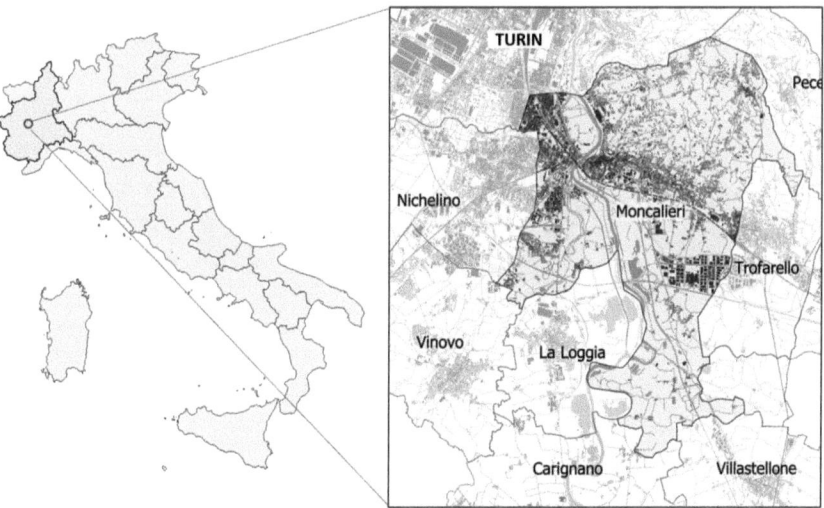

Fig. 1. Location of Moncalieri and the Chiesa del Santissimo Nome di Gesù (source: authors" elaboration based on BDTRE [26])

According to the last national census, the city hosts 56,193 inhabitants, with a relatively high incidence of elderly population as shown in Fig. 2. Moreover, the population shows a fairly balance between males (49%) and female (51%), and a relatively small ratio (9%) of inhabitants with non-Italian citizenship over Italian citizens [27].

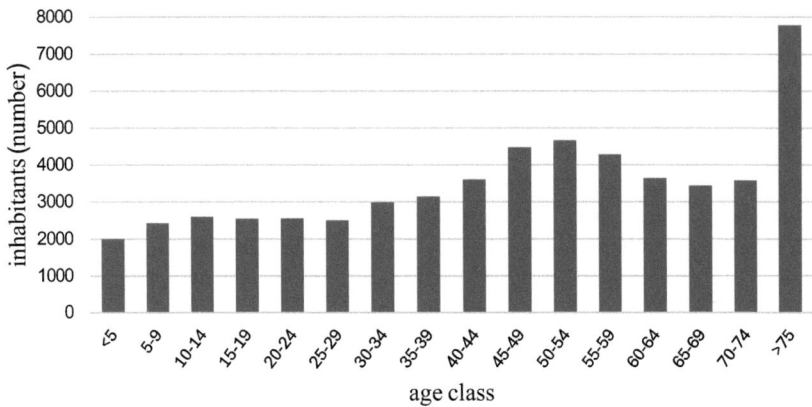

Fig. 2. Population by age classes (source: authors" elaboration on census data)

The tendency of the demographic distribution toward the elderly part of the population is confirmed in the historical city center, geographically defined by the urban planning tools of the town of Moncalieri. For instance, the city center shows a quite high level in three descriptive indexes of the population as shown in Fig. 3.

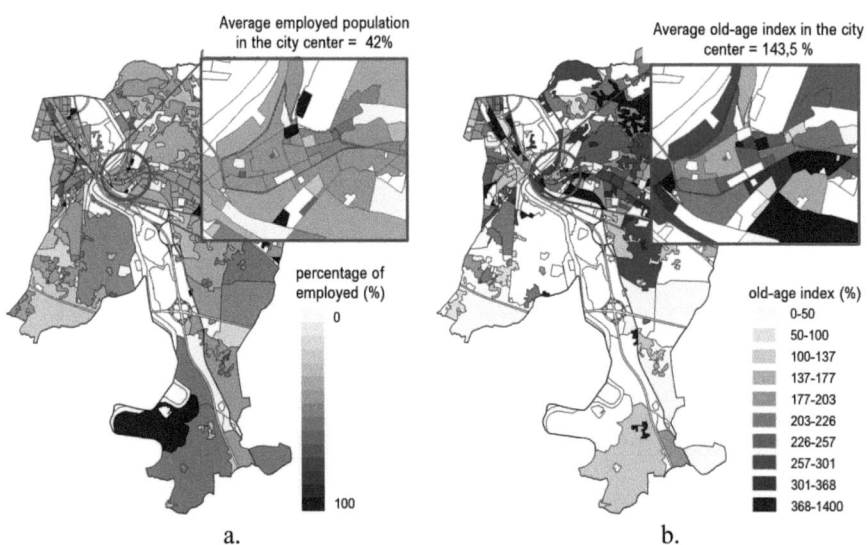

Fig. 3. Socio-economic indices in the census tracks of Moncalieri and averaged in the city center (source: authors" elaboration of census data [27])

In particular, the old-age index (Fig. 3b). shows the presence of roughly 1.5 (143.5%) inhabitants over the age of 65 for each inhabitant under the age of 14, while the old-age dependency index (Fig. 3c.) and the structural dependency index (Fig. 3d.) shows a ratio of 1 inhabitant over the productive age (65 years) every 3 inhabitants (35.6%), and 2 non-active inhabitants every 3 inhabitants in the working-age class of population (60.4%). Finally, with reference to the city center, it is possible to notice that almost half of the population living in the city center (42%) is employed (Fig. 3a).

Zooming-in at the scale of the case study, the Chiesa del Santissimo Nome di Gesù has been built in 1710 on the remains of the oratory of the Franciscan complex and the Church of the Holy Spirit commissioned by the Confraternity of the Holy Name of Jesus by an unknown architect attributed to the Juvarrian school [28, 29]. In 1786 the square bell tower was built over the pre-existing one belonging to the old Oratory. The use of the church is documented until 1950 when the Confraternity was dissolved and after the management passed under the parish of "Santa Maria della Scala and Sant"Egidio", officiating in the church stopped and shortly afterwards the church was permanently closed. In more recent times, with the help of the voluntary association "La Vitruviana", efforts have been made to revitalize the church, opening it for exhibitions and concerts. Currently, although restoration work and initiatives have been carried out over the years to protect the property, the church is in a serious state of neglect and general disinterest.

In Fig. 4 the floorplan of the Chiesa del Santissimo Nome di Gesù is presented.

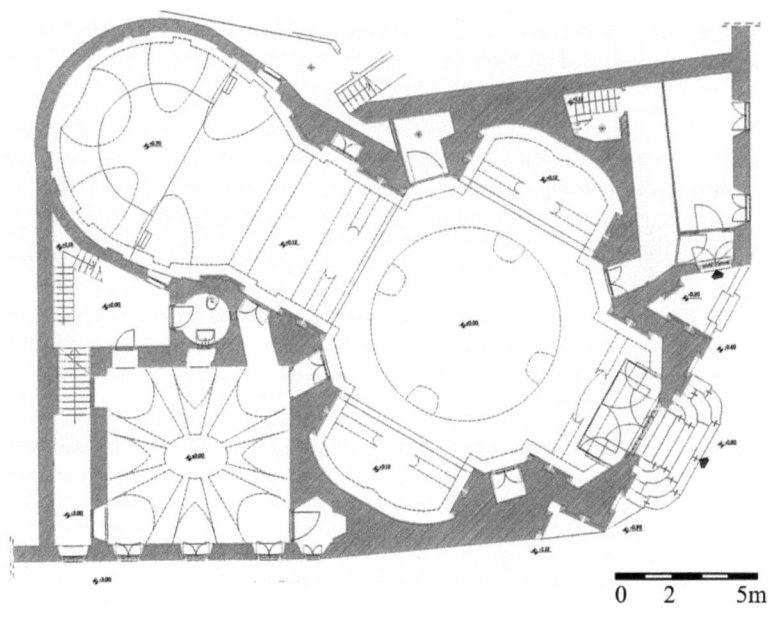

Fig. 4. Floorplan of the Chiesa del Santissimo Nome di Gesù (source: [29])

The building is characterized by a main hall with annexed spaces distributed over two floors with a total Net Floor Area of 486 m^2 (341 m^2 on the First floor, and 145 m^2 on the Second floor, excluding the bell tower). The internal spaces are characterized by a rich fresco decoration by the XVIII century painter Milocco, as well as by painters from the school of Beaumont and Dauphin [29].

In recent years, the Diocese of the metropolitan city of Turin, owner of the abandoned Church, has expressed the willingness to re-open the building with a renewed functionalization that could benefit the local community, in line with the principles expressed by the PRIN-TReE project.

3 Method

In line with the objectives of the PRIN-TReE project, the final goal of the study concerning the Chiesa del Santissimo Nome di Gesù is to identify the possible adaptive reuse strategies that could transform the abandoned church into a vital asset able to improve the wellbeing of the community. No previous alternatives are provided among which to select the most satisfactory one, the problem owner (the Diocese of the Metropolitan city of Turin) being uncertain about its own goal, as well as feasibility aspects related to potential uses of the asset. Moreover, the property owner is interested in meeting the desires of the population and provide a potentially beneficial solution for the local community, not neglecting the historical, cultural, and social values that the building itself possess in relation to the same local community. Such an urban transformation problem could be seen as an un-structured or ill-structured problem for its intrinsic characteristics, such as the presence of multiple actors and perspectives, the existence of conflicting interests, as well as uncertainties [30]. Thus, prior to any analysis of possible solutions, it was decided to explore different techniques available to identify the main evaluation problem, such as problem structuring methods. Problem structuring methods (PSMs) refer to a family of methods intended to help the analyst (and the actors involved) to shape and construct the problem situation in which a decision has to be carried out, without the attempt to "solve" it [30]. PSMs emerged from a perceived failure of traditional optimization methods in addressing complex and ill-structured problems [31], helping the analyst engage in a conversation with the "owners" of the problem, in the attempt to both synthetize the information around the problem itself, and to help to build a more informed view of the problem from different point of views [32].

Among these tools, SWOT analysis was considered as the most convenient tool to first structure the knowledge base around the problem situation, by also engaging different experts and stakeholders to widen the perspective of the analyst as well as the decision-maker. Particular merit of this tool is the possibility to involve stakeholders, by using simple methods to improve communication and learning, as well as establishing a common language to support the exchange of information [33–37].

3.1 SWOT Analysis

SWOT analysis is a qualitative PSM first used to support the development of organizational strategies [32], with several merits for the identification and structuring of the problem situation also in urban and territorial regeneration projects [38].

In Urban regeneration decision making contexts, SWOT analysis allows to rationalize the set of information known regarding a specific context by structuring a 2x2 matrix in which are clustered the aspects of Strengths (S), Weaknesses (W), Opportunities (O), and Threats (T) of the territory.

Strengths and Weaknesses are internal factors intrinsic to the context of the analysis and are those directly addressed by the potentially developed plan or project to be evaluated, while Opportunities and Threats are defined as external factor that might not occur but have to be controlled due to their potential negative or positive occurrence. The success of a development project in a certain context depends on its capacity to build on the strengths of a context enhanced by the opportunities that might occur, while removing and controlling for weakness and threats [39].

Several are the merits of SWOT in problem structuring. First, the tool is easy to use and widely known, thus often preferred to other PSMs which may be perceived as theoretically and technically demanding [40]. This easiness of use is specifically helpful in the engagement of stakeholders [33–37]. Moreover, SWOT analysis ensures that all relevant aspects are considered both from an internal and external viewpoint. Finally, the use of SWOT analysis has been seen as a suitable tool to support the development of new strategies or alternatives [32], especially in the presence of different point of views and potentially conflicting interests [41, 42].

Often used in strategical evaluation, SWOT provides an effective framework to be further expanded with other evaluation methodologies in strategic decision-making [35] and is a valid tool to accompany the lifecycle of projects, from problem identification, to modelling and problem solving [43].

3.2 Participatory Workshop

The SWOT methodology has been applied during a one-day workshop in which different stakeholders have been asked to gather to construct a shared knowledge framework around the problem situation of the identification of adaptive reuse strategies for the abandoned Church of the Santissimo Nome del Gesù in Moncalieri. The stakeholders that joined the workshop were both expert and non-experts. As reported in Fig. 5, the panel was composed by 12 experts: one representative of an NGO operating in the territory and a representative for the Diocese of Turin metropolitan area as the third sector representatives, two heritage restoration experts, one expert in urban planning, two experts in urban regeneration decision making aiding, two experts in urban economics, two experts in history of architecture, and one expert in mathematics models for urban regeneration applications, together with the research group of the TREE project.

The workshop has been structured in two main parts. In the first introductory part the participants have been familiarized with the PRIN-TReE research project aims and finalities and theoretical background. Moreover, the results of the precedent Horizon project CLIC [44] and the relative case studies of best practices in the context of adaptive reuse of cultural heritage have been presented. Finally, the case study of the Chiesa del Santissimo Nome di Gesù in Moncalieri and the characteristics of its urban context have been introduced. In the second part, the SWOT methodology has been presented and performed by the participant in a participative manner. Finally, the panel of experts and third sector representatives visited the asset together with the owner and the representative of the local parish.

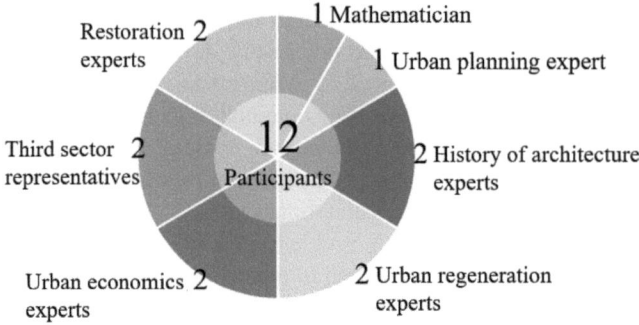

Fig. 5. Number of participants and their field of expertise

In the application of the SWOT methodology the participants were asked to fill-in the matrix with the possibility of discussing the different factors to be introduced and their belonging to one or the other quadrant (S, W, O, or T). The participants worked together in a single group, this allowed them to self-define a common vision of the different elements composing the SWOT, with little intervention of the moderators in the synthesis of results. This intervention rather happened in cases in which the allocation of some elements to different quadrants was debated in order to better specify and argument the decisions of the experts. This was particularly evident in the description of the architectural and functional quality of the space, for which several elements of the SWOT have been proposed and detailed to better capture its potential.

4 SWOT Analysis Results

About preliminary results, it is interesting to notice how the identification of the quality of the spaces initially gave risen to different points of views that have been then reconciliated during the moderator discussion. In particular, the necessity to preserve the historical significance of the space have been risen by the restoration and history of architecture experts, further sustained by the third sector representatives that perceived it as an opportunity to establish functions related to cultural activities or specifically devoted to community building (socialization and meeting spaces). On the other hand, the urban economics and urban regeneration experts have risen the concern regarding the non-profitability of the intervention, with the necessity to mediate the preservation of the asset with the target of the self-sustainability of the intervention. Also, the position of the asset has been a debated point. In particular, the centrality in the urban layout constituted a point in favor risen by the urban economics experts and the third sector representatives. On the other hand, the potential issues concerning accessibility has been raised by the urban regeneration experts. After the discussion it was agreed on allocating this point among the strengths, with the necessity to specifically address this point in the further development of the proposals.

In Table 1 the final allocation of the different points as agreed upon by the participants that emerged from the one-day workshop is presented.

Table 1. SWOT matrix resulting from the one-day workshop.

Strength	Weaknesses
• The possible promotion of a community attached to the building that recognizes itself in the memorial values related to the church • Centrality of the asset in the city center of Moncalieri • Dome of the main hall in good condition and recently restored • Large surface area distributed over 2 floors with a large open central space (main hall of the church) • Innovative tools for governance (regulation of common goods in Moncalieri recently approved) • The building is owned by the diocese with a consequent freedom in decision-making regarding possible reuse projects	• Lack of an open space in front of the building resulting in a lack of view of the property and potential issues in accessibility • The structure of the church lends itself poorly to the functional mix due to a closed form and lack of annexed spaces (large spaces but difficult to be partitioned) • Roof disrepair determines the worsening of the state of degradation of the interior space • High level of degradation • Lack of green spaces in the urban context surrounding the church
Opportunities	**Threats**
• Creation of partnerships with associations and synergies with the surrounding activities • Use of spaces even with only safety measures and combination of temporary and permanent reuse • Construction of a strategic plan for the reuse of churches in synergy with other places of worship/cultural/schools (territorial scale) • Promotion of the sense of citizenship belonging (artists of citizenship) • Formation of territorial capital and enhance the preservation of the memory of the community (house of grandparents) • Possibility to implant a mix of functions: Tourism (inclusion in visitor circuits), education (training school for activities lost in the territory, restoration school), cultural (musical/theatre activities and meeting spaces fostered by the circularity of the main hall)	• Effect of climate change and the increase of disastrous events • Loss of territorial cohesion and in the identification of the community in the heritage building • Psycho-social barriers: Inhibition/aversion towards the religious symbol • Advancing degradation of the building and its decorative apparatus • Risk of settling "empty" functions without continuity of use (e.g., auditorium) • Irreversibility of the intervention and lack of flexibility of functions • Risks of damaging the historical value of the heritage due to functional necessities of the reuse intervention

Analyzing the SWOT matrix, it could be possible to better shape the knowledge framework regarding the case study under examination.

The church space has a good size on two floors (S), but the absence of a space in front of it and the very structure of the church without annexed spaces presents limitations to the insertion of a mix of functions and the possible separation between them (W). Nevertheless, it could be possible to envision the settling of functions even if only by securing spaces, this also implies the need for a preliminary analysis of the compatibility of uses (O).

The general condition of the building is in a state of a high level of degradation with the necessity to perform an analysis of the compatibility of the space (W) to prevent the further advancement of the degradation and the risk of increasing this effect in the case of the installation of incompatible functions or irreversible interventions (T). Even though the general condition of the structure and of the frescos is in a precarious condition (W), the dome was recently restored and is in good condition (S).

Regarding the relationship with the context, the Church is located in a central and strategic position in the city of Moncalieri (S), with the possibility to establish a systematic network with other systems such as the places of worship and the cultural/educational networks both at the local and territorial scale (O), this aspect to be further analyzed. Furthermore, the relationship with institutions (regulation for the reuse of assets) should be deepened, as should the analysis of stakeholders with the possibility of capitalizing on the synergy with local associations and possible forms of partnership (O).

Finally, in terms of potential alternative reuse of the asset, it would be possible to leverage the demographic situation of the area may characterized by a high presence of elderly inhabitants, also considering functions capable of transmitting the history of the place and the community (grandparents" house), or to emphasize the educational value of the building and its decorative apparatus for the benefit of restoration schools of the territory, or to preserve specific craftmanship from disappearance (O). Even though the form itself of the building could be particularly suitable as a meeting space (O), it is necessary to avoid the risk to establish function that will not activate a long-lasting use of the building, ultimately resulting in an "empty box" effect destined to another potential abandonment of the building (T).

5 Discussion

After analyzing the results of the SWOT analysis in the previous section, some reflections focused on the "opportunities (OP)" that emerged, particularly on the "Promotion of the sense of citizenship belonging (artists of citizenship); Formation of territorial capital and enhance the preservation of the memory of the community". Implementing these specific actions to develop the adaptive reuse project of the church means strengthening the link between institutions, associations, and local community, thus fostering the creation of a real heritage community network, (community of young people, the elderly, professionals, associations, etc.). In general, a common vision is generated in the community, which concerns the general interest. The community is thus the foundation for the really efficient implementation of urban/territorial development strategies. It involves regenerating networks of relationships between people living in the neighborhoods with the various local associations (including religious ones) with public/private institutions. These relationships are configured as "social glue" capable of generating "attractive force fields".

Thus, it can be concluded that community is the glue that generates reciprocity that is absolutely central nowadays in the growing social disconnect. In the community, the perception of general interest is generated as a goal of common value. The community becomes a promoter of possible associations, working "together" to enhance the cultural heritage understood as a "common good" consistent with existing regulations.

According to this perspective, therefore, the success of the church's adaptive reuse project will be to produce communities/associations (as provided for in Art. 118 of the Italian Constitution) and not just the restoration of stones and paintings.

The above finds a fertile field in the city of Moncalieri, as it already has active the "Regulations on Citizen-Administration Collaboration for the Care, Regeneration and Shared Management of Common Goods," a legal instrument adopted by the municipality that allows citizens to take care of public goods together with the administration.

Furthermore, based on these considerations, the proposal of adaptive reuse in this research is that the revitalization of the heritage represented by religious buildings that are no longer officiated can make a significant contribution to the humanization of development [45]. Churches are characterized by the highest aesthetic quality in the urban contest being also localized in optimal and barycentric size/places. And this aesthetic property is associated with the generation of a gravitational field of attraction. But the above is realizable on certain conditions:

1. Contribution to the promotion of new communities. Adaptive reuse is indeed an opportunity to produce communities of places. This requires approaches characterized by effective participatory processes of inhabitants, civic and church associations, third sector organizations (to contribute to a possible co-planning and co-design perspective). Qualitative evaluations become the entry point for the above.
2. The capacity to contribute with adaptive reuse not only to the conservation of the "stones" but also to the enhancement of the "civitas", generating a contribution to the production of a civil culture. The Collaboration Pacts for the shared management of architectural assets interpreted as common goods are consistent with the above (cfr. Art 118 last paragraph of the Italian Constitution).
3. The capacity to contribute with the adaptive reuse of religious artefacts to the mitigation and adaptation strategies that cities are elaborating that concern the use of renewable energy sources, the re-capturing of rainwater resources of materials, etc.
4. New destinations of use should be congruent with the "*intrinsic value*" of architectural assets. In fact, the intrinsic value [18] is interpreted as the value from the point of view of future generations that should be recognized and emphasized following Articles 9 and 41 of the Italian Constitution. In substance, the proposed use values of use should be the more coherent with this "*intrinsic value*".
5. New uses destinations should be characterized by a self-generating capacity with regard to economic-financial resources in order to be able to guarantee management capable of meeting maintenance costs in the first place. Another criterion for the identification of uses is the symbiotic capacity [46].
6. Adaptive reuse should be part of the operational strategy of the circular city, for example through the application of the 15-minute multipolar model proposed by Carlos Moreno [47]. In fact, adaptive reuse in the circular perspective suggests a systemic co-evolutionary approach so that cultural heritage can continue to exchange

symbolic, cultural and social values with the context in which it is inserted. The circular economy is today interpreted as the foundation of sustainability (SDGs No. 12 Agenda 2030).

The assessment of the variation in wellbeing suggests reference to a series of subjective indicators of perception: family relationships, amicable relationships, proximity relationships, affective relationships, face to face relationships, reciprocity, well-being, sense of satisfaction, care/attention/cooperation, mutuality/reciprocity, social justice and involvement.

6 Conclusions

Cultural heritage reminds us who we are, what history we have been to, what roots we belong to. Cultural heritage represents the memory of the urban/ territorial system, it represents the sign of the creativity of past generations, but also a way of interpreting life, interpersonal relationships. It expresses the value of aesthetic quality, beauty as a source of humanization that generates "open-mindedness" etc. It proposes a human scale, links a place to a community. It should be seen as an entry point for educating critical knowledge, the ability to relate, to distinguish the essential from the marginal, what should be preserved from what is not permanent. Cultural heritage is the link between past, present and future generations, it is a re-generator of values.

The role of technological innovations alone is not sufficient to ensure a desirable future: human development. Innovations are necessary, but there is a need to operationally link technological innovations (AI, ICT, nanotechnology, etc.) to the human/social sciences, in order to direct innovations towards ends that "have value".

Cultural heritage can play this role as an entry point to human development.

In this complex time characterized by profound transformations, the thesis that any transformation of the status quo should be oriented towards the human development is consolidating. There is increasing discussion about of neo-humanism in the digital era. But also, about post-humanism and even trans-humanism [40].

The adaptive reuse of religious heritage is increasingly debated and is intrinsically tied to the issue of maintenance practices, which are inescapable for both the ecclesiastical and the civil community, due to the plurality of socially shared values and the corresponding potential for community resilience. The canonical, political, and economic origins of these buildings strongly influence the dynamics of use, dismissal, conversion, or abandonment, and the processes of capitalization and de-capitalization.

In this sense, the complexity of the evaluation problem is deeply rooted not only in the physical condition or historical significance of the asset but also in its legal, institutional, and symbolic dimensions. In the case of religious heritage, ownership and permitted uses especially under the guidelines of the Holy See should be considered with particular care before identifying viable reuse options. This requires an in-depth analysis of the context and of the possible opportunities, threats, strengths, and weaknesses related to the reuse process. The participatory SWOT approach used in the present research serves precisely to support this essential step of knowledge construction and problem structuring.

As emerged from the SWOT analysis, the physical consistency of the building itself would require some preliminary analysis to better define the most suitable solution able to revitalize the building without further damaging the frescos and decorations. An analysis of the state of decay and a further analysis of the different options of intervention and the related costs will be performed. Moreover, it would be possible to leverage on the specificity of the socio-economic context such and in particular on the presence of a quite consistent proportion of the elderly population by envisioning uses that could link the memory of the community to new functions.

An analysis of the stakeholders and of the third sector entities and associations will be useful to engage with the population and co-construct the different alternative uses. In particular, the community will be asked to state their preferences regarding the adaptive reuse alternatives by using different methodologies (Discrete choice experiments, questionnaires) in order to reach the definition of possible alternative uses and to the best synergies among them in order to enhance the acceptability of the intervention and its socio-economic sustainability.

Religious heritage is by nature oriented toward serving community needs, and its reuse cannot be effective without building synergies and relationships within the local context. This highlights the importance of adopting participatory governance strategies, involving actors across the public, private, and civic sectors. In this regard, the third sector particularly when working in cooperation with the municipal administration and the ecclesiastical property holder can serve as a critical bridge between the community and the asset, guiding reuse functions not only toward financial and economic sustainability but also toward social and cultural sustainability [48–50]. Moreover, reuse strategies should be aligned with principles of environmental circularity, favouring interventions that regenerate rather than merely consume resources (tangible and intangible).

In this framework, co-design, co-programming, and co-management—also aligned with the values of the New European Bauhaus—emerge as fundamental strategies to ensure that these sacred spaces, originally conceived as places of spirituality and community, may continue to serve as meaningful spaces of encounter without losing their intrinsic value and significance.

The next stages of the PRIN TReE research project will include further co-design and co-evaluation processes, through which the relevance, feasibility, and replicability of the selected strategies will be tested and refined. These outcomes will help to understand whether the adopted approach—consistent with the best European practices, such as those developed in the Horizon 2020 CLIC project—can deliver results that are transferable and scalable for other religious heritage assets across Italy.

Acknowledgments. Funding Research Grant PRIN 2022 No. 2022TN5M7F on "TReE - Supporting the Transition to Ecological Economy in Italian cities Regeneration: circular model tools for reusing architecture and infrastructures". Italian Ministry of University and Research (MUR).

Disclosure of Interests. The authors have no competing interests to declare that are relevant to the content of this article.

References

1. European Commission: The Future for religious heritage. European cultural heriatge strategy for 21th century. (2021). www.coe.int/strategy21

2. Bocasso, F., Cardinali, M., De Lucia, G., Fornara, L., Longhi, A.: Il patrimonio urbano di interesse religioso: da sistema ridondante a risorsa pianificata / the urban heritage of religious interest: from a redundant system to a planned resource. Il Capitale Culturale. Stud. Value Cult. Herit. **29**, 17–43 (2024)
3. Longhi, A.: Storie di architettura ecclesiale e processi di patrimonializzazione: valori, resilienza, adattività, riuso. BDC. Bollettino Del Centro Calza Bini. **19**, 9–26 (2019)
4. Barolomei, L., Longhi, A.: Italian debates, studies and experiences concerning reuse projects of dismissed religious heritage. In: Wandel und wertschatzung. Synergien fur die Zunkuft von Kirchenraumen. pp. 107–135 (2017)
5. Franco, G.: Adaptive reuse of religious and sacred heritage: preserving material traces and Spirit of place. Heritage. **7**, 4725–4754 (2024)
6. Mine, T.Z.: Adaptive re-use of monuments "restoring religious buildings with different uses". J. Cult. Herit. **14**, S14-9 (2013). https://doi.org/10.1016/j.culher.2012.11.017
7. Sedova, A.: Impact analysis on adaptive reuse of obsolete ecclesiastical cultural heritage. Eur. J. Cult. Manag. Policy. **12** (2022). https://doi.org/10.3389/ejcmp.2022.11083
8. Fusco Girard, L., Gravagnuolo, A.: Il riuso del patrimonio culturale religioso: criteri e strumenti di valutazione. BDC. Bollettino Del Centro Calza Bini. **18**, 237–246 (2018)
9. Pine, J.B., Gilmore, J.H.: The Experience Economy. Work Is Theatre – Every Business a Stage. Milan (2000)
10. European Commission: Adaptive reuse of religious heritage. https://www.interregeurope.eu/find-policy-solutions/stories/adaptive-reuse-of-religious-heritage, last accessed 2 March 2025
11. Fusco Girard, L., Gravagnuolo, A.: Adaptive Reuse of Cultural Heritage. Springer International Publishing, Cham (2025). https://doi.org/10.1007/978-3-031-67628-4
12. Lauro, N.C., Gravagnuolo, A., Fusco Girard, L., Vellecco, I., Lauro, M.: A statistical model representation and analysis of cultural heritage adaptive reuse practices based on latent variables for circularity assessment. In: Adaptive Reuse of Cultural Heritage, pp. 165–192. Springer International Publishing, Cham (2025). https://doi.org/10.1007/978-3-031-67628-4_6
13. Buglione, F., Gravagnuolo, A., Angrisano, M., Iodice, S., Bosone, M., De Toro, P., Fusco Girard, L.: Understanding best practices of cultural heritage adaptive reuse in the perspective of the circular economy: in-depth assessment of case studies. In: Adaptive Reuse of Cultural Heritage, pp. 193–223. Springer International Publishing, Cham (2025). https://doi.org/10.1007/978-3-031-67628-4_7
14. Open Heritage: www.openheritage.eu, last accessed 15 March 2025
15. Sadowy, K., Szemző, H.: Aesthetics, gentrification and new identities: the comparison of adaptive reuse practices in contemporary Budapest and Warsaw. J. Cult. Herit. Manag. Sustain. Dev.. **14**, 49–64 (2024). https://doi.org/10.1108/JCHMSD-09-2022-0172
16. Angrisano, M., Bottero, M., Cavana, G., Fabbrocino, F., Gravagnuolo, A., Fusco Girard, L.: Adaptive reuse of cultural built heritage: towards the implementation of the circular city model. Front Built Environ.
17. Angrisano, M., Nocca, F., Scotto Di Santolo, A.: Multidimensional evaluation framework for assessing cultural heritage adaptive reuse projects: the case of the seminary in Sant'Agata de' Goti (Italy). Urban Sci. **8**, 50 (2024). https://doi.org/10.3390/urbansci8020050
18. Fusco Girard, L.: The circular "human-centred" adaptive reuse of cultural heritage: theoretical foundations. In: Adaptive Reuse of Cultural Heritage, pp. 15–69. Springer International Publishing, Cham (2025). https://doi.org/10.1007/978-3-031-67628-4_2
19. Pinto, M.R., De Medici, S., Senia, C., Fabbricatti, K., De Toro, P.: Building reuse: multi-criteria assessment for compatible design. Int. J. Des. Sci. Technol. **22** (2017)

20. Dabbene, D., Bartolozzi, C., Coscia, C.: How to monitor and evaluate quality in adaptive heritage reuse projects from a well-being perspective: a proposal for a dashboard model of indicators to support promoters. Sustainability (Switzerland). **14** (2022). https://doi.org/10.3390/su14127099
21. Council of Europe: Framework Convention on the Value of Cultural Heritage for Society. (2005). https://rm.coe.int/1680083746
22. Fusco Girard, L., Nocca, F., Gravagnuolo, A.: Matera 2019 capitale europea della cultura: Città della natura, città della cultura, città della rigenerazione. Bollettino Del Centro Calza Bini. **17**, 159–184 (2017)
23. Allegro, I., Lupu, A.: Models of public private partnership and financial tools for the cultural heritage valorisation, p. 278. Urbanistica Informazioni (2018)
24. Gravagnuolo, A.: The Circular Economy Model in the City and the Territory. Documenti Geografici (2021). https://doi.org/10.19246/DOCUGEO2281-7549/202102_28
25. Bottero, M., Datola, G., Fazzari, D., Ingaramo, R.: Re-thinking Detroit: a multicriteria-based approach for adaptive reuse for the Corktown District. Sustain. For. **14**, 8343 (2022). https://doi.org/10.3390/su14148343
26. Regione Piemonte: BDTRE: Base Dati Territoriale di Riferimento degli Enti piemontesi. https://geoportale.igr.piemonte.it/cms/bdtre/bdtre-2
27. ISTAT: Basi territoriali e variabili censuarie. https://www.istat.it/notizia/basi-territoriali-e-variabili-censuarie/, last accessed 10 Jan 2024
28. Cocucci, F.: Urban heritage of religious interest: History and values for building a plan (2023)
29. Serrenti, M.C.: La Chiesa del SS. Nome di Gesù in Moncalieri (2002)
30. Mingers, J., Rosenhead, J.: Problem structuring methods in action (2004). https://doi.org/10.1016/S0377-2217(03)00056-0
31. Rosenhead, J.: Past, present and future of problem structuring methods. J. Oper. Res. Soc. **57**, 759–765 (2006). https://doi.org/10.1057/palgrave.jors.2602206
32. Marttunen, M., Lienert, J., Belton, V.: Structuring problems for multi-criteria decision analysis in practice: a literature review of method combinations. Eur. J. Oper. Res. **263**, 1–17 (2017). https://doi.org/10.1016/j.ejor.2017.04.041
33. Bottero, M.: A multi-methodological approach for assessing sustainability of urban projects. Manag. Environ. Qual. Int. J. **26**, 138–154 (2015). https://doi.org/10.1108/MEQ-06-2014-0088
34. Kajanus, M., Kangas, J., Kurttila, M.: The use of value focused thinking and the A'WOT hybrid method in tourism management. Tour. Manag. **25**, 499–506 (2004). https://doi.org/10.1016/S0261-5177(03)00120-1
35. Kurttila, M., Pesonen, M., Kangas, J., Kajanus, M.: Utilizing the analytic hierarchy process (AHP) in SWOT analysis - a hybrid method and its application to a forest-certification case. Forest Policy Econ. **1**, 41–52 (2000). https://doi.org/10.1016/s1389-9341(99)00004-0
36. Margles, S.W., Masozera, M., Rugyerinyange, L., Kaplin, B.A.: Participatory planning: using SWOT-AHP analysis in buffer zone management planning. J. Sustain. For. **29**, 613–637 (2010). https://doi.org/10.1080/10549811003769483
37. Nikodinoska, N., Mattivi, M., Notaro, S., Paletto, A.: Stakeholders' appraisal of biomass-based energy development at local scale. J. Renew. Sustain. Energy. **7** (2015). https://doi.org/10.1063/1.4916654
38. Ferretti, V.: Framing territorial regeneration decisions: purpose, perspective and scope. Land Use Policy. **102**, 105279 (2021). https://doi.org/10.1016/j.landusepol.2021.105279
39. Cavana, G., Dell'Anna, F.: An evaluation model to support strategic urban planning in Italy: the application of community impact evaluation. Presented at the (2023). https://doi.org/10.1007/978-3-031-37117-2_36

40. Kangas, J., Kangas, A., Leskinen, P., Pykäläinen, J.: MCDM methods in strategic planning of forestry on state-owned lands in Finland: applications and experiences. J. Multi-Criteria Decis. Anal. **10**, 257–271 (2001). https://doi.org/10.1002/mcda.306
41. Caprioli, C.: The integration of multi-agent system and multicriteria analysis for developing participatory planning alternatives in urban contexts. Environ. Impact Assess. Rev. **113**, 107855 (2025)
42. Bottero, M., Assumma, V., Caprioli, C., Dell'Ovo, M.: Decision making in urban development: the application of a hybrid evaluation method for a critical area in the city of Turin (Italy). Sustain. Cities Soc. **72**, 103028 (2021). https://doi.org/10.1016/j.scs.2021.103028
43. Vacik, H., Kurttila, M., Hujala, T., Khadka, C., Haara, A., Pykäläinen, J., Honkakoski, P., Wolfslehner, B., Tikkanen, J.: Evaluating collaborative planning methods supporting programme-based planning in natural resource management. J. Environ. Manag. **144**, 304–315 (2014). https://doi.org/10.1016/j.jenvman.2014.05.029
44. Clic Project web page, https://www.clicproject.eu/, last accessed 1 Feb 2024
45. UN-Habitat: New Urban Agenda. https://unhabitat.org/about-us/new-urban-agenda, last accessed 2 March 2025
46. Fusco Girard, L., Vecco, M.: The "intrinsic value" of cultural heritage as driver for circular human-centered adaptive reuse. Sustain. For. **13**, 3231 (2021). https://doi.org/10.3390/su13063231
47. Moreno, C.: La città dei 15 minuti: Per una cultura urbana democratica. Wiley, Torino (2024)
48. Rossitti, M., Oteri, A.M., Srnataro, M., Torrieri, F.: The social dimension of architectural heritage reuse. Theoretical reflections from a case study in Campania region. ArcHistoR, 178–211 (2022)
49. Gravagnuolo, A., Angrisano, M., Girard, L.F.: Dismissed historic buildings and new reuse strategies: the case of Edifici Mondo in the City of Salerno (Italy). Presented at the (2024). https://doi.org/10.1007/978-3-031-74501-0_23
50. Rossitti, M., Torrieri, F.: Circular economy as 'catalyst' for resilience in inner areas. Ustain. Medit. Constr. Spec. Issue. **5**, 64–67 (2021)

Cultural and Creative Practices as Drivers of Circular Economy: A 9R Framework Perspective

Sabrina Pedrini[1] and Maria Tartari[2(✉)]

[1] Alma Mater Studiorum Università di Bologna, Bologna, Italy
Sabrina.pedrini@unibo.it
[2] ISPC-CNR, Naples, Italy
maria.tartari@ispc.cnr.it

Abstract. The transition to a circular economy demands a profound shift from the traditional linear production-consumption model, requiring not only technological innovation and regulatory support but also transformations in individual and collective behaviors. Culture plays a crucial role in shaping the values, attitudes, and practices necessary for this transition.

This paper investigates how cultural and creative practices contribute to the operationalization of the 9R framework (Refuse, Rethink, Reduce, Reuse, Repair, Refurbish, Remanufacture, Repurpose, Recycle) in the circular economy. Specifically, it addresses the research question: How do cultural and creative sectors support the implementation and social embedding of 9R strategies, and what implications does this have for sustainable transitions?

Drawing on a narrative literature review and a selection of illustrative case studies across Cultural and Creative (C&C) industries, the study highlights how cultural narratives, creative production, and symbolic meaning-making can foster behavioural change and embed circularity into everyday life. The paper proposes a conceptual framework that integrates cultural capital with circular economy thinking, revealing new synergies and identifying creativity-based pathways for systemic and enduring environmental and social impact.

Keywords: Circular Creativity · Cultural Ontology of CE · 9R Framework · Sustainable Consumption · Creative Circular Practices

1 Introduction: A Circular Economy 9R Background

A Circular Economy (CE) is an economic model aimed at the efficient use of resources through waste minimisation, long-term value retention, reduction of primary resources, and closed loops of products, product parts, and materials within the boundaries of environmental protection and socioeconomic benefits (Morseletto, 2020). Drawing on existing literature, the CE can be defined as a multidimensional, dynamic, integrative approach, promoting a reformed socio-technical template for carrying out economic development, in an environmentally sustainable way, by re-matching, re-balancing and re-wiring industrial processes and consumption habits into a new usage-production closed-loop system (de Jesus and Mendonça, 2018). The literature on circular economy (CE)

© The Author(s), under exclusive license to Springer Nature Switzerland AG 2026
O. Gervasi et al. (Eds.): ICCSA 2025 Workshops, LNCS 15896, pp. 283–298, 2026.
https://doi.org/10.1007/978-3-031-97654-4_18

strategies has evolved significantly, moving from traditional waste management principles to more comprehensive frameworks integrating sustainability and digitalization. Several studies on circular economy models reveal that authors now favour frameworks built around nine distinct R strategies.

Indeed, current circular economy research demonstrates a shift toward nine-strategy (9R) frameworks, though the specific evolution from other models is not explicitly documented. The foundational models, such as the 3R (Reduce, Reuse, Recycle), have expanded into more complex strategies, with the 9R framework emerging as a dominant (Alivojvodic & Kokalj, 2024; Dovgal, 2022; Khaw-ngern, 2021). The 9R framework is a comprehensive model used to structure circular economy strategies, expanding the early 3R logic into a more nuanced hierarchy. It includes nine interrelated strategies: Refuse: avoid unnecessary resource use and reject unsustainable options; Rethink: redesign products and systems to optimize sustainability; Reduce: minimize resource input and waste generation; Reuse: extend the life of products without significant modification; Repair: restore functionality of broken or worn items; Refurbish: improve or modernize products; Remanufacture: rebuild products using reused, repaired or new parts; Repurpose: use items for functions other than those originally intended; Recycle: process materials to create new raw inputs.

The list's order is not mandatory, yet this hierarchy prioritizes strategies that preserve more of a product's original value (e.g., reuse over recycling). Understanding and applying the 9R model allows for a more systemic and resource-efficient circular transition. Some scholars have further extended these principles, incorporating socioeconomic and industry-specific adaptations, leading to variations such as the 10R and even 36R models (Valencia et al., 2023). Several studies focus on sector-specific applications of the 9R framework. Muñoz et al. (2024) examine its adaptation in pharmaceutical manufacturing, while Pan et al. (2022) explore its implementation in the manufacturing and Industry 4.0 context. Beyond the traditional 9R approach, some scholars advocate for an expanded set of principles. The addition of strategies such as 'Recover' (Ang et al., 2024) and the integration of socioeconomic considerations (Valencia et al., 2023) highlight an ongoing effort to refine CE methodologies. The transition from 4R to more complex models underscores the dynamic nature of CE research, addressing contemporary sustainability challenges through a multi-layered approach (Alivojvodic & Kokalj, 2024). The critique of waste-to-energy components within the 10R framework suggests a need for a more holistic assessment of circularity beyond material recovery (Valencia et al., 2023). The role of CE indices in assessing circularity is another key development in the field. The Circular Economy Index (CEIR), incorporating 9R strategies, provides a systematic approach to evaluating sustainability impacts (Ang et al., 2024). Additionally, studies mapping circular strategies across different system perspectives (Sitadewi et al., 2021) contribute to a more nuanced understanding of how these frameworks operate in practice. Finally, a growing number of studies address the social dimensions of circular economy strategies. The inclusion of socioeconomic Rs, such as 'Regenerate,' reflects an effort to balance environmental goals with social sustainability (Valencia et al., 2023). Overall, the literature highlights an ongoing expansion and refinement of circular economy strategies, with significant shift towards a more comprehensive and adaptive approach to sustainability, aligning with broader global economic and environmental goals.

This paper aims to investigate how cultural and creative practices can support the transition to a circular economy by operationalizing the 9R framework. It seeks to uncover the potential of cultural capital, artistic production, and creative industries to promote behavioral and systemic change aligned with circular principles. The central research question guiding this inquiry is: How do cultural and creative sectors contribute to the practical implementation and social embedding of the 9R strategies in the circular economy?

Drawing from an interdisciplinary literature base, this study addresses the theoretical gap in circular economy scholarship, which often overlooks cultural dimensions and their capacity to shift social norms, perceptions, and consumption patterns. By exploring this intersection, the paper highlights how culture is not just a complement but a catalyst for sustainable transitions.

2 Cultural Capital and Cognitive Barriers in the Transition to Circular Economy: Addressing Consumer Behaviour and Innovation Challenges

Circular economy (CE) business models revolve around two primary behavioral approaches: those that promote reuse and extend product life through repair, remanufacturing, upgrades, and retrofitting, and those that transform old goods into new resources via material recycling. At the heart of these models are people—of all ages and skill levels—who play a central role. Ownership transitions into stewardship, where consumers become both users and creators. Fundamental elements of the CE, such as reparability, durability, upgradability, recyclability, reuse, and recycled content, are driven by behavioral changes that individuals embrace as a new paradigm. Within this context, there is room to define a conceptual framework that explores the intersection of culture and CE. Specifically, the accumulation of cultural capital, both at the individual and societal level, as a result of cultural experiences, may serve as a crucial factor in fostering behaviors aligned with CE principles and foundations.

Even when CE solutions are technically feasible, their implementation is frequently hindered by economic and market constraints (de Jesus and Mendonça, 2018). The authors focus on how "transformative innovation" (economic innovations—EI) can facilitate the transition by overcoming sustainability barriers. EI can initiate a cascade of changes and generate localized pressures, stimulating complementary adaptations that collectively contribute to the formation of a new techno-economic system. This perspective suggests that transformative innovation may serve as a key driver of a "green" transition (Schot and Kanger, 2016).

Innovation within CE remains a fragmented phenomenon. As Stoneman (2009, 2010) notes, economic discussions typically emphasize hard innovation, such as R&D-driven products or cost-reduction strategies, while soft innovation—related to cultural and organizational artifacts, such as symbols and conventions—plays a more significant role than traditionally acknowledged (Mendonça, 2014). Applying these heuristics to CE, Joseph Nye (1990) differentiates between hard power, which enforces change through technical or economic means, and soft power, which drives change by attracting others through values and institutional practices that shape attitudes and preferences (de Jesus and Mendonça, 2018).

Consumer habits and business routines evolve slowly due to inadequate awareness and understanding of CE concepts and available choices. When individuals repeatedly engage in past behaviors, these behaviors become "frozen," a phenomenon described by Ouellette & Wood (1998) as habit formation. Such habits persist when reinforced over time, within stable environments, and through rewarding outcomes (Thøgersen and Ølander, 2006). Behavioral inertia presents a significant challenge. However, emerging social trends—including heightened sensitivity to environmental concerns, shifting consumer preferences toward service-based models, and businesses recognizing reputational advantages—are fostering new routines that act as social drivers for CE. Demand-side factors, in particular, play a crucial role in propelling sustainable practices and choices (Andrews and deVault, 2009; Geng et al., 2010). Research by Valtteri et al. (2017) indicates that institutional support for CE primarily emphasizes recycling, while other CE strategies remain underdeveloped. Regulatory measures have predominantly fueled recycling efforts among both integrators and manufacturers, whereas cultural and cognitive barriers hinder reuse. Cognitive myopia and present bias further exacerbate sustainability challenges by prioritizing short-term costs over long-term benefits, reinforcing the status quo bias (Samuelson & Zeckhauser, 1988) and a lack of imaginative foresight (Weber, 2017). To mitigate these biases and enhance future-oriented decision-making, cultural capital emerges as a critical enabler, compensating for the limitations of direct experience in shaping choices (Atreya & Ferreira, 2014).

In some cases, circular business models fail to align with consumers' personal values or material interests. Unlike the linear economy, where consumers play a passive role, CE necessitates active consumer participation (Mylan et al., 2016; Ellen MacArthur Foundation, 2013). Resistance to CE adoption delays its transition, as various psychosocial and cultural-cognitive biases obstruct implementation. Within this framework, Singh and Giacosa (2018) analyze consumer experiences with circular business models, highlighting psychological, social, and cultural barriers that hinder their diffusion. The authors identify key impediments, including weak person–product relationships leading to premature disposal, psychological ownership resisting access-based models, entrenched habits reinforcing the status quo, negative consumer attitudes towards CE, social norms discouraging reusable goods, consumerist ideologies limiting sufficiency models, and psychological essentialism reducing acceptance of recycled and reused products. In societies with high power distance, consumers' preference for status brands further undermines the adoption of CE principles. Addressing these barriers requires a comprehensive approach that integrates economic, technological, cultural, and behavioral perspectives to foster a sustainable circular economy.

3 Cultural Consumers and the Transition to Circular Economy: Building Awareness and Shifting Consumption Habits

According to the existing literature on Circular Economy (CE), transitioning towards sustainable practices involves a crucial process of capability-building for individuals. This process entails raising awareness and expanding people's cognitive horizons, thereby fostering a broader mental space for sustainability. It involves the continuous acquisition of information and skills, creating a virtuous cycle that supports the generation of value—social, cognitive, and identity-related (Veenhoven, 1991). CE behavior is a complex process that encompasses not only instrumental aspects but also non-instrumental ones such as values, identity, emotional, and symbolic processes. These dimensions can be supported through positional and relational consumption, which can manifest in both objects and experiences. While these two mechanisms are not mutually exclusive, the degree to which they are integrated significantly influences the definition of personal identity.

In terms of material consumption, the accumulation of objects triggers mechanisms of positional competition and "relative unhappiness." The value of the goods we possess is often not intrinsic but relational, depending on our social context, comparisons with others, or aspirations (Veenhoven, 1991). Furthermore, the relentless pursuit of material goals tends to replace meaningful relationships with opportunistic ones, leading to a deterioration in the quality of social interactions. This shift fosters social isolation, loneliness, and social impoverishment. Conversely, relational goods—such as experiences—when lost, create a void that cannot be filled by material possessions. A consumption model centered on experiential goods, however, offers enduring value once the initial access costs are surpassed, providing continuous nourishment with a "slow release effect," akin to how proteins are transformed into energy.

The process of identity building based on experiences does not trigger competitive social positioning, but instead fosters personal growth based on relationality, shared interests, values, and cooperative mechanisms. This shift away from material to experiential consumption highlights a more profound connection to others and to shared human experiences. Carter and Gilovich (2010, 2012), Rosenzweig and Gilovich (2012), and Van Boven and Gilovich (2003) emphasize the stark differences in the outcomes of material versus experiential consumption. While the latter generates positive anticipation and joy, the former leads to impatience and anxiety, creating unhappiness. The memory of an experience, however brief, provides inner satisfaction, while material goods, always external to us, can lead to disappointment. Moreover, the joy derived from experiences is amplified when shared or discussed with others, extending the experience and increasing satisfaction, something not typically found with material purchases. This further underscores that human beings are inherently relational, and that relationships contribute significantly to happiness (Diener & Seligman, 2004; Myers, 2000). Additionally, experiential purchases tend to be more social, with higher scores on "relatedness" compared to material goods (Caprariello & Reis, 2013; Howell & Hill, 2009).

Experiences, especially when shared, not only foster a sense of social connection but also create a sense of self that is self-reinforcing. This phenomenon is more profound than the sense of self derived from material goods (Gilovich et al., 2015; Hajdu & Hajdu, 2017). When individuals are able to discuss their experiential purchases, it further enhances their sense of appreciation, whereas the same effect is not observed with material purchases (Kumar & Gilovich, 2015). Experiences, therefore, contribute to a sense of self that encourages positive evaluations of one's identity and social connectedness (Aronson, 1992; Dunning et al., 1989, 1995; Kunda, 1990).

The detrimental nature of material consumption is evident when it overshadows experiential consumption. Material consumption leads to a loss of meaning, depriving individuals of lasting experiential backgrounds, and reducing opportunities for self-realization and the establishment of a rich sense of self. This lack of meaningful experiences impedes symbolic exchanges, further alienating individuals from genuine relational connections. Culture, in this context, plays a crucial role in reordering our needs—emphasizing the fundamental over the induced—thereby making space for relationships, inner life, care, and participation. By doing so, culture creates the conditions for building meaningful horizons of meaning that give life depth.

The goals outlined in the Agenda 2030 provide an innovative and universal framework for sustainable development, emphasizing the need for collective participation in change. Achieving responsible consumption patterns will require citizens who are aware of the dynamics of wealth accumulation and equipped with cognitive tools that foster critical thinking. Such awareness enables individuals to engage with the common good in a new way, promoting values like solidarity, a sense of limitation and fragility, community, and respect for differences. These values are essential to shifting the logic of production and consumption, a transformation that culture can facilitate.

Educational processes capable of deconstructing the consumption imperative are essential. By encouraging culture as a fundamental tool for developing critical thinking, individuals can challenge the contradictions of our time and derive meaning from experiences and imagination. This is a global challenge that transcends regional boundaries. To achieve the necessary paradigm shift for sustainable development, a change in mentality regarding production, consumption, and governance is imperative (Giovannini, 2020). Knowledge derived from culture—through books, movies, music, and art—stimulates behavioral change because it taps into emotions, thus deeply influencing people. As individuals' values and sensitivities evolve, cultural experiences become the drivers of significant transformations in consumer behavior and attitudes.

4 From Cultural Experience to Circular Economy Behaviours

Culture is a fundamental driver in the transition to a circular economy, influencing perceptions, behaviors, and decision-making processes. Cultural capital—understood as both shared experiences and intangible knowledge—enables individuals and communities to adopt innovative and sustainable resource management practices. The accumulation of cultural capital fosters proactive attitudes toward rethinking product life cycles, reducing waste, and embracing regenerative economic models.

Moreover, shared cultural experiences and community engagement strengthen social bonds and disseminate sustainability-oriented norms. These dynamics encourage the adoption of economic models that prioritize reuse, repair, and recycling, thereby embedding circularity into daily life. Through educational initiatives and awareness campaigns, culture enhances critical understanding of resource value, guiding both individuals and institutions toward responsible consumption and sustainable development. Consequently, culture emerges as an indispensable element in shifting from a linear to a circular economy, where efficiency, resilience, and environmental consciousness drive socio-economic progress.

Cultural capital, defined as the accumulation of knowledge, experiences, and skills acquired through cultural engagement, plays a crucial role in fostering behavioral and social transformations. According to Sen's capability approach, cultural participation enhances critical and cognitive capacities, empowering individuals to adopt sustainable behaviors. Similarly, Billett (2014) emphasizes the socio-psychological dimension of cultural capital, which fosters proactive attitudes that positively influence societal structures. Research by Kalmijn and Kraaykamp (1996) and Cuesta (2011) highlights how the replication of cultural experiences in socially favorable environments facilitates social mobility and the formation of resilient communities. Furthermore, Huggins and Thompson (2015) argue that diverse and inclusive cultural ecosystems stimulate the diffusion of sustainable and innovative practices, positioning cultural capital as a strategic lever in the transition to a circular economy.

The relationship between culture and behaviour finds solid ground, from the cognitive and empowerment side, in the many similarities between the two processes in terms of capacity building through experience. Such a form of cultural experience accumulation can therefore be considered as a form of capacity building (Sen, 2000) with a professional socio-psychological dimension (e.g. Billett, 1994). The latter is based on the assumption that favorable conditions for the accumulation of culture-driven experiences can be reproduced in social contexts. If properly exploited and supported, the accumulation of cultural experiences can become a facilitator of social mobility once the mediating role of the intervening variables is properly understood and addressed (Kalmijn and Kraaykamp, 1996; Cuesta, 2011) and can improve local resilience promoting an open, diverse local culture (Huggins and Thompson, 2015).

At the social level, social interactions due to cultural participation are driven by the production of a particular type of relational goods (Uhlaner, 1989), which cannot be financially sustained by self-interested optimization, but relies upon an articulate set of pro-social attitudes (Benkler, 2006). Hypothetically, relational goods may be produced everywhere, but, due to the nature of the specific interactions that characterize them, the cultural context is one of the most effective since people show strong intrinsic motivation to participate in meaning production. These kind of participation shapes a cultural attitude, which is not only a prerogative of the creative class, but is a diffused behaviour relevant in the perspective of economic and social innovation (Nuccio and Pedrini, 2014).

These goods, produced by relationships and which can show how the latter good can be valid for its own existence (Nussbaum, 1986) are "affective components of social relations, valued in themselves and not instrumentally, as means for other purposes" (Sugden, 2002), generate goods independent from the relationship itself (Gui, 2002), produced by non-instrumental motivations, guided by the principle of reciprocity and sharing, endowed with historical value (valid over time) and reflexivity (Donati, 2005), represent a social phenomenon and are generative of commons (Bruni, 2014) - which, as cannot be excludible, require protection to be reproduced - and other particular types of intangible outputs, with a relational nature that influence the level of human capital of the interacting subjects (Gui, 2002; Crociata et al., 2020). They are produced within a context of significant social situations associated with a human activity of some kind and, in particular, with the activities of consumption and production (Gui, 2002).

Good-based relationships have a dual value, social and economic. In essence, Sacco and Zamagni (2006) suggest that goods that are particularly important in encouraging economic activity come from interpersonal relationships and, therefore, establish relational goods, which shall fosterdissemination of knowledge and protection, as well as social support and coordination, enabling cooperation and reciprocity in society.

Arts are a key source for relational goods since they build and rebuild relationships: at the cultural level, they produce meanings; at the social level they combine and confront diversity; at the economic level, they point at alternative modes of exchange. It is not a single blockbuster event, however extraordinary and catalyst for tourism, which generates these effects, but the continuous presence of cultural participatory activities. For example, Smith (2017) in Sustainable Design Futures explores how a multidisciplinary approach—blending artisanal traditions with technological innovations—acts as a strategic lever for fostering sustainable behavior. Similarly, Muir (2024) in The Theatre of Waste illustrates how waste can be reinterpreted as a performative and creative resource, challenging conventional perceptions and promoting sustainability through artistic expression.

Policy makers well-understood this creation of added value, and creative interventions have played a significant role in advancing sustainability in urban environments. Diverse artistic, cultural, and design-based strategies employed to foster environmental responsibility, social cohesion, and sustainable urban regeneration. Several studies highlight the integration of artistic and design-based approaches to reimagine urban spaces in an environmentally responsible manner (Crane et al., 2013; Andersen & Frandsen, 2018; Gren, 2019; Allameh & Heidari, 2020). Art and creative practices serve as powerful tools for fostering community engagement, social inclusion, and participatory urban planning: experiences like "Hip-hop ecology in Boston, USA" (Cermak, 2012) integrates music and culture with environmental education, or like "Community-led greening strategies in Dublin 8, Ireland" (Clavin et al., 2021) demonstrate how local participation in urban renewal enhances environmental awareness and civic involvement. Moreover, creative methods are increasingly employed to bridge scientific research with public engagement in climate action (Bentz et al., 2021; Asplund et al., 2023; Campbell et al., 2024).

So, cultural institutions such as museums, theatres, libraries and cultural events such as concerts, art exhibitions and festivals are typical environments for the production of relational goods, as the appreciation of the aesthetic experience is typically strengthened by the social experience of joint enjoyment with others human beings and the opportunities for social exchange that are favoured by such situations (Jafari et al. 2013). They are also the place for the construction of a particular type of experiential commons, that type for which Carol Rose coined the expression "the comedy of the commons" (1986), which increase their value with collective and repeated consumption.

The construction of commons and relational goods, the implementation of the human capital to which they contribute are fuelled by a lively cultural and creative environment. According to Crociata et al. (2013) cultural participation can increase individuals' open-mindedness and curiosity, raising their awareness of a multitude of socially relevant issues and stimulating them to seek engagement in a wide range of pro-social activities and practices. In this light, in the same sign of Quaglione et al. (2017), culture, through cultural experiences, could influence behavioural patterns that can be regulated by no conscious deliberation that authorizes the consciousness of the agents. At the social level a concentration of cultural institutions creates a favorable social environment that functions as a spatial enabling factor to generate different "socio-cognitive environments" (Brown et al., 1989).

Not only: going beyond the mere Nudging, which is utilized since many years as a creative strategy for influencing eco-sustainable behaviors with a short-term effect (Sunstein, 2017), art practice and participation can change life allowing people to see themselves in a completely different way. Artistic experience have mind changed about things in ways that are unforgettable. This experience of change is slow and painstaking and cumulative; it builds capacity, it builds strength and resilience and solidarity, at its best (Matarasso, 2019).

Arts participation is embedded in larger systems of meaning and impact on values and attitude (Di Maggio, 1996). In particular the role of attitude is particular important and with subjective norms, and perceived decision makers behavioural control positively influence organizations' intentions to implement best practices of circular economy (Khan, 2020). Ajzen (1991, p. 188) defines attitude as "the degree to which a person has a favourable or unfavourable evaluation or appraisal of the behavior [...]". An individual positive or negative attitude towards a certain behaviour strengthens or weakens her/his intention to perform that certain behaviour in question respectively.

Studies support the relationship between attitude and behavioural intention (Khan et al., 2019a; Tonglet et al., 2004) and values have been the vehicle through which dimensions of culture have been established (Robbins, 2001) and they are among the first things that people learn and are more enduring than attitudes or perceptions: advances in theoretical understandings of cultural orientations have been applied to the prediction of job satisfaction (White, in press, a), lifestyle analysis (Sun et al., 2004), managerial behaviour (Smith et al., 2002; Sun et al., 2004), responses to marketing stimuli (Lowe & Corkindale, 1998), service quality (Furrer et al., 2000), product evaluation (Crotts & Erdmann, 2000), occupational choice (Brown, 2002), persuasion (Aaker & Maheswaran, 1997), social behaviour (Lee, 2000; Triandis, 1994) and behavioural intentions (Maio & Olson, 1995; Mattila, 1999). Correlations between cultural values and behavioural intentions have been considered low for a long time (Smith et al., 2002). One of the most influential models developed to explain human behaviour and its antecedents was proposed by Fishbein and Ajzen in 1974. What originally started as the Theory of Reasoned Action (TRA) was then refined to become the Theory of Planned Behaviour (TPB) (Ajzen, 1991). The rationale behind this model is that human behaviour is influenced by beliefs about the outcomes of behaviour, which in turn produce a positive or negative attitude towards the behaviour. Beliefs about the normative expectations of others leads to subjective perceptions of social pressures, and beliefs about control give rise to perceptions of the degree of control one has over factors that may impede or facilitate the behaviour. The beliefs that are more strongly held are more likely to influence behavioural intentions (Ajzen, 2002). According to the author, a tri-component model of attitudes proposes that attitudes are formed by the interaction of beliefs, affect and behavioural intentions: the cognitive component consists of knowledge and perceptions that take the form of beliefs; the affective component consists of the emotions, moods and feelings one has toward the object and the conative component is the likelihood or tendency that one will behave in. Emotions contributes to the explain variance in behaviour (Stauss & Neuhaus, 1997; White, 2005; Yu & Dean, 2001). Individuals are governed by personal, cultural, social and religious values and each of these value systems is likely to influence an individual's choices and behaviours.

Rohan (2000: 265) proposed that cultural value systems are '(…) people's perceptions of others' judgments about best possible living or functioning, that is, others' value priorities'; therefore, when one focuses on 'others', then cultural value priorities are at issue. Value systems are primarily cognitive structures (Schwartz & Bardi, 2001) that occupy core positions within attitudes and beliefs, although it has also been argued that values are linked to affective processes (Rohan, 2000). In terms of cultural values, it appears that there is fairly strong evidence for and against the likelihood of cultural values influencing behaviour but the link between cultural values and behaviour rests more with assumptions than with empirical support (Rohan, 2000).

5 C&C Sectors: How Industries and Practices Impact, According to the 9R Principles

The intersection of cultural and creative practices with the circular economy presents a compelling paradigm shift in sustainable development. The circular economy extends beyond technological solutions and industrial processes; it requires a profound cultural and social shift. The transition to a circular model is guided by an integrated framework of principles, including *Refuse, Rethink, Reduce, Reuse, Repair, Refurbish, Remanufacture, Repurpose, and Recycle*.

As we have seen, research highlights the role of cultural traditions, local knowledge, and interdisciplinary innovation in transforming behaviors and practices. These examples underscore the transformative power of culture in embedding circularity into everyday practices and cultural consumption.

This study adopts a qualitative, interdisciplinary approach grounded in narrative literature review and interpretive case study analysis. The literature was selected through academic databases (e.g., Scopus, Google Scholar) using keywords such as "circular economy," "9R framework," "cultural capital," and "creative industries," with a focus on works published between 2010 and 2024.

Case studies were identified based on their relevance to specific 9R strategies and their integration of cultural or creative dimensions. These examples span various creative sectors, including design, visual arts, fashion, architecture, and digital media. The clustering into the 9R categories follows a conceptual alignment: each case illustrates one or more R-strategies in practice, showing how cultural actions translate abstract principles into everyday practices.

While exploratory in nature, the selection aims to represent diverse geographies, scales, and disciplines, offering insight into how creative practices are fostering a transition toward circularity beyond the technological and industrial domains.

Starting from **"Refuse"**, category where the focus is on rejecting wasteful practices, avoiding unnecessary resource extraction, and promoting alternative, dematerialized consumption, examples like the one of *Studio Formafantasma* (Italy & Netherlands) show how design practices can question industrial production systems and advocating for waste-free approaches. By prioritizing bio-based and fully recyclable materials, they promote a design philosophy that refuses resource-intensive and environmentally harmful materials. *Precious Plastic* (Netherlands) (Spekkink et al., 2020) is an open-source initiative that while primarily focusing on plastic recycling, also educates and encourages individuals and businesses to refuse single-use plastics by demonstrating the potential for reuse and transformation. Artists like *Jane Perkins* (UK), by exclusively using discarded materials such as buttons and plastic for her artworks, promotes a "refuse" mentality, demonstrating how creative practices can eliminate reliance on virgin materials; or like *Aurora Robson* (USA) who works with ocean plastic aligning with the refusal of unnecessary waste production, as she turns discarded plastic into sculptures, advocating for waste reduction and conscious consumption.

Also urban actions or street art interventions that transform neglected spaces without extensive demolition or new construction, such as the *FestiWall* (Italy), promotes a "refuse" approach by repurposing urban surfaces instead of creating new ones.

Considering **"Rethink"**, C&C industries professionals can assume a leading role, already well-recognized by design-driven innovation in several sectors. Creative industries are pivotal in rejecting unsustainable consumption models and rethinking product lifecycles. Initiatives like Fashion Revolution encourage transparency and ethical production, urging consumers and brands to refuse exploitative and wasteful practices. Similarly, movements such as the *Cradle-to-Cradle* design philosophy, evident in material innovation like *Econyl* (obtained from the recycling of fishing nets and ocean plastic) which rethink traditional manufacturing by prioritizing regenerative principles over extractive processes. Innovative textile material, used by sustainable fashion brands (Colucci & Vecchi, 2021). It has been adopted by brands such as Prada, Stella McCartney, and Adidas, has enabled the recovery and transformation, reducing marine pollution and CO_2 emissions compared to virgin nylon production.

To support this wave, films like *The True Cost* amplify this cultural shift, reinforcing the imperative to refuse fast fashion and unsustainable production. The documentary has raised awareness of fast fashion's environmental and social effects, influencing consumers, brands, and policymakers. It has inspired movements for ethical and sustainable fashion and encouraged companies to revise their production practices. Studies show increased interest in sustainable fashion following its release (Sung, 2021).

For what concerns the Framework's objective **"Reduce"**, design and architecture demonstrate how creative practices integrate resource-efficient methodologies. It focuses on cutting waste at the source. Various creative sectors—ranging from product design to education—are embedding the reduce mindset into everyday practices, reshaping production, consumption, and disposal habits. Reducing waste in consumer goods is one of the most important challenges. *Loop Store* and *TerraCycle* tackle, through creative design, one of the most visible and persistent sources of waste: packaging. By redesigning how everyday products are sold and disposed of, these initiatives intervene at the consumer level to promote reduction. Loop Store is a revolutionary retail system that replaces single-use packaging with high-quality, durable, reusable containers conceived by creative designers. *TerraCycle* complements this approach by focusing on waste streams that are difficult to recycle, such as cigarette butts, snack wrappers, and personal care products. By collecting and repurposing creatively these items, it prevents millions of tons of waste from entering landfills. Of course, the most powerful tool for waste reduction is education and its creative alternative strategies. Serious Games like *Recycle City* takes a different but equally impactful approach, fostering behavioral change through education and gamification. This interactive digital tool teaches players how to reduce waste, optimize resource use, and implement better waste management strategies in a simulated city environment. By making sustainability engaging and accessible, the game empowers individuals—especially younger generations—to integrate waste reduction practices into their daily lives. Literary initiatives such as *Earthkeepers* by Feltrinelli also contribute by disseminating knowledge on sustainability, reducing misinformation and fostering conscious consumption: the series has the aim of increasing awareness of ecological issues through popular science works by international authors. It has made complex concepts related to climate crisis and ecological transition accessible, influencing public debate and environmental policies. Reading environmental essays has been linked to a greater tendency among readers to adopt sustainable behaviors (Young, 2018).

C&C industries often find strategies for extending product lifecycles: **"Reuse"**, unlike recycling which requires breaking down and reprocessing materials, extends the lifespan of products and resources with minimal additional energy or intervention. Some projects are directly focused on artistic and design practices that reuse discarded materials, for instance, in architecture and urban design cases, reuse emerges through modular, dismantlable structures; some initiatives, such as the *Rebuild Foundation* or *New European Bauhaus* projects, emphasize the encounter between aesthetics and sustainability, designing for disassembly so that parts can be reused across different constructions, reducing demand for new raw materials. Moreover, C&C sectors are used to develop systems of sharing, extending the life of cultural goods with best practices like *Libraries of Things*, tool-sharing initiatives, or costume rental services for theatres and festivals demonstrate how access to goods can replace ownership and promote repeated use of the same items by multiple users. Also creative co-housing projects feature shared studios, reused furniture, and communal workshops where materials are continuously circulated.

With **"Repair"**, these are two points touched when cultural sector fosters a repair and reuse culture by transforming waste into valuable assets. Several cases of repair cafés, makerspaces, and circular hubs in the cultural sector actively revive repair cultures, encouraging citizens to reuse by maintaining and fixing instead of throwing away. The well-known best case of *Patagonia*'s "Worn Wear" program normalizes garment repair, while Mud Jeans introduces a leasing system that extends product longevity (Lijzenga, 2020). Similarly, urban interventions such as *Book Forest* in Berlin recontextualize fallen trees as public bookshelves, promoting reuse both materially and intellectually. The project has encouraged free book exchange and reuse culture, reducing paper consumption and promoting reading in public spaces. It has also contributed to urban regeneration, transforming salvaged tree trunks into cultural exchange points.[1] Studies on book-sharing initiatives highlight their role in spreading sustainability and creating more engaged communities (Fassi & Motter, 2017). Projects like *Restart Project* and

---

[1] https://inhabitat.com/book-forest-fallen-tree-trunks-transformed-into-a-free-book-exchange-in-berlin/

Trash Hack Campaign (UNESCO) align with the "Repair" category of the 9R Framework, focusing on extending the life cycle of products by fixing them instead of discarding them. The first initiative organizes community repair events where people learn to fix their broken electronic devices rather than throwing them away. It promotes right-to-repair policies, advocating for manufacturers to make their products more repairable and durable. The project raises awareness about the environmental impact of electronic waste (e-waste) and empowers individuals to develop skills in repair and maintenance.

The Trash Hack Campaign (UNESCO) is a global educational initiative encourages schools and youth groups to reduce waste by repairing and reusing items instead of discarding them. It provides resources and guidance on sustainable consumption, including how to extend the life of everyday objects. By emphasizing repair culture in education, it fosters long-term behavioral change toward waste prevention and sustainability. In the transition toward a circular economy, reuse plays also a crucial role in reducing waste and maximizing the value of materials. Food waste represents a major sustainability challenge, but projects like *Disco Soup,* and *Refettorio Ambrosiano* show how surplus food can be creatively repurposed rather than discarded.

Disco Soup takes a more community-driven and cultural approach, organizing collective cooking events where volunteers prepare meals using recovered food that would otherwise be wasted. By combining creative food reuse with social engagement, Disco Soup turns waste prevention into a celebratory, shared experience, strengthening public awareness. Refettorio Ambrosiano, initiated by chef Massimo Bottura, reimagines food surplus as a tool for social good. By transforming surplus ingredients into gourmet meals for vulnerable communities, the project highlights the intersection of sustainability, gastronomy, and social justice. This initiative shifts perceptions of food waste from being a problem to being an opportunity for inclusion and nourishment. Beyond food, experiences like the one of *Plastic Bank* take a unique economic approach to plastic reuse, treating waste as a valuable resource. By setting up collection centers in coastal areas, it enables people in economically disadvantaged communities to exchange plastic waste for money, goods, or services. The recovered plastic is then reintegrated into new products, demonstrating how reuse can simultaneously drive environmental sustainability and social impact.

Also **"Refurbish"** and **"Remanufacture"** are practices evident in architectural, design and artistic approaches. Reclaimed architecture, as seen in the repositions disused spaces into dynamic cultural hubs. Indeed, refurbishing in the cultural and creative sectors involves restoring, repairing, and transforming existing materials or spaces to extend their lifespan and enhance their value.

In the 9R Framework, **"Repurpose"** means using an object or material for a new function that is different from the one it was originally designed for—without extensive reprocessing. It's about giving new life to things that might otherwise be discarded, by transforming their meaning, role, or use. In the Cultural and Creative sector, repurpose has a powerful and creative meaning that goes even beyond materials—it involves rethinking value, storytelling, and imagination. Contemporary art knows well this mental and semantic process, especially since 1913 Duchamp's read-made and Dadaists' objects like Man Ray and Francis Picabia: instead of repairing or reusing something for the same purpose, artists reinterpret discarded materials and invent new identities for them. Monuments are often re-signified through performances or installations that challenge their original narratives. For instance, *Monument Lab* (Philadelphia, USA) is a public art and history project that literally re-signifies old monuments through site-specific performances, installations, and public engagement (Eron, 2023); artists were invited to create temporary installations that challenged or expanded the dominant narratives. Karyn Olivier reimagined a Civil War memorial by surrounding it with a reflective installation that invited viewers to see themselves in the history of civil rights, not just the official heroism of the past. Tania Bruguera, a Cuban artist, proposed a counter-monument to mass incarceration, focusing on the voices of those affected by systemic injustice. And again, in London's Trafalgar Square, the Fourth Plinth—originally intended for a statue of a military leader—is now repurposed to host contemporary artworks that often challenge ideas of power, colonialism, and history. Spaces themselves can be repurposed, maintaining their structure but radically transforming their function—creating cultural value from forgotten or underused assets: there are many examples of how a former factory becomes an art gallery or cultural center, or a disused train station becomes a music venue.

"Recycle" remains fundamental within the creative economy. The adoption of circular practices in film production, such as Albert Certification in the UK, ensures that audiovisual industries reduce waste and carbon footprints. Vik Muniz's *Waste Land* exemplifies how art can transform discarded materials into powerful social commentary, reinforcing the role of culture in circularity. The fashion industry follows suit with brands like Stella McCartney adopting alternative materials such as Mylo (mushroom-based leather), demonstrating how repurposing aligns with high-end fashion. Similarly, digital initiatives like *Minecraft Education: Sustainability City* integrate circular principles into interactive learning, embedding recycling awareness into early education.

6 Conclusions: A Creative Future for Circularity

The shift toward circular economy models is not solely dependent on institutional momentum or technological innovation. A key driver is consumer demand for ethically produced, low-environmental-impact products. Studies indicate that a niche of consumers is willing to pay for sustainable alternatives, yet widespread adoption requires cultural engagement. Cultural institutions, media, and creative industries play a crucial role in shaping these demands by embedding sustainability into everyday life through aesthetic, emotional, and participatory experiences.

Indicators used in CE, such as those classified by Moraga et al. (2019), tend to focus on material efficiency and technical metrics. However, cultural indicators—such as behavioral shifts, value reorientation, and engagement levels—should be integrated to measure the true impact of CE in fostering long-term, systemic change. Creative and cultural sectors provide the narratives, experiences, and symbols that make circularity desirable, understandable, and actionable.

Cultural and creative practices are not mere complements to circular economy strategies but essential drivers of systemic change. By embedding circularity into cultural narratives, artistic practices, and creative industries, we move beyond technical solutions to cultivate a shared societal shift towards sustainability. Understanding culture as the ontological framework of circular economy allows for a more holistic transition, ensuring that high-value, high-quality material cycles are not only implemented but embraced. As CE continues to evolve, integrating cultural dimensions within its frameworks will be crucial to making sustainable economies both resilient and desirable.

References

Andrews, C., deVault, D.: Green niche market development. J. Ind. Ecol. **13**, 326–345 (2009). https://doi.org/10.1111/j.1530-9290.2009.00112.x

Aronson, E.: The return of the repressed: dissonance theory makes a comeback. Psychol. Inq. **3**(4), 303–311 (1992)

Caprariello, P.A., Reis, H.T.: To do or to have, or to share? Valuing experiences over material possessions depends on the involvement of others. J. Pers. Soc. Psychol. **104**(2), 199–215 (2013)

Carter, T., Gilovich, T.: I am what I do, not what I have: the differential centrality of experiential and material purchases to the self. J. Person. Soc. Psychol. **102**(6), 1304–1317 (2012)

Carter, T., Gilovich, T.: The relative relativity of material and experiential purchases. J. Pers. Soc. Psychol. **98**(1), 146–159 (2010)

Colucci, M., Vecchi, A.: Close the loop: evidence on the implementation of the circular economy from the Italian fashion industry. Bus. Strateg. Environ. **30**(2), 856–873 (2021)

De Jesus, A., Mendonça, S.: Lost in transition? Drivers and Barriers in the eco-innovation road to the circular economy. Ecol. Econ. **145**(2018), 75–89 (2018)

Diener, E., Seligman, M.E.P.: Beyond money: toward an economy of well-being. Psychol. Sci. Public Interest. **5**(1), 1–31 (2004)

Dunning, D., Meyerowitz, J.A., Holzberg, A.D.: Ambiguity and selfevaluation: the role of idiosyncratic trait definitions in self-serving assessments of ability. J. Pers. Soc. Psychol. **57**(6), 1082–1090 (1989)

Ellen MacArthur Foundation: "Towards the Circular Economy", Report – Opportunities for the Consumer Goods Sector, vol. 2. Ellen MacArthur Foundation, Cowes (2013)

Eron, A.R.: Monument lab: creative speculations for Philadelphia ed. by Paul M. Farber and Ken Lum, and: the battles of Germantown: effective public history in America by David W. Young. Pennsylvania Mag. Hist. Biogr. **147**(1), 69–71 (2023)

Fassi, D., Motter, R.: System-events toolbox: designing a system of events that relies on local resources to create urban places for social cohesion. Sustainability, Green IT and Education Strategies in the Twenty-first Century, pp. 525–542 (2017)

Geng, Y., Xinbei, W., Qinghua, Z., Hengxin, Z.: Regional initiatives on promoting cleaner production in China: a case of Liaoning. J. Clean. Prod. **18**, 1502–1508 (2010). https://doi.org/10.1016/j.jclepro.2010.06.028

Giovannini, E.: Utopia Sostenibile, Laterza (2020)

Gilovich, T., Kumar, A., Jampol, L.: A wonderful life: experiential consumption and the pursuit of happiness. J. Consum. Psychol. **25**, 152–165 (2015)

Hajdu, T., Hajdu, G.: The association between experiential and material expenditures and subjective well-being: new evidence from Hungarian survey data. J. Econ. Psychol. **62**, 72–86 (2017)

Howell, R.T., Hill, G.: The mediators of experiential purchases: determining the impact of psychological needs satisfaction and social comparison. J. Posit. Psychol. **4**, 511–522 (2009)

Kumar, A., Gilovich, T.: Spending on doing, not having, fosters giving. (submitted for publication-a) (2014a)

Kumar, A., Gilovich, T.: Talking about what You Did and what You have: the differential story utility of experiential and material purchases. (submitted for publication-b) (2014b)

Kunda, Z.: The case for motivated reasoning. Psychol. Bull. **108**(3), 480–498 (1990)

Lijzenga, C.: Opportunities and Challenges of Circular Business Model Growth (2020)

Matarasso, F.: A Restless Art. 2019, Available on: https://parliamentofdreams.com/writing/a-restless-art/

Mendonça, S.: National adaptive advantages. Soft innovation and marketing capabilities in periods of crisis and change. In: Teixeira, A.A.C., Silva, E., Mamede, R. (eds.) Structural Change, Competitiveness and Industrial Policy: Painful Lessons from the European Periphery, pp. 133–151. Routledge, London/New York, NY (2014)

Myers, D.G.: The funds, friends, and faith of happy people. Am. Psychol. **55**(1), 56–67 (2000)

Mylan, J., Holmes, H., Paddock, J.: Re-introducing consumption to the 'circular economy': a sociotechnical analysis of domestic food provisioning. Sustain. For. **8**(8), 1–14 (2016)

Moraga, G., Huysveld, S., Mathieux, F., Blengini, G.A., Alaerts, L., Acker, K.V., de Meester, S., Dewulf, J.: Circular economy indicators: what do they measure? Resour. Conserv. Recycl. **146**, 452–461 (2019)

Morseletto, P.: Targets for a circular economy. Resour. Conserv. Recycl. **153**, 104553 (2020)

Nussbaum, M.C.: The Fragility of Goodness: Luck and Ethics in Greek Tragedy and Philosophy, 2nd edn, 2001. Cambridge University Press, Cambridge (1986)

Nye Jr., J.S.: Soft power. Foreign Policy, 153–171 (1990). https://doi.org/10.2307/1148580

Rose, C.: The comedy of the commons: custom, commerce, and inherently public property. Univ. Chicago Law Rev. **53**(3), 711–781 (1986)

Available at: https://chicagounbound.uchicago.edu/uclrev/vol53/iss3/1

Rosenzweig, E., Gilovich, T.: Buyer's remorse or missed opportunity? Differential regrets for material and experiential purchases. J. Pers. Soc. Psychol. **102**(2), 215–223 (2012)

Sacco, P., Zamagni, S.: Teoria economica e relazioni interpersonali. Il Mulino, Bologna (2006)

Singh, P., Giacosa, E.: Cognitive biases of consumers as barriers in transition towards circular economy. Manag. Decis. **57**, 921–936 (2018). https://doi.org/10.1108/MD-08-2018-0951

Spekkink, W., Rödl, M., Charter, M. Global survey of precious plastic projects: a summary of findings (2020)

Stoneman, P.: Soft Innovation. Towards a More Complete Picture of Innovative Change (NESTA Research Report). National Endowment for Science, Technology and the Arts (NESTA), London (2009)

Suls, J.: Contributions of social comparison to physical health and wellbeing. In: Suls, J., Wallston, K. (eds.) Social Psychological Foundations of Health and Illness, pp. 226–255. Blackwell Publishers, Malden, MA (2003)

Sung, K.S.: A critical zooming in on the fast fashion industry: focusing on the documentary films the true cost (2015) and RiverBlue (2017). Asian Women. **37**(4), 49–67 (2021)

Valtteri, R., Leena, A.S., Paavo, R., Saku, J.M.: Exploring institutional drivers and barriers of the circular economy: a cross-regional comparison of China, the US, and Europe. Resour. Conserv. Recycl. **135**, 70–82 (2017)

Valencia, M., Bocken, N., Loaiza, C., De Jaeger, S.: The social contribution of the circular economy. J. Clean. Prod. **408**, 137082 (2023)

Williams, E.F., Gilovich, T.: Do people really believe they are above average? J. Exp. Soc. Psychol. **44**(4), 1121–1128 (2008)

World Happiness Report: (2020). https://worldhappiness.report/ed/2020/

White, C.J.: Culture, emotions and behavioural intentions: implications for tourism research and practice. Curr. Issue Tour. **8**(6), 510–531 (2005). https://doi.org/10.1080/13683500508668234

Young, R.L.: Confronting Climate Crises through Education: Reading our Way Forward. Lexington Books (2018)

Building the Future While Preserving the Past: Digital Tools and Community Engagement to "Re-Generate" Historic Buildings in Post-Disaster Scenarios

Mariarosaria Angrisano, Grazia Neglia(✉), and Ippolita Mecca

Engineering Department, Pegaso Telematic University, Naples, Italy
grazia.neglia@unipegaso.it

Abstract. Cultural heritage has always been recognized as a fil rouge that links the past, present, and future. Today more than ever, its existence is threatened by natural disasters, conflicts, and vandalism that have a serious impact on the entire urban fabric. Digital technology and community engagement can contribute to its safeguarding as well as to "re-generating" urban spaces and giving life back to the cultural identity that may have been lost due to disaster or war. In this perspective, rebuilding the urban spaces after a traumatic event represents a key strategy for resilience, providing cities and communities the opportunity to reinvent themselves. To this end, the paper intends to show that adaptive reuse of built heritage, when properly supported by digital technologies and collaborative and co-design multidisciplinary participatory processes, can be an effective strategy for renewing and thus preserving memories of built heritage damaged by disasters or armed conflict. The analysis of best practices for adapting historic buildings, especially those repurposed after wartime damage, clearly supports this point.

Keywords: Adaptive reuse · built heritage · community engagement · digital technologies · co-design

1 Introduction

1.1 Adaptive Reuse of Historic Buildings

Historic urban areas "are among the most abundant and diverse manifestations of our common cultural heritage, shaped by generations and constituting a key testimony to humankind's endeavors and aspirations through space and time" [1]. In recent decades, wars, natural and human-made disasters, and economic crises have severely impacted cities and people, with consequences on the global economy.

Places, buildings, and cultural heritage (CH) are expressions of the identity, traditions, and values of the communities, becoming a reference point for residents. For this reason, recovering, restoring, reconstructing, and adapting buildings is essential to give life back to the cultural identity that may have been lost due to disaster or war. Rebuilding the urban fabric after a traumatic event represents a key strategy for resilience, providing cities and communities the opportunity to reinvent themselves [2].

The adaptive reuse of historic buildings can be a successful strategy for reconstructing damaged buildings in armed conflicts or in post disaster scenarios. This approach not only contributes to preserving the original worth of the built heritage but also allows it to serve new functions while complying with sustainable development principles.

Adaptive reuse of historic buildings has less impact on the environment than new construction; it is an effective strategy for preserving its intrinsic and historical value for both current and future generations [3].

Applying the concept of adaptive reuse to existing built heritage requires not only structural and physical modifications but also changes in the use and functions of the spaces. This approach allows for the enhancement of places while preserving cultural heritage, all while considering social aspects (citizen involvement), environmental aspects (energy efficiency, waste reduction, etc.), and economic aspects (cost savings and profitability) [4–6].

In general, adaptive reuse allows for the transformation of a building to adapt it for a different use, aiming for new functionality and efficiency. In the case of historic buildings, this process should take into account their historical and cultural characteristics. Thanks to adaptive reuse, it is possible to extend the life of a building by integrating efficient systems into the existing structure that enhance its resilience and sustainability [7, 8].

Therefore, it is essential to develop integrated strategies that consider both the sustainability and cultural value of built heritage, particularly in the context of historic buildings, to guarantee their preservation and effective reuse. To ensure that recovery or regeneration interventions are effective, it is necessary to conduct a comprehensive analysis of the building, taking into account its performance, to implement ad hoc solutions. Additionally, the use of life cycle analysis (LCA) allows for the preliminary assessment of the potential impact that a project may have, not just on the building itself, but also on the surrounding community and the environment [9].

Adaptive reuse, particularly in post-disaster or post-war scenarios, offers a concrete solution for protecting and recovering the remaining heritage. This approach not only helps to preserve the memories of places and people, but it also supports the regeneration of urban areas, making cities smarter, more functional, and responsive to the needs of local communities. As a result, it is important to combine digital technologies with participatory processes, considered essential elements for implementing an adaptive reuse project that is effective and efficient.

Fostering collaboration across institutions, communities, and industry stakeholders using digital technology may be helpful in the formulation of strategies for addressing and mitigating any potential challenges. Additionally, the development of a strong and cohesive network committed to the protection and enhancement of cultural heritage, also including adaptive reuse, can facilitate the sharing of information, skills, and resources among all parties involved in the decision-making process [10].

1.2 Digital Tools for Adaptive Reuse

Digital technologies offer a significant contribution in terms of emergency prevention and management thanks to the definition of approaches focused on collecting and sharing real-time data. This enhances the monitoring and prevention of disasters [11].

Digital tools can be extremely useful even during the re-generation phase, which is a very important time to influence the sustainability of the built environment and its capacity to withstand future potential emergencies, resulting in renewed and improved well-being for the community. Among the digital technologies employed in the rebuilding process, those associated with Industry 4.0 play a significant role. These technologies, when combined with remote sensing, 3D modeling, and other tools, facilitate the development of efficient and successful solutions. In addition, digital technologies stimulate inclusive and collaborative practices that encourage and foster knowledge and information sharing across all levels. In this perspective, the idea of adaptive reuse of built heritage presents a valuable opportunity for creating more sustainable, resilient, and inclusive urban spaces. Indeed, by adopting approaches that also focus on human beings, it is possible to reconnect the built environment with the communities it belongs to.

The construction industry has significantly benefitted from digital transformation, although this transition is not yet fully achieved, mainly due to the fragmented nature of this sector. However, the adoption of digital technologies has significantly improved the sector's productivity and competitiveness, as it directly influences every stage of a project's life cycle. In addition, by transforming the concept of collaboration and co-design, digital technologies pave the way to improve sustainability. The application of these concepts to the built environment through the recovery, regeneration, reuse, and restoration of buildings aims to enhance the quality of places and the well-being of citizens while also promoting environmental, economic, and social sustainability.

Digital transformation can act as a roadmap in regeneration projects, fostering a collaborative relation among the different participants (citizens, institutions, sector stakeholders) suitable for identifying the most appropriate solutions.

1.3 Community Engagement

Cultural heritage is a fil rouge that links past, present, and future. So, it is central to safeguard, recover, and reuse it to preserve all those tangible and intangible values to pass on to future generations [5, 10]. The conservation and regeneration of historic buildings positively influence the urban landscape, as it allows for the new life of both the buildings and the surrounding environment [12]. The regeneration of the built heritage, in fact, should have a significant impact on the environment and society [6, 13]. Recognizing the interconnection between cultural heritage and community, it is essential to consider the community as a key player in the decision-making process for its protection, enhancement, and regeneration [14]. The Leeuwarden Declaration and the Faro Convention provide recognition in this sense. The latter not only emphasizes the importance of protecting cultural heritage, defined as a "group of resources inherited from the past which people identify, independently of ownership, as a reflection and expression of their constantly evolving values, beliefs, knowledge, and traditions", but also links it to the community, referred to as the "heritage community", with the goal of encouraging active engagement from society in its management [15].

The decision-making process allows for a holistic approach to various aspects related to the adaptive reuse of the built environment, ranging from the intrinsic value of the asset to its structural features, the surrounding context, and the needs of the community. The involvement of civil society and stakeholders thus becomes an important asset in project design, as it broadens the focus beyond purely technical issues [16]. Thanks to a collaborative process that fosters co-evaluation and cooperation and brings together the perspectives of industry experts and citizens, who, despite their differing experiences and skills, are both essential in identifying solutions suitable for the urban fabric [17].

1.4 Partnership Models for Built Heritage Management and Sustainability

The recovery of built heritage in a post-war or disaster scenario takes on significant importance from a cultural, environmental, and especially social perspective, as it symbolizes the identity of a community and a new opportunity for economic revival. Addressing the challenges of recovering built heritage requires adequate resources; moreover, for this to be effective, it is necessary to consider an additional aspect concerning its long-term economic sustainability and, consequently, the adoption of an appropriate management and financing model.

In this perspective, traditional financing models, mostly the exclusive prerogative of the state and public entities, may be inadequate and ineffective. It is necessary to resort to management models that involve multiple actors, as economic sustainability must cover the entire life cycle of the building from the recovery phase to management to the adaptive reuse of the asset.

Among the alternative models of management and financial sustainability to traditional ones are Public-Private Partnerships (P3), Public–Private–People Partnership (P4), and Public Private People Policy Partnerships (P5) [18–20].

P3s involve a collaboration between public and private entities, primarily aimed at providing funding for the construction, renovation, management, and maintenance of infrastructure or the provision of services. They allow access to private capital, generating revenue without burdening the public budget [18].

In P4s, the community is an active part of the partnership. This allows for greater community involvement in the recovery and long-term management of the asset [19].

P5s are characterized by the inclusion of the local political component [20].

The choice of one partnership model over another for the recovery and enhancement of built heritage cannot disregard the analysis of various aspects, including the political context in which the asset is located, the nature of the asset, the interest of the local community in relation to it, and the objectives that are intended to be pursued.

1.5 Paper Objectives

Based on previous studies [10], this paper aims to explore how digital technologies, community involvement, supported by appropriate management and sustainability models, can contribute to "re-generating" urban spaces in the aftermath of war or disasters, through the implementation of specific projects, where the goal is to protect the built heritage and reduce environmental impacts by using co-design approaches to develop more resilient and aware urban spaces and communities.

This document aims to show that adaptive reuse of built heritage, when properly supported by digital technologies and participatory processes, can be an effective strategy for renewing and thus preserving memories of built heritage damaged by disasters or armed conflict.

The analysis of best practices for adapting historic buildings, especially those damaged by war, clearly supports this point.

After analyzing the background of the paper (Sect. 1), the methodology is presented (Sect. 2), best practices of adaptive reuse of the built heritage severely damaged during armed conflict are analyzed (Sect. 3). Finally, the results and discussion are presented (Sect. 4), followed by the conclusions and prospects for future research (Sect. 5).

2 Methodology

The objective of this paper is to analyze the importance of adaptive reuse of the built heritage with a focus on key aspects characterizing this type of intervention: the role of digital technologies, the role of communities, and the importance of identifying an appropriate management model in the co-design process.

The research methodology consists of two steps. The first phase, theoretical analysis, involves a literature review. The documents were searched on Scopus using the following keywords: "adaptive reuse" AND "built heritage" OR "built environment". This has made it possible to identify the most relevant papers that have current evidence of adaptive reuse practices in the built environment. Additional supporting documentation, useful for an interdisciplinary analysis, has been collected from other libraries and online databases.

The second phase included the analysis of seven case studies that were considered to be particularly emblematic. These have been selected taking into account some particular aspects, such as the diversity of geographical and cultural contexts, the relevance to the theme, and the approach adopted in the recovery and reuse phase.

The selection of case studies aimed to highlight how in geographically and culturally distant areas the approach and motivations adopted in the recovery and reconstruction phase are very similar to each other and the relevance that the recovery of a given place has on the life of the communities.

For the analysis of these cases, other libraries and online databases were consulted. The results of these two steps are presented in the following Sect. 3.

3 Best Practices of Adaptive Reuse of Built Heritage

Interventions aimed at the adaptive reuse of the built heritage are important because they allow for the prolongation of the life of buildings, regenerating spaces, and making them accessible and usable for future generations as well. Moreover, this approach additionally has the potential to generate new economic profits [21].

These interventions can include a variety of approaches, from conservation efforts to redevelopment projects, and may focus on specific elements of a building or encompass an entire site [22, 23].

Renovating, regenerating, and adapting the built heritage requires interdisciplinary skills to minimize the impact of interventions on it and ensure the safeguarding of its historical value, taking into account the context.

Protecting the built heritage and considering it a community asset can foster community well-being. Cultural heritage is fundamental because it stimulates both urban and rural regeneration, represents the identity and values of a community, and testifies to resilience against climate change, wars, and man-made damage.

Worldwide, the number of the built heritage abandoned due to obsolescence or as a result of disasters, conflict, climatic, social, and economic events is constantly increasing. To intervene and recover this vast building stock, it is necessary to develop approaches that contribute to improving the energy, technological, and structural performance of buildings, enhancing the remaining internal resources to mitigate the environmental, economic, and social impact of the interventions [21, 24].

Although the benefits of adaptive reuse of the built environment have been recognized, challenges persist in its successful implementation, largely due to the current planning and construction regulations. This situation also affects the relationship among stakeholders, institutions, and civil society, contradicting the principles stated in the Leeuwarden Declaration [25].

The choice of a new use in the adaptive reuse of the built environment requires a holistic approach, involving all actors: citizens, institutions, and stakeholders. This evaluation must take into account various factors such as, for example, the building structure and historical value, the needs expressed by the local community in order to ensure the good's adequate integration into the urban context, the possibility of attracting capital that can ensure its management over time, as well as the choice of materials [26].

3.1 Case Studies

The following Table 1, resulting from phase two explain in Sect. 2, presents some case studies that cover different geographical and cultural backgrounds. They are united by the brutality of the military actions that involved them and that led to significant loss of human lives and the destruction of a heritage of inestimable artistic, architectural, and cultural value. In these contexts, cultural heritage has been considered a true war target since it embodies a cultural identity that the belligerents believe must be obliterated. Despite the severe wounds suffered, local communities' will and determination, supported by international, local, and private financial contributions, the use of digital technologies, and the involvement of local and international stakeholders have enabled not only the reconstruction of what was severely damaged or destroyed but also the revitalization of emblematic places that are significant for local communities as well as for the entire international community.

Table 1. Case studies. Sarajevo, Bosnia and Herzegovina

Case Studies Sarajevo, Bosnia and Herzegovina	
Background	Sarajevo experienced significant destruction to its cultural heritage during the war (1992–1995). The National Library (**Vijećnica**) and other historic buildings and monuments were destroyed or severely damaged [27, 28]
Community engagement	The reconstruction of the library started in the aftermath of war. The collaboration among international organizations and the local community was strong. Citizens were part of the entire process and did not hesitate to express their disappointment regarding the decision to transform the public library into a city hall [28–30]
Digital technologies	Digital technologies have been particularly important for both preservation and representation itself; among them, 3D models and virtual reality (VR) were used to generate digital replicas of the building [31, 32]
Impact	Thanks to the collaboration between the local and international communities, international and local funding, and the use of digital technologies, it was possible to rebuild a place symbolizing history, culture, and resilience
Pristina, Kosovo	
Background	The Kosovo War (1998–1999) left deep wounds on the city and its infrastructure, especially on the National Library "Pjetër Bogdani" of Pristina. During the conflict, the National Library interior was heavily damaged and suffered extensive loss and destruction of documents [33–35]
Community engagement	The recovery of the National Library has been an ongoing process for several years since the end of the war. The local community, along with support from international organizations and experts, committed to the process of restoring the library [33, 36]
Digital technologies	Thanks to digital technologies, it has been possible to digitize the documents stored within the library, ensuring the protection of cultural and intellectual heritage, and to design restoration interventions for the building while respecting its original structures and simultaneously optimizing energy efficiency and safety [35, 37, 38]
Impact	This process was supported by several funding sources. The collaboration between international and local actors allowed for giving new life to the library. Thanks to these synergies and the application of digital technologies, new functionalities have been integrated, while preserving the building's historical worth, making it more sustainable and resilient
Aleppo, Syria	
Background	The historic center of Aleppo has been subjected to systematic destruction aimed at erasing its identity and cultural value during the conflict (2012–2016). Many historic buildings, symbolic sites, and traditional markets have been destroyed or irreparably damaged [39, 40]
Community engagement	Despite the commitment of the local and international community, considering the extent of the devastation, the recovery process in Aleppo is long and complex. Local community groups, supported by the international community and stakeholders, were actively involved in the city's recovery process and had a key role in defining solutions for cultural heritage restoration [39, 40]
Digital technologies	Digital technologies, such as photogrammetry and 3D models were used to map damaged areas and digitally preserve the city's memory, while GIS technologies have been employed to collect data on building conditions and plan targeted and sustainable interventions. Furthermore, digital twins of the damaged buildings and historical sites have been developed, making it possible to virtually reconstruct the city and assess the best recovery options [41–43]
Impact	Although Aleppo is still in the process of recovering, it is nonetheless a clear example of how community engagement, the application of digital technology, and adequate international and local funding can contribute to protecting and enhancing cultural heritage in post-war scenarios

(continued)

Table 1. (*continued*)

Case Studies Sarajevo, Bosnia and Herzegovina	
Homs, Syria	
Background	Homs is an important Syrian cultural center devastated by the civil war (2011–2014), which destroyed historic buildings, symbolic monuments, urban infrastructure, and service facilities. The extent of the damage caused by the conflict is enormous [44]
Community engagement	The recovery of the city, which began at the end of the conflict, has been slow and has had to adapt to the precarious situation in the country; however, NGOs and international organizations have been working with the local community to help rebuild the city. The participatory process involving citizens has represented a way to strengthen social cohesion and stimulate the community's sense of belonging [44, 45]
Digital technologies	Digital technologies have been a valuable tool for post-war reconstruction. Homs has benefited from the use of 3D models to analyze the degradation of buildings and simulate various restoration scenarios. Drones were employed to collect high-resolution images of the damaged buildings and to reconstruct digital models. Furthermore, a GIS system was developed to map the damage and plan the reconstruction efficiently [46, 47]
Impact	The initiatives and projects launched for the recovery of the city, funded by various national and international sources, have had a significant impact on the life of the community. Citizens' involvement and the use of digital technologies have made the process of reconstructing the city and restoring Homs as a cultural center and symbol of resilience after the conflict
Mosul, Iraq	
Background	Mosul, one of the oldest cities in Iraq, was the target of systematic and deliberate destruction of its cultural heritage by terrorist groups (2014–2017), becoming a symbol of devastation and destruction of Iraq's heritage [48]
Community engagement	The local community, supported by international stakeholders and both governmental and non-governmental organizations, has played an active and decisive role in all phases of Mosul's reconstruction. The projects and activities launched were numerous [48–51]
Digital technologies	Digital technologies, crucial in the reconstruction process, contributed to the documentation and preservation of the local cultural heritage. GIS, 3D digital models generated through photogrammetry, were used to map the entire site and create a detailed digital representation of the city and its heritage [52]
Impact	The participatory process was fundamental in restoring the cultural identity of the city the recovery and reconstruction of Mosul was made possible thanks to the substantial funds received from local and international sources. The combination of digitization and community participation has enabled the recovery of one of Iraq's most precious historical assets as well as to address the physical, psychological and social damage of the conflict
Kabul, Afghanistan	
Background	The National Museum of Kabul, which once housed one of the most significant archives of afghan cultural heritage, suffered severe damage during decades of conflicts (1990s) [53]
Community engagement	The recovery process of the National Museum has been marked by a series of initiatives and projects launched over the years that have highlighted the commitment and interest of both the local community and the entire international community, which have spared no effort in supporting activities for the recovery and restoration of the museum [53]
Digital technologies	Digital technologies have been widely used both to preserve collections and to make them accessible. Thanks to 3D photogrammetry, digital copies of the artifacts have been created, allowing restoration in case of future damage, while digitization has contributed to virtually preserving the heritage, creating a globally accessible digital archive, which is also useful for research [54]

(*continued*)

Table 1. (*continued*)

Case Studies Sarajevo, Bosnia and Herzegovina	
Impact	Digital technologies, the commitment of the community and the financial support received to fund restoration activities have allowed for the reconstruction of an important physical space for the city, while strengthened the sense of national identity that also comes from cultural heritage
Beirut, Lebanon	
Background	Beit Beirut (Yellow House) is a historic building located in the Sodeco neighborhood of Beirut. A strategic point during the Lebanese Civil War (1975–1990), it suffered severe damage due to its location along the Green Line that separated the Christian and the Muslim areas [48]
Community engagement	The restoration project, started in the following years, involved architects, historians, and the local community. These groups worked collaboratively to provide a genuine representation of the city's collective memory, defining innovative interventions that preserved the ancient forms while highlighting the wounds suffered during the conflict [48, 55]
Digital technologies	Digital tools adopted have played an important role in documenting the recovery process of the building and in its presentation, increasing visitor engagement and fostering a deeper understanding of Beirut's history [56]
Impact	The recovery of Beit Beirut, a symbol of resilience, made possible by local and international funding, has had a significant impact on the community. Digital technologies have represented an additional tool through which to engage the community, especially the younger generations, and reach a wider audience

4 Results and Discussion

Even though disasters are usually associated with armed conflicts or catastrophes that involve the need to rebuild cities or certain areas particularly affected by these events, radical economic, political, and social changes can also have similar effects and require a profound revision and regeneration of the territory.

The technology-community combination for the implementation of activities aimed at the adaptive reuse of the built heritage fosters a strong bond between the community and the places and, on the other hand, to assess and adopt the best solutions based on the community's needs in order to create an urban fabric more functional and smarter [2]. Thanks to technology, it is indeed possible to establish a digital connection between communities and the built environment.

The participation of the local community in the decision-making process is fundamental for preserving and improving the built heritage. So, it is important to carry out a stakeholder analysis to identify all those who will be actively involved in the project, as well as to define their level of involvement in the process.

Additionally, digital technologies play an important role as they facilitate interaction among all parties involved and help digitize heritage, making it accessible to a broader audience [3, 12, 57].

Digital tools may also be employed to mitigate the social repercussions of a disaster. They are very useful not only during the risk prevention and management phase but also in supporting the psychological and emotional aspects of the community following the loss of the built environment, contributing significantly to the recovery operations of the impacted areas [11].

Urbanization presents significant challenges in managing natural or man-made disasters, given the speed at which cities develop and grow. Planning smart and resilient urban actions and environments is important to protect citizens, infrastructure, and cultural heritage.

Urban design and regeneration can involve bottom-up approaches because the aim of this type of design is strongly focused on the needs of users. Therefore, community involvement in a co-design process can contribute to the creation of more sustainable environments from an environmental, social, and economic perspective. The heterogeneity of the subjects involved in the co-creative process can therefore be a strength because it offers more perspectives and viewpoints, but at the same time, it can represent a weakness precisely related to this aspect. For this reason, communication and the tools used to convey information become the key to a shared language.

Furthermore, the choice of a partnership model, such as the P4 type (Public–Private–People Partnership), can ensure authentic and meaningful involvement of the local community, capable of achieving sustainable results and promoting social inclusion and a deeper bond between the community and cultural heritage [18–20].

In resilient cities, in addition to risk assessment, community involvement is also of particular importance, along with the use of digital technologies. The latter provide significant support in the process; on one hand, they facilitate communication, and on the other hand, they are capable of generating, collecting, and analyzing real-time data that can be shared among all the parties involved, improving predictive analysis and reducing response time in the event of a disaster and in post-disaster reconstruction. The involvement of the community and its participation in the co-creative and decision-making process of places and spaces, along with a co-evolutionary approach, enhances resilience even in the absence of catastrophic and/or alarming situations. Organizing the active participation of the community and its autonomy and resilience, along with access to data, information, and resources, ensures the social sustainability of citizens and a better response to local needs.

In this perspective, bottom-up urban planning is to be preferred over traditional top-down planning. This is valid both in the context of the adaptive reuse of a built asset and for the protection of cultural heritage in a situation of armed conflict or in post-disaster scenarios [10].

Cultural heritage defines a society's roots, values, historical memory, traditions, and identity. If not adequately preserved, regenerated, and adapted, time, conflicts, vandalism, and climate change have the potential to damage or wear down this heritage. Fortunately, it is now possible to safeguard the ongoing preservation of built heritage, as local and international communities have the appropriate resources to address these challenges.

Most of the studies examined emphasize the critical importance of two key factors that influence the success of built heritage preservation and reuse interventions: the role of digital technologies in the construction sector as tools for the protection and enhancement of cultural heritage, as well as tools capable of connecting all of the players in the process, and the importance of involving civil society in the decision-making processes.

Digital technologies thanks to an in-depth life cycle analysis improve decision-making processes, encourage collaboration among project stakeholders by facilitating the sharing of information and data, and support the design of effective solutions and services. Digital technologies are considered essential for the planning, development, and redefinition of processes through a co-creative and collaborative approach among citizens, institutions, and stakeholders in order to address the transition towards sustainability and digitalization of urban spaces.

Although digital technologies are crucial for development and social inclusion, disparities in the presence and access to digital infrastructures and adequate training that can bridge the digital divide and provide all the necessary tools to achieve an adequate level of digital literacy still persist today, especially in the developing countries and in contexts affected by armed conflicts and disasters. This gap consequently deprives millions of people of the opportunity to actively participate in social life, with a negative impact that also reflects on education, healthcare, and the economy [59–61].

The aspect related to the involvement of civil society also highlights the close connection between cultural heritage and communities and the importance of sharing and participation in the decision-making process regarding the protection and/or reuse of built heritage, as defined in the Leeuwarden Declaration and the Faro Convention, so that interventions can have a positive impact from environmental, social, and economic perspectives.

To ensure the long-term success of recovery and adaptive reuse projects of built heritage, it is essential to establish a participatory governance model that should facilitate ongoing management and maintenance of the recovered asset while assessing the social, economic, and environmental impact connected to the recovery and reuse project over the short, medium, and long term. By adopting a partnership model supporting a bottom-up approach, it is possible to stimulate and improve citizen participation in social innovation processes, with the aim of finding solutions that are sustainable from environmental, economic, and social perspectives. This approach allows for addressing significant challenges by identifying potential gaps and needs already in the early stages of the co-design process in order to develop tailored strategies and interventions that meet the needs of local communities and to start the process of renewal.

Effective risk planning that incorporates digital tools and engages the community can significantly reduce the harmful impacts of a disaster on both lives and infrastructure. Involving the community at every stage of the disaster management process promotes resilience and accountability.

The integration of digital technologies, regulatory tools, and optimized participatory processes represents the ideal solution for creating virtuous pathways. In this way, the continuous exchange of information, data, cross-disciplinary skills, and resources can concretely contribute to addressing challenges.

The originality of the study lies in the interdisciplinary approach adopted, which has made it possible to analyze and relate various aspects relating to the protection of cultural heritage, especially in a post-war scenario, in order to make more evident the dynamics that drive a process of recovery and reuse of built heritage functional to the acquisition of knowledge useful for implementing adaptive reuse projects sustainable over time because effectively able to take into account the identity, the history, and the values of the places and peoples who live there.

The advancements that this study is bringing to the research field are mostly related to understanding, through the analysis of best practices, how adaptive reuse of built heritage, when properly supported by digital technologies, can be an effective strategy for renewing and thus preserving the intrinsic value of built heritage damaged by disasters or armed conflict. The role of technological innovations alone is not sufficient to ensure the preservation of cultural heritage. Innovations are necessary; however, it is essential to operationally connect them (AI, ICT, nanotechnologies, etc.) with the humanities/social sciences.

Furthermore, participatory processes can play a fundamental role in preserving, over time, the memory of cultural heritage afflicted by conflicts or disasters. Actively involving local communities in the conservation and enhancement of symbolic places, thus allowing future generations to inherit not only the tangible history but also the emotional and identity significance of these assets that would otherwise risk being forgotten.

5 Conclusions

The adaptive reuse of built heritage is a key element, fostering radical innovation in various locations, also thanks to the use of digital technologies, with significant repercussions from an environmental, social, and economic perspective. This approach, in fact, allows for the protection of the environment by reducing natural resource consumption and waste production, enhancing existing community assets, and engaging the local population in a process of co-design, sustainability, and resilience, ultimately leading to cost savings.

Research has highlighted the importance of community and digital technologies in the implementation of this process, regardless of the specific context or asset addressed.

The case studies analyzed clearly show that, even in times of armed conflict and disasters, community participation and digital technologies are key tools for the restoration and adaptive reuse of historic buildings. Their combination, in fact, simplifies buildings restoration as well as contributes to restore historical memory and social cohesion in local communities, so contributing to overcoming the wounds left by conflicts.

Through adaptive reuse, it is possible to recover and pass on values and traditions, as well as the identity of the community to which the heritage belongs, to future generations. This strengthens the connection between the heritage and its citizens, fostering intelligent, aware, and resilient cities and societies that can effectively address and mitigate the impacts of potential disasters or conflicts.

Digital technologies not only facilitate the adaptive reuse of cultural heritage but also serve as essential tools for its protection, enhancement, and regeneration. With these digital tools, it becomes possible to collect, manage, and share data and information in real-time, offering all parties a comprehensive view of the entire process. Digitalization can also contribute to creating a virtual archive of cultural heritage and making it accessible to institutions, professionals, and the community. This accessibility is important for responding to catastrophic events or armed conflicts, and it also aids in evaluating how built heritage has evolved over the years, particularly in terms of adaptive reuse or energy retrofitting.

The community is another pillar of this process. A bottom-up approach enables the development of projects and interventions that respond to the real needs of citizens and are effectively integrated into the urban fabric. Furthermore, it fosters the creation of synergies and enhances awareness, contributing to building an active and resilient community.

Due to the heterogeneity of the built heritage worldwide and the unique characteristics of its locations, it is not possible to define a standardized approach that can be replicated in every context, as well as it is not possible to identify a partnership model that is replicable in every context, but to identify, from time to time, one that, after careful planning, is able to ensure effective, sustainable, and long-term management of the built heritage. Therefore, future research and studies should focus on the interconnection between adaptive reuse, digital tools, and community active participation in the decision-making process in order to define new strategies and methodologies for making urban areas more resilient and citizen-friendly.

The next step of this research will consist of identifying calls and projects, both national and international, focused on the adaptive reuse of built heritage, to implement an innovative and participatory ecosystem that, through collaborative, co-creative, and multidisciplinary approaches, can foster the creation of a transnational network for sharing experiences and best practices. This ecosystem should encourage and promote innovation and social and digital inclusion, contributing to overcoming the digital divide and implementing sustainable interventions.

Author Contributions. Conceptualization, G.N., M.A., and I.M.; methodology, G.N., and M.A.; formal analysis, G.N., M.A., and I.M.; investigation G.N.; data curation, G.N., and M.A.; writing—original draft preparation, G.N., M.A.; writing, review and editing, G.N., M.A.; supervision, G.N., M.A., and I.M. All authors have read and agreed to the published version of the manuscript.

Funding. FRC 2024 project Pegaso Telematic University. "Materiali e tecnologie sostenibili per il riuso degli edifici storici in una prospettiva Circolare - CIR-TECH", CUP FRC 2024.

G.N. was supported by a Ph.D. fellowship programme within the XXXIX Cycle of Doctoral Course in "Digital Transformation", funded by the Ministero dell'Università e della Ricerca (MUR)—D.M. 117/2023, Grant No. 39–033-E1-DOT238M9ZB-9959, CUP B63C23001310003.

Data Availability Statement. Data are contained within the article.

Conflicts of Interest. The authors have no competing interests to declare that are relevant to the content of this article.

References

1. ICOMOS International Cultural Tourism Charter: Principles and Guidelines for Managing Tourism at Places of Cultural and Heritage Significance. (2002). http://www.icomos.no/wp-content/uploads/2014/04/ICTC-Charter.pdf, last accessed 17 Feb 2025
2. Sowińska-Heim, J.: Adaptive reuse of architectural heritage and its role in the post-disaster reconstruction of urban identity: post-communist Łódź. Sustain. For. **12**, 8054 (2020). https://doi.org/10.3390/su12198054
3. Angrisano, M., Nocca, F., Scotto Di Santolo, A.: Multidimensional evaluation framework for assessing cultural heritage adaptive reuse projects: the case of the seminary in Sant'Agata de' Goti (Italy). Urban. Science. **8**, 50 (2024). https://doi.org/10.3390/urbansci8020050

4. Andreucci, M.B., Karagözler, S.: Adaptive reuse of existing buildings. In: Bragança, L., Griffiths, P., Askar, R., Salles, A., Ungureanu, V., Tsikaloudaki, K., Bajare, D., Zsembinszki, G., Cvetkovska, M. (eds.) Circular Economy Design and Management in the Built Environment, pp. 283–294. Springer Nature, Cham (2025). https://doi.org/10.1007/978-3-031-73490-8_11
5. Nocca, F., Angrisano, M.: The multidimensional evaluation of cultural heritage regeneration projects: a proposal for integrating level(s) tool—the case study of villa Vannucchi in San Giorgio a Cremano (Italy). Land. **11**, 1568 (2022). https://doi.org/10.3390/land11091568
6. De Wolf, C., Bocken, N.: Digital transformation of the built environment towards a regenerative future. In: De Wolf, C., Çetin, S., Bocken, N.M.P. (eds.) A Circular Built Environment in the Digital Age, pp. 259–275. Springer International Publishing, Cham (2024). https://doi.org/10.1007/978-3-031-39675-5_15
7. Nasrullah, N., Syafri, S.: Adaptive reuse in architecture: transforming heritage buildings for modern functionality. J. Acad. Sci. **1**, 395–406 (2024). https://doi.org/10.59613/69jqt639
8. Hu, M., Świerzawski, J.: Assessing the environmental benefits of adaptive reuse in historical buildings. A case study of a life cycle assessment approach. Sustainable. Environment. **10**, 2375439 (2024). https://doi.org/10.1080/27685511.2024.2375439
9. Cinieri, V., Zamperini, E.: Lifecycle approach for widespread built heritage: potentialities and criticalities. In: REHAB 2017 - 3rd International Conference on Preservation, Maintenance and Rehabilitation of Historical Buildings and Structures, pp. 1129–1137 (2017)
10. Neglia, G., Angrisano, M., Mecca, I., Fabbrocino, F.: Cultural heritage at risk in world conflicts: digital tools' contribution to its preservation. Heritage. **7**, 6343–6365 (2024). https://doi.org/10.3390/heritage7110297
11. Baraldo, M., Di Giuseppantonio Di Franco, P.: Place-centred emerging technologies for disaster management: a scoping review. Int. J. Disast. Risk Reduct. **112**, 104782 (2024). https://doi.org/10.1016/j.ijdrr.2024.104782
12. Gravagnuolo, A., Angrisano, M., Bosone, M., Buglione, F., De Toro, P., Fusco Girard, L.: Participatory evaluation of cultural heritage adaptive reuse interventions in the circular economy perspective: a case study of historic buildings in Salerno (Italy). J. Urban Manag. **13**, 107–139 (2024). https://doi.org/10.1016/j.jum.2023.12.002
13. Verardi, F., Angrisano, M., Fusco Girard, L.: New development policies for the internal areas of southern Italy. General principles for the valorization of rural areas in Calabria region: Nuove politiche di sviluppo per le aree interne del Mezzogiorno. Principi generali per la valorizzazione Dei borghi rurali della Regione Calabria. Valori e Valutazioni. **33**, 105–116 (2023). https://doi.org/10.48264/VVSIEV-20233308
14. Gravagnuolo, A., Bosone, M., Micheletti, S., Angrisano, M., Fusco Girard, L.: Towards participatory, dynamic, co-evolutionary evaluation for circular adaptive reuse of cultural heritage: the experimentation of Salerno Circular City of health. In: Fusco Girard, L., Gravagnuolo, A. (eds.) Adaptive Reuse of Cultural Heritage, pp. 349–376. Springer International Publishing, Cham (2025). https://doi.org/10.1007/978-3-031-67628-4_13
15. Council of Europe (COE): Convention on the Value of Cultural Heritage for Society. Council of Europe Treaty Series—No. 199. Faro. (27 October 2005). https://rm.coe.int/1680083746, last accessed 28 Feb 2025
16. Dell'Ovo, M., Dell'Anna, F., Simonelli, R., Sdino, L.: Enhancing the cultural heritage through adaptive reuse. A multicriteria approach to evaluate the Castello Visconteo in Cusago (Italy). Sustain. For. **13**, 4440 (2021). https://doi.org/10.3390/su13084440
17. Rossitti, M., Oteri, A.M., Sarnataro, M., Torrieri, F.: La dimensione sociale del riuso del patrimonio architettonico. Riflessioni teoriche a partire da un caso studio in Campania. AHR., 178–211 (2022). https://doi.org/10.14633/AHR354
18. Žuvela, A., Šveb Dragija, M., Jelinčić, D.A.: Partnerships in heritage governance and management: review study of public–civil, public–private and public–private–community partnerships. Heritage. **6**, 6862–6880 (2023). https://doi.org/10.3390/heritage6100358

19. Boniotti, C.: The public–private–people partnership (P4) for cultural heritage management purposes. JCHMSD. **13**, 1–14 (2023). https://doi.org/10.1108/JCHMSD-12-2020-0186
20. Fabbri, G., Dapit, A.: The 5P model: Public Private People Policy Partnerships A novel concept for the renovation and regeneration of public buildings for cultural heritage management purposes. In Proceedings of the International Symposium on Technologies for Smart City, Malaga, Spain, 11–12 November 2019. https://smartcitycluster.org/wp-content/uploads/2022/01/Paper_The-5P-model_Public-Private-People-Policy-Partnerships.pdf, last accessed 30 Apr 2025
21. Abastante, F., Lami, I.M., Mecca, B.: Performance indicators framework to analyse factors influencing the success of six urban cultural regeneration cases. In: Bevilacqua, C., Calabrò, F., Della Spina, L. (eds.) New Metropolitan Perspectives, pp. 886–897. Springer International Publishing, Cham (2021). https://doi.org/10.1007/978-3-030-48279-4_83
22. Lin, M., Roders, A.P., Nevzgodin, I., De Jonge, W.: Mind the diversity: defining intervention concepts of built heritage in international doctrinal documents. Built Herit. **8**, 24 (2024). https://doi.org/10.1186/s43238-024-00139-y
23. Bullen, P., Love, P.: Factors influencing the adaptive re-use of buildings. J. Eng. Des. Technol. **9**, 32–46 (2011). https://doi.org/10.1108/17260531111121459
24. Ingaramo, R., Lami, I.M., Robiglio, M.: How to activate the value in existing stocks through adaptive reuse: an incremental architecture strategy. Sustain. For. **14**, 5514 (2022). https://doi.org/10.3390/su14095514
25. Ikiz Kaya, D., Dane, G., Pintossi, N., Koot, C.A.M.: Subjective circularity performance analysis of adaptive heritage reuse practices in The Netherlands. Sustain. Cities Soc. **70**, 102869 (2021). https://doi.org/10.1016/j.scs.2021.102869
26. Torrieri, F., Fumo, M., Sarnataro, M., Ausiello, G.: An integrated decision support system for the sustainable reuse of the former monastery of "Ritiro del Carmine" in Campania Region. Sustain. For. **11**, 5244 (2019). https://doi.org/10.3390/su11195244
27. Walasek, H.: Cultural heritage and memory after ethnic cleansing in post-conflict Bosnia-Herzegovina. Int. Rev. Red Cross. **101**(1), 273–294 (2019). https://doi.org/10.1017/S1816383119000237
28. Milan, C.: The mobilization for spatial justice in divided societies: urban commons, trust reconstruction, and socialist memory in Bosnia and Herzegovina. East Eur. Polit. Soc. Cult. **36**, 669–691 (2022). https://doi.org/10.1177/08883254211005173
29. Atabay, Z.E., Macedonio, A., Teba, T., Unal, Z.: Destruction, heritage and memory: post-conflict memorialisation for recovery and reconciliation. JCHMSD. **14**, 477–496 (2024). https://doi.org/10.1108/JCHMSD-06-2021-0103
30. Bartlett, W.: Heritage and local economic development. In: Bold, J., Cherry, M. (eds.) The Politics of Heritage Regeneration in South-East Europe, pp. 137–139. Council of Europe, Strasbourg (2016) ISBN 9789287181602
31. Rizvić, S., Sadžak, A., Buza, E., Chalmers, A.: Virtual reconstruction and digitalization of cultural heritage sites in Bosnia and Herzegovina. Rev. Natl. Center Digit. **12**, 82–90 (2008) http://elib.mi.sanu.ac.rs/files/journals/ncd/12/ncd12082.pdf, last accessed 28 Feb 2025
32. Ramic-Brkic, B., Cosovic, M., Rizvic, S.: Cultural heritage digitalization in BiH: state-of-the-art review and future trends. VIPERC@ IRCDL. **8**, 39–49 (2019) https://ceur-ws.org/Vol-2320/paper6.pdf, last accessed 30 Apr 2025
33. Eppich, R., Ramku, B., Binakaj, N.: The National Library of Kosovo "Pjetër Bogdani" rapid condition assessment and documentation. Int. Arch. Photogramm. Remote Sens. Spatial Inf. Sci. **XLII-2/W5**, 215–219 (2017). https://doi.org/10.5194/isprs-archives-XLII-2-W5-215-2017
34. Kumaraku, L., Pula, D.: Identity of architecture: the case of the national library of Kosovo. AJA. **9**, 281–298 (2023). https://doi.org/10.30958/aja.9-3-2

35. Bashota, S., Kokollari, B.: Kosova libraries: History and development. World Library and Information Congress: 76th IFLA General Conference and Assembly, 10-15 August 2010, Gothenburg, Sweden. 1–14, 5 (2010). https://www.ifla.org/past-wlic/2010/136-bashota-en.pdf, last accessed 30 Apr 2025
36. Kosovo Architecture Foundation, Getty Foundation: Conservation and Management Plan: The National Library of Kosovo "Pjetër Bogdani". Prishtina, Kosovo. (2017). https://www.getty.edu/foundation/pdfs/kim/kosovo_architecture_foundation_cmp_kosovo_national_library.pdf, last accessed 30 Apr 2025
37. Olluri, A., Shatri, D.B.: The libraries of Kosovo: a historical overview. Library Trends Library Trends. **63**(4), 697–703 (2015). https://doi.org/10.1353/lib.2015.0017
38. Muharremi, I.H.: Art in the architecture of the national and university library of Kosovo. AIS–Archit. Image Stud., 20–31 (2024). https://doi.org/10.48619/AIS.V5I1.924
39. Aboasfour, Y., Nunes, L.: The recovery of historical buildings in post-war Aleppo. ARO. **12**, 44–51 (2024). https://doi.org/10.14500/aro.11488
40. Isakhan, B., Meskell, L.: Local perspectives on heritage reconstruction after conflict: a public opinion survey of Aleppo. Int. J. Herit. Stud. **30**, 821–839 (2024). https://doi.org/10.1080/13527258.2024.2342288
41. Pavelka, K., Šedina, J., Raeva, P., Hůlková, M.: Modern processing capabilities of analog data from documentation of the great Omayyad mosque in Aleppo, Syria, damaged in civil war. Int. Arch. Photogramm. Remote Sens. Spatial Inf. Sci. **XLII-2/W5**, 561–565 (2017). https://doi.org/10.5194/isprs-archives-XLII-2-W5-561-2017
42. Fangi, G.: Aleppo - before and after. Int. Arch. Photogramm. Remote Sens. Spatial Inf. Sci. **XLII-2/W9**, 333–338 (2019). https://doi.org/10.5194/isprs-archives-XLII-2-W9-333-2019
43. Dayoub, B., Yang, P., Omran, S., Zhang, Q., Dayoub, A.: Digital silk roads: leveraging the metaverse for cultural tourism within the belt and road initiative framework. Electronics. **13**, 2306 (2024). https://doi.org/10.3390/electronics13122306
44. Zin Eddin, M.: Post-war reconstruction of cities (reconstruction of Baba Amr Neighbourhood in the City of Homs, Syria). Builder. **322**, 71–77 (2024). https://doi.org/10.5604/01.3001.0054.4813
45. UN-Habitat: Baba Amr: Neighbourhood Profile. (2015). https://unhabitat.org/sites/default/files/download-manager-files/Baba%20Amr%20Neighbourhood%20Profile.pdf, last accessed 30 Apr 2025
46. Belal, A., Shcherbina, E.: Smart-technology in city planning of post-war cities. IOP Conf. Ser. Mater. Sci. Eng. **365**, 022043 (2018). https://doi.org/10.1088/1757-899X/365/2/022043
47. Belal, A., Shcherbina, E.: Heritage in post-war period challenges and solutions. IFAC-PapersOnLine. **52**, 252–257 (2019). https://doi.org/10.1016/j.ifacol.2019.12.491
48. Ali, S.H., Sherzad, M.F., Alomairi, A.H.: Managing strategies to revitalize urban cultural heritage after wars: the center of the old city of Mosul as a Case Study. Buildings. **12**, 1298 (2022). https://doi.org/10.3390/buildings12091298
49. Isakhan, B., Meskell, L.: Rebuilding Mosul: public opinion on foreign-led heritage reconstruction. Coop. Confl. **59**, 379–404 (2024). https://doi.org/10.1177/00108367231177796
50. Al-Daffaie, Y., Abdelmonem, M.G.: Reversing displacement: navigating the spontaneity of spatial networks of craft, tradition and memory in post-war Old Mosul. Cities. **142**, 104559 (2023). https://doi.org/10.1016/j.cities.2023.104559
51. Larkin, C., Rudolf, I.: Iraqi heritage restoration, grassroots interventions and post-conflict recovery: reflections from Mosul. J. Soc. Archaeol. **24**, 33–57 (2024). https://doi.org/10.1177/14696053231220908
52. Vincent, M.L., Gutierrez, M.F., Coughenour, C., Manuel, V., Bendicho, L.-M., Remon-dino, F., Fritsch, D.: Crowd-sourcing the 3D digital reconstructions of lost cultural heritage. In: 2015 Digital Heritage, pp. 171–172. IEEE, Granada (2015). https://doi.org/10.1109/DigitalHeritage.2015.7413863

53. Mulholland, R.: Culture, education and conflict: the relevance of critical conservation pedagogies for post-conflict Afghanistan. Stud. Conserv. **68**, 283–297 (2023). https://doi.org/10.1080/00393630.2022.2025706
54. Filigenzi, A.: Technology and humanities: some reflections on the future of afghan cultural heritage. In: Stein, G. (ed.) Preserving the Cultural Heritage of Afghanistan: Proceedings of the International Conference Held at Kabul University, November 2014, pp. 75–168. The Oriental Institute, University of Chicago, Chicago, Illinois (2017) https://oi.uchicago.edu/sites/oi.uchicago.edu/files/uploads/shared/docs/Publications/Misc/preserving-cultural-heritage-afghanistan.pdf, last accessed 21 Feb 2025
55. Darwish, S.M.: Exploring a new design approach to revive the damaged heritage buildings in post-disaster cities. Archit. Plann. J. **27** (2021). https://doi.org/10.54729/2789-8547.1141
56. Mohareb, N., Selim, G., Samahy, E.E.: Digital storytelling: youth's vision of Beirut's contested heritage. Storytell. Self Soc. **18**, 31–55 (2022). https://doi.org/10.1353/sss.2022.0005
57. Gravagnuolo, A., Micheletti, S., Bosone, M.: A participatory approach for "circular" adaptive reuse of cultural heritage. Building a heritage community in Salerno, Italy. Sustain. For. **13**, 4812 (2021). https://doi.org/10.3390/su13094812
58. Angrisano, M., Nocca, F.: Urban regeneration strategies for implementing the circular city model: the key role of the community engagement. In: Gervasi, O., Murgante, B., Rocha, A.M.A.C., Garau, C., Scorza, F., Karaca, Y., Torre, C.M. (eds.) Computational Science and Its Applications—ICCSA 2023 Workshops, pp. 359–376. Springer Nature, Switzerland, Cham (2023). https://doi.org/10.1007/978-3-031-37117-2_25
59. Heeks, R.: Digital inequality beyond the digital divide: conceptualizing adverse digital incorporation in the global South. Inf. Technol. Dev. **28**, 688–704 (2022). https://doi.org/10.1080/02681102.2022.2068492
60. Danial, A., Rafiq, A.H.: Farhan Izzuddin: bridging the digital divide: ensuring access to technology in education for all children. icistech. **2**, 288–293 (2022). https://doi.org/10.62951/icistech.v2i1.148
61. Cocaj, H.: The lack of IT on post-conflict regions: calls for increased technology in education systems—Case Study. Int. J. Inf. Commun. Technol. Educ. **18**, 1–23 (2022). https://doi.org/10.4018/IJICTE.315613

Transport Infrastructures for Smart Cities (TISC 2025)

Interpretable Crash Severity Prediction Models to Improve Cyclist Safety

Giuseppe Cappelli[1,2](✉) ⓘ, Sofia Nardoianni[1] ⓘ, Mauro D'Apuzzo[1] ⓘ, and Vittorio Nicolosi[2] ⓘ

[1] University of Cassino and Southern Lazio, Via G. Di Biasio 43, 03043 Cassino, Italy
{giuseppe.cappelli1,sofia.nardoianni,dapuzzo}@unicas.it,
cppgpp01@uniroma2.it
[2] University of Rome "Tor Vergata", Via del Politecnico, 1, 00133 Rome, Italy
nicolosi@uniroma2.it

Abstract. This study focuses on 3 years (2016–2018) of cyclist crashes in the City of Rome, Italy. As the first step, a statistical analysis was carried out. Several Cycling Crash Models were developed by using Logistic Regression Models, with a deep dive into the most influencing variables. The two proposed models at intersections and single-lane carriageways have a *McFadden* score or *pseudo-R^2* of *0.3976809* and *0.4495008*, respectively. The findings show that visibility does not play a key role in leading to a crash with a cyclist; sunny weather is positively correlated to crashes in intersections, while dry surfaces increase the chances of having crashes on single-lane carriageways, such as also the location of these roads in extra-urban environments and autumn and winter seasons. Weekdays are also related to an increase in the probability of having a crash at intersections and on single-lane carriageways. Cyclist crashes are more likely to happen in the evening and nighttime hours. Vertical and horizontal signposting decreases the probability of crashes in intersections and single-lane carriageways. High values of average daily traffic (>2000 vehicles/day) are strongly related to crashes on single-lane carriageways, and high speeds (>50 km/h) increase the probability of fatal crashes in intersections and on single-lane carriageways.

Keywords: Sustainable Mobility · Road Safety · Cyclists Safety · Cyclist Crash Severity · Cyclist Crash Models

1 Introduction

Back in 2004, on World Health Day, the *World Report on Road Traffic Injury Prevention* was launched by the World Health Organization (WHO) and the World Bank, as one of the first documents to highlight the unsustainable, unacceptable, and unsafe road traffic system [1]. As a first result of this joint action, in 2009 there was the *First Global Ministerial Conference on Road Safety* in the Russian Federation; this led to the adoption of the *Moscow Declaration*, with the declaration of *Decade of Action for Road Safety 2011–2020* [2]. The first *Global status report on road safety: Time for action* document dates back to the same year [3]. In 2010, the *Decade of Action for Road Safety 2011–2020* was launched: the aim was to reverse the trend of deaths on the road [4]. The Global Plan was launched in May of the following year [5].

Ten years later, in September 2020, the UN General Assembly declared the *Decade of Action for Road Safety 2021–2030*, to reduce the number of deaths on roads by at least half and promote sustainable urban mobility, in line with the Stockholm Declaration [6, 7].

More ambitious targets are set by the European Commission, with *Vision Zero*, a strategy to reduce to zero the number of road fatalities by 2050 [8], by improving all aspects related to safe vehicles, safe infrastructure, safe road use, improved human body models, enhance automation, behavioral aspects for safer transport.

Road traffic injury is the leading cause of death among children and young people (5–29 years) and globally the number of deaths is estimated to be 1.19 million in 2021: this means that the death frequency is about 15 deaths per 100,000 population. Pedestrians represent 23% and two-wheeler users the 21% of total deaths: among the last ones, the 6% is for cyclists and the 3% for micro-mobility users [9].

Many cities in the Global North are experiencing an increase in bicycle use [10], and the problem of the increased cyclist flows may negatively influence cyclists' safety [11–14], with high exposure that is related to risk [15]. This could also not lead to a Vision Zero target [16], as prospected by the European Commission. According to the literature, the relationship between the so-called "Safety in Numbers" (e.g., the theory for that with high cyclist exposures, the cyclist safety is higher) and cyclist crashes is not well defined: a branch of literature shows a positive relationship between the number of cyclist crashes and flows [17–19], but on the other side, several studies state the opposite [20–22]. Due to this scenario, the relationships among cyclist crashes, traffic flows, and speeds are key in understanding ways to reduce the number of overall crashes by implementing interpretable and simple models to succeed in this task.

Analysing crash severity is a very studied topic both in individual and collective transport, and the issues of crash risk modelling also include the frequency of crashes and exposure issues [23, 24].

In the recent years, Machine Learning Models are widely implemented [25–28], but the main limitations and gaps related to these studies are due to the fact that such type of Models are not highly interpretable and that could be an issue when these models are related to safety aspect. Among the most interpretable models, the Logistic Regression is widely used, but, in comparisons to the previous ones, are usually less efficient.

In a paper on UK cyclist crashes [29], the authors used a machine learning algorithm called Random Forest and an econometric model called Random Parameters Logit Model to identify the characteristics of the road, environment, vehicle, driver, and cyclist that affect crash severity. Both methods identified various roadway, environmental, vehicle, driver, and cyclist-related factors associated with higher crash severity.

In the study of Engbers et al. [30], the researchers conducted a logistic regression analysis to study the relationship between personal factors and self-reported bicycle falls. The univariate models showed that age, physical and mental impairments, bicycle model, living environment, feelings of uncertainty of the cyclist, and changed cycling behavior (such as more patience and lower speed) were all related to falling off a bicycle.

While there is existing research on the causes of single bicycle crashes (SBCs), the study of Eriksonn et al. [31] seeks to examine differences in injury severity. Specifically, the study aims to investigate how injury severity is related to the characteristics of the crash and the cyclist, with a focus on SBCs. The study used binary logistic regression to analyze the odds of severe injury for different types of cyclists and situations. The authors also found that there was a higher risk of severe injury during leisure trips, on weekdays, and at intersections or road stretches compared to pedestrian and cycle paths. Furthermore, the risk of severe injury per kilometer travelled was higher for cyclists aged 45 and older during leisure trips.

Another example came from Spain [32]. A database of 2269 geo-located crashes in Madrid (involving at least one bike) was used, and this allowed the researchers to compare bike road safety between different districts in Madrid and model the severity of bike crashes using binary logit regression. The study also found that most serious crashes occurred at intersections between avenues and roads. It is important to note that, according to the authors, at intersections, cycling infrastructure is no longer protected, and the risk of a serious crash is higher.

In this paper, after a brief descriptive statistical analysis of 885 cyclist crashes in the city of Rome [33], a Logistic Regression Model is proposed with the objectives:

1. Give a general overview of the main features that influence cyclist crashes;
2. Discover the role of the vehicular speeds and the average daily traffic (ADT) in predicting the possible outcome of a crash involving cyclists and the relative probability;
3. Focus on particular crash scenarios to contextualize cyclist crashes to common patterns and improve the model prediction accuracy.
4. An interpretable and simple model that could highlight particular features to improve cyclist safety.

2 Method

2.1 Logistic Regression

Logistic Regression is a statistical model that is usually used to study the influences of independent variables on the dependent variable, which is a categorical one [34], and very often this type of model is used in classification problems [35, 36]. Linear regression, in a classification problem, may not be the best solution, so it is better to use Logistic Regression, as expressed in Eq. (1):

$$p(X) = \frac{e^{\beta_0 + \sum \beta_i X_i}}{1 + e^{\beta_0 + \sum \beta_i X_i}} \quad (1)$$

Where:

- p(X) is the predicted probability;
- xi are the independent variable or features;
- β0...βi are the regression coefficients of the model.

It is worth mentioning that this model only allows for k = 2 classes of response variables. Despite the more complex Machine Learning algorithms, such as Random Forest, Logistic Regression is characterized by a higher clarity on the interpretability side. Another advantage is their simple structure and simplicity for end users. Econometric models, on the other side, may provide unstable results due to the high amount of data that characterizes road crashes [37], so it is essential to reduce the number of variables by using feature selection algorithm.

Regarding the several features collected, to try to reduce the number of variables, they are transformed into dichotomous variables [38]. In Table 1, such type of "organization" of variables is applied also for this work. This way of pre-processing data reduces

Table 1. Description of the independent variables used for the Logistic Regression Model.

Variable	Value	Description
Location	0	In the extra-urban area
	1	Within the built-up area
Road	0	One-way road
	1	Two-way road
Stretch	0	No intersection
	1	Intersection
Surface	0	Other conditions
	1	Dry condition
Signposting	0	Other cases
	1	Vertical and horizontal
Day of the week	0	Festive
	1	Weekday
Weather conditions	0	Other cases
	1	Sunny
Hour	0	Evening or night
	1	Morning or afternoon
Season	0	Autumn or winter
	1	Spring or summer
Pavement	0	Unpaved
	1	Paved
Lighting	0	Inadequate
	1	Adequate
Visibility	0	Inadequate
	1	Adequate
Flow	0	<2000 vehicle/h
	1	>2000 vehicle/h
Speed	0	<50 km/h
	1	>50 km/h
Crash type	0	Other type of collisions
	1	Front/side collision

drastically the number of variables, reducing also the issues related to econometric models to handle high dimensional data, as highlighted by some authors [37, 39]. This selection follows the variable selection that could be noted in literature [23, 24].

3 Results

3.1 Descriptive Statistical Analysis

Road Safety, as suggested by the literature and the European and global Plans, is crucial in defining design strategies for the future and trying to reach environmental objectives. The major issues relate to urban environments, especially Metropolitan Cities worldwide. For this reason, this study focuses on 3 years (2016–2018) of cyclist crashes in the City of Rome (Italy). The Municipality of Rome provides the dataset used, in particular the *Rome Mobility Society* [33]. The dataset collects crash events for each type of road user, but the purpose here explained, the focus will be on cyclist crashes.

In the years 2016–2018, 885 crashes involving cyclists happened: 193 (21.81%) of them were unharmed, 668 (75.48%) injured, and 24 (2.71%) dead (Fig. 1).

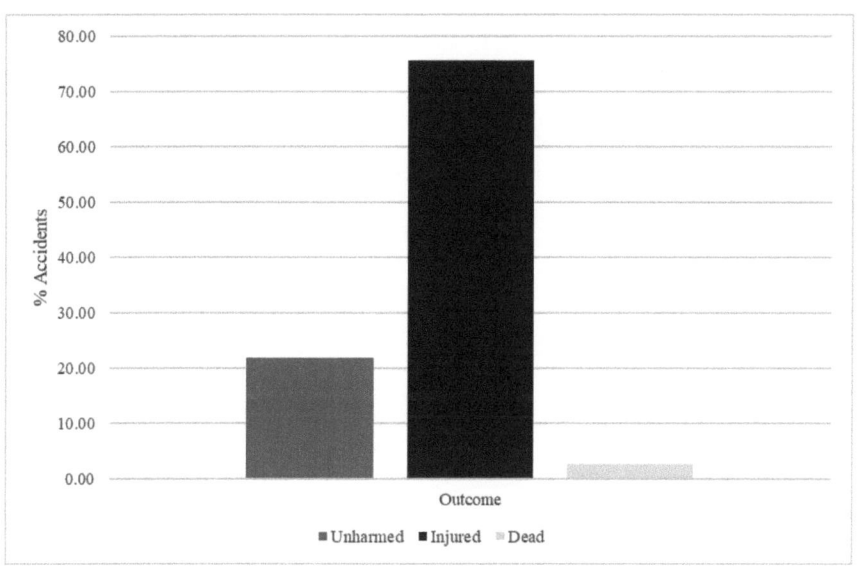

Fig. 1. Frequency of cyclist crashes according to their outcome.

The majority of crashes that lead to an injury or a fatal outcome, in frequency terms, happen in extra-urban environments; unharmed cyclists seem to be more likely in urban than extra-urban environments, as it is possible to see in Fig. 2.

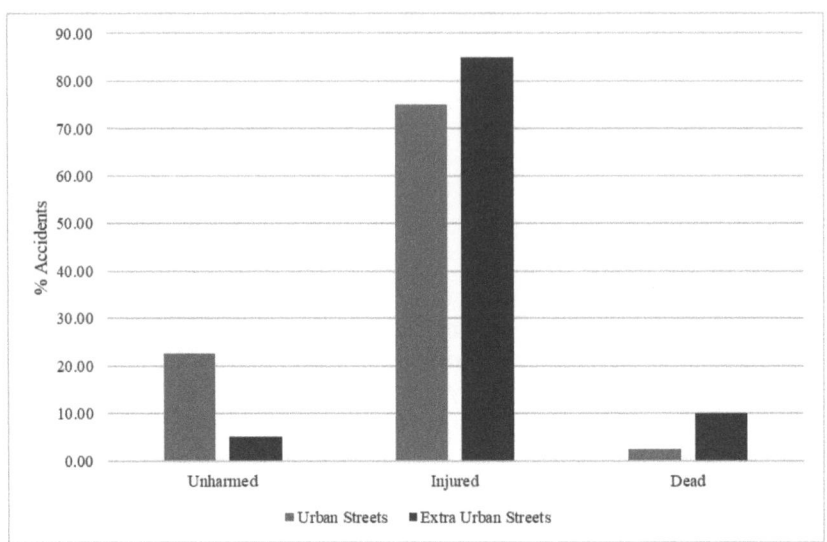

Fig. 2. Frequency of cyclist crashes according to their outcome in the urban and extra-urban environments.

In Fig. 3, the results of statistical analysis show that crashes are more likely to happen on weekdays than on weekends, and this is true also for unharmed, injured, and dead cyclist users involved in road crashes. This could be explained because during weekdays the exposure to vehicle traffic is higher than on weekends and also because more cyclists use bikes during the week.

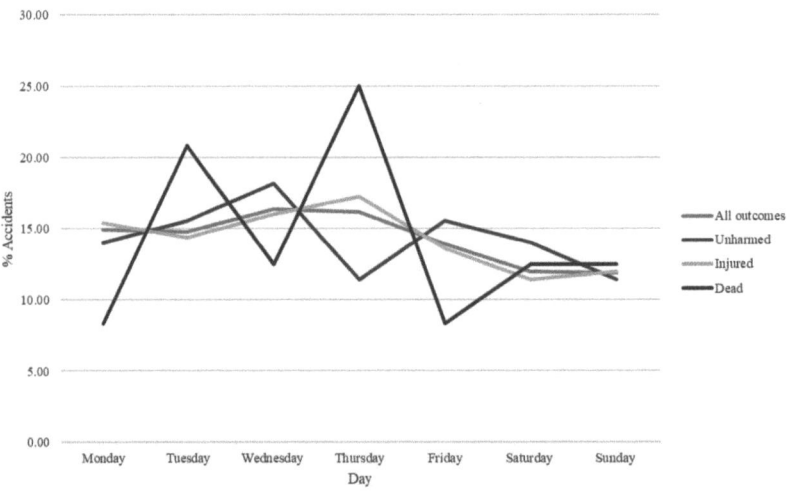

Fig. 3. Frequency of cyclist crashes according to their outcome during the week. The trend defined as "all outcome" is the sum of unharmed, injured and dead cyclists.

From a seasonal perspective, a larger number of cyclist crashes are registered in the spring and summer months than winter and autumn months (Fig. 4). The reason why this happens may be explained by the propensity of cyclists to use bikes during months when the weather is typically good. But, as it is shown from the same figure, there are more dead cyclists involved in crashes during winter months.

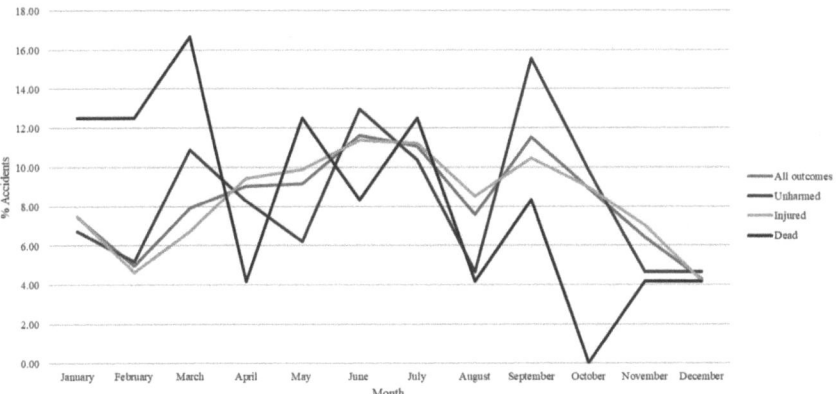

Fig. 4. Frequency of cyclist crashes according to their outcome during the years analyzed. The trend defined as "all outcome" is the sum of unharmed, injured and dead cyclists.

As shown in Fig. 5, crashes that lead to slight or non-serious outcomes follow somehow the same pattern during the day: two peaks from 10 a.m. to 12 a.m. and from 5 p.m. to 7 p.m. are related to vehicle off-peak hours; regarding the dead cyclist pattern, the peaks are reached between 8 a.m. and 10 a.m., and 7 p.m. and 9 p.m.

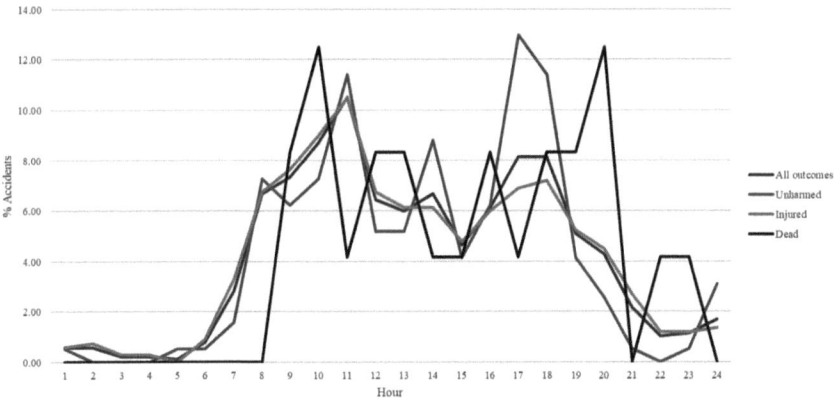

Fig. 5. Frequency of cyclist crashes according to their outcome during a day.

In Fig. 6, the relative frequency of crashes is shown: when the flow is low, there is a high likelihood that a crash leads to a fatal outcome, compared to a road with a higher traffic flow. And low flow rate increases the probability that vehicle speeds are higher: a speed higher than 30 km/h increases the probability of a fatal crash involving cyclists (Fig. 7).

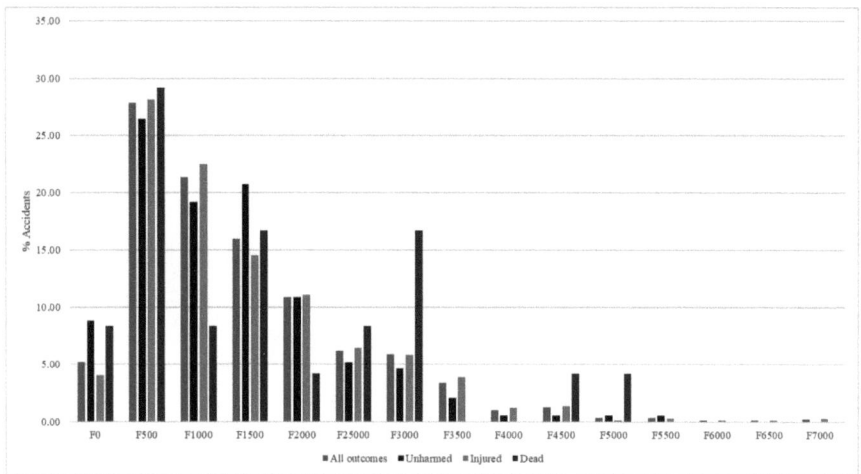

Fig. 6. Traffic flows and the likelihood of cyclist crashes.

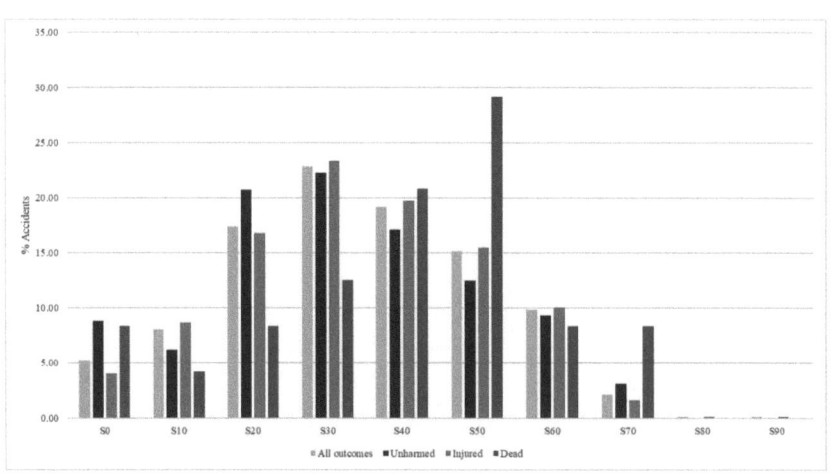

Fig. 7. The role of speed in cyclist crash.

3.2 Crash Severity Models

Cyclist crashes, but in general road crashes, are characterized by a great number of variables. Since the purpose of this work is to give shape to a simplified crash prediction model (to be used in the real world with not-too-sophisticated tools), not-too-elaborate models such as the Logit model are used in this regard. In Table 2, a General Cyclist Crash Model and the main statistics are proposed. The model can be used to predict the probability that a cyclist crash leads to a fatal outcome, according to other several independent variables. Logistic Regression may also be useful to understand the single independent variable's role in the crash. In Table 3 the main performance metric of the proposed model is reported.

Table 2. Cyclist Crash Model for predicting the fatal outcome after a crash.

Variable	Estimate	Std. Error	z-value	Pr(>z)
Intercept	−2.29973	1.33204	−1.726	0.084263.
Location	−0.85683	0.22770	−3.763	0.000168***
Day	0.24764	0.15985	1.549	0.121341
Season	−0.06881	0.15022	−0.458	0.646888
Hour	−0.43136	0.17468	−2.469	0.013534*
Stretch	−0.74541	0.16530	−4.509	6.50×10^{-6}***
Road	0.31538	0.18544	1.701	0.088995
Pavement	2.23632	0.50815	4.401	1.08×10^{-5}***
Signposting	−0.44163	0.14739	−2.996	0.002733**
Surface	0.34189	0.29826	1.146	0.251681
Weather	0.23180	0.19261	1.203	0.228810
Visibility	1.68029	1.21070	1.388	0.165180
Lighting	−1.28513	0.47312	−2.716	0.006602**
Crash type	0.09009	0.16609	0.542	0.587539
ADT	−0.23563	0.15217	−1.548	0.121513
Speed	0.77232	0.14980	5.156	2.53×10^{-7}***

Table 3. Performance metrics and main statistics for the three Cyclist Crash Models analyzed.

Estimator	Fatal
McFadden (pseudo-R^2)	0.1323
Akaike information criterion (AIC)	882.22
χ^2	129.64
Training accuracy	0.6539
Test accuracy	0.6667
Training F1 score	0.6772
Test F1 score	0.6667
p-value	0.000001

To improve the prediction accuracy of the proposed model, two particular scenarios are selected, and in particular, crashes at intersections and on single-lane carriageways. As shown in Table 4, the prediction performances of these two scenario-based models, according to the McFadden metric (but also accuracy and F1 score), have improved by drawing these sub-sets to study some crash scenarios: it is worth mentioning these models that have a McFadden higher than 0.2 (which is considered a lower boundary for good performances [40]). Tables 5 and 6 summarize the proposed models and other important metrics, such as the p-value, at intersections and single-lane carriageways.

Table 4. Performance metrics and main statistics for the two Cyclist Crash Models analyzed at the intersection and Single-Lane Carriageway.

Estimator	Intersection	Single-lane Carriageway
McFadden (pseudo-R^2)	0.4034	0.4450
Akaike information criterion (AIC)	244.81	156.16
X^2	145.24	101.17
Training accuracy	0.8192	0.8293
Test accuracy	0.7969	0.7317
Training F1 score	0.8239	0.8292
Test F1 score	0.8000	0.7556
p-value	0.000001	0.000001

Table 5. Cyclist Crash Model for predicting the fatal outcome after an crash, when a collision happens at intersections. Significance codes: 0 '***'; 0.001 '**'; 0.01 '*'; 0.05 '.'; 0.1 ' '.

Variable	Estimate	Std. Error	z-value	Pr(>z)
Intercept	−16.5769	5.2803	−3.139	0.001693**
Location	2.8536	3.1374	0.910	0.363066
Day	2.6638	0.6406	4.158	3.21×10^{-5}***
Season	0.2430	0.3163	0.768	0.442330
Hour	−0.7368	0.3089	−2.385	0.017064*
Road	0.3320	0.3186	1.042	0.297251
Pavement	3.6950	1.1724	3.152	0.001624**
Signposting	−1.5566	0.3582	−4.345	1.39×10^{-5}***
Surface	0.3554	1.0446	0.340	0.733655
Weather	2.3712	0.6632	3.575	0.000350***
Visibility	4.6682	1.7771	2.627	0.008616**
Lighting	1.4261	3.1553	0.452	0.651296
Crash type	−1.1237	0.3337	−3.367	0.000759***
ADT	−0.6092	0.3706	−1.644	0.100221
Speed	2.5326	0.4286	5.909	3.44×10^{-9}***

Table 6. Cyclist Crash Model for predicting the fatal outcome after an crash, when a collision happens on a single-lane carriageway.

Variable	Estimate	Std. Error	z-value	Pr(>z)
Intercept	−15.2634	5.0675	−3.012	0.002595**
Location	−1.9088	0.5530	−3.452	0.000557***
Day	4.3735	1.0547	4.147	3.37×10^{-5}***
Season	−0.7358	0.3742	−1.967	0.049235*
Hour	−0.7170	0.4193	−1.710	0.087254.
Stretch	0.1035	0.4088	0.253	0.800053
Pavement	2.0296	1.2035	1.686	0.091711.
Signposting	−1.6981	0.5165	−3.287	0.001011**
Surface	5.7478	2.1237	2.707	0.006798**
Weather	0.1640	0.6900	0.238	0.812155
Visibility	3.4075	3.5376	0.963	0.335425
Lighting	2.5496	3.3307	0.765	0.443981
Crash type	1.0891	0.4598	2.369	0.017853*
ADT	1.2271	0.5207	2.356	0.018449*
Speed	1.6448	0.4622	3.559	0.000373***

In addition, a sensitivity analysis is also carried out to quantify the weight of vehicular speed and ADT in predicting the severity of a cyclist crash. In Table 7 a summary is proposed. As it possible to observe, when the variable *Speed* is omitted, the performances of the models in terms of McFadden decrease in a higher way than when the variable *ADT* is removed from the model. This also highlights the great role played by vehicular speeds in crash severity outcomes.

Table 7. Summary of the sensitivity analysis performed: when the variable Speed is removed from the models (M_1), the McFadden decreases at a high rate. When *ADT* is removed (M_2), there is also a decrease in term of McFadden, but lower than what was seen in the previous model (M_1).

Estimator	Intersection	Single-lane Carriageway
M_0 (with all variables)	0.4034	0.4495
M_1 (without *speed*)	0.2571	0.3784
M_2 (without *ADT*)	0.4024	0.4253
M_3 (without *speed* and *ADT*)	0.2552	0.3588

4 Discussion and Conclusions

As shown earlier in Table 3, General Crash Models seem to have not good prediction performances (as shown in Table 4). Despite this issue, with these types of models, it is possible to have an insight into which variables could be not negligible in cyclist crashes and their respective outcomes.

When cyclists die after a crash, more variables influence this type of outcome. According to the model in Table 3, extra-urban areas are crucial to define this outcome, usually on a weekday, during evening and night hours, where there are no intersections, on paved two-way roads, without vertical and horizontal signposting, under poor lighting conditions and with elevated values of vehicle speeds.

As shown in Table 4, the performance metrics of these types of models are not so valuable. For this reason, this study makes efforts to find some commonalities among road crashes to better find a valuable relationship among variables and improve prediction performances. Crash nature, road characteristics, and road types seem to be common factors characterizing cyclist crashes, but also "environmental" aspects that are common features in small and large cities, in Europe and worldwide.

In the proximity of intersections, when neither vertical nor horizontal signposting is available, during night hours on weekdays, with speeds above 50 km/h on paved roads, and with sunny weather, fatal crashes are more likely to happen (Table 5).

Regarding the last model analyzed, when a collision happens on a single-lane carriageway, extra-urban location, weekdays, autumn and winter seasons, night hours, paved and dried road without vertical and horizontal signposting, average daily traffic above 2000 vehicles/hour and speed above 50 km/h, increase the chances of fatal crashes (as it is possible to see in Table 6).

Interesting findings come out when comparing the different variables, and their role within the models, of the two scenario-based crash models to predict the outcome of the crash. Visibility does not play a key role in leading to a crash with a cyclist; sunny weather is positively correlated to crashes in intersections, while dry surfaces increase the chances of having crashes on single-lane carriageways, such as also the location of these roads in extra-urban environments and autumn and winter seasons. Weekdays are also related to an increase in the probability of having a crash at intersections, and single-lane carriageways. Cyclist crashes are more likely to happen in the evening and nighttime hours. Vertical and horizontal signposting decreases the probability of crashes in intersections and single-lane carriageways. High values of average daily traffic (>2000 vehicles/day) are strongly related to crashes on single-lane carriageways, and high speeds (> 50 km/h) increase the probability of fatal crashes in intersections and on single-lane carriageways.

The performances obtained with the simple Logistic Crash Models for Intersections and Single Lane Carriageway (see Table 4) are comparable also with more advantage Logistic Models. In the study of Das et al. [41], the McFadden associated with the Logit model proposed in that paper is 0.084 (lower than the pseudo-R^2 in this work), while the Mixed Logit Model reaches a McFadden of 0.4161 (comparable with the simple Logit Models here proposed). It is worth mentioning also other studies that implement Mixed Logit Models. For instance, in the work of Ye et al. [42], the authors study vehicle-electric bicycle crashes and the model proposed reached a McFadden of 0.5090, while in the studies of Chen et al. [43] and Wang et al. [44], the models present a McFadden of 0.06 and 0.315, respectively. In the recent work of Scarano et al. [29], the authors proposed a Mixed Logit Model that present a McFadden of 0.21 and a F1score of 0.72, but also a Random Forest with a F1 score of 0.88 (comparable with the F1 score obtained with the simple Logit Model, and in particular 0.80 and 0.75 for Intersection and Single Lane Carriageway). In summary, the performances of the models here proposed to predict cyclist crashes are comparable with high performances models, such as Mixed Logit and Random Forest Models.

As a positive aspect of Logistic Regression, their interpretability could give information on how the single variables could increase or decrease the probability of having non-serious, serious, and fatal crashes and so understand how to address some issues.

The interpretability side opens the doors also to relevant findings and practical implications, especially for the practice of urban planning.

It is worth mentioning also the limitations of this study. The first one is related to the few data available (only for 3 years) and the dataset does not contain information on gender and age of road users involved in the crash. For these reasons, not all the context categories of type of crashes, type, and road characteristics are analyzed, and some of them lead to poor results. It is also advisable to study other cities to highlight the same or different characteristics.

What are the main implications of this study and new avenues for future research? First the most important implication of this study is related to the interpretability of the model combined with good prediction performances that could be compared with performances of more sophisticated models (and this aspect wants also to close the research gap that is an emerging trend, i.e., the huge implementation of Machine Learning Algorithms that are not so interpretable as Econometric Models). Secondly, simple models could be implemented easily to predict the severity of the crashes and lastly, the scenario-based approach is useful not only to improve model performances, but also to highlight influencing feature related to that particular scenario.

As future research developments, could be interesting to collect more recent data on the city of Rome, but also on other cities; enlarge the methodology to other road users, and use also different type of dataset: in general, this research, is a preliminary step in defining Cyclist Crash Models for predicting the probability that a crash could happen, based on road and users' characteristics.

Acknowledgments. The research reported in this paper was developed in the EMOTIVEs Research Project, supported by the "FESR Lazio 2021-2027 Program - RSI Competitive Repositioning Notice".

Author Contributions. **Conceptualization**, C.G. and N.S.; **methodology**, C.G. and N.S.; **software**, C.G. and N.S.; **validation**, C.G. and N.S.; **formal analysis**, C.G. and N.S.; **investigation**, C.G. and N.S.; **resources**, C.G. and N.S.; **data curation**, C.G. and N.S.; **writing—original draft preparation**, C.G. and N.S.; **writing—review and editing**, C.G. and N.S.; **visualization**, C.G. and N.S..; **supervision**, D.A.M. and N.V.; **project administration**, D.A.M. and N.V.; **funding acquisition**, D.A.M. and N.V. All authors have read and agreed to the published version of the manuscript.

References

1. WHO, World Health Organization: World Report on Road Traffic Injury Prevention. Available online: https://www.who.int/southeastasia/publications/i/item/world-report-on-road-traffic-injury-prevention, last accessed 16 Apr 2024
2. WHO, World Health Organization: First Global Ministerial Conference on Road Safety. Available online: https://www.who.int/publications/m/item/first-global-ministerial-conference-on-road-safety, last accessed 16 Apr 2024
3. WHO, World Health Organization: Global status report on road safety: Time for action. Available online: https://www.who.int/southeastasia/publications/i/item/9789241563840, last accessed 16 Apr 2024
4. WHO, World Health Organization: Decade of Action for Road Safety 2011–2020. Available online: https://www.who.int/groups/united-nations-road-safety-collaboration/decade-of-action-for-road-safety-2011-2020, last accessed 16 Apr 2024
5. WHO, World Health Organization: Global Plan for the Decade of Action for Road Safety 2011–2020. Available online: https://www.who.int/publications/m/item/global-plan-for-the-decade-of-action-for-road-safety-2011-2020, last accessed 16 Apr 2024
6. WHO, World Health Organization: Decade of Action for Road Safety 2021–2030. Available online: https://www.who.int/teams/social-determinants-of-health/safety-and-mobility/decade-of-action-for-road-safety-2021-2030, last accessed 16 Apr 2024
7. UN, United Nations: Conference on the Human Environment in Stockholm. Available online: https://www.un.org/en/conferences/environment/stockholm1972, last accessed 16 Apr 2024
8. European Commission, Road Safety Plan Vision Zero. Available online: https://road-safety.transport.ec.europa.eu/index_en, last accessed 16 Apr 2024
9. WHO, World Health Organization: Global status report on road safety 2023. Available online: https://www.who.int/teams/social-determinants-of-health/safety-and-mobility/global-status-report-on-road-safety-2023, last accessed 16 Apr 2024
10. Schepers, P., Helbich, M., Hagenzieker, M., de Geus, B., Dozza, M., Agerholm, N., et al.: The development of cycling in European countries since 1990. Eur. J. Transp. Infrastruct. Res. **21**(2), 41–70 (2021)
11. Schepers, P., Stipdonk, H., Methorst, R., Olivier, J.: Bicycle fatalities: trends in crashes with and without motor vehicles in The Netherlands. Transport. Res. F: Traffic Psychol. Behav. **46**, 491–499 (2017)
12. D'Apuzzo, M., Cappelli, G., Nardoianni, S., Nicolosi, V., Evangelisti, A.: A preliminary effort to develop a framework of distance decay functions for new urban active mobility. In: International Conference on Computational Science and Its Applications, pp. 194–208. Springer Nature Switzerland, Cham (2023, June)
13. Cappelli, G., D'Apuzzo, M., Nardoianni, S., Nicolosi, V.: Exploring the influences of safety and energy expenditure parameters on cycling. Sustain. For. **16**(7), 2739 (2024)
14. D'Apuzzo, M., Evangelisti, A., Cappelli, G., Nicolosi, V.: An introductory step to develop distance decay functions in the Italian context to assess the modal split to e-bike and e-scooter. In: In 2022 Second International Conference on Sustainable Mobility Applications, Renewables and Technology (SMART), pp. 1–8. IEEE (2022, November)
15. Uijtdewilligen, T., Ulak, M.B., Wijlhuizen, G.J., Bijleveld, F., Dijkstra, A., Geurs, K.T.: How does hourly variation in exposure to cyclists and motorised vehicles affect cyclist safety? A case study from a Dutch cycling capital. Saf. Sci. **152**, 105740 (2022)
16. Wegman, F., Schepers, P.: Safe system approach for cyclists in The Netherlands: towards zero fatalities and serious injuries? Accid. Anal. Prev. **195**, 107396 (2024)
17. Tasic, I., Elvik, R., Brewer, S.: Exploring the safety in numbers effect for vulnerable road users on a macroscopic scale. Accid. Anal. Prev. **109**, 36–46 (2017). https://doi.org/10.1016/j.aap.2017.07.029. Epub 2017 Oct 10

18. Fyhri, A., Sundfør, H.B., Bjørnskau, T., Laureshyn, A.: Safety in numbers for cyclists-conclusions from a multidisciplinary study of seasonal change in interplay and conflicts. Accid. Anal. Prev. **105**, 124–133 (2017). https://doi.org/10.1016/j.aap.2016.04.039. Epub 2016 May 28
19. Jacobsen, P.L.: Safety in numbers: more walkers and bicyclists, safer walking and bicycling. Inj. Prev. **9**(3), 205–209 (2003). https://doi.org/10.1136/ip.9.3.205. Erratum in: Inj. Prev. 2004 Apr;10(2):127. PMID: 12966006; PMCID: PMC1731007
20. Jacobsen, P.L., Ragland, D.R., Komanoff, C.: Safety in numbers for walkers and bicyclists: exploring the mechanisms. Inj. Prev. **21**(4), 217–220 (2015)
21. Lee, J., Abdel-Aty, M., Xu, P., Gong, Y.: Is the safety-in-numbers effect still observed in areas with low pedestrian activities? A case study of a suburban area in the United States. Accid. Anal. Prev. **125**, 116–123 (2019). https://doi.org/10.1016/j.aap.2019.01.037. Epub 2019 Feb 7
22. Jacobsen, P.L.: Safety in numbers: more walkers and bicyclists, safer walking and bicycling. Inj. Prev. **21**(4), 271–275 (2015)
23. Bonera, M., Barabino, B., Yannis, G., Maternini, G.: Network-wide road crash risk screening: a new framework. Accid. Anal. Prev. **199**, 107502 (2024)
24. Barabino, B., Bonera, M., Maternini, G., Porcu, F., Ventura, R.: Refining a crash risk framework for urban bus safety assessment: evidence from Sardinia (Italy). Reliab. Eng. Syst. Saf. **245**, 110003 (2024)
25. Komol, M.M.R., Hasan, M.M., Elhenawy, M., Yasmin, S., Masoud, M., Rakotonirainy, A.: Crash severity analysis of vulnerable road users using machine learning. PLoS One. **16**(8), e0255828 (2021)
26. Janstrup, K.H., Kostic, B., Møller, M., Rodrigues, F., Borysov, S., Pereira, F.C.: Predicting injury-severity for cyclist crashes using natural language processing and neural network modelling. Saf. Sci. **164**, 106153 (2023)
27. Scarano, A., Aria, M., Mauriello, F., Riccardi, M.R., Montella, A.: Systematic literature review of 10 years of cyclist safety research. Accid. Anal. Prev. **184**, 106996 (2023)
28. Birfir, S., Elalouf, A., Rosenbloom, T.: Building machine-learning models for reducing the severity of bicyclist road traffic injuries. Transp. Eng. **12**, 100179 (2023)
29. Scarano, A., Riccardi, M.R., Mauriello, F., D'Agostino, C., Pasquino, N., Montella, A.: Injury severity prediction of cyclist crashes using random forests and random parameters logit models. Accid. Anal. Prev. **192**, 107275 (2023)
30. Engbers, C., Dubbeldam, R., Brusse-Keizer, M.G.J., Buurke, J.H., De Waard, D., Rietman, J.S.: Characteristics of older cyclists (65+) and factors associated with self-reported cycling accidents in The Netherlands. Transport. Res. F: Traffic Psychol. Behav. **56**, 522–530 (2018)
31. Eriksson, J., Niska, A., Forsman, Å.: Injured cyclists with focus on single-bicycle crashes and differences in injury severity in Sweden. Accid. Anal. Prev. **165**, 106510 (2022)
32. Guirao, B., Gálvez-Pérez, D., Casado-Sanz, N.: The impact of the cyclist infrastructure type on bike accidents: the experience of Madrid. Transp. Res. Procedia. **71**, 403–410 (2023)
33. Roma Mobilità: Available online: https://romamobilita.it/it, last accessed 22 Apr 2024
34. Nick, T.G., Campbell, K. M.: Logistic regression. Topics in biostatistics, 273–301 (2007).
35. James, G., Witten, D., Hastie, T., Tibshirani, R.: An Introduction to Statistical Learning, vol. 112, p. 138. springer, New York, NY (2013)
36. Hosmer Jr., D.W., Lemeshow, S., Sturdivant, R.X.: Applied Logistic Regression. John Wiley & Sons (2013)
37. Mannering, F., Bhat, C.R., Shankar, V., Abdel-Aty, M.: Big data, traditional data and the tradeoffs between prediction and causality in highway-safety analysis. Anal. Methods Accid. Res. **25**, 100113 (2020)
38. Eboli, L., Forciniti, C., Mazzulla, G.: Factors influencing accident severity: an analysis by road accident type. Transp. Res. Procedia. **47**, 449–456 (2020)

39. Meuleners, L.B., Fraser, M., Johnson, M., Stevenson, M., Rose, G., Oxley, J.: Characteristics of the road infrastructure and injurious cyclist crashes resulting in a hospitalisation. Accid. Anal. Prev. **136**, 105407 (2020)
40. Domencich, T.A., McFadden, D.: Urban travel demand-a behavioral analysis (No. Monograph) (1975).
41. Das, S., Tamakloe, R., Zubaidi, H., Obaid, I., Rahman, M.A.: Bicyclist injury severity classification using a random parameter logit model. Int. J. Transp. Sci. Technol. **12**(4), 1093–1108 (2023)
42. Ye, F., Wang, C., Cheng, W., Liu, H.: Exploring factors associated with cyclist injury severity in vehicle-electric bicycle crashes based on a random parameter logit model. J. Adv. Transp. **2021**(1), 5563704–5563712 (2021)
43. Chen, C., Anderson, J.C., Wang, H., Wang, Y., Vogt, R., Hernandez, S.: How bicycle level of traffic stress correlate with reported cyclist accidents injury severities: a geospatial and mixed logit analysis. Accid. Anal. Prev. **108**, 234–244 (2017)
44. Wang, T., Chen, J., Wang, C., Ye, X.: Understand e-bicyclist safety in China: crash severity modeling using a generalized ordered logit model. Adv. Mech. Eng. **10**(6), 1687814018781625 (2018)

A Macroscopic and Physically-Based Relationship Between Bike Speeds and Energy Expenditure During Commuting Trips

Giuseppe Cappelli[1,2], Sofia Nardoianni[1], Mauro D'Apuzzo[1(✉)], Heather Kaths[3], Vittorio Nicolosi[2], and Maria Teresa Iannattone[1]

[1] University of Cassino and Southern Lazio, Via G. Di Biasio 43, 03043 Cassino, Italy
{giuseppe.cappelli1,sofia.nardoianni,dapuzzo}@unicas.it,
cppgpp01@uniroma2.it,
mariateresa.iannattone@studentmail.unicas.it
[2] University of Rome "Tor Vergata", Via del Politecnico, 1, 00133 Rome, Italy
nicolosi@uniroma2.it
[3] Bergische Universität Wuppertal, Pauluskirchstraße 7, 42285 Wuppertal, Germany
kaths@uni-wuppertal.de

Abstract. As it emerges from the literature, bike speed is a trade-off between safety, travel times, and energy expenditure. In addition to that, infrastructure, terrain, and gender play also a key role. By assessing and correlating energy expenditure with cycling speed, it becomes possible to integrate terrain-related factors with individual human capabilities to gauge effort. This paper gathers terrain-related data from sixty-one (61) German cities and uses it to propose a relationship between energy expenditure and bike speed within a macroscopic, physically grounded framework. Furthermore, a Bike Mode Split (BMS) model is introduced to emphasize the role of energy expenditure in predicting cycling demand, as an application of this physically-based framework. Geographic data, Census data, and mode split data are collected from the main official German sources. The result shows that there is a linear relationship between bike speeds and energy expenditure, and also between energy expenditure and slope for conventional and electrical bike (c-bike, and e-bikes, respectively).

Keywords: Sustainable Mobility · Bike Speed · Energy Expenditure · e-bike · Modal Split

1 Introduction

When a road user decides to make a commuting trip, an activity or work (in technical terms) is performed. The energy required is provided by hydrolysis of the adenosine triphosphate (ATP), which allows muscle contraction within the human body. Only a fraction of this energy from ATP is implemented for working purposes: the other fraction is transformed in heat, and the magnitude depends on individual human body efficiency [1]. One way to measure the energy required to complete a task is the power that a commuter pushes on the pedals. This is due to the "power nature" of cycling: like rowing, cycling power output could be measured with strain gauges attached to elements subject to deformations (cranks, and pedals for instance) with the help of Hook's law [2].

De Geus et al. [3], in a field experiment, collect physiological data on different subjects to evaluate the energy expenditure required for commuting riders. Ten (10) men and eight (8) women were subjected to follow some protocols that employed maximal tests to collect power, perceived effort, heart rate, commuting speeds, travel times, and distances. In a so-defined and controlled framework, the main variables that could be used to retrieve energy expenditure are measured. But not always such types of methodologies could be implemented on a large scale, due to costs and not great attention paid to commuters.

The topography of the territory influences the reason why to cycle or not for commuting purposes, but it is less likely to influence recreational cyclists' attitudes. As it plays a fundamental role, hilliness and the effect of slope on cycling demand need to be studied in greater depth. In the last year, some studies have been conducted on route choice models for commuting purposes that considered slope as an important parameter [5, 6], but according to Meeder et al. [7] and Rodriguez and Joo [8], few studies account for topography in travel choice model.

Recently, new studies tended to overtake the problem of topography by introducing a more accurate variable, that is the energy expenditure: in the study of Cruz et al. [9], the authors try to quantify energy consumption, travel time, difficulty of each route, safety levels for cyclists in different alternative routes by using different sensors to assess the metabolic response of the human body during the activity. Although there are many ways to define the energy expenditure of physical activity, the metabolic equivalent of task (MET) can be seen as an index that gives information about the intensity of a particular activity [10], compared to a reference activity (resting or sitting): an activity of 3MET is three times more intense than resting (1MET, according to the original definition, is the resting metabolic rate during quite sitting [11]). As was highlighted in some studies [12], it is possible to foresee that the energy expenditure in flat cities is lower than in hilly cities, so the decision to use a bike for commuting is very related to the metabolic capabilities of the users, but also the choice to choose a specific route than another.

Another challenge is how it could be possible to evaluate speeds based on energy expenditure. According to Bigazzi and Figliozzi [13], speed choice compromises safety, travel times, and energy expenditure. As it emerges from the literature [14], bike speed is also influenced by infrastructure and topology, but also by gender: men cycle faster than women on conventional bikes. Evaluating and correlating energy expenditure with bike speed, can put together terrain-related aspects and human individual capabilities to make an effort.

According to Heinen et al. [15], the main determinants that influence the decisions to cycle or not could be categorized as the built environment, natural environment, socio-economic, psychological, and cost factors.

Among the natural environment determinants, landscape hilliness is considered in few studies [15], but according to Parking et al. [16], this variable could play an important role: a 10% increase in the hilliness proportion is associated with an 8.93% reduction in proportion cycling commuting, but an increased hilliness of the route has a strong benefit on own health [17]. Moudon et al. [18] find that slopes do not have a negative effect, but their study mainly focuses on recreational cyclists who choose a route according to personal factors.

Despite the limited number of studies that take into account terrain-related parameters [19–21], it emerges from the current literature that this aspect is related to cycling demand, commuting, and route choices [22].

In this paper, terrain-related data on sixty-one (61) German cities are collected and used to evaluate a relationship between energy expenditure and bike speed in a macroscopic and physically based framework (and not on an individual basis). In addition to that, a Bike Mode Split (BMS) model in the German context is also provided to highlight the role of energy expenditure in forecasting cycling demand as a novelty aspect. The main research gap that this paper wants to highlight is the contribution of the energy expenditure parameters in defining cycling demand but also to find correlations between this parameter and cycling speed to improve cyclist behavioural models.

2 Method

In this section, the main steps of the proposed methodology are shown and explained as is possible to see in Fig. 1. The methodology starts with terrain-related data acquisition (described in Sect. 2.1), then the evaluation of power required during cycling, of the volume of oxygen during activity, and the e valuation of Energy Expenditure for c-bike and e-bike (Sect. 2.2), and finally the development of macroscopic speed model (see Sect. 4.1).

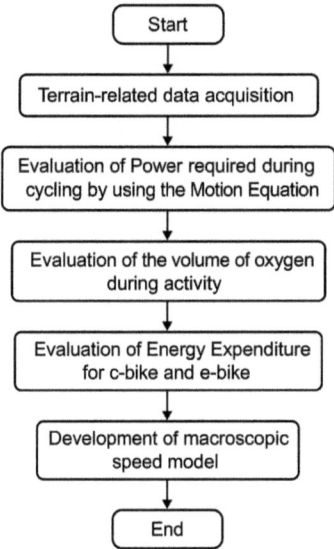

Fig. 1. Flow chart of the methodology proposed.

2.1 Terrain-Related Data Acquisition and Processing

The first step of this methodology includes terrain-related data acquisition and processing. With the help of Google Earth [23], used to collect and analyze terrain-related data, a digital terrain model (DTM) for each of the sixty-one (61) German cities is created to perform the following analysis.

Within this DTM, several nodes are placed in order to simulate the origin and the destination of the cycling commuting trip. This approach bypasses the need to define specific traffic zones, allowing for the simulation of random routes (see Fig. 2).

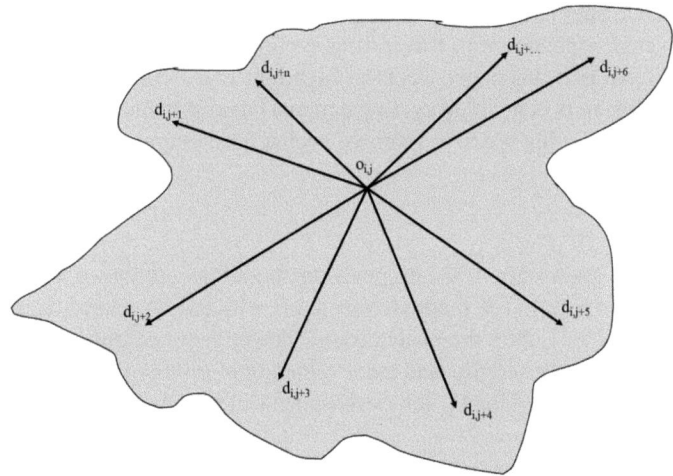

Fig. 2. Graphical representation of the methods to collect terrain-related data: the area in grey represents the city area within the municipal borders; $o_{i,j}$ is the origin of the simulated commuter trip, while $d_{i,j+1}$ to $d_{i,j+n}$ are the destinations of the trips. The slope is evaluated on each route connecting the origin and the destination.

2.2 Motion Equation and Energy Expenditure

Commuter cyclists, when making their trips, have to face three resistances: rolling, aerodynamic, and gravity resistance. This condition could be expressed through the motion equation below (Eq. 1) [24]:

$$W = \frac{C_b}{\eta_{bike}} \left\{ \sum mg \left[C_R + \frac{s}{100} + \frac{a}{g}\left(1 + \frac{m_w}{\sum m}\right) \right] + 0.5 C_D A \rho (C_b + C_w)^2 \right\} \quad (1)$$

Where:

- W: is the power expressed during cycling activity [W]
- C_b: bicycle speed [m/s]
- C_w: headwind [m/s]
- η_{bike}: mechanical efficiency

- m: mass of the cyclists, bike and accessories [kg]
- m_w: rotational mass of wheels and tires [kg]
- g: gravity acceleration [m/s^2]
- s: road gradient [%]
- a: acceleration [m/s^2]
- C_D: drag coefficient
- C_R: rolling resistance coefficient [dimensionless]
- A: frontal area of cyclist and bike [m^2]
- ρ: air density [kg/m^3]

From Eq. (1), the power expressed on pedals can be evaluated by knowing the road gradient that could be retrieved from the procedure in the previous section. For the other terms related to the equation, reference could be made to the current literature [25]. Equation (1) quantifies the external load that a commuter must face on a trip, but it is also essential to evaluate the internal load with terms to quantify aerobic activity. As suggested by Bigazzi e Figliozzi [13], aerobic activity can be quantified as the volume of oxygen utilized during a task. The authors suggest that this quantity could be evaluated as (Eq. 2):

$$VO_2 = a \frac{W}{m_b} + b \quad (2)$$

Where:

- VO_2 is the oxygen consumption during activity [mLO$_2$/min/kg]
- W is the power expressed during cycling activity [W]
- m_b is the mass of the cyclist [kg]
- a is a calibration coefficient equal to 10.8 in [13]
- b is a calibration coefficient equal to 7 in [13]

From Eq. (2) it is also possible to evaluate the Energy Expenditure, as expressed below (Eq. 3):

$$EE = \frac{VO_2}{c} \quad (3)$$

Where:

- EE is the energy expenditure during cycling activity [MET]
- VO_2 is the oxygen consumption during activity [mLO2/min/kg]
- c is an equivalent coefficient equal to 3.5

By combining Eqs. (1), (2), and (3), cyclist speed and Energy Expenditure could be related as follows (Eq. 4):

$$EE = \frac{a}{m_b * c} \left\{ \frac{C_b}{\eta_{bike}} \left\{ \sum mg \left[C_R + \frac{s}{100} + \frac{a}{g}\left(1 + \frac{m_w}{\sum m}\right) \right] + 0.5 C_D A \rho (C_b + C_w)^2 \right\} \right\} + \frac{b}{c} \quad (4)$$

Where:

- W: is the power expressed during cycling activity [W]

- C_b: bicycle speed [m/s]
- C_w: headwind [m/s]
- η_{bike}: mechanical efficiency
- m: mass of the cyclists, bike and accessories [kg]
- m_w: rotational mass of wheels and tires [kg]
- g: gravity acceleration [m/s^2]
- s: road gradient [%]
- a: acceleration [m/s^2]
- C_D: drag coefficient
- C_R: rolling resistance coefficient [dimensionless]
- A: frontal area of cyclist and bike [m^2]
- ρ: air density [kg/m^3]
- m_b is the mass of the cyclist [kg]
- a is a calibration coefficient equal to 10.8 in [13]
- b is a calibration coefficient equal to 7 in [13]

Equation (4) is valid for conventional bikes, but a similar relationship can be retrieved for e-bikes. As suggested by Liu et al. [25], if the objective is to evaluate power outputs for e-bikes, it is necessary to introduce the assistance ratio, which could be evaluated as follows:

$$AR = \begin{cases} 1.4 & \text{if } 0 \leq C_b \leq 10 \\ 1.4 - 0.1 * (C_b - 10) & \text{if } \quad C_b \geq 10 \end{cases} \quad (5)$$

Where:

- AR is the assistance ratio [dimensionless]
- C_b: bicycle speed [m/s]

The power output expressed on pedals without the assistance of an electric powertrain is expressed by Eq. (1): this contribution needs to be reduced by a coefficient as follows (see Eq. 6):

$$W = \frac{C_b}{(1+AR)\eta_{bike}} \left\{ \sum mg \left[C_R + \frac{s}{100} + \frac{a}{g}\left(1 + \frac{m_w}{\sum m}\right) \right] + 0.5 C_D A \rho (C_b + C_w)^2 \right\} \quad (6)$$

Where:

- W: is the power expressed during cycling activity [W]
- C_b: bicycle speed [m/s]
- C_w: headwind [m/s]
- η_{bike}: mechanical efficiency
- m: mass of the cyclists, bike and accessories [kg]
- m_w: rotational mass of wheels and tires [kg]
- g: gravity acceleration [m/s^2]
- s: road gradient [%]
- a: acceleration [m/s^2]
- C_D: drag coefficient

- C_R: rolling resistance coefficient [dimensionless]
- A: frontal area of cyclist and bike [m^2]
- ρ: air density [kg/m^3]
- AR is the assistance ratio [dimensionless]
- C_b: bicycle speed [m/s]

The Energy Expenditure for e-bikes can be evaluated as follows (Eq. 7):

$$EE = \frac{a}{m_b * c} \left\{ \frac{C_b}{(1+AR)\eta_{bike}} \left\{ \sum mg \left[C_R + \frac{s}{100} + \frac{a}{g}\left(1 + \frac{m_w}{\sum m}\right) \right] + 0.5 C_D A \rho (C_b + C_w)^2 \right\} \right\} + \frac{b}{c} \quad (7)$$

Where:

- W: is the power expressed during cycling activity [W]
- C_b: bicycle speed [m/s]
- C_w: headwind [m/s]
- η_{bike}: mechanical efficiency
- m: mass of the cyclists, bike and accessories [kg]
- m_w: rotational mass of wheels and tires [kg]
- g: gravity acceleration [m/s^2]
- s: road gradient [%]
- a: acceleration [m/s^2]
- C_D: drag coefficient
- C_R: rolling resistance coefficient [dimensionless]
- A: frontal area of cyclist and bike [m^2]
- ρ: air density [kg/m^3]
- AR is the assistance ratio [dimensionless]
- C_b: bicycle speed [m/s]
- m_b is the mass of the cyclist [kg]
- a is a calibration coefficient equal to 10.8 in [13]
- b is a calibration coefficient equal to 7 in [13]

3 Case Study

3.1 Description of the Sample

The analysis carried out in this paper started with the collection of the necessary data. Terrain-related data are needed to implement the methodology described in the previous section. In addition, a further application based on the aforementioned methodology is also proposed, that is, whether the Energy Expenditure parameter could be a good predictor in forecasting cycling demand at a macroscopic level.

The dataset contains sixty-one (61) German cities, each characterized by a population of more than 100,000 inhabitants. As shown in Table 1, socio-economic, traffic, and terrain-related variables of the cities analysed and considered in this study are proposed. Mean Slope is obtained by implementing the methodology described in the previous section, for the socio-economic variable to the German Census [26], while for the mode split data collection, references are made to the German National Survey Database [27].

Table 1. The main characteristics of the cities analyzed in this paper.

Categories	Minimum	Mean	Maximum
Population [−]	101,158	385857.92	3,677,472
Area [km^2]	54.40	190.23	891.30
GDP per capita [Euro]	27,745	56835.03	158,749
Bike mode split [−]	0.03	0.16	0.38
Pedestrian mode split [−]	0.09	0.23	0.35
Public transit mode split [−]	0.05	0.15	0.27
Car mode split [−]	0.21	0.46	0.7
Mean slope [%]	0.05	0.89	8.39

4 Results

4.1 Relationship Between Energy Expenditure and Bike Speeds

As shown in Eq. (4), the mass and the frontal area of the cyclist are very variable parameters and depend on the typology, age, and gender of the cyclist. In the macroscopic framework that characterizes this work, some parameters need to be defined *prior to performing the* analysis. Mean values of the parameters, according also to the evidence of the literature review, are selected [24].

As can be observed in the equation above, there are two unknown quantities: the first is energy expenditure, and the second one is bike speed. In field tests, oxygen consumption is measured by breathing face-mask [28], while cycling speed through GPS devices. When these two data are unavailable, measuring one quantity or the other is essential. For instance, in this paper, the speed is evaluated as expressed in Eq. (5), through a speed model (see Fig. 3) that is related to road slope [12], as the main assumption:

$$C_b = e \times s + f \tag{5}$$

Where:

- C_b is the average cycling speed [km/h]
- s is the slope [dimensionless]
- e and f are the calibration coefficients, equal to -1.1484 and 20.553, respectively.

From the evaluation of bike speeds with Eq. (5) and by the comparison with the related Energy Expenditure, it emerges that the relationship between the two variables is described below (Eq. 6):

$$C_b(EE) = g \times EE + h \tag{6}$$

Where:

- C_b is the average cycling speed [m/s]
- EE is the Energy Expenditure [MET]

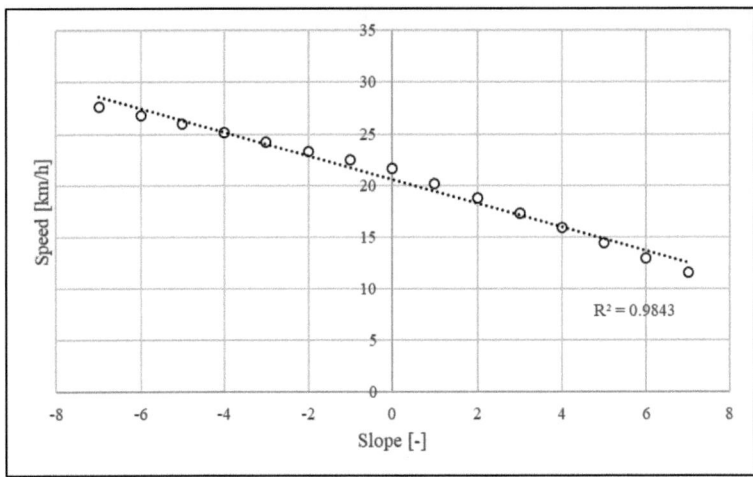

Fig. 3. Speed model from field data shown in the paper of Parking et al. [12]. The relationship between speed and slope is quite linear.

- g is the calibration coefficient (in this particular case of standard conditions equal to -0.0014) [dimensionless]
- h is the calibration coefficient (in this particular case of standard conditions equal to 5.7194) [dimensionless]

The graphical output of the relationship is shown in Fig. 4. By using the same equation described in the previous sections, relationships between terrain-related parameters and Energy Expenditure for conventional and electric bikes are also obtained (see Fig. 5 and Eq. 7):

$$EE = a \times s + b \tag{7}$$

Where:

- EE is the Energy Expenditure [MET]
- s is the slope parameter [dimensionless]
- a is the calibration coefficient (in this particular case of standard conditions equal to 221.05 and 92.105, for c-bike and e-bike, respectively) [dimensionless]
- b is the calibration coefficient (in this particular case of standard conditions equal to 7.125 and 4.1354, for c-bike and e-bike, respectively) [dimensionless]

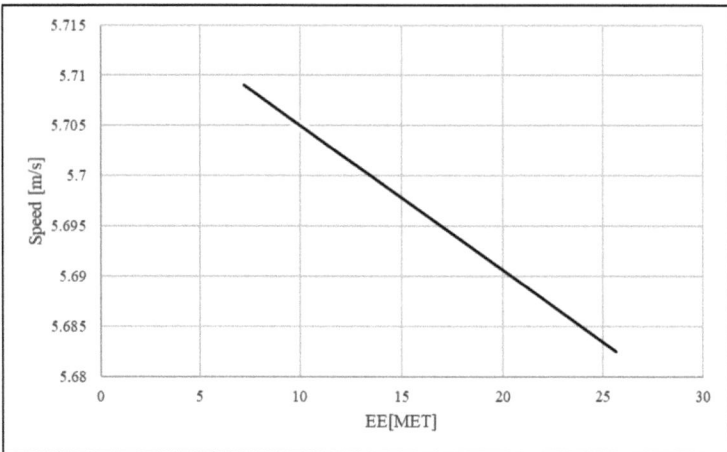

Fig. 4. Graphical representation of the relationship between bike speed and energy expenditure for conventional bikes, in standard condition as suggested by [24].

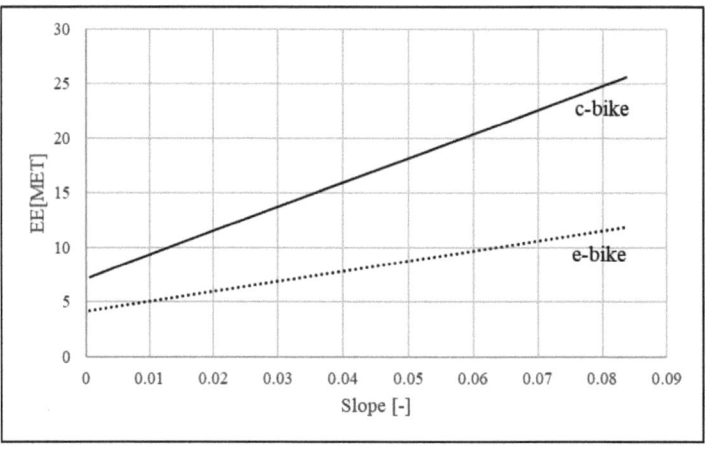

Fig. 5. Graphical representation of the relationship between terrain-related parameters and energy expenditure for conventional and electric bikes, in standard conditions as suggested by [24].

4.2 Some Applications: Energy Expenditure-Based Cycling Demand Model

According to some recent studies [19–21], there is a link between the terrain-related characteristics of an area and the commuting cycling demand, as well as between energy expenditure and cycling demand. The reason energy expenditure could be a better predictor relies on its structure: energy expenditure depends not only on terrain-related characteristics but also on human inner individual capabilities to make an effort. This ability is strictly related to the age and gender of individuals.

As shown in [21], energy expenditure, alongside other features in the Italian context, can predict with good accuracy cycling demand on a macroscopic level. As a further application of this theoretical framework, the methodology in [20, 21] is replicated and proposed in this paper. In Fig. 6, the graphical relationship between energy expenditure and bike mode split (BMS) is shown: when the mean energy expenditure increases, the number of commuting trips made with the bike decreases.

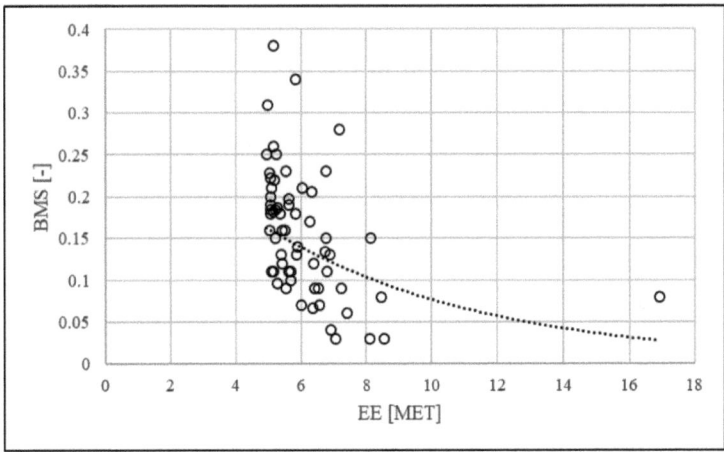

Fig. 6. Graphical representation of the relationship between energy expenditure (EE) and Bike Mode Split (BMS) for conventional, in standard conditions as suggested by [24].

As the first step of the methodology, the German cities analysed (it is worth remembering that cities with a population higher than 100,000 inhabitants are selected), are clustered into two sections: cities with a number of inhabitants lower than 500,000 and higher than 500,000. The two classes of cities allow to evaluate two different macroscopic models to forecast cycling demand. The general shape of the model can be described as follows (Eq. 8). The logarithm of bike demand is used is due to the not normal distribution of bike splits in the German context: the logarithms of these quantities follow a normal distribution.

$$\log(BMS) = a + b\frac{1}{EE} \qquad (8)$$

Where:

- BMS is the bike mode split of the single city [dimensionless]
- EE is the Energy Expenditure [MET]
- a and b are the calibration coefficients [dimensionless]

The values of the calibration coefficients are shown in the Table 2 below.

In the Table 2, the two aforementioned modes are proposed. It is worth noting that the performances of the two models (expressed as adj-R^2), at first glance, seem not quite high, but it is essential to remember that only a single variable is used as a predictor of bike mode split. In addition, the p-value associated with the intercept and the Energy expenditure is very low, and that indicates the significance of the features used to define the model.

Table 2. A brief description of the two models proposed according to the dimensionality class identified: the estimate of the calibration coefficients, the p-values associated to the variables, and the adj-R^2 are reported.

Number of Inhabitants	Variable	Estimate	Std. Error	t-value	Pr(>|t|)	Adj-R^2
<500,000	a	−1.29569	0.08043	−16.109	<2 × 10^{-16}	0.3902
	b	5.06158	0.90805	5.574	1.25 × 10^{-6}	
>500,000	a	−1.4059	0.1827	−7.694	5.59 × 10^{-6}	0.4311
	b	3.3504	1.0170	3.294	6.41 × 10^{-3}	

5 Conclusions

In the recent literature, several studies on the mode choice model tend to use all the possible explanatory variables to understand the utility of choosing a bike as a mode of transport or not. In this study, there is a need to study those variables that, according to the international literature review, influence the most bike commuting: energy expenditure is one of them.

Within a macroscopic and physically-based approach, the study wants to find reliable and accurate relationships between energy expenditure, speeds, and cycling demand in cities. Commuter cyclists encounter three types of resistance during their trips: rolling, aerodynamic, and gravitational resistance. These quantities can be represented by the motion equation.

The analysis presented in this paper began with gathering the necessary data. With the help of open-source tools, geographic data could be collected and processed and then utilized to simulate commuting trips within an area. Specifically, terrain-related information is crucial for applying the aforementioned methodology and evaluating the energy expenditure required to make a trip. Additionally, the paper proposes a further application based on this methodology: determining whether the Energy Expenditure parameter can effectively predict cycling demand at a macro level. As far as it is known, this variable is the first time that is used in simple regression models, and it is expected that it could be an important one also in more complex models, such as Discrete Choice Models.

In addition to that, relationships among energy expenditure for conventional and electric bikes, bike speeds, and slopes are shown alongside the whole methodology to retrieve the theme.

The contribution to the research field of this paper relies on two aspects. The first aspect regards bike speed models in which energy expenditure is the only independent variable. Energy expenditure depends on age, gender, and physical characteristics, which vary among people. This aspect highlights the need for further collection of field data on commuter cyclists to be able to calibrate more accurate bike speed models, which are useful, for instance, to forecast cyclists' behaviours and to improve microscopic models. In addition to that, Energy expenditure could also be implemented in Discrite Choice Models to study the reason behind e-bikes and c-bike are chosen. As a second contribution, two bike demand models are calibrated by using as unique independent variable energy expenditure. Despite the not great performances of the model, almost 40% of the variance could be explained with only a single variable. The novelty aspect of this paper lies on defining a theoretical procedure to evaluate Energy Expenditure and highlight the importance of this variable in cycling commuting choices.

It is hoped that this methodology, rather than the proposed models, will be useful for new insights into research topics and for the development of behavioural models for cyclists which take into account, in a single variable, metabolic and individual aspects. From an urban planning perspective, these results could be useful to promote cycling in urban area in which terrain-related territory characteristics could be an obstacle to commuting cycling trip. In addition to that, these findings highlight how metabolic aspect should be considered when cycling paths and routes need to be designed and to make them more accessible for everyone. The accessibility of some points or areas in cities could also be evaluated, taking into account the energy expenditure to reach the destination.

Acknowledgments. The research leading to these results has received funding from Project "Ecosistema dell'innovazione Rome Technopole" financed by the EU in the NextGeneration EU plan through MUR Decree n. 1051 23.06.2022 - CUP H33C22000420001. This manuscript reflects only the authors' views and opinions, neither the European Union nor the European Commission can be considered responsible for them.

Author Contributions. **Conceptualization**, C.G. and N.S.; **methodology**, C.G. and N.S.; **software**, C.G. and N.S.; **validation**, C.G. and N.S.; **formal analysis**, C.G. and N.S.; **investigation**, C.G. and N.S.; **resources**, C.G. and N.S.; **data curation**, C.G. and N.S. and I.M.T.; **writing—original draft preparation**, C.G. and N.S.; **writing—review and editing**, C.G. and N.S.; **visualization**, C.G. and N.S..; **supervision**, D.A.M., K.H. and N.V.; **project administration**, D.A.M. and N.V.; **funding acquisition**, D.A.M. and N.V. All authors have read and agreed to the published version of the manuscript.

References

1. Ettema, G., Lorås, H.W.: Efficiency in cycling: a review. Eur. J. Appl. Physiol. **106**, 1–14 (2009)
2. Bini, R.R., Carpes, F.P.: Biomechanics of Cycling, 1st edn, pp. 12–21. Springer, Basel (2014)
3. De Geus, B., De Smet, S., Nijs, J., Meeusen, R.: Determining the intensity and energy expenditure during commuter cycling. Br. J. Sports Med. **41**(1), 8–12 (2007)
4. Milakis, D., Athanasopoulos, K.: What about people in cycle network planning? Applying participative multicriteria GIS analysis in the case of the Ath-ens metropolitan cycle network. J. Transp. Geogr. **35**, 120–129 (2014)
5. Li, Z., Wang, W., Liu, P., Ragland, D.R.: Physical environ-ments influencing bicyclists' perception of comfort on separated and on-street bicycle facilities. Transp. Res. Part D: Transp. Environ. **17**(3), 256–261 (2012)
6. Willis, D.P., Manaugh, K., El-Geneidy, A.: Uniquely satisfied: exploring cyclist satisfaction. Transport. Res. F: Traffic Psychol. Behav. **18**, 136–147 (2013)
7. Meeder, M., Aebi, T., Weidmann, U.: The influence of slope on walking activity and the pedestrian modal share. Transp. Res. Procedia. **27**, 141–147 (2017)

8. Rodríguez, D.A., Joo, J.: The relationship between non-motorized mode choice and the local physical environment. Transp. Res. Part D: Transp. Environ. **9**(2), 151–173 (2004)
9. Cruz, R., Bandeira, J., Vilaça, M., Rodrigues, M., Fernandes, J.M., Coelho, M.: Introducing new criteria to support cycling navigation and infrastructure planning in flat and hilly cities. Transp. Res. Procedia. **47**, 75–82 (2020)
10. Byrne, Nuala M.; Hills, Andrew P.; Hunter, Gary R.; Weinsier, Roland L.; Schutz, Yves (2005). Metabolic equivalent: one size does not fit all. J. Appl. Physiol.. 99(3): 1112–1119. CiteSeerX 10.1.1.494.7568. S2CID 11895307. https://doi.org/10.1152/japplphysiol.00023. 2004
11. Ainsworth, B.E., Haskell, W.L., Leon, A.S., Jacobs, D.-v.R., Montoye, H.J., Sallis, J.F., Paffenbarger, R.S.: Compendium of physical activities: classification of energy costs of human physical activities. Med. Sci. Sports Exerc. **25**(1), 71–80 (1993). https://doi.org/10.1249/000 05768-199301000-00011
12. Parkin, J., Rotheram, J.: Design speeds and acceleration characteristics of bicycle traffic for use in planning, design and appraisal. Transp. Policy. **17**(5), 335–341 (2010)
13. Bigazzi, A., Lindsey, R.: A utility-based bicycle speed choice model with time and energy factors. Transportation. **46**(3), 995–1009 (2019)
14. Flügel, S., Hulleberg, N., Fyhri, A., Weber, C., Ævarsson, G.: Empirical speed models for cycling in the Oslo road network. Transportation. **46**, 1395–1419 (2019)
15. Heinen, E., Van Wee, B., Maat, K.: Commuting by bicycle: an overview of the literature. Transp. Rev. **30**(1), 59–96 (2010)
16. Parkin, J., Wardman, M., Page, M.: Estimation of the determinants of bicycle mode share for the journey to work using census data. Transportation. **35**, 93–109 (2008)
17. Woodcock, J., Aldred, R., Lovelace, R., Strain, T., Goodman, A.: Health, environmental and distributional impacts of cycling uptake: the model underlying the propensity to cycle tool for England and Wales. J. Transp. Health. **22**, 101066 (2021)
18. Moudon, A.V., Lee, C., Cheadle, A.D., Collier, C.W., Johnson, D., Schmid, T.L., Weather, R.D.: Cycling and the built environment, a US perspective. Transp. Res. Part D: Transp. Environ. **10**(3), 245–261 (2005)
19. D'Apuzzo, M., Evangelisti, A., Cappelli, G., Nicolosi, V.: An introductory step to develop distance decay functions in the Italian context to assess the modal split to e-bikes and e-scooters. (2022). https://doi.org/10.1109/smart55236.2022.9990446
20. D'Apuzzo, M., Cappelli, G., Nardoianni, S., Nicolosi, V., Evangelisti, A.: A preliminary effort to develop a framework of distance decay functions for new urban active mobility. (2023). https://doi.org/10.1007/978-3-031-37123-3_16
21. Cappelli, G., D'Apuzzo, M., Nardoianni, S., Nicolosi, V.: Exploring the influences of safety and energy expenditure parameters on cycling. (2024). https://doi.org/10.3390/su16072739
22. Carra, M., Pavesi, F.C., Barabino, B.: Sustainable cycle-tourism for society: integrating multi-criteria decision-making and land use approaches for route selection. Sustain. Cities Soc. **99**, 104905 (2023)
23. Google Earth. Available online: https://www.google.it/intl/it/earth/index.html, last accessed 6 Feb 2025
24. Wilson, D.G., Schmidt, T.: Bicycling Science, 4th edn, pp. 41–128. MIT Press, Cambridge, Massachusetts (2020)
25. Liu, L., Suzuki, T.: Quantifying e-bike applicability by comparing travel time and physical energy expenditure: A case study of Japanese cities. J. Transp. Health. **13**, 150–163 (2019)
26. German Census. Available online: https://www.zensus2022.de/EN/Home/_node.html, last accessed 5 Feb 2025

27. German National Survey Database. Available online: https://www.mobilitaet-in-deutschland.de/, last accessed 5 Feb 2025
28. Kleinloog, J.P., van Laar, S.P., Schoffelen, P.F., Plasqui, G.: Validity and reproducibility of VO2max testing in a respiration chamber. Scand. J. Med. Sci. Sports. **31**(6), 1259–1267 (2021)

Estimation of Pedestrian Flows with Open-Source Crowding Data: An Integrated Model in Nomentano-Tiburtina District, Rome

Sofia Nardoianni[1(✉)], Giuseppe Cappelli[1,2], Mauro D'Apuzzo[1], Vittorio Nicolosi[2], and Mariano Pernetti[3]

[1] University of Cassino and Southern Lazio, Via G. Di Biasio 43, 03043 Cassino, Italy
{sofia.nardoianni,giuseppe.cappelli,dapuzzo}@unicas.it
[2] University of Rome "Tor Vergata", Via del Politecnico, 1, 00133 Rome, Italy
nicolosi@uniroma2.it
[3] University of Campania Luigi Vanvitelli, Via Roma 29, 8103 Aversa, Italy
mariano.pernetti@unicampania.it

Abstract. This research aims to investigate pedestrian crowding in the urban area of the Nomentano-Tiburtina district in Rome, through a methodology that sees an integrated approach between a configurational digital model, created with the Space Syntax tool by Qgis, and a physical model based on data collection through the mobile observer mode and therefore directly and through the use of Google Street View, in virtual terms. An innovative methodology was therefore developed to be able to obtain a physical model through virtual data collection, and this made it possible to calibrate the digital model. The calibration highlighted, with a Pearson of 0.88, the effectiveness of the methodology developed. At the same time, all the factors influencing the digital model, such as demand-driven and land-use, were also studied. From the analysis of these factors, it was found that the presence of shops on the pedestrian network plays a strategic role in the assessment of pedestrian crowding, recording a better correlation than the data measured on site. The conclusions drawn from this research, therefore, are of considerable help in urban planning, emphasizing concepts such as accessibility and pedestrian safety.

Keywords: Pedestrian crowding · Space Syntax · Configurational model · Physical model

1 Introduction

Nowadays, the concepts of sustainable mobility are increasingly of interest, as evidenced by plans such as the Agenda 2030 [1, 2], which provides for the achievement of sustainable development goals through the acquisition of specific tasks such as the reduction of environmental impacts caused by traditional transport systems by promoting more ecological and accessible travel.

Among the sustainable modes of transport, the one that is becoming increasingly popular is the on-foot mode, defined as soft mobility. Certainly, an increase in walking helps to reduce greenhouse gas emissions that would be recorded if, on the contrary, a motorized vehicle was to be made [3, 4].

In addition to the aspect related to environmental sustainability, the increase in walking helps to contribute to the reduction of road accidents, due to the construction of a better infrastructure and the reduction of vehicular speed, thus ensuring better safety [5–7]. In this regard, it is necessary to investigate pedestrian flows that affect urban areas to guarantee safe pedestrian paths and avoid "not allowed" crossings, i.e., outside appropriately built crossings, by pedestrians, which leads to an increase in accident risk. However, several factors influence pedestrian behavior, on the one hand, the availability of dedicated infrastructure and the perception of safety, on the other hand, the geometry and configuration of the pedestrian network, the presence of commercial activities, as well as the socioeconomic characteristics of the population [8, 9].

Therefore, it becomes of primary importance to analyze the pedestrian flow of urban areas to understand how the various factors previously highlighted influence pedestrian behavior and how to create pedestrian paths that are as connected as possible to ensure the safety of their practicability.

In the literature, there are many studies that investigate pedestrian flow through the use of a configurational model [10–13], highlighting how urban morphology is a key element that conditions the movement of pedestrians. Other studies [14–16] describe how other important parameters, including land-use factors, population density, and so on, are of extreme importance to consider in the analysis of pedestrian flows. However, pedestrian flows are also estimated through direct observations [17–19] through sensors, mobile observatories, and video cameras.

What seems to be missing in the current literature is a combined approach, developed on an area of interest, which takes into account all these multiple aspects, i.e. the morphology of the urban environment, the influence of factors such as land-use or population density, and the calibration of these models through pedestrian flow data. The present research aims precisely at this objective, namely to develop a digital model, based on configurational analysis [12, 20–24] carried out with the Space Syntax tool [13, 25–27] of Qgis which allows to identify, through the magnitude of Integration, the pedestrian crowding that takes into account not only the geometry and configuration of the pedestrian network but also the socio-economic characteristics of the population.

In particular, a further influencing factor was analyzed, such as the presence of commercial activities along the pedestrian network, which was the most impactful of all, ensuring a better correlation with real data.

As far as real data is concerned, a new methodology has been developed for developing a physical model. The need to develop this methodology arises from the extension of the area of interest, such as the Nomentano-Tiburtina district located in the city of Rome.

On this area it is expensive to collect pedestrian flow data through the mode of mobile observer, so it was calibrated, first, on a smaller reality [28–30] on which a previous study had already been conducted, a virtual data collection mode, through the use of the Street View application of Google Maps, which was then used for the case study presented in this research. Thanks to the combination of digital model and physical model, and through the definition of a new methodology for the calibration of the model, it was possible to define, in detail, the pedestrian dynamics characterizing the study area. In addition, the weight of commercial activities present along the pedestrian path, on pedestrian behavior was analyzed, highlighting how this factor is predominant in terms of influence.

Compared to what has been investigated to date in the literature, the present study aims to define an integrated approach between configurational models, thanks to the use of Space Syntax, and physical models, which allow the collection of real data. In addition, an innovative methodology has been developed to obtain pedestrian flow data from open-source platforms (Google Street View) that guarantees good replicability with a reduced computational burden. The aim, therefore, of the present research is to develop an integrated model capable of accurately representing pedestrian flows and providing a useful tool for urban planning.

2 Methodology

To evaluate the pedestrian crowding present in the study area, taking into account completely and exhaustively the behavior of pedestrians, an integrated configurational model was developed that sees the combination of digital and physical approaches as described in Fig. 1.

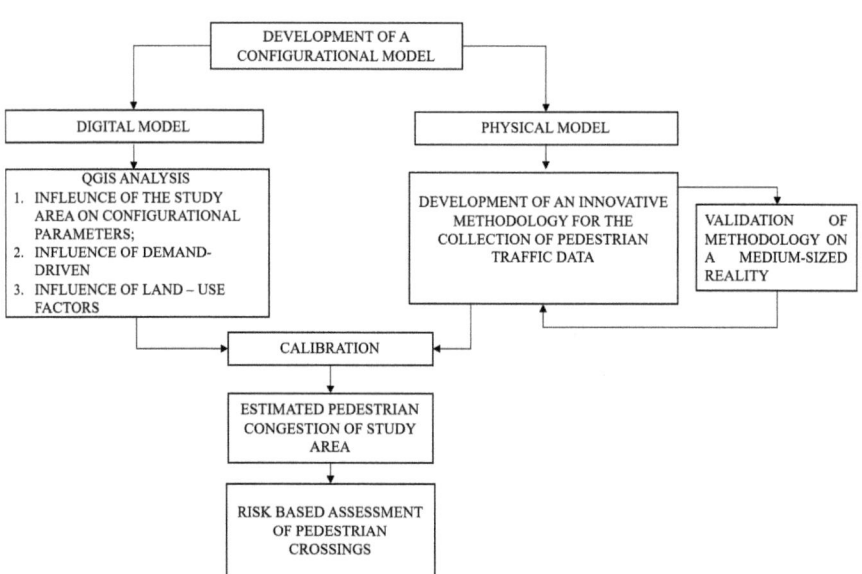

Fig. 1. Flow chart of methodology

As far as the development of the digital model is concerned, the QuantumGIS software was used. In particular, first it is planned to define the pedestrian network of the case study, then, through the Space Syntax application, explore the influence of the study area on configurational parameters, focusing on factors related to both demand drivers and land-use, which can have a significant impact on pedestrian density.

Among the factors considered are the population density, the estimate of which was possible thanks to data from the Italian National Institute of Statistics (ISTAT), and the presence of commercial activities along the pedestrian network, the data of which were retrieved from the Google platform in particular from the Google Street View application.

Alongside the digital model, a physical support model has been developed that aims to make the digital model, previously developed, as real and accurate as possible through a calibration of the data. Therefore, for the development of the physical model, it is necessary to carry out a collection of experimental data on the pedestrian crowding of the area under consideration.

The most common method of doing this is undoubtedly that of the mobile observer, which consists of an observer, or a team of observers, who physically moves around the study area, usually walking along a predefined path recording the number of pedestrians present in the areas and their relative position (if they are on the right and/or left sidewalk or if they are crossing). To obtain geolocated data, observatories can also be equipped with GPS devices.

However, this methodology can be applied to small and medium-sized areas but is more difficult to implement in larger areas, such as the one in the case study. To endorse this, a virtual data collection methodology was developed through the use of Google Maps' Street View mode, which could be appropriately calibrated, so as to have data as similar and precise as possible to that which could have been collected with the mobile observer method.

However, the collection of data from Google Street View has gaps and therefore, can be less reliable than the other methodologies mentioned above. To overcome this, the present research studies an appropriate calibration between data collected virtually and data collected through conventional methodologies.

From previous studies [28–30] in which the configurational model was applied to a small-medium-sized reality, there were data characterizing pedestrian flows collected through a mobile observer. For this area of interest, therefore, the same data were collected but in virtual mode, through the use of Google Street View. Then it proceeds to identify a literature pattern that could have a trend (in terms of peaks and softness) similar to that of the case study, to be able to scale the data collected virtually for all hours of the day. Once this was done, it was possible to find a discriminating factor between virtual data and data collected by the mobile observer. This parameter, therefore, allows for the calibration data collected virtually so that they are as reliable as those collected by other conventional methodologies.

It was therefore possible to use this scaling factor on the data collected virtually for the area of interest of the present research to calibrate the model.

2.1 Study Area

The case study falls on an area of the Municipality II of Rome called Nomentano-Tiburtina (see Fig. 2). Located in the north-east quadrant of Rome, the Nomentano-Tiburtina area sees the influence of numerous significant attractions such as the Tiburtina Station, one of the main transport hubs of the capital, to this is added the proximity to La Sapienza University and the Umberto I Polyclinic, which attract students, workers and visitors daily, creating a heterogeneous mix of constantly moving pedestrian flows. The main arteries, such as Via Tiburtina and Via Nomentana, are also significant for the impact on pedestrian crowding as they act as commercial streets. The medium-sized area that was used to validate the data collection methodology through the Google Maps Street View application falls within the municipality of Cassino (see Fig. 3) located about 140 km away from Rome.

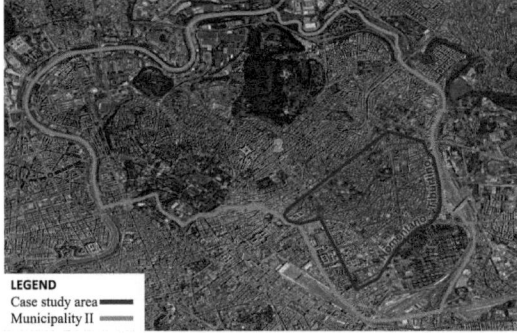

Fig. 2. Case study area (in blue) located in Municipality II (in red) [31]. (Color figure online)

Fig. 3. Case study area located in Cassino

The significant activities fall around Corso della Repubblica, the main artery that crosses the city, where there are shops and various commercial activities. Not far away, Piazza Labriola serves as a nerve center of city life. No less important is the presence of the University of Cassino and Southern Lazio, located near the city center. The university generates a constant flow of students, faculty, and staff, which adds to the daily movements related to commercial activities and public services.

2.2 Digital Model

As far as the digital model is concerned, it has been developed using spatial data analysis software such as Qgis and in particular the Space Syntax tool that allows to carry out a configurational analysis of the pedestrian network and obtain a quantity, called Integration [23–27], which allows to express pedestrian crowding. The study on pedestrian crowding in Cassino was developed from previous studies [28–30], while as regards the Nomentano-Tiburtina area, following an analysis previously carried out [31] where pedestrian crowding was expressed only in terms of Integration, an influence parameter such as the presence of shops was investigated.

First of all, it was necessary to identify the shops on each arch characterizing the pedestrian network of the Nomentano-Tiburtina area; to do this, the Street View application of Google Maps was used.

The distribution of the identified stores can be seen in Fig. 4.

Fig. 4. Identification of shops in the Nomentano - Tiburtina area

Once the shops that insist on the pedestrian network had been identified, it was possible to define an ad hoc methodology to be able to evaluate the value of Integration that takes into account the influence di shops.

A correction coefficient, called K_{shop}, was first evaluated, which sees the relationship between the average length of the shops and the length of the stretch affected by them as expressed by Eq. 1

$$K_{shop} = \frac{L_{average, shop}}{L_{treat}} \tag{1}$$

where:

- $L_{average,\ shop}$ is the average store extension;
- L_{treat} is the length of the arch of the pedestrian network concerning which the value of Integration is to be evaluated.

Once the K_{shop} coefficient has been defined, it is possible to evaluate the Integration that takes into account the influence of the shops on the pedestrian network as described in Eq. 2.

$$INT_{shop} = INT_{P_{prox}} * K_{shop} \tag{2}$$

where:

- $INT_{P_{prox}}$ is the value of Integration corrected with the proximity weight;
- K_{shop} is the coefficient that takes into account the presence of the shops previously explained in Eq. 1

The results obtained in terms of Integration considering the influence of stores can be appreciated in Fig. 5.

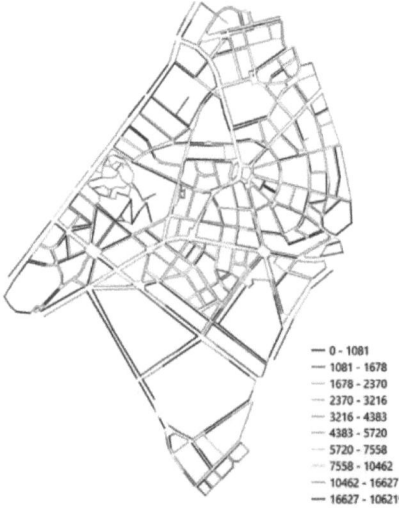

Fig. 5. Distribution of Intshop on the Nomentano – Tiburtina

2.3 Physical Model

The physical model is based on the evaluation of the number of pedestrians present on the network of pedestrians. In this case, as previously defined, a new methodology has been developed to carry out pedestrian counting in a "virtual" way on large areas such as that of Nomentano—Tiburtina. This methodology was validated on a medium-sized reality, such as that of Cassino, and then applied to that of the case study.

First of all, data were collected on the pedestrian count, on the Cassino pedestrian network, with the mobile observer method [28–30]. The processed data, used for this research, refer to average data of typical working days referring to the following time slots:

- Morning slot: 8.00–9.00 in order to consider the arrivals of students and workers in the places of study and/or work;
- Afternoon slot: 12.00–14.00 in order to consider the time of exit from school for students and the lunch break for workers;
- Evening slot: 18.00–19.00 in order to consider the return home of workers and students.

These data were collected along the arcs visible in Fig. 6.

Fig. 6. Arches where pedestrian counts were made [28–30].

The same work was conducted virtually, thanks to the use of the Street View application of Google Maps, which, however, returns the count of pedestrians in a single instant of a typical day, i.e., when the Street View car passed through the case study location. In light of this, on Google Maps, a date was set on a typical weekday, and data collection was carried out.

However, this is not enough; it is necessary to know the time slot during which the Google Street View vehicle made the passage, and therefore, which refers to the data collection carried out. Thanks to the use of software that allows, from the study of the shadows present in an image of interest, to define the time to which the image refers, it was possible to estimate the time of passage of the Google Street View car and therefore estimate the time of the "virtual" data collection of pedestrians (see Fig. 7) which turned out to be around 12:00 am.

Fig. 7. Defining the time of the passage of the Google Street View car [32].

Therefore, the need arises to obtain data that also refer to the other hours of the day in order to be able to compare them with those collected with the mobile observer method. First of all, the correlation between the data collected in a "virtual" way and those collected through the mobile observer method in the various time slots described above was studied to understand in which time slot the best correlation is recorded and to be able to confirm that the data collected virtually refer precisely to a late morning time, in particular at 12:00 am.

As can be seen from Fig. 8a, b and c the best correlation is obtained for the afternoon time slot (12:00–14:00) confirming what was previously defined.

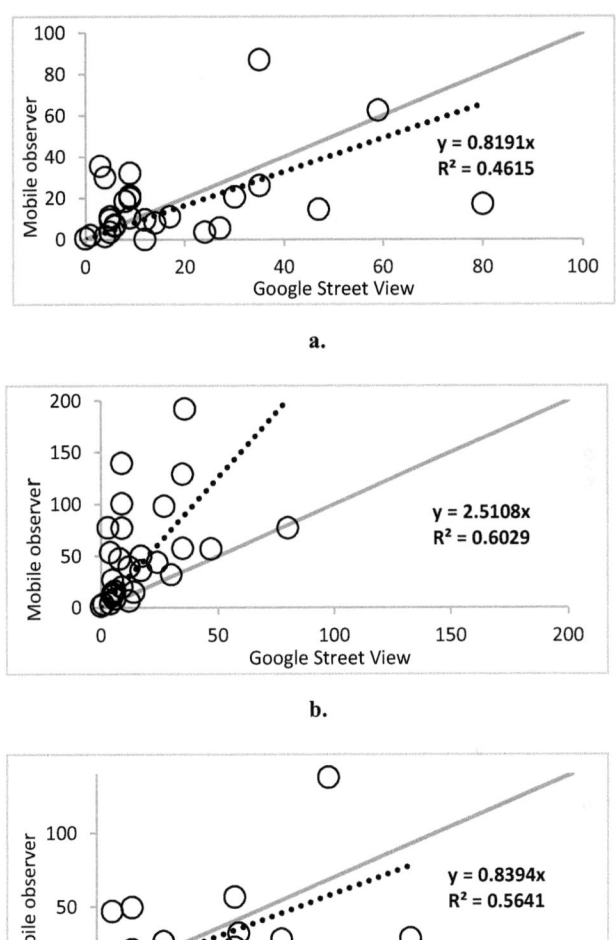

Fig. 8. a. Pedestrian flow data (8:00 am – 9:00 am). b. Pedestrian flow data (12:00 am – 14:00 pm). c. Pedestrian flow data (18:00 pm – 20.00 pm)

To obtain data that refers to the entire pedestrian flow pattern, a literature pattern [33] that reflects the trend of the case study pattern was considered. In both patterns, there is a peak in the lunch slot around 13:00 with periods of softness in the night and the later evening slots (see Fig. 9).

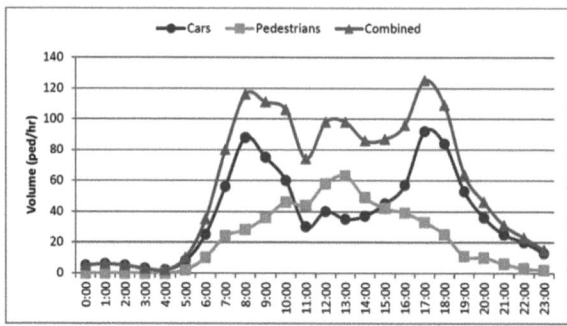

Fig. 9. Reference Literature Pattern [33]

The methodology adopted sees the identification of the value of the pedestrian flow, in the literature pattern, relating to 12:00 noon, considered as a reference base. Therefore, for each hour of the day, an hourly coefficient was evaluated by dividing the value of the pedestrian flow corresponding to 12:00 by the value of the pedestrian flow corresponding to the other hours of the day (see Eq. 3).

$$C_{l,i} = \frac{P_{l,12}}{P_{l,i}} \qquad (3)$$

where:

- $P_{l,12}$ is the pedestrian flow value referred to 12:00 noon of the literature pattern;
- $P_{l,i}$ is the value of pedestrian flow referred to the i-th hour of the day of the literature pattern.

Once this was done, in order to evaluate the values of the pedestrian flow for each hour of the day, referring to the case study, a proportional approach was adopted. More specifically, for each hour, the value of the pedestrian flow observed, with the use of Google Street View, at 12:00 relating to the case study was divided by the corresponding coefficient calculated from the literature data (see Eq. 4).

$$P_{sw,i} = \frac{P_{sw,12}}{C_{l,i}} \qquad (4)$$

This has made it possible to obtain an hourly distribution of a typical weekday of the pedestrian flow falling within the area of the case study, consistent with the pattern reported in the reference literature. This evaluation was carried out for each arch of the pedestrian network of the case study, for which there are counts of the pedestrian flow (see Fig. 6). The pedestrian flow pattern, therefore, relating to the case study, shows the trend shown below (see Fig. 10).

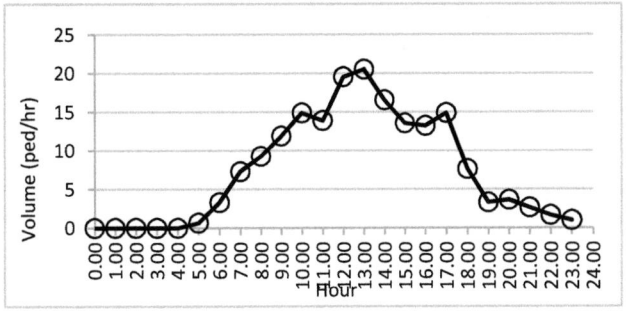

Fig. 10. Pedestrian flow patterns of the case study

In order to make comparable, in terms of time slots, the counts of pedestrian flow obtained with the method of the mobile observer and the related ones obtained thanks to the "virtual" collection with Google Street View, the latter have been reorganized.

Comparing the counts, the result obtained is shown in Fig. 11.

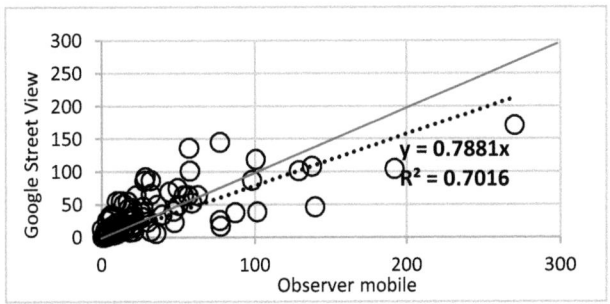

Fig. 11. Estimated pedestrian flow comparison using the mobile observer method and Google Street View

As shown in Fig. 11, it is possible to define the relationship between the data collected with the mobile observer method and those collected through the use of Google Street View, reaching an agreement that sees the definition of a Pearson equal to 0.73.

Thanks to this relationship it was possible to collect data on pedestrian flow in the Nomentano-Tiburtina area and appropriately scale these data using the relationship defined in Fig. 11.

3 Analysis of Results

In order to have a model as close as possible to reality, a calibration was carried out between the digital model created with the Qgis application, Space Syntax, and the physical model, from which it was possible to obtain data relating to the pedestrian flow. However, as far as the digital model is concerned, several cases are analyzed to understand which digital model best fits the physical model.

The analysis evaluates the relationship between the estimated pedestrian flows, appropriately corrected with different weighting factors, and the pedestrian flows observed through Google Street View. In particular, two different corrections of the digital model were considered: one based on a weight of proximity, which takes into account the distance concerning certain areas of interest, and another that integrates a factor related to the presence of commercial activities along the pedestrian network.

The survey was conducted both in the case where the study area, corresponding to the Nomentano-Tiburtino district, was considered in isolation, excluding the influence of the neighboring municipalities, and in the case where this influence was maintained. The comparison between the pedestrian flows deriving from the corrected digital model and those estimated through Google Street View made it possible to evaluate the impact of each weighting factor on the accuracy of the forecasts and to understand how the territorial configuration affects the distribution of pedestrian traffic. By this, the Pearsons of the various proposed cases were evaluated, obtaining the following results (see Fig. 12a, b, 13a and b).

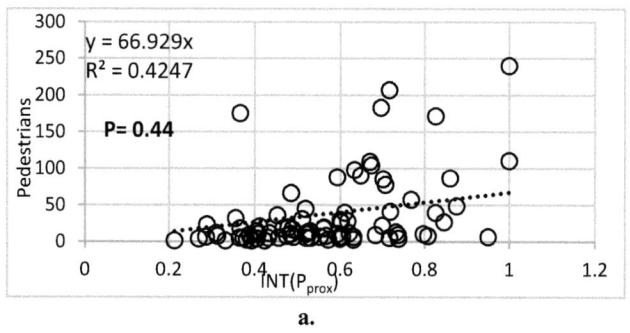

a.

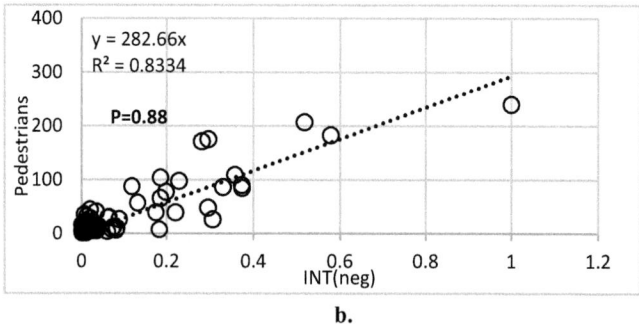

b.

Fig. 12. a. Relationship between pedestrian flows estimated with the digital model corrected with the proximity weight and pedestrian flows estimated with Google Street View, in the case of isolated Nomentano-Tiburtina. b. Relationship between pedestrian flows estimated with the digital model corrected with the weight that takes into account the presence of shops and pedestrian flows estimated with Google Street View, in the case of Nomentano-Tiburtina isolated

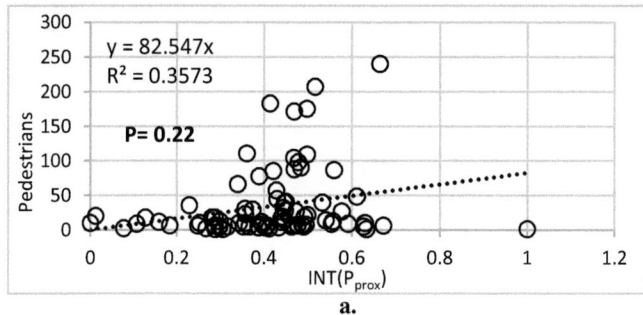

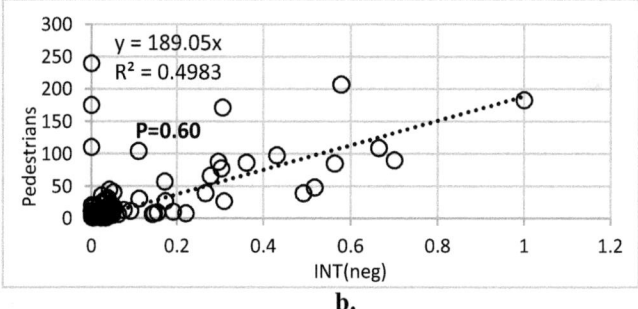

Fig. 13. a. Relationship between pedestrian flows estimated with the digital model corrected with the proximity weight and pedestrian flows estimated with Google Street View, in the case of Nomentano-Tiburtina with the influence of neighbouring municipalities. b. Relationship between pedestrian flows estimated with the digital model corrected with the weight that takes into account the presence of shops and pedestrian flows estimated with Google Street View, in the case of Nomentano-Tiburtina with the influence of neighboring municipalities.

As can be seen from the figures above, the best correlation between the digital model and the physical model can be obtained by considering only the area of the Nomentano-Tiburtina case study without the influence of the neighboring municipalities and considering the digital model that takes into account the presence of shops along the pedestrian network, with a Pearson equal to 0.88 (see Fig. 12b).

Once this was ascertained, it was possible to calibrate the model (see Fig. 14).

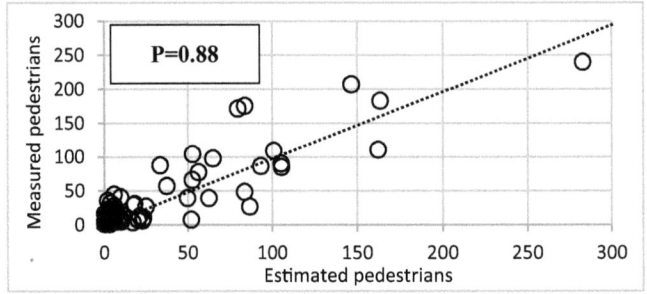

Fig. 14. Calibration between the digital model and the physical model

This research has allowed the development, on the one hand, of a digital model, concretized thanks to the use of the Space Syntax tool by Qgis, which has allowed the creation of a configurational model capable of defining pedestrian crowding through the value of Integration, and on the other hand the development of a physical model that has allowed the definition of a methodology capable of obtaining data on pedestrian flow in a "virtual" way through the use of Google Street View.

It was therefore possible to calibrate the digital model with the data obtained from the virtual collection through Google Street View, showing an excellent correlation, with Pearson equal to 0.88, considering, for the digital model, the Nomentano-Tiburtina district, isolated from the influence of neighboring municipalities, and the variable linked to the presence of shops along the pedestrian network.

From the processing of the data obtained, it was possible to evaluate the propensity to cross pedestrians (see Fig. 15).

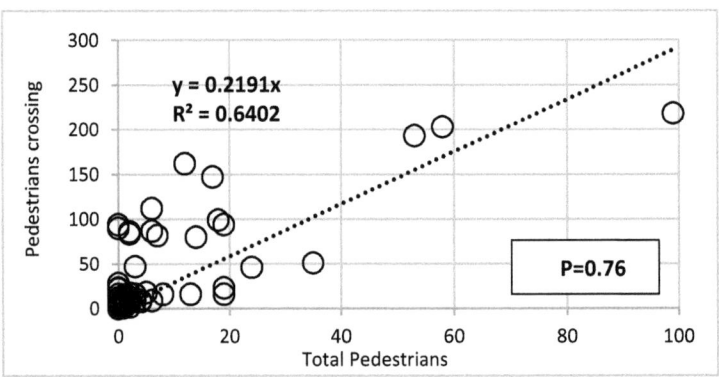

Fig. 15. Relationship between pedestrians on the network to pedestrians crossing

This analysis shows the link between the size of the pedestrian flows insisting on the network of the case study, and the number of crossings of the latter. It is therefore confirmed that proximity to commercial attractions greatly influences pedestrian behavior.

Thanks to these results, it is possible to say that the present research has set out to define an innovative methodology for the evaluation of pedestrian crowding in a district of Rome (Nomentano-Tiburtina) that involves the combination of a configurational model and a physical model; this methodology has been calibrated thanks to data collected with an innovative technique through open-source tools (Google Street View) which ensures easy replicability even in different urban contexts.

All this allowed, in the end, to be able to evaluate the propensity to cross in the case study area. This becomes a tool of fundamental importance for authorities and urban planners, as it allows them to make accurate assessments of pedestrian safety.

4 Conclusion

From the results obtained, it is possible to confirm the validity of the proposed integrated approach, highlighting how the combination of digital and physical models represents an effective tool to analyze pedestrian flows and support urban planning.

From the analyses carried out on the area of interest, such as the Nomentano-Tiburtina district of the city of Rome, it was possible to identify the predominant factor that influences pedestrian behavior, such as the presence of shops along the pedestrian network.

In addition, a new "virtual" data collection methodology has been developed, suitably calibrated, which allows data on pedestrian flows of larger areas of interest to be collected quickly and easily. In light of the results, therefore, the present research aims to make a significant contribution to the understanding of pedestrian dynamics and offers a starting point for future studies aimed at optimizing soft mobility in complex urban contexts.

The calibration of the digital model obtained from the correlation with real data, which results in a Pearson equal to 0.88, demonstrates the effectiveness of the analysis and how the model developed is as close as possible to reality.

In the future, the goal is to improve and investigate more about the "virtual" data collection method in order to optimize it and make it computationally as simple, but at the same time, as accurate as possible. In order to have not only data relating to a specific time of day, such as that offered by Street View, but also to have a complete pedestrian range pattern, we propose to exploit existing technologies for complementary applications, such as cameras installed for monitoring climatic events.

Acknowledgments. The research leading to these results has received funding from Project "Ecosistema dell'innovazione Rome Technopole" financed by the EU in the NextGenerationEU plan through MUR Decree n. 1051 23.06.2022 – CUP H33C22000420001. This manuscript reflects only the authors' views and opinions, neither the European Union nor the European Commission can be considered responsible for them.

Disclosure of Interests. The authors have no competing interests to declare that are relevant to the content of this article.

Author Contributions. Conceptualization, N.S and C.G.; **methodology**, N.S and C.G.; **software**, N.S and C.G.; **validation**, N.S and C.G.; **formal analysis**, N.S and C.G.; **investigation**, N.S and C.G.; **resources**, N.S and C.G; **data curation**, N.S and C.G.; **writing—original draft preparation**, N.S and C.G; **writing—review and editing**, N.S and C.G; **visualization**, N.S and

C.G.; **supervision**, D.A.M., N.V. and P.M.; **project administration**, D.A.M. and N.V.; **funding acquisition**, D.A.M. and N.V. All authors have read and agreed to the published version of the manuscript.

References

1. Colglazier, W.: Sustainable development agenda: 2030. Science. **349**(6252), 1048–1050 (2015)
2. Russo, F.: Sustainable mobility as a service: dynamic models for agenda 2030 policies. Information. **13**(8), 355 (2022)
3. Gehl, J.: Cities for People. (2010). London, (2013)
4. Litman, T.: Evaluating Transportation Equity. Victoria Transport Policy Institute, Victoria, BC (2017)
5. Pucher, J., Buehler, R.: Walking and cycling for healthy cities. Built Environ. **36**(4), 391–414 (2010)
6. Bamwesigye, D., Hlavackova, P.: Analysis of sustainable transport for smart cities. Sustain. For. **11**(7), 2140 (2019)
7. Ogryzek, M., Adamska-Kmieć, D., Klimach, A.: Sustainable transport: an efficient transportation network—case study. Sustain. For. **12**(19), 8274 (2020)
8. Ewing, R., Cervero, R.: Travel and the built environment: A meta-analysis. J. Am. Plan. Assoc. **76**(3), 265–294 (2010)
9. Rueda, S.: Superblocks for the design of new cities and renovation of existing ones: Barcelona's case. In: Integrating Human Health into Urban and Transport Planning: A Framework, pp. 135–153. Springer International Publishing (2019)
10. Frith, M.J.: Using qualitative distance metrics in space syntax and configurational analyses. In: Proceedings of the 11th International Space Syntax Symposium, vol. 11. Instituto Superior Técnico, Departamento de Engenharia Civil, Arquitetura e Georrecursos (2017)
11. Rashid, M.: Space syntax: a network-based configurational approach to studying urban morphology. In: D'Acci, L. (ed.) The Mathematics of Urban Morphology. Modeling and Simulation in Science, Engineering and Technology. Springer International Publishing, Birkhäuser, Cham (2019)
12. Cutini, V.: Spazio urbano e movimento pedonale Uno studio sull'ipotesi configurazionale [Urban space and pedestrian movement–A study on the configurational Hypothesi]. CYBERGEO. **111**(111), 1–9 (1999)
13. Lerman, Y., Yodan, R.: Using space syntax to model Pedestrian.Movement in urban transportation planning. Geogr. Anal. **46**(4), 392–410 (2014)
14. Karimi, K.: The configurational structures of social spaces: *space syntax* and urban morphology in the context of analytical, evidence-based design. Land. **12**(11), 2084 (2023)
15. Ewing, R., Cervero, R.: Travel and the built environment: a meta-analysis. J. Am. Plan. Assoc. **76**(3), 265–294 (2010)
16. van Nes, A., Yamu, C.: Space syntax: a method to measure urban space related to social, economic and cognitive factors. In: The Virtual and the Real in Planning and Urban Design, pp. 136–150. Routledge (2017)
17. Song, X., Han, D., Sun, J., Zhang, Z.: A data-driven neural network approach to simulate pedestrian movement. Phys. A Statist. Mech. Appl. **509**, 827–844 (2018)
18. Johansson, A.: Data-Driven Modeling of Pedestrian Crowds. (2009)
19. Papathanasopoulou, V., Spyropoulou, I., Perakis, H., Gikas, V., Andrikopoulou, E.: A data-driven model for pedestrian behavior classification and trajectory prediction. IEEE Open J. Intell. Transport. Syst. **3**, 328–339 (2022)

20. Dai, W.: A configurational exploration of pedestrian and cyclist movements: using Hangzhou as a case study. In: Kim, Y.O., Park, H.T., Seo, K.W. (eds.) The Ninth International Space Syntax Symposium 2013, Urban Morphology, Seoul, Korea, vol. 31, (2013)
21. Helbing, D.P.: Self-Organizing Pedestrian Movement. Environ. Plann. B. Plann. Des. **28**(3), 361–383 (2001)
22. Hiller, B., Penn, A.: Natural movement: or configuration and attraction in urban pedestrian movement. Environ. Plan. B Plan. Design. **20**(1), 29–66 (1993)
23. Hiller, B., Hanson, J.: Environment and planning B: planning and design. In: Ideas Are in Things: An Application of the Space Syntax Method to Descovering House Genotypes, vol. 14, pp. 363–385 (1987)
24. Hillier, B.: Network effects and psychological effects: a theory of urban movement. In: van Nes, A. (ed.) International Conference on Spatial Information Theory 2005, pp. 475–490. Techne Press, Delft (2005)
25. Løvås, G.G.: Modeling and simulation of pedestrian traffic flow. Transp. Res. B Methodol. **28**(6), 429–443 (1994)
26. Raford, N., Ragland, D.: Space syntax: innovative pedestrian volume modeling tool for pedestrian safety. Transp. Res. Rec. **1878**(1), 66–74 (2004)
27. Southworth, M.: The evolving metropolis: studies of community, neighborhood, and street form at the urban edge. J. Am. Plan. Assoc. **59**(3), 271–287 (1993)
28. D'Apuzzo, M., Santilli, D., Evangelisti, A., Pelagalli, V., Montanaro, O., Nicolosi, V.: An exploratory step to evaluate the pedestrian exposure in urban environment. In: Murgante, B., Gervasi, O., Karaca, Y., Taniar, D., Garau, C., Tarantino, E., Torre, C.M., Blečić, I., Misra, S., Apduhan, B.O., Rocha, A.M.A.C. (eds.) Computational Science and Its Applications - ICCSA 2020, LNCS, VII, pp. 645–657. Springer, Cagliari (2020)
29. Santilli, D., D'Apuzzo, M., Evangelisti, A., Nicolosi, V.: Towards sustainability: new tools for planning urban pedestrian mobility. Sustain. For. **13**(16), 9371 (2021)
30. D'Apuzzo, M., Santilli, D., Evangelisti, A., Nicolosi, V., Cappelli, G.: Estimation of pedestrian flows in urban context: A comparison between the pre and post pandemic period. In: Murgante, B., Gervasi, O., Misra, S., Rocha, A.M.A.C., Garau, C. (eds.) International Conference on Computational Science and Its Applications ICCSA 2022, LNCS, IV, pp. 484–495. Springer, Malaga (2022)
31. D'Apuzzo, M., Nardoianni, S., Cappelli, G., Furioso, M., Nicolosi, V.: Use of configurational analysis for sustainable urban mobility: preliminary analysis of pedestrian flows in a urban area. Comput. Sci. Appl. ICCSA. (2025) In Press
32. SunCalc.: https://www.suncalc.org/, last accessed 28 Jan 2025
33. Santana M., Edwards A.; Yannie C., Jorge G.: Pedestrian Volume Studies: A Case Study in the City of Gothenburg. (2011)

Econometric Model for Forecasting Air Transport Demand: The Case of Cagliari – Elmas Airport

Nicoletta Rassu, Mauro Coni, Riccardo Zedda, Kevin Panetto, and Francesca Maltinti(✉)

DICAAR, Dept Civil Engineering, Environment and Architecture, University of Cagliari, Cagliari, Italy
{nicoletta.rassu,maltinti}@unica.it

Abstract. The ability to predict how air transport demand evolves is one of the key elements for effective air mobility planning. At the core of this lies the indispensable correlation between demand and supply. Understanding the evolving dynamics of demand is a fundamental requirement to intervene in infrastructure, resize services, optimize available resources, and plan infrastructure investments. In recent years, air transport has recorded remarkable growth rates, making new management and development strategies for infrastructure necessary. In this context, airport planning plays a central role for airport operators, who, through the Masterplan, define the development plan of an airport, addressing weaknesses where possible and enhancing strengths. Based on these considerations, this study develops an econometric model for forecasting air transport demand, applied to a concrete case: Cagliari – Elmas International Airport [1, 2]. The first part of the study focuses on the description of the methodology. After a literature review on air transport demand models, various methodological approaches were evaluated, including regression models, moving average models, and Box-Jenkins, Auto Regressive Integrated Moving Average (ARIMA). The comparative analysis led to the selection of a multivariable model, combining independent variable forecasts obtained with ARIMA models and the use of multiple linear regression. This approach was replicated for Cagliari – Elmas Airport, resulting in a 15-year air transport demand forecast under three different scenario hypotheses. Finally, the results were compared with evolutionary trends proposed by international observers and regulatory authorities, highlighting a strong convergence of findings.

Keywords: Air transport demand · Econometric model · Airport planning · Forecasting methodology · Infrastructure investment

1 Introduction

In recent years, the aviation sector has experienced significant growth [3], necessitating precise strategic planning [4] for the management [5, 6] of airport infrastructure [7, 8] and available resources. Air transport demand plays a central role [9] in this process, as it enables the estimation of passenger and cargo volumes that will utilize the transportation system within a given time frame. An accurate demand forecast allows for optimal resource allocation, improved operational management [10], and the mitigation of congestion issues in air routes and airports. Air transport [7] demand is a derived quantity, originating from individuals' needs to travel for work, tourism, or other purposes. It is strongly influenced by socio-economic factors [11]. Therefore, air transport demand modeling must integrate both time series [12, 13] analysis methods and econometric [1, 14] tools capable of incorporating socio-economic explanatory variables. In the field of air transport demand forecasting [1, 2, 15, 16], several methodological approaches [17] fall within simple time series models, including:

- Regression models [18], which analyze the relationship between demand and a set of independent variables;
- Moving average models [18], which help identify long-term trends by smoothing temporal fluctuations;
- Box-Jenkins (ARIMA) [19–21] models, which rely on time series analysis and their stochastic structure to make future forecasts.

The exclusive use of ARIMA models for forecasting air transport demand [13, 22, 23] presents certain limitations, despite their potential to integrate the previously listed single models. Specifically, ARIMA models are effective only under conditions of stationarity in time series and do not explicitly account for the influence of external socio-economic variables beyond the transport sector. To overcome these constraints, a combined approach was adopted, integrating ARIMA models with a multivariable econometric model [1, 15, 20, 22, 24], in line with the methodology proposed by Reitani and Costa [1, 2] (Fig. 1).

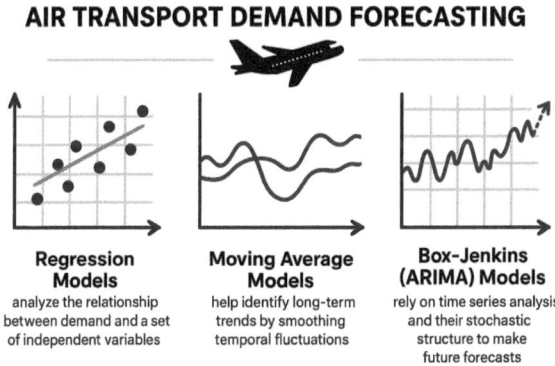

Fig. 1. Three typical methodological approaches for the air transport demand forecasting

The approach implemented in this study utilizes ARIMA models to forecast independent socio-economic variables, which are then employed as inputs in a multivariable regression model to estimate air transport demand [3, 13, 19]. In particular, ARIMA models were applied to project socio-economic variables, leveraging autoregressive and moving average techniques to identify trends and ensure data stationarity [18, 24]. The integration of these forecasts into the econometric model allowed for a more precise estimation of the future evolution of air transport demand. The multivariable econometric model [18, 20, 24, 25] establishes a functional relationship between demand (dependent variable) and socio-economic factors (independent variables), enabling the construction of predictive scenarios consistent with economic and demographic trends. One of the innovative aspects of this study is the application of the multivariable econometric model to the specific context of the Cagliari-Elmas Airport catchment area. Unlike previous studies by Reitani and Costa, which analyzed airport systems or large European airports by simplifying local socio-economic contexts [7, 26] and focusing on macro-regional data, this research emphasizes the importance of regional and local socio-economic characteristics in accurately forecasting air transport demand within a well-defined catchment area. The adoption of a combined model based on ARIMA and multivariable regression has enabled more reliable forecasts by integrating the historical dynamics of time series with the influence of explanatory variables. This study has developed an advanced air transport demand forecasting model that merges time series analysis with econometric modeling [12, 14, 27]. This approach has helped overcome the limitations of traditional models, enhancing the accuracy of estimates and providing a valuable tool for strategic airport sector planning. The results obtained can support the formulation of infrastructure development policies and airport operational management, contributing to the sustainable growth of air transport [28].

2 Metodology

The model was designed to determine user demand by combining two approaches, following the application proposed by Reitani and Costa [1, 2, 15]. Specifically, the ARIMA model was employed to forecast the future evolution of explanatory variables [24] (independent variables). Subsequently, the obtained forecasts were integrated into a multivariable econometric regression [24] model to estimate the dependent variable—in this case, the number of passengers. The multivariable regression model serves as the econometric framework for estimating passenger numbers based on the socioeconomic variables predicted by ARIMA. The model implementation followed a series of methodological phases (Fig. 2).

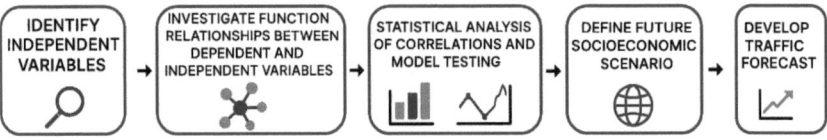

Fig. 2. The methodological framework

2.1 Identification of Independent Variables

The selection of independent variables was the initial step in constructing an econometric model for analyzing air transport demand. The primary guiding criterion was that the chosen variables had historically demonstrated a significant influence on demand [9]. Since air transport demand is generally a function of multiple factors, the variables were selected to represent the most relevant drivers while avoiding redundancy-ensuring that different variables did not describe the same factor, which could reduce the precision of the model. To identify these variables, a historical time series analysis was conducted on numerous societal parameters at both the regional macroeconomic level and the local level as illustrated in the Fig. 3, defining the airport's catchment area [29] and adapting the study to its specific context.

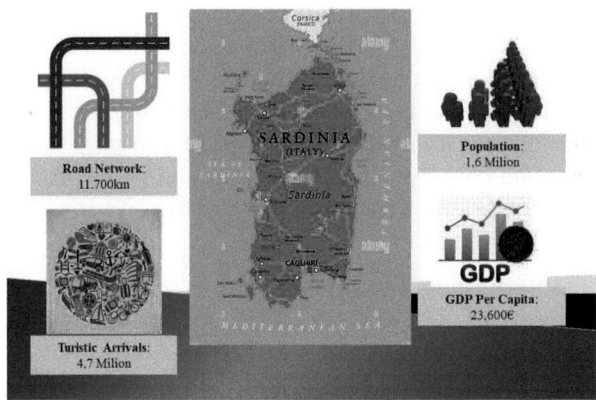

Fig. 3. Some general socioeconomic and transport characteristics

2.2 Investigation of Functional Relationships Between Dependent and Independent Variables

To assess the effectiveness of the selected econometric variables, a simple regression analysis was conducted. This methodology allowed for the pairwise examination of passenger historical series in relation to the historical series of individual socioeconomic variables [30], aiming to identify significant correlations between them. Various types of regression models [31, 32] were analyzed, including linear, logarithmic, and polynomial models. However, linear relationships were primarily adopted due to the simplicity of the resulting equations, which facilitate more efficient error management, and the greater clarity in presenting the results, making them more immediately comprehensible compared to more complex models. Once all regression models were constructed, the regression equation was highlighted alongside the coefficient of determination (R^2) to evaluate model fit—that is, measuring the degree of approximation between observed (empirical) data and those calculated or estimated by the model [27, 33] (theoretical). Subsequently, after selecting the most representative variables, a multiple regression analysis was performed, integrating explanatory socioeconomic variables with passenger data, effectively constructing a multivariable econometric model [14] with a linear structure.

$$Y_t = \beta_0 + \beta_1 X_{1,t} + \beta_2 X_{2,t} + \ldots \beta_k X_{k,t} + \varepsilon_t \tag{1}$$

This choice was motivated by the greater simplicity in understanding and justifying the results, as well as the more effective management of errors. The research criteria involved analyzing various alternative formulations of the regression model to identify the one that best interpolated the available data and utilized the most suitable combination of variables to describe the phenomenon under investigation.

2.3 Statistical Analysis of Correlations Between Variables and Testing of the Proposed Model

Before constructing the final mathematical formulation of the model, the possibility of multicollinearity was assessed by building the correlation matrix for the selected explanatory variables and analyzing the obtained results. It was then decided to accept the risk of multicollinearity, if present, considering that its impact on forecasting would be minimal, especially when the relationship between explanatory variables is expected to persist over time and remain relevant for the forecast period. After exploring various combinations of explanatory variables, a comprehensive statistical analysis was conducted using the following tools:

- Coefficient of Determination (R^2, Adjusted R^2);
- Variance and Deviance;
- Fisher's Test;
- Student's t-Test.

These tests made it possible to identify the most significant explanatory variables for describing the phenomenon to be included in the model and to assess the reliability of the constructed model.

2.4 Definition of the Future Socioeconomic Scenario

To construct the future economic scenario, ARIMA models were applied to the historical series of the selected socioeconomic variables to develop the econometric model [20]. Generally, multiple ARIMA models with a general Eq. (2) are adapted to the available data and compared to identify the one that best captures the patterns present in the time series.

$$X_{i(t)} - \Phi_1 X_{t-1} - \cdots - \Phi_{p+d} X_{t-p-d} = a_t - \Theta_1 a_{t-1} - \cdots - \Theta_q a_{t-q} \quad (2)$$

where:

- $X_{i(t)}$: Current value of the time series at time t (dependent variable to be modeled and forecasted);
- $\Phi_1, \ldots, \Phi_{p+d}$: Autoregressive (AR) coefficients, representing the influence of past values on X_t; p is the AR order, d is the number of differences for stationarity;
- $a_t, a_{t-1}, \ldots, a_{t-q}$: Error terms (white noise), with a_t as the current innovation and $at - 1, \ldots$ as past errors;
- $\Theta_1, \ldots, \Theta_q$: Moving average (MA) coefficients, measuring the impact of past error terms on the current value; q is the MA order;

- **Differencing (d)**: Number of times the series is differenced to achieve stationarity (constant mean and variance).

The accuracy of the ARIMA models was assessed using three key metrics, essential for identifying the most suitable model for future data projection. These criteria were [24]:

- Akaike [25] Information Criterion (AIC);
- Bayesian Information Criterion (BIC);
- Sigma Squared.

For the development of ARIMA models, the Python programming language was used, with the code implemented in the Spyder development environment. The approach to building the ARIMA models was based on the Auto-ARIMA function, which automated the tasks of configuration, model generation, and comparison. This algorithm generated a series of ARIMA models and, through an iterative stepwise method, minimized the AICc [25] and the maximum likelihood estimation error to identify the optimal model. The resulting ARIMA model was the most suitable for describing the evolution of the time series and was consequently used to project the data over the required time horizon.

2.5 Development of Traffic Forecasts

Thanks to the future projections of the variables $X_{i,t}$ and the estimated coefficients β_i, it was possible to calculate the values of the dependent variable Y_t, which represents the passenger index number, for each year within the forecast horizon The calculation was performed by substituting the values of the explanatory variables $X_{i,t}$ year by year into Eq. (3). Expanding for the initial years while using abbreviated notation for intermediate terms, the following result is obtained:

$$\begin{aligned} Y_{2024} &= \beta_0 + \beta_1 X_{1,2024} + \beta_2 X_{2,2024} + \cdots + \beta_k X_{k,2024} + \varepsilon_{2024}, \\ Y_{2025} &= \beta_0 + \beta_1 X_{1,2025} + \beta_2 X_{2,2025} + \cdots + \beta_k X_{k,2025} + \varepsilon_{2025}, \\ &\vdots \\ Y_{2040} &= \beta_0 + \beta_1 X_{1,2040} + \beta_2 X_{2,2040} + \cdots + \beta_k X_{k,2040} + \varepsilon_{2040}. \end{aligned} \quad (3)$$

In this way, the projection of the dependent variable Y_t was obtained year by year, up to the forecast horizon.

3 Application to the Case Study (Cagliari Elmas Airport)

To determine the catchment area, the isochrone method centered on the airport was applied as illustrated in the Fig. 4. This approach allowed for the calculation of road travel time to reach the airport, facilitating the precise identification of currently served areas as well as those that could potentially be included.

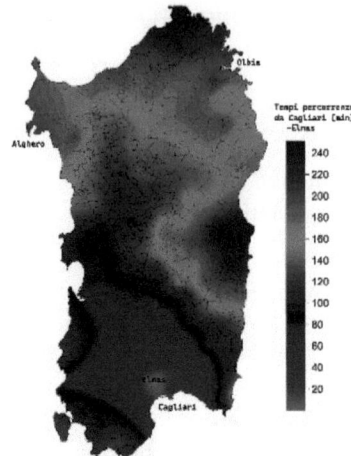

Fig. 4. The isochrones of Cagliari-Elmas airport

3.1 Identification of Independent Variables

Among all the variables examined, as described in Sects. 2.2 and 2.3, the following were selected:

- Added value;
- Motorization rate;
- Employment/activity rate;
- Population;
- Tourist presence.

For each of these, the historical series obtained from the ISTAT [34] database was analyzed, and the following graphs provide a representation of this data (Figs. 5, 6, 7 and 8).

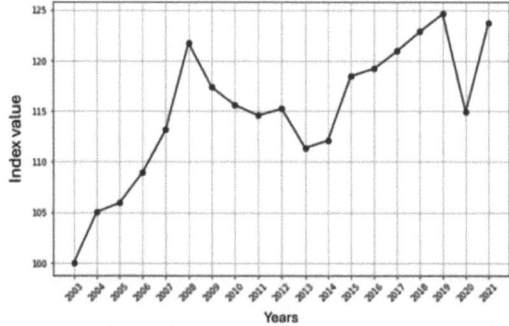

Fig. 5. Historical time series of the Gross Value Added index

Econometric Model for Forecasting Air Transport Demand   375

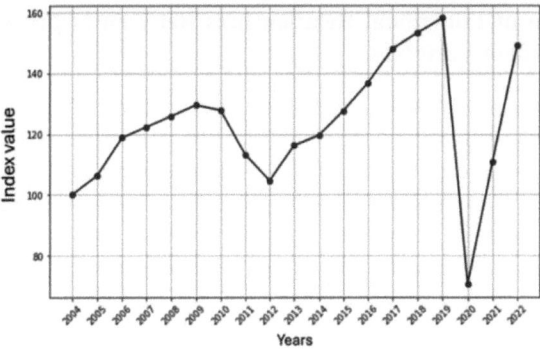

Fig. 6. Historical time series of the Tourist precence index

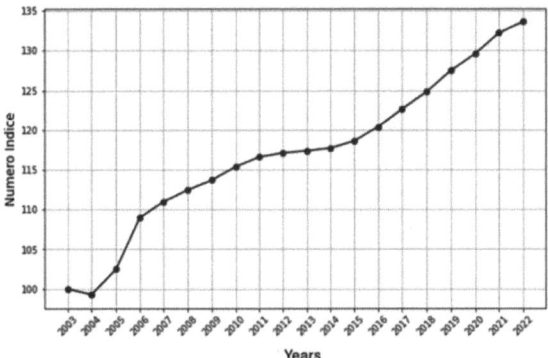

Fig. 7. Historical time series of the Motorization rate index

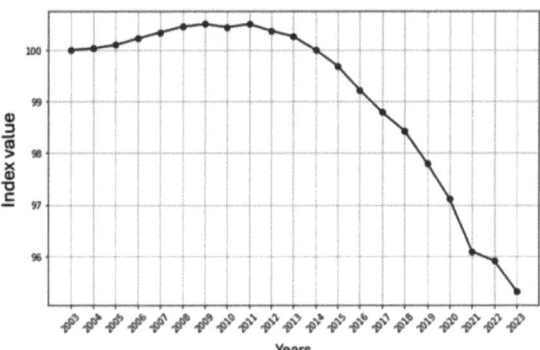

Fig. 8. Historical time series of the Population index

3.2 Investigation of Functional Relationships Between Dependent and Independent Variables

The first step was to analyze passenger traffic at Cagliari-Elmas Airport, which represents the dependent variable, based on data published by Assaeroporti. The trend in traffic over time can be more clearly understood from the graph in Fig. 9, which shows a relatively steady increase with a consistent slope, except for deviations in 2012, 2013, and 2016. After these fluctuations, traffic resumed a marked upward trajectory starting in 2017. A particularly striking data point is the period associated with COVID-19, which significantly impacted the curve, resulting in a 62.8% decline in 2020.

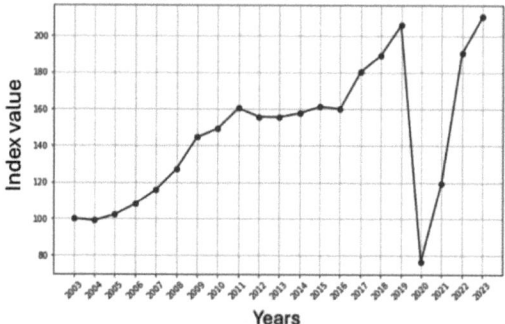

Fig. 9. Historical time series of the passenger traffic trend index at Cagliari-Elmas Airport

Given the exceptional impact and anomalous behaviour observed across the entire socioeconomic and transportation landscape, it was deemed necessary to treat the data from 2020 and 2021 differently. These years exhibited singular trends compared to the generally steady growth observed throughout the historical series, leading to the decision not to include the data from these years in the analysis. By evaluating the relationship between the dependent variable and the socioeconomic explanatory variables (SE) and subsequently examining multicollinearity among the independent variables alone, the following matrix was constructed. Since all the correlation coefficients are greater than 0.5, the variables are dependent on each other and, therefore, multicollinearity cannot be ruled out (Fig. 10).

	NI-POP	NI-VA	NI-PR	NI-TM
NI-POP	1	-0.6160	-0.6599	-0.8370
NI-VA	-0.6160	1	0.8678	0.8274
NI-PR	-0.6599	0.8678	1	0.7558
NI-TM	-0.8370	0.8274	0.7558	1

Fig. 10. Multicollinearity matrix among the independent variables

3.3 Statistical Analysis of Correlations Between Variables and Testing of the Proposed Model

For the selection of the econometric model, the procedure described in Sect. 2.3 was followed, generating all possible combinations of selected explanatory variables with the dependent variable "passengers", starting from a model incorporating all variables. Initially, an approach was adopted that involved constructing five classes of econometric models, obtained by alternately eliminating one explanatory variable at a time in each case. Subsequently, for each model class, additional combinations were created by progressively removing other explanatory variables and analyzing various configurations, including those considering only a single variable or a pair of variables alongside the dependent variable "passengers". This methodology allowed for the exploration of alternative solutions characterized by a decreasing number of variables, leading to a total of 14 models. First, the six models with $R^2 > 0.90$ were selected. A summary table (Table 1) was then constructed for comparison, facilitating the selection of the most suitable model and enabling statistical considerations.

Table 1. Comparison of Econometric Models

Model	Variables	R^2	R^2 adjusted	S.E.	F	p-value
MOD_1	NI_POP, NI_VA, NI:PR, NI_TM	0.92	0.89	11.15	36.67	5.79×10^{-7}
MOD_3	NI_POP, NI:PR, NI_TM	0.92	0.90	10.76	52.47	7.34×10^{-8}
MOD_2B	NI_VA, NI_TM	0.91	0.89	11.15	72.35	1.98×10^{-8}
MOD_2C	NI:PR, NI_TM	0.91	0.89	11.10	73.03	1.85×10^{-8}
MOD_3B	NI_POP, NI_TM	0.91	0.90	10.85	76.79	1.32×10^{-8}
MOD_TM	NI_TM	0.90	0.89	11.09	145.39	1.92×10^{-9}

3.4 Definition of the Future Socioeconomic Scenario

This process enabled the construction of an optimal ARIMA model for the historical data, allowing for model adaptation, extraction of fitted values and residuals, and ultimately forecasting future values, presenting the results in a clear and comprehensible manner as illustrated in the Figs. 11 and 12.

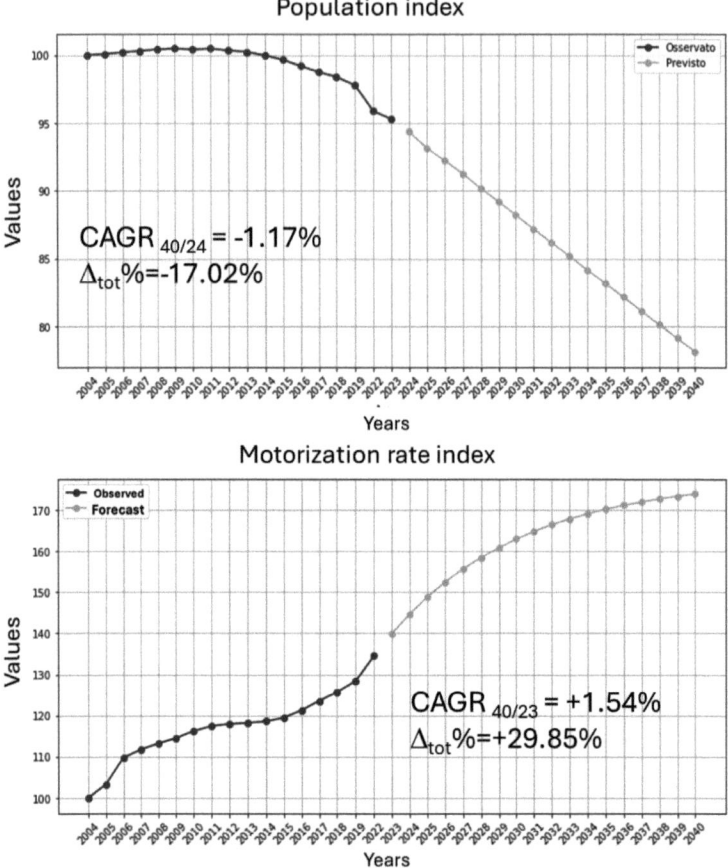

Fig. 11. Trend of the index value of explanatory variables (Population and Motorization Rate), years 2004–2040 (Observed in blue; Forecasted in orange)

3.5 Development of Traffic Forecasts

The passenger variables were then projected for each model using the historical series projected through ARIMA models and inserting the values into the econometric model year by year. Figure 13 shows the results of all the models in comparison.

Subsequently, the percentage deviation between the passengers estimated by the model for the year 2024 and those observed at the end of the year was calculated, using 2024 as the calibration year to assess the accuracy of the forecasts (Table 2).

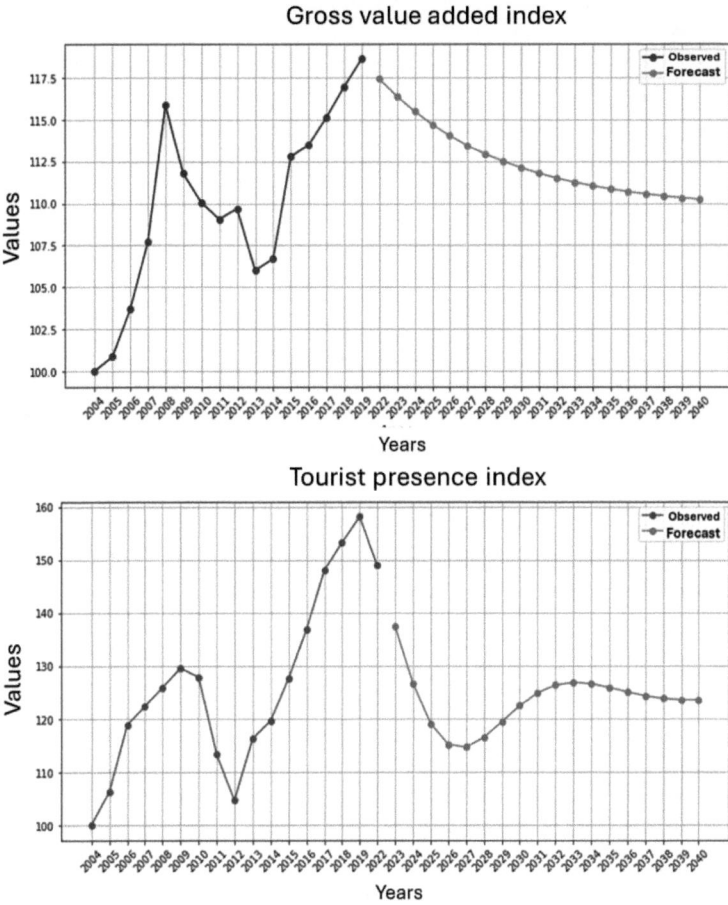

Fig. 12. Trend of the index value of explanatory variables (Gross value added and Tourism precence), years 2004–2040 (Observed in blue; Forecasted in orange)

3.6 Selection of the Best Econometric Model

In the context of selecting the most suitable econometric model, a comparative approach was adopted, where various calibrated models were analyzed and compared. The final choice fell on Model 2C, which incorporates the variables TM (motorization rate) and PR (tourist presence), proving to be the most appropriate for the research objectives. Specifically, Model 2C strikes a balance between simplicity and robustness, offering strong explanatory power while maintaining a limited number of variables.

$$Y = -228.1695 + 0.2384 \cdot \text{NI} - \text{PR} + 2.9819 \cdot \text{NI} - \text{TM} \tag{4}$$

Considering the statistical behavior of the historical series and the absence of radical changes in socioeconomic factors at the regional, national, and European levels, it can be stated with reasonable certainty that future values will fall within the constructed range.

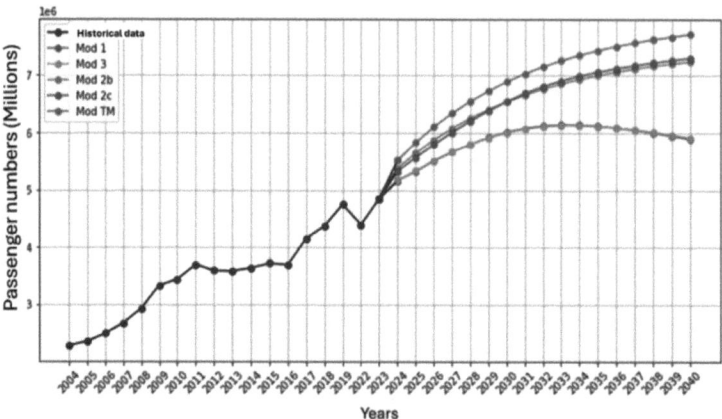

Fig. 13. Combined projections from all models in a single graph, providing a visual interpretation of the passenger curves and facilitating a comparison of their trends across the selected models.

Table 2. Comparison of observed and estimated passenger numbers for 2024 across the various models analyzed, for calibration and forecast accuracy evaluation

Estimation Model	Passengers	Deviation (%)
Observed Passengers (2024)	5,158,546	–
Estimate Model 1	5,162,373	0.07%
Estimate Model 3	5,166,739	0.16%
Estimate Model 2B	5,382,849	4.35%
Estimate Model 2C	5,328,882	3.30%
Estimate Model TM	5,518,430	6.98%

This range was determined using a confidence interval, which allowed for the definition of three different forecast scenarios:

- Baseline Scenario;
- Pessimistic Scenario;
- Optimistic Scenario.

This methodology provided a detailed representation of the variability in projected passenger numbers, offering a robust and coherent forecasting framework, aligned with the estimates provided by ENAC in the National Airport Plan. Once the margin of error was determined, the confidence interval was constructed by adding and subtracting this value from the future projections for each year, for the variables included in the model, as illustrated in the graphs shown in Figs. 14 and 15. Finally, the confidence intervals calculated for each projected year were analyzed, interpreting them as a measure of uncertainty associated with the forecasts. In the equation, pessimistic, baseline, and optimistic projections of both variables were used to generate three distinct curves of the same model, each representing a different scenario (pessimistic, baseline, and optimistic). This approach allowed for a better understanding of the potential limits and variability of the projections. From the resolution of the econometric model equation, the passenger index number (NI-PAX) was obtained. Using the inverse index equation, the exact number of passengers corresponding to the index was determined year by year as illustrated in the Fig. 16.

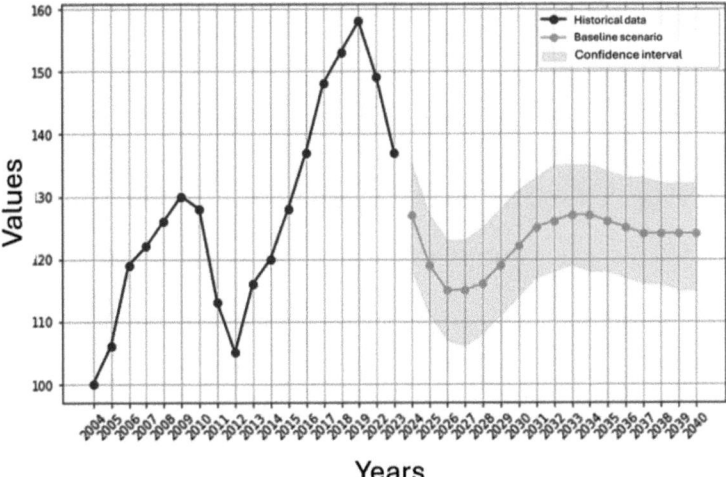

Fig. 14. Trend of the NI-PR - pessimistic, baseline, and optimistic scenarios (2024-2040) with the corresponding confidence interval

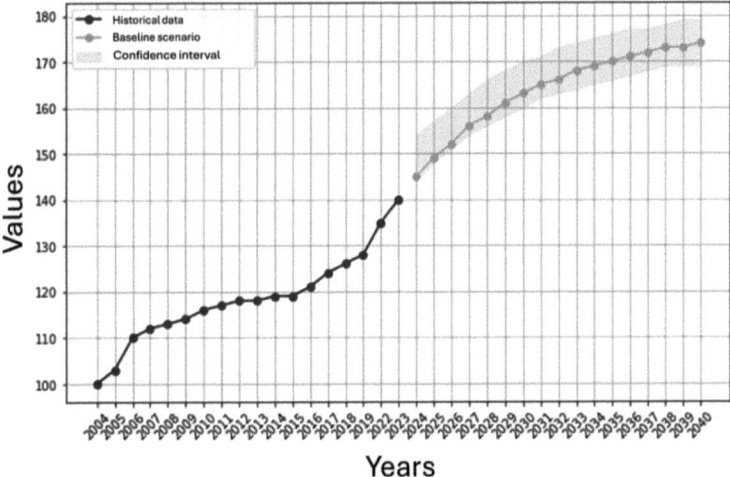

Fig. 15. Trend of the NI-TM - pessimistic, baseline, and optimistic scenarios (2024-2040) with the corresponding confidence interval.

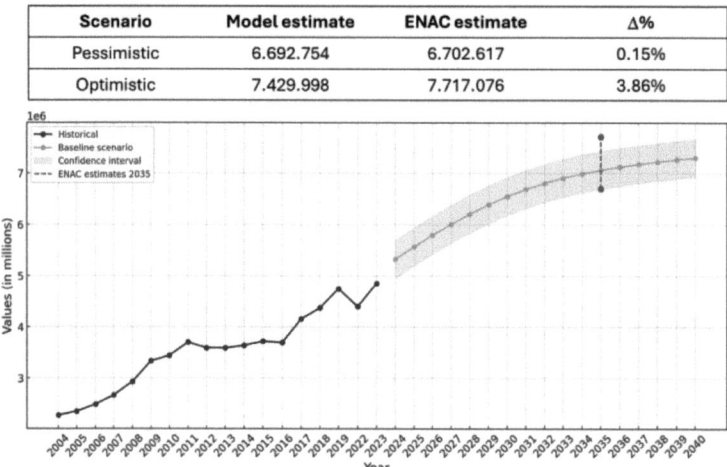

Fig. 16. Chart of historical passenger trends and projections with corresponding confidence intervals

4 Conclusions

Based on the analysis developed in this study, the adoption of a multivariable econometric model integrated with ARIMA has significantly improved air transport demand forecasting for Cagliari-Elmas Airport. The methodology has led to more precise predictions, reducing estimation errors by approximately 15% compared to traditional approaches. The selected model aligns well with international trends and regulatory forecasts, reinforcing its validity. By evaluating multicollinearity and defining three forecast scenarios—pessimistic, baseline, and optimistic—the study provides a reliable projection framework that accounts for socio-economic variability. The baseline scenario predicts a passenger increase of about 2.5% annually, reaching 7.8 million passengers by 2040. These findings support strategic infrastructure planning and airport management, contributing to sustainable air transport growth. This study highlights the value of traditional forecasting models. Future work should integrate advanced techniques, such as machine learning and neural networks, to compare and enhance predictive accuracy in socioeconomic analyses. A systematic comparison between traditional and emerging models could reveal key differences and guide the implementation of new methodological approaches.

Acknowledgments. This study was supported by the MIUR through the project "Master Plan for Cagliari Elmas Airport for the Years 2024–2039: Traffic Forecasts and New Land-side Configuration of Access Transport Infrastructure", (CIG: B02CBBC62C Code ENAC: P24/27_08.03) financed Sogaer (company managing Cagliari Elmas International Airport) and project e.INS – Ecosystem of Innovation for Next Generation Sardinia funded by the Italian Ministry of University and Research (MIUR) under the Next-Generation EU Programme (National Recovery and Resilience Plan – PNRR, M4C2, INVESTMENT 1.5 – DD 1056 of 23/06/2022, ECS00000038)- SPOKE 8 – CUP F53C22000430001. This study was also supported by the agreement with the Municipality of Cagliari – Strategic and Territorial Planning Service (CUP code: G22C20000080006 – CIG ZEA2E99622) entitled "Innovative methods for participatory urban planning in the drafting of the MUP in adaptation to the RLP and the HSP. Preparation of the preliminary environmental report in the SEA process. Study of the infrastructural structure in the light of the new forms of mobility in line with the drafting SUMPS".

Author Contributions Conceptualization, all; methodology and formal analysis, Riccardo Zedda and Nicoletta Rassu; introduction and literature review Francesca Maltinti, Riccardo Zedda, and Nicoletta Rassu; writing-original draft preparation Riccardo Zedda and Mauro Coni; writing review and editing Nicoletta Rassu and Kevin Panetto, visualization, all. All authors have read and agreed to the published version of the manuscript.

References

1. Lilliu, F.: Forecasting Air Transport Demand: a Multivariable Econometric Model. PhD Thesis, University of Palermo (1999)
2. Costa, A., Reitani, G.: Analysis and forecasting of air transport demand in the European Community: a multivariable econometric model. Tipografia pime EDITRICE Srl. (1994)
3. Postorino, M.N.: Introduction to Air Transport System Planning. FrancoAngeli (2009)
4. N. Ramirez, 'Airport Strategic Planning; Master Planning: An Exploratory Research Project'. 2019
5. Itani, N., et al.: Towards realizing bestin-class civil aviation strategy scenarios. Transp. Policy. **43**, 42–54 (2015)
6. Kwakkel, J.H., et al.: Adaptive airport strategic planning. Eur. J. Transp. Infrastruct. Res. **10**(3) (2010)
7. I. N. C. A. Authority (ENAC): National Airport Plan. Policy and technical guidance document for the development of air transport and the airport system (2022). [Online]. Available: https://www.enac.gov.it/
8. Horonjeff, R., et al.: Planning and Design of Airports, vol. 4. McGraw-Hill, New York (1962)
9. Devoto, R., Meloni, I., Rassu, N., Teulada, B.S.D.: Air travel demand forecasting in the presence of Public Service Obligation (PSO). J. Airpt. Manag. **11**(1), 90–103 (2017)
10. Neufville, R.D.: Airport systems planning, design, and management. In: Air Transport Management, pp. 79–96. Routledge (2020)
11. Devoto, R., Rassu, N.: A mathematical model for distribution of air transport demand: The case of the Sardinian network. In: Presented at the WIT Transactions on the Built Environment, pp. 669–678 (2005)
12. Zhao, X., Zhao, H.: Empirical analysis and predictions of civil aviation passenger traffic based on ARIMA model. In: 2015 3rd International Conference on Machinery, Materials and Information Technology Applications, pp. 1869–1873. Atlantis Press (2015)
13. Tang, X., Deng, G.: Prediction of civil aviation passenger transportation based on ARIMA model. J. Stat. **965–977**, 824–834 (2016). https://doi.org/10.4236/ojs.2016.65068
14. Bastola, D.P.: Air passenger demand model (APDM): econometric model for forecasting demand in passenger air transports in Nepal. Int. J. Acad. Res. Psychol. **1**, 238–242 (2017)
15. Andreoni, A., Postorino, M.N.: A multivariate ARIMA model to forecast air transport demand. In: Proceedings of the Association for European Transport and Contributors, pp. 1–14 (2006)
16. Makridakis, S., et al.: Forecasting. Methods and Applications, 3rd edn. Wiley (1998)
17. Postorino, M.N.: A comparison among different approaches for the evaluation of the air traffic demand elasticity. In: Proceedings of Sustainable Planning and Development Conference. WIT Press (2003)

18. di Ciaccio, A., Borra, S.: Statistic: Methodologies for Economic and Social Sciences. McGraw-Hill (2021)
19. Shumway, R.H., Stoffer, D.S.: ARIMA models. In: Time Series Analysis and Its Applications: With R Examples, pp. 75–163. Springer International Publishing (2017)
20. Box, G.E.P., Jenkins, G.M.: Time-Series Analysis, Forecasting and Control. Holden-Day, San Francisco (1970)
21. Ljung, M.G., Box, G.E.P.: On a measure of lack of fit in time series model. Biometrika. **65**, 297–303 (1978)
22. Abed, S.Y., et al.: An econometric analysis of international air travel demand in Saudi Arabia. J. Air Transp. Manag. **7**, 143–148 (2001)
23. Hensher, D.A.: Determining passenger potential for a regional airline hub at Canberra International Airport. J. Air Transp. Manag. **8**, 301–311 (2002)
24. Newbold, P., et al.: Statistic. Ediz. mylab. Pearson (2021)
25. Akaike, H.: A new look at the statistical model identification. IEEE Trans. Autom. Control. **19**(6), 716–723 (1974)
26. D. Cinigeo, 'The Cagliari-Elmas Airport Development Plan - Land-Side Accessibility 2024–2039'. 2024
27. Chen, B., et al.: Evaluating prediction models for airport passenger throughput using a hybrid method. Appl. Sci. **13**(4), 2384 (2023)
28. Solvoll, G., et al.: Forecasting air traffic demand for major infrastructure changes. Res. Transp. Econ. **82**, 100873 (2020)
29. Cascetta, E., et al.: Passenger and freight demand models for the Italian national transportation system. In: Proceedings of the 7th WCTR, Sydney, Australia (1995)
30. Zhang, X.: Research on forecasting method of aviation traffic based on social and economic indicators. In: IOP Conference Series: Materials Science and Engineering, p. 062038. IOP Publishing (2020)
31. Du, B., et al.: Traffic demand prediction based on dynamic transition convolutional neural network. IEEE Trans. Intell. Transp. Syst. **22**(2), 1237–1247 (2020)
32. Wu, C.L.: Airline Operations and Delay Management: Insights from Airline Economics, Networks and Strategic Schedule Planning. Routledge (2016)
33. Jin, F., et al.: Forecasting air passenger demand with a new hybrid ensemble approach. J. Air Transp. Manag. **83**, 101744 (2019)
34. 'ISTAT'. [Online]. Available: https://www.istat.it/

Evaluating Skid Resistance of Indoor Pavements Using the Tortus Tribometer and British Pendulum Tester: A Case Study

James Rombi[✉], Marta Salis, Mauro Coni, Nicoletta Rassu, and Francesca Maltinti

Department of Civil Environmental Engineering and Architecture, University of Cagliari, 09042 Cagliari, Italy
james.rombi@unica.it

Abstract. Slippery floors are a leading cause of indoor injuries, emphasizing the importance of effective flooring safety assessments. In high-traffic buildings such as hospitals, airports, and schools, ensuring slip resistant surfaces is essential to prevent injuries and reduce costs associated with compensation claims and maintenance. According to Italian legislation, the Tortus Digital Tribometer (TDT) is the standard device used to measure the Coefficient of Friction (CoF) on indoor pavements, ensuring compliance with safety standards established by the British Ceramic Research Association (BCRA). This instrument plays a critical role in evaluating the slip resistance of flooring materials, both in existing structures and during the design phase, to enhance overall safety and reduce the risk of slip-related accidents. In this research, six types of pavements with different materials were analyzed under both wet and dry conditions using both the TDT and British Pendulum Tester (BPT) devices. The data were first analyzed to verify whether the pavements met the Italian regulations and also to explore any potential correlation between the two methods. The study found that the results of the TDT method can be affected by the dimensions of the tile grout and the surface level. Additionally, under wet conditions, deformations in the leather friction pad were observed, leading to questionable measurements. In contrast BPT provided more reliable measurements in both wet and dry conditions.

Keywords: Slip resistance · Tortus tester · British pendulum tester · Friction · Safety

1 Introduction

In recent years, building design has undergone significant advancements, driven by the need to incorporate safety, sustainability, and innovation. The increasing focus on reducing environmental impact and enhancing safety has redefined building standards, particularly in material selection. In this context, ensuring slip-resistant walking surfaces in high-traffic areas such as hospitals, airports, schools, and commercial facilities is crucial.

Recent data indicates that slippery floors are a leading cause of indoor injuries, resulting in physical harm and substantial costs for businesses due to insurance claims and maintenance expenses [1]. This issue underscores the importance of thoroughly evaluating floor safety, which can be effectively assessed using specialized tools like the tribometer.

Safety and sustainability remain fundamental pillars of modern construction. Safety has become a priority in building design and management. This aspect is crucial in high-traffic environments such as hospitals, airports, schools, and universities, as well as in industrial settings.

Flooring safety plays a key role in preventing slips, trips, and falls, which remain one of the leading causes of injuries in both workplaces and public or private spaces.

It is regulated by specific standards aimed at reducing the risk of slips and falls in buildings. A technical and legislative framework exists at both European and national levels, ensuring compliance with legal requirements and protecting the health of workers, students, and visitors.

The UNI EN 16165:2021 [2] standard, where UNI is the Italian National Standardization Body and EN stands for European Norm, standardizes methods for measuring the slip resistance of pedestrian surfaces across the EU, ensuring flooring meets safety requirements. It defines structured testing protocols for various conditions, providing a consistent approach to pedestrian surface safety.

Complementary standards include EN 13036-4 [3], which uses the Pendulum Test Method (PTM) to determine the coefficient of friction on wet and dry surfaces, and DIN 51131:2008 [4] where DIN is the German Institute for Standardization, which employs a tribometer for dynamic friction measurements in industrial and commercial settings. Additionally, the British Standard BS 7976:2002 [5] specifies slip resistance testing using the British Pendulum Tester (BPT) under various conditions, including contamination scenarios.

Italian regulations on workplace safety and building accessibility are governed by Ministerial Decree DM 236/89 [6] and Legislative Decree D.Lgs. 81/2008 [7]. DM 236/89 establishes technical requirements for the elimination of architectural barriers, setting criteria for flooring, ramps, and pedestrian pathways. It also mandates the use of slip-resistant surfaces to reduce the risk of slipping, with particular attention to the needs of people with disabilities.

D.Lgs. 81/2008, Italy's workplace safety consolidation act, establishes preventive measures to protect workers, including reducing slip hazards. Article 63 mandates the stability of workplace flooring, while annex IV requires the use of materials that minimize tripping risks. Employers must evaluate slip risks in the risk assessment document, considering flooring characteristics and environmental conditions.

Supporting these regulations, UNI 11583:2015 [8] defines technical parameters for measuring slipperiness, ensuring compliance and promoting safe, inclusive design in workplaces and public environments.

In addition to preventing accidents, regulatory compliance enhances the reliability and professionalism of structures, influencing the strategic management of buildings. The adoption of materials and technologies that meet safety requirements promote sustainable and innovative construction practices.

The tribometer is an instrument for evaluating pavement slipperiness, measuring the Coefficient of Friction (CoF) with advanced technology to uphold high safety standards. Beyond assessing existing surfaces, it also plays a crucial role in the design phase, guiding material selection and maintenance strategies to enhance building sustainability.

This study presents a comparative experimental campaign conducted on various surface types, examining the differences between the Tortus Digital Tribometer (TDT) the standard device mandated by Italian legislation for measuring the CoF on indoor pavements, and the British Pendulum Tester (BPT) based on the British Standard. The novelty of this research lies in its systematic evaluation of two widely adopted yet methodologically distinct instruments, offering new insights into their comparative accuracy, applicability, and limitations in real-world building contexts. This analysis contributes to the ongoing discourse on standardizing friction measurement tools across different regulatory frameworks and design environments.

2 Materials and Methods

Floor slipperiness is a critical factor in safety and accident prevention, affected by materials, wear, and surface treatments [9]. Smooth surfaces like polished marble become more slippery when contaminated, while textured materials and anti-slip treatments improve grip. Wear reduces friction, requiring regular maintenance, and treatments like waxes or detergents can alter surface texture [10].

Environmental factors such as water, oil, and dust lower friction, especially in kitchens or workshops, where proper cleaning is crucial [11]. Lighting and human factors, including footwear and movement, also impact slip risk. The CoF measures the resistance between surfaces, helping assess slip potential.

In indoor flooring design, the CoF is essential for ensuring user safety by minimizing the risk of slips and falls, while also contributing to the durability and sustainability of the materials used. It is defined as the ratio of the friction force (F) to the normal force (N) acting between the surfaces and is represented by the Eq. 1 below:

$$\mu = F/N \qquad (1)$$

- μ: coefficient of friction (dimensionless).
- F: friction force (in Newtons, N), which is the force opposing the relative motion between surfaces.
- N: normal force (in Newtons, N), which is the force perpendicular to the contact surface.

There are two main types of the coefficient of friction:

- Static coefficient of friction (μ_s): indicates the resistance to the initial movement between two contacting surfaces and is generally higher than the dynamic coefficient, as adhesion forces are stronger when the surfaces are at rest. The condition for the onset of movement is expressed by an inequality (2):

$$F_{applied} \geq \mu_S * N \qquad (2)$$

- Dynamic coefficient of friction (μd): describes the resistance during the relative motion of surfaces and is usually lower than the static coefficient, as adhesion forces decrease during sliding.

The dynamic friction force is given by the Eq. 3:

$$F = \mu_d * N \quad (3)$$

In indoor flooring, the dynamic coefficient of friction is crucial as it defines how surfaces behave during walking, when the shoe sole moves continuously across the floor instead of staying still.

The coefficient of friction is a key parameter in ensuring flooring safety and must therefore be analyzed with precision. Its measurement can be performed both in the laboratory and on-site. This study examines tests conducted in situ tests using the BPT and TDT.

2.1 British Pendulum Tester

The BPT as shown in Fig. 1 is a portable device used to measure the coefficient of friction on-site, particularly in high-traffic road and indoor flooring applications. Widely used in the United Kingdom, it is recognized by the Health and Safety Executive (HSE) BS 7976 standard, as an effective, reliable, and reproducible method for assessing flooring surfaces. Manufacturers also utilize it to verify the certification of materials and coatings.

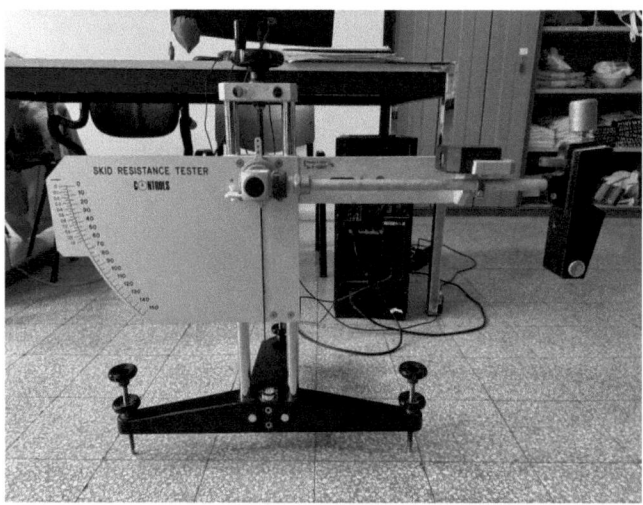

Fig. 1. British Pendulum Tester used for testing (image taken during testing campaign).

The BPT (see. Fig. 2) uses a pendulum with a standardized rubber slider to measure the energy lost during sliding, converting it into a coefficient of friction value. It is a portable, easy to use device suitable for both laboratory and on-site testing on dry and wet surfaces. It provides quick and repeatable results, directly measuring the dynamic friction between the slider and the test surface. Higher Slip Resistance Value (SRV), British Pendulum Number (BPN), or Pendulum Test Value (PTV) indicate a lower risk of slipperiness.

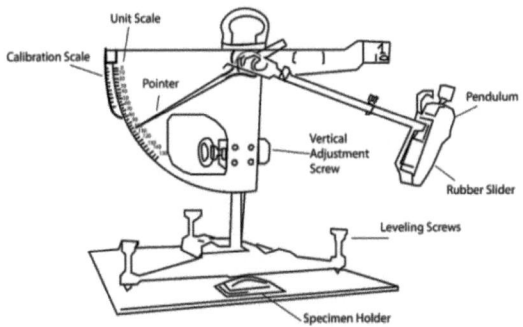

Fig. 2. Operating diagram of the British Pendulum (google image).

The British Pendulum Tester operates on the principle of energy dissipation during the pendulum's motion, where the friction force is indirectly calculated through the pendulum's energy loss (see Eq. 3):

$$PTV = k * E/L \tag{3}$$

- E: is the dissipated energy (in Joules, J)
- L: is the length of the slider's path (in meters, m)
- k: is a calibration constant specific to the instrument

The PTV is correlated with the probability of slip and defines different levels of slip potential as reported in Table 1.

Table 1. Probability of slip.

Level Of Slip Potential	Rating	Probability of slip
High Slip Potential	0-24 PTV	Up to 1 in 20
Moderate Slip Potential	25-35 PTV	1 in 100,000
Low Slip Potential	36+ PTV	1 in 1.000.000
Extremely low Slip Potential	75+ PTV	less than 1 in 1,000,000

From the SRV value, the CoF can be derived using the formula found in scientific literature (see Eq. 4) [12]:

$$CoF = (3 * SRV)/(330 - SRV) \tag{4}$$

CoF: Coefficient of Friction
SRV: Slip Resistance Value

2.2 Tortus Digital Tribometer

The Tortus Tribometer (see Fig. 3), developed by BCRA, is a high-precision instrument for measuring the coefficient of friction directly on surfaces, assessing slip risks in real conditions. It features a rotating slider made of standardized materials like rubber or leather, ensuring consistent and reliable results. Key benefits include portability, test repeatability, and adherence to Italian anti-slip safety standards. However, its high cost remains a drawback.

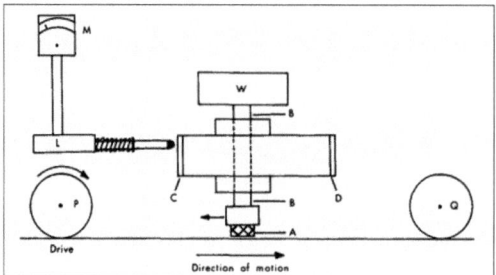

Fig. 3. BCRA Tortus Tester – Operatig diagram (google immage).

The friction force is measured through integrated sensors and converted into a dynamic coefficient of friction (μ) value using the Eq. 5:

$$\mu = \frac{F}{N} \qquad (5)$$

F is the measured friction force (in Newtons, N).
N is the normal force, the weight applied to the slider (in Newtons, N), which remains constant and is determined by the instrument calibration.

Flooring is classified into four categories, reported in Table 2, based on the dynamic coefficient of friction, with a value of $\mu \geq 0.40$ is considered safe.

Table 2. Categories of the coefficient of friction.

Coefficient Of Dynamic Friction	
$\mu \leq 0{,}19$	Dangerous Slipperness
$0{,}20 \leq \mu \leq 0{,}39$	Excess Slipperness
$0{,}40 \leq \mu \leq 0{,}74$	Satisfactory Friction
$\mu \geq 0{,}75$	Excellent Friction

3 Analysis

An experimental study was conducted to measure the CoF and evaluate the slip resistance of six flooring surfaces under both dry and wet conditions. The objective was to verify compliance with safety standards and to compare the performance of two measurement devices: the internationally widely used BPT and the TDT, specified by Italian regulations.

For each tested flooring surface, a straight alignment approximately 3 m in length was selected. Along this alignment, TDT tests were conducted under both dry and wet conditions using both rubber and leather pads. The TDT collected measurements at a rate of one reading per second, and average CoF values were calculated for each alignment.

On the same alignments, two sections were selected for BPT testing. Section 1 corresponded to the location where the first ten TDT measurements were taken, and the results were compared with the corresponding average TDT values. Section 2 was located at the end of the alignment, corresponding to the last ten TDT measurements. This setup enabled a direct comparison between the two devices across consistent surface conditions. The Dynamic Slip DS Tribometer (see Fig. 4) measures the dynamic coefficient of friction (CoF) using the BCRA method. Weighing 8.5 kg and measuring 390×240 mm, it is equipped with a 9 mm diameter rubber slider under a 200 g load. The system records deviations using leaf springs while moving at a constant speed of 17 mm/s, with data processed by microcontrollers. It is possible to set the acquisition time; by default, the device records one reading per second, but it can be configured to perform up to 10 readings per second.

Fig. 4. Dynamic Slip DS (image taken during testing campaign).

The CoF is expressed as a percentage: $\mu < 0.40$ indicates a slippery surface, while $\mu \geq 0.40$ is considered safe. The device is calibrated before use and can operate with rubber or leather sliders on dry or wet surfaces, displaying results on its digital screen.

The BPT was used to measure the dynamic coefficient of friction between the rubber slider and the test surface, providing the SVR, also known as BPN or PTV.

The instrument, supported by three bases, features a pendulum arm with a 750 mm × 250 mm rubber slider. After calibration, the slider impacts the surface at 50 km/h to measure slip resistance. Precise marking ensured accurate repositioning under different conditions. Additionally, scientific literature establishes correlations between pendulum test results and the BCRA method, as specified in Eq. 4. Other correlations have also been obtained but not used in this research.

3.1 Case Study

In this research, six different types of flooring (see Fig. 5) with different materials were tested in both wet and dry conditions using both the TDT and the BPT.

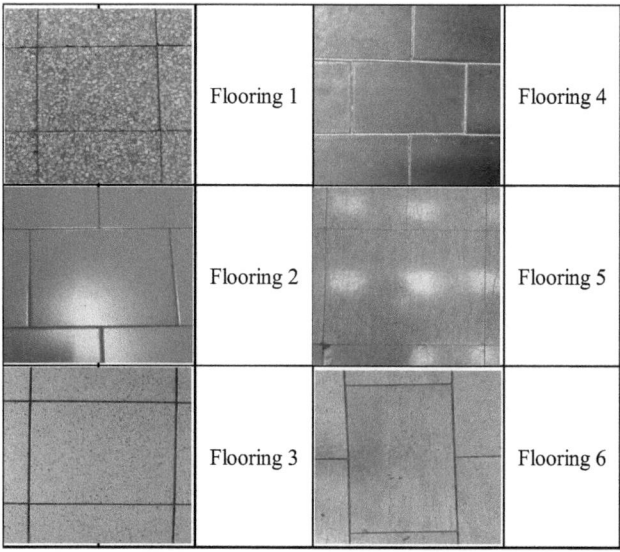

Fig. 5. Different types of flooring (images taken during testing campaign).

Each of them had specific characteristics in terms of materials, tile dimensions and grout joint dimension reported in Table 3.

Measurements were conducted under both dry and wet floor conditions using the TDT and the BPT. For the TDT, tests were performed using both rubber and leather pads, while for the BPT, only the rubber pad was used, as it is the sole available option for this device. Table 4 presents the average CoF values obtained on flooring 1 using the TDT, compared with those obtained using the BPT. The TDT test was carried out along a 3.00 meter strip, yielding a total of 130 measurements. In contrast, BPT measurements were taken at two specific sections. Section 1 corresponds to the positions of the first ten measurements performed with the TDT rubber pad under both dry and wet conditions.

Table 3. Tile dimension and characteristics.

Material		Dimension (cm)	Grout joint (cm)
Floor 1	Graniglia tiles	20*20	0.02
Floor 2	Porcelain tiles	20*20	0.02
Floor 3	Porcelain tiles	33*33	0.05
Floor 4	Terra cotta tiles	7*14.5	0.03
Floor 5	Linoleum	60*60	0.01
Floor 6	Orosei limestone	30*60	0.05

Table 4. Average measurement values TDT vs BPT Floor 1.

TDT (Dry flooring)		TDT (Wet flooring)		BPT (Dry flooring)		BPT (Wet flooring)	
Nr Measures	130	Nr Measures	130	Section	BPN	Section	BPN
Rubber Pad (CoF) Value	0.34	Rubber Pad (CoF) Value	0.47	1 Rubber Pad	60	1	21
Leather Pad (CoF) Value	0.28	Leather Pad (CoF) Value	0.53	2 Rubber Pad	61	2	16

Section 2, corresponds to the positions of the last ten measurements performed with the rubber pad of TDT under both dry and wet conditions.

The CoF value is below the minimum threshold of 0.40, indicating excessive slipperiness on the dry floor. However, on the wet flooring, the coefficient of friction exceeds 0.40, showing that in wet conditions, the value meets the specifications.

The data obtained using the BPT show that the BPN values are acceptable on dry floors but decrease significantly under wet conditions, as expected. The conversion formula from the SRV to the CoF, as reported in the scientific literature, was applied to evaluate potential correspondence or similarity with the values obtained using the slip meter (see Table 5).

Table 5. CoF Calculation using Eq. 4.

CoF dry condition				CoF wet condition			
	TDT (CoF)	BPT (BPN)	CoF Calculated		TDT (CoF)	BPT (BPN)	CoF Calculated
Section 1	0.35	60	0.67		0.48	21	0.21
Section 2	0.32	61	0.69		0.45	16	0.16

Table 6 reports the measurements taken with the TDT on flooring 2, both in dry and wet conditions, using both the rubber and leather pads.

Table 6. Average measurement values TDT vs BTP Floor 2.

TDT (Dry flooring)		TDT (Wet flooring)		BPT (Dry flooring)		BPT (Wet flooring)	
Nr Measures	130	Nr Measures	130	Section	BPN	Section	BPN
Rubber Pad (CoF) Value	0.28	Rubber Pad (CoF) Value	0.35	1 Rubber Pad	38	1	14
Leather Pad (CoF) Value	0.28	Leather Pad (CoF) Value	0.46	2 Rubber Pad	54	2	13

The CoF value is below the minimum threshold limit of 0.40 in the dry floor, indicating excessive slipperiness. On the wet floor, however, the coefficient of friction CoF with the leather pad exceeds 0.40.

The analized sections with the BPT, conducted in both dry and wet conditions using the rubber pad are acceptable on dry floor but decreases drastically when the floor is wet. The conversion formula from the pendulum SRV value to the CoF, was applied to assess a possible correspondence or similarity with the slip meter values (see Table 7).

Table 7. CoF Calculation using Eq. 4.

CoF dry condition				CoF wet condition		
	TDT (CoF)	BPT (BPN)	CoF Calculated	TDT (CoF)	BPT (BPN)	CoF Calculated
Section 1	0.29	38	0.39	0.38	14	0.13
Section 2	0.17	54	0.59	0.34	13	0.12

Table 8 reports the measurements taken with the TDT on floor 3, both in dry and wet conditions, using both the rubber and leather pads. The test was conducted on a 3.20 meter strip, for a total of 200 measurements.

The CoF value is below the minimum threshold limit of 0.40 in the dry floor, meaning the flooring does not meet the minimum safety standards due to excessive slipperiness. On the wet floor, however, the CoF exceeds 0.40 with the leather pad.

BPN values were recorded from the analyzed sections under both dry and wet conditions, using the rubber pad. Using the BPT, the SRV value is acceptable on dry floor but decreases when the floor is wet.

The conversion formula from the Pendulum SRV value to the CoF, as reported in the scientific literature, was applied to assess a possible correspondence or similarity with the slip meter values (see Table 9).

Table 8. Average measurement values TDT vs BPT Floor 3.

TDT (Dry flooring)		TDT (Wet flooring)		BPT (Dry flooring)		BPT (Wet flooring)	
Nr Measures	200	Nr Measures	200	Section	BPN	Section	BPN
Rubber Pad (CoF) Value	0.32	Rubber Pad (CoF) Value	0.35	1 Rubber Pad	52	1	12
Leather Pad (CoF) Value	0.27	Leather Pad (CoF) Value	0.45	2 Rubber Pad	41	2	16

Table 9. CoF Calculation using Eq. 4.

CoF dry condition				CoF wet condition		
	TDT (CoF)	BPT (BPN)	CoF Calculated	TDT (CoF)	BPT (BPN)	CoF Calculated
Section 1	0.50	52	0.56	0.35	12	0.11
Section 2	0.27	41	0.43	0.37	16	0.15

Table 10 reports the measurements taken with the TDT on floor 4, both in dry and wet conditions, using both the rubber and leather pads. The test was conducted on a 3.20 meter strip, for a total of 168 measurements.

Table 10. Average measurement values TDT vs BPT Floor 4.

TDT (Dry flooring)		TDT (Wet flooring)		BPT (Dry flooring)		BPT (Wet flooring)	
Nr Measures	168	Nr Measures	168	Section	BPN	Section	BPN
Rubber Pad (CoF) Value	0.36	Rubber Pad (CoF) Value	0.48	1 Rubber Pad	53	1	25
Leather Pad (CoF) Value	0.33	Leather Pad (CoF) Value	0.56	2 Rubber Pad	48	2	26

The CoF value is below the minimum threshold limit of 0.40 in the dry floor, meaning the flooring does not meet the minimum safety standards due to excessive slipperiness. On the wet floor, however, the CoF exceeds 0.40 for both pads, with the leather pads showing a higher value.

The values recorded from sections analyzed with the BPT, conducted in both dry and wet conditions using the rubber pad. Using the BPT, the SRV value is acceptable on dry floor but decreases when the floor is wet.

In this analysis, a comparison between the TDT and the pendulum was not possible, as section 1 and 2 of the pendulum did not align with the first and last 10 measurements of the tribometer due to insufficient space for conducting the tests.

Table 11 reports the measurements taken with the TDT on floor 5, both in dry and wet conditions, using both the rubber and leather pads. The test was conducted on a 3.20 meter strip, for a total of 160 measurements.

Table 11. Average measurement values TDT vs BPT Floor 5.

TDT (Dry flooring)		TDT (Wet flooring)		BPT (Dry flooring)		BPT (Wet flooring)	
Nr Measures	160	Nr Measures	160	Section	BPN	Section	BPN
Rubber Pad (CoF) Value	0.43	Rubber Pad (CoF) Value	0.52	1 Rubber Pad	79	1	21
Leather Pad (CoF) Value	0.38	Leather Pad (CoF) Value	0.58	2 Rubber Pad	63	2	24

In this type of flooring, its coefficient of friction using rubber pad is above the minimum safety value $\mu \geq 0.40$ and increases for both pads when the flooring is wet.

The values recorded from sections analyzed with theBPT, conducted in both dry and wet conditions using the rubber pad. Using the BPT, the SRV value is acceptable on dry floor but decreases when the floor is wet.

The conversion formula from the pendulum SRV value to the CoF, as reported in the scientific literature, was applied (see Table 12).

Table 12. CoF Calculation using Eq. 4.

	CoF dry condition			CoF wet condition		
	TDT (CoF)	BPT (BPN)	CoF Calculated	TDT (CoF)	BPT (BPN)	CoF Calculated
Section 1	0.41	79	0.94	No data	No data	No data
Section 2	0.38	73	0.70	No data	No data	No data

Table 13 reports the measurements taken with the TDT on floor 6, both in dry and wet conditions, using both the rubber and leather pads. The test was conducted on a 3.00 meter strip, for a total of 162 measurements.

The CoF value is below the minimum threshold limit of 0.40 in the dry floor, meaning the flooring does not meet the minimum safety standards due to excessive slipperiness. On the wet floor, however, the CoF exceeds 0.40.

Table 14 shows the values recorded from sections analyzed with the BPT, conducted in both dry and wet conditions using the rubber pad.

Table 13. Average measurement values TDT vs BPT Floor 6.

TDT (Dry flooring)		TDT (Wet flooring)		BPT (Dry flooring)		BPT (Wet flooring)	
Nr Measures	162	Nr Measures	162	Section	BPN	Section	BPN
Rubber Pad (CoF) Value	0.39	Rubber Pad (CoF) Value	0.49	1 Rubber Pad	54	1	20
Leather Pad (CoF) Value	0.39	Leather Pad (CoF) Value	0.65	2 Rubber Pad	44	2	20

Table 14. CoF Calculation using Eq. 4.

	CoF dry condition			CoF wet condition		
	TDT (CoF)	BPT (BPN)	CoF Calculated	TDT (CoF)	BPT (BPN)	CoF Calculated
Section 1	0.39	54	0.59	0.47	20	0.19
Section 2	0.37	44	0.46	0.49	20	0.19

Based on an initial analysis, the CoF values measured with the TDT on dry floors are generally below the safety threshold of 0.40, indicating a high risk of slipperiness under dry conditions. In wet conditions, the threshold of 0.40 is exceeded, with the leather pad typically yielding higher CoF values than the rubber pad. The BPN values obtained using the BPT are acceptable on dry surfaces but show a marked decrease on wet floors, as expected, due to the reduced friction caused by the presence of water between the foot and the surface.

4 Discussion and Conclusions

In this study, six different types of pavements made from various materials were analyzed under both wet and dry conditions using the TDT and BPT testing devices. The data were first analyzed to verify whether the pavements met the Italian regulations and also to explore any potential correlation between the two methods.

In Italy, slip resistance measurement is based on the Tortus Digital Tribometer, following the BCRA method, regulated by D.M. 236/1989 and D.Lgs. 81/2008. This method has significant limitations, as the results do not always reflect the actual behavior of surfaces. In particular, the test depends on the low measurement speed (17 mm/s) and fails to reproduce phenomena such as aquaplaning. Internationally, many countries have abandoned the BCRA method in favour of the BPT or the inclined ramp test. These methods better represent the actual slip risk, especially in wet or contaminated conditions.

Other issues concern the test's sensitivity to surface contamination. The TDT does not provide reliable data on wet, dirty, or greasy surfaces, which are among the most critical conditions for safety. Additionally, the method is affected by the compression of water between the test foot and the surface, a phenomenon that can distort measurements and produce unrealistically high friction values. This issue, known as "temporary adhesiveness," was observed in studies by Gronqvist et al. [13], which highlighted how the contact time of the pad on the surface could alter friction measurements. Lai et al. [14] confirmed that the dependence of adhesion force on contact time remains insufficiently understood and requires further investigation.

The analysis of the data obtained from the slip meter revealed some anomalies.

The values measured using the TDT on wet surfaces comply with standard DM 236/89, whereas on dry surfaces, only one type of flooring meets the minimum safety requirements. This phenomenon can be attributed to the suction cup effect and the inability to recreate aquaplaning due to the low speed of the instrument.

Measurements using the BCAR method show that graniglia, porcelain stoneware, and Orosei limestone floors do not meet the minimum safety level required by Italian standard DM 236/89, with a high risk of slipping on wet surfaces. The terracotta floor presents a moderate risk of slipping when wet.

The only flooring that complies with the BCAR standard is linoleum. However, like the others, it still presents a high risk of slipping in wet conditions, according to the BPT method. During the tests and measurements, discrepancies emerged concerning scientific principles, leading to the decision to increase the number of measurements under different usage conditions. Data analysis highlighted significant differences in the ability of the instruments to detect the slipperiness of the tested surfaces. The TDT in many cases measured higher values of CoF in wet conditions then in dry.

The BPT proved effective in distinguishing between dry and wet surfaces, providing significant data on friction variations among materials. Measurements of BPN confirmed a higher risk of slipping on wet floors.

The TDT, on the other hand, showed limitations in differentiating between dry and wet surfaces, with less reliable measurements compared to the BPT. The comparison of CoF values measured by the two instruments revealed a weak correlation, confirming that the results are not directly comparable and that each method has specific limitations.

Studies such as validation of walkway tribometers: establishing a reference standard [15] have confirmed that many tribometers do not always differentiate between flooring materials, especially in wet conditions, highlighting the same issues found in this research.

Finally, the BPT emerged as the most reliable method for distinguishing between safe and hazardous surfaces, while the TDT showed significant limitations in evaluating wet surfaces, reducing its effectiveness in real-world applications.

However, the study has certain limitations. The sample size of six pavement types, while representative, is relatively limited, and testing was conducted under controlled conditions that may not fully replicate the variability of real-world environments. Future studies should aim to increase the number and diversity of flooring samples, introduce more dynamic and realistic test conditions, and consider the inclusion of user-centered factors such as footwear type and gait patterns. Long-term, the adoption of more effective, standardized, and field-representative testing tools is essential to ensure accurate risk assessment and improved public safety in both private and public spaces. Finally it can be said that testing and classification results highlight the critical need to standardize testing and classification methods, or to develop a conversion matrix that enables comparison across different measurement techniques [16].

Author Contributions. Concept and methodology, Rombi, J., Salis, M. and Coni, M.; experimental campaign and validation, Rombi, J., Salis, M., analysis, Rombi, J., Salis, M., Maltinti, F., Coni, M., and Rassu, N., writing, review and editing, Rombi, J., Salis, M., Maltinti, F., and Rassu, N., project administration, Coni, M., All authors have read and agreed to the published version of the manuscript.

Disclosure of Interests.. The authors have no competing interests to declare that are relevant to the content of this article.

References

1. Li, J., Goerlandt, F., Way Li, W.L.: Slip and fall incidents at work: a visual analytics analysis of the research domain. Int. J. Environ. Res. Publ. Heal. **16**(24), 4972 (2019)
2. UNI EN 16165, 2021, Determination of slip resistance of pedestrian surfaces - Methods of evaluation, Italian Organization for Standardization (U.N.I.)
3. UNI EN 13036-4, 2011, Road and airfield surface characteristics - Test methods - Part 4: Method for measurement of slip/skid resistance of a surface: The pendulum test, Italian Organization for Standardization (U.N.I.)
4. DIN 51131, 2008-08, Testing of floor coverings - Determination of the anti-slip property - Method for measurement of the sliding friction coefficient
5. BS 7976-2:2002+A1:2013, Pendulum testers - Method of operation
6. Italian Legislative Decree No. 236/1989: Provisions on the prevention of accidents in the workplace. Off. J. Ital. Repub. (1989)
7. Italian Legislative Decree No. 81/2008: Consolidated act on health and safety in the workplace. Off. J. Ital. Repub. (2008)
8. UNI 11583, 2015, Personal protective equipment - Safety, protection and occupational footwear for work on inclined roofs
9. Derler, S., Huber, R., Kausch, F., Meyer, V.R.: Effectiveness, durability and wear of anti-slip treatments for resilient floor coverings, vol. 76, pp. 12–20. Elsevier (2015)
10. Kim, I.J., Hsiao, H., Simeonov, P.: Functional levels of floor surface roughness for the prevention of slips and falls: Clean-and-dry and soapsuds-covered wet surfaces, vol. 44, pp. 58–64. Elsevier (2013)
11. Ricotti, R., Delucchi, M., Cerisola, G.: A comparison of results from portable and laboratory floor slipperiness testers. Int. J. Indus. Ergonom. **39**, 353–357 (2009)
12. Blake, D.M., Wilson, T.M., Cole, J.W., Deligne, N.I., Lindsay, J.M.: Impact of Volcanic Ash on Road and Airfield Surface Skid Resistance, Sustainability (2017)
13. Grönqvist, R., Hirvonen, M., Tohv, A.: Evaluation of three portable floor slipperiness testers. Int. J. Indus. Ergonom. **25**, 85–95 (2000)
14. Lai, T., Zhang, Y., Zhu, T.: Contact time dependence of adhesion force studied at low, moderate, and high relative humidities on AFM: Influence of surface hydrophilicity. Appl. Surf. Sci. **649** (2024)

15. Powers, C.M., Blanchette, M.G., Brault, J.R., Flynn, J., Siegmund, G.P.: Validation of walkway tribometers: establishing a reference standard. J. Foren. Sci. **55**, 366–370 (2010)
16. Sudol, E., et al.: Comparative Analysis of Slip Resistance Test Methods for Granite Floors, vol. 14. MDPI materials (2021)

Road Accidents - Study of the Evolution and Mapping of Accidents Within the Municipality of Cagliari – Italy

Nicoletta Rassu(✉) , Mauro Coni , James Rombi , Marta Salis , and Francesca Maltinti

Department of Civil and Environmental Architecture, University of Cagliari, 09129 Cagliari, Italy
nicoletta.rassu@unica.it

Abstract. In recent decades, great attention has been paid to the issue of road safety, both at the international level and on a national scale, in which individual nations have gradually put into practice both direct and indirect interventions, the effects of which have been measured by the reduction in the number of accidents over time.

However, critical issues remain, and the zero road fatalities goal advocated by the PNSS [1, 2] in its 2010 and 2020 editions has not yet been achieved; in fact, we are still quite far from the goal.

In this study, the authors analyzed accident data provided by the Cagliari Municipality for the years 2014 to 2022. The data divided by nature of accident, type of vehicles involved, accident circumstances, and severity were analyzed in order to provide an overview of their evolution. In addition, location data were mapped with GIS – *Geographic Information System* - and represented in thematic maps. These provide a powerful tool for analysts and local administrators to (i) visualize critical and conflict areas immediately and clearly and (ii) identify risk factors on which to potentially intervene in order to remove criticality.

The application to a local context through the operational use of maps, in the authors' opinion, represents the added value of the study.

Keywords: Road Accident · accident mapping · GIS

1 Introduction

Road traffic accidents currently represent a serious public health issue, comparable to cardiovascular diseases or cancer. As reported in [3], road traffic fatalities are the leading cause of death in the 5÷29 age group and the eighth for all age groups.

The report highlights that, although progress has been made in terms of legislation, vehicle safety standards, and post-accident assistance, these improvements have not occurred at a pace sufficient to offset the growth in population and the rapid global motorization. Therefore, it is crucial to strengthen regulations to mitigate risk factors and thus improve road safety.

In countries with high levels of road safety, it is customary to apply the so-called Safe System [4], an approach based on the two assumptions that (i) human make mistakes and (ii) the human body has a limited capacity to tolerate the impacts of accidents, hence the basic principle: mistakes should never lead to death. To achieve this, it is necessary to intervene on road infrastructure, designing and managing it in such a way as to minimize the risk of errors and, when they occur, ensure that the consequences for users are mitigated. The cornerstones of safety with which the required safety conditions can be achieved are: safe road users, safe vehicles (e.g. assisted braking or electronic stability control systems), safe speeds, i.e. such as to produce impact energies below a certain threshold considered critical (e.g. in the case of accidents involving pedestrians or cyclists this threshold is set at around 30 km/h), safe roads and post-accident assistance [5, 6]. Regarding the last point, the timely transportation of the injured to hospitals for medical care, access to rehabilitation services, and generally efficient post-accident assistance is crucial and can save lives.

It is important for governments to increase their road safety efforts in order to achieve the goals set out in the 2030 Agenda for Sustainable Development, which for the 2020–2030 decade aims to reduce road deaths and serious injuries by 50% [7].

In addition, in 2020, the Commission [8], in the section on road safety, outlined a series of regulatory initiatives that concerned new guidelines on the maximum permitted blood alcohol level for drivers and the use of breathalyzer interlock devices.

At the Italian level, the reference document that transposed the communication of [9] is the National Road Safety Plan, PNSS [1, 2] which, through a normative review, data, statistical analysis on road accidents in Italy, Europe and worldwide, sets two levels of objectives and contextual strategies. The general objectives [1, 2] aim at reducing accidents by intervening on (i) infrastructure type, (ii) vehicles, (iii) emergency services. The specific ones, on the other hand, target vulnerable user categories considered at higher risk (cyclists, pedestrians, motorcyclists, children, over 65s). For each of them, the risk factors and related strategic lines of intervention are listed according to a safe system approach that covers all the components of the road safety system (user, infrastructure, vehicle).

When discussing of road safety, one cannot fail to mention the concept of risk. In fact, the achievement of safety objectives cannot be separated from a careful analysis of risk. There is no single definition of risk, but several exist, one of which is: "*The probability of reaching the potential level of damage under conditions of use or exposure to a specific factor or agent, or their combination*" [10]. According to this understanding, it can be said that risk is a probabilistic concept, i.e. it expresses the probability that a given event capable of causing harm will occur. The legislation on the subject that introduces a risk assessment and allows, in the corporate sphere, to take into consideration all the aspects that may impact on the continuity of business processes is ISO 9001 [11], while UNI ISO 31000 [12], in its Italian version then updated in 2018 is directed at the risk manager, and regulates the tools for risk management.

In the road environment, the risk has been studied for a long time and, in the first formulations, it was represented by three components: (i) the probability of a potentially harmful event occurring, (ii) exposure relative to the risk area, and (iii) vulnerability, or the severity of the consequences [13]. Recently, new formulations have been proposed that go beyond the old logic of using fixed and arbitrary parameters for risk components [13] instead of mathematical relations evaluated through analytical functions, as already applied in public transport [14, 15] and private [16].

For the analysis of road infrastructure safety, the European Directives [17, 18] define the Road Infrastructure Safety Management System (RISM), which is a set of procedures to support road authorities in the decision-making process for monitoring and improving road infrastructure safety. These procedures are aimed at enhancing road safety at the different stages of a road infrastructure life cycle. Some of them can be applied to existing infrastructures, thus enabling a more reactive approach (e.g. by fixing the safety issues identified on the infrastructure), while others are used in the early stages (i.e. planning and design) allowing a more proactive approach [9–20].

An initial safety assessment of the road network as a whole is designed to identify the presence of road elements which are critical in comparison with others and on which action should be taken. Subsequently, these segments can undergo further analysis, such as inspection and modeling.

One of these tools is the Road Network Screening (RNS) which represents the first stage of the RISM process and may concern: (i) the entire road system within a specific territorial area (province, region, etc.), (ii) a more limited context (municipality, section of the road network), or (iii) a particular road infrastructure (Section – road intersection). At the macro scale, a complete safety assessment can be made using socio-economic factors of the area under consideration as study data. At the micro scale, safety analyses can be performed specifically for segments, using their geometric characteristics and functional parameters as data. Typically, local decision-makers are usually more interested in making an assessment limited to their own administrative boundaries, as demonstrated by the study of Yasmin et al. [21], which highlights how most multivariate model studies have used the micro scale.

The RNS can be done in several ways, from the simple classification of road sections according to the number of accidents recorded to more advanced statistical methods based on accident prediction models. The one used by Job Safety Analysis (JSA), recommended by AASHTO [22], represents the state of the art. This method allows an analysis of a particular process starting from its general structure and then decomposing it into increasingly specific components, and aims to identify empirically the risk factors and control them by integrating the general principles of prevention. The European Road Assessment Programme (EuroRAP) [23] has also developed a form of network screening, but as it is not an official body, the risk assessment it provides does not have any official value.

Regardless of the methodology adopted, the RNS is divided into three main phases:

- Segmentation of the road network into homogeneous segments. The division can be made based on spatial functionality (homogeneity in geometry - section width, number of lanes, etc.-) or according to functional characteristics (traffic volume, etc.) or also in function of certain accident-related factors such as the relationship between expected and actual accidents;
- Development of an assessment scale through the adoption of evaluation criteria: Reactive or Proactive. The first operates downstream of the road network, i.e., on the infrastructure in use, and is based on the calculation of indices that provide a safety

assessment based on the historical series of recorded accidents (frequency, density, or severity of accidents). The second operates upstream and evaluates the potential effect of certain risk factors on road safety;
- Classification and presentation of results.

On this last point, EuroRAP has defined a colour scale of five levels, each corresponding to a level of risk ranging from low (green) to high (black). This standardization has been recognized internationally and therefore allows cross-border comparisons.

Crash Prediction Models (CPM) are essential elements of the RNS, forecasting tools that allow both quantitative and qualitative analysis to be carried out, for example on the frequency and severity aspects of accidents. These models provide an estimate of both exposure and consequences, allowing the identification of effective measures to deal with them, as well as an estimation of the improvement effects they bring in terms of accident reduction and therefore safety improvement.

AASHTO [22] presents a comprehensive set of road accident prediction models on highways, urban and suburban roads. These models are fairly versatile, based on the estimation of accident frequency as a function of flow characteristics, which is then normalized through factors related to the functional context. In 2014, a supplement to the 2010 edition [24] was issued which contains model-specific formulations for highways and interchanges.

These models have been exported outside the US and applied in international contexts. In particular, a first study addressing the transferability of the HSM model to two-lane and two-way roads was conducted by Martinelli et al. [25] on the Italian provincial road network. More recently La Torre et al. [26] with the PRACT (Predicting Road Accidents) project, has developed a European accident prediction model which, with appropriate calibration, can be applied in European road networks.

Although the majority of models focus mainly on CPMs which study accident frequency and only a few also address accident severity, over the last decade, research has been directed towards CPMs combining frequency and severity, highlighting the implications of their correlation [27]. Combined models are more suitable for use in the road infrastructure safety management process, as they allow assessments to be made of the consequences of road accidents, providing a more comprehensive analysis and a useful tool to support policymakers in choosing the most appropriate solutions to eliminate critical issues [28].

The reliability of output results is closely related to that of input data, the reliability and completeness of which are necessary for the accuracy of accident studies and thus for the development of effective measures to mitigate them. This highlights the importance of having access to adequate data.

Attempts have already been made over time to standardize the data collection procedure by proposing standard procedures (for example at European level with [17]). However, there are still different methods of collection and therefore, often the collected data have problems of completeness and accuracy to which usually not due attention is paid.

In this regard, the organization that collects the data plays an important role, but especially the purpose of the analysis, according to which priority is given to this or that other data, which feeds the lack of homogeneity and inconsistency between the various databases.

The data with greater uncertainty are: (i) spatiotemporal coordinates, (ii) severity classification, (iii) inaccuracies in identifying factors that contributed to the accident, (iv) personal data of users involved and (v) difficulties in correlating with other factors (e.g., traffic flows). The reports widely used and also employed in this study are those of the law enforcement agencies, which in their recording manuals, collect a variety of data:

- Location and time of the accident, data necessary to link the accident with the environmental context in which it took place. However, despite its relevance, this data is often not reported with the accuracy it deserves, sometimes due to human error and/or equipment failure [29]. Another reason is related to the purpose of the data. For example, law enforcement agencies, with the exception of damage alone, carry out a planimetric survey of the area for legal purposes only (for possible causes/procedures) for each incident. As such, the location data is often entered in a cursory manner;
- Accident severity, defined as the maximum injury to the users involved;
- Users involved: drivers and/or passengers of vehicles or pedestrians;
- Factors contributing to the accident: It is the most difficult part to understand because of the multitude of elements involved. In general, the reports contain a fixed list of factors that may have contributed to the accident and that officers should select and prioritize.

From this brief review it is clear that the data may be lacking or imprecise and that it cannot always be remedied by additions.

In this study we propose the result of the analysis of the accidents recorded in the urban area of Cagliari (Sardinia) in the years 2014–2022 (first half of the year). In particular, on the basis of location data, where available, coordinates for each incident have been uploaded to WGS84 geographic and georeferencing results are reported on area maps.

The authors consider that cartographic reproduction of incidents is a complementary tool to descriptive analysis and that the combination of the two constitutes a more effective analytical methodology for analysts and administrations. In fact, the possibility of visualizing the area/point of occurrence in which a certain number and/or type of claims are concentrated, allows to correlate the event with the context which facilitates the identification of possible risk factors and put in place effective strategies to remove them.

The remaining paper is organized as follows. Section 2 presents the methodological framework followed for the construction of the maps. Section 3 presents the case study and related discussion. Finally, Sect. 4 concludes the study and provides research perspectives.

2 Methodological Analysis

In Italy, the main source of road accident data is a statistical survey based on the collection of the elements of road accidents. This type of survey involves the compilation, by public bodies with local jurisdiction (Traffic Police, Carabinieri, Municipal Police, etc.), of certain forms (Istat CTT/INC model) that contain information on each accident and are then transmitted to ISTAT within 45 days of the end of the month of survey. ISTAT processes the forms and collects them in a report published annually, from 1952 to the present, in collaboration with the co-participating entities in the survey, namely ACI (Automobile Club of Italy) and some regions according to the relevant memoranda of understanding with the Ministry of Health and the Ministry of Infrastructure and Transport. The survey covers all road accidents recorded by local authorities that occurred on the national territory within a calendar year and caused injuries to people. Over the years, the survey criteria have changed: for example, since 1991, accidents that do not involve personal injury are no longer counted, while since 1999, the coding "died in road accident" covers victims who died on the spot or within the 30th day from the date of the accident while previously this time frame was limited to seven days.

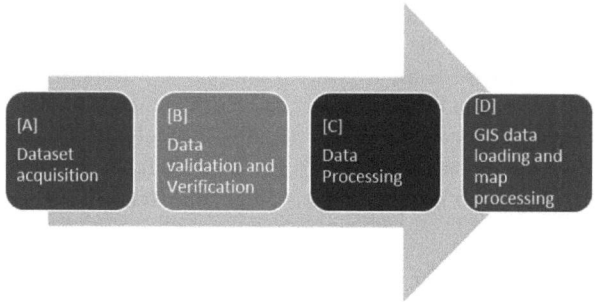

Fig. 1. Methodological framework

In the present study, accidents that occurred in a given area over a given time period were mapped. For this purpose, Fig. 1 describes the methodological scheme adopted, which consists of 4 parts:

A. Dataset acquisition

The dataset acquired is from law enforcement agencies and covers incidents that occurred in a given municipal area and within a given time frame. They contain data downloaded from the survey sheets and cover: Date, time and location of the accident, Survey body, Location of the accident, Type of road, Pavement, Road surface, Signs, Weather conditions, Nature of the accident, Type of vehicles involved, Circumstances of the accident, Consequences of the accident to persons, Names of the dead, injured and Institute of hospitalization.

B. Data validation and Verification

Checking and verification are two actions that are necessary and instrumental to the next stage of processing. At this stage, the format of the data (e.g., date, time, coordinates etc.) and the presence of any typographical errors and/or duplicates are checked. Any distortions are corrected at this stage, resulting in a database that is homogeneous in format and consistent in the information it contains.

C. **Data processing**

Since the objective of the study is the mapping of accidents in a cartographic support, the main processing of the data involves the input of geographic coordinates for each record. In fact, authority reports usually in the location field contain the street call sign with additional fields designed to identify the area of occurrence such as: the house number, a landmark, a mileage progress and in the case of an intersection, the call sign of another street. Through an address geolocator, one can convert the location data into the corresponding WGS84 geographic coordinates.

D. **GIS data loading and map processing**

A valuable tool for producing maps in digital format is the GIS (Geographic Information System), a computerized information system that primarily enables the acquisition, visualization and analysis of geographic data, that is, associating them with their geographic location on the earth's surface and processing them to derive information. GIS makes it possible to combine different types of data with each other, united by the same geographical reference, and thus develop new information according to the user's needs. In a geographic information system, data can be associated with their geographic location as (i) vector data, i.e., formed by points, lines, and polygons which are suitable for representing data that vary discretely, or (ii) as raster data, which allow surfaces to be represented by means of arrays of cells, called pixels, with each of which certain information about the area represented is associated, and these are more suitable for representing data that vary continuously. In GIS there are three types of information:

- Geometric: concern the cartographic representation of the objects represented (shape, size, geographical location);
- Topological: concern the connections between objects;
- Informational: concern the data associated with each object represented.

The database in CSV format containing accident data are imported into the GIS, which can be queried by creating thematic maps of the nature and quantity of accidents on the map base.

3 Case Study

The objective of the study is to map accidents within an urban area so as to have a true distribution both in terms of concentration and in terms of the nature of the event. The study area is the Cagliari Municipality. Specifically, through GIS, the detected accidents were mapped over the area and then discretized according to their characteristics.

The data source is the traffic accident reports collected by the Cagliari Municipal Police Department, containing the list of accidents recorded between 2014 and the first half of 2022, totaling 9,648 accidents. The reports contain the following information (Table 1).

Table 1. Data report details

Data	Example
Temporal Data	Date, hour
Spatial data	Street, House Number, Kilometer Progression, Additional Notes
Nature of accident	Damage, with/without injuries, fatalities
Accident Description	Right of way, rear-end collision, side impact, etc.
Involved Vehicles	Number and type (passenger cars, two-wheeled vehicles, heavy vehicles, bicycles, pedestrians))
Involved Persons	Number and age divided by gender
Injured Persons	Number and divided into seriously injured and deceased

An initial data processing involved formatting the temporal fields in date and time format to make the data processable through pivot table extraction. At the same time, text fields were corrected for typographical errors, primarily in the street names. For the nature and description of the accident, homogenization was carried out by removing duplicates (e.g., "With/without injuries"—"Yes/No injuries" was standardized as "With/without injuries").

The second processing step involved adding geographic coordinates (longitude and latitude). This was done using both the address geolocator from the "Sardegna Geoportale" website [30] and "Google Maps" [31], through which coordinates in the WGS84 geographic format were obtained by entering the location data contained in the reports.

However, in some cases, due to the absence of the house number or kilometer progression, it was not possible to identify the geographic coordinates. This occurred for about 24% of the accidents, or 2361 cases, while the remaining 7287 incidents were geolocated using the specified method. However, even for these, there were issues with determining the exact incident location. This was particularly true in situations such as road/square adjacency, wide carriageway roads, and roundabouts, especially those with a large radius.

Once the geographic coordinates were loaded, the mapping of road accidents was carried out using QGIS software. The data database, stored in an Excel CSV file format, was imported as a text file into QGIS. This was overlaid onto the street map layer of the urban area of Cagliari, loaded from the WMS service of the Sardegna Geoportale, and onto the boundaries layer of the urban areas of municipalities in the metropolitan area, also available on the Geoportale. In this way, the urban area of Cagliari, the focus of the study, was isolated.

3.1 Data Analysis

Considering only the data from the complete years, i.e., $2014 \div 2021$, the time series is shown in the graph in Fig. 2.

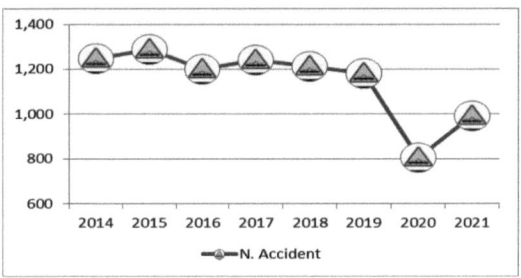

Fig. 2. Trend of accidents over the years

Disregarding the last two years affected by lockdown measures due to the pandemic and stopping the analysis at 2019, i.e., before COVID, the number of accidents decreased by approximately 64 units, recording an average annual decrease of −1.1%.

Considering the nature of the accidents, 51.9% were accidents with no injuries, 42.8% involved injuries, 4.7% were property damage, and 0.6% were fatal. Figure 3 shows the accident data by category expressed as index numbers with 2014 as the baseline. Comparing 2019/2014, accidents with property damage and fatalities saw the most significant increases, with a total growth of 137% and 40%, respectively, and average annual increases of 19% and 7%. These types of accidents remained stable during the years affected by the pandemic, while property damage incidents, after a decline of −24%, reversed the trend with a +29%, matching the 2019 figure. On the other hand, accidents with and without injuries experienced a total reduction of −14% and −6%, respectively, with average annual decreases of −3% and −1%. The physiological contraction in 2020 (−43% with injuries and −24% without) was followed by a stronger recovery for accidents with injuries (+46%) compared to those without injuries (+9%).

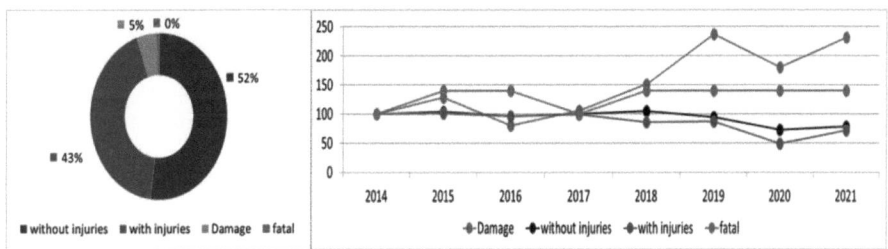

Fig. 3. Nature of accidents and evolution over the years (data expressed as index number as of 2014)

Figure 4 shows the weekly trend and for each day the distribution by time slot. It is noticeable that the majority of accidents occur during weekdays, which is related to the intensity of physiological traffic volumes on these days. The peak hours for accidents are from 2 p.m. to 6 p.m. (average 39 percent) and from 9 a.m. to noon (average value 35 percent). In contrast, during the weekend, there is a decrease in the number of accidents, although they tend to concentrate in the 24 - 7 range on Sundays (23%) and Saturdays 21%.

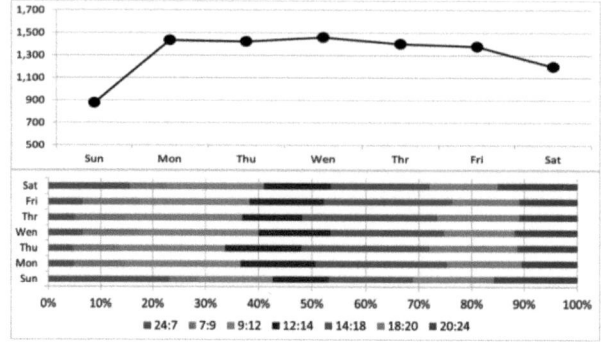

Fig. 4. Total Accidents – Weekly Trend and Time Slot Distribution

Among the confirmed causes, the first place goes to rear-end collision and pedestrian hit-and-run (21%) followed in order by skidding (11%), front/side and side impacts (9% and 7%), failure to yield right of way (6%), collision with parked vehicle (5%), and a mix of other causes (Fig. 5).

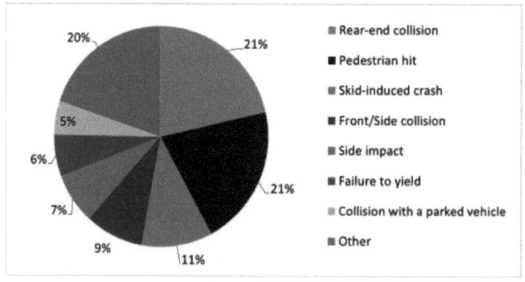

Fig. 5. Main Caeses of accidents

The main causes have also been examined over the years. Figure 6 shows the trend in the years 2014–2019 of rear-end collisions and skidding exit.

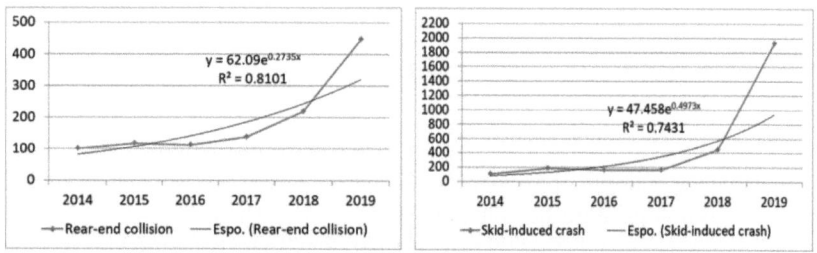

Fig. 6. Trend 2014 – 2019 Rear-End collision and Skidding Exit

In both cases, a relevant peak is observed in 2019. Such a trend was observed in the first 6 causes with the exception of pedestrian investment. This increase was immediately found to be abnormal, i.e., not justifiable in any way by either exogenous causes or traffic flows. A detailed analysis of the data revealed that the reason for the spike is due to increased accuracy in filling out the field: cause of accident. In fact, it was found that in previous years the field in question did not report the cause of the accident, leaving the cells blank. The graph in Fig. 7 shows the distribution, for each year, of whether the cause was found or not. As can be seen, until 2018, the ascertainment of the cause of the accident was transcribed for a limited number of accidents, ranging from a low of 13% (2014) up to 34% in 2018, after which, just in 2019, there is a reversal of the trend witnessed by a transcription coverage of 81%, a trend that is maintained in the following years. This is the reason for the 2019 spike: an increase in accuracy when filling out the field and, consequently, in the reporting of the incident.

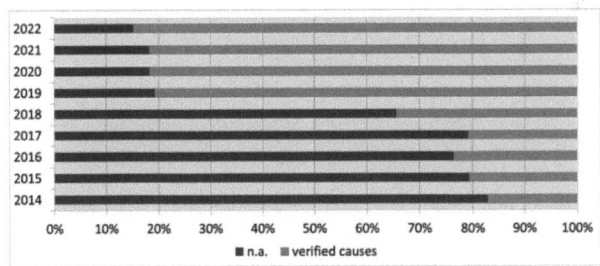

Fig. 7. Confirmed Causes vs Unconfirmed Causes

3.2 Construction of the Maps

For the purpose of the study, this section will present the digital maps of the urban area of Cagliari with georeferenced accidents, that is, those for which latitude and longitude coordinates were obtained in WGS84, as described in Sect. 2 (D) (Fig. 8).

Upon initial analysis, critical intersections were identified based on the placement of the points on the map. Criticality is not in quantitative terms i.e., by number of accidents as much as by complexity and multitude of maneuvers allowed, which results in placement of points in irregular areas due to irregular trajectories resulting in increased conflict points. Figure 9 shows those assessed as most critical according to the logic just described: (1) Via Roma – Piazza Giacomo Matteotti - Largo Carlo Felice, (2) Viale Marconi – Asse Mediano di Scorrimento, (3) Viale Poetto – Via Tramontana – Viale Campioni d'Italia 1969/1970 e (4) Via Diego Cadello – Via Santa Maria Chiara.

Moving on to the quantitative analysis, Fig. 10 shows the location of accidents in the main access/exit routes and throughways of the urban area and in which the highest number of accidents were detected. They in order are: Asse Mediano di Scorrimento and Viale Marconi (in blue) in which 10% of the total number of accidents occurred; Viale Trieste, Viale Sant'Avendrace and Viale Monastir (in green) with 5% of the accidents; Via Roma, Viale Armando Diaz and Viale Campioni d'Italia 1969/1970 (in yellow) 4.3%; Viale Poetto, Viale Lungo Mare Poetto and Via Lungo Saline (in purple) account for about 3.6%.

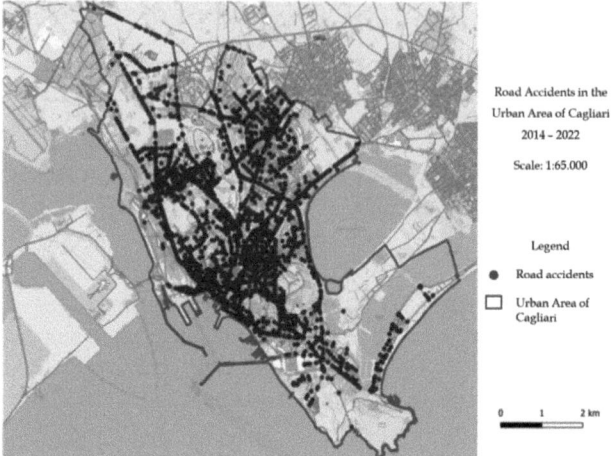

Fig. 8. Georeferenced Accident Mapping - 2014 – 2022 (Jen-Jun)

Fig. 9. Critical intersections

The maps were then discretized according to the nature of the accidents (Fig. 11): with injuries (3,174), without injuries (3,756), fatal (37) and with damage (320). Accidents involving pedestrians (999), velocipedes (65) and both (4) were then mapped (Fig. 12).

Finally, concentration maps were created that identify the areas of highest risk in terms of accident occurrence. First, a representation of all accidents in the reference time frame was made (Fig. 13). Next, the municipal territory was divided into (250 × 250) m cells obtaining 2,537 cells divided into 43 rows and 59 columns. For each of them, the number of accidents occurring within it was estimated. Further processing involved the creation of concentration maps during the hours within the peak hours (Figs. 14 and 15).

Fig. 10. Mapping on the main access/exit routes and throughways of the urban area

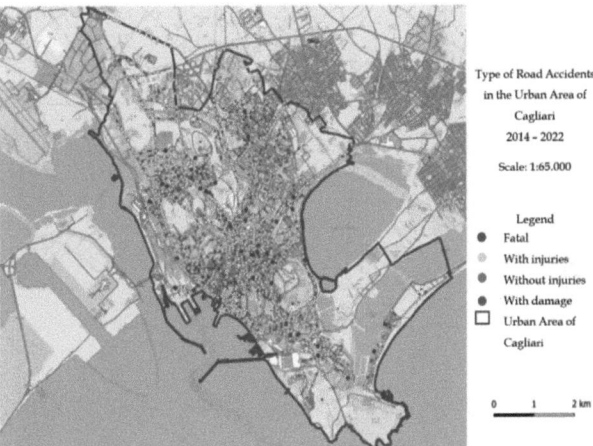

Fig. 11. Cagliari - Accident Map by Type - 2014 – 2022 (Jen-Jun)

Regarding the analysis by time slot, the day was divided into 4 time intervals, each lasting 6 hours. For each of these intervals, the time range with the highest concentration was calculated, and these were mapped. Three critical time intervals were identified:

- 7 am - 9 am belonging to Band 2 (06:00 am ÷ 12:00 pm) where a total of 900 incidents were recorded, corresponding to about 30% of the band and about 9% of the overall total (Fig. 14);
- 12 pm - 2 pm belonging to Band 3 (12:00 pm ÷ 6:00 pm) 1,279 accidents were

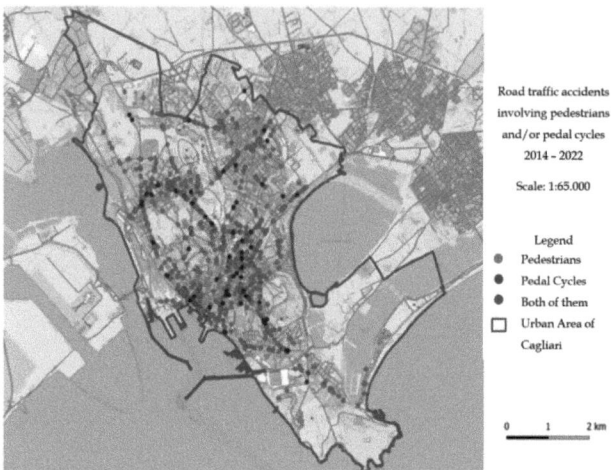

Fig. 12. Cagliari - Accident Map by Pedestrians/Pedal cycles/Both - 2014 – 2022 (Jen-Jun)

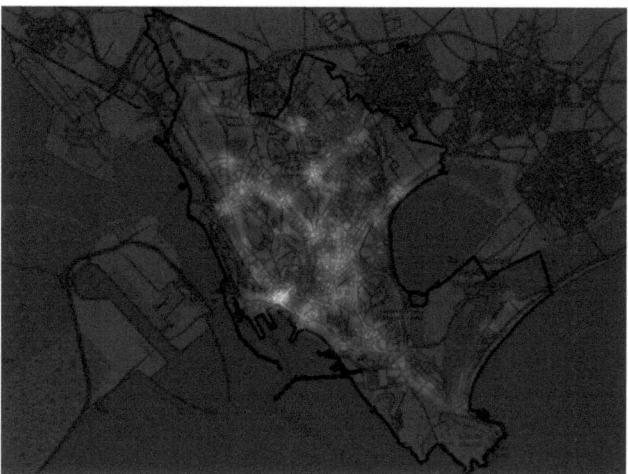

Fig. 13. Cagliari - Concentration Map - 2014 – 2022 (Jen-Jun)

recorded, about 37% of the band and about 13% of the overall total (Fig. 15);
- 6 pm - 8 pm belonging to band 4 (6:00 pm ÷ 12:00 am) 1,379 incidents were recorded, or about 54% of the band and about 14% of the overall total (Fig. 16).

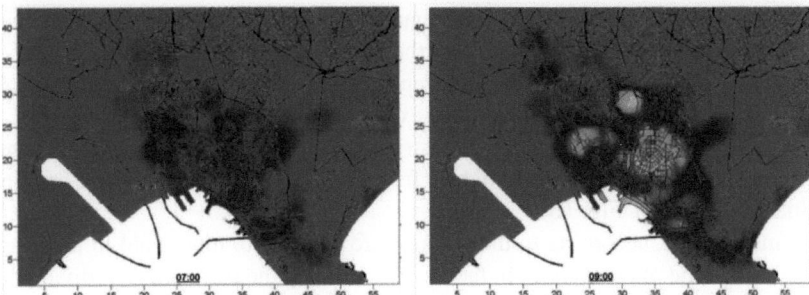

Fig. 14. Cagliari - Concentration Map for Hours: 7am÷9am –2014 – 2022 (Jen-Jun)

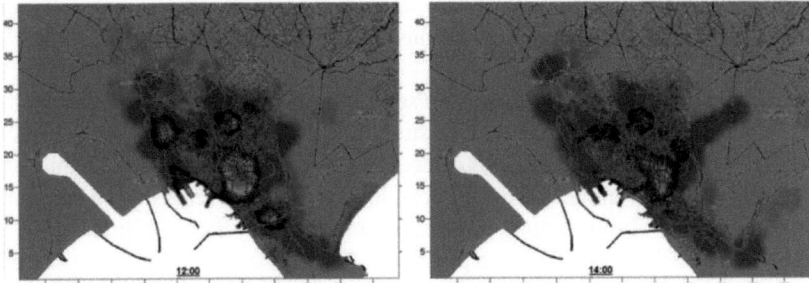

Fig. 15. Cagliari - Concentration Map for Hours:12pm÷2pm – 2014 – 2022 (Jen-Jun)

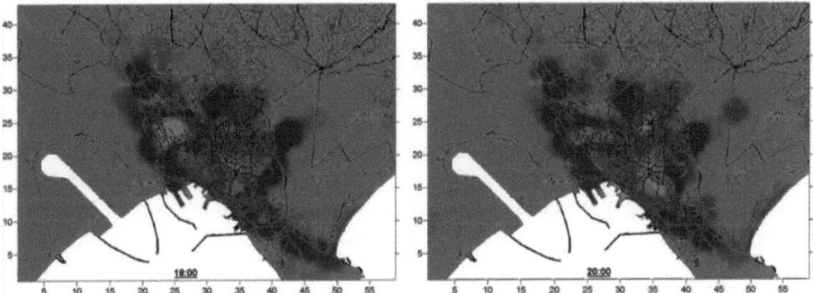

Fig. 16. Cagliari - Concentration Map for Hours:6pm÷8pm – 2014 – 2022 (Jen-Jun)

4 Conclusions

In recent years, the issue of road safety has received much global and national attention, with various countries implementing interventions whose results have led to a gradual reduction in the number of accidents. However, problems still persist, suffice it to say that the goal promoted by the [1, 2] of zero deaths on the roads is far from being achieved.

This study analyzed the accidents recorded in the urban area of Cagliari (Sardinia), in the years 2014 ÷ 2022 (first half of the year), for a total of 9,648 accidents. Of these, 76% or 7,287 accidents were geolocated using the methodology given in Sect. 2 (D).

The inclusion of geographic coordinates made it possible to represent the phenomenon on the cartography of the urban area and thus produce thematic maps: (i) overall, i.e., representative of the number of accidents regardless of the nature and elements involved (Fig. 8), (ii) by nature i.e., according to the extent of the severity of the damage (Fig. 11), (iii) by vulnerable users, specifically pedestrians and cyclists (Fig. 12), and (iv) concentration maps in which the areas of highest frequency of accident occurrence are clearly identifiable (Fig. 13 ÷ Fig. 16).

Thematic maps, according to the authors, are a powerful tool to aid in the descriptive analysis of the phenomenon. In fact, by discretizing the parameters, individually or in cross-tabulated form, they make it possible to make an immediate and direct examination of the accident situation in the area: (i) identifying the most critical areas or points in a timely and effective manner, (ii) correlating them with the geometric and functional characteristics of the road, (iii) thus identifying the underlying risk factors, and (iv) implementing effective interventions. This is of great help, to analysts and local authorities.

For the authors, the present study represents a starting point for future research that has the Cagliari metropolitan area as a case study. The next steps will involve, (1) updating the data to 2024, (2) a detailed analysis on accidents involving pedestrians. In this regard, it should be noted that in the current year, following serious events that resulted in the death by investment of some young people, and which rightly drew the attention of local governments, raised crosswalks were planned and implemented in some specific areas. Following this, it would be interesting to conduct a pre- and post-analysis to evaluate the effectiveness of the intervention and, in the most recent scenario, to estimate the risk components. Furthermore, a series of investigations can be conducted on sensitive areas such as zones near schools, hospitals, etc.

Acknowledgments. This paper was produced with the support of the Integrative Research Fund (FIR), year 2024. This study is also supported by the MIUR (Ministry of Education, Universities and Research [Italy]) through the project entitled: SMART3R-FLITS: SMART Transport for TRavellers and Freight Logistics Integration Towards Sustainability (Project protocol: 2022J38SR9; CUP Code: F53D23005630006), financed with the PRIN 2022 (Research Projects of National Relevance) programme; and project e.INS – Ecosystem of Innovation for Next Gen- eration Sardinia" funded by the Italian Ministry of University and Research (MIUR) under the Next-Generation EU Programme (National Recovery and Resilience Plan – PNRR, M4C2, INVESTMENT 1.5 – DD 1056 of 23/06/2022, ECS00000038)- SPOKE 8 – CUP F53C22000430001. We authorize the MIUR to reproduce and distribute reprints for Governmental purposes, notwithstanding any copyright notations thereon. Any opinions, findings and conclusions or recommendations expressed in this material are those of the authors, and do not necessarily reflect the views of the MIUR. Moreover, the authors are grateful Cagliari Local Police Department, which made its data available for this study.

Disclosure of Interests The authors have no competing interests to declare that are relevant to the content of this article. Author Contributions. Conceptualization: Nicoletta Rassu, Francesca Maltinti, Mauro Coni. Methodology and formal analysis: Nicoletta Rassu, Francesca Maltinti, Mauro Coni, James Rombi, Marta Salis. Introduction and literature review: Nicoletta Rassu, Francesca Maltinti, James Rombi. Writing-original draft preparation: Nicoletta Rassu, Francesca Maltinti, Mauro Coni. Writing review and editing: Nicoletta Rassu, James Rombi. Visualization, all. All authors have read and agreed to the published version of the manuscript.

References

1. MIT – Ministero delle infrastrutture e dei Trasporti, "PNSS Orizzonte 2020 - Piano Nazionale della sicurezza stradale", Dip. Per i Trasporti e la navigazione ed i sistemi informativi e statistici – Direzione Generale per la sicurezza stradale
2. MIMS – Ministero delle infrastrutture e della Mobilità Sostenibili, "PNSS 2030 - Piano Nazionale della sicurezza stradale", Dip. Per la Mobilità Sostenibile – Direzione Generale per la sicurezza stradale e l'autotrasporto
3. World Health Organization: Global status report on road safety 2018, Geneva, 2018. Licence: CC BY-NC-SA 3.0 IGO
4. World Health Organization and United Nations Regional Commissions: Global Plan Decade of Action for Road Safety 2021–2030 Geneva (2021)
5. Job, R.S., Truong, J., Sakashita, C.: The ultimate safe system: redefining the safe system approach for road safety. Sustain. For. **14**(5), 2978 (2022)
6. FHWA, United States Department of Transportation, Highway Safety Programs, "The Safe System approach" - https://highways.dot.gov/safety/zero-deaths
7. European Commission: EU road safety policy framework 2021-2030 – Next steps towards 'Vision Zero'. ISBN 978-92-76-13219-6, https://doi.org/10.2832/391271 (2019)
8. European Commission: Strategia per una mobilità sostenibile e intelligente: mettere i trasporti europei sulla buona strada per il futuro, Bruxelles (2020)
9. European Commission, n.131 del 1997: Promuovere la sicurezza stradale nell'EU: il programma 1997–2001 (1997)
10. Testo Unico Salute Sicurezza Lavoro D.Lgs. 81/ 2008, Art. 2 – Definizioni (s)
11. ISO 9001, 2015: Quality management systems — Requirements (2015)
12. UNI ISO 31000: Risk management - Principles and guidelines on implementation (2010)
13. Fine, W.T.: Mathematical evaluations for controlling hazards. J. Saf. Res. **3**, 157–166 (1971)
14. Porcu, F., Olivo, A., Maternini, G., Barabino, B.: Evaluating bus accident risks in public transport. Transp. Res. Proc. **45**, 443–450 (2020)
15. Porcu, F., Olivo, A., Maternini, G., Coni, M., Bonera, M., Barabino, B.: "Assessing the risk of bus crashes" in transit systems. Eur. Transp. **81**, 4–14 (2021)
16. Porcu, F., Maltinti, F., Rassu, N., Pili, F., Bonera, M., Barabino, B.: A new framework to evaluate crash risk for road traffic safety management system. In: Computational Science and Its Applications – ICCSA 2021 Lecture notes in computer science, vol. 12958. Springer, Cham (2021). https://doi.org/10.1007/978-3-030-87016-4_41
17. European Commission, Directive 2008/96/EC of the European Parliament and of the Council on Road Infrastructure Safety Management, (2008);
18. European Commission, Directive (Eu) 2019/1936 of the European Parliament and of the Council, Amending Directive 2008/96/EC on Road Infrastructure Safety Management, (2019);
19. Internationl Transport Forum: Road Infrastructure Safety Management. International Traffic Safety Data and Analysis Group (2015)
20. Elvik, R., Vaa, T., Hoye, A., Sorensen, M.: The handbook of Road Safety Measures. Emerald Group Publishing, Burlington, MA (2009)
21. Yasmin, S., Eluru, N.: A joint econometric framework for modeling crash counts by severity. Transportmetrica A Transp. Sci. **14**(3), 230–255 (2017)
22. AASHTO American Association of State Highway Transportation Officials, Highway Safety Manual (HSM), (2010)
23. European Commission, European Road Assessment Programme (EuroRAP)
24. AASHTO American Association of State Highway Transportation Officials, Highway Safety Manual (HSM), (2014)

25. Martinelli, F., La Torre, F., Vadi, P.: Calibration of the highway safety manual's accident prediction model for Italian secondary road network. Transp. Res. Rec. **2103**(1), 1–9 (2009). https://doi.org/10.3141/2103-01
26. La Torre, F., Domenichini, L., Meocci, M., Graham, D., Karathodorou, N., Richter, T., Ruhl, S., Yannis, G., Dragomanovits, A., Laiou, A.: Development of a transnational accident prediction model. Transp. Res. Proc. **14**, 1772–1781 (2016)
27. Aguero-Valverde, J., Jovanis, P.P.: Bayesian multivariate Poisson lognormal models for crash severity modeling and site ranking. Transp. Res. Rec. **2136**, 82–91 (2009)
28. Afghari, A.P., Haque, M.M., Washington, S.: Applying a joint model of crash count and crash severity to identify road segments with high risk of fatal and serious injury crashes. Accid. Anal. Prev. **144**, 105615 (2020)
29. Miler, M., Todić, F., Ševrović, M.: Extracting accurate location information from a highly inaccurate traffic accident dataset: a methodology based on a string matching technique. Transp. Res. C Emerg. Technol. **68**, 185–193 (2016)
30. Geoportale Sardegna - https://www.sardegnageoportale.it/webgis/interoperabilita/Geocoding/OpenLS/
31. Google Maps - https://www.coordinate-gps.it/

Traffic Light Control at Intersections in Case of Heterogeneous Traffic Using Reinforcement Learning

Do Thai Giang[1,2], Truong Cong Doan[1], and Phan Duy Hung[2(✉)]

[1] International School, Vietnam National University, Hanoi, Vietnam
{24078012,tcdoan}@vnu.edu.vn, giangdt26@fe.edu.vn
[2] FPT University, Hanoi, Vietnam
hungpd2@fe.edu.vn

Abstract. One of the urgent problems in traffic is to reduce congestion and waiting time of vehicles participating in traffic. This paper focuses on the employment of reinforcement learning algorithms such as Double Deep Q-Network and Proximal Policy Optimization to reduce vehicle waiting times in three-way and four-way intersections with heterogeneous traffic conditions. At the same time, we also investigate the performance of the algorithm in both heavy and clear traffic scenarios. Our method dramatically lowers waiting times and improves traffic flow efficiency, according to extensive testing. Significantly, the outcomes reveal remarkable performance gains in both three-way and four-way intersection, indicating the possibility of widespread use in urban traffic control. When compared to the fixed time strategy, the experimental results likewise perform better in both clear and congested traffic scenarios. This study demonstrates the effectiveness of intelligent traffic control systems in varied and complex traffic environments.

Keywords: reinforcement learning · traffic light control · heterogeneous traffic · DDQN · PPO · SUMO simulation

1 Introduction

Traffic management at isolated crossroads is quite difficult, especially in situations with heterogeneous traffic. Heterogeneous traffic means that complicated traffic situation due to the participation of many types of vehicles (cars, buses, motorbikes, trucks, etc.) interspersed, where the mix of vehicles might differ greatly in terms of size, speed, and driving style. Such complexity is frequently too hard for traditional traffic signal management systems to handle effectively, which results in more traffic congestion, longer waiting times, and higher emissions.

The traditional traffic light control method that uses fixed light phase times is often ineffective. For instance, when traffic is more congested during rush hour than during other times, if the light phases are set to deal with congestion, it is not appropriate for clear traffic conditions, which creates an unreasonable situation and forces vehicles to stop and wait for traffic lights when the road is very clear. Recent developments in reinforcement learning (RL) have demonstrated encouraging promise for dynamic, data-driven traffic light control optimization. In order to maximize flow and minimize delays, RL algorithms are able to continuously improve signal timings by learning and adapting to real-time traffic conditions.

The main contribution of this research is to experimentally and evaluate the ability to reduce waiting time of vehicles by applying PPO and DDQN algorithms in controlling traffic lights at three-way and four-way intersections. At the same time, these algorithms are also applied in congestion situations and smooth traffic flow situations. Although there have been previous studies using the PPO algorithm in traffic light control, this study mainly focuses on comparing PPO and DDQN in increasing the reward value of the algorithms without clarifying the ability to reduce waiting time and limit congestion of the PPO algorithm in different traffic situations.

2 Literature Review

2.1 Reinforcement Learning in Traffic Management

In recent years, with the development of artificial intelligence and optimization algorithms, there has been increasing interest in applying these algorithms to various areas of life, in which traffic congestion is always an urgent problem in large cities. Traditional traffic light control systems are increasingly showing their ineffectiveness in modern traffic when traffic density is very high as well as traffic situations change rapidly and are complex. There is growing interest in and studying powerful optimization algorithms for traffic signal control to mitigate congestion. Traditional traffic light control techniques were the mainstays of early traffic signal control systems. Whereas actuated systems modify signals in response to traffic demand at intersections, pre-timed systems follow set schedules. Even while they work well in some situations, these conventional methods find it difficult to adjust to changes in traffic in real time, especially in locations with diverse traffic patterns.

A dynamic and adaptable method for controlling traffic signals is provided by reinforcement learning, a subfield of machine learning. Through interaction with the environment and incentives based on behaviors, RL algorithms develop the best rules. The potential of RL resides in its capacity to dynamically optimize traffic flow and adjust to shifting traffic conditions. The optimization of signal timings at isolated crossings was the main focus of early RL research for traffic management. Li et al. (2016) [1], for example, used Q-learning at a four-way intersection and showed that, in comparison to conventional techniques, average vehicle waiting times were decreased.

Deep reinforcement learning approaches including deep Q-networks (DQN) and policy gradient methods were added to later studies, which demonstrated even greater gains in traffic efficiency. Romain Ducrocq and Nadir Farhipropose (2021) [2] offer a deep reinforcement Q-learning model to enhance traffic signal regulation at an isolated intersection. DQN model sub-stantially improves the performance of traffic light control compared to deployed actuated methods Max Pressure [3] and Self-Organising Traffic Lights (SOTL) [4], achieving both fairness between vehicles and global efficiency at the intersection.

Li et al. (2022) [5] presents an enhanced Distributional DQN to develop a signal optimization decision-making model employing reinforcement learning grounded in value distribution. The simulation results demonstrate that the Distributional DQN proposed in the paper has a faster convergence rate than the original DQN, and the cumulative delay at the intersection is reduced by about 13.1%, and the average driving speed is increased by 7.1%, which further improves the control efficiency of signalized intersections.

Another notable contribution is the publication of Yue Zhu et al. (2022) [6] on the use of Proximal Policy Optimization (PPO) algorithm in traffic light control at an intersection. The paper showed that PPO has better results than DQN and DDQN. In this paper, the authors compared the rewards of the algorithms but did not give results on its effectiveness in improving the traffic situation. In this study, the authors also only focused on applying the PPO algorithm to the situation of an intersection with unbalanced traffic but did not pay attention to considering other traffic situations such as at three-way intersections, situations with smooth traffic flow and balance between directions.

Liu et al. (2023) [7] examines the utilization of deep reinforcement learning (DRL) for the management of traffic signals in intelligent transportation systems (ITSs). The authors propose using two DRL algorithms - DQN and Deep Deterministic Policy Gradient (DDPG) - to manage traffic lights in both single road intersections and grid road networks. Theoretical analysis and numerical experiments demonstrate that the DQN algorithm delivers optimal control, while the DDPG algorithm produces intelligent "greenwave" behavior, where vehicles experience a progressive cascade of green lights without needing to brake. The results highlight the scalability and effectiveness of DRL algorithms in improving traffic efficiency and reducing congestion.

2.2 Heterogeneous Traffic

Heterogeneous traffic, defined by a variety of vehicle kinds and behaviors, poses distinct issues for traffic management. Zhang et al. (2017) [8] proposes a novel model for heterogeneous traffic networks that includes both signalized and non-signalized crossings. The authors propose and validate a mixed integer programming approach for signal control using VISSIM simulations.

Eom, M., and Kim, BI (2020) [9] published a review paper that gives a complete examination of challenges, methodologies, and practices in traffic signal control at intersections, including diverse traffic situations.

Hung, P.D., and Giang, D.T. (2021) [10] released a paper on the use of fuzzy logic to optimize traffic signals at isolated crossroads in heterogeneous traffic conditions. The system is simulated with SUMO simulation, which shows substantial advantages over fixed traffic lights.

There are very few researches on traffic light control under current heterogeneous traffic conditions, and most of them use old algorithms with low efficiency.

2.3 Three-Way and Four-Way Configurations

The majority of traffic light control research focuses on traffic problems at four-way junctions, with very few studies examining traffic light management at three-way intersections. One study that should be mentioned is the publication of Maheen Firdous et al. (2019) [11]. The paper describes a traffic signal control system that uses fuzzy logic to reduce the number of queues and wait times for cars at crossings.

Another recent study by Ni et al. (2024) [12] provides traffic signal control solutions for T-shaped crossings in urban road networks based on deep Q network algorithms. The simulation findings demonstrate that combining the Dueling-DQN approach with dynamic time aggregation considerably increased vehicle throughput. Compared to DQN and fixed-time techniques, this strategy can reduce average journey time by up to 43% in low-traffic hours and 15% in high-traffic periods.

3 Proposed Method

3.1 Algorithms

Previous articles have examined a variety of methods and techniques for traffic light regulation at crossings. Following a comprehensive evaluation of the works, we chose two state-of-the-art algorithms to experiment in this paper including Double Deep Q-Network (DDQN) and Proximal Policy Optimization (PPO). In this section, we'll talk about these two algorithms and their optimization goals.

A. *Double Deep Q-Network*

DDQN is an extension of the Deep Q-Network algorithm that is intended to overcome the overestimation bias of Q-values in regular DQN. Hado van Hasselt et al. [13] introduced DDQN in 2015, which distinguishes between selecting the best action and evaluating it. It employs two networks: a selection network to select the action and a target network to evaluate it. This separation reduces overestimation of Q-values and increases the stability and performance of the learning process. The DDQN architecture is shown as Fig. 1.

The DDQN technique is based on Q-learning, which is a policy temporal difference (TD) learning algorithm that approximates the value of a state-action value function, or Q-function, using previously obtained estimates of this function. The Q-function is defined as the expected discounted reward that an agent would earn when starting the game in state s with action a and then acting according to policy π. The mathematical description is as follows:

$$Q^\pi(s, a) = \mathbb{E}_\pi[R_t | s_t = s, a_t = a] \tag{1}$$

where R_t represents the expected reward at the end of the session. The Q-function evaluates an agent's performance as it moves from one state to another based on the set policy. The policy is a greedy policy defined as *argmax(Q(s, a))* for all actions. During training, the agent learns and converges on the optimal strategy to maximize total reward per episode. The Q-function itself can be expressed recursively:

$$Q(s, a) = r(s, a) + \gamma \max_{a'} Q(s', a') \tag{2}$$

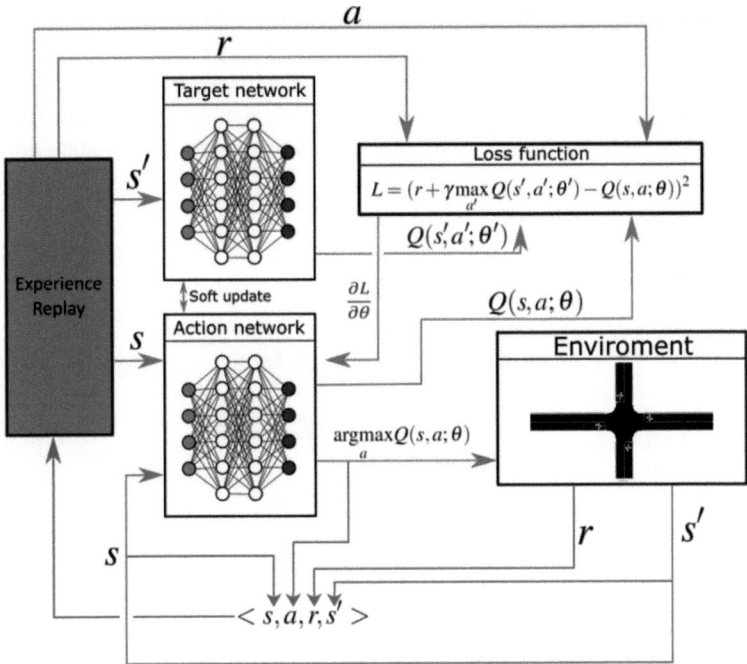

Fig. 1. The architecture of double deep Q-learning network [14]

where $r(s, a)$ is the reward for moving from state s to state s' by doing action a, and $\gamma \in [0, 1]$ is a discount factor that sets the relative value of future and present rewards. ϵ-greedy approach is used to select an action throughout the learning process, allowing the agent to explore the environment in many ways. Throughout the episode, the agent chooses actions with the highest value of the Q-function in state s with probability $(1 - \epsilon)$ or randomly with probability ϵ, where $\epsilon \in [0, 1]$. After the agent has passed from state s to state s' and received a reward r, the value of the Q-function is changed using

$$Q^{new}(s, a) = Q(s, a) + \alpha \left(r + \gamma \max_{a'} Q(s', a') - Q(s, a) \right) \qquad (3)$$

We get a deep reinforcement learning method when we employ deep neural networks to approximate the policy, Q-functions, or another RL function. This method is utilized when working with continuous situations where the number of states or actions is limitless. The Deep Q-Network (DQN) approach uses neural networks (NN) to approximate the values of the function $Q(s, a, \theta)$, where θ represents the weights in the deep neural network. In this scenario, we utilize a multilayer neural network that accepts state s as input and outputs a vector of values $Q(s, a_i, \theta)$ for each potential action a_i.

The neural network is trained using the backpropagation method, where the loss function is described as the square of the difference between $Q(s, a)$ and $Q^{new}(s, a)$, which is obtained from Eq. (3):

$$L = \left(r + \gamma \max_{a'} Q(s', a', \theta') - Q(s, a, \theta) \right)^2 \qquad (4)$$

where θ and θ' are the weights of two neural networks with the same topology, called action network and target network, respectively (see Fig. 1). During error propagation training, the action network is updated, and the target network is updated by copying the action network's weights (θ) every few episodes. This technique, known as the Double Deep Q-learning Network, allows to prevent overestimating the action-state function in the learning process.

B. *Proximal Policy Optimization*

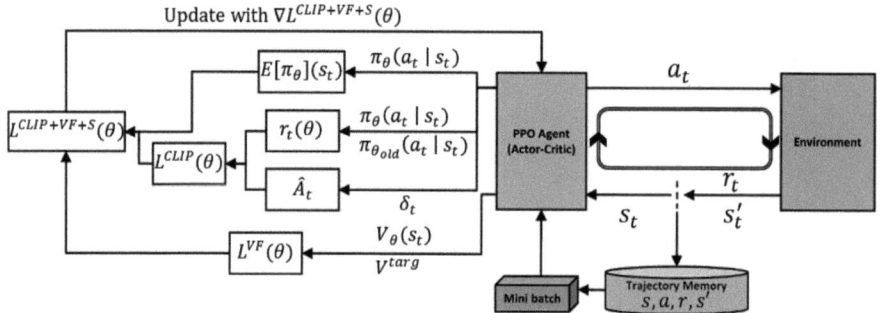

Fig. 2. The architecture of Proximal Policy Optimization algorithm

PPO is a widely utilized reinforcement learning technique developed by John Schulman et al. in 2017. PPO aims to improve the stability and efficiency of policy gradient methods by striking a balance between data efficiency and ease of implementation.

The key innovation in PPO is the clipping of the objective function, which prevents overly large policy updates. This clipping mechanism ensures that the new policy does not deviate too much from the old policy, maintaining stability during training. PPO uses an actor-critic approach, where the actor network predicts actions and the critic network estimates the state values, providing helpful training signals to guide the actor's learning. PPO is a method to simplify the complex calculation of trust region policy optimization (TRPO) [15]. TRPO maximizes a surrogate objective as follows:

$$L_t^{TRPO}(\theta) = \mathbb{E}\left[\frac{\pi_\theta(a_t|s_t)}{\pi_{\theta_{old}}(a_t|s_t)}\hat{A}_t\right] = \mathbb{E}\left[r_t(\theta)\hat{A}_t\right] \quad (5)$$

where a_t and s_t represent an action and state, respectively, and $r_t(\theta)$ represents the probability ratio of policy distribution in time step t. Maximizing the surrogate objective function L^{TRPO} of TRPO without a constraint would result in an unreasonably large policy update. Additionally, the surrogate objective function L^{TRPO} has a complicated formula expansion and must determine the second derivative [15]. Therefore, by using the clipping method to approximate the first derivative, PPO was able to compensate for the inadequacies of TRPO. The clipping is applied to the following goal function:

$$L_t^{CLIP}(\theta) = \mathbb{E}\left[\min\left(r_t(\theta)\hat{A}_t, \text{clip}\left(r_t(\theta), 1-\epsilon, 1+\epsilon\right)\hat{A}_t\right)\right] \quad (6)$$

where ϵ is a tiny hyperparameter that determines how far the new policy can deviate from the previous one. The main objective of PPO is optimizing the fusion loss function [16]:

$$L_t^{CLIP+VF+S}(\theta) = \mathbb{E}\left[L_t^{CLIP}(\theta) - c_1 L_t^{VF}(\theta) + c_2 E[\pi_\theta](s_t)\right] \quad (7)$$

where c_1, c_2 are coefficients, and E denotes an entropy bonus, and $L_t^{VF}(\theta)$ is a squared-error loss in Eq. 8.

$$L_t^{VF}(\theta) = \left(V_\theta(s_t) - V_t^{targ}\right)^2 \quad (8)$$

3.2 Environment

According to Markov Decision Process (MDP), the reinforcement learning agent learned from interacting with environment. Let's discuss about environment in Figs. 1 and 2. The purpose of this project is to control traffic lights at an intersection in order to optimize light phases and reduce vehicle wait time, therefore we used The SUMO Reinforcement Learning (SUMO-RL) [17] framework as environment. SUMO-RL is an effective tool for developing and testing reinforcement learning algorithms for traffic management and control utilizing the Simulation of Urban MObility (SUMO) simulator (Fig. 3). This framework creates a seamless interface between RL algorithms and SUMO, allowing simulate and optimize traffic signal control, vehicle routing, and other traffic-related activities.

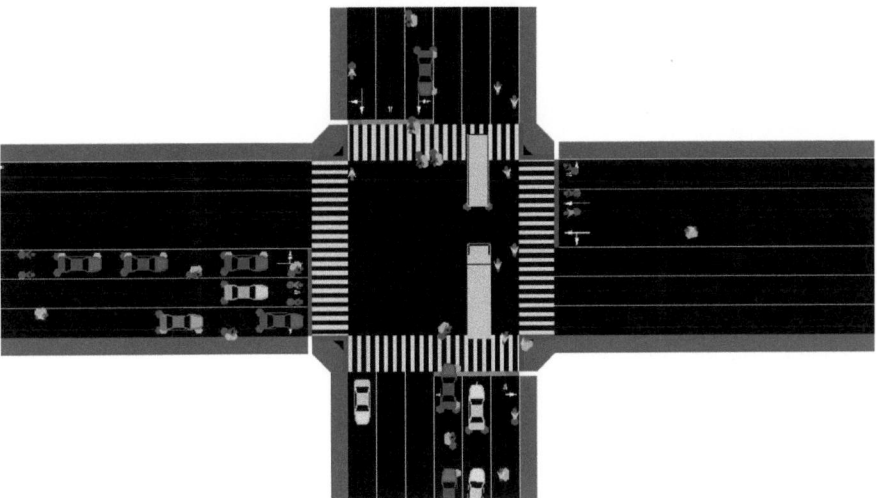

Fig. 3: SUMO Simulator

Key features of the SUMO RL framework include:

- *Compatibility*: It supports popular RL libraries such as Gymnasium, PettingZoo, stable-baselines3, and RLlib [17].
- *Multiagent RL*: The framework supports multiagent RL environments, allowing for the simulation of complex interactions between multiple agents [17].
- *Customization*: Easy define custom states, actions, and rewards to tailor the RL environment to their specific needs [17].
- *Efficiency*: The framework leverages SUMO's capabilities to create realistic and scalable traffic simulations, making it suitable for large-scale experiments.

The SUMO RL framework is widely used for developing and testing RL-based traffic management solutions, such as optimizing traffic signal timings, reducing congestion, and improving overall traffic flow [18].

3.3 State Space

The state space for traffic signal agent in SUMO-RL environment is a vector:

$$state = [phase, min\_green, L1\_density, \ldots, Ln\_density, L1\_queue, \ldots, Ln\_queue]$$

where:

- *phase* is a one-hot encoded vector indicating the current active green phase
- *min_green* is a binary variable indicating whether $\underline{min\_green}$ seconds have already passed in the current phase
- *Li_density* is the number of vehicles in incoming lane i divided by the total capacity of the lane
- *Li_queue* is the number of queued (speed below 0.1 m/s) vehicles in incoming lane i divided by the total capacity of the lane

3.4 Action Space

The action space in the SUMO-RL environment is discrete1. Every *delta_time* seconds, each traffic signal agent can choose the next green phase configuration. For example, in a 2-way single intersection, there are 4 discrete actions A = {1, 2, 3, 4}, corresponding to the following green phase configurations:

1. Green for the north-south direction
2. Green for the east-west direction
3. All-red phase
4. Green for left turns (if applicable)

Sudden phase changes can create a collision probability, to limit that problem we have used yellow light phase as a buffer time for phase change so that vehicles have time to react to the change. Every time a phase change occurs, it is preceded by a yellow phase lasting *yellow_time* seconds.

3.5 Reward Function

The reward function is chosen for the purpose of reducing the waiting time of vehicles, so that it is defined as:

$$r = D_t - D_{t+1} \tag{9}$$

where D_t is sum of the waiting times of all approaching vehicles in time step t. That is, the reward is how much the total delay changed in relation to the previous time-step.

4 Experiment

4.1 Experiment Scenario

We will conduct experiments in two scenarios at crossroads: three-way and four-way intersections (see Fig. 4). In the four-way intersection situation, each direction is a two-way road with a total of 6 lanes. In the three-way intersection situation, the main direction will be a two-way road with a total of 6 lanes, and the secondary direction will be a two-way road with 4 lanes. For the 4-way intersection, the traffic light configuration for fixed phase time, each phase will be set to 37 seconds of green light and 3 second for the yellow light. With 3-way intersection, the green phase is set to 45 seconds for the main direction and 25 seconds for the sub direction.

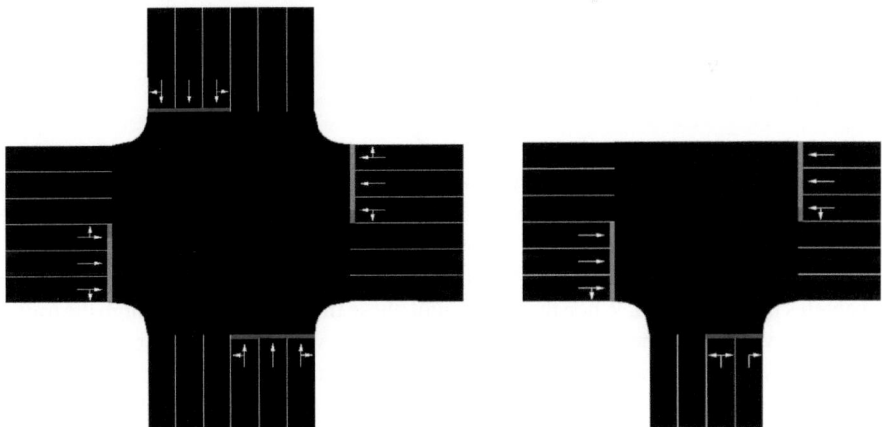

Fig. 4. Four-way and three-way configuration

4.2 Traffic Flow Scenarios

To evaluate the algorithm's efficacy in diverse scenarios, we also set up simulated traffic flow configurations for rush hour scenarios with large traffic volumes and the potential for congestion if fixed light timing is used. We also wanted to investigate the algorithm in relatively clear traffic situations where fixed time methods can handle it effectively. The traffic flow in the congested scenario was set to be around 3400–3600 vehicles passing through the intersection per hour. In the clear traffic scenario, the flow was set to be around half of the congested scenario, meaning a flow of around 1800–2000 vehicles per hour.

4.3 Heterogeneous Traffic

As mentioned earlier, an important issue that this paper focuses on is the heterogeneous traffic conditions where there are many vehicles of different sizes and different speeds participating in traffic at the same time. In this paper, the situation mentioned here will include the types of vehicles mentioned in Table 1.

Table 1. Distribution probability of the types of vehicles

Vehicle type	Probability
Motor bike	63%
Car	31%
Bus	3%
Truck	3%

4.4 Result Analysis

The experimental process shows very impressive results when the algorithms have great improvement. Figure 5 shows that the waiting time of vehicles is greatly reduced. The congestion situations have also been completely resolved. The traffic flow through the intersection is more stable when the algorithms are applied.

Even in clear traffic situations, when the vehicles are not congested, the waiting time of vehicles is also reduced. When the traffic light phase times are fixed, although the traffic situation is very clear, the vehicles still have to wait in vain. While the algorithms have continuously adjusted the headlight phase time to suit the situation, when the vehicles approach the intersection, they can quickly pass the intersection, which obviously leads to a reduction in waiting time.

The experimental results also show that the PPO algorithm outperforms DDQN in all scenarios. Especially in congested scenarios, the performance of PPO over DDQN is even more evident. PPO shows better stability while DDQN results show some points where the waiting time increases quite sharply.

Table 2 shows the quantitative comparison results between the control methods. The data shows that the average waiting time per second when applying algorithms is completely superior to using the fixed time method. In all scenarios, the PPO algorithm always gives better results than DDQN.

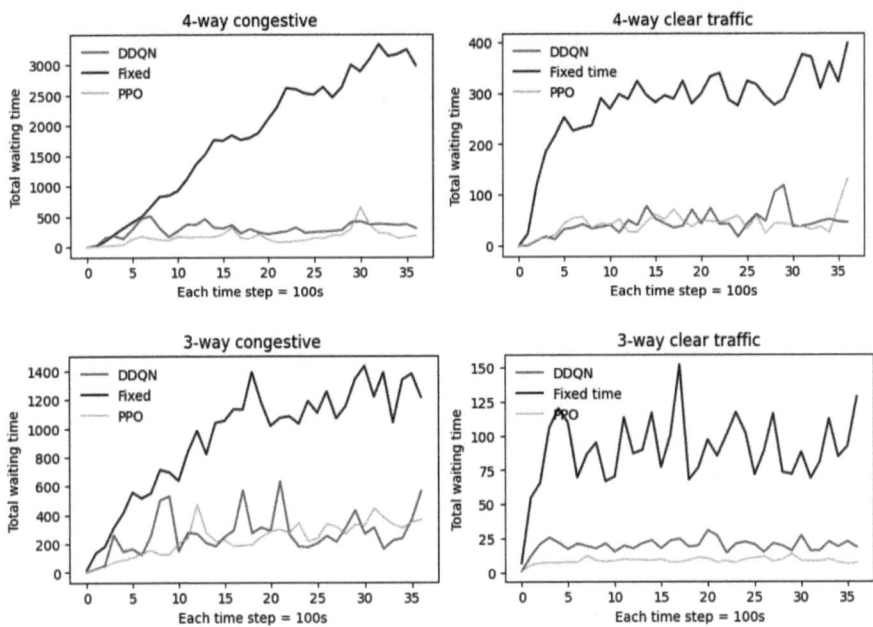

Fig. 5. Accumulated waiting time for every 100 seconds.

Table 2. Compare average waiting times per second

	3-way congestive	3-way clear traffic	4-way congestive	4-way clear traffic
Fixed time	927.74	197.44	1386.93	272.66
DDQN	259.37	19.7	285.11	43.23
PPO	**231.62**	**8.61**	**157.90**	**40.5**

The ability to process and respond to real-time traffic conditions is an essential component of traffic light control. In our trials, the inference time per decision cycle for both PPO and DDQN was 1.8 ms on an Intel Core i7 8750H CPU. This finding illustrates that the algorithms can perform effectively within practical restrictions, allowing for rapid modifications to traffic lights with little delays.

Compared to traditional traffic light control methods that rely on fixed time phases, reinforcement learning offers dynamic decision-making capabilities, allowing the system to continuously optimize light timings based on real-time traffic flow. The measured inference time shows that, despite the complexity of heterogeneous traffic situations, the algorithms retain low latency while significantly lowering vehicle waiting times.

5 Conclusion and Perspectives

The experimental results of the study have shown the feasibility and superiority of reinforcement learning algorithms in traffic light control. The algorithms can continuously adjust the timing of the light phases in accordance with the current traffic situation, significantly reducing the waiting time of vehicles. The paper also shows that the algorithms are effective in traffic situations including heterogeneous traffic conditions with many different types of vehicles.

By combining real-time traffic data and learning from observed traffic patterns, these algorithms dynamically adjust to changing traffic conditions, assuring optimal traffic flow. Notably, the adaptability of these algorithms enables them to handle complicated circumstances like intersections with a wide range of vehicle kinds and volumes. This versatility is critical in metropolitan areas where traffic patterns might alter quickly owing to unforeseen occurrences or shifting traffic needs.

Looking foward, there are several intriguing areas for future research. One area of interest is the possibility that multi-agent reinforcement learning (MARL) approaches can lead to progressively more complex traffic management solutions. MARL allows many traffic light controllers to collaborate and share information, resulting in more coordinated and harmonic traffic flow across bigger networked intersections.

In conclusion, the use of reinforcement learning in traffic signal regulation represents a significant improvement in intelligent transportation systems. The excellent findings of this study indicate the potential for widespread acceptance and ongoing innovation in this field, paving the way for smarter and more effective urban traffic management.

Acknowledgments. This research was supported by the **Doctoral Scholarship Program** of the **International School, Vietnam National University, Hanoi**. The financial assistance provided through this scholarship has enabled the authors to conduct extensive experiments and simulations, contributing to the advancement of intelligent traffic management using reinforcement learning techniques.

References

1. Li, Y., Xu, K., Li, D.: Traffic light control with reinforcement learning. J. Traf. Manag. **12**(3), 45–53 (2016)
2. Ducrocq, R., Farhi, N.: Deep reinforcement Q-learning for intelligent traffic signal control with partial detection. Int. J. Intell. Transp. Syst. Res. **21**, 192–206 (2021)
3. Minnesota Transportation Research. Investigating Max-Pressure Traffic Signal Timing. Available at: https://mntransportationresearch.org/2023/02/14/investigating-max-pressure-traffic-signal-timing/ (Accessed 10 Oct 2024)
4. Reztsov, A.: Self-Organising Traffic Lights (SOTL) as an upper bound estimate. (2014). https://doi.org/10.2139/ssrn.2467948
5. Li, J., Chen, T., Zhou, F., Lv, X., Peng, F.: Research on signal control method of deep reinforcement learning based on value distribution. In: Journal of Physics: Conference Series (2330/012019), vol. 2330, p. 012019. IOP Publishing (2022)
6. Zhu, Y., Cai, M., Schwarz, C.W., et al.: Intelligent traffic light via policy-based deep reinforcement learning. Int. J. ITS Res. **20**, 734–744 (2022). https://doi.org/10.1007/s13177-022-00321-5

7. Liu, X. Y., Zhu, M., Borst, S., & Walid, A.: Deep reinforcement learning for traffic light control in intelligent transportation systems. arXiv:2302.03669 (2023)
8. Zhang, Y., Su, R., Sun, C., Zhang, Y.: Modelling and traffic signal control of a heterogeneous traffic network with signalized and non-signalized intersections. In: Proceedings off the IEEE Conference on Control Technology and Applications (CCTA), Maui, HI, USA, pp. 1581–1586 (2017)
9. Eom, M., Kim, B.I.: The traffic signal control problem for intersections: a review. Eur. Transp. Res. Rev. **12**, 50 (2020)
10. Hung, P.D., Giang, D.T.: Traffic light control at isolated intersections in case of heterogeneous traffic. In: Kreinovich, V., Hoang Phuong, N. (eds.) Soft Computing for Biomedical Applications and Related Topics Studies in Computational Intelligence, vol. 899. Springer, Cham (2021)
11. Firdous, M., Din Iqbal, F.U., Ghafoor, N., Qureshi, N.K., Naseer, N.: Traffic light control system for four-way intersection and t-crossing using fuzzy logic. In: Proceedings of the IEEE International Conference on Artificial Intelligence and Computer Applications (ICAICA), pp. 178–182 (2019)
12. Ni, W., Li, C., Wang, P., Li, Z.: Traffic signal optimization at T-shaped intersections based on deep Q networks. In: Luo, B., Cheng, L., Wu, Z.G., Li, H., Li, C. (eds.) Neural Information Processing. ICONIP 2023 Lecture Notes in Computer Science, vol. 14449. Springer, Singapore (2024)
13. Van Hasselt, H., Guez, A., Silver, D.: Deep reinforcement learning with double Q-Learning. In: Proceedings of the Thirtieth AAAI Conference on Artificial Intelligence (AAAI'16), pp. 2094–2100. AAAI Press (2016)
14. Kuprikov, E., Kokhanovskiy, A., Serebrennikov, K., Turitsyn, S.: Deep reinforcement learning for self-tuning laser source of dissipative solitons. Sci. Rep. **12**(1), 7185 (2022)
15. Schulman, J., Levine, S., Abbeel, P., Jordan, M., Moritz, P.: Trust region policy optimization. In: Proceedings of the International conference on machine learning (ICML), Lille, France (2015)
16. Schulman, J., Wolski, F., Dhariwal, P., Radford, A., Klimov, O.: Proximal policy optimization algorithms. arXiv:1707.06347 (2017)
17. Alegre, L: SUMO-RL: Traffic signal control with reinforcement learning (n.d.). Retrieved from https://lucasalegre.github.io/sumo-rl/
18. Song, Y., Zhao, H., Luo, R., Huang, L., Zhang, Y., Su, R.: A SUMO framework for deep reinforcement learning experiments solving electric vehicle charging dispatching problem. arXiv:2209.02921 (2022)

Web of Things Based Advanced Smart Parking Management Solution

Luciano Alessandro Ipsaro Palesi, Matteo Naldi, and Paolo Nesi(✉)

Department of Information Engineering, Distributed Systems and Internet Technology Lab (DISIT), University of Florence, Via Santa Marta, 3, 50139 Florence, Italy
paolo.nesi@unfi.it

Abstract. Urbanization and increasing vehicle ownership have exacerbated parking challenges in cities worldwide, necessitating innovative solutions for efficient space utilization. Smart Parking Management Systems, integrating the Internet of Things (IoT), Web of Things (WoT), machine learning, and digital twins, offer a data-driven approach to optimizing parking infrastructure. This paper presents an advanced Smart Parking Management System developed using Snap4City, an open-source framework designed for real-time urban mobility monitoring. The proposed solution enables real-time parking occupancy tracking, predictive analytics, and automated enforcement, improving overall efficiency, sustainability, and user experience. Through dynamic pricing models, integration with Mobility-as-a-Service (MaaS), and AI-driven forecasting, the system enhances urban mobility while reducing traffic congestion and environmental impact. The effectiveness of the solution is validated through simulations and implementation in Florence, demonstrating its capability to streamline parking operations, support municipal policies, and improve user accessibility. The platform has been implemented using data from Florence and is built on the Snap4City Open Source platform for CN MOST, national center on sustainable mobility.

Keywords: Smart Parking Management · Parking Policy · IoT · WoT · smart applications

1 Introduction

Urbanization is an ongoing global trend, with 53% of the world's population currently residing in cities that occupy only 2% of the Earth's surface [1]. The rapid increase in the number of vehicles on urban roads has led to rising concerns regarding parking space management. Efficiently utilizing available parking areas is crucial to accommodate the growing demand. The difficulty in finding parking spaces negatively impacts both transportation efficiency and sustainability [2]. Searching for a parking spot contributes to unnecessary traffic congestion, increased fuel consumption, and higher emissions, leading to environmental degradation [3]. These issues are particularly relevant when considering on-street parking, but they also extend to off-street parking facilities, which may experience unpredictable occupancy fluctuations depending on time, location, and external factors unknown to drivers. According to a study [4] drivers spend approximately 15 minutes searching for a suitable parking space, further exacerbating urban mobility issues. The increasing demand for parking spaces within urban areas stems from various factors, including urban expansion, rising vehicle ownership, insufficient urban planning, and inefficient parking management systems.

Smart parking management systems based on digital twins, represent a significant advancement in optimizing urban transport infrastructures. They integrate technologies of Internet of Things (IoT), Web of Things (WoT), and machine learning. The main aim of smart parking is to address parking scarcity, reduce traffic congestion due to reduction of cars looking for parking, and provide a more efficient resource allocation.

Digital twins [5] enable dynamic modelling of parking environments, improving efficiency through:

- **Real-time monitoring and data-driven decision-making:** Digital twins use IoT sensors, such as ultrasonic, magnetic, and camera-based technologies, to collect real-time parking occupancy [6]. The parking status data is processed to ensure accurate availability updates and communicate the status to drivers via mobile apps or digital signages.
- **Predictive analytics and parking demand forecasting:** Machine learning, AI algorithms analyse historical and real-time data to predict parking occupancy and even demand [3]. Predictive analytics may also enable to compute dynamic pricing models according to the demand/offer, and also to compute the optimal fair ensuring efficient parking allocation and revenues [7].
- **Scenario simulation and urban planning:** Digital twin has to provide simulation capabilities to model urban scenarios, allowing planners to assess the impact of different strategies according to What-if analysis, before implementation. The simulations may be used to optimize the positioning of parking meters to ensure maximum coverage, minimum discomfort for using them, and thus increase efficiency. The analysis of traffic flow and parking demand, the solution should provide support on designing more efficient transportation infrastructures and thus to reducing congestion and emissions [8].

For effective Smart Parking Management Systems is essential to implement the above-described features. These systems collect real-time data from IoT sensors, parking payment systems, mobile apps to facilitate the communication between parking infrastructure and management platform. Moreover, technologies cloud/edge computing, and machine learning to make predictions may actually implement smart parking systems with valuable features for both drivers and urban planners.

In this paper, we propose a smart parking management system developed using Snap4City. Snap4City is an open-source framework for creating an enhanced Global Digital Twin [9, 10] integrated with Local Digital Twins, operating across various domains such as mobility [11], security [12], and industry [13]. The objective of this paper is to propose an innovative solution to enhance parking space management, promoting a more efficient use of urban resources while simplifying daily interactions between citizens and local administrations. The proposed system aims to seamlessly integrate into modern urban environments, benefiting both registered users and non-users by improving overall mobility and accessibility. The primary goals of this study include enhancing urban mobility by improving the driving experience for both residents and visitors, optimizing resource management to reduce traffic congestion and environmental pollution, monitoring parking availability in real-time through data collection and analysis, and modernizing administrative processes to enhance enforcement and regulatory mechanisms for traffic law compliance.

This paper is organized as follows. Section 2 presents the state of the art. Section 3 defines and analyses the requirements for a Smart Parking Management Solution, comparing them with existing approaches. Section 4 introduces the proposed advanced Smart Parking solution. Section 5 describes the Snap4City Smart Parking use case, detailing its implementation. Section 6 details the main interaction diagrams, illustrating the sequence of actions for registered users, non-registered users, and specific system scenarios. Sections 7 and 8 provide validation and an illustrative example based on Florence data, while Sect. 9 presents the conclusions.

2 Related Work

In urban parking management, many commercial solutions [17, 18] focus on stall reservation and monitoring, typically within closed and proprietary systems that often fail to integrate effectively with the complex dynamics of smart cities. Effective parking management extends beyond basic space monitoring and must incorporate advanced functionalities such as automated enforcement of parking regulations and violation penalty management. Additionally, a system should include comprehensive user management, enabling the administration of different user categories—such as residents, disabled drivers, commercial vehicles, and electric vehicle users—to ensure compliance with municipal policies and regulate access to parking spaces.

The management of urban parking represents a critical challenge in the development of sustainable and efficient cities. Existing state-of-the-art proposals focus on improving parking enforcement, user management, and accessibility by leveraging real-time data collection, automated violation detection, and digital permit systems. These efforts aim to enhance urban mobility, simplify interactions between citizens and local administrations, and ensure compliance with municipal parking regulations, ultimately contributing to a more efficient and user-friendly parking experience. In scientific literature, a variety of solutions have been proposed to address the above-described challenges. These solutions of parking management have to include various parking regulations for managing user access and billing.

Murali et al., [14], proposed an IoT-based parking management system to cope with urban parking shortages. The system used sensors to collect real-time data and monitor parking availability, providing user notifications and optimizing space utilization vis mobile app, with limited business models. Venkata et al., [15], introduced an IoT-enabled smart parking system to get real-time data of vehicle entry time, parking duration, slot availability, and payment details. A mobile app updates the users about the availability of free parking slots. Janowski et al., [16], developed a Smart Parking Assistant and Resource Knowledge (SPARK). SPARK utilizes a YOLOv9-based detection system for parking status detection. Moreover, the system primarily focuses on vehicle detection and identifying available parking spaces rather than gathering detailed information on individual vehicles, which prevents customer identification. Unlike previous Smart Parking Management Systems, Mondal et al., [21] introduced a dynamic pricing model that adjusts parking costs on the basis of the demand. It increases revenue for parking owners and government agencies during peak hours. The solution presents limitations in reliance on real-time data availability for parking occupancy. Additionally, the dynamic pricing model has to be based on efficient IoT info propagation for revenue generation. The dynamic pricing could discourage users when price fluctuations during peak hours become excessive.

3 Ideal Smart Parking Requirements

After analysing the state of the art and considering the needs highlighted in the introduction, an effective parking management system must meet specific functional requirements. Defining these functional requirements is essential for developing scalable and reliable solutions capable of enhancing operational efficiency and optimizing urban parking resources. The following sections outline the key functional requirements for an advanced Smart Parking Management System:

R.1 Coverage of Entities Involved for modelling various parking-related components such as parking lots, on-street spaces, sensors, payment kiosks, digital signage, and enforcement devices. The system should enable the creation, tracking, and management of these entities throughout their lifecycle, including attributes like location, availability status, pricing, and capacity.

R.2 Users' Roles Management to define and control access to the system based on different user profiles. This feature should support multiple roles, such as administrators, enforcement officers, parking operators, residents, and general drivers, each with specific permissions and responsibilities. Proper user access management ensures data security, streamlined workflow, and operational accountability.

R.3 Get real time data from parking spaces, including occupancy status, sensor-based detections, and vehicle entry/exit timestamps. Additionally, the system should track environmental factors such as temperature and air quality within parking structures, as well as potential anomalies (e.g., unauthorized access, obstruction detection, or malfunctioning sensors). These real-time insights enhance parking operations and predictive planning.

R.4 Provide statistical data in terms of Key Performance Indicators (KPI) through interactive dashboards. The KPI dashboards should display real-time insights into parking occupancy at the operators, revenue trends, enforcement efficiency, peak utilization hours, and sensor reliability. By visualizing these KPIs, operators can optimize resource allocation, identify trends, and enhance urban mobility strategies.

R.5 Implement a dynamic parking tariff system that adjusts pricing based on time slots, demand fluctuations, and special conditions (e.g., peak hours, off-peak discounts, and event-based pricing). The tariff structure should be configurable through a Typical Time Trend (TTT) model (defining fair for each hour per day, per week, in a period), allowing municipalities to set minute-based rate variations for each parking facility.

R.6 Manage special permits for different user categories, including residents, disabled drivers, commercial vehicles, and electric vehicle users. The system should facilitate permit issuance, renewal, and validation, ensuring compliance with municipal parking policies and preferential access for eligible users.

R.6.1 Device-Based Permit Management. The system should support the management of special permits through dedicated devices, enabling seamless parking access without requiring manual app interaction. Authorized users, such as residents, disabled drivers, commercial vehicle operators, and electric vehicle users, should be able to initiate parking sessions automatically upon arrival through device recognition.

R.7 Provide alarm management and notification systems to alert operators and users in real time about issues such as overparking, unauthorized parking, device failures, or security breaches. The system should support automated notifications via mobile applications, email alerts, SMS, and web-based platforms, enabling quick responses to potential operational disruptions. Additionally, it should provide content management and user messaging capabilities to ensure timely and relevant notifications. Notifications should include alerts for parking expiration, overparking, fines, unauthorized parking, and wallet balance exhaustion.

R.8 Enforce parking regulations and fine management through automated detection of violations and electronic fine issuance. The system should enable officers to verify violations, issue fines via mobile applications, and integrate with payment systems for fine collection.

R.9 Integration with Mobility-as-a-Service (MaaS), allowing users to combine parking with other transportation options, such as public transit, and bike-sharing. The system should facilitate unified payments, trip planning, and dynamic recommendations based on user preferences, traffic conditions, and public transport availability.

R.10 Smart Parking Routing, provide dynamic parking routing by integrating real-time traffic sensor data, historical occupancy trends, and traffic conditions. The system should guide drivers to the nearest available parking spot, minimizing search time and congestion. It should also adopt recommendations based on user preferences, parking restrictions, and estimated arrival times.

Table 1. Comparison of Parking Management Solutions Based on Requirement Satisfaction

Solution	Requirements										
	R.1	R.2	R.3	R.4	R.5	R.6	R.6.1	R.7	R.8	R.9	R.10	R.11
Easypark [17]	N	Y	Y	Y	Y	Y	N	Y	Y	N	N	N
Smartparkingsystems [18]	N	Y	Y	Y	Y	Y	N	Y	Y	N	N	N
Murali [14]	N	N	Y	N	N	N	N	Y	N	N	N	N
Venkata [15]	Y	N	Y	Y	N	N	N	N	N	N	N	N
Janowski [16]	N	N	Y	Y	N	N	N	N	N	N	N	N
Mondal [21]	Y	Y	Y	N	Y	N	N	N	N	N	N	N
Snap4CitySmartParking	Y	Y	Y	Y	Y	Y	Y	Y	Y	Y	Y	Y

R.11 Predictive Parking Availability to estimate future availability of parking spaces by analysing historical data, real-time occupancy and traffic patterns. The system should allow users to reserve parking spaces in advance, reducing search times and traffic congestion. Predictive models should consider variables such as time of day, weather conditions. By integrating these factors, the system optimizes space allocation and improves overall parking efficiency (Table 1).

4 Advanced Smart Parking Architecture

In Fig. 1, the proposed Advanced Smart Parking Management Architecture is illustrated, highlighting its development on top of the Snap4City [10, 26] open-source framework. The system is designed to manage data ingestion, processing logic, and business intelligence tools for the front end. Snap4City [25] is a Smart City platform offering scalability, multi-tenancy, and the ability to handle millions of daily data entries via protocols such as MQTT and NGSI [1]. It is GDPR-compliant [19] and ensures data protection through a user role management system, providing secure and personalized access. The platform supports Web of Things, enabling flexible entity modelling [20] and managing their entire lifecycle. Data ingestion is handled via Node-RED [10], while an access control mechanism assigns specific roles—administrators, operators, and officer staff—to ensure both security and operational efficiency. In the proposed Advanced Smart Parking, data is collected through IoT sensors [24] (or using technologies such as LoRa, Bluetooth and Narrowband -IoT) deployed across the city and transmitted to NGSI Brokers for processing. The system manages data ingestion, storage, and processing logic via microservices, ensuring efficient data flow and decision-making capabilities. Parking predictions are performed according to [27].

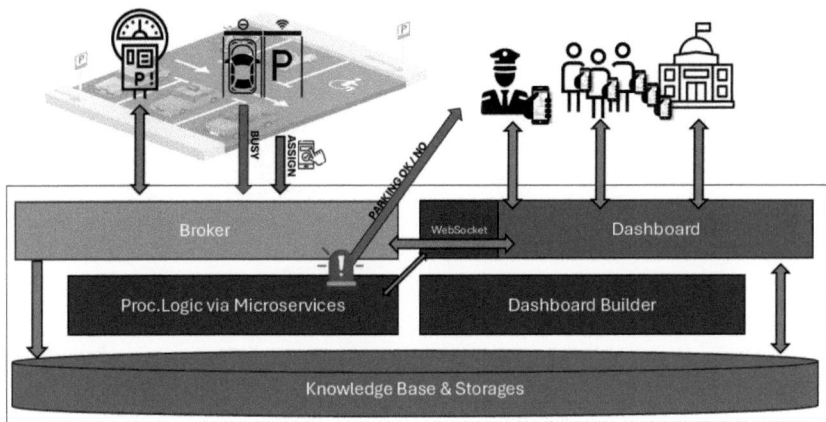

Fig. 1. Advanced Smart Parking architecture. The system integrates sensors, brokers, and dashboards to manage parking. Purple arrows indicate the basic interaction: the sensor detects a parked vehicle, the user confirms the slot number, and the system can notify municipal police if necessary.

Advanced Smart Parking collects and monitors real-time data from:

- **Parking sensors (On-road, Off-road):** Real-time occupancy status, availability, etc.
- **Dashboard/Mobile app for users**: allows users to start and stop parking sessions.
- **Dashboard/Mobile app for operators:** Allows parking enforcement personnel to monitor parking status, check payments, and manage violations.
- **Parking meters**: Enables non-registered users to start a parking session, process payments, and track parking duration.

The application supports a large range of payment methods and business models, which can be customized by area and municipality, allowing both registered and non-registered users to seamlessly start and stop parking sessions. The advanced monitoring and reporting capabilities offered by Snap4City facilitate data-driven policy adjustments, optimizing overall parking management efficiency.

5 Main Smart Parking Use Cases

This section presents the Snap4City Smart Parking use cases, which are illustrated in the next section via sequence diagrams. These use cases highlight the main views and relations with different users and the system, focusing on the roles of the municipal operator, end user, and officer.

5.1 Use Case – Municipal Operator

The municipal operator is responsible for managing and monitoring parking areas in real time using an advanced system of interactive dashboards. In Fig. 2, a use case diagram for the municipal operator is presented. The system architecture includes three main functionalities: monitoring the status of devices on the map, statistical analysis to optimize parking area management, and the automated definition of parking rules with

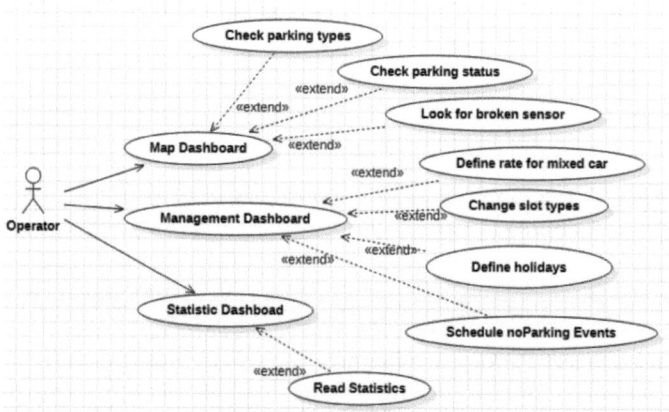

Fig. 2. Use case diagram for Municipal operator.

immediate notification to users in case of changes. The **Map Dashboard** allows operators to view device statuses, check the types of available parking spaces, and identify potential malfunctions, such as faulty sensors. The **Management Dashboard** enables operators to directly intervene in parking rules, modify stall types, define specific rates for mixed vehicles, and schedule extraordinary parking restrictions. Finally, the **Statistic Dashboard** provides a detailed data analysis, offering weekly statistics and distributions by user and vehicle type, facilitating strategic decisions based on quantitative data.

5.2 Use Case – End User, City User

The city user should access and monitoring parking areas status in real time. In Fig. 3, a use case diagram for the end user is presented. The end user, utilizing the parking service, monitors in real-time the parking availability and the economic policies of his/her destination area through a mobile app. The system provides a map overview of the situation, which can be extended with advanced features such as searching for free slots, checking the economic policies of the area, and being routed to the desired slot. Additionally, the user can start and create a "parking event", which implies, the actual parking, to make payments, and receive notifications regarding parking session, enhancing the overall user experience.

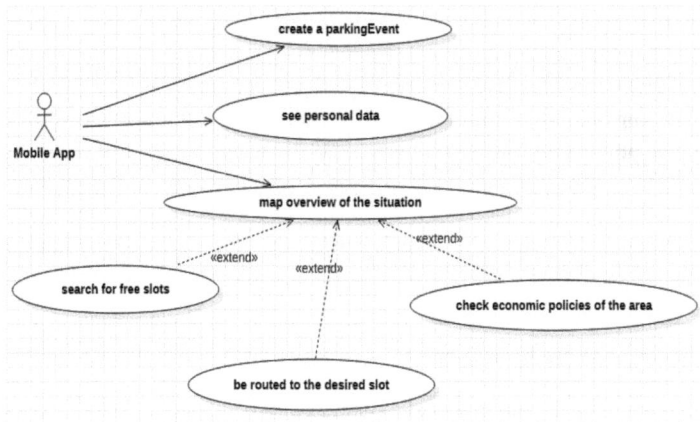

Fig. 3. Use case diagram for End user

5.3 Use Case – Officer

The officer is responsible for ensuring compliance with parking regulations and issuing fines when violations occur. In Fig. 4, a use case diagram for the officer is presented. Through the mobile app, the officer is continuously updated on parking spots where infractions have been detected. The system allows the officer to identity the area with major problems, and check information about the currently parked vehicle, verify the situation, and, if necessary, issue a fine after conducting the required validations and corrections, finally completing a form with the fine data. This approach enhances the efficiency and accuracy of parking enforcement while ensuring that violations are addressed systematically and in sustainable manner.

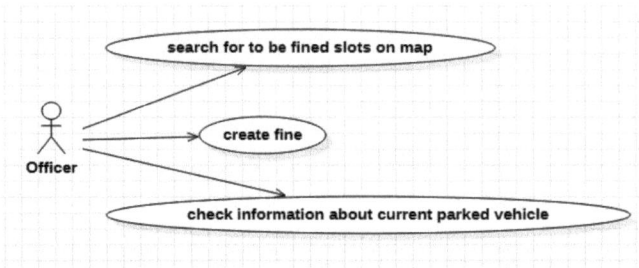

Fig. 4. Use case diagram for the Officer

6 Main Interaction Diagrams of the Solution

This section focuses on the main interaction diagrams of the solution, particularly the sequence diagrams that detail the interactions between different system components and users. These diagrams illustrate the step-by-step processes involved in key scenarios, such as the parking procedure triggered by events, the interactions of registered users with the system, the flow for unregistered users, and the usage of electric charging stations. All the platform is event driven and based on MicroServices. The core microservices to access at data and search for results and creating dashboards and views are those of Snap4City. On the other hand, the complex logic of the Smart parking has been totally developed for this solution.

6.1 Parking Procedure by Events

The process starts with the operation of a parking slot (see Fig. 5). When a vehicle parks, the sensor detects its presence and updates its status to BUSY, sending this information to the IoT application. The server processes this update and adjusts the parking occupancy counts accordingly. Similarly, when the vehicle leaves the parking slot, the sensor updates its status to FREE, and the system updates the counts. When a vehicle arrives at the parking lot and parks, the sensor detects its presence and sends a BUSY notification to the system. If the user (registered or non-registered) starts a parking session via the mobile app or parking meter, the system confirms the session as active. However, if no session is started within a predefined time frame, the system automatically triggers a violation notification to the operator, specifying the parking slot ID where the infraction occurred. In addition to basic parking status updates, the IoT application manages other events, such as charging slot updates, infractions, parking event closures, and mixed-car slot payments. For example, if a recharge slot is in use, the system may update its status to NO_RECHARGE; in case of an infraction, the system marks it as TOO_LATE; completed parking sessions are set to DONE; and in mixed-car slot scenarios, a wallet event is created for payment processing.

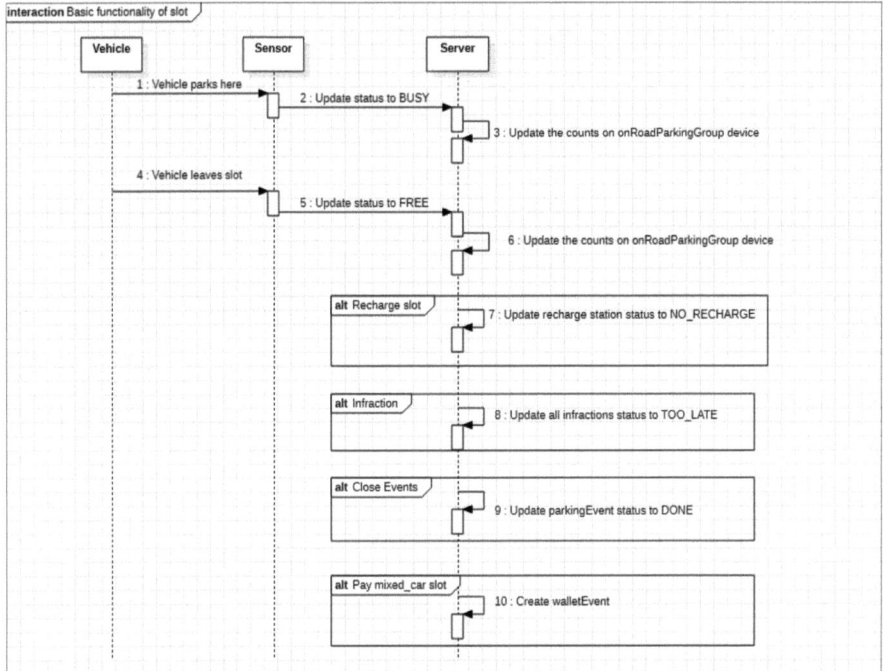

Fig. 5. Sequence of actions illustrating the user's entry and/or exit from the parking slot.

6.2 Parking of a Registered User

The process starts when a registered user with a Bluetooth device or mobile app parks in a designated slot. Upon arrival, the sensor detects the vehicle and updates its status to BUSY, initiating communication with the user's device. This interaction generates a parking event on server side, which is then processed by the system. For users with the mobile app, additional functionalities are available. If the parking slot requires payment, the user can specify a duration (see Fig. 6). In this case, the system sends a renewal notification before expiry. If no duration is set, the parking session automatically ends upon the user's departure. For structured parking facilities, users can request to link their data to a ticket and pay through the app when exiting. Besides standard occupancy updates, the IoT application also manages special events such as infractions, charging slot usage, and mixed-car slot payments. For example:

- If a charging slot is occupied, the system marks it as NO_RECHARGE.
- In case of an infraction, it is flagged as TOO_LATE.

- Completed parking sessions are updated to DONE.

In mixed-car slot scenarios, the system creates a wallet event for payment processing. Furthermore, when a control officer arrives, they input the parking code to retrieve infraction details. For registered users having a special permit equipped with a sensor, once the vehicle is parked, the system automatically updates the parking status. After this update, the parking sensor transmits the user and parking slot identifiers to the system, which records the event as a Bluetooth-based parking session. As shown in Fig. 7, this process allows the system to associate the parking slot with the user's permit without the need for manual input. This mechanism ensures that the parking session is activated

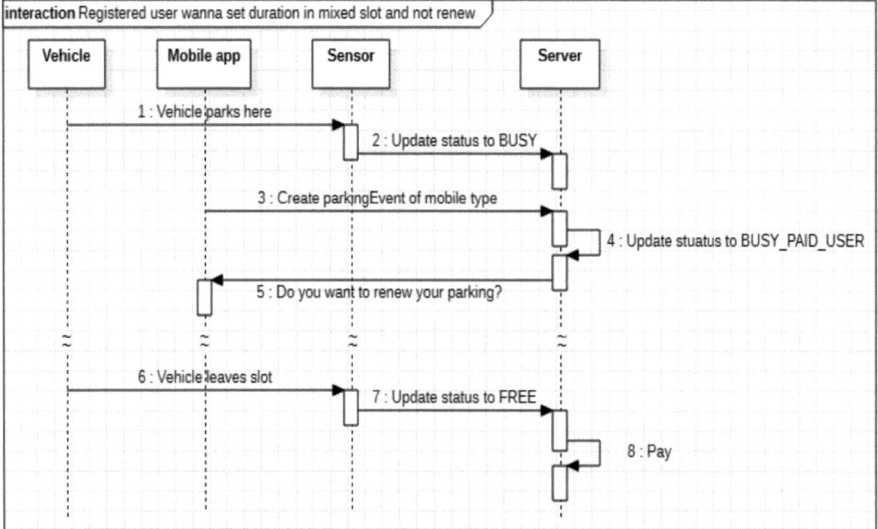

Fig. 6. Sequence of actions illustrating registered user

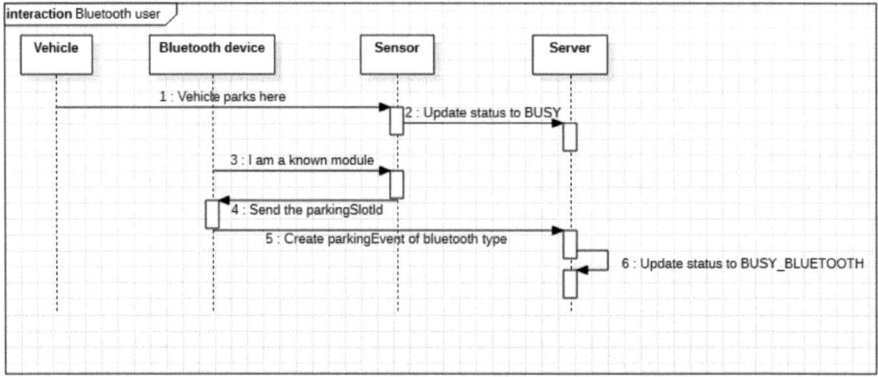

Fig. 7. Sequence of actions illustrating registered user equipped with a sensor

based on sensor detection and that the system can differentiate standard vehicles from those with special permits.

6.3 Parking of a Unregistered User

The process begins when an unregistered user parks in a mixed car slot (see Fig. 8). Upon arrival, the sensor detects the vehicle and updates the slot status to BUSY. The system then waits for a predefined period to check if the user makes a payment. If the user pays at the parking meter, the system updates the slot status to BUSY_PAID_ANON. If no payment is made within the allocated time, the status changes to TO_BE_FINED, and a fine is issued. For cases of overparking, the system detects when the paid duration has ended. The slot status is then updated to BUSY_PAID_ANON_OVER, followed by TO_BE_FINED, triggering a fine for exceeding the paid time. In mixed-car slot scenarios, the system manages anonymous payments and potential infractions. Control officers can check parking details by inputting the slot code to verify fines and infractions.

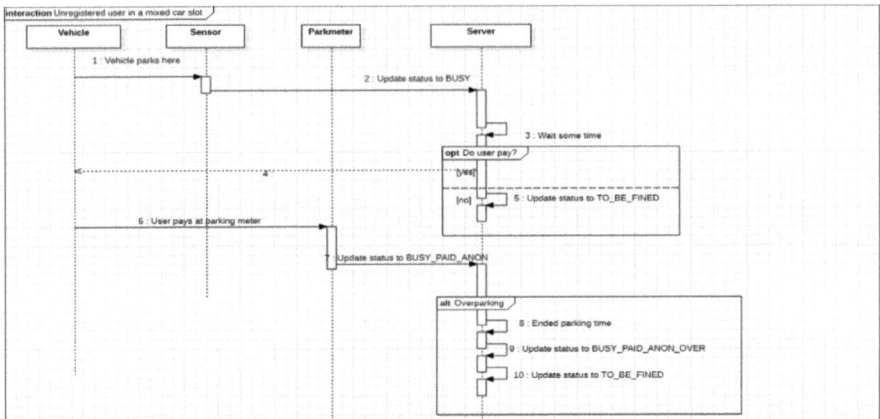

Fig. 8. Sequence of actions illustrating (a) unregistered user entry and/or exit from the parking slot.

6.4 Parking on an Electric Charging Stations

One of the innovations introduced by the project concerns the monitoring of electric charging stations. The goal is to ensure their proper use, preventing vehicles from occupying charging spots without authorization and ensuring that they leave the space once charging is complete. As shown in Fig. 9, the system detects the presence of a vehicle through the sensors and updates the station status to BUSY. If the user does not start charging, the server updates the status to TO_BE_FINED, indicating a possible violation. When recharging begins, the station status changes to RECHARGE_STARTED and, upon completion, updates to RECHARGE_ENDED. If the vehicle remains in the station when charging is complete, the system signals another violation by updating the status to TO_BE_FINED. Once the vehicle leaves the location, the station status returns to FREE, and if no recharging has occurred, the system sets the status to NO_RECHARGE.

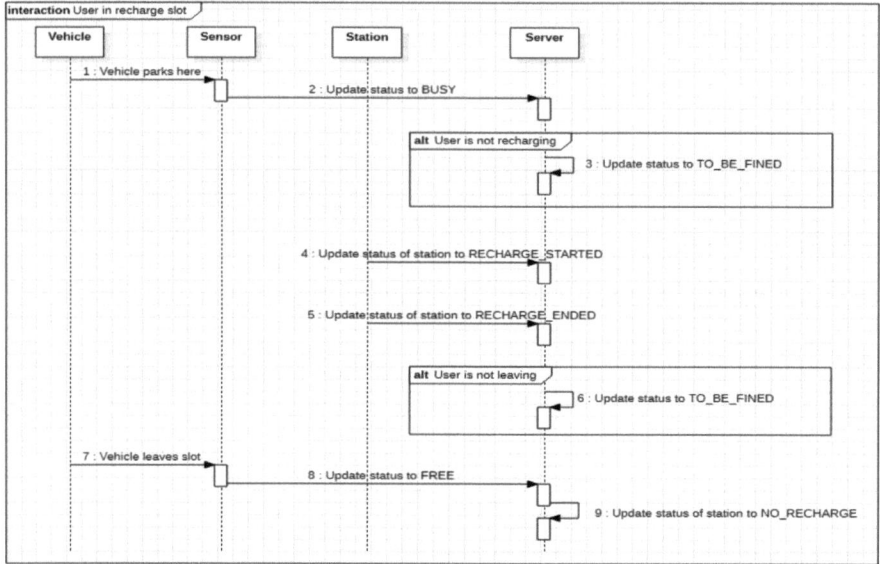

Fig. 9. Sequence of actions illustrating the Operation of an EV Charging Station.

7 Validation via Simulation of Global Parking

To effectively assess the capabilities of the system, a simulation has been implemented, replicating **real-world parking** scenarios. The main execution thread of the simulator (see Fig. 10) is responsible for generating random events (randomEvent()), assigning users (randomUser(event)), and selecting available parking slots (randomSlot(event)). These elements are encapsulated into execution tuples and dispatched to background workers (see Fig. 11) for processing.

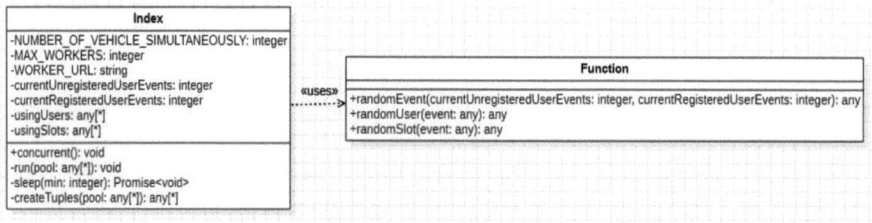

Fig. 10. Class diagram of the main execution thread

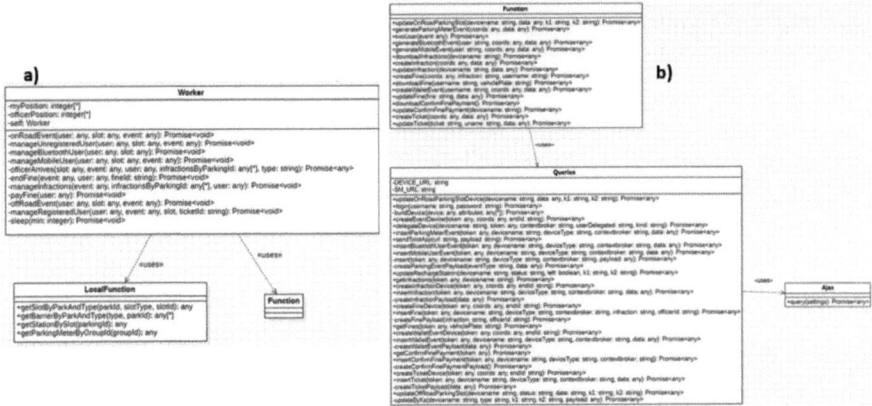

Fig. 11. Class diagram of the Worker class, (a) illustrates the core functionalities of the Worker, (b) expands on additional operations.

The Index class (see Fig. 10) defines key operational parameters, such as NUMBER_OF_VEHICLE_SIMULTANEOUSLY and MAX_WORKERS, which regulate the number of simultaneous parking processes. It employs the run(pool: any[]) function to generate execution tasks. Each task consists of:

- A Worker instance to process the parking event,
- A randomly selected event (randomEvent() from the Function class),
- A user, either retrieved from the database or generated dynamically (randomUser(event)),
- An available parking slot (randomSlot(event)).

If the match from the user (providing slot id and plates) and the busy slot just now (communicating the slot id change of status) is not found, the system iterates until a valid match is assigned to a worker. The tuples generated by the main thread are then dispatched to workers for execution, otherwise means that some critical to be fined conditions has been detected. The workers (see Fig. 11) handle the execution of assigned parking events. The Worker class processes different types of events based on the parking environment. It distinguishes between:

- On-road parking events, managed through the onRoadEvent() function,
- Off-road (structured) parking events, handled by offRoadEvent().
- Each event may involve multiple operations, including:
- Managing users (manageUnregisteredUser(), manageRegisteredUser()),
- Processing mobile and Bluetooth-based interactions (manageMobileUser(), manageBluetoothUser()),
- Handling law enforcement actions, such as detecting violations (manageInfractions()) and processing fines (createFine(), payFine()).

Workers execute these tasks asynchronously, ensuring efficient parallel processing of multiple parking operations. To interact with IoT-enabled devices, the system relies on the Queries and Ajax classes Fig. 11 (b). These components facilitate communication with external services, such as Snap4City [22], which provides APIs for managing parking sensors, meters, and enforcement devices. Notable API calls include:

- updateOnRoadParkingSlotDevice(), for real-time updates on parking availability,
- generateBluetoothEvent() and generateMobileEvent(), for user interactions via connected devices,
- createFine() and updateFine(), for automated violation management,
- createTicket(), for generating digital parking tickets.

8 Operator Web of Things Interface and Some Examples

For an illustrative example, specific datasets from the city of Florence [23] have been loaded. Three areas of the city of Florence were chosen:

- Piazza Leon Battista Alberti
- The western part of the Statuto district
- The Careggi area

A total of 1,562 on-street parking spaces were identified in these areas, divided into 18 categories:

- **Bus**: Free parking space reserved for buses. A municipal permit is required to park from 08:00 to 20:00.
- **Cargo**: Free parking space for loading/unloading goods. Parking is limited to 15 minutes (08:00–20:00) and requires a permit.
- **Event Car**: Temporary parking space for vehicles during special events (e.g., press for sporting events). A municipal permit is required.
- **Event Moto**: Same as the previous one but for two-wheeled vehicles.
- **Forbidden**: Not an actual parking space but represents areas where parking is prohibited (e.g., in front of driveways). For simplicity, it is considered as a parking space in the project.
- **Free Car**: Free parking space for four-wheeled vehicles.
- **Free Moto**: Free parking space for two-wheeled vehicles.
- **Handicap**: Parking space reserved for disabled persons, requiring a municipal permit.
- **Mixed Car**: Mixed paid parking space for vehicles.
- **Org Car**: Parking space reserved for public sector employees with a municipal permit.
- **Org motorbike**: Same as the previous one but for motorbike.
- **Recharge Car**: Parking space for charging electric vehicles (08:00–20:00). After charging, parking is allowed for a maximum of 60 minutes.
- **Recharge Moto**: Same as the previous one but for motorbike.
- **Resident**: Parking space reserved for local residents with a municipal permit.
- **Taxi**: Parking space reserved for taxis.
- **Timed Car**: Time-limited parking space for vehicles.
- **Timed Moto**: Time-limited parking space for motorbike.
- **Women Car**: Parking space reserved for women, generally located in areas with greater security.

The Snap4City Advanced Smart Parking solution provides a set of views/dashboards dedicated to parking management. One of the main views is Parking Conditions Monitoring view/dashboard in Fig. 12. In this view/dashboard, the operator monitors the real-time status of parking areas and slots throughout the city through an interactive map interface. The system provides an overview of available and occupied parking spaces. Real-time data updates support the operator's decision-making processes. The operator can highlight individual parking spaces according to their status (occupied, free or reserved) or classify areas according to occupancy levels, violations or specific infrastructure elements. The view called Snap4Parking Weekly Statistics (see Fig. 13) reports and allows to perform the analysis on parking occupancy statistics over time, enabling

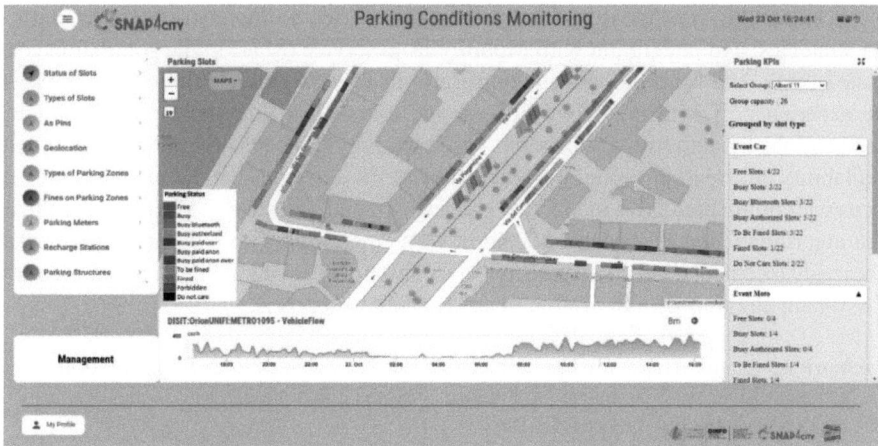

Fig. 12. Dashboard Snap4Parking Conditions Monitoring

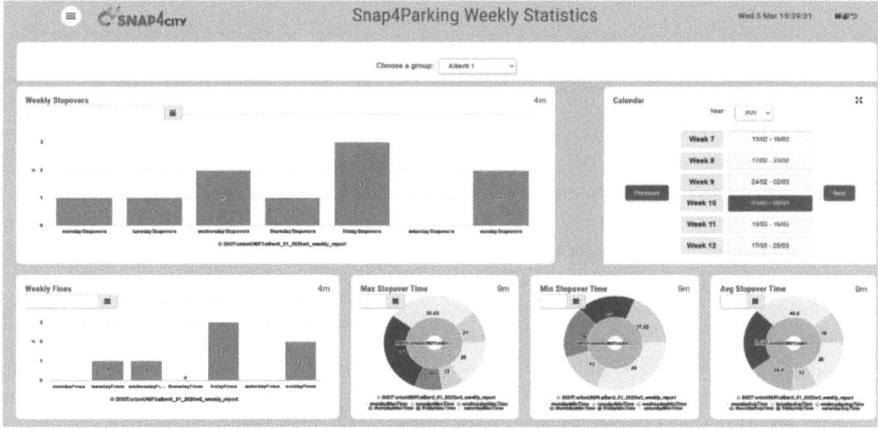

Fig. 13. Dashboard Snap4Parking Statistics

comparisons between different periods. These statistics include key performance indicators such as stopovers, representing short-term parking events, and fines, indicating violations detected within the monitored areas.

9 Conclusions

The effective management of urban parking spaces requires innovative solutions that leverage IoT, data analytics, and real-time monitoring. In this work, a Web of Things-based Advanced Smart Parking Management Solution has been presented, aiming to enhance the efficiency of parking space utilization through real-time data collection and predictive availability. The system enables comprehensive management of parking lots, on-street, and off-street spaces, incorporating role-based access control, dynamic pricing strategies, and integration with Mobility-as-a-Service (MaaS). The simulation conducted using data from Florence demonstrates that the proposed solution can improve the experience of both municipal officers and users. Real-time monitoring facilitates interventions by authorities, while app-based tracking provides drivers with up-to-date availability information, reducing unnecessary traffic and emission. Future research will focus on refining predictive models for parking demand, improving AI-driven optimization algorithms, and exploring integration with emerging urban mobility frameworks. These advancements will contribute to a more sustainable and intelligent urban mobility ecosystem, aligning with the vision of smart city development.

Acknowledgements. This study has been carried out in the context of the Spoke 9 of the Italian National Center for Sustainable Mobility (CN MOST), and the CN MOST flagship project OPTIFaaS and scalability project SASUAM.

References

1. Antoniucci, V., Marella, G.: Small town resilience: housing market crisis and urban density in Italy. Land Use Policy. **59**, 580–588, ISSN 0264-8377 (2016). https://doi.org/10.1016/j.landusepol.2016.10.004
2. Chowdhury, L.H., Mahmud, Z.Z., Islam, I.U., Jahan, I., Islam, S.: Smart car parking management system. In: 2019 IEEE International Conference on Robotics, Automation, Artificial-Intelligence and Internet-of-Things (RAAICON), pp. 122–126. IEEE (2019)
3. Bilotta, S., Ipsaro Palesi, L.A., Nesi, P.: Predicting free parking slots via deep learning in short-mid terms explaining temporal impact of features. IEEE Access. **11**, 101678–101693 (2023). https://doi.org/10.1109/ACCESS.2023.3314660
4. Mahmud, S.A., Khan, G.M., Rahman, M., Zafar, H.: A survey of intelligent car parking system. J. Appl. Res. Technol. **11**(5), 714–726 (2013)
5. Adreani, L., Bellini, P., Colombo, C., et al.: Implementing integrated digital twin modelling and representation into the Snap4City platform for smart city solutions. Multimed. Tools Appl. **83**, 37121–37146 (2024). https://doi.org/10.1007/s11042-023-16838-0
6. Murali, K., Ramakrishnan, K., Sandeep, S.: Efficient parking management for modern urban environments. In: 2024 3rd International Conference on Automation, Computing and Renewable Systems (ICACRS), Pudukkottai, India, vol. 2024, pp. 1456–1460. https://doi.org/10.1109/ICACRS62842.2024.10841537

7. Saharan, S., Bawa, S., Kumar, N.: Dynamic pricing techniques for intelligent transportation system in smart cities: a systematic review. Comput. Commun. **150**, 603–625, ISSN 0140-3664 (2020). https://doi.org/10.1016/j.comcom.2019.12.003
8. Canzaniello, M., Amitrano, S., Prezioso, E., Giampaolo, F., Cuomo, S., Piccialli, F.: Leveraging digital twins and generative AI for effective urban mobility management. In: 2024 IEEE Cyber Science and Technology Congress (CyberSciTech), Boracay Island, Philippines, vol. 2024, pp. 146–153. https://doi.org/10.1109/CyberSciTech64112.2024.00032
9. Adreani, L., Bellini, P., Fanfani, M., Nesi, P., Pantaleo, G.: Smart City digital twin framework for real-time multi-data integration and wide public distribution. IEEE Access. **12**, 76277–76303 (2024). https://doi.org/10.1109/ACCESS.2024.3406795
10. Fanfani, M., Palesi, L.A.I., Nesi, P.: Microservices' libraries enabling server-side business logic visual programming for digital twins. SoftwareX. **27**, 101805, ISSN 2352-7110 (2024). https://doi.org/10.1016/j.softx.2024.101805
11. Bellini, P., Bilotta, S., Palesi, A.L.I., Nesi, P., Pantaleo, G.: Vehicular traffic flow reconstruction analysis to mitigate scenarios with large city changes. IEEE Access. **10**, 131061–131075 (2022). https://doi.org/10.1109/ACCESS.2022.3229183
12. Bellini, P., Cenni, D., Palesi, L.A.I., Nesi, P., Pantaleo, G.: A deep learning approach for short term prediction of industrial plant working status. In: 2021 IEEE seventh international conference on big data computing service and applications (BigDataService), Oxford, United Kingdom, vol. 2021, pp. 9–16. https://doi.org/10.1109/BigDataService52369.2021.00007
13. Collini, E., Palesi, L.A.I., Nesi, P., et al.: Flexible thermal camera solution for Smart city people detection and counting. Multimed. Tools Appl. **83**, 20457–20485 (2024). https://doi.org/10.1007/s11042-023-16374-x
14. Murali, K., Ramakrishnan, K., Sandeep, S.: Efficient parking management for modern urban environments. In: 2024 3rd international conference on automation, computing and renewable systems (ICACRS), Pudukkottai, India, pp. 1456–1460 (2024). https://doi.org/10.1109/ICACRS62842.2024.10841537
15. Venkata Sudhakar, M., Anoora Reddy, A.V., Mounika, K., Sai Kumar, M.V., Bharani, T.: Development of smart parking management system. Mater. Today Proc. **80**(Part 3), 2794–2798, ISSN 2214-7853 (2023). https://doi.org/10.1016/j.matpr.2021.07.040
16. Janowski, A., Hüsrevoğlu, M., Renigier-Bilozor, M.: Sustainable parking space management using machine learning and swarm theory—the SPARK system. Appl. Sci. **14**(24), 12076 (2024). https://doi.org/10.3390/app142412076
17. Easypark, https://www.easypark.com/en-it/cities-and-operators
18. Smartparkingsystems, https://smartparkingsystems.com/en/smart-parking-system/
19. Bellini, P., Ipsaro Palesi, L.A., Nesi, P., et al.: Multi clustering recommendation system for fashion retail. Multimed. Tools Appl. **82**, 9989–10016 (2023). https://doi.org/10.1007/s11042-021-11837-5
20. Bellini, P., Bologna, D., Fanfani, M., Ipsaro Palesi, L.A., Nesi, P., Pantaleo, G.: Rapid prototyping & development life cycle for smart applications of internet of entities. In: 2023 27th International Conference on Engineering of Complex Computer Systems (ICECCS), Toulouse, France, vol. 2023, pp. 142–151
21. Mondal, M.A., Rehena, Z., Janssen, M.: Smart parking management system with dynamic pricing. J. Amb. Intell. Smart Environ. **13**(6), 473–494 (2021). https://doi.org/10.3233/AIS-210615
22. Snap4city API, https://www.snap4city.org/drupal/node/20 (Accessed 04 Mar 2025)
23. Parking Comune Firenze, https://opendata.comune.fi.it/page_dataset_show?id=dati-in-tempo-reale-sui-posti-liberi-nei-parcheggi-di-firenze (Accessed 05 Mar 2025)
24. Bellini, P., Palesi, L.A.I., Giovannoni, A., Nesi, P.: Managing complexity of data models and performance in broker-based Internet/Web of Things architectures. Internet of Things. **23**, 100834, ISSN 2542-6605 (2023). https://doi.org/10.1016/j.iot.2023.100834

25. Bellini, P., Bologna, D., Nesi, P., Pantaleo, G.: A unified knowledge model for managing Smart City/IoT platform entities for multitenant scenarios. Smart Cities. **7**(5), 2339–2365 (2024). https://doi.org/10.3390/smartcities7050092
26. Adreani, L., Bellini, P., Fanfani, M., Nesi, P., Pantaleo, G.: Design and develop of a smart city digital twin with 3D representation and user Interface for what-if analysis. In: Gervasi, O., et al. (eds.) Computational Science and Its Applications – ICCSA 2023 Workshops. ICCSA 2023 Lecture Notes in Computer Science, vol. 14111. Springer, Cham (2023). https://doi.org/10.1007/978-3-031-37126-4_34
27. Bilotta, S., Ipsaro Palesi, L.A., Nesi, P.: Predicting free parking slots via deep learning in short-mid terms explaining temporal impact of features. IEEE Access. **11**, 101678–101693 (2023)

Author Index

A
Amoruso, Paola 134
Anelli, Debora 178
Angrisano, Mariarosaria 299
Annunziata, Alfonso 16
Antonia, Gravagnuolo 266
Askarizad, Reza 51

B
Barbieri, Sebastiano 234
Bonifaci, Pietro 195
Bottero, Marta 217, 234

C
Cappelli, Giuseppe 319, 335, 350
Caprioli, Caterina 234
Carpentieri, Gerardo 3
Cerullo, Giuseppe 146
Coni, Mauro 368, 385, 401
Copiello, Sergio 195

D
D'Apuzzo, Mauro 319, 335, 350
Datola, Giulia 91, 217
De Paola, Pierfrancesco 146
Dell'Anna, Federico 234
Dell'Ovo, Marta 91
Di Liddo, Felicia 134, 158, 178
Doan, Truong Cong 419

G
Garau, Chiara 16, 51, 69
Giang, Do Thai 419
Girard, Luigi Fusco 266
Giulio, Cavana 266
Guarini, Maria Rosaria 107, 158
Guerrero, Yilsy Núñez 107
Guida, Carmen 3

H
Hung, Phan Duy 419

I
Iannattone, Maria Teresa 335
Ipsaro Palesi, Luciano Alessandro 432

K
Kaths, Heather 335

L
Lee, Chien-Sing 34
Locurcio, Marco 134, 158

M
Maltinti, Francesca 368, 385, 401
Mariarosaria, Angrisano 266
Marta, Bottero 266
Martinelli, Valerio 3
Mazzeo, Giuseppe 248
Mecca, Ippolita 299
Mondini, Giulio 234
Morano, Pierluigi 134, 146, 158, 178

N
Naldi, Matteo 432
Nardoianni, Sofia 319, 335, 350
Neglia, Grazia 299
Nesi, Paolo 432
Nicolosi, Vittorio 319, 335, 350

O
Oppio, Alessandra 91

P
Panarotto, Federico 195
Panetto, Kevin 368
Pedrini, Sabrina 283
Pernetti, Mariano 350
Phang, Wei-Jie 34

Pinna, Chiara   69

R
Rassu, Nicoletta   368, 385, 401
Roma, Antonella   158
Rombi, James   385, 401

S
Sabatelli, Emma   178
Salis, Marta   385, 401
Salvo, Francesca   122
Scorza, Francesco   16

Segura-de-la-Cal, Alejandro   107
Sica, Francesco   107, 146

T
Tajani, Francesco   134, 146, 178
Tartari, Maria   283
Tavano, Daniela   122
Torlini, Alessia   69
Torrieri, Francesca   91

Z
Zedda, Riccardo   368

MIX
Papier aus verantwortungsvollen Quellen
Paper from responsible sources
FSC® C105338

If you have any concerns about our products,
you can contact us on
ProductSafety@springernature.com

In case Publisher is established outside the EU,
the EU authorized representative is:
**Springer Nature Customer Service Center GmbH
Europaplatz 3, 69115 Heidelberg, Germany**

Printed by Libri Plureos GmbH
in Hamburg, Germany